Microsoft Works 4/4.5 for Windows 95
Illustrated Standard Edition

Microsoft® Works 4/4.5 for Windows® 95
Illustrated Standard Edition

Michael Halvorson

COURSE
TECHNOLOGY

ONE MAIN STREET, CAMBRIDGE, MA 02142

an International Thomson Publishing company I(T)P®

Cambridge • Albany • Bonn • Boston • Cincinnati • London • Madrid • Melbourne • Mexico City
New York • Paris • San Francisco • Singapore • Tokyo • Toronto • Washington

Microsoft® Works 4/4.5 for Windows® 95—Illustrated is published by Course Technology.

Managing Editors:	Marjorie Hunt, Nicole Jones Pinard
Product Managers:	Ann Marie Buconjic, Mary-Terese Cozzola, Jennifer Thompson
Production Editors:	Donna Gridley, Seth Andrews
Contributing Authors:	Linda Ericksen, Mary-Terese Cozzola
Composition House:	GEX, Inc.
QA Manuscript Reviewers:	Alex White, Edward Notosoehardjo, John Bosco
Text Designer:	Leslie Hartwell
Cover Designer:	John Gamache

© 1998 by Course Technology— I(T)P.

For more information contact:
Course Technology
One Main Street
Cambridge, MA 02142

ITP Europe
Berkshire House 168-173
High Holborn
London WCIV 7AA
England

ITP GmbH
Königswinterer Strasse 418
53227 Bonn
Germany

Nelson ITP, Australia
102 Dodds Street
South Melbourne, 3205
Victoria, Australia

ITP Asia
60 Albert Street, #15-01
Albert Complex
Singapore 189969

ITP Nelson Canada
1120 Birchmount Road
Scarborough, Ontario
Canada M1K 5G4

ITP Japan
Hirakawacho Kyowa Building, 3F
2-2-1 Hirakawacho
Chiyoda-ku, Tokyo 102
Japan

International Thomson Editores
Seneca, 53
Colonia Polanco
11560 Mexico D.F. Mexico

All rights reserved. This publication is protected by federal copyright law. No part of this publication may be reproduced, stored in a retrieval system, or transmitted in any form or by any means, electronic, mechanical, photocopying, recording, or otherwise, or be used to make any derivative work (such as translation or adaptation), without prior permission in writing from Course Technology.

Trademarks

Course Technology and the open book logo are registered trademarks of Course Technology.

I(T)P   The ITP logo is a trademark under license.

Some of the product names in this book have been used for identification purposes only and may be trademarks or registered trademarks of their respective manufacturers and sellers.

Disclaimer

Course Technology reserves the right to revise this publication and make changes from time to time in its content without notice.

0-7600-6024-X

Printed in the United States of America

2 3 4 5 6 7 8 9 10 BM 02 01 00 99 98

Exciting New Illustrated Products

The Illustrated Projects® Series: The Quick, Visual Way to Apply Computer Skills

Looking for an inexpensive, easy way to supplement almost any application text and give your students the practice and tools they'll need to compete in today's competitive marketplace? Each text includes more than 50 real-world, useful projects—like creating a resume and setting up a loan worksheet—that let students hone their computer skills. These two-color texts have the same great two-page layout as the Illustrated Series.

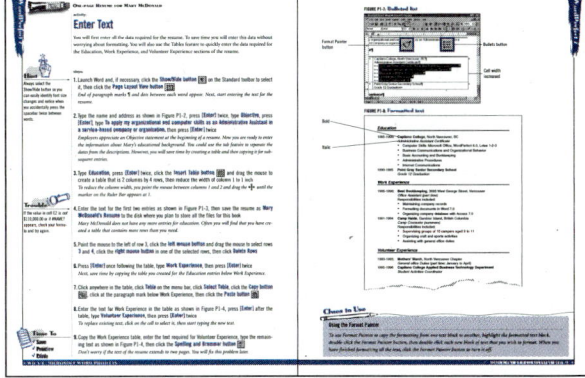

Illustrated Projects titles are available for the following applications:

- Microsoft Access
- Creating Web Sites
- Microsoft Excel
- World Wide Web
- Microsoft Office Professional
- Adobe PageMaker
- Microsoft Publisher
- Corel WordPerfect
- Microsoft Word

Illustrated Interactive® Series: The Safe, Simulated Way to Learn Computer Skills

The Illustrated Interactive Series uses multimedia technology to teach computer concepts and application skills. Students learn via a CD-ROM that simulates the actual software and provides a controlled learning environment in which every keystroke is monitored. Plus, all products in this series feature the same step-by-step instructions as the Illustrated Series. An accompanying workbook reinforces the skills that students learn on the CD.

Illustrated Interactive titles are available for the following applications:*

- Microsoft Office 97
- Microsoft Access 97
- Microsoft Word 97
- Microsoft PowerPoint 97
- Microsoft Excel 97
- Computer Concepts

*Standalone & networked versions available. Runs on Windows 3.1, 95, and NT. CD only version available for Computer Concepts and Office 97.

CourseKits™: Offering You the Freedom to Choose

Balance your course curriculum with Course Technology's mix-and-match approach to selecting texts. CourseKits provide you with the freedom to make choices from more than one series. When you choose any two or more Course Technology products for one course, we'll discount the price and package them together so your students pick up one convenient bundle at the bookstore.

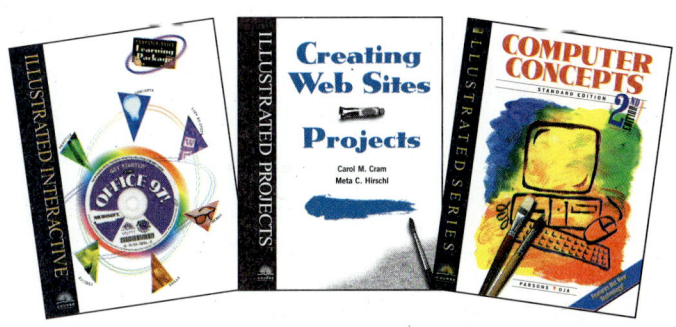

Contact your sales representative to find out more about these Illustrated products.

Preface

Welcome to *Microsoft Works 4/4.5 for Windows 95 — Illustrated Standard Edition*. This highly visual book offers new users a hands-on introduction to Microsoft Works 4 and 4.5 and also serves as an excellent reference for future use.

Organization and Coverage

Microsoft Works 4/4.5 for Windows 95 — Illustrated Standard Edition contains thirteen units that cover basic Works skills. In these units students learn how to design, build, edit, and enhance Works documents, spreadsheets, and databases. The book thoroughly covers Works wordprocessing, spreadsheet, charting, database, telecommunications, and draw features, as well as its integration capabilities. We've also added an Upgrader's Appendix which introduces students to the new features of Works 4.5.

Approach

What makes the Illustrated approach so effective at teaching software skills? It's quite simple. Each skill is presented on two facing pages, with the step-by-step instructions on the left page, and large screen illustrations on the right. Students can focus on a single skill without having to turn the page. This unique design makes information extremely accessible and easy to absorb, and provides a great reference for after the course is over. This hands-on approach also makes it ideal for both self-paced or instructor-led classes.

Lessons: Information Displays

The basic lesson format of this text is the "information display," a two-page lesson that is sharply focused on a specific task. This sharp focus and the precise beginning and end of a lesson make it easy for students to study specific material. Modular lessons are less overwhelming for students, and they provide instructors with more flexibility in planning classes and assigning specific work. The units are modular as well and can be presented in any order.

Each lesson, or "information display," contains the following elements:

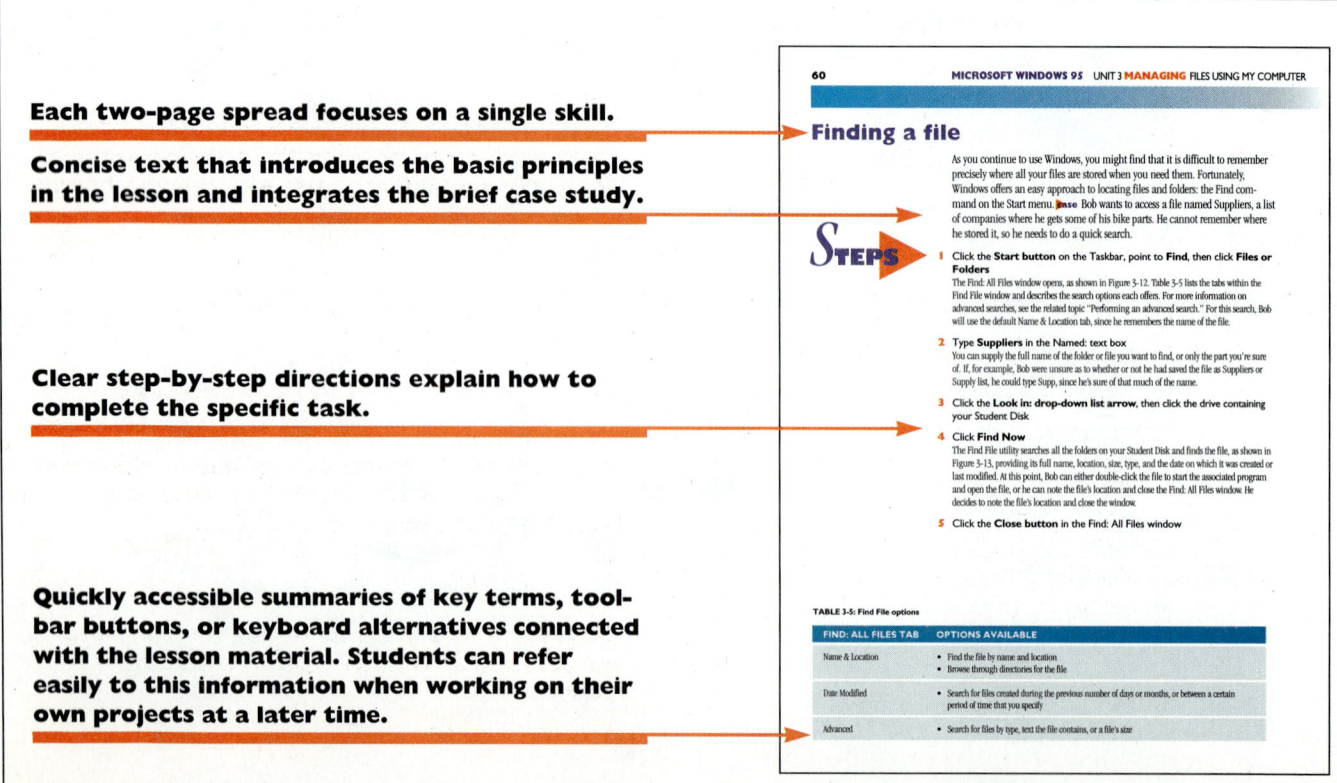

Each two-page spread focuses on a single skill.

Concise text that introduces the basic principles in the lesson and integrates the brief case study.

Clear step-by-step directions explain how to complete the specific task.

Quickly accessible summaries of key terms, toolbar buttons, or keyboard alternatives connected with the lesson material. Students can refer easily to this information when working on their own projects at a later time.

Additional Features

The two-page lesson format featured in this book provides the new user with a powerful learning experience. Additionally, this book contains the following features:

- "Read This Before You Begin Microsoft Works 4" page — This page provides essential information for both students and instructors.
- Windows 95 Overview — The Microsoft Windows 95 section provides an overview so students can begin working in the Windows environment right away.
- Real-World Case — The case study used throughout the textbook is designed to be "real-world" in nature and representative of the kinds of activities that students will encounter when working with Works. With a real-world case, the process of solving the problem will be more meaningful to students.
- CourseHelp — CourseHelp consists of interactive movies that help students to understand the major concepts in Works. A camera icon next to a lesson paragraph indicates that a CourseHelp movie is available.
- End-of-Unit Material — Each unit concludes with a Task Reference that summarizes the various methods used to execute each of the skills covered in the unit. The Task Reference is followed by a Concepts Review that tests students' understanding of what they learned in the unit. The Concepts Review is followed by a Skills Review, which provides students with additional hands-on practice of the skills they learned in the unit. The Skills Review is followed by Independent Challenges, which pose case problems for students to solve. The Independent Challenges allow students to learn by exploring, and develop critical thinking skills. Visual Workshop that follow the Independent Challenges also help students to develop critical thinking skills. Students are shown completed output and are asked to recreate it from scratch.

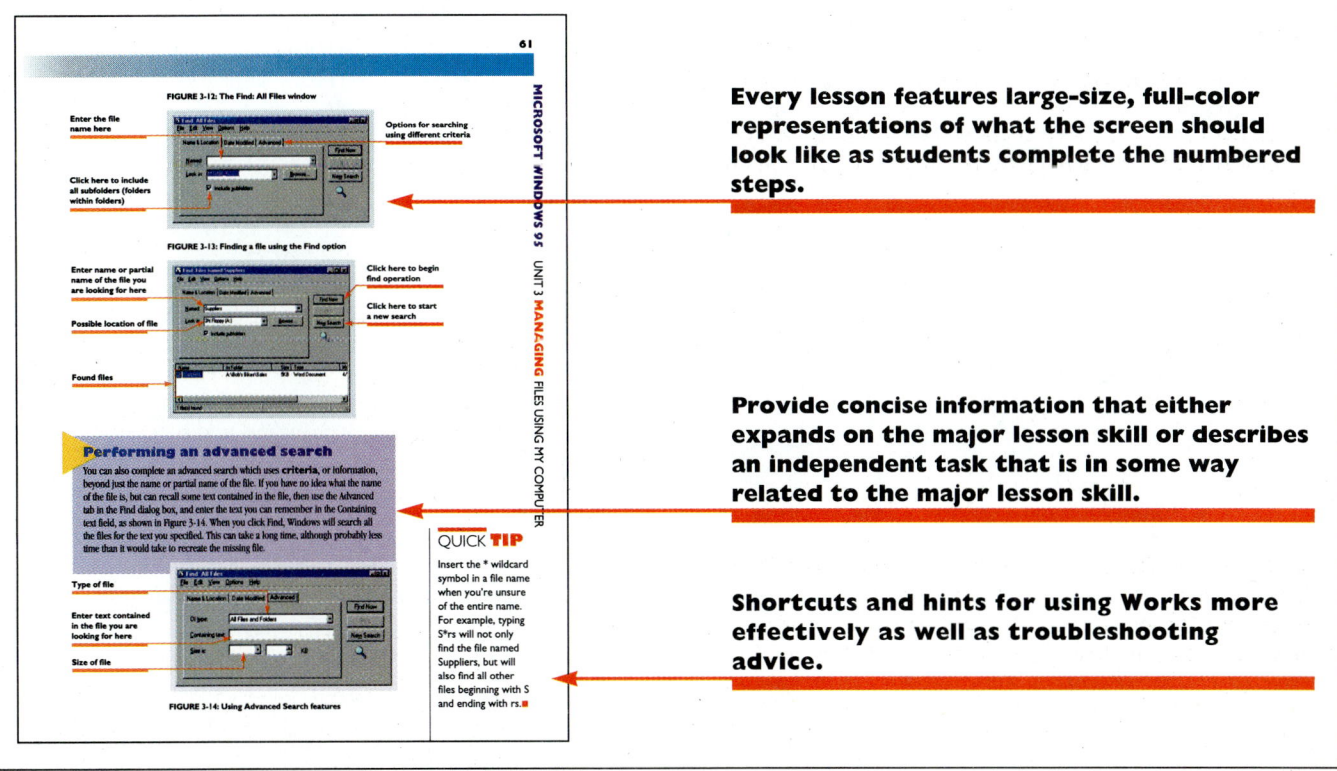

Instructor's Resource Kit

The Instructor's Resource Kit is Course Technology's way of putting the resources and information needed to teach and learn effectively into your hands. With an integrated array of teaching and learning tools that offer you and your students a broad range of instructional options, we believe this kit represents the highest quality and most cutting edge resources available to instructors today. Many of these resources are available at www.course.com. The resources available with this book are:

CourseHelp

CourseHelp is a student reinforcement tool offering online step-by-step annotated tutorials that are accessible directly from the Start menu in Windows 95. These on-screen "slide shows" help students understand the most difficult concepts in a specific application. Students are encouraged to view a CourseHelp before completing that lesson. This text includes the following CourseHelp slideshows:

- Moving and Copying Data
- Copying and Moving Cell Entries
- Displaying Data as a Chart
- Planning a Database
- Understanding Mail Merge

Student Disk

To use this book students must have a Student Disk. See the inside front or inside back cover for more information on the Student Disk. Adopters of this text are granted the right to post the Student Disk on any stand-alone computer or network.

www.course.com

We encourage students and instructors to visit our Web site at www.course.com to find articles about current teaching and software trends, featured texts, interviews with authors, demos of Course Technology's software, Frequently Asked Questions about our products, and much more. This site is also where you can gain access to the Faculty Online Companion for this text — see below for more information.

Course Online Faculty Companion

Available at www.course.com this World Wide Web site offers Course Technology customers a password-protected Faculty Lounge where you can find everything you need to prepare for class. These periodically updated items include lesson plans, solutions to end of unit material, additional problems, updates and revisions to the text, links to other Web sites, and access to Student Disk files. This site will continue to evolve throughout the semester. Contact your Customer Service Representative for the site address and password.

Instructor's Manual

Quality assurance tested and includes:

- Solutions to all lessons and end-of-unit material
- Detailed lecture topics with teaching tips
- Extra Independent Challenges
- Transparency Masters
- Student Files
- CourseHelp

Course Test Manager

Designed by Course Technology, this cutting edge Windows-based testing software helps instructors design, administer, and print tests and pre-tests. A full-featured program, Course Test Manager also has an online testing component that allows students to take tests at the computer and have their exams automatically graded.

Brief Contents

	From the Illustrated Series	v
	Preface	vi
	Microsoft Windows 95	W 1
	Read This Before You Begin Microsoft Windows 95	W 2
UNIT 1	Getting Started with Windows 95	W 3
UNIT 2	Managing Files, Folders, and Shortcuts	W 27
	Microsoft Works 4 for Windows 95	WK 1
	Read This Before You Begin Microsoft Works 4 for Windows 95	WK 2
UNIT 1	Getting Started with Microsoft Works 4 for Windows 95	WK 3
UNIT 2	Creating a Document with the Word Processor	WK 27
UNIT 3	Enhancing a Document's Appearance	WK 51
UNIT 4	Getting Started with Desktop Publishing	WK 73
UNIT 5	Building a Spreadsheet	WK 95
UNIT 6	Working with Spreadsheet Functions	WK 123
UNIT 7	Creating Charts with the Spreadsheet	WK 145
UNIT 8	Building a Database	WK 167
UNIT 9	Working with an Existing Database	WK 193
UNIT 10	Creating Database Reports	WK 217
UNIT 11	Exploring Telecommunications	WK 235
UNIT 12	Creating Illustrations with Draw	WK 255
UNIT 13	Combining Works Applications	WK 275
	Glossary	WK 293
APPENDIX	Upgrading to Microsoft Works 4.5	AP 1
	Glossary/Index	IN 1

Contents

	From the Illustrated Series	*v*
	Preface	*vi*
	Microsoft Windows 95	**W1**
	Read This Before You Begin *Microsoft Windows 95*	**W2**
UNIT 1	**Getting Started with Windows 95**	**W3**
	Starting Windows and viewing the desktop	W 4
	More about operating systems	W 5
	Using the mouse	W 6
	Starting a program	W 8
	Resizing a window	W 10
	More about sizing windows	W 11
	Using menus and toolbars	W 12
	Using dialog boxes	W 14
	Using scroll bars	W 16
	Getting Help	W 18
	More about Help	W 19
	Closing a program and shutting down Windows	W 20
	Closing programs and files with the Close button	W 21
	Task Reference	W 22
	Concepts Review	W 23
	Skills Review	W 24
	Independent Challenges	W 25
UNIT 2	**Managing Files, Folders, and Shortcuts**	**W 27**
	Formatting a disk	W 28
	Creating and saving a Paint file	W 30
	Working with multiple programs	W 34
	Understanding file management	W 36
	Viewing files and creating folders with My Computer	W 38
	Moving and copying files using My Computer	W 40
	Using Edit commands to copy and move files	W 41
	Viewing files and renaming folders with Windows Explorer	W 42
	Quick View	W 43
	Deleting and restoring files	W 44
	Important note about deleting files on a floppy disk	W 45
	Managing files on the desktop	W 46
	Adding shortcuts to the Start menu	W 47
	Task Reference	W 48
	Concepts Review	W 49
	Skills Review	W 52
	Independent Challenges	W 53

	Read This Before You Begin Microsoft Works 4 for Windows 95	WK 2
UNIT 1	**Getting Started with Microsoft Works 4 for Windows 95**	*WK 3*
	Starting Microsoft Works 4 for Windows 95	WK 4
	Starting a Works tool	WK 6
	Switching to other Windows programs	WK 7
	Using dialog boxes	WK 8
	Moving around a dialog box	WK 9
	Using toolbars	WK 10
	Using the Works Help system	WK 12
	Searching for specific topics	WK 13
	Using a TaskWizard	WK 14
	Saving a File	WK 16
	More about filenames	WK 17
	Closing a file and exiting Works	WK 18
	Task Reference	WK 20
	Concepts Review	WK 21
	Skills Review	WK 23
	Independent Challenges	WK 24
	Visual Workshop	WK 26
UNIT 2	**Creating a Document with the Word Processor**	*WK 27*
	Planning a document	WK 28
	Opening a file	WK 30
	Entering text in a document	WK 32
	Editing a document	WK 34
	Using the ruler	WK 35
	Moving text in a document	WK 36
	Viewing CourseHelp	WK 37
	Using the Spelling Checker	WK 38
	Using the Thesaurus	WK 39
	Viewing a document	WK 40
	Normal view vs. Page Layout view	WK 41
	Printing your document	WK 42
	Task Reference	WK 44
	Concepts Review	WK 45
	Skills Review	WK 46
	Independent Challenges	WK 48
	Visual Workshop	WK 50
UNIT 3	**Enhancing a Document's Appearance**	*WK 51*
	Changing font type and size	WK 52
	Where do fonts come from?	WK 53
	Changing font style	WK 54
	Changing alignment	WK 56
	Changing line spacing	WK 57
	Changing margin settings	WK 58
	Changing the paper source, size, and orientation	WK 59

	Changing paragraph style	WK 60
	Changing tab stops	WK 61
	Inserting manual page breaks	WK 62
	Inserting headers and footers	WK 64
	Task Reference	WK 66
	Concepts Review	WK 67
	Skills Review	WK 69
	Independent Challenges	WK 70
	Visual Workshop	WK 72
UNIT 4	**Getting Started with Desktop Publishing**	*WK 73*
	Creating multiple columns	WK 74
	Creating a multicolumn table	WK 75
	Placing borders around text	WK 76
	Inserting WordArt	WK 78
	Inserting ClipArt	WK 80
	Inserting footnotes	WK 82
	Printing endnotes	WK 83
	Replacing text	WK 84
	Using the find command	WK 85
	Verifying page layout and printing	WK 86
	Task Reference	WK 88
	Concepts Review	WK 89
	Skills Review	WK 90
	Independent Challenges	WK 92
	Visual Workshop	WK 94
UNIT 5	**Building a Spreadsheet**	*WK 95*
	Starting the Works Spreadsheet Tool	WK 96
	Entering numbers and labels	WK 98
	Saving your work	WK 100
	Using the Spelling Checker	WK 100
	Changing column width and row height	WK 102
	Dragging column and row borders	WK 103
	Using formulas	WK 104
	How Works calculates formulas	WK 105
	Editing the spreadsheet	WK 106
	Making changes with the Replace command	WK 107
	Changing alignment and number format	WK 108
	Changing the number format	WK 109
	Changing font and font style and adding borders	WK 110
	Adding shading to cells	WK 111
	Printing the spreadsheet	WK 112
	Adding headers and footers	WK 113
	Task Reference	WK 114
	Concepts Review	WK 115
	Skills Review	WK 117
	Independent Challenges	WK 119
	Visual Workshop	WK 122

UNIT 6	**Working with Spreadsheet Functions**	*WK 123*
	Learning about functions	WK 124
	Planning to use functions	WK 125
	Using the SUM function	WK 126
	Building formulas with the Easy Calc command	WK 127
	Using date and time functions	WK 128
	Using statistical functions	WK 130
	Mathematical functions	WK 131
	Using financial functions	WK 132
	Using the Mortgage and Loan Analysis TaskWizard	WK 133
	Using text functions	WK 134
	Sorting rows and printing	WK 136
	Sorting by more than one column	WK 137
	Task Reference	WK 138
	Concepts Review	WK 139
	Skills Review	WK 140
	Independent Challenges	WK 142
	Visual Workshop	WK 144
UNIT 7	**Creating Charts with the Spreadsheet**	*WK 145*
	Planning a chart	WK 146
	Creating a chart	WK 148
	Changing the chart type	WK 150
	Adding a subtitle and gridlines	WK 152
	Changing the chart legend	WK 153
	Changing fonts and colors	WK 154
	Pasting a spreadsheet table into the Word Processor	WK 156
	Working with tables in the Word Processor	WK 157
	Pasting a chart into the Word Processor	WK 158
	Establishing a link between documents	WK 159
	Task Reference	WK 160
	Concepts Review	WK 161
	Skills Review	WK 162
	Independent Challenges	WK 164
	Visual Workshop	WK 166
UNIT 8	**Building a Database**	*WK 167*
	Planning a database	WK 168
	Creating Fields	WK 170
	Building a data-entry form	WK 172
	Using the Customers or Clients TaskWizard	WK 173
	Entering data into fields	WK 174
	Adding records to the database	WK 176
	Working in List view	WK 177
	Editing data in fields	WK 178
	Managing fields	WK 180
	Changing the alignment in a field	WK 181
	Changing font size and style	WK 182
	Adding shading and borders to fields	WK 183

	Printing the database	WK 184
	Adding headers and footers	WK 185
	Task Reference	WK 186
	Concepts Review	WK 187
	Skills Review	WK 188
	Independent Challenges	WK 190
	Visual Workshop	WK 192
UNIT 9	**Working with an Existing Database**	***WK 193***
	Opening an existing database	WK 194
	Adding ClipArt to a database form	WK 196
	Working with ClipArt objects	WK 197
	Using field entries in formulas	WK 198
	Sorting database records	WK 200
	Filtering a database	WK 202
	Using advanced filters	WK 204
	Protecting a database	WK 206
	Printing envelopes from a database	WK 208
	Task Reference	WK 210
	Concepts Review	WK 211
	Skills Review	WK 212
	Independent Challenges	WK 214
	Visual Workshop	WK 216
UNIT 10	**Creating Database Reports**	***WK 217***
	Creating a new report	WK 218
	Adding summary information	WK 220
	Viewing a report in Print Preview	WK 222
	Editing in Report view	WK 224
	Printing a report	WK 226
	Opening an existing report	WK 227
	Task Reference	WK 228
	Concepts Review	WK 229
	Skills Review	WK 231
	Independent Challenges	WK 232
	Visual Workshop	WK 234
UNIT 11	**Exploring Telecommunications**	***WK 235***
	Planning a telecommunication session	WK 236
	What is a modem?	WK 237
	Starting the Communications tool	WK 238
	Setting communications parameters	WK 240
	What is baud rate?	WK 241
	Connecting to a remote computer	WK 242
	Searching an online database	WK 244
	Sending e-mail on the Internet	WK 246
	Ending your telecommunication session	WK 248
	Using the Easy Connect dialog box	WK 249

	Task Reference	WK 250
	Concepts Review	WK 251
	Skills Review	WK 252
	Independent Challenges	WK 253
	Visual Workshop	WK 254

UNIT 12 — Creating Illustrations with Draw — WK 255

Starting Draw	WK 256
Working with the Draw tools	WK 258
Creating a drawing	WK 260
Adding text to a drawing	WK 262
Saving and formatting a drawing	WK 264
Printing a drawing	WK 266
Editing ClipArt in Draw	WK 267
Task Reference	WK 268
Concepts Review	WK 269
Skills Review	WK 270
Independent Challenges	WK 271
Visual Workshop	WK 274

UNIT 13 — Combining Works Applications — WK 275

Creating a cover letter	WK 276
Inserting an illustration	WK 278
Inserting spreadsheet data	WK 280
Inserting database fields	WK 282
Printing a form letter	WK 284
Task Reference	WK 286
Concepts Review	WK 287
Skills Review	WK 288
Independent Challenges	WK 290
Visual Workshop	WK 292

APPENDIX — Upgrading to Microsoft Works 4.5 — AP 1

What's new in Works 4.5	AP 2
Find out more about Works 4.5 on the Works home page	AP 3
Using new Works templates	AP 4
Exploring new templates for civic and volunteer projects	AP 6
User Defined Templates help with planning and writing	AP 7
Exploring new templates for home and education productivity	AP 8
Exploring new clip art	AP 10
Learning about Internet Explorer	AP 12
Connecting to the Internet	AP 13
Practice using Internet Explorer	AP 14
The Works Forum	AP 14
Visual Workshop	AP 16

WINDOWS 95 TABLES

Table 1-1: Elements of the Windows desktop	W 4
Table 1-2: Common mouse pointer shapes	W 7
Table 1-3: Basic mouse techniques	W 7
Table 1-4: Start menu categories	W 8
Table 1-5: Common Windows Accessories	W 9
Table 1-6: Typical items on a menu	W 13
Table 1-7: Typical items in a dialog box	W 15
Table 1-8: Using scroll bars in a window	W 17
Table 2-1: Formatting options	W 29
Table 2-2: Paint Toolbox tools	W 31
Table 2-3: File/folder selection techniques	W 41

WORKS 4 TABLES

Table 1-1: Examples of documents you can create with Works	WK 4
Table 1-2: Interface elements common to all Works tools	WK 6
Table 1-3: Useful toolbar buttons and their functions	WK 11
Table 2-1: Elements in Word Processor document window	WK 31
Table 2-2: Useful keys for moving the insertion point around a document	WK 33
Table 2-3: Buttons found only on the Word Processor toolbar	WK 37
Table 3-1: Font and style formatting samples	WK 53
Table 3-2: Alignment icons on the toolbar	WK 57
Table 4-1: Keyboard shortcuts for selecting text blocks	WK 77
Table 5-1: Toolbar buttons unique to the Spreadsheet tool	WK 96
Table 5-2: Spreadsheet file formats included in the Save As Type list box	WK 101
Table 5-3: Methods for selecting spreadsheet cells	WK 103
Table 5-4: Useful mathematical operators	WK 105
Table 5-5: Useful Spreadsheet header and footer codes	WK 113
Table 6-1: Categories of Spreadsheet functions	WK 125
Table 6-2: Works date and time functions	WK 129
Table 6-3: Works statistical functions	WK 130
Table 6-4: Useful financial functions	WK 132
Table 6-5: Useful text functions	WK 135
Table 7-1: Chart types available in Works and common use of each	WK 147
Table 7-2: Common charting terms	WK 149
Table 7-3: Charting buttons on Chart Accessory toolbar	WK 151
Table 8-1: Field Formats	WK 171
Table 8-2: Toolbar buttons unique to the Database	WK 173
Table 8-3: Useful keys for working with database fields	WK 175
Table 8-4: Useful keys for editing text on the entry bar	WK 179
Table 9-1: Useful mathematical operators (listed in order of evaluation)	WK 199
Table 10-1 Statistical calculations available in database reports	WK 221
Table 11-1: Useful toolbar buttons	WK 238
Table 12-1: Drawing tools in the Draw accessory	WK 256
Table A-1: Overview of User Defined Templates	AP 5
Table A-2: Internet Explorer toolbar buttons	AP 13

Microsoft® Windows® 95

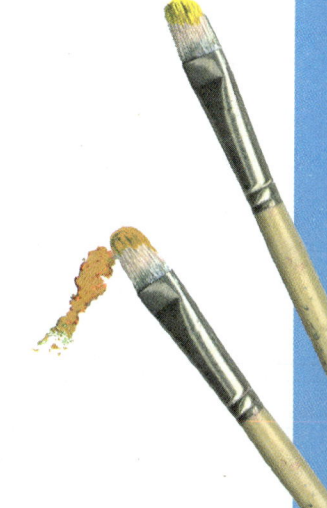

UNIT 1   **Getting Started with Windows 95**

UNIT 2   **Managing Files, Folders, and Shortcuts**

Read This Before You Begin
Microsoft Windows 95

To the Student

To complete the step-by-step lessons, Skills Reviews, and Independent Challenges in this book, you will need a blank, unformatted disk. Once this disk is formatted, it is referred to as the Work Disk. See your instructor or technical support person for further information.

Additional materials, designed especially for you are available on the World Wide Web. Go to http://www.vmedia.com/cti/.

Using Your Own Computer

If you are going to work through this book using your own computer, you need a computer system running Microsoft Windows 95 and a blank disk. *You will not be able to complete the step-by-step lessons in this book using your own computer until you have your own blank disk.*

To the Instructor

To complete the step-by-step lessons, Skills Reviews, and Independent Challenges in this book, your students must have a blank, unformatted disk. After they format this disk, it is referred to as the Work Disk.

The instructions in this book assume a standard installation of Microsoft Windows 95. It is also assumed that the students know which drive and directory contain the Work Disk. It's important that you provide disk location information before the students start working through the units.

UNIT 1

OBJECTIVES

- Start Windows and view the desktop
- Use the mouse
- Start a program
- Resize a window
- Use menus and toolbars
- Use dialog boxes
- Use scroll bars
- Get Help
- Close a program and shut down Windows

Getting Started
WITH WINDOWS 95

Microsoft Windows 95 is an **operating system** that controls the basic operation of your computer and the programs you run on it. Windows has a **graphical user interface** (GUI) which means you can use pictures (called **icons**) in addition to words to carry out tasks and operations. Windows 95 also helps you organize the results of your work (saved as **files**) and coordinates the flow of information among the programs, files, printers, storage devices, and other components of your computer system. ▶ This unit introduces you to basic skills that you can use in all Windows programs. ▶

Starting Windows and viewing the desktop

Microsoft Windows 95 is an operating system designed to help you get the most out of your computer. For more information about operating systems, see the related topic "More about operating systems." You can use Windows 95 to run **programs**, also known as **applications**, which are software tools you use to accomplish tasks. When you first start Windows, you see the **desktop**, which is the area on your screen where you organize your computer work. See Figure 1-1. The small pictures you see on the desktop are called icons. Icons represent a program you use to carry out a task, or a document, or a set of files or documents. The **My Computer** icon represents a program you use to organize the files on your computer. The **Recycle Bin** icon represents a storage area for deleted files. Below the desktop is the **taskbar**, which shows you the programs that are running (at the moment, none are running). At the left end of the taskbar is the **Start button**, which you use to start programs, find files, access Windows Help and more. Use Table 1-1 to identify the icons and other key elements you see on your desktop. ▶ If Windows 95 is not currently running, follow the steps below to start it now.

1. **Turn on your computer and monitor**
   Windows automatically starts, and the desktop appears as shown in Figure 1-1. If you are working on a network at school or at an office, you might see a password dialog box. If so, continue to step 2.

2. **Type your password, then press [Enter]**
   If you don't know your password, see your instructor. Once the password is accepted, the Windows desktop appears on your screen, as shown in Figure 1-1.

TABLE 1-1: Elements of the Windows desktop

DESKTOP ELEMENT	DESCRIPTION
Icon	Picture representing a task you can carry out, a program you can run, or a document
Mouse pointer	Arrow indicating the current location of the mouse on the desktop
Taskbar	Area that identifies any programs currently open (that is, running); by default, the taskbar is always visible
Start button	Provides main access to all Windows operations and programs available on the computer

FIGURE 1-1: Windows desktop

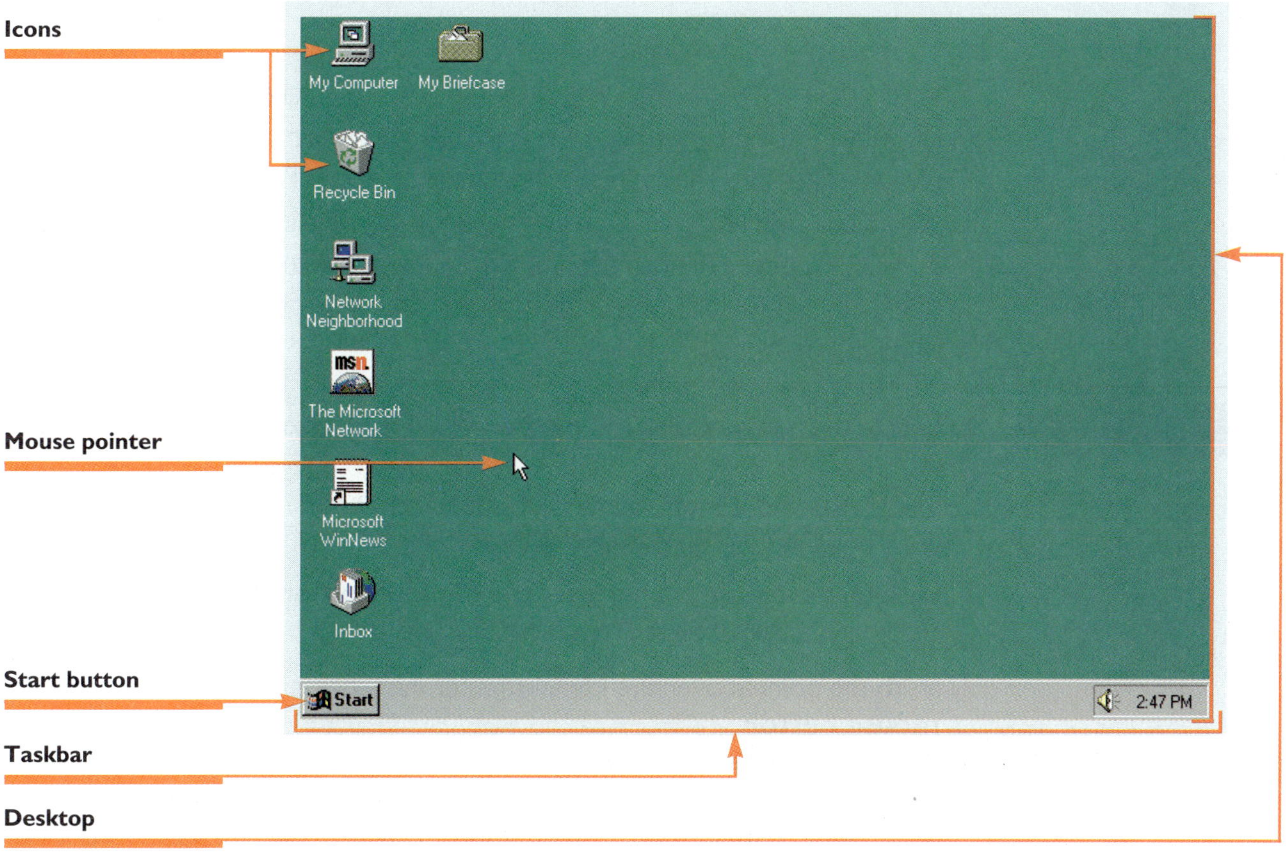

Icons

Mouse pointer

Start button

Taskbar

Desktop

WINDOWS 95 UNIT 1 **GETTING STARTED**

More about operating systems

Windows 95 is one of several operating systems. The operating system you use depends to some degree on the kind of computer you are using. For example, an Apple Macintosh computer uses an operating system that only runs on Macintosh computers. Other computers might run other operating systems such as UNIX and OS/2. Each operating system has its own unique features and benefits, causing different user communities to prefer one over the others based on their computing needs. Before Windows, many personal computers ran an operating system called MS-DOS. This character-based operating system required that you enter commands very carefully when you used the computer. With the development of Windows (and more powerful computers), personal computers can now run programs that take advantage of a graphical user interface. As a result computers have become easier to use.

Using the mouse

The **mouse** is a handheld input device that you roll on a smooth surface (such as your desk or a mousepad) to position the mouse pointer on the Windows desktop. When you move the mouse, the **mouse pointer** on the screen moves in the same direction. The buttons on the mouse, shown in Figure 1-2, are used to select icons and commands. You also use the mouse to select options and identify the work to be done in programs. Table 1-2 shows some common mouse pointer shapes. Table 1-3 lists the five basic mouse actions. ▶ Begin by experimenting with the mouse now.

1. **Locate the mouse pointer ⌁ on the Windows desktop and then move the mouse across your desk**
   Watch how the mouse pointer moves on the desktop in response to your movements. Practice moving the mouse pointer in circles, and then back and forth in straight lines.

2. **Position the mouse pointer over the My Computer icon**
   Positioning the mouse pointer over an icon is called **pointing**.

3. **With the pointer over the My Computer icon, press and release the left mouse button**
   Unless otherwise indicated, you will use the left mouse button to perform all mouse operations. Pressing and releasing the mouse button is called **clicking**. When you position the mouse pointer over an icon and then click, you **select** the icon. When an icon is selected, both it and its title are highlighted. Practice moving an icon by **dragging** it with the mouse.

4. **With the icon selected, press and hold down the left mouse button, then move the mouse down and to the right and release the mouse button**
   The icon becomes dimmed and moves with the mouse pointer. When you release the mouse button, the icon relocates on the desktop. Next, you will use the mouse to display a pop-up menu.

5. **Position the mouse pointer over the My Computer icon, then press and release the right mouse button**
   Clicking the right mouse button is known as **right-clicking**. Right-clicking an item on the desktop displays a **pop-up menu**, as shown in Figure 1-3. This menu displays the commands most commonly used for the item you have clicked.

6. **Click anywhere outside the menu to close the pop-up menu**
   Now use the mouse to open a window.

7. **Position the mouse pointer over the My Computer icon, then press and release the left mouse button twice quickly**
   Clicking the mouse button twice quickly is known as **double-clicking**. Double-clicking this icon opens a window. The My Computer window displays additional icons that represent the drives and system components that are installed on your computer.

8. **Click the Close button ☒ in the upper-right corner of the My Computer window**

FIGURE 1-2: The mouse

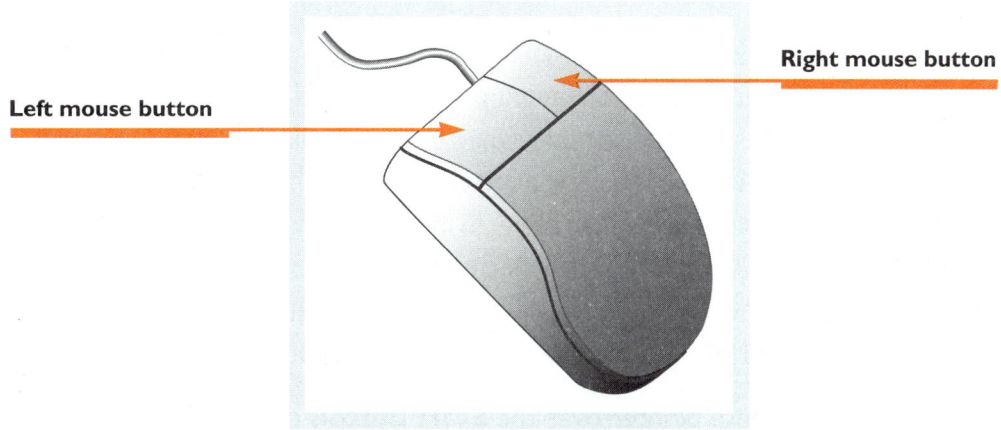

FIGURE 1-3: Displaying a pop-up menu

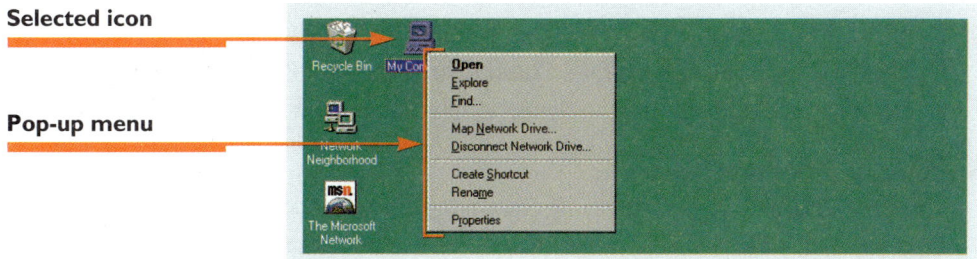

TABLE 1-2: Common mouse pointer shapes

SHAPE	USED TO
▷	Select items, choose commands, start programs, and work in programs
I	Position mouse pointer for editing or inserting text; called the insertion point or cursor
⧖	Indicate Windows is busy processing a command
↔	Change the size of a window; appears when mouse pointer is on the border of a window

TABLE 1-3: Basic mouse techniques

TECHNIQUE	WHAT TO DO
Pointing	Move the mouse to position the mouse pointer over an item on the desktop
Clicking	Press and release the left mouse button
Double-clicking	Press and release the left mouse button twice quickly
Dragging	Point to an item, press and hold the left mouse button, move the mouse to a new location, then release the mouse button
Right-clicking	Point to an item, then press the right mouse button

Starting a program

Clicking the Start button on the taskbar displays the all-important Start menu. You use the Start menu to start a program, find a file, or display help information. Table 1-4 describes the **default** categories of items available on this menu that are installed with Windows 95. As you become more familiar with Windows you might want to customize the Start menu to include additional items that you use most often. ▶ Begin by starting the **WordPad** program, an Accessory that comes with Windows 95. You can use WordPad to create and edit simple documents. See Table 1-5 for a description of other popular Windows Accessories.

1. **Position the mouse pointer over the Start button on the taskbar, then click**
   The Start menu appears. Next, you need to open the Programs submenu.

2. **Point to Programs**
   An arrow next to a menu item indicates a **cascading menu**. Pointing at the arrow displays a submenu from which you can choose additional commands, as shown in Figure 1-4.

3. **Point to Accessories**
   This is the Accessories menu, containing several programs to help you complete day-to-day tasks. You want to Start WordPad, which should be at the bottom of the list.

4. **Click WordPad**
   The WordPad program opens and a blank document window appears, as shown in Figure 1-5. WordPad is a simple word processor provided with Windows 95 that you can use to write and edit documents. Note that when a program is open, a program button appears on the taskbar indicating that it is open. An indented button indicates the program that is currently active. Leave the WordPad window open for now, and continue to the next lesson.

TABLE 1-4: Start menu categories

CATEGORY	DESCRIPTION
Programs	Opens programs included on the Start menu
Documents	Opens documents most recently opened and saved
Settings	Allows user preferences for system settings, including control panels, printers, Start menu, and taskbar
Find	Locates programs, files, and folders not included on the Start menu
Help	Displays Windows Help information by topic, alphabetical index, or search criteria
Run	Opens a program or file based on a location and filename that you type or select
Shut Down	Provides options to shut down the computer, restart the computer in Windows mode, restart the computer in MS-DOS mode, or log on to the system as a different user

FIGURE 1-4: Cascading menus

Arrow indicates cascading menu will open

Cascading menus

WordPad program

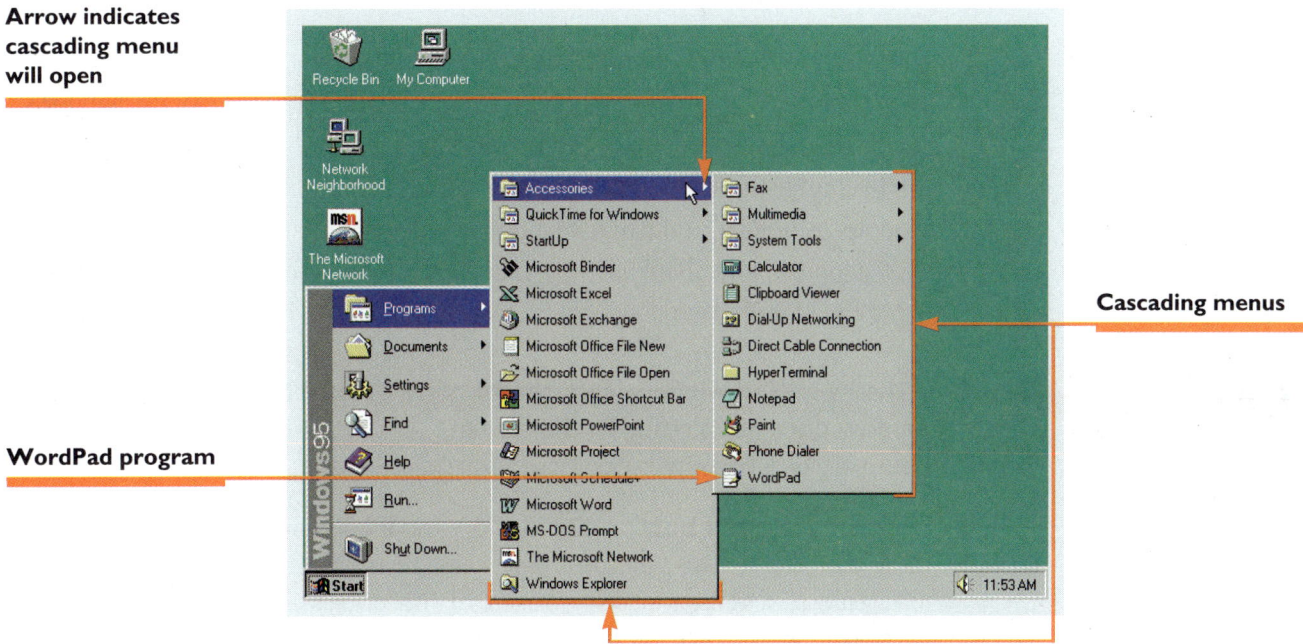

FIGURE 1-5: WordPad document window

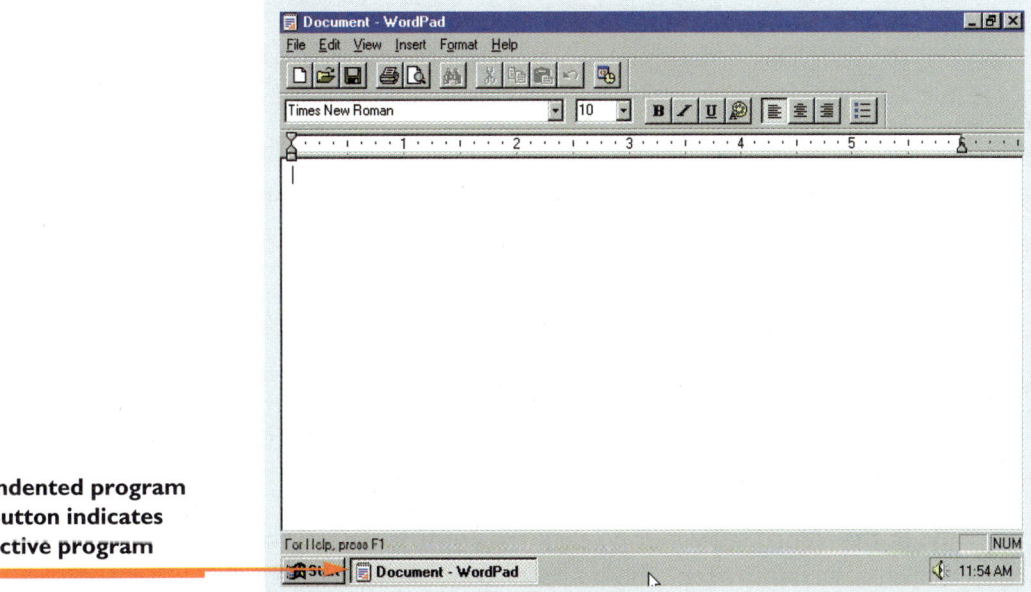

Indented program button indicates active program

TABLE 1-5: Common Windows Accessories

ACCESSORY	DESCRIPTION
Calculator	Use to add, subtract, divide, and multiply numbers
Paint	Use to draw and edit graphic images
WordPad	Use to create and edit documents

Resizing a window

The Windows desktop can quickly get cluttered with icons and windows. One of the ways to keep your desktop organized is by changing the size of the windows. Each window is surrounded by a standard border and sizing buttons that allow you to change the size of windows by minimizing, maximizing, and restoring windows as needed. You can also drag a window's border to size it. See the related topic "More about sizing windows" for more information. ▶ Practice sizing the WordPad window now.

1. **In the WordPad window, click the Maximize button, if the WordPad window does not already fill the screen**
   When a window is **maximized**, it takes up the whole screen.

2. **Click the Restore button in the WordPad window**
   The Restore button returns a window to its previous size, as shown in Figure 1-6. The Restore button only appears when a window is maximized. In addition to minimizing, maximizing, and restoring windows, you can also change the dimensions of any window. Next, experiment with changing the dimensions of the WordPad window.

3. **Position the pointer on the right edge of the WordPad window until the pointer changes to ⇔, then drag to the right**
   The width of the window increases. You can size the height and width of a window by dragging any of the four sides individually. You can also size the height and width of the window simultaneously by dragging the corner of the window.

4. **Position the pointer in the lower-right corner of the WordPad window, as indicated in Figure 1-6, then drag down and to the right**
   The height and width of the window are increased at the same time. You can also position a restored window wherever you wish on the desktop by dragging its title bar.

5. **Click the title bar on the WordPad window and drag up and to the left**
   The window is repositioned on the desktop. At times, you might wish to close a program's window, yet keep the program running and easily accessible. You can accomplish this by minimizing a window.

6. **In the WordPad window, click the Minimize button**
   When you **minimize** a window, it shrinks to a program button on the taskbar, as shown in Figure 1-7. The WordPad program is still open and running; however, it is not active.

7. **Click the WordPad program button on the taskbar to restore the window to its previous size**
   The WordPad program is now **active**; this means that any actions you perform will take place in this window. Next, return the window to its full size.

8. **Click the Maximize button in the upper-right corner of the WordPad window**
   The window fills the screen. Leave the WordPad window maximized and continue with the next lesson.

FIGURE 1-6: Restored WordPad window

Title bar

Sizing buttons

Drag here to size both height and width

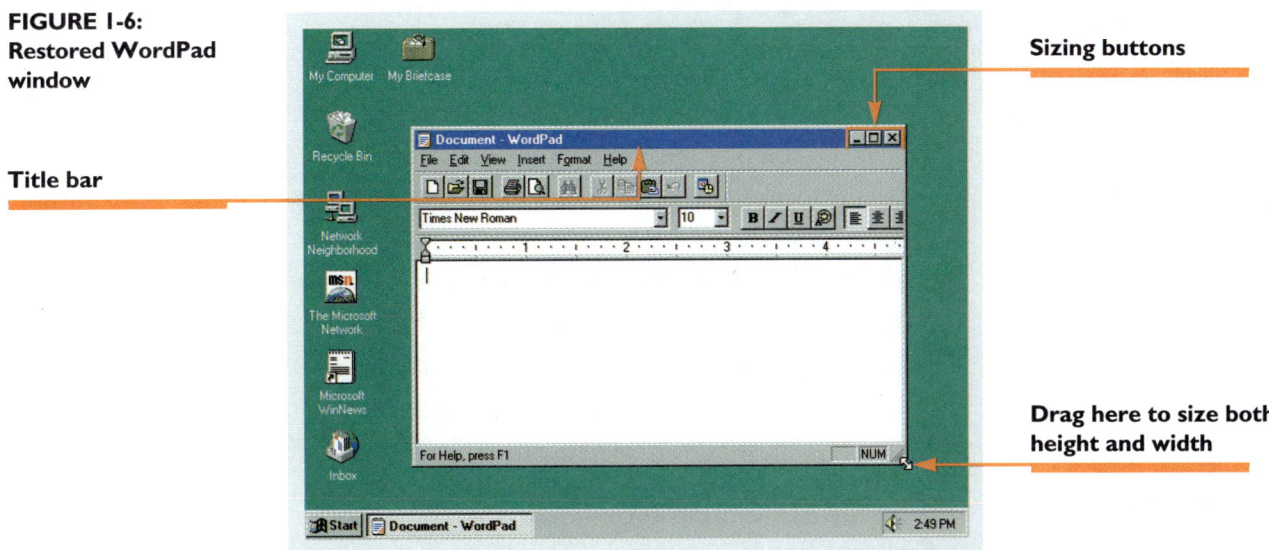

FIGURE 1-7: Minimized WordPad window

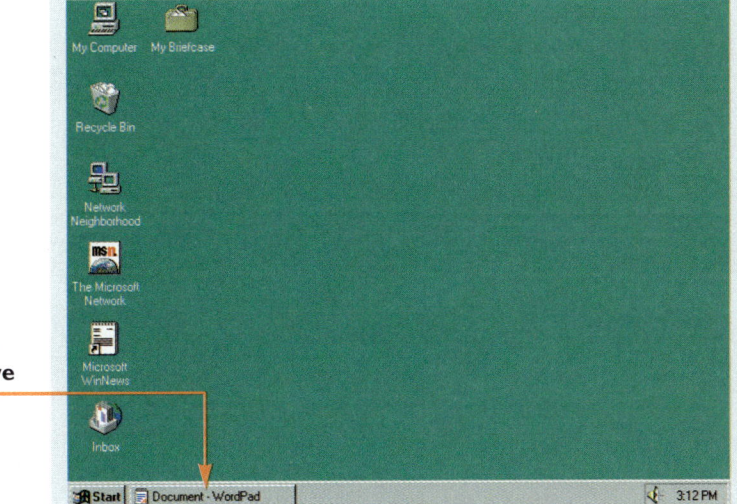

Indicates program is running but not active

More about sizing windows

Many programs contain two sets of sizing buttons: one that controls the program window itself and another that controls the file which can be a document, spreadsheet, database, or presentation window within the program. The program sizing buttons are located in the title bar; the file sizing buttons are located below them in the menu bar. See Figure 1-8. When you minimize a file window within a program, the file window is reduced to an icon in the lower-left corner of the program window. The size of the program window remains intact.

Program window sizing buttons

File window sizing buttons

FIGURE 1-8: Program and file window sizing buttons

Using menus and toolbars

A **menu** is a list of commands that you use to accomplish certain tasks. You've already used the Start menu to start WordPad. Each Windows program also has its own set of menus, which are located on the **menu bar** along the top of the program window. The menus organize commands into groups of related operations. See Table 1-6 for examples of what you might see on a typical menu. Some of the commands found on a menu can also be carried out by clicking a button on a **toolbar**. Toolbar buttons provide you with convenient shortcuts for completing tasks. ▶ Open the Control Panel program, then use a menu and toolbar button to change how the window's contents are displayed.

1. **Click the Start button on the taskbar, point to Settings, and then click Control Panel**
   The Control Panel window contains icons for various programs that allow you to specify your preferences for how your computer environment looks and performs.

2. **Click View on the menu bar**
   The View menu appears, displaying the View commands, as shown in Figure 1-9. When you click a menu name, a general description of the commands available on that menu appears in the **status bar**. On a menu, a check mark identifies a feature that is currently selected (that is, the feature is **enabled**). To disable the feature, you click the command again to remove the check mark. A bullet mark can also indicate that an option is enabled. To disable this option, however, you must select another option in its place. In the next step, you will select a command.

3. **On the View menu, click Small Icons**
   The icons are now smaller than they were before, taking up less room in the window. You can also use the keyboard to access menu commands. Next, open the View menu by pressing [Alt] on the keyboard and then the underlined letter of the menu on the menu bar.

4. **Press and hold [Alt], then press [V] to open the View menu, then release both keys**
   The View menu appears. Notice that a letter in each command is underlined. You can select these commands by pressing the underlined letter. Now, select a command using the keyboard.

5. **Press [T] to select the Toolbar command**
   The Control Panel toolbar appears below the menu bar. This toolbar includes buttons for the commands that you use most frequently while you are in the Control Panel program. When you position the mouse pointer over a button, the name of the button – called a **ToolTip** – is displayed. Pressing a button displays a description of the button in the status bar. Use the ToolTip feature to explore a button on the toolbar.

6. **On the Control Panel toolbar, position the pointer over the Details button ▦, as shown in Figure 1-10, then click**
   See the TROUBLE? on the next page if you don't see a Details button. The Details view includes a description of each Control Panel program. If you were to click the View menu now, you would see that the Details command is now checked.

FIGURE 1-9: View menu on Control Panel menu bar

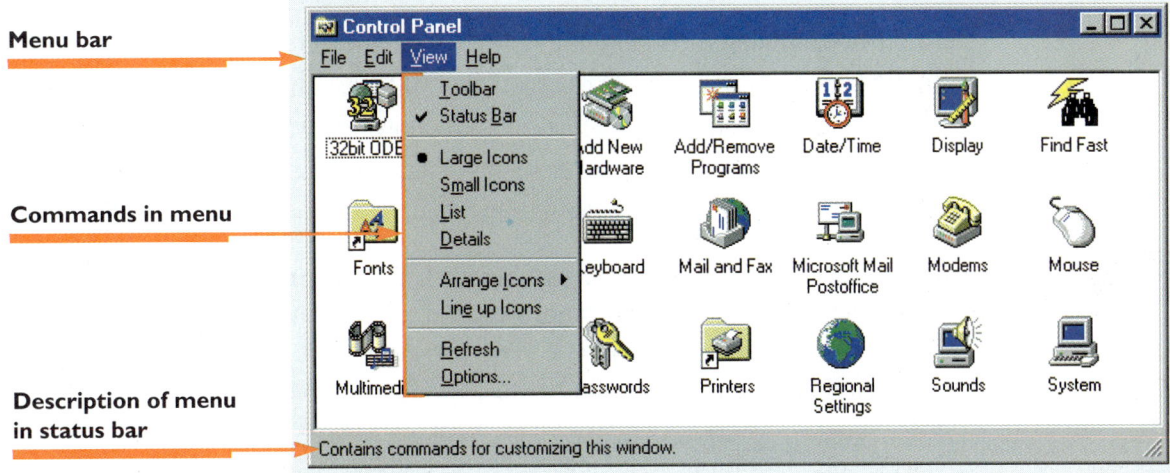

- Menu bar
- Commands in menu
- Description of menu in status bar

FIGURE 1-10: Control Panel toolbar

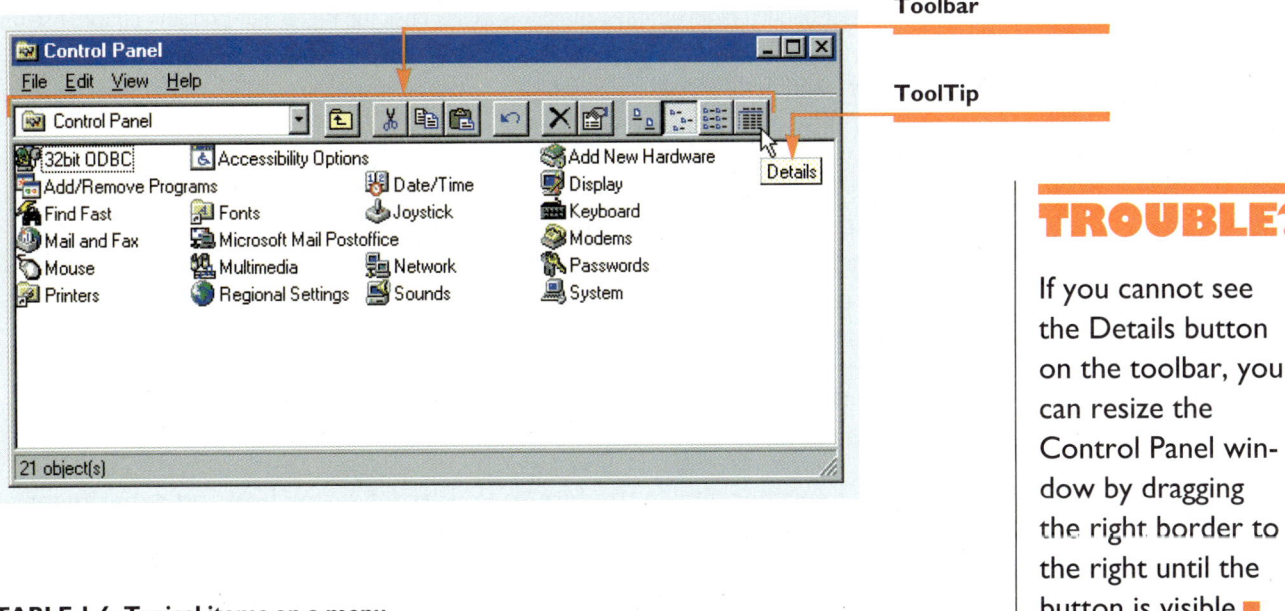

- Toolbar
- ToolTip

TROUBLE?

If you cannot see the Details button on the toolbar, you can resize the Control Panel window by dragging the right border to the right until the button is visible.■

TABLE 1-6: Typical items on a menu

ITEM	DESCRIPTION	EXAMPLE
Dimmed command	A menu command that is not currently available	Line up Icons
Ellipsis	Choosing this menu command opens a dialog box that allows you to select different or additional options	Options...
Triangle	Choosing this menu command opens a cascading menu containing an additional list of menu commands	Arrange Icons ▶
Keyboard shortcut	A keyboard alternative for executing a menu command	Select All Ctrl+A
Underlined letter	Pressing the underlined letter executes the menu command	Refresh

Using dialog boxes

A command from a menu that is followed by an ellipsis (...) requires more information before it can complete its task. When you select this type of command a **dialog box** opens for you to specify the options you want. See Figure 1-11 and Table 1-7 for some of the typical elements of a dialog box. ▶ Practice using a dialog box to control your mouse settings.

1. In the Control Panel window, double-click the **Mouse icon** (you might need to resize the Control Panel window to find this icon)
   The Mouse Properties dialog box opens, as shown in Figure 1-12. The options in this dialog box allow you to control the way the mouse buttons are configured, select the types of pointers that are displayed, choose the speed of the mouse movement on the screen, and specify what type of mouse you are using. **Tabs** at the top of the dialog box separate these options into related categories.

2. Click the **Buttons tab** if it is not the frontmost tab, then in the Button configuration area click the **Left-handed radio button** to select it
   If the Left-handed radio button is already selected, click the Right-handed radio button. Use this option to specify which button is primary (controls the normal operations) and which is secondary (controls the special functions, such as context-sensitive pop-up menus). Next, select an option which shows pointer trails when you move the mouse.

3. Click the **Motion tab**, then in the Pointer trail area click the **Show pointer trails** check box to select it
   This option makes the mouse pointer easier to see on certain types of computer screens such as laptop computers. The slider feature, located below the check box, lets you specify the degree to which the option is in effect, in this case, the length of the pointer trail.

4. Drag the **slider** below the check box all the way to the right
   As you move the mouse, notice the longer pointer trails.

5. Click the other tabs in the Mouse Properties dialog box and experiment with the options that are available in each category
   Finally, you need to select a command button to carry out the options you've selected. The two most common command buttons are OK and Cancel. Clicking OK accepts your changes and closes the dialog box; clicking Cancel leaves the settings intact and closes the dialog box. The third command button in this dialog box is Apply. Clicking the Apply button accepts the changes you've made and keeps the dialog box open so that you can select additional options. Because you might share this computer with others, it's important to return the dialog box options back to the original settings.

6. Click **Cancel** to leave the original settings intact and close the dialog box

FIGURE 1-11: Dialog box elements

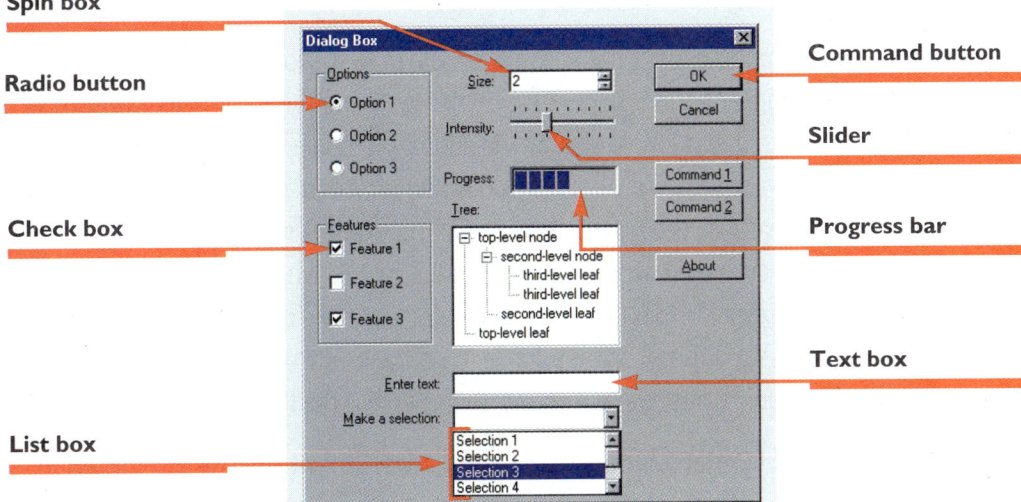

- Spin box
- Radio button
- Check box
- List box
- Command button
- Slider
- Progress bar
- Text box

FIGURE 1-12: Mouse Properties dialog box

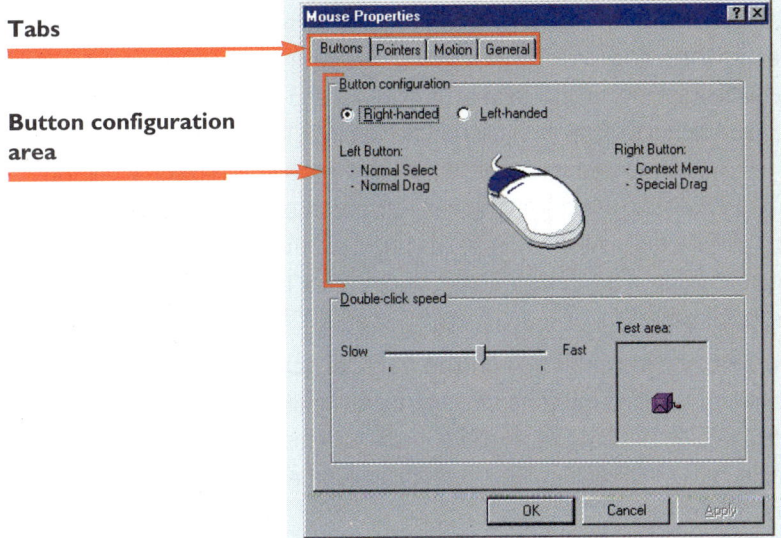

- Tabs
- Button configuration area

QUICK TIP

You can also use the keyboard to carry out commands in a dialog box. Pressing [Enter] is the same as clicking OK; pressing [Esc] is the same as clicking Cancel.

TABLE 1-7: Typical items in a dialog box

ITEM	DESCRIPTION	ITEM	DESCRIPTION
Check box	Clicking this square box turns a dialog box option on or off	List box	A box containing a list of items; to choose an item, click the list arrow, then click the desired item
Text box	A box in which you type text	Spin box	Allows you to scroll or type numerical increments
Radio button	Clicking this small circle selects a single dialog box option	Slider	Allows you to set the degree to which an option is in effect
Command button	Clicking this button carries out a command in a dialog box	Progress bar	Indicates how much of a task is completed

Using scroll bars

When you cannot see all of the items available in a window, scroll bars will appear on the right and/or bottom edges of the window. Using the scroll bars, you can move around in a window to display the additional contents of the window. There are several ways you can scroll in a window. When you need to scroll only a short distance, you can use the scroll arrows. Clicking in the scroll bar above or below the scroll box scrolls the window in larger increments, while dragging the scroll bar moves you quickly to a new part of the window. See Table 1-8 for a summary of the different ways to use scroll bars. ▶ With the Control Panel window in the Details view, you can use the scroll bars to view all of the items in this window.

1. **In the Control Panel window, click the down scroll arrow, as shown in Figure 1-13**
   Clicking this arrow moves the view down one line. Clicking the up arrow moves the view up one line at a time. So that you can better explore other scrolling features in this lesson, you will resize the window to show fewer items.

2. **Drag the bottom border of the Control Panel window up so that only 6 or 7 items appear in the window**
   Notice that the scroll box appears smaller than in the previous step. The size of the scroll box changes to reflect the amount of items available, but not displayed in a window. For example, a larger scroll box indicates that a relatively small amount of the window's contents is not currently visible; therefore you need to scroll only a short distance to see the remaining items. A smaller scroll box indicates that a relatively large amount of information is currently not visible. To see the additional contents of the resized window, you can click in the area below the scroll box in the vertical scroll bar.

3. **Click the area below the scroll box in the vertical scroll bar**
   The view moves down one window full of information; for example, you see another 6 or 7 items further down in the window. Similarly, you can click in the scroll bar above the scroll box to move up one window full of information. Next, you will display the information that appears at the very bottom of the window.

4. **Drag the scroll box all the way down to the bottom of the vertical scroll bar**
   The view displays the items that appear at the very bottom of the window. Similarly, you can drag the scroll box to the top of the scroll bar to display the information that appears at the top of the window.

5. **Drag the scroll box all the way up to the top of the vertical scroll bar**
   This view displays the items that appear at the top of the window. Next, you will explore the horizontal scroll bar, so you can see all of the icons near the right edge of the window.

6. **Click the area to the right of the scroll box in the horizontal scroll bar**
   The far right edge of the window comes into view. Next, you will redisplay the left edge of the window.

7. **Click the area to the left of the scroll box in the horizontal scroll bar**

8. **Resize the Control Panel window so that the scroll bars no longer appear**

FIGURE 1-13: Control Panel window in Details view

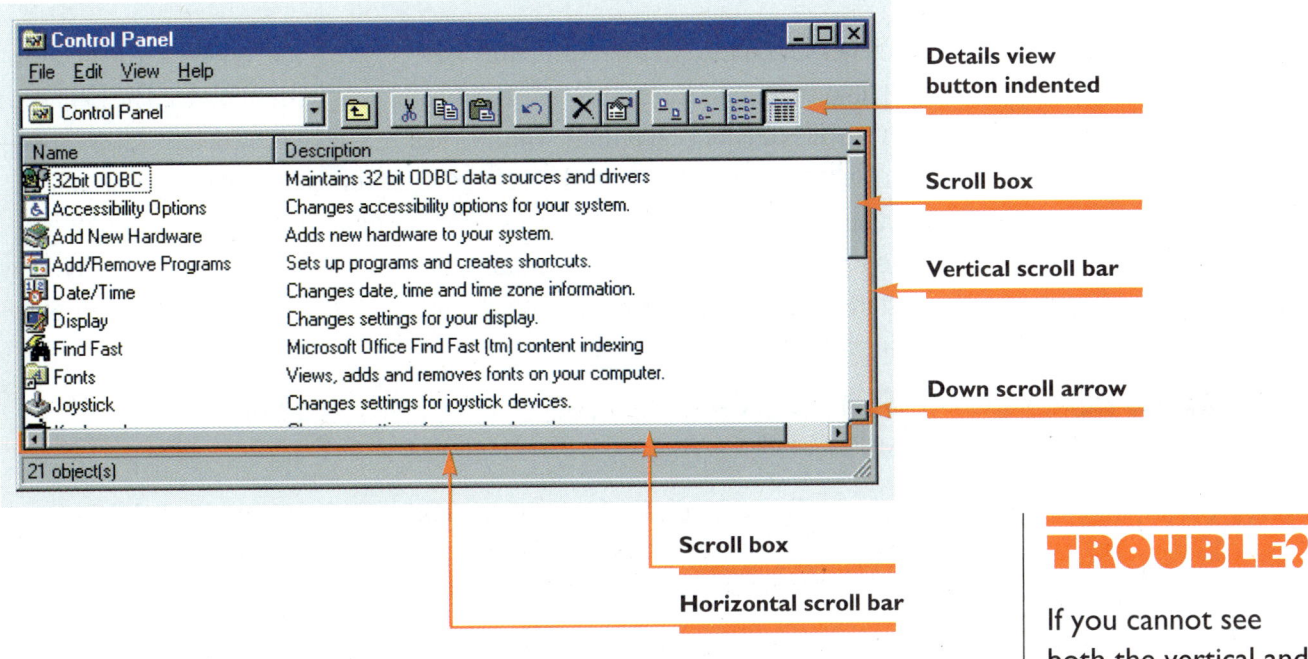

TROUBLE?

If you cannot see both the vertical and horizontal scroll bars, make the window smaller (both shorter and narrower) until both scroll bars appear. ■

TABLE 1-8: Using scroll bars in a window

TO	DO THIS
Move down one line	Click the down arrow at the bottom of the vertical scroll bar
Move up one line	Click the up arrow at the top of the vertical scroll bar
Move down one window	Click in the area below the scroll box in the vertical scroll bar
Move up one window	Click in the area above the scroll box in the vertical scroll bar
Move up a greater distance in the window	Drag the scroll box up in the vertical scroll bar
Move down a greater distance in the window	Drag the scroll box down in the vertical scroll bar
Move a short distance side to side in a window	Click the left or right arrows in the horizontal scroll bar
Move to the right one screenful	Click in the area to the right of the scroll box in the horizontal scroll bar
Move to the left one screenful	Click in the area to the left of the scroll box in the horizontal scroll bar
Move left or right a greater distance in the window	Drag the scroll box in the horizontal scroll bar

Getting Help

Windows 95 comes with a powerful online Help system that allows you to obtain help information in several ways, depending on your current needs. The Help system provides guidance on many Windows features, including detailed steps for completing a procedure, definitions of terms, lists of related topics, and search capabilities. You can also receive assistance in a dialog box; see the related topic "More about Help" for more information. ▶ In this lesson, you'll get Help on how to start a program. You'll also get information on the taskbar. You start the online Help system from the Start menu.

1. **Click the Start button on the taskbar, then click Help**
   The Help Topics dialog box opens, as shown in Figure 1-14. Verify that the Contents tab is selected.

2. **Click the Contents tab if it isn't the frontmost tab, double-click How To...** in the list box, then double-click **Run Programs**
   The Help window displays a selection of topics related to running programs.

3. **Click Starting a program, then click Display**
   A Windows Help window opens. At the bottom of the window, you can click the Related Topics button to display a list of topics that may also be of interest. Some help topics also allow you to display additional information about important words; these words are identified with a dotted underline.

4. **Click the dotted underlined word taskbar**
   A pop-up window appears with a definition of the underlined word.

5. **Read the definition, then click anywhere outside the pop-up window to close it**

6. **Click the Help Topics button to return to the Help Topics window**
   You can use the Find tab to search for a specific word or phrase for which you want to display help topics. As you type the word or phrase in the first list box, any available words that match appear in the second list box. In the next step, search for help topics on the word "taskbar."

7. **Click the Find tab, then in the first list box, type taskbar**
   Two word matches are displayed in the second list box, as shown in Figure 1-15. The third list box displays help topics related to the selected word.

8. **In the third list box, click Customizing the taskbar or Start menu, then click Display**
   The Help window that appears lists the steps for completing this task. Close the Windows Help window for now.

9. **In the Windows Help window, click the Close button ☒ in the upper-right corner of the window**
   Clicking the Close button closes the active window.

FIGURE 1-14: Help Topics dialog box

Click this tab to display an alphabetical index of Help topics

Click this tab to search for words and phrases in the Help topics

Prints contents of help topic on a printer connected to your computer

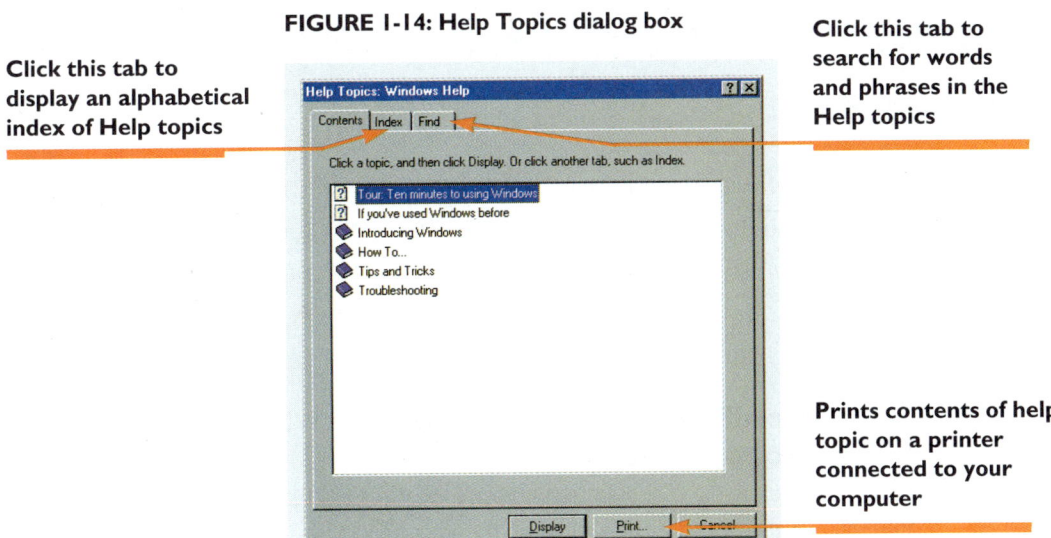

FIGURE 1-15: Find tab in Help Topics dialog box

Type the word you are searching for here

Lists word matches

Lists the help topics for word matches

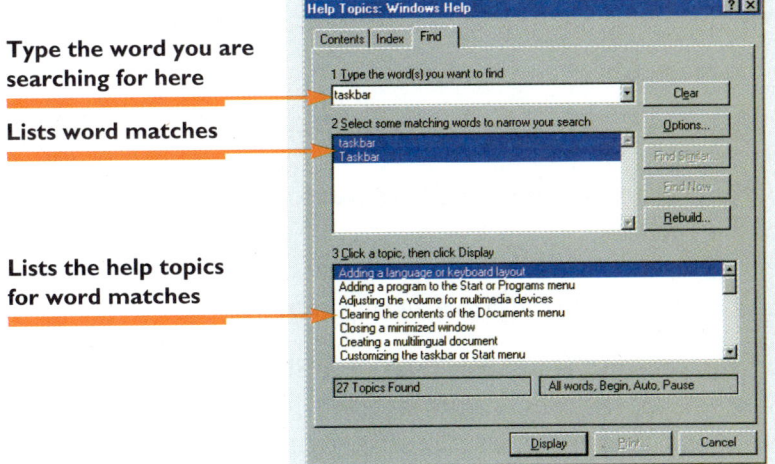

More about Help

To receive online help in a dialog box, click the Help button in the upper-right corner of the dialog box. The mouse pointer changes to . Click the Help pointer on the item for which you need additional information. A pop-up window provides a brief explanation of the selected feature. You can also click the right mouse button on an item in a dialog box. Then click the What's This? button to display the help explanation. In addition, when you click the right mouse button in a help topic window, you can choose commands to annotate, copy, and print the contents of the topic window. From the Help pop-up menu, you can also choose to have topic windows always appear on top of the currently active window, so you can see help topics while you work.

Closing a program and shutting down Windows

When you are finished working with Windows, close all the open programs and windows, and then exit Windows using the Shut Down command on the Start menu. Do not turn off the computer while Windows is running; you could lose important data if you turn off your computer too soon. ▶ Close all your active programs and exit Windows.

1. Click the **WordPad program button** on the taskbar to make the WordPad program active

   To close a program and any of its currently open files, you select the Exit command on the File menu. You can also click the Close button in the program window. See the related topic "Closing programs and files with the Close button" for more information. If you have made any changes to the open files, you will be prompted to save your changes before the program quits. Some programs also give you the option of choosing the Close command on the File menu. This command closes the active file but leaves the program open, so you can continue to work in it. In the next step, you will quit the WordPad program and return to the Windows desktop.

2. Click **File** on the menu bar, then click **Exit**

3. If you see a message asking you to save changes to the document, click **No**

4. In the Control Panel window, click the **Close button** ☒ in the upper-right corner of the window

   The Control Panel window closes. *Complete the remaining steps to shut down Windows and your computer only if you have been told to do so by your instructor.*

5. Click the **Start button** on the taskbar, then click **Shut Down**

   The Shut Down Windows dialog box opens, as shown in Figure 1-16. In this dialog box, you have the option to shut down the computer, restart the computer in Windows mode, restart the computer in MS-DOS mode, or log on to the computer as another user.

6. Verify that the first option, "Shut down the computer?," is selected

7. If you are working in a lab click **No**; if you are working on your own machine or if your instructor told you to shut down Windows, click **Yes** to exit Windows and shut down the computer

FIGURE 1-16: Shut Down Windows dialog box

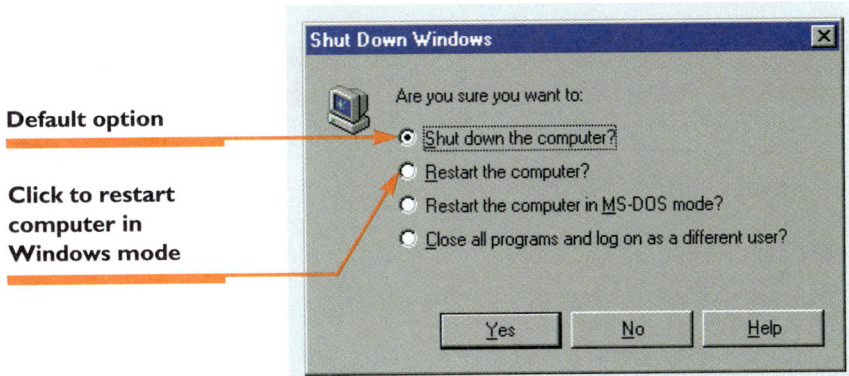

Default option

Click to restart computer in Windows mode

Closing programs and files with the Close button

You can also close a program and its open files by clicking the Close button  on the title bar in the upper-right corner of the program window. If there is a second set of sizing buttons in the window, the Close button that is located on the menu bar will close the active file only, leaving the program open for continued use.

QUICK TIP

Some programs allow you to close multiple files simultaneously by pressing [Shift], then clicking File on the menu bar. Click Close All to close all open files at once.

TASK REFERENCE

TASK	MOUSE/BUTTON	MENU	KEYBOARD
Change the size of a window in one direction	Drag a window border		
Change the size of a window in two directions	Drag a corner of the window		
Choose a command		Click the menu name on the menu bar, then click the command	Press [Alt], press the underlined key in the menu name, then press the underlined key in the command
Close a program	Click the Close button in the title bar of the program window	Click File, Exit	[Alt] [F4]
Display help information		Click Start, Help	
Display help information in a dialog box	Click the Help button in the dialog box, then click the item for which you want information		Select an item and press [F1]
Display a pop-up menu	Click the right mouse button		Press [Shift] [F10]
Exit Windows		Click Start, Shut Down	
Maximize a window	Click the Maximize sizing button		
Minimize a window	Click the Minimize sizing button		
Move a window	Drag the title bar		
Restore the window to its previous (not maximized) size	Click the Restore sizing button		
Start a program	Double-click the icon or shortcut that represents the program	Click Start, Programs	[Ctrl] [Esc] (displays Start menu)

CONCEPTSREVIEW

Without referring to the unit material, identify each of the items in Figure 1-17.

1.
2.
3.
4.
5.
6.
7.
8.
9.
10.
11.
12.
13.

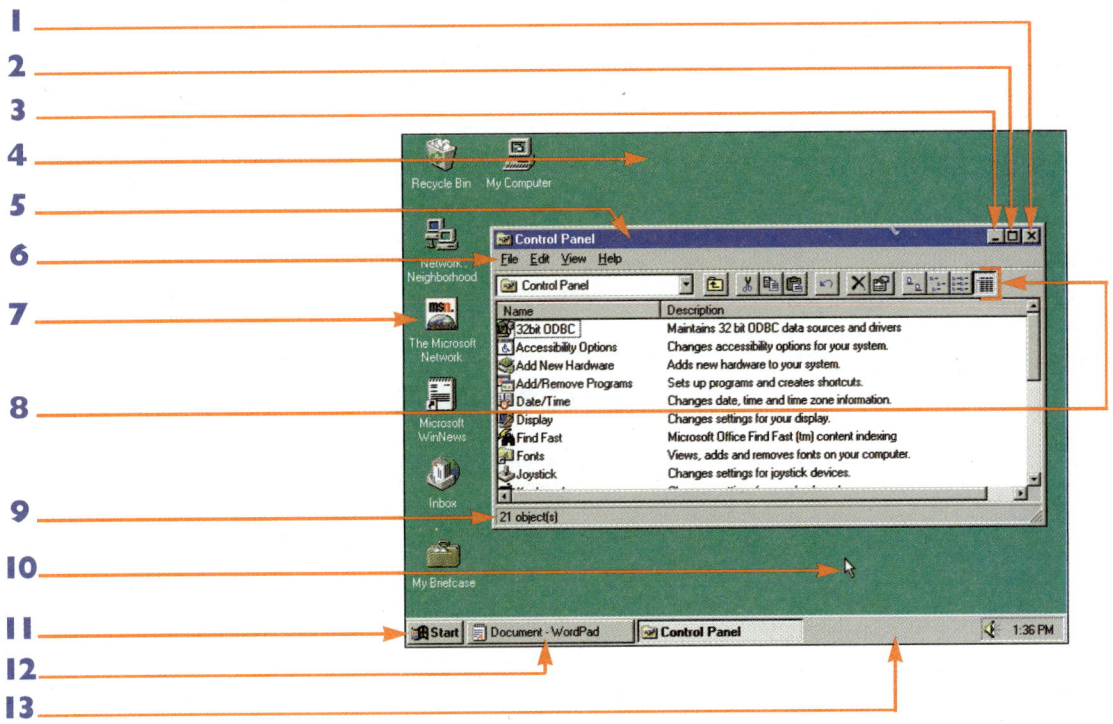

FIGURE 1-17

Match each of the statements with the term it describes.

14. Shrinks a window to a button on the taskbar
15. Displays the name of the window or program
16. Displays list of programs you can run
17. Requests more information that you supply before carrying out command
18. Displays Start button and currently open programs
19. Lets you point to and make selections
20. Graphic representation of program you can run

a. Start button
b. Dialog box
c. Taskbar
d. Mouse
e. Title bar
f. Minimize button
g. Icon

Select the best answer from the list of choices.

21. The acronym GUI means
    a. Grayed user information
    b. Group user icons
    c. Graphical user interface
    d. Group user interconnect

22. Which of the following is NOT provided by an operating system?
    a. Programs for organizing files
    b. Instructions to coordinate the flow of information among the programs, files, printers, storage devices, and other components of your computer system
    c. Programs that allow you to specify the operation of the mouse
    d. Spell checker for your documents

23 The small pictures that represent items such as programs are called

a. Icons

b. Windows

c. Buttons

d. Pointers

24 All of the following are examples of using a mouse, EXCEPT

a. Clicking the Maximize button

b. Pressing [Enter]

c. Double-clicking to start a program

d. Dragging the My Computer icon

25 The term for moving an item to a new location on the desktop is

a. Pointing

b. Clicking

c. Dragging

d. Restoring

26 Which of the following does NOT appear on the Start menu?

a. Help

b. Accessories

c. Programs

d. Settings

27 The Maximize button is used to

a. Return a window to its previous size

b. Expand a window to fill the computer screen

c. Scroll slowly through a window

d. Run programs from the Start menu

28 What appears if a window contains more information than can be displayed in the window?

a. Program icon

b. Cascading menu

c. Scroll bars

d. Check box

29 A window is active when its title bar is

a. Highlighted

b. Dimmed

c. Checked

d. Underlined

30 A toolbar provides access to a program's functions with

a. Buttons

b. Scroll bars

c. Commands

d. Status bars

31 You can exit Windows by

a. Selecting the Shut Down command from the Start menu

b. Double-clicking the Program Manager control menu box

c. Clicking File, then clicking Exit

d. Double-clicking the Control Panel application

SKILLS REVIEW

1 Start Windows and identify items on the screen.

a. Turn on the computer, if necessary.

b. After Windows loads, try to identify as many items on the desktop as you can, without referring to the lesson material. Then compare your results with Figure 1-1.

2 Practice dragging, maximizing, restoring, sizing, and minimizing windows.

a. Drag the Recycle Bin icon to the bottom of the desktop.

b. Double-click the My Computer icon to open the My Computer window.

c. Maximize the window, if it is not already maximized.

d. Restore the window to its previous size.

e. Size the window by dragging the window borders until you see both horizontal and vertical scroll bars.

f. Size the window until the horizontal scroll bar no longer appears.

g. Click the Minimize button. Now try restoring the window.

3 Run a program.

a. Click the Start button on the taskbar, then point to Programs.

b. Point to Accessories, then click Calculator.

c. Minimize the Calculator program.

4. Practice working with menus and dialog boxes.
   a. Click the Start button on the taskbar, then point to Settings, then click Control Panel.
   b. Click View on the menu bar, then click Toolbar twice to practice hiding and displaying the toolbar.
   c. Double-click the Display icon.
   d. Click the Appearance tab.
   e. Write down the current settings you see in this dialog box.
   f. Try out different selections in this dialog box to change the colors on your desktop and click the Apply button.
   g. Return the options to their original settings and click OK to close the dialog box.

5. Use online Help to learn more about Windows.
   a. Click the Start button on the taskbar, then click Help.
   b. Click the Contents tab.
   c. Double-click Introducing Windows.
   d. Double-click each of the following topics (click Help Topics to return to the Contents window after reading each topic):
      - Welcome, then A List of What's New, then A new look and feel
      - Getting Your Work Done, then The basics
      - Keyboard Shortcuts, then General Windows keys
      - Using Windows Accessories, then For General Use
      - Using Windows Accessories, then For Writing and Drawing

6. Close all open windows.
   a. Click the Close button to close the Help topic window.
   b. Click File on the menu bar, then click Exit to close the Control Panel window.
   c. Click Calculator in the taskbar to restore the window.
   d. Click the Close button in the Calculator window to close the Calculator program.
   e. Click the Close button in the My Computer window to close the window.
   f. If you are instructed to do so by your instructor, use the Shut Down command on the Start menu to exit Windows. Otherwise, be sure all windows and programs are closed and you have returned the desktop to its original appearance as it appeared before you began this unit.

INDEPENDENT CHALLENGE 1

Microsoft Windows 95 provides an extensive help system designed to help you learn how to use Windows effectively. In addition to step-by-step instructions, there are also tips that you can try to gain even greater confidence as you become acquainted with Windows features. In this challenge, you start Help, double-click Tips and Tricks, then double-click Tips of the Day. Read each of the following topics (click Help Topics to return to the Contents window after reading each topic):

- Getting your work done
- Personalizing Windows
- Becoming an expert
- Optional: If you have a printer connected to your computer, click the Print button to print the tips described in each Help topic window.
- Close all the Help topic windows and return to the desktop.

INDEPENDENT CHALLENGE 2

Use the skills you have learned in this unit to create a desktop that looks like the desktop in Figure 1-18. It's OK if your desktop contains more items than in this figure.

FIGURE 1-18

- Calculator program minimized
- Scroll bars in Control Panel window

- Large icons in Control Panel window
- Rearranged icons

Be sure to return your settings and desktop back to their original arrangement when you complete this challenge.

INDEPENDENT CHALLENGE 3

At times it may be necessary to change the format of the clock and date on your computer. For example, if you work with international clients it might be easier to display the time in military (24-hour) time and display the date with the day before the month. You can also change the actual time and date on your computer, such as when you change time zones. Follow these guidelines to explore the Clock feature in Windows.

- Open the Control Panel window.
- Double-click the Regional Settings icon.
- Click the Date tab to change the time to show a 24-hour clock rather than a 12-hour clock.
- Click the Time tab to change the date to show the day before the month (e.g., 30/3/96).
- Change the time to one hour later using the Date/Time icon in the Control Panel window (you can also double-click the displayed time in the lower-right corner of the taskbar).
- Observe the effect of these changes, and then return the settings back to the original time and formats.

The Calculator is a Windows program provided on the Accessories menu. You can use it to help you with calculations that you might need to perform while using the computer. Follow these guidelines to explore the Calculator:

- Start the Calculator program (from the Accessories menu).
- Determine how many months you have to work to earn an additional week of vacation if you work for a company that provides one additional day of paid vacation for every 560 hours you work.
(Hint: First multiply 560 times 5 days, then divide the answer by the number of hours you work in a month.)
- Determine how many years you must work to earn enough money to pay for your favorite car in cash.

INDEPENDENT CHALLENGE 4

You can customize many Windows features to suit your needs and preferences. One way you do this is to change the appearance of the taskbar on the desktop. In this challenge, try the guidelines described below to explore the different ways you can customize the appearance of the taskbar.

- Position the pointer over the top border of the taskbar. When the pointer changes shape, drag upwards an inch or so. Increasing the size of the taskbar gives you more room to display more minimized programs. Use this feature when you have many minimized programs at once. Resize the taskbar back to its original size.
- Click the Start button on the taskbar, then point to Settings, and click Taskbar.
- On the Taskbar Options tab, practice clicking different options and observe their effects in the preview area of the dialog box.
- Return the options to their default settings or click Cancel.

UNIT 2

OBJECTIVES

▶ Format a disk

▶ Create and save a Paint file

▶ Work with multiple programs

▶ Understand file management

▶ View files and create folders with My Computer

▶ Move and copy files using My Computer

▶ View files and rename folders with Windows Explorer

▶ Delete and restore files

▶ Manage files on the desktop

Managing
FILES, FOLDERS, AND SHORTCUTS

ow you are ready to explore the file management features of Windows 95. ▶ In this unit you will learn how to format a floppy disk, so that you can permanently store your work. You will then create and save files using a drawing program called Paint. Next, you will learn how to use the Clipboard to copy and paste your work from one program to another. Then you will learn two methods for managing the files you create: using My Computer and Windows Explorer. Finally, you will learn how to work more efficiently by managing files directly on your desktop. ▶

Formatting a disk

When you use a program, your work is temporarily stored in your computer's random access memory (RAM). When you turn off your computer, the contents of RAM are erased. To store your work permanently, you must save your work as a file on a disk. You can save files either on an internal **hard disk** (which is built into your computer, usually drive C) or on a removable 3.5 or 5.25 inch **floppy disk** (which you insert into a drive on your computer, usually drive A or B). Before you can save a file on a floppy disk, you must prepare the disk to receive your file by first **formatting** the disk. To complete the steps below, you need a blank disk or a disk containing data you no longer need. Formatting erases all data on a disk, so be careful which disk you use.

1 **Place a blank, unformatted disk in drive A:**
If your disk does not fit in the drive A, try drive B and substitute drive B wherever you see drive A.

2 **Double-click the My Computer icon on the desktop**
The My Computer window appears, as shown in Figure 2-1. This window displays all the drives and printers that you can use on your computer; depending on your computer system, your window might look different. You can use My Computer for managing your files as well as for formatting your disk. You will learn more about My Computer later in this unit. For now, locate the drive that contains the disk you want to format in the My Computer window.

3 **Right-click the 3½ Floppy (A:) icon**
This icon is usually the first icon in the upper-left corner of the window. Clicking with the right mouse button displays a pop-up menu of commands that apply to using drive A, including the Format command.

4 **Click Format on the pop-up menu**
The Format dialog box opens, as shown in Figure 2-2. In this dialog box, you specify the capacity of the disk you are formatting and the kind of formatting you want to do. See Table 2-1 for a description of formatting options.

5 **Click the Full radio button then click Start**
Windows is now formatting your disk. By selecting the Full option, you ensure that the disk can be read by your computer. Once a disk is formatted you will not need to format it again. After the formatting is complete, you see a summary about the size of the disk. Now that the disk is formatted, you are ready to save files on it. From now on, we will refer to this disk as your **Work Disk**. Before you continue with this unit, close each of the open dialog boxes.

6 **Click Close in the Format Results dialog box, then click Close in the Format dialog box**
You can keep the My Computer window open for now; you will return to it later in this unit.

FIGURE 2-1:
My Computer window

Drive containing disk

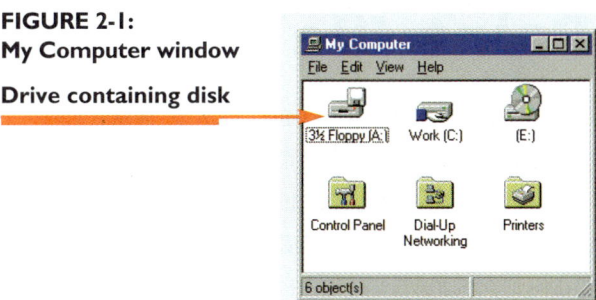

FIGURE 2-2:
Format dialog box

Click to format a new, blank disk

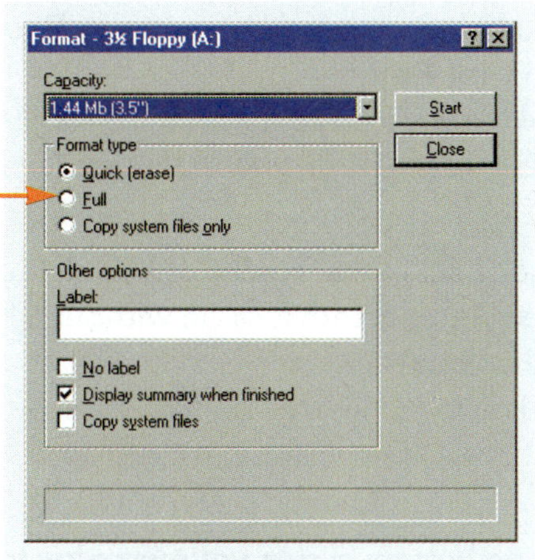

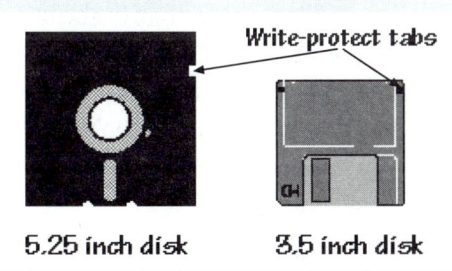

FIGURE 2-3:
Write-protect tabs

TROUBLE?

Windows cannot format a disk if it is write-protected, therefore, you need to remove (on a 5.25 disk) or move (on a 3.5 disk) the write-protect tab to continue. See Figure 2-3 to locate the write-protect tab on your disk.

TABLE 2-1: Formatting options

OPTION	DESCRIPTION
Capacity	Click the Capacity list arrow to specify the amount of information your disk is made to hold; for a high-density disk, choose 1.44 Mb, for double-density disks, choose 720Kb
Quick (erase)	Choose this option if your disk contains files that you want to erase; it takes less time than the Full option
Full	Choose this option if you are using a new, blank disk; this option initializes, as well as formats, the disk, requiring more time to complete than the Quick option
Copy System Files Only	Use this option when you want to make the disk you are formatting **bootable**; this means you will be able to start Windows from this disk (You will seldom use this option)
Label	Choose this option to give your disk a name; this will help you keep track of the files you save on a disk

Creating and saving a Paint file

Most of your work on a computer involves creating files in programs. When you use a program, you can use many of the Windows skills you have already learned. In this lesson, you'll work with **Paint**, a drawing program located on the Accessories submenu that you use to create simple graphics. ▶ Launch Paint and create a file that contains the simple logo shown in Figure 2-6 (located in the continuation of this lesson). Then you'll save the file to your Work Disk.

1. Click the **Start button** on the taskbar, point to **Programs**, point to **Accessories**, then click **Paint**

   The Paint program window opens. If the Paint window does not fill your screen, click the Maximize button. To create the circle in the logo, you first need to select the best tool for drawing circles.

2. Click the **Ellipse tool** ⭕ in the Toolbox at the left of the window, then click the **third fill style** to create a circle without a border (the styles appear below the Toolbox)

   See Table 2-2 for a description of the Toolbox tools. Next, you'll select a color for the inside of the circle. You do this with the right mouse button, even though you will draw the circle with the left mouse button.

3. With the right mouse button, click a **yellow color** from the color palette, and in the drawing window, hold down **[Shift]** with the left mouse button as you drag to create a filled circle that is about two inches across

   Remember to use the left mouse button to drag the circle, not the right mouse button. A yellow circle appears in the drawing window. Holding the [Shift] key while you drag with the Ellipse tool creates a perfect circle. If you don't like what you've drawn, you can start over by clicking Undo on the Edit menu. Next, you will create a dark blue, curving line. You use the left mouse button to select the color for lines.

4. With the left mouse button, click a **dark blue color**, then click the **Curved Line tool** and drag across the middle of the circle

   As you drag, be sure the line extends to both edges of the circle completely. A line extends across the circle. To create curves in the line as shown in Figure 2-6, you will drag the ends of the line up and down slightly.

5. With the Curved Line tool, click and drag near the left end of the line up about one-half inch (see Figure 2-4), and again click and drag near the right end of the line down about one-half inch

   A curved line appears across the circle.

6. Click the **Fill With Color tool**, then click below the curved line

   The blue color fills the bottom of the circle. Next, you will add the text for the logo.

7. Click the **Text tool** A to select it, then in a blank area just below and to the left of the circle, drag a thin rectangle that is about three inches long and type **New Directions**

   By starting slightly to the left of the circle, your text will appear centered below the graphic. To improve the appearance of the text, you will apply new formatting with the Text toolbar. Continue with Step 8 to display the Text toolbar, if it is not already displayed.

FIGURE 2-4: Filled circle

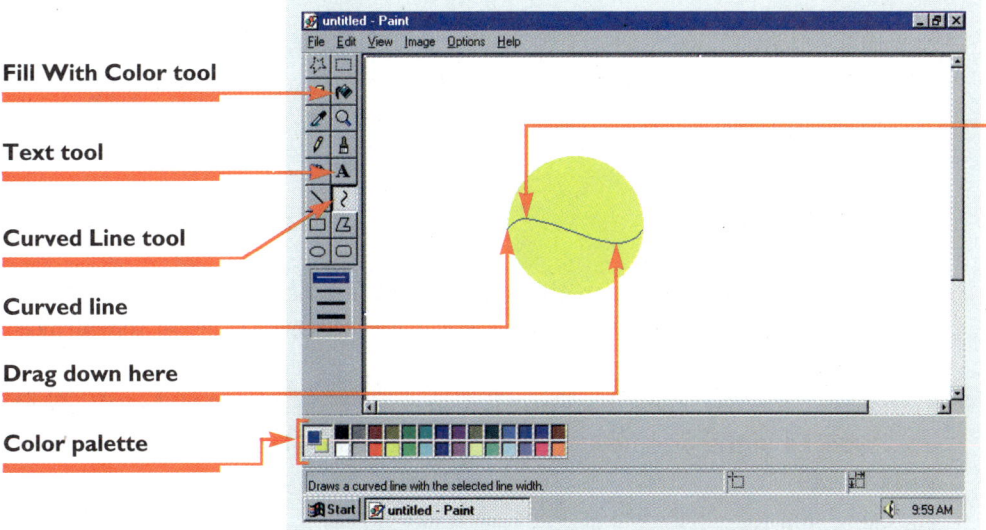

TROUBLE?

If the blue fill color fills the circle completely, choose Undo from the Edit menu and redraw the curved line, making sure it extends all the way to both edges of the circle.

TABLE 2-2: Paint Toolbox tools

TOOL	DESCRIPTION	TOOL	DESCRIPTION
Free-Form Select	Selects a free-form section of the picture to move, copy, or edit	Airbrush	Produces a circular spray of dots
Select	Selects a rectangular section of the picture to move, copy, or edit	Text	Inserts text into the picture
Eraser/Color Eraser	Erases a portion of the picture using the selected eraser size and foreground color	Line	Draws a straight line with the selected width and foreground color
Fill With Color	Fills closed shape or area with the current drawing color	Curve	Draws a wavy line with the selected width and foreground color
Pick Color	Picks up a color off the picture to use for drawing	Rectangle	Draws a rectangle with the selected fill style; also used to draw squares by holding down [Shift] while drawing
Magnifier	Changes the magnification; displays list of magnifications under the toolbar	Polygon	Draws polygons from connected straight-line segments
Pencil	Draws a free-form line one pixel wide	Ellipse	Draws an ellipse with the selected fill style; also used to draw circles by holding down [Shift] while drawing
Brush	Draws using a brush with the selected shape and size	Rounded Rectangle	Draws rectangles with rounded corners using the selected fill style; also used to draw rounded squares by holding down [Shift] while drawing

Creating and saving a Paint file, continued

Now that you've created the logo, you can add formatting to enhance its appearance and then save the file to your Work Disk.

8. Click **View** on the menu bar, then click **Text Toolbar**
   The Text toolbar appears, as shown in Figure 2-5. With the Text toolbar displayed, you can modify the appearance of text in the graphic.

9. In the Text toolbar, click the **Font list arrow**, then click **Arial** in the Font box, type **14** in the Size box, then click the **Bold button** and the **Italic button**
   The text is formatted with the font, size, and effects you selected.

10. Click the **Rectangle tool** and drag a rectangle that surrounds both the circle and the text below it
    A dark blue rectangle appears around the entire logo, as shown in Figure 2-6. Now that your logo is complete, you are ready to save it to a file on your Work Disk.

11. Click **File** on the menu bar, then click **Save As**
    The Save As dialog box opens, as shown in Figure 2-7. In this dialog box you give your work a filename and specify where you want the file saved. You specify the location first.

12. Click the **Save In list arrow**, and click **3½ Floppy (A:)** (or whichever drive contains your Work Disk), then click the **Save as type list arrow** and click **16 color Bitmap**
    The drive containing your Work Disk is now active. This means that the file you save will be saved on the disk in this drive.

13. Double-click the text in the File Name box, type **My first Paint file,** then click **Save**
    Your logo is now saved as a Paint file with the name "My first Paint file" on your Work Disk in drive A. When you name a file, you can type up to 255 characters (including spaces and punctuation) in the File Name box. You can use both upper and lowercase. Next, you will modify the logo and save the changed logo with a new name.

14. Click a **light blue color** on the color palette, then click the **Fill With Color tool** and click the **bottom half of the circle**
    The bottom of the circle fills with the light blue color. To save this modified logo in a new file (so you can keep the original unchanged), you can use the Save As command. (If you wanted to save a change in the original file, you can use the Save command.)

15. Click **File** on the menu bar, then click **Save As**
    The Save As dialog box opens. Because Windows "remembers" where you last saved a file, you do not need to specify a location this time. Enter a new filename to create a new file.

16. With the text in the File Name box selected, type **My second Paint file,** then click **Save**
    Your revised logo is now saved as a new Paint file with the name "My second Paint file" on your Work Disk. The original file closes automatically when you use the Save As command. There are now two Paint files on your Work Disk.

FIGURE 2-5: Text toolbar

Font box

Size box

Italic button

Underline button

Bold button

FIGURE 2-6: Completed logo

Rectangle tool

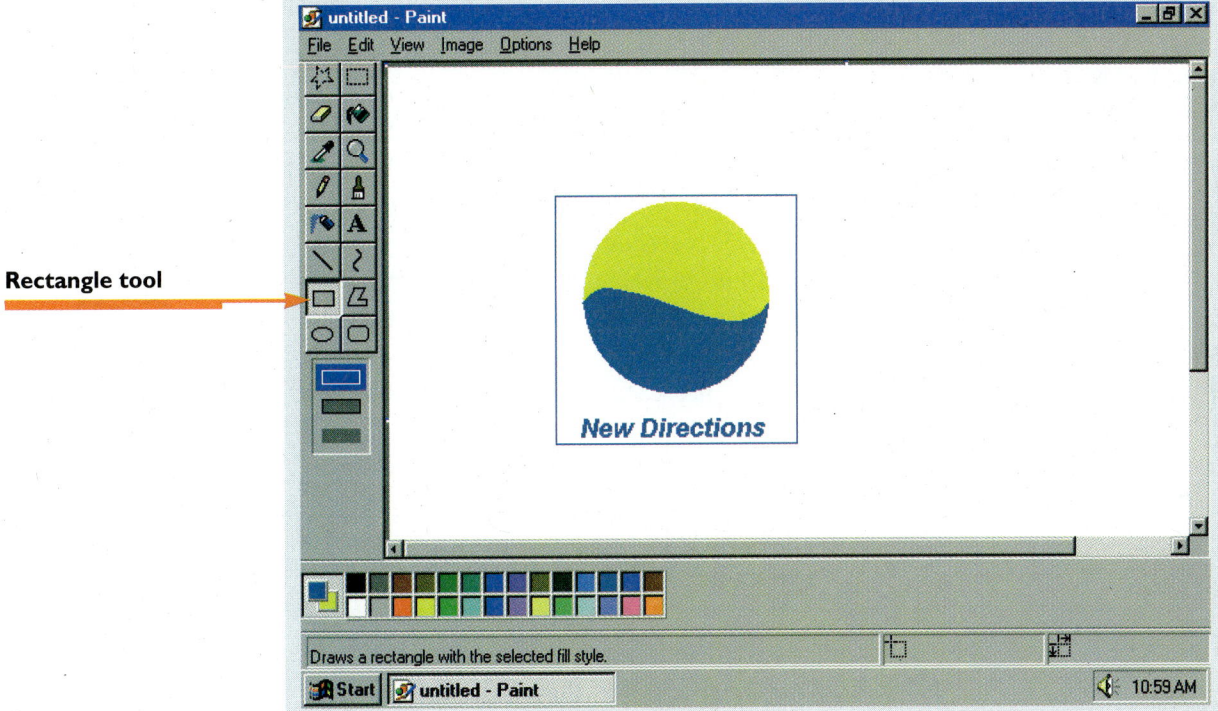

FIGURE 2-7: Save As dialog box

Click to select a new location for a file

Existing files (if any) appear in list

Enter filename

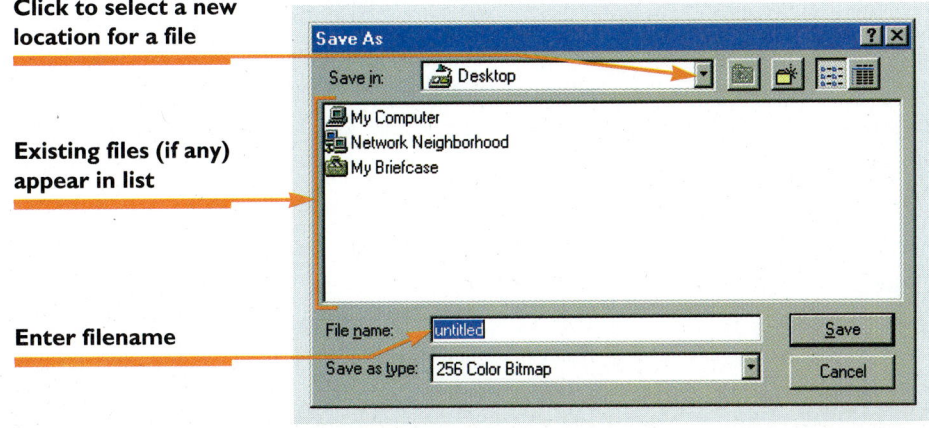

QUICK TIP

If the filename is not already selected in the File name box, you can double-click the text to select it quickly.

WINDOWS 95 UNIT 2 **MANAGING** FILES, FOLDERS, AND SHORTCUTS

Working with multiple programs

Occasionally, you might want to work with more than one program at a time. For example, perhaps you have created a graphic file that you want to include with text in a document file. With Windows 95 you can copy objects onto the Clipboard. The **Clipboard** is a temporary area in your computer's memory for storing text or graphics. Once you place something on the Clipboard, you can paste it into other locations. Using the taskbar or keyboard, you can switch to another program quickly so that you can paste the contents of the Clipboard into another file without closing the original program. ▶ Next, you will copy the logo graphic you created in the previous lesson into a WordPad document.

1. Click the **Start button** on the taskbar, point to **Programs,** point to **Accessories**, then click **WordPad**
   The WordPad program window opens. If the WordPad program window does not fill your screen, click the Maximize button. The blinking **insertion point**, also called the **cursor**, indicates where the text you type will appear.

2. In the WordPad window, type **This is the new logo I created for our company brochure.**, then press **[Enter]** twice
   Pressing [Enter] once places the insertion point at the beginning of the next line. Pressing [Enter] again creates a blank line between the first line of text and the graphic you will copy from the Paint program.

3. Click the **Paint program button** on the taskbar
   The Paint program becomes the active program in the window. Next, you will select the logo graphic in the Paint window.

4. Click the **Select tool** 🔲, then drag a rectangle around the entire graphic
   When you release the mouse button, the dotted rectangle indicates the contents of the selection. The next action you take will affect the entire selection.

5. Click **Edit** on the menu bar, then click **Copy**
   The selected logo graphic is copied to the Clipboard. When you copy an object onto the Clipboard, the object remains in its original location, and is also available to be pasted into another location. Now you will switch to the WordPad window using the keyboard.

6. Press and hold down **[Alt]**, press **[Tab]** once, then release **[Alt]**
   A box appears, as shown in Figure 2-8, indicating which program will become active when you release the Alt key. If you have more than two programs open, you press the Tab key (while holding down [Alt]) until the program you want is selected. The WordPad program becomes the active program in the window.

7. Click **Edit** on the menu bar, then click **Paste**
   The contents of the Clipboard, in this case the Paint graphic, are pasted into the WordPad window at the location of the insertion point.

8. Click **File** on the menu bar, then click **Save As**, and save the file to your Work Disk with the name **My WordPad file**
   Be sure to select the Work Disk in the Save In box before naming the file.

9. Click the **Close buttons** in both the WordPad and Paint programs to close the open files and exit the programs
   You return to the desktop and the My Computer window.

FIGURE 2-8: Using the keyboard to switch between programs

Indicates which program will become active

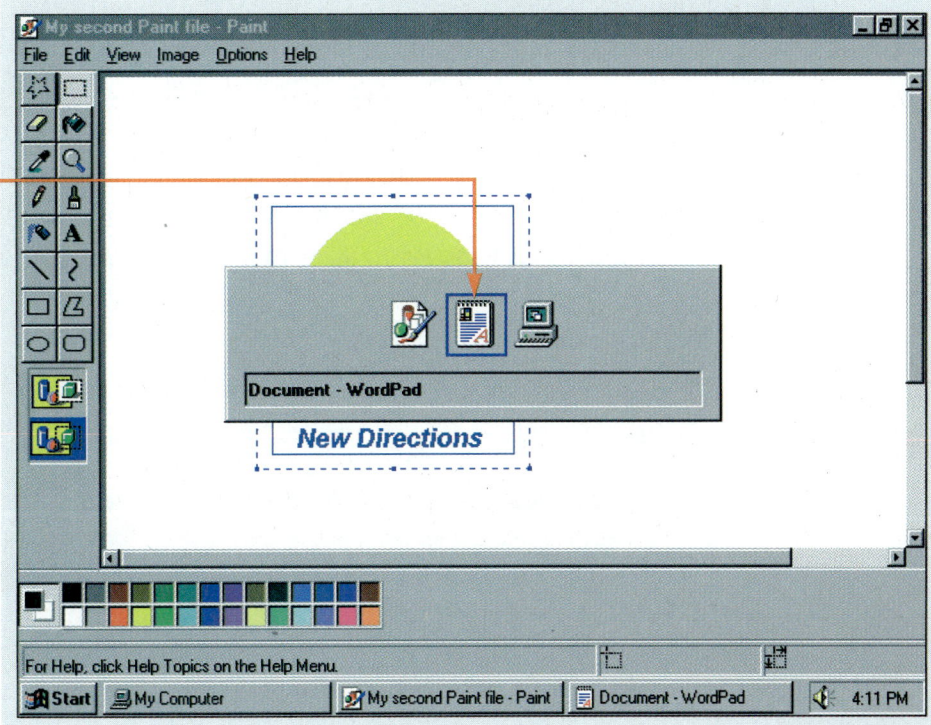

TROUBLE?

If you make the wrong program active, hold down [Alt] and press [Tab] to redisplay the box. Then (while holding down [Alt]), press [Tab] to move the selection box from program to program. When the program you want to make active is selected, then release both keys.

Understanding file management

After you have created and saved numerous files while working in various programs, it can be a challenge to keep track of all of your files. Fortunately, Windows 95 provides the tools you need to keep everything organized so you can quickly locate the files you need. There are two main tools for managing your files: My Computer (which you have already opened when you formatted your Work Disk) and Windows Explorer. You'll learn more about Windows Explorer later in this unit.

No matter which tool you use, Windows 95 gives you the ability to:

- **Create folders in which you can save your files**
  Folders are areas on your disk (either a floppy disk or a hard disk) in which you can save files. For example, you might create a folder for your documents and another folder for your graphics. Folders can also contain additional folders, so you can create a more complicated structure of folders and files, called a **hierarchy**. See Figure 2-9 for an example of your Work Disk hierarchy.

- **Examine the hierarchy of files and folders**
  When you want to see the overall structure of your folders and files, you can use either My Computer or Windows Explorer. By examining your file hierarchy with these tools, you can better organize your files by adding new folders, renaming folders, deleting folders, and adjusting the hierarchy to meet your needs. Figures 2-10 and 2-11 illustrate sample hierarchies for your Work Disk, one using My Computer and the other using Windows Explorer.

- **Copy, move, delete, and rename files**
  For example, if you decide that a file belongs in a different folder, you can move the file to another folder. You can also rename a file if you decide a new name is more descriptive. If you want to keep a copy of a file in more than one folder, you can copy files to new folders. With the same files in two different folders, you can keep track of previous versions of files, so that they are available in the event of data loss. You can also delete files you no longer need, as well as restore files you delete accidentally.

- **Locate files quickly with the Windows 95 Find feature**
  With Find you can quickly locate files by providing only partial names or by other factors, such as by file type (for example, a WordPad document, a Paint graphic, or a program) or by the date the file was created or modified.

- **Preview the contents of a file without opening the file in its program**
  For example, if after locating a particular file, you want to verify that it is the file you want, you can use the Preview feature to quickly look at the file. The Preview feature saves you time because you do not need to wait for the program to open the file. Other options help you get additional information about your files so you can better organize your work.

FIGURE 2-9: Sketch of Work Disk hierarchy

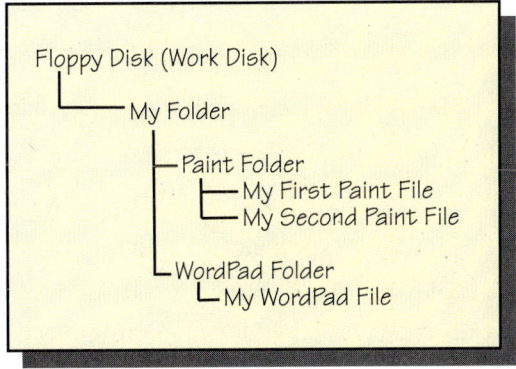

FIGURE 2-10: Sample hierarchy in My Computer

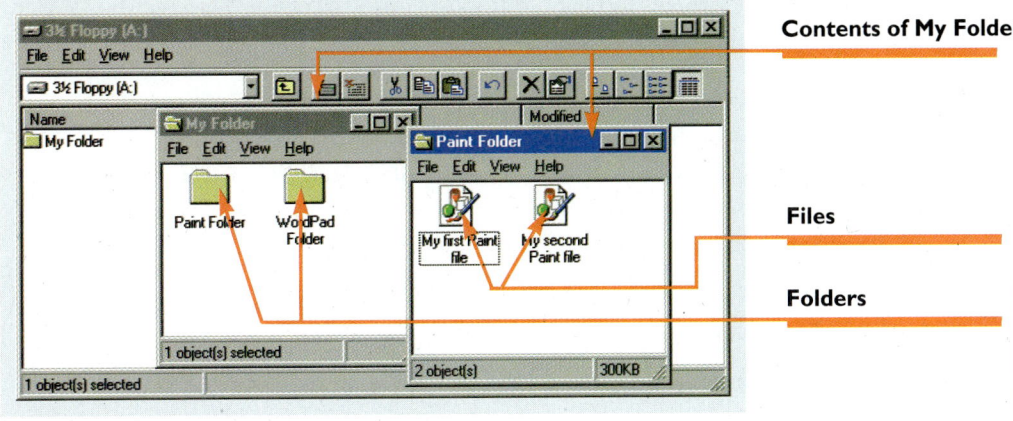

FIGURE 2-11: Sample hierarchy in Windows Explorer

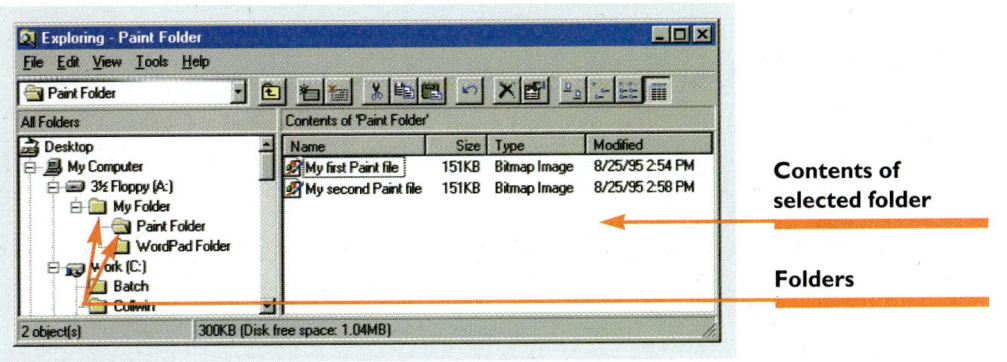

QUICK TIP

To browse My Computer using a single window (rather than the multiple windows you see in Figure 2-10) click View on the menu bar, then click Options. In the Options dialog box, click the Folder tab, then click the second radio button, which lets you browse the contents of a folder using a single window that changes as you open each folder. ■

WINDOWS 95 UNIT 2 **MANAGING** FILES, FOLDERS, AND SHORTCUTS

Viewing files and creating folders with My Computer

The My Computer window displays the contents of the selected drive or folder. When you double-click a drive or folder, its contents appear in a new window. Begin by using My Computer to move around in the system's file management hierarchy and then create a new folder on your Work Disk that will contain the files you create. First, you need to turn on the My Computer toolbar if it is not currently displayed. See Figure 2-12 if you're not sure what the toolbar looks like.

1. **Click the Maximize button in the My Computer window, if My Computer does not already fill the screen**
   If your toolbar is visible, skip Step 2 and continue with Step 3.

2. **Click View on the menu bar, then click Toolbar**

3. **Click the drive list arrow, then click the drive icon for your hard disk**
   Now you are ready to view the hierarchy of your hard drive. You can do this using any one of the four view buttons on the My Computer toolbar.

4. **Click the Details button on the My Computer toolbar**
   In addition to the drive and folder icons, Details view also displays the type of drive or folder, the amount of total available space on the hard disk, and the remaining free space, as shown in Figure 2-12. The List button provides a slightly smaller amount of information, but still mostly text-based. Let's try viewing the files and folders using a more graphical view.

5. **Click the Large Icons button on the My Computer toolbar**
   This view offers less information but provides a large, clear view of the contents of the disk.

6. **Click the Small Icons button on the My Computer toolbar**
   This view provides the same amount of information as the large icons except that the icons are smaller and take up less space in the window. Next, you want to display the contents of My Computer again, so that you can choose another drive.

7. **Click the Up One Level button on the My Computer toolbar**
   Clicking the Up One Level button displays the next level up the file hierarchy, in this case My Computer. Now, you are ready to create a folder on your Work Disk so you need to select the drive that contains your Work Disk.

8. **Double-click the 3½ Floppy (A:) icon (or B if that drive contains your Work Disk)**
   You can now create a folder that will contain the files you create in this unit.

9. **Click File on the menu bar, point to New, then click Folder**
   A new folder is created on your Work Disk. Finally, give the folder a unique name.

10. **Type My Folder and press [Enter]**
    Verify that the contents contained in the window are the same as those shown in Figure 2-13. Depending on the selections used by the previous user, your window might not match the one in the illustration. If you wish, you can match the illustration by resizing the window, displaying the toolbar, and clicking the Details button.

Toolbar

FIGURE 2-12: Using Details view to examine the hard disk

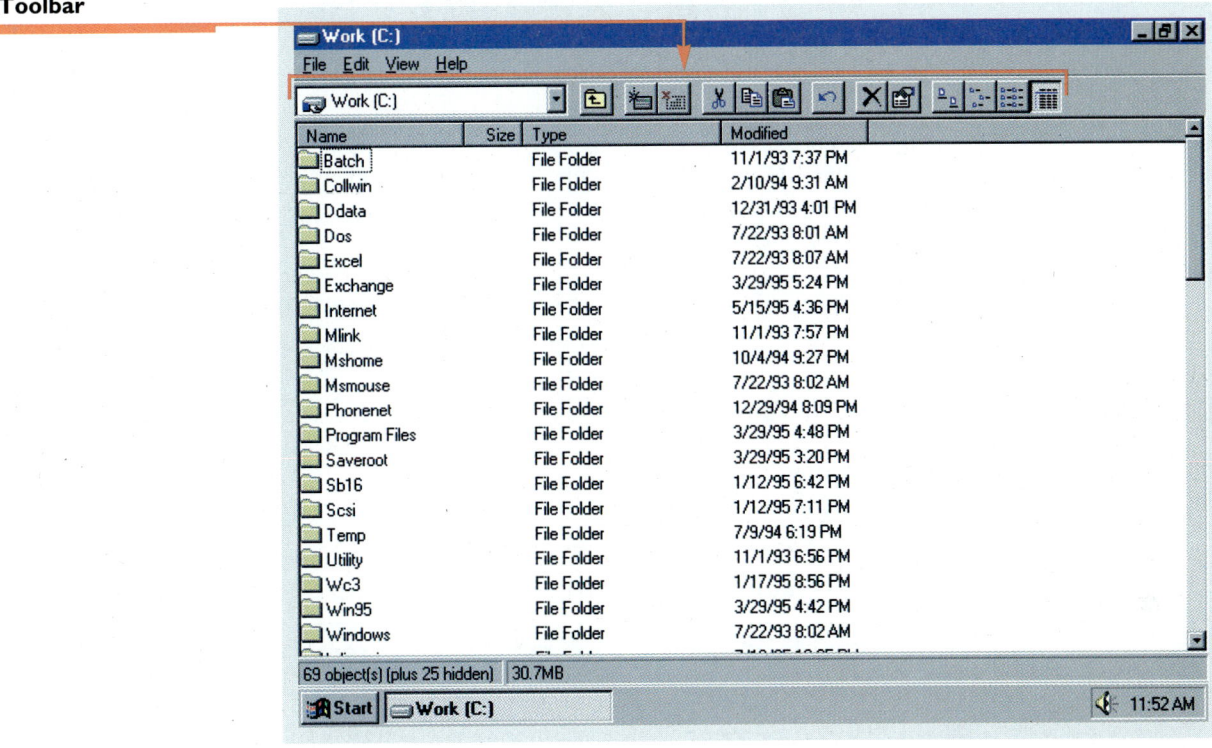

FIGURE 2-13: New folder in A: window

New folder

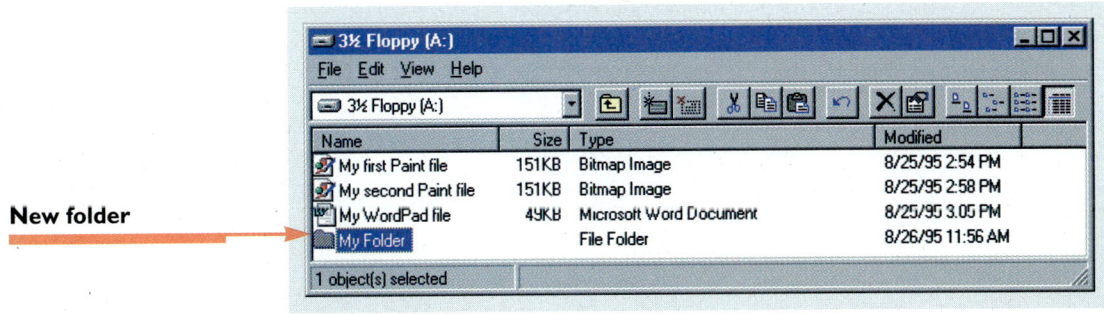

Moving and copying files using My Computer

At times you might want to change the hierarchy of your files within a particular drive. For example, to better organize your files, you might decide to place files in a folder whose name reflects the name of a project or the program in which the file was created. My Computer allows you to quickly move or copy files and folders to another location. ▶ In this lesson you will create two folders within the folder you created in the previous lesson. Then you will move the appropriate files into these new folders.

1. **Double-click the My Folder to open it**
   The My Folder window opens. Before you can create a folder, you have to make sure you are creating it in the right place—in this case within the My Folder. Now you will create two folders, one named Paint Folder and the other named WordPad Folder.

2. **Right-click in an empty area of the My Computer window (away from files, folder, and buttons)**

3. **Point to New in the pop-up menu, then click Folder**
   A new folder appears in the My Computer window. Next, you'll name it.

4. **Type Paint Folder, then press [Enter]**
   Now you need to repeat these steps to create another folder.

5. **Repeat Steps 2-4 to create a folder named WordPad Folder**
   Compare your My Folder window to Figure 2-14. Next, you will move the Paint files to the Paint Folder, removing them from the original location at the root of drive A:.

6. **In the 3½ Floppy (A:) window, click My first Paint file, then press [Shift] and click My second Paint file, then drag both files on top of the Paint Folder icon in the My Folder window**
   Windows displays the Moving window which shows the names of the files being moved and how much of the move operation is complete. See Table 2-3 for a description of the different file selection techniques. Instead of dragging files or folders to a new location, you can use the cut, copy, and paste commands on the Edit menu or the Cut, Copy, and Paste toolbar buttons. See the related topic "Using Edit commands to copy and move files" for more information. Next, you will move the WordPad file to the WordPad folder.

7. **Click My WordPad file to select it, then drag the file over the WordPad Folder icon and release the mouse button**
   The My WordPad file is moved to the WordPad Folder. Next, you will close all of the open windows including the 3½ Floppy (A:) window.

8. **Click the Close buttons in all open windows**
   All open windows are closed and you return to the Windows desktop.

FIGURE 2-14: Contents of My Folder

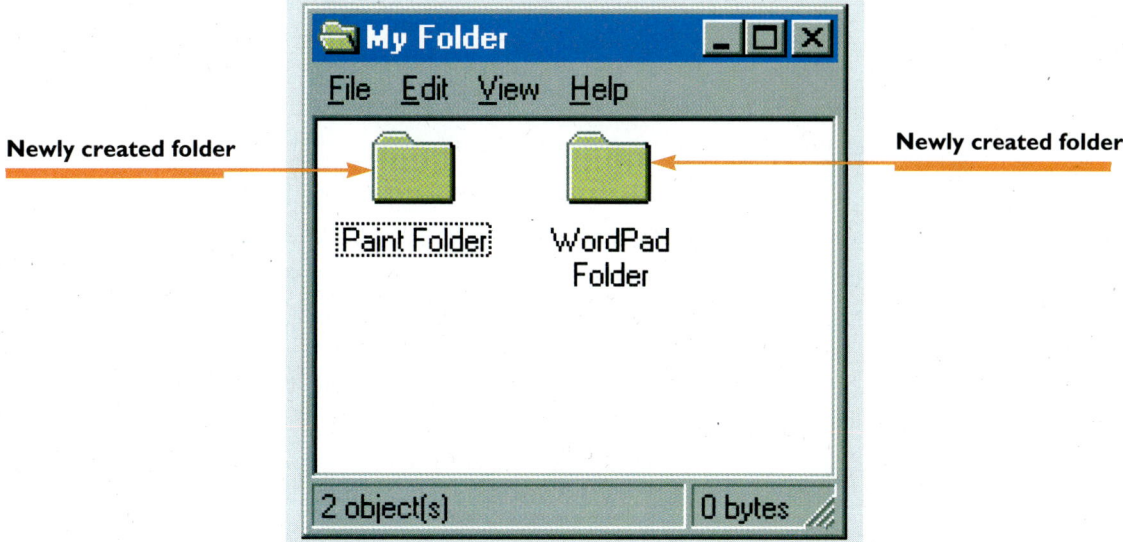

Newly created folder → Paint Folder

Newly created folder → WordPad Folder

Using Edit commands to copy and move files

An alternative to dragging files is to use the Cut, Copy, or Paste commands on the Edit menu or the Cut, Copy and Paste buttons on the toolbar. The Cut and Copy commands or Cut and Copy buttons  place the selected files on the Clipboard. Once on the Clipboard, the files can be pasted into the destination folder with the Paste command or Paste button . Be sure to select the destination folder before you paste your files. You can also use keyboard shortcuts to cut, copy, and paste files. See the Quick Tip for more information.

TABLE 2-3: File/folder selection techniques

TO SELECT THIS	USE THIS TECHNIQUE
Individual objects not grouped together	Click the first object you want to select, then press [Ctrl] as you click each additional object you want to add to the selection
Objects grouped together	Click the first object you want to select, then press [Shift] as you click the last object in the list of objects you want to select; all the objects listed between the first and last objects are selected

QUICK TIP

To cut a selected file, you can press [Ctrl] [X]. To copy a selected file, you can press [Ctrl] [C]. To paste a selected file, you can press [Ctrl] [V].

Viewing files and renaming folders with Windows Explorer

You've seen how to view, copy, and move files and create folders with My Computer. Windows 95 also provides another tool, Windows Explorer, that is particularly useful when you need to establish a hierarchy or move and copy files between multiple drives. You can also use Windows Explorer to view files without opening them. See the related topic "Quick View" for more information. ▶ In this lesson, you will copy a folder from your Work Disk onto the hard drive, and then rename it.

1. **Click the Start button, point to Programs, click Windows Explorer, then click the Maximize button in the Windows Explorer window**
   The Windows Explorer window appears, as shown in Figure 2-15. You can see right away that unlike My Computer, the window is divided into two sides called **panes**. The left pane displays the drives and folders on your computer. The right pane displays the contents of the drive or folder selected in the left pane. A plus sign next to a folder in the left pane indicates there are additional files or folders located within a drive or folder. A minus sign indicates that all folders of the next level of hierarchy are displayed.

2. **In the left pane, right-click the hard drive icon, then click Properties on the pop-up menu**
   The Properties dialog box opens with the General tab the frontmost tab. Here, you see the capacity of your hard drive and how much free space you have available. After you've examined the properties of your hard drive you can close this window.

3. **Click the Close button in the Properties dialog box**
   Next, you will use Windows Explorer to examine your Work Disk.

4. **In the left pane double-click the 3½ Floppy (A:) icon**
   The contents of your Work Disk are displayed in the right pane as shown in Figure 2-16. The plus sign next to My Folder indicates that it contains additional folders. Try expanding My Folder in the next step.

5. **In the left pane click the plus sign next to My Folder**
   The folders contained within the My Folder now appear in the left pane.

6. **In the left pane click the WordPad folder**
   The contents of the WordPad folder appear in the right pane of Windows Explorer. In the next step, you'll copy the WordPad folder to the hard drive in order to have a backup copy for safe keeping.

7. **In the left pane, drag the WordPad Folder on top of the icon for the hard drive then release the mouse button**
   The WordPad folder and the file in it are copied to the hard disk. Check to see if the copy of this folder is on the hard drive.

8. **In the left pane, click the icon representing your hard drive**
   The WordPad Folder should now appear in the list of folders in the right pane. You might have to scroll to find it. Now let's rename the folder so you can tell the original folder from the backup.

9. **Right-click the WordPad Folder in the right pane, click Rename in the pop-up menu, then type Backup WordPad Folder and press [Enter]**
   Leave the Windows Explorer window open and continue with the next lesson.

FIGURE 2-15: Windows Explorer window

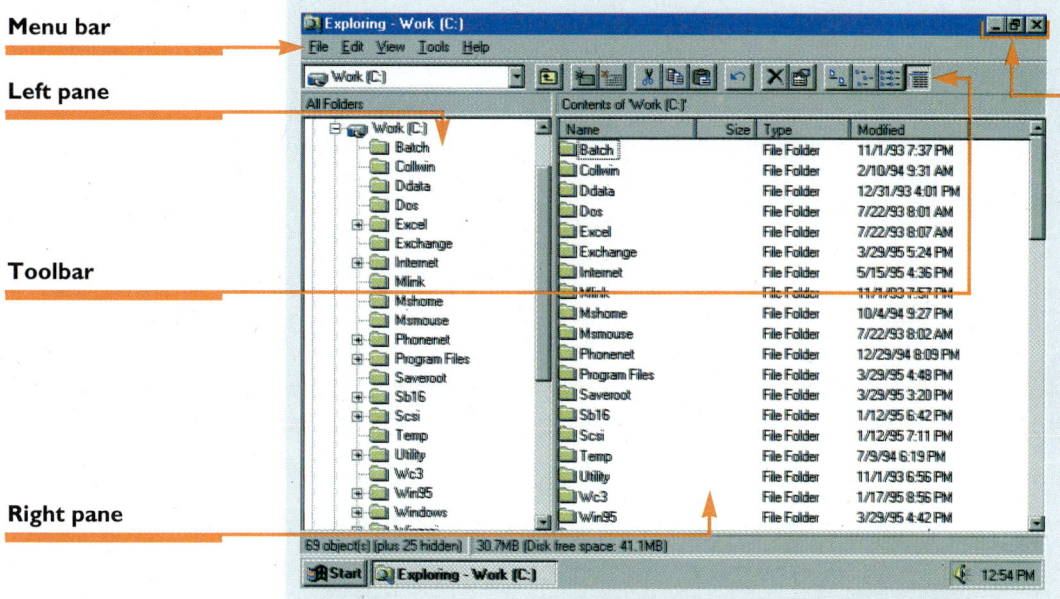

- Menu bar
- Left pane
- Toolbar
- Right pane
- Sizing buttons

FIGURE 2-16: Contents of your Work Disk

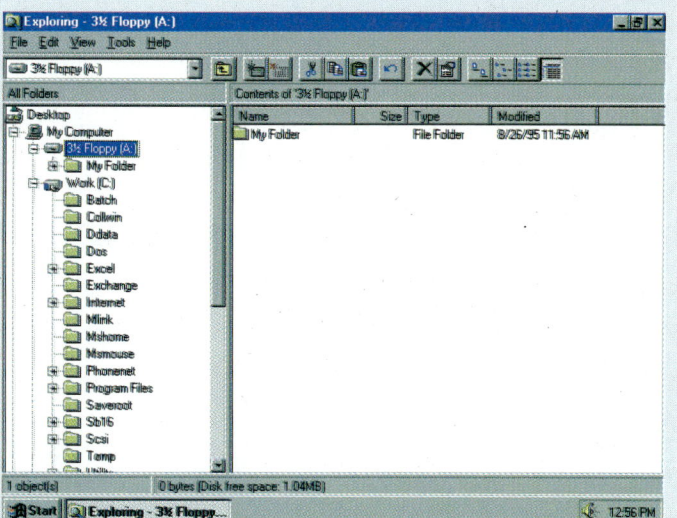

Quick View

At times you might want to preview a document to get an idea of what is in the file before opening it. It is much faster to preview the document using either My Computer or Windows Explorer than opening the program in which the file was created, then opening the file. To preview the file, simply right-click the selected file, then click Quick View on the pop-up menu. A preview of the file appears in the Quick View box. If the Quick View command does not appear on the pop-up menu, it means that this feature was not installed on your computer; see your instructor or technical support person for additional information.

QUICK TIP

To rename a file using the keyboard, select the file then press [F2] and type the new name. To rename a file using menus, select the file, click Edit on the menu bar, click Rename, then enter the new name.

Deleting and restoring files

To save disk space and to manage your files more effectively, you should delete files you no longer need. Because all files deleted from your hard drive are stored in the Recycle Bin (until you remove them permanently), you can restore files you might have deleted accidentally. See the related topic "Important note about deleting files" for more information. ▶ There are many ways to delete files in Windows 95. In this lesson, you'll use two different methods for removing files you no longer need. Then you will learn how to restore a deleted file.

1. **Click the Restore button on the Windows Explorer title bar**
   Now you should be able to see the Recycle Bin icon on your desktop. If you can't see it, resize or move the Windows Explorer window until it is visible.

2. **Drag the folder called Backup WordPad Folder from the right pane to the Recycle Bin on the desktop**
   The folder no longer appears in the Windows Explorer window because you have moved it to the Recycle Bin. The Recycle Bin looks as if it contains paper. If you see an "Are you sure you want to delete" confirmation box, click No and see the Trouble? on the next page. Next, you will examine the contents of the Recycle Bin.

3. **Double-click the Recycle Bin icon on the desktop**
   The Recycle Bin window appears, as shown in Figure 2-17. Depending upon the number of files already deleted on your computer, your window might look different. The folder doesn't appear in the Recycle Bin window but the file does. Use the scroll bar if you can't see it. Next, you'll try restoring a deleted folder.

4. **Click Edit on the Recycle Bin menu bar, then click Undo Delete**
   The Backup WordPad folder is restored and should now appear in the Windows Explorer window. You might need to move or resize your Recycle Bin window if it blocks your view of the Windows Explorer window. Next, you can delete the Backup WordPad folder for good using a Windows Explorer toolbar button.

5. **Click the Backup WordPad Folder in the left pane, then click the Delete button ⊠ on the Windows Explorer toolbar**
   The Confirm Folder Delete dialog box opens as shown in Figure 2-18.

6. **Click Yes**
   When you are sure you will no longer need files you've moved into the Recycle Bin, you can empty the Recycle Bin. You won't do this now, in case you are working on a computer that you share with other people. But, when you're working on your own machine, simply right-click the Recycle Bin icon, then click Empty Recycle Bin in the pop-up menu.

   Leave both the Recycle Bin and the Windows Explorer windows open and continue to the next lesson.

FIGURE 2-17: Contents of Recycle Bin

File you just deleted

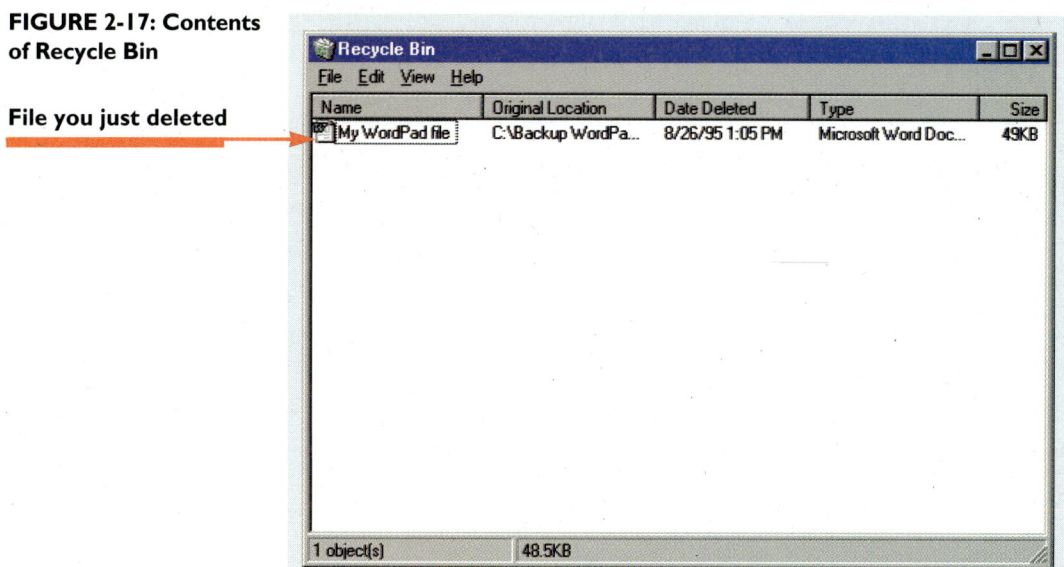

FIGURE 2-18: Confirm Folder Delete dialog box

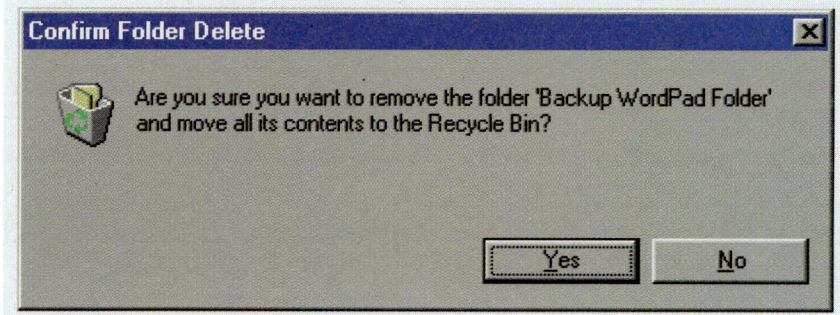

Important note about deleting files on a floppy disk

You cannot restore files deleted from a floppy disk. Once a file on a floppy disk is sent to the Recycle Bin, it is permanently removed from the floppy disk and cannot be retrieved.

TROUBLE?

If you are unable to recycle a file, it might be because your Recycle Bin is full, or too small, or the properties have been changed so that files are not stored in the Recycle Bin, they are deleted right away. Right-click the Recycle Bin icon, then click Properties on the pop-up menu to change the settings for storage and capacity.

QUICK TIP

You can also restore a file or folder by dragging it out of the Recycle Bin and into a new location (for example to a floppy disk).

Managing files on the desktop

You've now learned two different tools for managing files in Windows 95: My Computer and Windows Explorer. There is yet another Windows 95 feature you can use to make it easier to access files, folders, or programs you frequently use. A pop-up menu on the Windows desktop allows you to create folders and shortcuts on the desktop itself. **Shortcuts** are icons that point to an object that is actually stored elsewhere in a drive or folder. When you double-click a shortcut, you open the object without having to find its actual location. ▶ In this lesson, you will create a shortcut to the My WordPad file. Creating shortcuts to files you use frequently and placing them on the desktop allows you to work more efficiently. See the related topic "Adding shortcuts to the Start menu" for more information on using Windows 95 more efficiently.

1. In the left pane of the Windows Explorer window, click the **WordPad folder**
   You need to select the file you want to create a shortcut to, first.

2. In the right pane, right-click the **My WordPad file**
   A pop-up menu appears as shown in Figure 2-19.

3. Click **Create Shortcut** in the pop-up menu
   The file named Shortcut to My WordPad file appears in the right pane. Now you need to move it to the desktop so it will be at your fingertips whenever you need it. If you drag it using the left mouse button you will copy it to the desktop. If you drag it using the right mouse button you will have the option to copy or move it. Let's try dragging it using the *right* mouse button.

4. Right-drag the **Shortcut to My WordPad file** to an empty area of the desktop
   When you release the mouse button a pop-up menu appears.

5. Click **Move Here** in the pop-up menu
   A shortcut to the My WordPad file now appears on the desktop as shown in Figure 2-20. When you double-click this shortcut icon, you will open both WordPad and the My WordPad file document. Now let's delete the shortcut icon in case you are working in a lab and share the computer with others. Deleting a shortcut does not delete the original file or folder to which it points.

6. On the desktop, click the **Shortcut to My WordPad file** and press **[Delete]**; click **Yes** to confirm the deletion
   The shortcut is removed from the desktop and now appears in the Recycle Bin; however, the file itself remains intact in the WordPad folder. (See the Windows Explorer window to make sure it's still there.)

7. Close all open windows

FIGURE 2-19: Pop-up menu

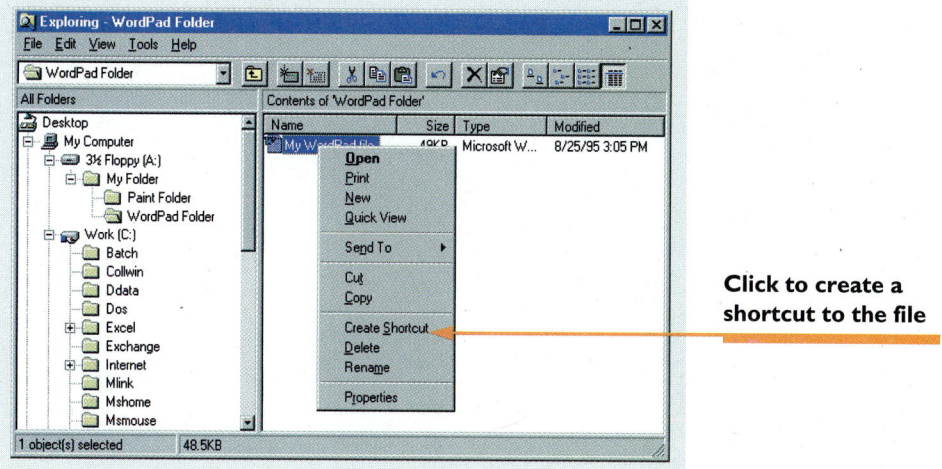

Click to create a shortcut to the file

FIGURE 2-20: Shortcut on desktop

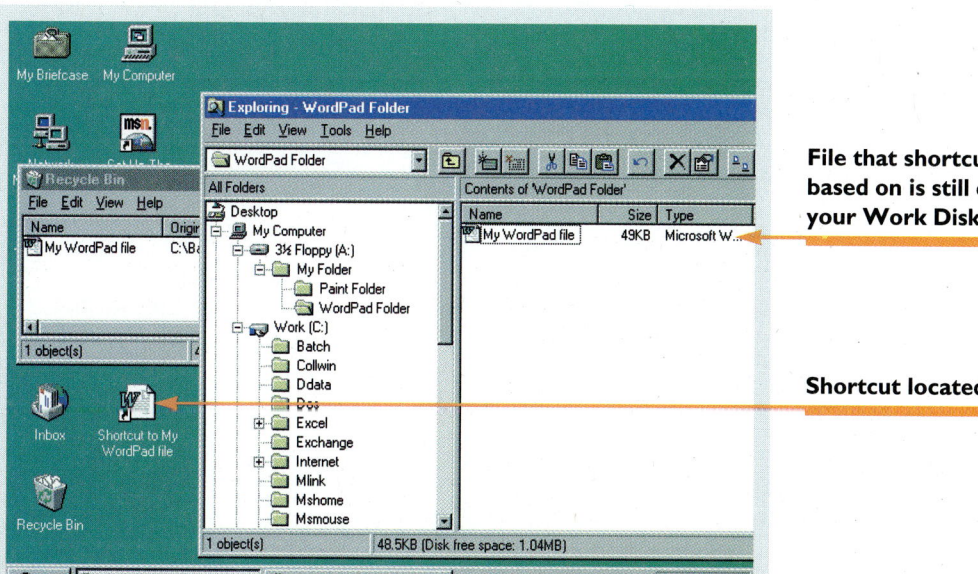

File that shortcut is based on is still on your Work Disk

Shortcut located here

Adding shortcuts to the Start menu

If you do not want your desktop to get cluttered with icons, but you would still like easy access to certain files, programs, and folders, you can create a shortcut on the Start menu or any of its cascading menus. Drag the file, program, or folder that you want to add to the Start menu from the Windows Explorer window to the Start button. The file, program, or folder will appear on the first level of the Start menu.

QUICK TIP

Windows 95 enables you to customize your desktop to suit your work habits. For example, you can create a folder on the desktop that you can use to store all of your shortcuts. You can even create a shortcut folder on the desktop.

TASK REFERENCE

TASK	MOUSE/BUTTON	MENU	KEYBOARD
Close selected folder and all its parent folders			Press [Shift] while clicking the Close button
Copy a file/folder	Press [Ctrl] while dragging the file or folder to its new location		
Copy to the Clipboard	📋	Click Edit, Copy	[Ctrl] [C]
Create a new folder (in My Computer or Windows Explorer)		Click the right mouse button, click New, Folder	
Create a shortcut	Press [Ctrl] [Shift] while dragging the file or folder to the desktop	Click the right mouse button, click Create Shortcut	
Cut to the Clipboard	✂	Click Edit, Cut	[Ctrl] [X]
Delete a file/folder	Drag the file/folder to the Recycle Bin	Click File, Delete	[Del]
Format a disk		Right-click icon containing disk, click Format	
Move a file/folder		Drag the file/folder to its new location	
Open a file		In a program, click File, Open	
Paste from the Clipboard	📋	Click Edit, Paste	[Ctrl] [V]
Rename a file	Click the file to select it, then click it again to display an insertion point	Right-click the file, click Rename	[F2]
Save a file (for the first time or with a new name)		Click File, Save As	
Save changes in a previously saved file		Click File, Save	
Switch between open programs	Click the program button on the taskbar		Press [Alt] [Tab] to display each open program
View a folder up one level	📁		[Backspace]

CONCEPTS REVIEW

Label each of the elements of the Windows Explorer window shown in Figure 2-21.

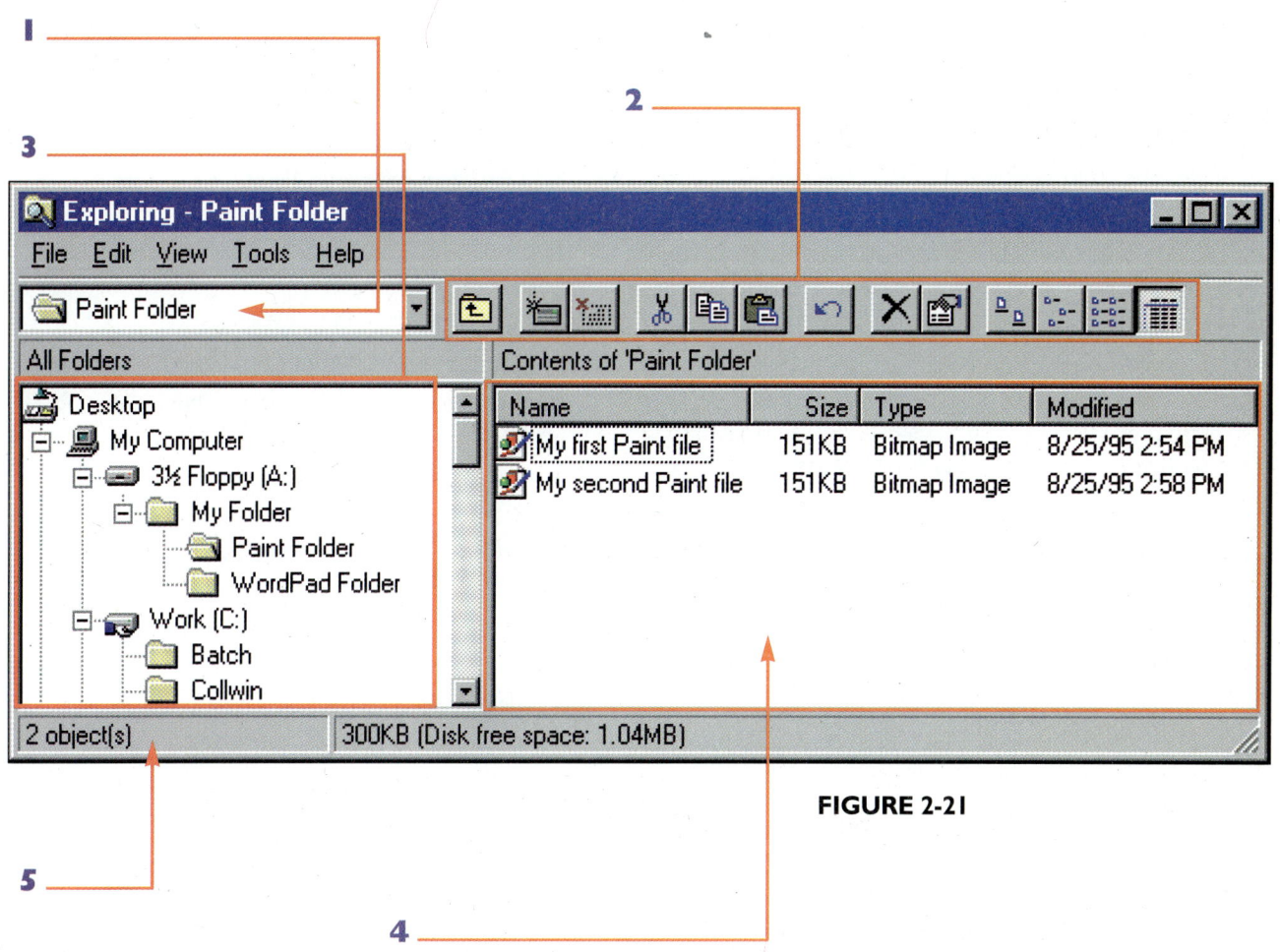

FIGURE 2-21

Match each of the descriptions with the correct term.

6. Permanent storage of your work in programs
7. Temporary location of your work as you use a program
8. Temporary location of information you wish to paste into another program
9. Storage area for organizing files or folders by type, project, or whatever you wish
10. Structure of files and folders revealing organization of a disk

a. RAM
b. Folders
c. Files
d. Hierarchy
e. Clipboard

Select the best answer from the list of choices.

11. To prepare a floppy disk to receive your files, you must first do which of the following?
    a. Copy work files to the disk
    b. Format the disk
    c. Erase all the files that might be on the disk
    d. Place the files on the Clipboard

12. To view the contents of a folder, you can use which of the following tools?
    a. The desktop
    b. Windows Explorer
    c. My Computer
    d. Either b or c

13. You can use the My Computer program to
    a. create a drawing of your computer.
    b. view the contents of a folder.
    c. customize the Start menu.
    d. determine what programs begin automatically when you start Windows.

14. While you are working in a program, where is your work stored?
    a. On a hard drive
    b. In RAM
    c. In the monitor
    d. On the Clipboard

15. What is the correct sequence for starting the Paint program?
    a. Double-click the Paint shortcut on the desktop
    b. Click Start, Programs, Accessories, Paint
    c. Click Start, Programs, Paint
    d. Click Start, Accessories, Paint

16. Which of the following best describes the WordPad program?
    a. A program for pasting in graphics
    b. A program for performing complex financial analysis
    c. A program that is a simple text editor for creating basic documents
    d. A program for creating graphics

17. For most Windows programs, the Save As command is located on which menu?
    a. File
    b. Edit
    c. Help
    d. Save

18. Which of the following is NOT a way to move files from one folder to another?
    a. Opening the file and using the Save As command to save the file in a new location.
    b. In My Computer or the Windows Explorer, drag the selected to the new folder.
    c. Use the Cut and Paste commands on the Edit menu while in the My Computer or the Windows Explorer windows.
    d. Use the [Ctrl] [X] and [Ctrl] [V] keyboard shortcuts while in the My Computer or the Windows Explorer windows.

19 Which of the following is a way to rename the selected file in either the My Computer window or the Windows Explorer window?

   a. Click Edit on the menu bar, then click Rename.
   b. Click File on the menu bar, then click Rename.
   c. Click the Rename button on the toolbar.
   d. You can only rename files in the program in which the file was created.

20 In which of the following can you view the hierarchy of drives, folder, and files in a split pane window?

   a. The Windows Explorer window
   b. The Programs window
   c. The My Computer window
   d. The WordPad window

21 For which of the following tasks would you NOT use Windows Explorer?

   a. Copying files or folders
   b. Moving files or folders
   c. Deleting files or folders
   d. Working in programs to create documents

22 In the Properties dialog box for your hard drive, you can see

   a. how much of the total capacity is being used and how much is free.
   b. what programs are being used.
   c. what programs are taking up the most space.
   d. all of the files and folders stored on the hard drive.

23 To display the Properties dialog box for one of your drives, you need to

   a. select the drive, then click Properties on the File menu.
   b. right-click on the desired drive, then click Properties from the shortcut menu.
   c. select the drive, then click Properties on the View menu.
   d. double-click on the desired drive.

24 If you are positive that you will not need to restore a file, you can delete it using the keyboard by pressing

   a. [Shift][End]
   b. [Delete]
   c. [Shift][Delete]
   d. [Ctrl][Delete]

25 To restore files that you have sent to the Recycle Bin,

   a. click File, then click Empty Recycle Bin.
   b. click Edit, then click Undo Delete.
   c. click File, then click Undo.
   d. you cannot retrieve files sent to the Recycle Bin.

26 To open the Recycle Bin,

   a. click Start, Programs, Recycle Bin.
   b. double-click the Recycle Bin icon.
   c. click Start, Accessories, Recycle Bin.
   d. click Start, Recycle Bin.

27 In Windows Explorer, a plus sign next to a drive or folder means

   a. the drive or folder is currently being used.
   b. the drive or folder is at full capacity.
   c. there are additional files or folders located within the folder or drive.
   d. this drive or folder cannot be used at this time.

28 To copy instead of move a file from one folder to another, drag while pressing

   a. [Shift]
   b. [Alt]
   c. [Tab]
   d. [Ctrl]

29 To select files that are not grouped together, select the first file, then

   a. press [Shift] while selecting the second file.
   b. press [Alt] while selecting the second file.
   c. press [Ctrl] while selecting the second file.
   d. click on the second file.

30 To select a group of files listed together,

   a. select the first file, then drag until all the files in the list are selected.
   b. select the first file, then press [Shift] while selecting the last file in the list.
   c. select the first file, then press [Ctrl] while selecting the last file in the list.
   d. select the first file, then press [Alt] while selecting the last file in the list.

SKILLS REVIEW

1. Format a disk.
   a. Insert a new blank disk in a drive.
   b. Open My Computer and use the right mouse button to click on the drive.
   c. Format the disk using the Format command on the pop-up menu. Check that the capacity and format type are correct.

2. Create a WordPad file.
   a. Launch WordPad.
   b. Type a short description of your artistic abilities and press [Enter] several times to create extra space between the text and the graphic you are about to create.
   c. Insert your Work Disk in the appropriate disk drive, then save the document as My New Document to the My Folder on your Work Disk.
   d. Minimize the WordPad program.

3. Create and save a Paint file.
   a. Launch Paint.
   b. Create your own unique, colorful design using several colors. Use a variety of tools. For example, create a filled circle and then place a filled square inside the circle. Use the Text button to create a text box in which you type your name.
   c. Save the picture as My Art to the My Folder on your Work Disk.
   d. Select the entire graphic and copy it onto the Clipboard.
   e. Switch to the WordPad program.
   f. Place the insertion point below the text and paste the graphic into your document.
   g. Save the changes to your WordPad document.
   h. Switch to the Paint program.
   i. Using the Fill With Color button, change the color of a filled area of your graphic.
   j. Save the revised graphic with a new name, My Art2 to the My Folder on your Work Disk.
   k. Select the entire graphic and copy it to the Clipboard.
   l. Switch to the WordPad program and above the picture type "This is an improved graphic."
   m. Select the old graphic by clicking the picture, then paste the new contents of the Clipboard. The new graphic replaces the old graphic that was selected.
   n. Save the changed WordPad document with a new name, My Second Document to the My Folder on your Work Disk.
   o. Exit the Paint and WordPad programs.

4. Manage files and folders with My Computer.
   a. Open My Computer.
   b. Be sure your Work Disk is in either drive A or drive B.
   c. Double-click the drive icon that contains your Work Disk to prepare for the next step.

5. Create new folders on the Work Disk and on the hard drive.
   a. Create a folder called My Review Folder on your Work Disk by clicking File, New, then clicking Folder.
   b. Open the folder to display its contents in a separate window.
   c. Create another folder (at the root of C on the hard drive) called My Temporary Folder.
   d. In the My Review Folder window, click File, New, then click Folder. Create two new subfolders (under My Review Folder), one called Documents and the other called ArtWork.
   e. In the My Computer window, double-click the drive C icon to display the contents of your hard drive in a new window.

6. Move files to the new folders in the My Review Folder.
   a. Open the ArtWork folder on your Work Disk.
   b. From the root of the Work Disk, drag the two Paint files into the ArtWork folder window on your Work Disk. Close the ArtWork folder window.
   c. Open the Documents folder on your Work Disk.
   d. From the root of the Work Disk, drag the two WordPad files into the Documents folder window on your Work Disk. Close the Documents folder window.
   e. Close all of the open windows in My Computer.

7. Copy files to the My Temporary Folder on the hard drive.
   a. Open the Windows Explorer.
   b. Copy the four WordPad and Paint files from the folders on the Work Disk to the My Temporary Folder.

8. Delete files and folders.
   a. Drag the My Temporary Folder to the Recycle Bin icon.
   b. Click the My Review Folder and press [Del]. Then confirm that you want to delete the file.
   c. Double-click the Recycle Bin icon and restore the My Temporary Folder and its files. Delete the folder again.

9. Create a shortcut that opens Windows Explorer.
   a. Use Windows Explorer to locate the Windows folder on your hard drive. In the right side of the window, scroll through the list of objects until you see a file called Explorer.
   b. Drag the Explorer file to the desktop.
   c. Close the Windows Explorer.
   d. Double-click the new shortcut to test the shortcut for starting Windows Explorer. Then close the Explorer again.
   e. Delete the shortcut for Windows Explorer. Then use the Start button to verify that the Windows Explorer program is still available on the Programs menu.

INDEPENDENT CHALLENGE 1

It is important to develop a sound, organized plan when you manage files and folders. Practice your skills by organizing the following list of names into a coherent and logical hierarchy. Begin by identifying folders. In each folder, identify the files you could expect to find in them. Sketch a hierarchical structure like the one you would see in the right side of a Windows Explorer window.

- Projects
- My Resume
- Recommendation letter
- First Qtr Bulletin
- Marketing
- Finance
- Sales 95
- Sales 96
- Personal
- Employee Profile article
- Sales 94
- Project Plan Second Qtr
- Project Plan First Qtr
- Sales Summary
- Performance Review 1996

INDEPENDENT CHALLENGE 2

It is important to develop a sound, organized plan when you manage files and folders. Practice your skills by organizing the following list of names into a coherent and logical hierarchy. Begin by identifying folders. Then in each folder, identify the files you could expect to find in them. Sketch the series of windows containing the folders and files you would display using My Computer. For example, one of the windows might represent the contents of a folder designated for non-work related files.

- Projects
- My Resume
- Recommendation letter
- First Qtr Bulletin
- Marketing
- Finance
- Sales 95
- Sales 96
- Personal
- Employee Profile article
- Sales 94
- Project Plan Second Qtr
- Project Plan First Qtr
- Sales Summary
- Performance Review 1996

INDEPENDENT CHALLENGE 3

On your computer's hard drive (at the root of C:), create a folder called My Review Folder. Then using the files on your Work Disk, create the file hierarchy indicated below. Follow these guidelines to create the files you need to place in the correct folders.

1. Create a new file using WordPad that contains a simple list of things to do. Save the file as To Do List.
2. Create two copies of any WordPad files and rename them New WordPad Article and Copy of Article.
3. Copy any Paint file and rename the copy Sample Logo.
4. Copy the To Do List, and rename the copy Important.

After you have placed the files in their correct folders, copy the My Review Folder (and its contents) to your Work Disk. Then on your hard drive, delete the My Review Folder. Using the Recycle Bin icon, restore the file called Important. To remove all your work on the hard drive, delete this file again.

FIGURE 2-22

My Review Folder
- ➥Projects
  - ➥To Do List
  - ➥Communications (folder)
    - ➥New WordPad Article
    - ➥Copy of Article
  - ➥Graphics (folder)
    - ➥Sample Logo
    - ➥Important

INDEPENDENT
CHALLENGE 4

To make working with files on a floppy disk easier, create a shortcut to a Windows Explorer window that displays the contents of a disk in the drive that currently contains your Work Disk. (*Hint:* Open Windows Explorer as shown in Figure 2-23 and drag the icon representing your floppy drive to the desktop). Next, capture a picture of your desktop (with the new shortcut) onto the Clipboard by pressing the [Prnt Scrn] key (located on the upper-right side of your keyboard). With the picture on the Clipboard, open the Paint program and paste the contents of the Clipboard into the drawing window as shown in Figure 2-24. Save the Paint file as My Desktop Picture on your Work Disk. Finally, delete the shortcut.

FIGURE 2-23

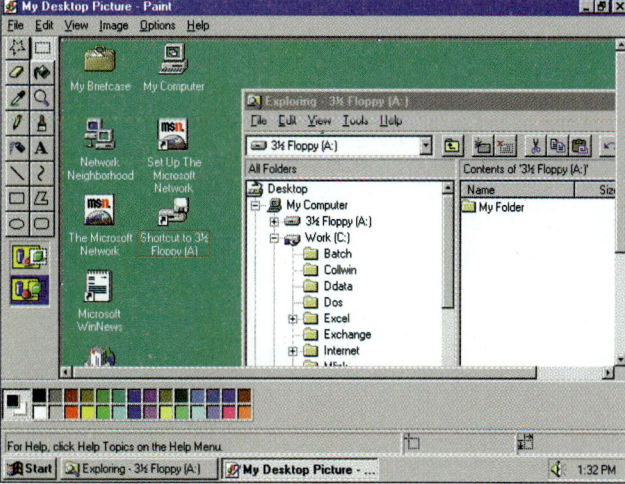

FIGURE 2-24

Microsoft® Works 4 for Windows® 95

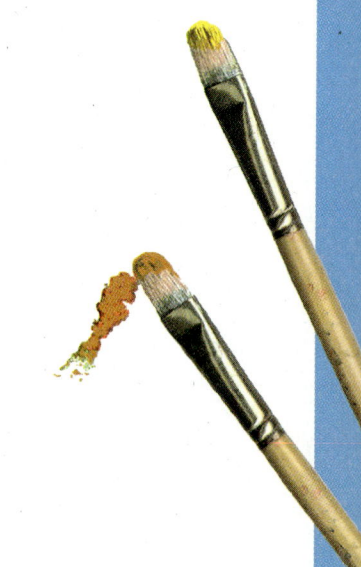

UNIT 1	Getting Started with Microsoft Works 4 for Windows 95
UNIT 2	Creating a Document with the Word Processor
UNIT 3	Enhancing a Document's Appearance
UNIT 4	Getting Started with Desktop Publishing
UNIT 5	Building a Spreadsheet
UNIT 6	Working with Spreadsheet Functions
UNIT 7	Creating Charts with the Spreadsheet
UNIT 8	Building a Database
UNIT 9	Working with an Existing Database
UNIT 10	Creating Database Reports
UNIT 11	Exploring Telecommunications
UNIT 12	Creating Illustrations with Draw
UNIT 13	Combining Works Applications

Read this Before You Begin
Microsoft Works 4 for Windows 95

To the Student

The exercises and examples in these units feature several ready-made Works document files which are contained on the Student Disk provided to your instructor. To complete the step-by-step exercises in this book, you must have a Student Disk. Your instructor will either provide you with your own copy of the Student Disk or will make the Student Disk files available to you over a network in your school's computer lab. See your instructor or technical support person for further information.

Any time you see a camera icon, you know an interactive movie, a CourseHelp, is available on that topic. To start a CourseHelp, click the Start button on the taskbar, point to Programs, point to CourseHelp, then click Works 4 Illustrated. From the CourseHelp opening screen, click the topic that relates to the lesson.

Using Your Own Computer

If you are going to work through this book using your own computer, you need a computer system running Microsoft Windows 95, Microsoft Works 4 for Windows 95, CourseHelp installed on your computer, and a Student Disk. *You will not be able to complete the step-by-step lessons and exercises in this book using your own computer until you have your own Student Disk.* This book assumes the default settings under a standard installation of Microsoft Works 4 for Windows 95.

To the Instructor

Bundled with the instructor's copy of this book is the Student Disk, which contains all the files your students need to complete the step-by-step exercises in this book. Adopters of this text are granted the right to distribute the files on the Student Disk to any student who has purchased a copy of the text. The data files to be used with the text are stored in 2 folders on the Student Disk. Before students can work through the book, the files contained in each folder below should be transferred to one of 2 high density 3.5 inch disks. **DISK 1** contains data files for use in units 1–5 and **DISK 2** contains data files for use in units 6–13. You can make the data files available to students on 2 high density 3.5 inch disks; you may choose to make this disk available to students, having them copy the data files themselves onto 2 separate high density disks; or you may post the files to network or standalone workstations. The book assumes that students will be working through the units using files of 2 high density 3.5 inch disks, each disk containing the files from the appropriate folder above. This disk division minimizes the possibility that students will not run out of disk space as they alter, create, and save data files in the units. *NOTE: the above folders contain Windows 95 filenames. You will need to perform the copy operations on a Windows 95 computer in order to avoid truncated filenames.* The instructions in this book assume that the students know which drive and directory contain the Student Disk files, so it's important that you provide disk location information before the students start working through the units. You also need to provide instructions about where students should save their modified files. We assume that students will save all files to their Student Disk in the My Works Files folder they create in Unit 1 of the Works section.

As an adopter of this book you will receive the CourseHelp disk and the Student Disk. The CourseHelp disk contains a README.DOC file with detailed instructions for installing CourseHelp on standalone machines or on a network. Once installed, students can access CourseHelp movies by clicking the Start button, pointing to Programs, Pointing to CourseHelp, then clicking Works 4 Illustrated.

UNIT 1

OBJECTIVES

▶ Start Microsoft Works 4 for Windows 95

▶ Start a Works tool

▶ Use dialog boxes

▶ Use toolbars

▶ Use the Works Help system

▶ Use a TaskWizard

▶ Save a file

▶ Close a file and exit Works

Getting Started
WITH MICROSOFT WORKS 4 FOR WINDOWS 95

Now that you have learned the basics of Windows 95, you will begin working with Microsoft Works 4 for Windows 95, a multipurpose or **integrated software package** that includes word processor, spreadsheet, database, and communications programs, as well as several supporting accessories. (Works programs and accessories are collectively called **tools** in the software.) ▶case This unit introduces you to Outdoor Designs, a company that sells kits for recreational products. Outdoor Designs uses Works to write memos and reports, manage inventory and sales data, and track customers. You have just been hired as a summer intern for Outdoor Designs. Sue Ellen, the sales manager, asked you to become familiar with Works and prepare a letterhead template that employees can use for their correspondence. Start building your skills now. ▶

Starting Microsoft Works 4 for Windows 95

You start Works by clicking the Windows Start button and clicking the Microsoft Works 4 program icon, or by double-clicking the Shortcut to Microsoft Works 4 icon on the Windows desktop if one was created during installation. Once started, Works displays the Works Task Launcher dialog box, where you can open existing Works files, launch time-saving TaskWizards, or start one of the four Works tools. **case** Sue Ellen asked you to start Works and learn about the documents you can create with this integrated software package. Table 1-1 lists a few projects you can build with Works.

1. **Click the Start button on the lower-left corner of the screen**
   The menu of folders shown in Figure 1-1 opens above the Start button. (Figure 1-1 also shows the Shortcut to Microsoft Works 4 icon on the Windows desktop, an alternate method for starting Works.)

2. **Point to the Programs folder, then point to the Microsoft Works 4.0 program folder**
   (As you learned in "Getting Started with Windows 95," to point to an item you simply move the mouse pointer over the item.) After a moment, the programs in the Microsoft Works 4 folder appear on a submenu. To run one of these programs, you simply click the program icon.

3. **Click the Microsoft Works 4.0 program icon**
   The Works Task Launcher dialog box shown in Figure 1-2 opens. If this is the first time the Works software has been used, you may see an introductory dialog box instead. In that case, read the contents of the dialog box, then close the dialog box to display the Works Task Launcher. Note that as you use the Works program, your screen may not exactly match the figures in this book. Video adapters and monitors differ from system to system and affect the Works display. Slight display differences should not affect your work in this book.

The Task Launcher is your pathway to the Works TaskWizards, Existing Works documents, and the four Works programs or tools. To switch among these three categories, click the tabs at the top of the dialog box. Tabs often appear in Works dialog boxes, and you can click them to switch quickly from one category to another. Table 1-1 lists the four Works tools and a few of the useful documents you can create with them.

TABLE 1-1: Examples of documents you can create with Works

WORKS TOOL	DOCUMENTS
Word Processor	Memo, letter, multicolumn newsletter, term paper, letterhead with art
Spreadsheet	General ledger, expense report, sales figures, 3-D pie charts
Database	Customer database, music collection, commission reports, form letters
Communications	Electronic mail, stock quotes, on-line research, document distribution

FIGURE 1-1: Two methods for starting Works for Windows 95

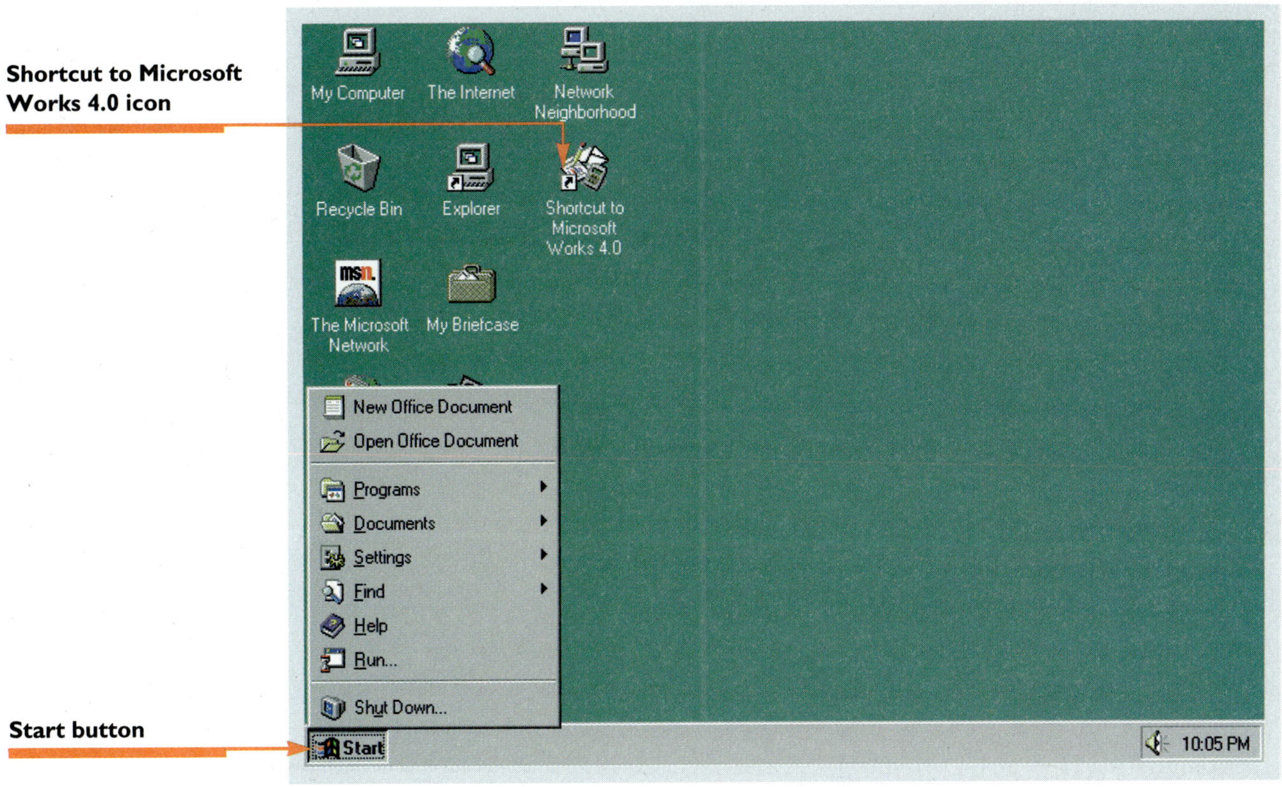

Shortcut to Microsoft Works 4.0 icon

Start button

FIGURE 1-2: Works Task Launcher dialog box

Tabs

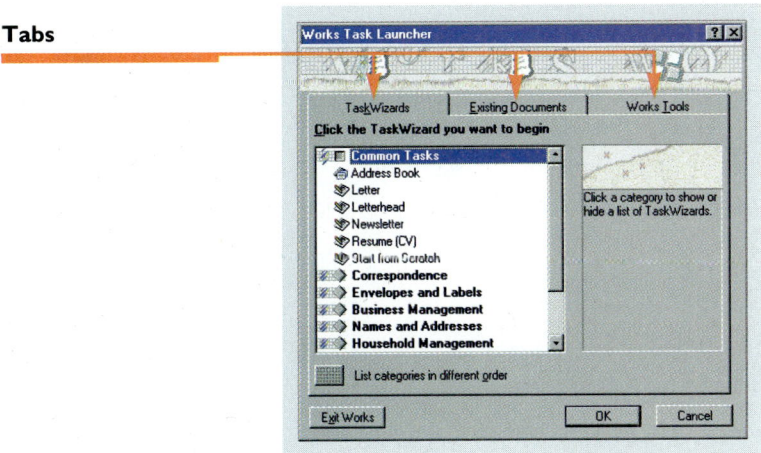

TROUBLE?

If you have trouble locating or starting the Works program, or don't see the Works Task Launcher dialog box, the program may not be properly installed on your computer. Ask your instructor or technical support person for assistance.

Starting a Works tool

From the Works Task Launcher, you can start the Works Word Processor, Spreadsheet, Database, or Communications tools. Each Works tool has a similar graphic interface. After you learn how to use the buttons, menus, and toolbars in one Works tool, you'll know how to use the interface elements in all Works tools. Table 1-2 lists some interface elements common to all Works tools. To learn to start other programs while you work with Works, see the related topic, "Switching to other Windows programs." ▶case Start the Works Word Processor now to practice the techniques you'll use throughout this book. After you get your feet wet, you'll use the Word Processor to create an Outdoor Designs letterhead that the entire company can use.

1. **Click the Works Tools tab** in the Works Task Launcher dialog box
   The four Works programs shown in Figure 1-3 appear in the Works Tools tab. To create a new document with one of these tools, you click a button in this dialog box.

2. **Click the Word Processor button** to start the Works Word Processor
   The Works Task Launcher closes, and the Works Word Processor opens in a window, as shown in Figure 1-4. The Works Word Processor manipulates text-based documents, such as memos, newsletters, and term papers. The Works Word Processor is the electronic equivalent of paper, typewriter, eraser, dictionary, and thesaurus.

   Use Figure 1-4 to identify the Word Processor's elements. Refer to Table 1-2 to identify the interface elements you'll use in your Outdoor Designs projects.

TABLE 1-2: Interface elements common to all Works tools

ELEMENT	DESCRIPTION
Menu bar	Area under title bar containing menu names. Each menu opens to provide access to a group of Word Processor commands
Toolbar	Row of list boxes and command buttons beneath the menu bar
Document window	Window containing the program's workspace
Scroll bars	Horizontal and vertical bars at the bottom and right edge of the window, used to view parts of a document not currently displayed in the window
Toggle indicators	Indicators for Num Lock, Caps Lock, and Insert toggle keys
Sizing buttons	Minimize, Maximize, and Close buttons for Works program window and each document window
Help buttons	Two buttons that provide on-line help for the open Works tool

FIGURE 1-3: Works Task Launcher dialog box

Word Processor button

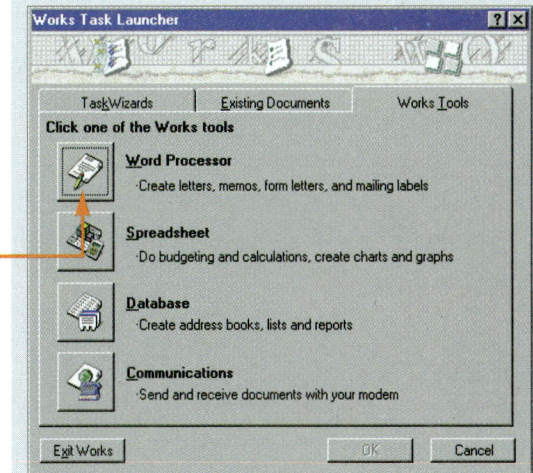

FIGURE 1-4: Typical elements in the Word Processor

Menu bar

Toolbar

Document window

Scroll bars

Toggle indicators

Sizing buttons

Help buttons

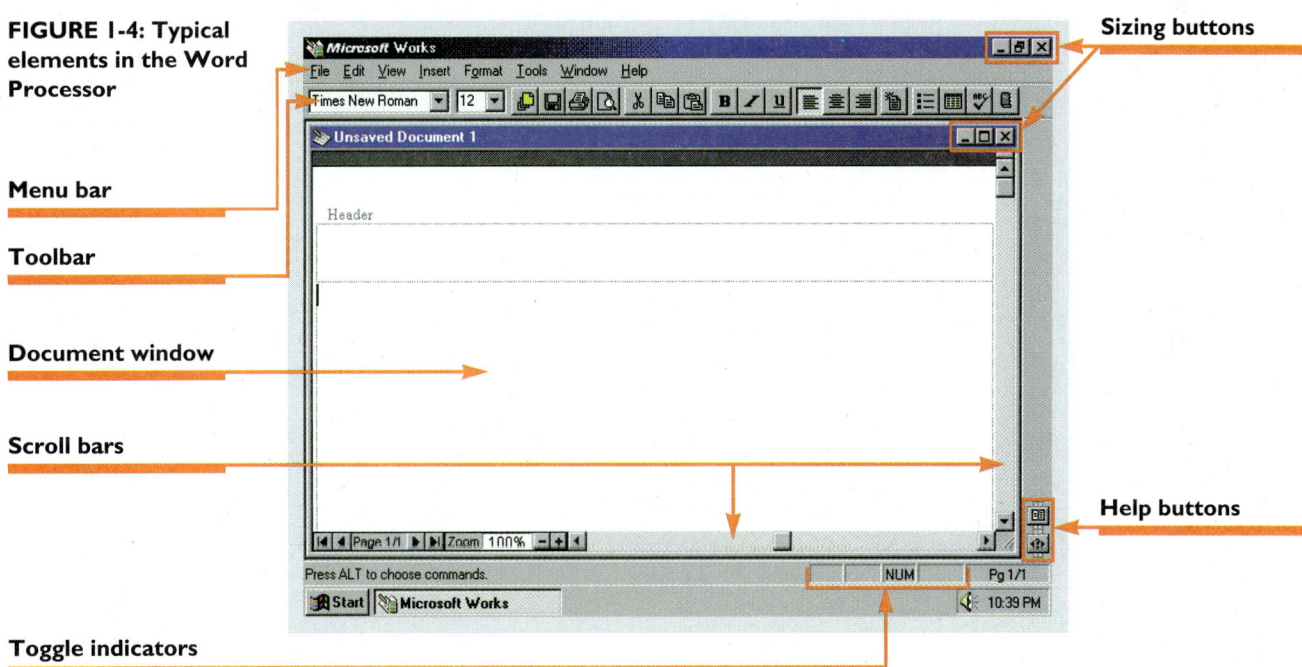

Switching to other Windows programs

As you learned in "Getting Started with Windows 95," you can run more than one Windows program at once and use the taskbar to switch between them. This feature is available in Works, too; it lets you switch back to Windows or another program while you work with Works. To start another program while you work with Works, simply click the Start button and point to the program icon representing the program you want to run. To switch to a program that is running, simply click the program name on the taskbar.

To quickly exit the Word Processor and quit Works, hold down [Alt] and press [F4].

Using dialog boxes

As in other Windows programs, in Works you choose commands from menus to execute them. If Works needs information to carry out a command, it displays a **dialog box** that presents available options. The related topic, "Moving around a dialog box," provides tips for working with a dialog box. **case** Build your dialog box skills now, so they come more easily when you begin creating your first Outdoor Designs document.

1. **Click Format on the menu bar**
   The Format menu opens. It includes useful commands for changing the style and presentation of text in the Word Processor.

2. **Click Font and Style on the Format menu**
   The Format Font and Style dialog box shown in Figure 1-5 opens. The dialog box lets you choose the font, style, size, color, and position of text in the Word Processor. The Sample rectangle shows you a sample of what text in the Word Processor will look like when you click OK. Take a moment to identify the dialog box options shown in Figure 1-5.

3. **Press and hold the list arrow in the Font list box to scroll up to the top of the box**
   The font names in the Font list box scroll vertically; the Arial font is near the top of the list. (Your font list may differ from the list shown in Figure 1-5.)

4. **Click Arial in the Font list box**
   Arial is highlighted in the Font list box and also appears in the Font text box above the Font list box. The font of the text in the Sample rectangle changes to Arial.

5. **Click the Bold and Italic check boxes under Style, then scroll and click 16 in the Size list box**
   A check mark appears in each check box, and the text in the Sample rectangle changes to bold and italic. A 16 displays in the Size text box, and the size of the text in the Sample rectangle changes to 16 points. (A point is $\frac{1}{72}$ of an inch.)

6. **Click the Color list box, then click Blue**
   After the first click, the Color list box displays the available colors. When you choose Blue, the color of the text in the Sample rectangle changes to blue.

7. **Click Superscript under Position**
   The Position indicator changes from Normal to Superscript. You're finished experimenting with the options in this dialog box. Now discard your font and style selections.

8. **Click the Cancel command button**
   The Format Font and Style dialog box closes without saving your new selections.

FIGURE 1-5: Format Font and Style dialog box

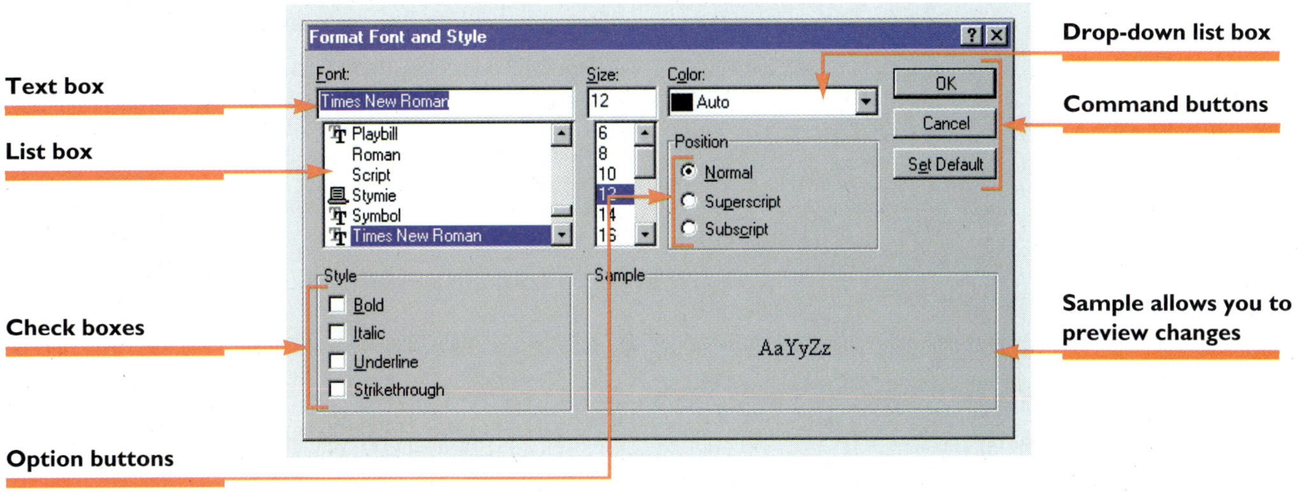

- Text box
- List box
- Check boxes
- Option buttons
- Drop-down list box
- Command buttons
- Sample allows you to preview changes

Moving around a dialog box

If a dialog box contains several options, you can press [Tab] to move from one option to the next. For example, to move from the Font list box to the Size list box shown in Figure 1-6, you would press [Tab]. (You can also move backward by holding down [Shift] and pressing [Tab].) If the highlighted section in the dialog box contains more than one option (as does the Position group of option buttons), you can press the direction keys to move from one option to the next.

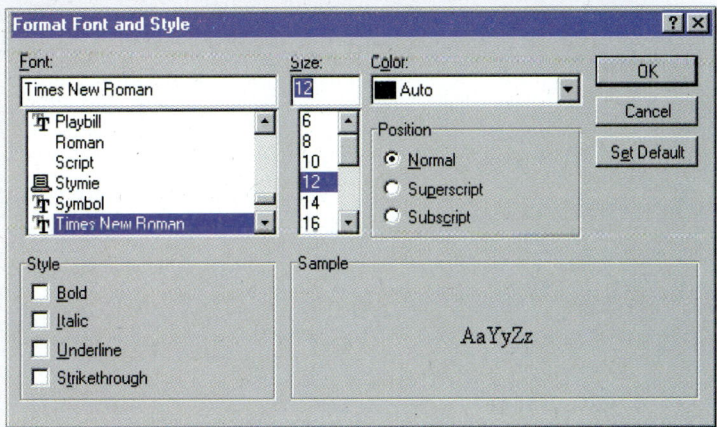

FIGURE 1-6: Press [Tab] in a dialog box to move from one option to the next

To move a dialog box, drag its title bar to the desired location.

Using toolbars

A **toolbar** is a customizable set of buttons and list boxes, located below the menu bar of a Works tool. Toolbars provide rapid access to the most commonly used Works commands. Buttons on Works toolbars are often easier to remember than menu and keyboard commands because the buttons graphically represent the tasks they accomplish. Table 1-3 lists the toolbar buttons found in most Works tools. **case** You'll use toolbars often in your work at Outdoor Designs, so practice using them now. The Word Processor tool should still be open on your screen.

1. **Type Mississippi**
   The word "Mississippi" appears in the document window. As you type, the blinking cursor or **insertion point** moves to the right.

2. **Double-click Mississippi**
   Now the word "Mississippi" is highlighted or **selected**, as shown in Figure 1-7. Before you can work with text in a Works tool, you need to select it. You'll learn more about selecting text in Unit 2.

3. **Click the Bold button** 🅱 **on the toolbar**
   The Bold button is highlighted, making it appear **indented**, and the style of the selected text changes to bold. Clicking the Bold button is much quicker than clicking the Format menu and then clicking Font and Style; both have the same effect.

4. **Click** 🅱 **again**
   The Bold button is no longer indented, and the style of the selected text returns to normal.

5. **Click the Center-align button** ≣ **on the toolbar**
   The Center-align button appears indented and the selected text is aligned at the center of the document. Notice that alignment buttons function like option buttons: when the Center-align button is pushed in, the Left-align button pops out.

6. **Click the Center-align button** ≣ **on the toolbar again**
   The Center-align button is no longer indented and the selected text once again aligns at the document's left margin.

7. **Click the Cut button** ✂
   The word "Mississippi" disappears from the document. You'll learn more about using the Cut and Paste commands in Unit 2.

FIGURE 1-7: Toolbar buttons can speed up your work

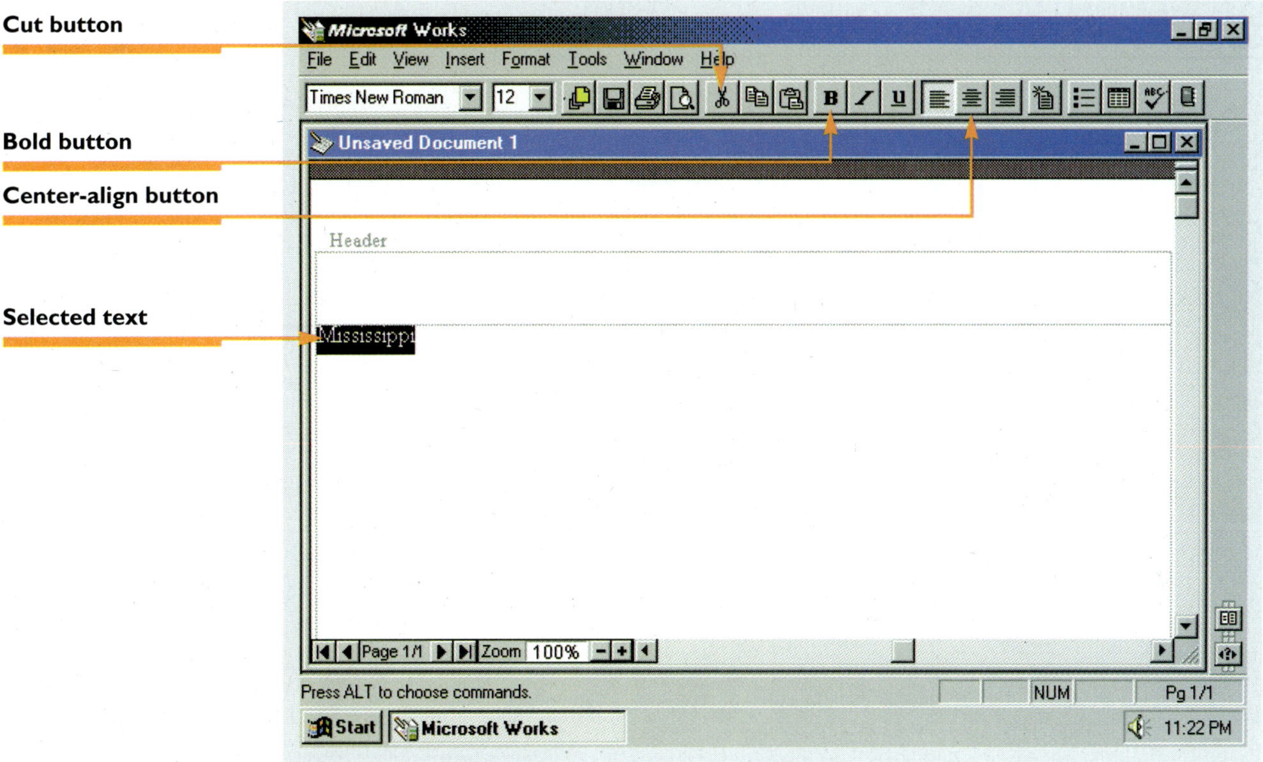

- Cut button
- Bold button
- Center-align button
- Selected text

TABLE 1-3: Useful toolbar buttons and their functions

TOOLBAR BUTTON	FUNCTION
	Displays Works Task Launcher dialog box
	Saves current document to disk
	Prints current document
	Shows how current document will look printed
	Cuts selected text
	Copies selected text
	Pastes selected text
	Changes style of selected text to bold
	Changes style of selected text to italic
	Changes style of selected text to underline
	Opens the default Works address book

To learn the function of a button or list box on the toolbar, point to it. After a moment, the tool's name appears in a yellow pop-up box.

Using the Works Help system

If you have a question about a Works feature or procedure, you can use the program's **Help system** to get an answer. The Help system explains the current tool and lets you review basic skills, run a step-by-step tutorial, or search for help on a specific topic. The related topic, "Searching for specific topics," offers more information on this Help system feature. You can access the Help system by clicking one of the two Help buttons on the lower-right of your screen, or you can choose a command on the Help menu. **case** As an eager summer intern, you take pride in learning about Works on your own. Use the Help system now to learn how to delete highlighted text in the Word Processor.

1. Click the **Help button** near the lower-right corner of the Works screen
   The on-line Help system shown in Figure 1-8 opens in a window. The Help system displays a list of topics about the open tool and several buttons that let you navigate the reference information available to you. The Index button displays a dialog box you can use to search for specific topics, the Shrink Help button closes the Help system, the Menu button returns you to the top list of topics, and the Back button lets you scroll in reverse order through the topics you have examined. Because you are working with the Word Processor, the topics listed in the Help system relate to the Word Processor. Find out more about correcting mistakes with the Word Processor.

2. Click the **Correct mistakes arrow** in the Help window
   A list of topics related to correcting mistakes opens in the Help window. To learn more about deleting highlighted text (text selected in a block), click at topic.

3. Click **To delete a block of text** in the Help window
   A Step-by-Step tab appears in the Help window, containing instructions you can follow to delete a highlighted text block in the Word Processor. One word in the instructions ("Highlight") is underlined and displayed in green type. This format indicates you can click the word with the mouse to get its definition.

4. Click **Highlight** in the first step to see highlighting defined.
   Works defines the term in a yellow text box.

5. Click the **text box** when you finish reading it to close the box
   Works closes the box. Now look for additional information on the subject.

6. Click the **More Info tab** in the Help window to learn more about deleting with the Word Processor
   Works displays a series of related topics in the Help window. To read about a topic, simply click the button associated with it.

7. Click the **Shrink Help button** to close the Help system
   The Help system closes and the Word Processor window returns to normal.

FIGURE 1-8: Works Help window

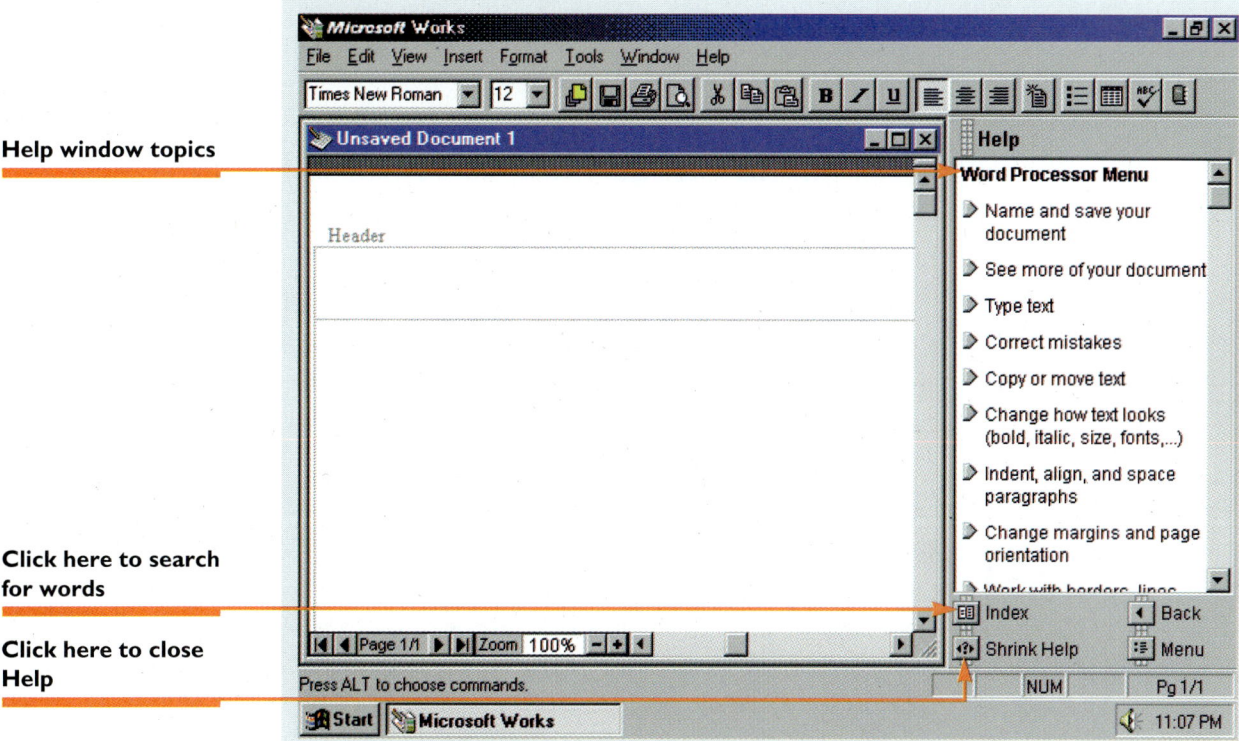

Help window topics

Click here to search for words

Click here to close Help

Searching for specific topics

To search for a particular word in the Works Help system, click the Index button  in the lower-right corner of your screen or in the Help window. When you click the button, Works opens a dialog box you can use to type search phrases, as shown in Figure 1-9. To use the search index, type the word you want to look for in the first text box, and watch Works attempt to find a match in the list box below. When you see the topic you want to read, click the description and review the documentation in the Help window. When you finish using the Help Index, click Close **and** shrink the Help window.

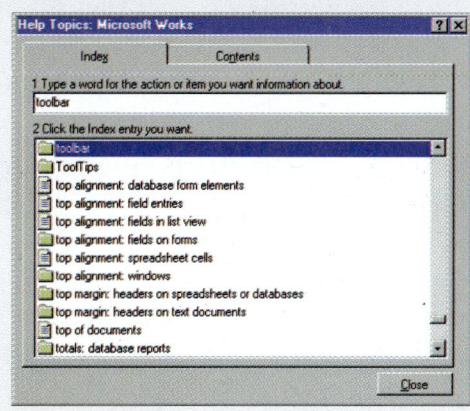

FIGURE 1-9: Index tab

QUICK TIP

To remove Help buttons from the right margin and make more room, click Help on the menu bar, then click Hide Help. ■

Using a TaskWizard

A **TaskWizard** is an automated tool that structures and formats a document for you. Works' dozens of TaskWizards give you a head start on managing addresses, tracking inventory, mailing form letters and other common tasks. ▶case Sue Ellen asked you to create a company letterhead that Outdoor Designs' employees can use for their mailings and correspondence. Create a simple letterhead file now with the Letterhead TaskWizard.

1. Click the **Task Launcher button** on the toolbar
   The Works Task Launcher dialog box opens, giving you access to new and existing projects.

2. Click the **TaskWizards tab**
   Names of available TaskWizards appear in a list box, grouped in categories. To display available TaskWizards in a category that is not currently open, click the square button to the left of the category name. Now start the Letterhead TaskWizard in the Common Tasks category.

3. Double-click **Letterhead** in the TaskWizard list box, then click **Yes**
   The window shown in Figure 1-10 opens. It describes the Letterhead TaskWizard and presents three style choices for the document. You make your selection by clicking one of the three large buttons and then clicking the Next button.

4. Click the **Simple button**, then click **Next**
   The TaskWizard displays a screen with five buttons you can use to customize the letterhead's contents. You'll customize the Letterhead section.

5. Click the **Letterhead button**
   A Works window gives you the option to either design your own letterhead or use your pre-printed letterhead stationary. You'll design your own, using the Works Contemporary style.

6. Click the **I want to design my own.** option button if it is not already selected, click **Next**, then click the **Contemporary** option button and click **Next**
   Works displays a window where you can specify a name to be used in your letterhead. You specify a company name, not a personal name, so that others in the company can use this letterhead.

7. Type **Outdoor Designs** in the Company name text box, click **Next**, type **1820 Big Timber Drive** in the Address Line 1 text box, press **[Tab]** twice, type **Seattle, WA 98109** in the City, State/Province, Postal Code text box, and click **Next**
   A screen prompts you for your business phone numbers.

8. If it is not checked, click the **Work Phone number check box**, type **(206) 555-3333**, then click the **Fax number check box** if it is not checked, and type **(206) 555-3344**
   Outdoor Designs' phone numbers replace the placeholder text in the text boxes, so customers can contact the company. Now you are ready to finish building the letterhead.

9. Click **Next**, click **OK**, click **Create It!**, then click **Create Document**
   The TaskWizard opens a new document window and creates the Outdoor Designs letterhead. After a moment, the letterhead shown in Figure 1-11 appears in a window.

FIGURE 1-10: Opening screen of the Letterhead TaskWizard

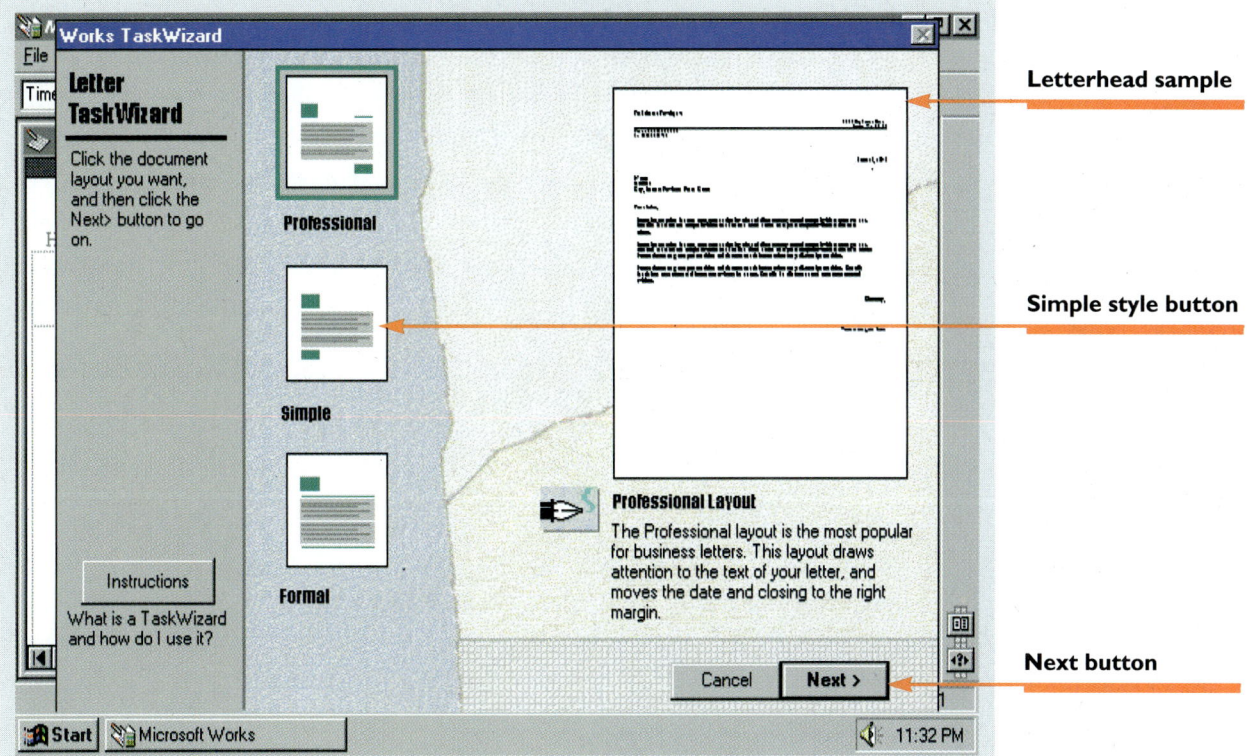

FIGURE 1-11: Completed Outdoor Designs letterhead

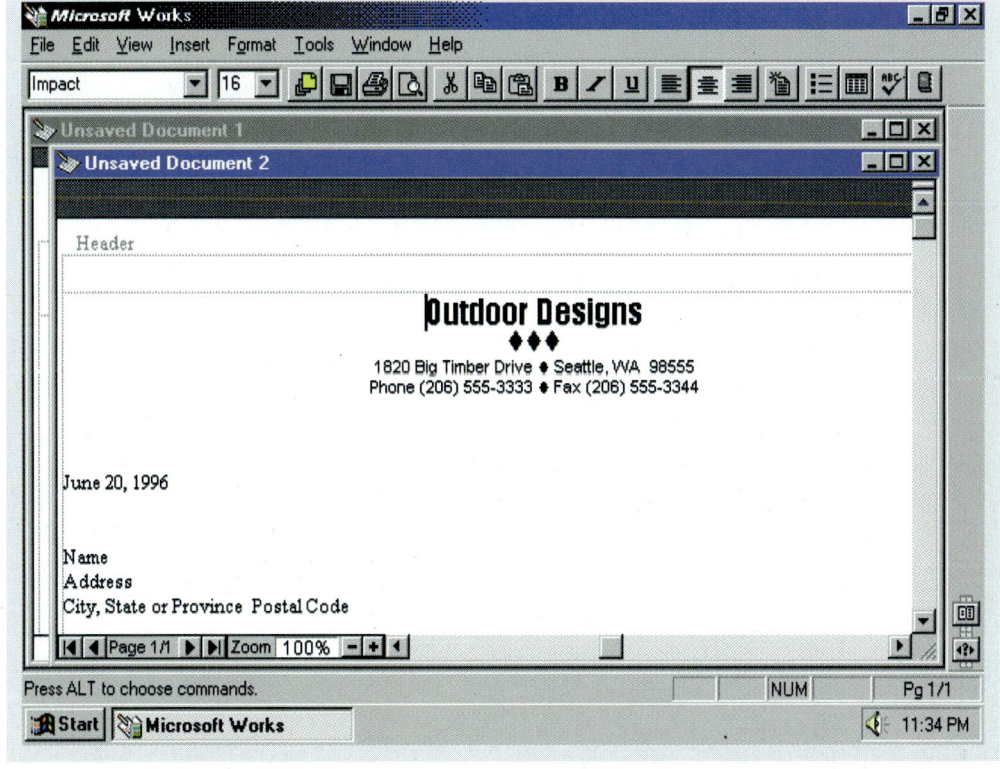

QUICK TIP

Press [Esc] or click Cancel to cancel the TaskWizard and return to your document. If you don't want the document the TaskWizard created, press [Ctrl][F4], then click No to discard your changes. ■

Saving a file

To keep a permanent copy of a document you must **save** it on disk with the Save or Save As command on the File menu. When you save a document on disk you must also assign it a unique **filename** so you can identify it later. For more information on working with filenames in Works, see the related topic, "More about filenames." Before you name a document, Works gives it a temporary filename beginning with the words "Unsaved Document." **case** Sue Ellen asked you to save the letterhead file on your Student Disk so others in your workgroup can use the file later.

1 Place your **Student Disk** in the appropiate drive
In this lesson and throughout the rest of this book, you'll be instructed to place your Student Disk in the appropriate drive. You can load your files from any disk location, including a disk in drive A or B, a hard disk, or a network drive. If you have questions about the location of your practice files, check with your instructor.

2 Click **File** on the menu bar, then click **Save As**
The Save As dialog box shown in Figure 1-12 opens. Take a moment now to identify the elements of the dialog box, using the figure for guidance.

3 Type **Outdoor Letterhead**
The filename Outdoor Letterhead appears in the File name text box. Now you need to indicate which drive contains your Student Disk.

4 Click the **Save in list box**, then click the letter of the drive that contains your **Student Disk**
The names of files on your Student Disk appear in the list box. To keep your Student Disk organized, save your new files in a special folder you'll create now for all projects you complete.

5 Click the **Create New Folder button** in the Save As dialog box, type **My Works Files**, then press **[Enter]** when the folder's name appears in the list box
Works creates a new folder on your Student Disk named "My Works Files." Now open the new folder so you can place your letterhead file in it.

6 Double-click the **My Works Files folder** to open it
My Works Files appears in the Save in list box, so you know it is the active folder.

7 Click **Save**
You save your letterhead file in the My Works Files folder, and the Save As dialog box closes. Note that the title bar of the letterhead document now includes the document's filename.

FIGURE 1-12: Save As dialog box

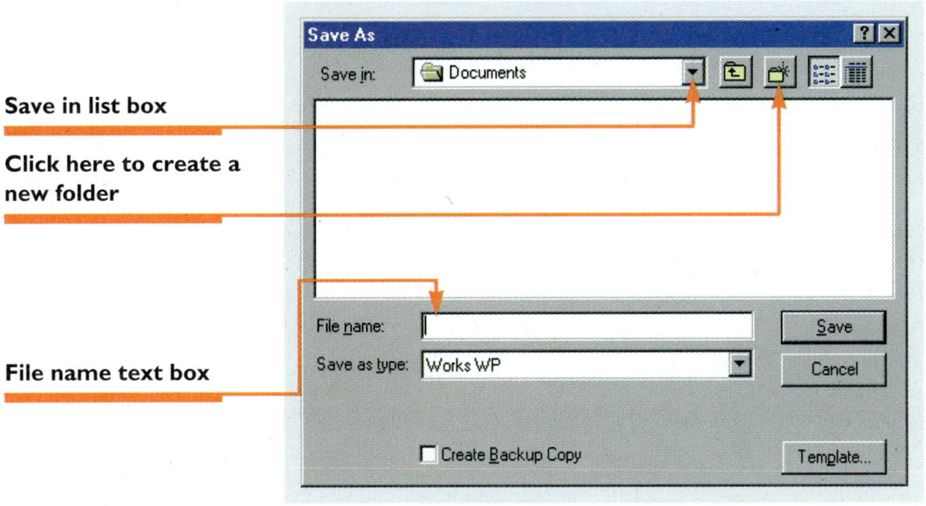

Save in list box

Click here to create a new folder

File name text box

More about filenames

A valid filename in Works may contain up to 255 characters, but descriptive filenames with fewer than 20 or so characters are easier to work with. You can use uppercase and lowercase letters in a filename, plus spaces and most symbols you can type on your keyboard. When you save your file, Works automatically associates a program type with it so that your programs can recognize and reload it later. (In previous versions of Works, filename extensions identified file types; these have been replaced by icons that appear next to filenames in the Open and Save As dialog boxes.) When you name your files, try to use clear names that you'll remember later.

QUICK TIP

For more information about working with files and folders, read the unit "Managing Files, Folders, and Shortcuts" earlier in this book.

TROUBLE?

For more information about your Student Disk, refer to the section called "Read This Before You Begin Microsoft Works 4."

Closing a file and exiting Works

After you save a document, you can safely close it and exit Works. To close a file, use the Close command on the File menu shown in Figure 1-13. When you complete all the work you want to get done in a given session, you quit or **exit** Works. ▶**case** Your day at Outdoor Designs is done, and you're ready to close your letterhead file and exit Works.

1. **Click File on the menu bar**
   Figure 1-13 shows the contents of the File menu. You use the Close command now to close the document with the highlighted title bar. This is known as the current or **active** document. (You can switch between document windows in Works by clicking the title bar of the document you want to activate and bringing it to the foreground.)

2. **Click Close to close the Outdoor Letterhead file**
   The Outdoor Letterhead document window closes. If you made changes to the file since you saved it, the Word Processor prompts you to save those changes. (You can save changes to your document at any time by clicking the Save command on the File menu.) Now you're ready to close Works.

3. **Click File on the menu bar, then click Exit Works**
   The Save changes dialog box shown in Figure 1-14 opens asking if you want to save changes you have made in the Unsaved Document 1 window. You only used this document window to practice using the toolbar, so you don't need to save these edits.

4. **Click No**
   The document window and the Works program both close.

FIGURE 1-13: Closing a document using the Close command

Click here to close the active document

Click here to exit Works

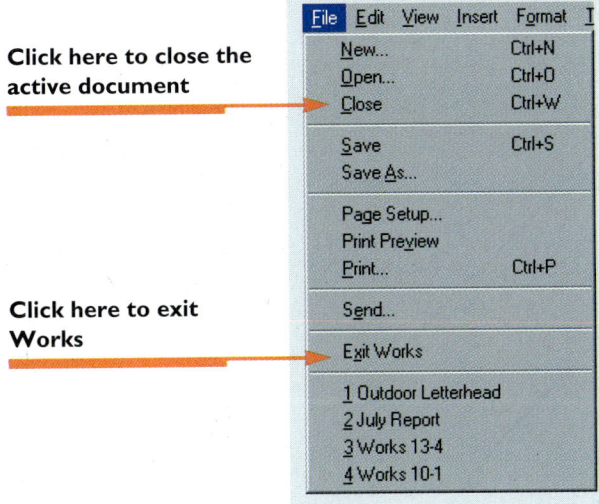

FIGURE 1-14: Works prompts you to save changes before closing a document

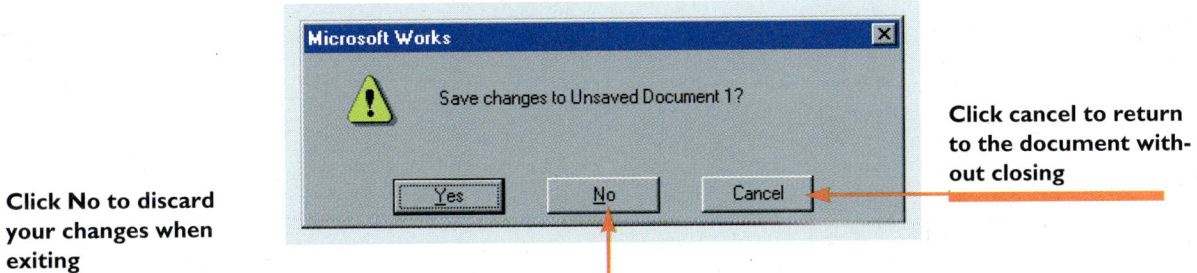

Click cancel to return to the document without closing

Click No to discard your changes when exiting

TROUBLE?

Be sure to exit Works and shut down Windows *before* you turn off your computer. If you do not, Works and Windows does not delete the temporary files they created, resulting in a cluttered hard disk.

TASK REFERENCE

TASK	MOUSE/BUTTON	MENU	KEYBOARD
Close Help		Click Help, Hide Help	[Alt][H],[H]
Exit Works		Click File, Exit Works	[Alt][F4]
Get Help		Click Help, Contents or Index	[Alt][H],[C] or [I]
Save a file under a new filename		Click File, Save as	[Alt][F][A]
Save a file under the current filename		Click File, Save	[Alt][F],[S]
Start a TaskWizard		Click File, New, then click TaskWizards tab	[Alt][F][N],[K]
Start a Works Tool	Click Works Tools tab in Works Task Launcher, then click a Tool button	Click File, New, then click Works Tools tab, then click a Tool button	[Alt][F],[N],[T]
Start Works	Click Start, point to Programs, point to Microsoft Windows 4.0 folder, then click Microsoft Works 4.0		[Alt][S],P, [Right Arrow], [Down Arrow] to Micorosft Works folder, [Right Arrow],[Down Arrow] to Microsoft Works 4.0 program icon, [Enter]

CONCEPTS REVIEW

Label each of the elements of the Works Task Launcher dialog box as shown in Figure 1-15.

1. _____
2. _____
3. _____
4. _____
5. _____
6. _____
7. _____

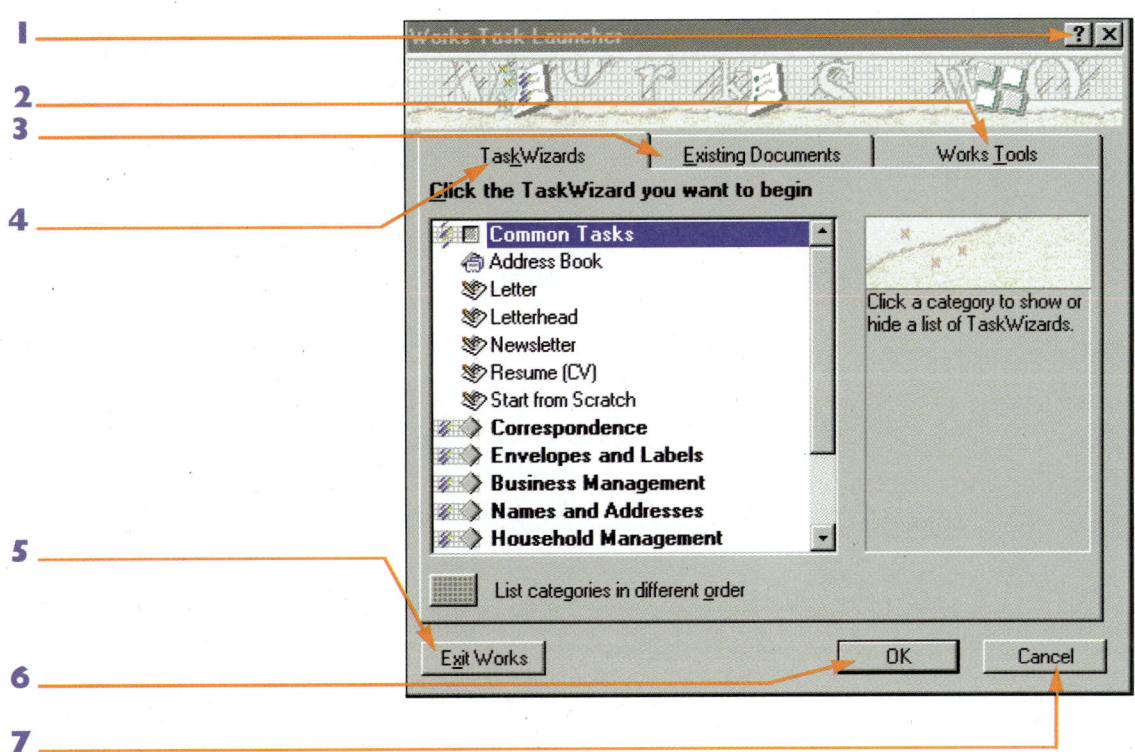

FIGURE 1-15

Match each document with the Works tool that creates it.

8 Electronic mail
9 Pie chart
10 Term paper
11 CD collection

a. Word Processor
b. Spreadsheet
c. Database
d. Communications

Select the best answer from the list of choices.

12 The phrase "Works is an integrated software package" means that
   a. Works can perform complex mathematical calculations
   b. Works contains useful tools that have been designed to work together
   c. Offices that use Works are politically correct
   d. Works can be used for communication

13 The Works Task Launcher allows you to
   a. Open existing documents
   b. Use a TaskWizard
   c. Choose a Works tool
   d. All of the above

14 The Word Processor is used primarily to
   a. Track expenses and create pie charts
   b. Write memos, letters, and mailing labels
   c. Download stock quotes
   d. Create address books, lists, and reports

15 The Spreadsheet is used primarily to
   a. Track expenses and create pie charts
   b. Write memos, letters, and mailing labels
   c. Download stock quotes
   d. Create address books, lists, and reports

16 The Database is used primarily to
   a. Track expenses and create pie charts
   b. Write memos, letters, and mailing labels
   c. Download stock quotes
   d. Create address books, lists, and reports

17 Each Works tool contains
   a. A menu bar
   b. Scroll bars
   c. A toolbar
   d. All of the above

18 Files saved in Microsoft Works
   a. Must be given a file name
   b. Are associated with the program tool and assigned an icon
   c. Should be given clear names that you will remember later
   d. All of the above

19 To use the Works Help System, you can
   a. Click the question mark in the upper-right corner of the dialog box, and then click the box option you need help with.
   b. Choose the Help menu and make a selection
   c. Click one of the Help buttons in the lower-right corner of the screen
   d. All of the above

SKILLS REVIEW

1 Start Works and open the Word Processing tool.
   a. Click the Start button on the Windows Desktop task bar.
   b. Point to Programs, then point to Microsoft Works.
   c. Click Microsoft Works 4.0.
   d. Click the Works Tool tab in the Works Task Launcher dialog box.
   e. Click Word Processor on the Works Tools tab.
   f. If the Help window is open, click the Shrink Help button.

2 Explore the Works document window.
   a. Click the File menu.
   b. Move the mouse over the other menus and notice the commands in each box.
   c. Click in the blank document area to close the menus.
   d. Click one of the Help buttons in the bottom-right corner of the screen.
   e. Click the Shrink Help button.
   f. Point to each button on the toolbar and read the corresponding ToolTip and description.
   g. Type your name in the blank document.
   h. Click the File Menu, then Click Exit.
   i. When a dialog box opens asking if you want to save changes to Document 1, click No.

3 Restart Works and explore the Spreadsheet window.
   a. Click the Start button on the Windows Desktop task bar.
   b. Point to Programs, then point to Microsoft Works.
   c. Click Microsoft Works 4.0.
   d. Click the Works Tool tab in the Works Task Launcher dialog box.
   e. Click Spreadsheet on the Works Tools tab.
   f. Click the Shrink Help button if necessary.
   g. Click the File menu.
   h. Move the mouse over the other menus and notice the commands in each box.
   i. Click in the blank spreadsheet area to close the menus.
   j. Click one of the Help buttons in the bottom-right corner of the screen.
   k. Click the Shrink Help button if necessary.
   l. Point to each button on the toolbar and read the corresponding ToolTip and description in the status bar.
   m. Click the File Menu, then Click Exit.
   n. When a dialog box opens asking if you want to save changes to Document 1, click No.

4 Use a Works TaskWizard.
   a. Start Works.
   b. On the TaskWizards tab, choose the Correspondence category.
   c. Choose the Certificate TaskWizard and click OK.
   d. In the Certificate Task Wizard dialog box, make sure that the Classic certificate is highlighted.
   e. Click the Create It! button.
   f. When the certificate appears on the screen, point the mouse to the space below the text "certify to all that" and click the mouse.
   g. Type your name.

5 Saving a Document.
   a. Click the File menu.
   b. Choose the Save As command.
   c. In the Save As dialog box, type the file name "Award."
   d. In the Save In dialog box, click the list arrow, then click the My Works Files folder on your Student Disk.
   e. Click the Save button.

6 Exit Works.
   a. Click on the File menu.
   b. Click on the Exit Works command.

INDEPENDENT CHALLENGE 1

To learn to use the Works help system, choose the Contents command from the Help menu. In the Help Topics dialog box, choose the Word Processor option, and then choose Word Processor Basics. Works provides many topics of interest to the new user. Explore the topics that are displayed and any other help topics that interest you.

INDEPENDENT CHALLENGE 2

You can use the help index to quickly find information on a particular topic. Once you have found the information, you can have Works print a copy of the help window. Use the Help Index to find the document "help: displaying Help topics." Click on any of the documents that result. Print the contents of the help topic you have chosen.

INDEPENDENT CHALLENGE 3

Microsoft Works contains a short tutorial, which you can complete in about 10 minutes. Choose Introduction to Works from the Help menu. Complete the Introduction to Works for Windows 95.

FIGURE 1-16

INDEPENDENT CHALLENGE 4

Works provides TaskWizards which you can use to complete complex tasks. Choose the Mortgage/Loan Analysis TaskWizard under the Household Management category. If you need help in the Works TaskWizard dialog box, click the Instructions button. Create the Standard Loan analysis. If the Help Window is open, shrink it, so that you can see the spreadsheet. Fill in the information as shown in Figure 1-17, using your own principal, interest, and duration. You can scroll around the spreadsheet to view the information. Use the Help button in the bottom right corner of the screen to get specific help on completing the TaskWizard.

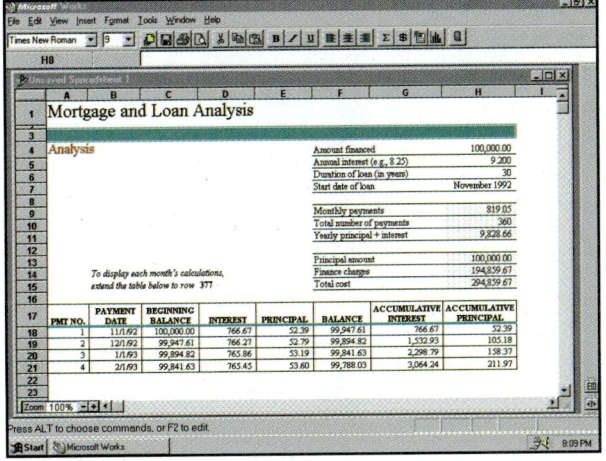

FIGURE 1-17

VISUAL WORKSHOP

Use the Works word processor to create a sign for a garage sale. Use a TaskWizard. Works provides Flyer TaskWizards under the Correspondence category. If you need help in the Works TaskWizard dialog box, click the Instructions button. Create the Jazzy Flyer. Use the Help button in the bottom-right corner of the screen to get specific help on completing the TaskWizard. When you are finished, exit from Works without saving changes to the document.

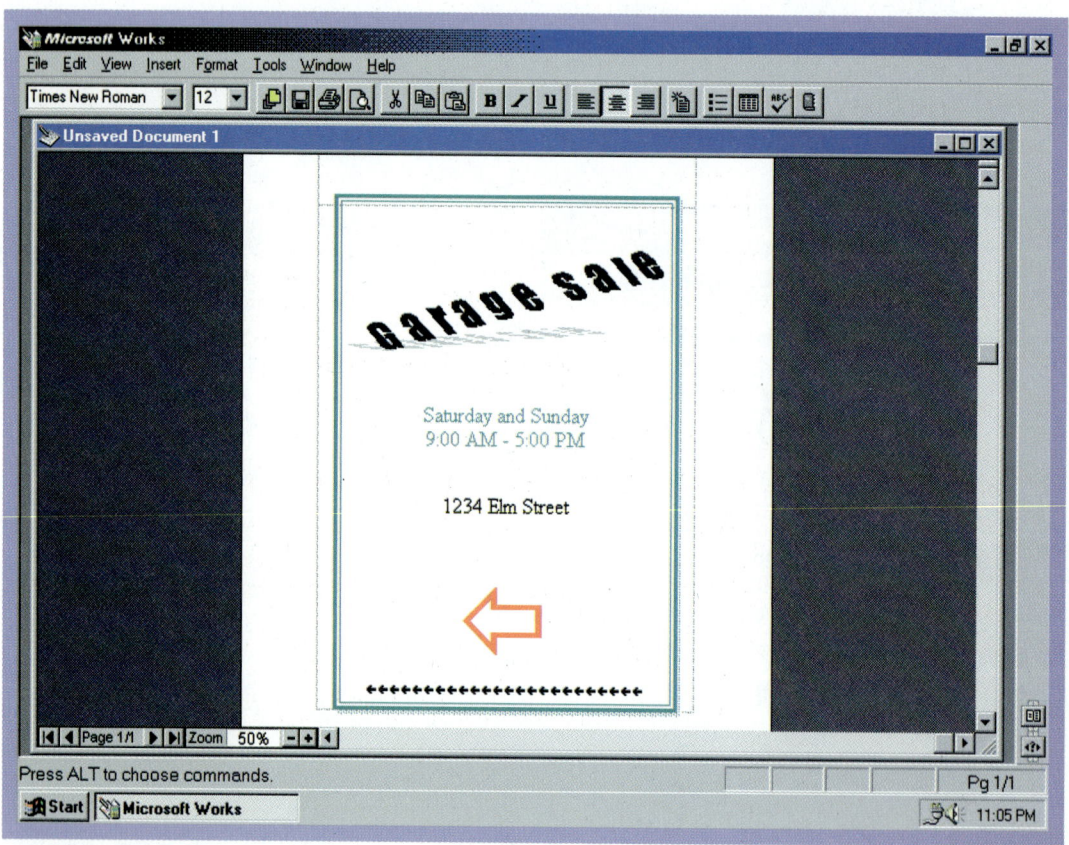

FIGURE 1-18

UNIT 2

OBJECTIVES

▶ Plan a document

▶ Open a file

▶ Enter text in a document

▶ Edit a document

▶ Move text in a document

▶ Use the Spelling Checker

▶ View a document

▶ Print your document

Creating A DOCUMENT WITH THE WORD PROCESSOR

In this unit you will continue to work with the Works Word Processor, the Works program used to create professional-looking memos, reports, research papers, and other text documents. **case** For your first assignment, Sue Ellen asks you to plan and create a memo to send to the company's sales representatives, reminding them that their monthly sales reports are due. More often than not, sales reps have been sending their reports late. She suggests that you put the memo on the letterhead you created in the last unit. To create the sales memo, you'll start the Word Processor, open the Outdoor Designs letterhead file, type the memo text, save it on disk, edit it, format it with the toolbar, view it in Print Preview, check its spelling, and finally print it. As you work on the memo, you'll learn word-processing skills that will help you each time you use the Works Word Processor. ▶

Planning a document

Before you begin to write any document, even a memo, you should outline its content and plan how you want it to look. You should consider who will read your document and what type of presentation will get your message across most clearly.

case Your first assignment at Outdoor Designs is to send a memo to all Outdoor Designs sales representatives, reminding them that their monthly sales reports are due and asking them to send the reports directly to you for processing. Before you begin typing your memo to sales reps, you should plan what you want to accomplish and how you'll accomplish it. Figure 2-1 shows a sample plan.

1 Determine the document's purpose
The purpose of your memo is twofold. Sue Ellen wants to make sure sales reps send their monthly sales reports on time. You want to introduce yourself to them.

2 Determine the document's content
You need to remind sales reps of the date that their reports are due to you. You tell them who you are and describe some of your job responsibilities. To give them an incentive to send their reports on time, you mention that you process commission checks based on their reports.

3 Determine the document's length
You decide to keep the memo short, no more than two paragraphs, to keep from boring the reps and to make sure they obtain the information they need quickly.

4 Determine the document's organization
A standard business letter format is a professional way to introduce yourself to the reps. On each letter, you'll include a rep's name and address, a salutation using first name only, the memo's body or main content, a closing, and your signature.

5 Determine how to create the document—from scratch or with a template
The Works TaskWizards help you create many types of documents, including letters. You could use a TaskWizard to create this letter, but because it's short, you open and add to the letterhead file you already created.

6 Determine the document's format
- Include headers and footers (text that prints at the top and bottom of every page).
- Change the margins (the space between the edges of the paper and the area in which you type).
- Add columns (separate text into vertical blocks).
- Use headings (titles that label and divide the document into sections).

Your short and simple letter doesn't need a lot of formatting to make it attractive and readable. The letterhead will add a graphical element, and the standard business letter style will include plenty of white space.

FIGURE 2-1: Notes for sales rep memo

> 1. Purpose
> Get sales reps to send their sales reports on time.
>
> 2. Content
> Introduce myself.
> Remind the reps that sales reports are due next week.
> Mention that their commission checks are based on these reports.
> Tell them that I'm responsible for processing their checks.
>
> 3. Length
> A two-paragraph memo
>
> 4. Organization
> Standard business letter
>
> 5. Create document
> Add to the Outdoor Designs letterhead
>
> 6. Formatting
> Standard business letter format

QUICK TIP

Depending on the length and complexity of your document, you might want to simply plan it in your head, rather than write a formal outline.

Opening a file

Loading an existing file into a Works program is called **opening** a file. Works offers two ways to open a file: you can choose the Open Existing File command from the File menu, or you can double-click the appropriate filename in the Existing Documents tab of the Works Task Launcher. **case** You plan to add the memo below the letterhead you created in the last unit. You open a copy of the letterhead file and type your memo in business letter form.

1. **Start Works from the Program Manager**
   The Works Task Launcher opens with three tabs from which to choose: TaskWizards tab, Existing Documents tab, Work Tools tab. When you click each tab, different options appear. For example, when you click the TaskWizards tab, you can choose from a wide range of documents that help you perform common tasks.

2. **Put your Student Disk in the appropriate drive**

3. **Click the Existing Documents tab**
   The Existing Documents tab becomes active, listing recently used Works documents. (Although you won't try it in this lesson, you can open files that appear in the Existing Documents tab by double-clicking their filenames in the list box.)

4. **Click Open a document not listed here**
   Remember that you can click the text of the button or the button itself to select it. The Open dialog box shown in Figure 2-2 opens. It contains a File name text box, a Look in list box, and a Files of type list box; your dialog box may look slightly different. These boxes let you specify the name, folder location, and type of file you want to open.

5. **Click the Look in list arrow, then click the name of the drive that contains your Student Disk**
   All the Works files on your Student Disk, including WKS 2-1, appear in the File Name list box.

6. **Double-click WKS 2-1**
   Double-clicking accomplishes the same thing as clicking WKS 2-1, then clicking Open. In fact, in any dialog box, you can double-click an option or you can click the option then click OK. After a moment the letterhead document opens in a window in the Word Processor, as shown in Figure 2-3. The document window contains several visual elements and controls to help you with word processing. Take a moment to identify the elements; refer to Table 2-1 for descriptions.

   Next you'll save the file with a different name in the My Works Files folder on your Student Disk. This keeps the original file intact in case you want to work through this lesson again.

7. **Click File on the menu bar, then click Save As**
   The Save As dialog box opens.

8. **Type Sales Rep Memo in the File name text box, then double-click the My Works Files folder in the Save in list box and press [Enter]**
   Works saves the new file, Sales Rep Memo, on your Student Disk in the My Works Files folder. The title bar changes to reflect the new name.

FIGURE 2-2: Open dialog box

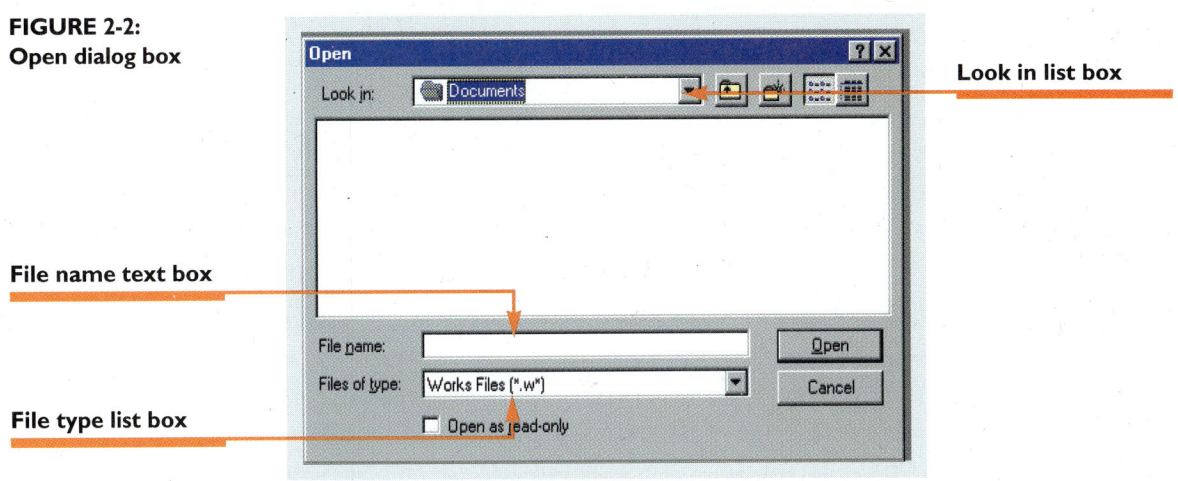

- Look in list box
- File name text box
- File type list box

FIGURE 2-3: Works Word Processor with WKS 2-1 file opened

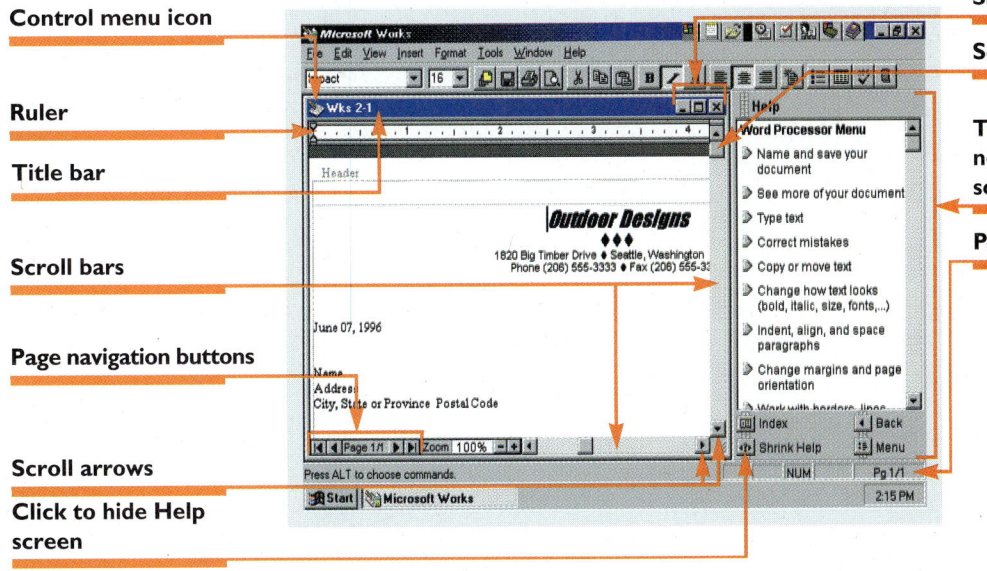

- Control menu icon
- Ruler
- Title bar
- Scroll bars
- Page navigation buttons
- Scroll arrows
- Click to hide Help screen
- Sizing buttons
- Scroll box
- The Help window may not be open on your screen
- Page number indicator

TROUBLE?

If the Help window appears on your screen, as shown in Figure 2-3, the previous user left Help open. Close Help by clicking the Shrink Help button  on the Help window.

QUICK TIP

To maximize the Word Processor document window, click the Maximize button in the upper-right corner of the document window.

TABLE 2-1: Elements in Word Processor document window

ELEMENT	DESCRIPTION
Control menu icon	Control menu box for the window, another way to size and close the window
Ruler	A ruler measuring the body of the document in inches (default)
Scroll box	Box in scroll bar showing approximate position in the document
Page number indicator	Numbers indicating the current page and the total pages in the document
Page navigation buttons	Buttons used to move through the document one or more pages at a time

WK 31

WORKS 4 UNIT 2 CREATING A DOCUMENT

Entering text in a document

The first step in creating a document is to **enter**, or type, the text that is the content of your document in the Word Processor document window. **case** You're ready to enter the content of the sales rep memo.

1. If necessary, click the **Shrink Help button** on the Help screen

2. Press **[↓]** 10 times, or as many times as necessary so that it rests on the word **Name**
   The Word Processor **cursor**, a blinking vertical bar indicating the insertion point, moves to the address template in the letter. The [↓] key is one of several keys that you can press to move the insertion point around the document. Table 2-2 describes these keys. You can also move the insertion point around the document by clicking the mouse. The Letterhead TaskWizard creates placeholders for the name, address, and salutation in your letter. You'll customize these before you type the memo text. Use the Backspace key to delete the placeholder text.

3. Press **[Backspace]** four times, then type **Pat Crenshaw**

4. Press **[↓]**, press **[Backspace]** seven times, type **1012 Hampton Parkway**, press **[↓]**, press **[End]**, press **[Backspace]** 36 times, then type **New York, New York 55555**
   When you use [Backspace] to delete several characters, hold down the Backspace key until you delete all the characters. Next you'll change the salutation. To get there, try navigating with the mouse instead of using the arrow keys.

5. Scroll down the document until you see **Dear John**, point to the right of the **n** in **John**, click, backspace to delete the name, then type **Pat**
   Note that when the pointer is over text it changes to the I-beam pointer.

6. Press **[↓]** twice, press **[End]**, delete the instruction **Start typing your letter here**, and type the memo's contents, shown in bold below
   Greetings from the Seattle office! The end of June is rapidly approaching, and I have been asked by our Sales Manager, Sue Ellen, to remind you that your monthly sales reports are due next week. Please send these directly to me at the address above. I have just been hired as the summer intern for the Outdoor Designs Sales and Marketing group and will be recording your sales data and processing your commission checks. [Enter] [Enter] I look forward to working with you throughout the summer!
   Your screen should now look like Figure 2-4 (the date on your document will differ, however). Note that when you press [Enter], the insertion point moves down one line and to the left margin, just like a typewriter carriage does when you press the Return key. Longer lines in the main paragraph **wrap** (continue on the next line) automatically when the insertion point reaches the right margin.

7. Press **[↓]** eight times, press **[End]**, then change the signature from **Your Name goes here** to your name
   In the rest of this unit, wherever you type your name, you'll see Melissa Cavenaugh in the figures.

8. Click the **Save button** on the toolbar
   Works saves the contents of your memo on disk.

FIGURE 2-4: Screen after sales rep memo has been entered

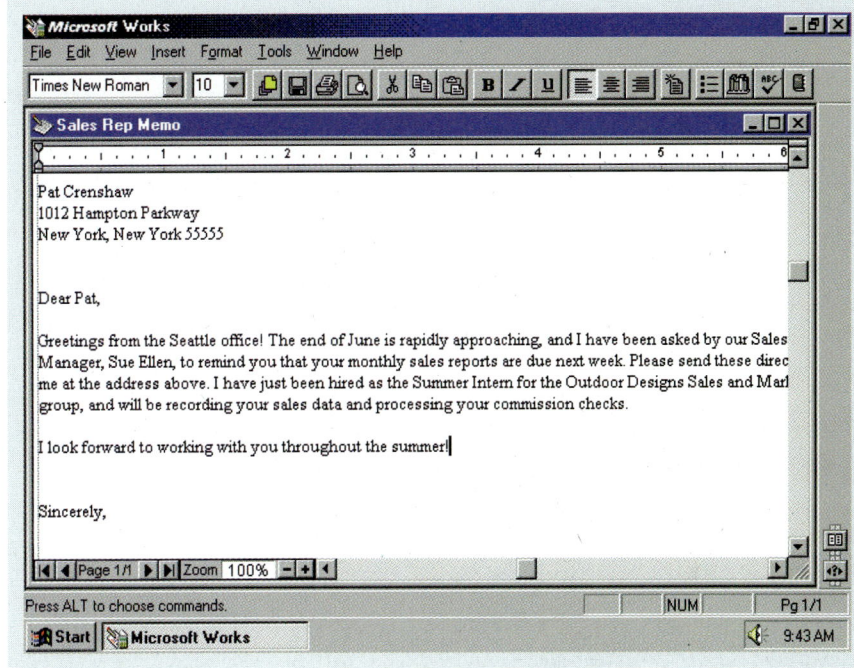

TABLE 2-2: Useful keys for moving the insertion point around a document

KEYBOARD KEY	MOVES INSERTION POINT
[Backspace]	Back one space, deleting previous character
[→]	One space to the right
[←]	One space to the left
[↑]	Up one line
[↓]	Down one line
[PAGE UP]	Up one page
[PAGE DOWN]	Down one page
[HOME]	To beginning of line
[END]	To end of line
[Ctrl][HOME]	To beginning of document
[Ctrl][END]	To end of document

TROUBLE?

The line wraps on your screen might not match the figure in this book exactly. Line wraps vary depending on the printer driver your particular machine uses.■

QUICK TIP

Save your work frequently to make sure you always have an up-to-date copy on disk.■

Editing a document

After you enter text in the Word Processor, you can **edit**, or modify, the text in several ways. In addition to pressing [Backspace] to delete individual letters, you can **select**, or highlight, all unwanted text at once, then press [Delete] to delete the entire selection. To select text, you either hold down [Shift] while pressing the arrow keys or **drag** over the text by positioning your mouse pointer to the left of the first character you want to delete, then clicking and holding down the mouse button while you move the pointer over the text you want to highlight. When you drag horizontally, you select characters. When you drag vertically, you select lines. To learn about another useful editing feature, the ruler, see the related topic, "Using the Ruler."

▶ **case** As you read the letter, you decide to make some edits.

1. **Click after the word these in the main paragraph**
   The insertion point moves from the bottom of the document window to the space after the word "these." Notice that when you move the mouse pointer into the document window, the pointer's shape changes to I, to help you place the insertion point exactly where you want it in the text. Now you'll change the word "these" to "them."

2. **Press [Backspace] twice, then type m**
   Now you decide to select the company name from the document.

3. **Click to the left of the letter O in Outdoor Designs**
   The insertion point blinks before the word "Outdoor." You'll use the [Shift] [→] key combination to select the company name one character at a time.

4. **Hold down [Shift] while you press [→] until the words Outdoor Designs and the blank space following them are selected, then release both keys**
   "Outdoor Designs" is selected, as shown in Figure 2-5.

5. **Press [Delete] to delete the selected text**
   The words "Outdoor Designs" disappear from the document. Notice that the text after the deleted words wraps back to fill the empty space. Now you'll select some text with the mouse.

6. **Position the pointer to the left of the S in Sue Ellen, click and hold down the mouse button while you drag across the name Sue Ellen and the comma and space after it, then release the mouse button.**
   The text "Sue Ellen" and the comma and the space after it, is selected.

7. **Press [Delete]**
   The name disappears from the document. As you read the edits you made, you decide you'd rather leave Sue Ellen's name in the memo.

8. **Press Edit on the menu bar, then press Undo Editing**
   The deleted text reappears in the document exactly how and where it was before you deleted it.

9. **Click the Save button 🖫 on the toolbar to save your edits**

FIGURE 2-5: Selected text

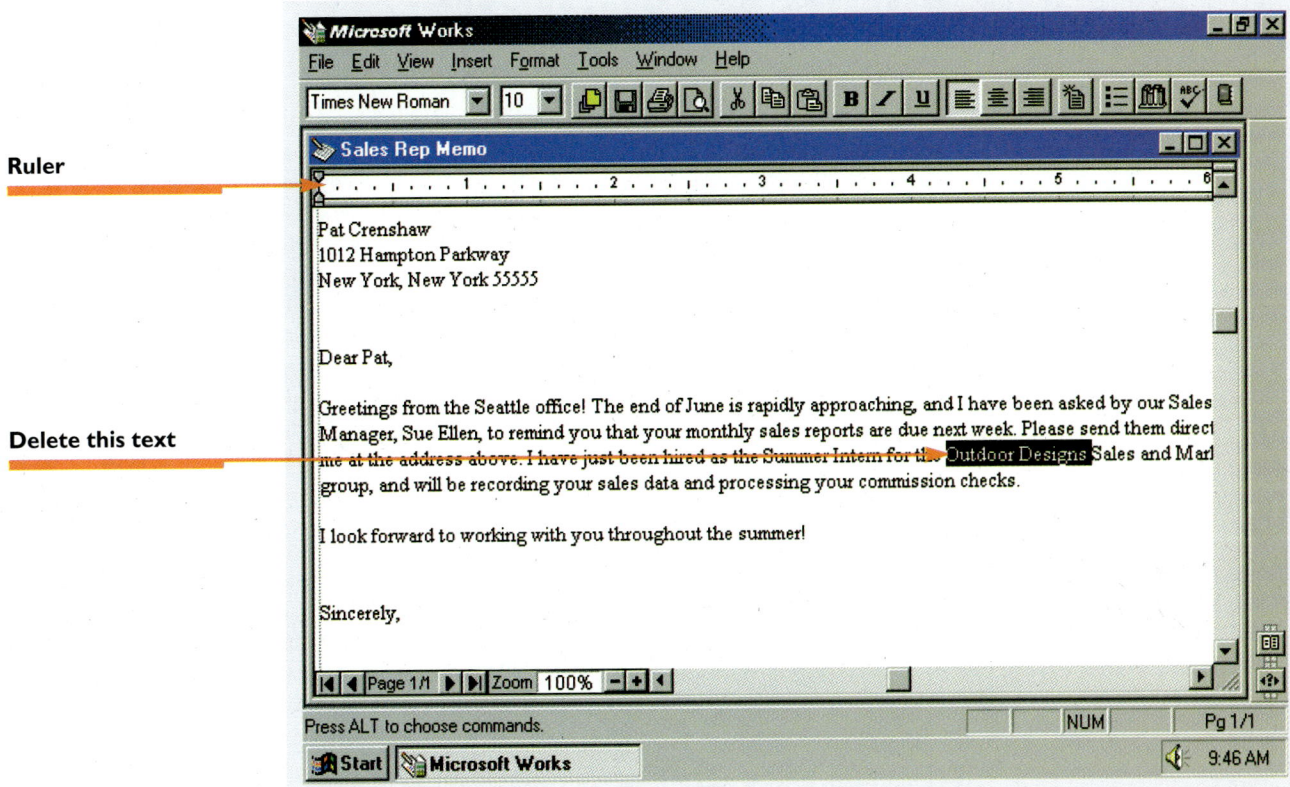

Ruler

Delete this text

Using the ruler

If you click View from the menu bar, then click Ruler, a measuring tool called a **ruler** appears. Below the title bar in the document window is a measuring tool called the **ruler**. The default ruler is marked with inch measures and contains symbols for left and right margins and tab stops in the document. The ruler gives you an idea of where your text will appear on the printed page and how big it will be. To remove the ruler and make more room for your document, choose the Ruler command from the View menu.

QUICK **TIP**

You can also press [Ctrl][Z] to undo your last edit.

WK 36   WORKS 4   UNIT 2 **CREATING** A DOCUMENT

Moving text in a document

Moving and Copying Data

Sometimes you want to move text from one part of your document to another. The Cut and Paste commands make this easy. You can **cut** (delete) selected text from your document, place it on the Windows **Clipboard** (a temporary storage area), and then **paste** (insert) it in a new location, as many times as you want until you cut or copy another selection. You can also use a technique, called **drag and drop,** in which you select the text you want to move, click it and drag it to its new location using the Drag pointer to place the text. You can **copy** (duplicate) text in the same ways. For more information, view the CourseHelp called "Moving and Copying Data" before completing the steps below. See the related material, "Viewing CourseHelp," to learn how to access CourseHelp. **case** While checking your letter, you notice that you might have used the wrong street address in the memo.

1. Click the **left scroll arrow** to display the left side of the memo, move the mouse pointer to the left of the street address **1012 Hampton Parkway**, then click in the **left margin**
   The line "1012 Hampton Parkway" is selected. When the mouse pointer crosses the left margin of the document, it changes to the line pointer, which you use to select entire lines with at once.

2. Click the **Cut button** on the toolbar
   The line is removed from the document and placed in the Clipboard. You look at the list of addresses and see that the street name is correct but the house number is 1210.

3. Click the **Paste button** on the toolbar
   The address is pasted back into the document from the Clipboard. You can use either the Cut and Paste commands, toolbar buttons, or any combination of these to produce identical results. Instead of typing the new number, you drag and drop the 12 in front of the 10.

4. In the same line, select the number **12** with the mouse, then position the pointer over the selected text
   The pointer changes to .

5. Click the highlighted text and while you hold down the mouse button, drag it to the beginning of the line, then release the pointer
   The insertion point blinks at the position where text will be dropped. See Figure 2-6. If the numbers are not in the right place, press [Ctrl][Z] to undo your change and try again.

   Next, you'll use the Copy button to place a copy of Sue Ellen's name at the bottom of the memo with cc: in front of it, indicating she'll receive a courtesy copy of the letter.

6. In the second line of the main paragraph, select **Sue Ellen** with the mouse, then click the **Copy button** on the toolbar
   A copy of the selected text is placed in the Windows Clipboard.

7. Press **[Ctrl][End]**
   The insertion point moves below your signature.

8. Type **cc:**, press **[Spacebar]**, then click
   The name "Sue Ellen" is pasted in the document from the Windows Clipboard.

9. Click the **Save button** on the toolbar

FIGURE 2-6: Text moved with drag and drop

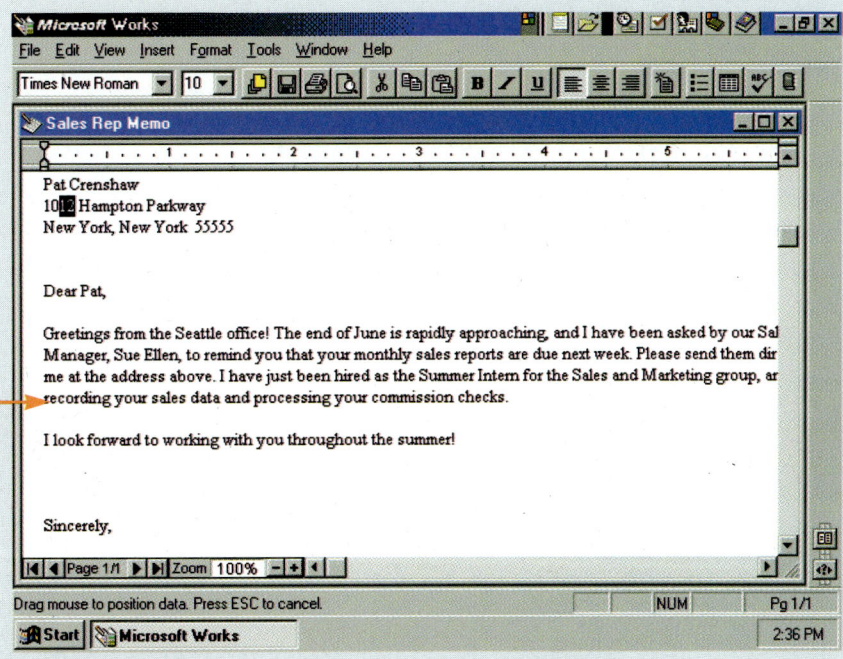

Left margin

Viewing CourseHelp

The camera icon on the opposite page indicates there is a CourseHelp available for this lesson. CourseHelps are on-screen "movies" that bring difficult concepts to life, to help you understand the material in this book. Your instructor received a CourseHelp disk and should have installed it on the machine you are using. To start CourseHelp, click the Start button, point to Programs, point to CourseHelp, then click Microsoft Works 4 Illustrated. In the main CourseHelp window, click the topic that corresponds to this lesson.

Because CourseHelp runs in a separate window, you can start and view a movie even if you're in the middle of completing a lesson. Once the movie is finished, you can click the Word program button on the taskbar and continue with the lessons, right where you left off. You can see a list of all the CourseHelps available with this book in the Preface. CourseHelp icons also appear in the table of contents.

TABLE 2-3: Buttons found only on the Word Processor toolbar

BUTTON	FUNCTION
	Format selected text with a predefined Easy Format
	Add a bulleted list to the document
	Insert a spreadsheet table in the document
	Check the spelling in the document

To cut selected text with the keyboard, press [Ctrl][X]; to copy selected text press [Ctrl][C]; to paste text press [Ctrl][V].

Using the Spelling Checker

The Spelling command checks your entire document for words that are misspelled, incorrectly hyphenated, incorrectly capitalized, repeated (such as "the the"), or not in its standard dictionary. When encountering one of these words, the Word Processor displays a dialog box where you can make corrections. Works also has a Thesaurus that you can use to find synonyms for repeated words; for more information about the Thesaurus, see the related topic, "Using the Thesaurus."

case As you entered and then edited the letter to sales reps, you might have made typos or other errors. You'll check your letter to make sure it is error free.

1. **Press [Ctrl][Home]**
   The insertion point blinks to the left of the words "Outdoor Designs" at the top of the page.

2. **Click Tools on the menu bar, then click Spelling**
   The Spelling command starts to check the spelling of words in the document, beginning at the insertion point. The Spelling Checker doesn't recognize the diamonds in the letterhead.

3. **Verify that a check mark is in the Always suggest check box**
   If the box is not checked, check it now. This feature prompts the Spelling Checker to suggest corrections for words it doesn't find in the dictionary.

4. **Click Ignore**
   The Spelling Checker skips the text design and highlights the word "Crenshaw." (If the Spelling Checker finds another word, that's OK; correct the word and the Spelling Checker highlights the next possible error.) You will choose to ignore this as well so other students in a lab setting can complete this lesson.

5. **Click Ignore then click OK**
   If you had chose to add the name "Crenshaw" the word would have been added to your **personal dictionary**, a special file on your hard disk that Works and other programs use to verify spelling. The next time you used the Spelling command, it would recognize the word "Crenshaw." Due to lab settings, you will not fix any other errors in your letter that the Spelling Checker identifies until you see the dialog box that notifies you that the spelling check is finished.

6. **On the line above the date of the memo, type have sum baloons**, select the line by clicking next to it in the left margin

7. **Click the Spelling button on the toolbar**
   Because you selected a text passage before running the Spelling Checker, Works checks only the selected text. The Spelling dialog box opens and suggests the correct spelling. See Figure 2-7.

8. **Click Change then click OK**
   The spelling changes and the spelling check ends. Note that the Spelling Checker did not flag the word "sum" as incorrect. The word should be "some," but the Spelling Checker could not determine the context of the phrase. This example demonstrates that although the Spelling Checker is useful, it cannot replace proofreading.

9. **Press [Delete]** to delete the selected line, press **[Enter]** to add a blank line, then click the **Save button** on the toolbar to save your changes

FIGURE 2-7: Spelling dialog box

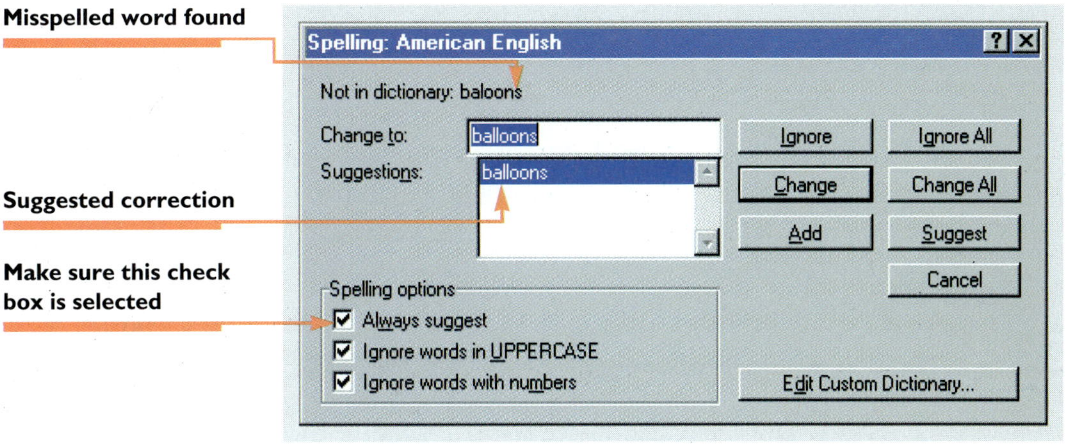

Misspelled word found

Suggested correction

Make sure this check box is selected

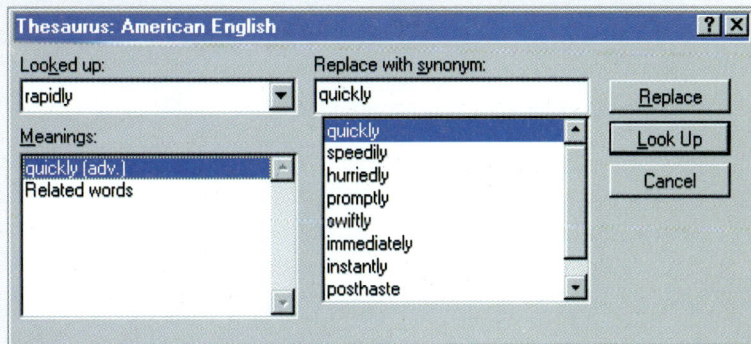

Using the Thesaurus

The Thesaurus lists one or more **synonyms** (words with a similar meaning) for the word you select. To use the Thesaurus, select a word for which you would like to see a list of synonyms, then click the Thesaurus command on the Tools menu to open the Thesaurus dialog box shown in Figure 2-8. It identifies one or more meanings for the selected word, then lists as many synonyms as it can find in the Replace with synonym list box. If you want to use one of the synonyms listed, click the synonym, then click Replace. The Thesaurus replaces the selected word with the synonym and closes the dialog box.

FIGURE 2-8: Works Thesaurus

The Works Spelling Checker uses a Houghton Mifflin dictionary that contains about 110,000 words. You can also use it in the Spreadsheet and Database programs.

Viewing a document

While you work on a document you can look at it in several views. **Normal view** shows your text with only some page elements visible, and not always where and how they'll print. **Page Layout view** shows all page elements, including margins, and where and how they'll print. In either view, you can zoom in on a detail or zoom out to see the entire page by clicking the plus and minus buttons in the Zoom Box at the bottom of the document window. When you are ready to print, use **Print Preview** to see your document exactly as it will appear on the printed page. In this view, you can easily check page margins and your document's overall appearance. For more information, see the related topic "Normal view vs. Page Layout view." ▶case Before you print the sales rep memo, you make sure it looks exactly as you want it by using the Zoom Box and the Print Preview command. You're currently viewing the memo at 100%.

1. **Click the minus button** ▭ **in the Zoom Box**
   The sales rep memo shrinks to 70% of its true size in the document window, so you see the document's left, right, and top margins at the same time. See Figure 2-9. If you were viewing your document at a value other than 100%, your memo might shrink to a different percentage.

2. **Click the plus button** ▭ **in the Zoom Box twice**
   The sales rep memo enlarges to 150% of its true size in the document window. This "up close" magnification lets you examine characters' shape, spacing between words, and other important details.

3. **Click** ▭
   The document view returns to normal.

4. **Click File on the menu bar, then click Print Preview**
   The Print Preview window opens, showing the sales rep memo as it will appear on the printed page. The right side of the screen contains several buttons. The top box tells you which page of your document you are viewing (in this case Page 1). The Previous and Next buttons are dimmed because the memo is only one page; in longer documents you would click these buttons to move from page to page. In Print Preview, you can use the mouse pointer to zoom in on your document.

5. **Move the mouse pointer over the document page**
   The pointer changes to the Zoom pointer ⌕, which you use to zoom in to closely examine parts of your letter in Print Preview. See Figure 2-10.

6. **Click the pointer anywhere in the top half of the memo**
   The top part of the document enlarges by 50% in the Print Preview window.

7. **Click the Outdoor Designs letterhead**
   The letterhead enlarges to full size (the size it will print) in the Print Preview window. (You know you are viewing the document in full size when the Zoom In button dims.)

8. **Click Zoom Out twice**
   The Print Preview window returns to 50% view, then standard (whole-page) view. The document looks good—you don't want to change anything before you print.

9. **Click Cancel**
   The Print Preview window closes and you return to the sales rep memo.

FIGURE 2-9: Sales rep memo in Page Layout view

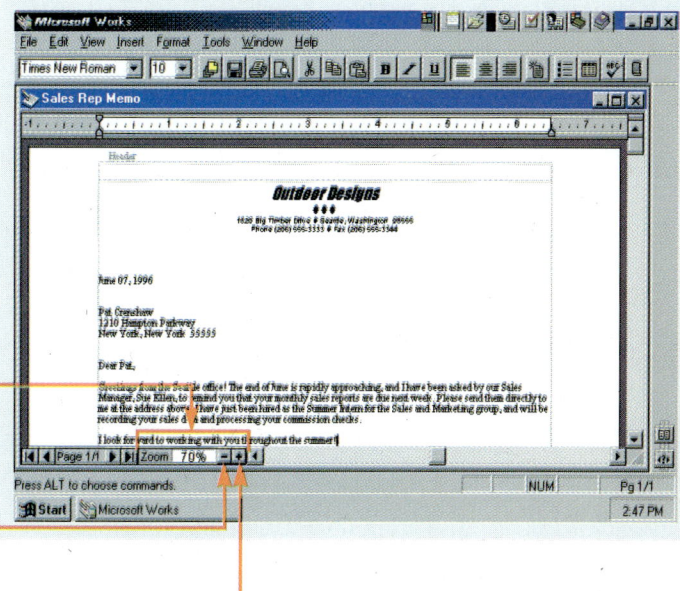

Zoom Box

Click to shrink document

Click to enlarge document

FIGURE 2-10: Sales rep memo in Print Preview

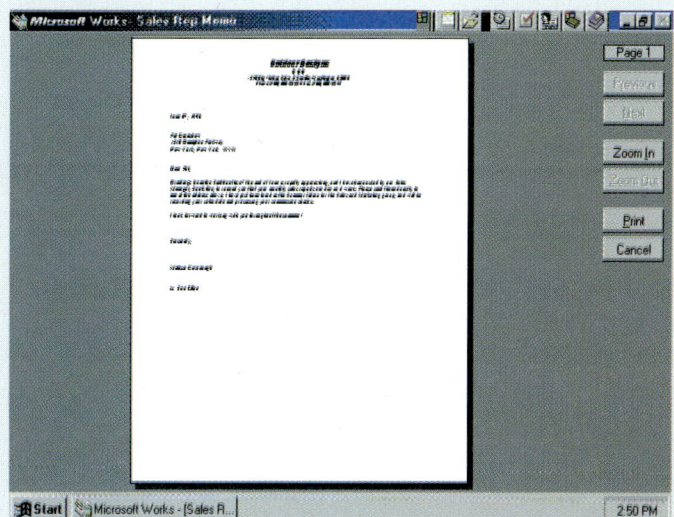

Normal view vs. Page Layout view

In addition to Print Preview, you can use the Normal and Page Layout commands on the View menu to change the way your document displays in the Word Processor. Page Layout view, the default document display, is similar to Print Preview in many ways—it shows the actual page you're working on, including margins, headers, footers, and columns. This view is especially useful when you are doing desktop publishing with Works. When you typed the sales rep memo, the Word Processor was in Page Layout view. In contrast, **Normal view** displays the document without margins, headers, footers, and columns. It is useful when you are outlining your thoughts and not yet terribly concerned with how your document looks on the page. You'll learn more about working with margins, headers, footers, and columns later in this book.

QUICK TIP

You can also preview your document by clicking the Print Preview button  on the toolbar.

Printing your document

After you preview your document with Print Preview, you can print it with the Print command. Special connectors, called **ports**, on the back of a computer can support one or more printers. To configure the settings in your printer, click the Properties button in the Print dialog box. Ask your instructor or technical support person for specific instructions on how to print using your classroom printer. **case** The completed sales rep memo is ready to print. After you print it, you're finished working for the day and can exit Works.

1. Take a moment to verify that your printer is online and properly connected to your computer

2. Click **File** on the menu bar, then click **Print**
   If the First-time Help dialog box opens, click OK to close it. The Print dialog box shown in Figure 2-11 opens. The Print dialog box lets you specify the number of copies of the document you want to print, the page range if you want to print part of a document, the type of document you are printing, whether you're using the advanced print merge feature, and whether printing should be best quality (the default) or draft quality.

   Figure 2-11 shows the default printer as an HP LaserJet 4 Plus connected to the LPT1: printer port. Your system's default printer is probably different. To configure the settings of the default printer, you can click the Properties button and change them in the Properties dialog box. (Your instructor might ask you to do this later.)

3. Click **Properties**
   The Properties dialog box opens. See Figure 2-12. The Properties dialog box lets you change paper size, orientation, graphics resolution, fonts, and other special options your printer supports. Your instructor will tell you if you need to adjust any settings.

4. Click **OK** to close the Properties dialog box, and then click **OK** to print the sales rep memo
   The Print dialog box closes and after a few moments the completed letter emerges from your printer. Congratulations! You've completed your first word processing session and your first assignment at Outdoor Designs. Now save your changes and exit Works.

5. Click the **Save button** 💾 on the toolbar to save your changes

6. Click **File** then click **Exit Works**
   The sales rep memo document and the Works program close.

FIGURE 2-11: Print dialog box

Your printer might be different

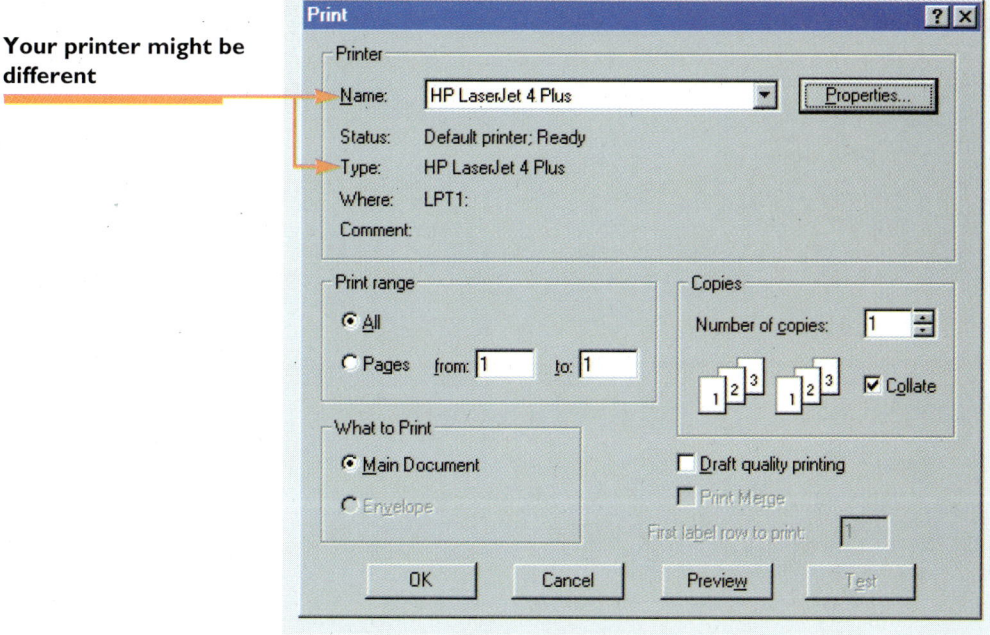

FIGURE 2-12: Properties dialog box

Your choices are based on the printer you're using

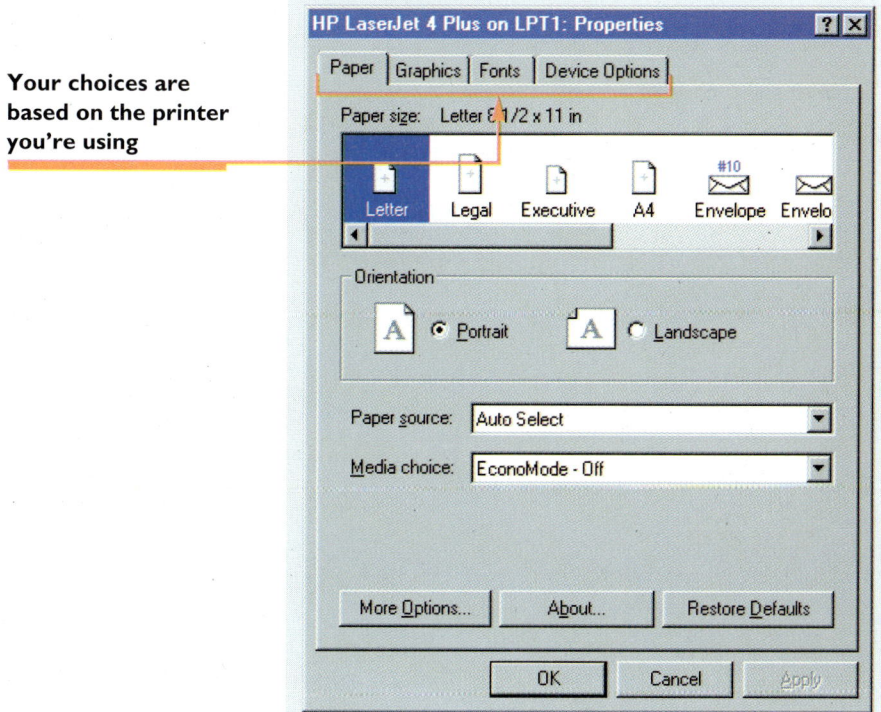

QUICK TIP

The Print button  on the toolbar is the fastest way to print the entire document in Works. However, it doesn't let you choose the number of copies, print range, or other special conditions.

TASKREFERENCE

TASK	MOUSE/BUTTON	MENU	KEYBOARD
Check spelling		Click Tools, Spelling	[F7]
Copy selected text		Click Edit, Copy	[Ctrl][C]
Cut selected text		Click Edit, Cut	[Ctrl][X]
Exit Works	Click Close button on title bar	Click File, Exit	[Alt][F], [X]
Maximize document window		Control menu, Maximize	
Maximize Works		Click document	[Alt][-], [X]
Move the insertion point to the end of a document	Drag the scroll box to the bottom of the vertical scroll bar		[Ctrl][End]
Open a file		Click File, Open	[Ctrl][O]
Paste text to document		Click Edit, Paste	[Ctrl][V]
Preview your document		Click File, Print Preview	[Alt][F], [V]
Run Thesaurus		Click Tools, Thesaurus	[Shift][F7]
Save a file		Click File, Save As	[Ctrl][S]
Undo an edit		Click Edit, Undo	[Ctrl][Z]

CONCEPTS REVIEW

Label each element of the Works Word Processor, shown in Figure 2-13.

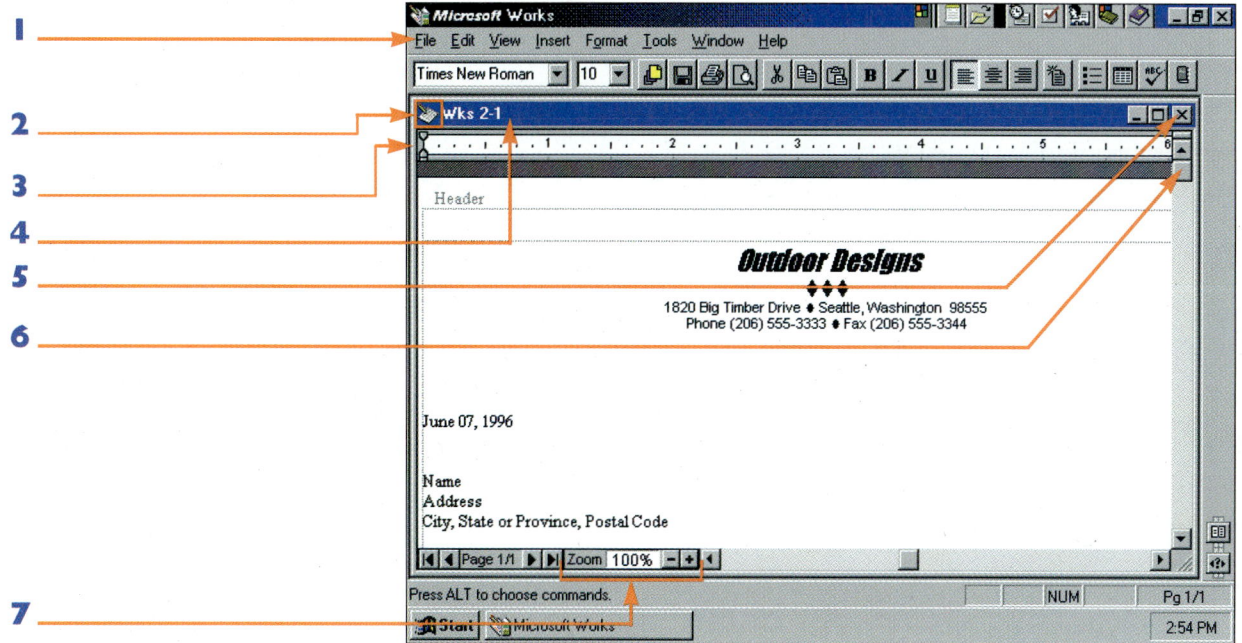

FIGURE 2-13

Match each button from the Word Processor toolbar with its function.

8. ✂
9. ABC✓
10. 📋
11. 💾
12. 🔍

a. Save the current document to disk
b. View the document in Print Preview
c. Copy the selected text to the Windows clipboard
d. Cut the selected text and place it in the Windows clipboard
e. Check the spelling in the document

Select the best answer from the list of choices.

13. Loading a file from disk into the Word Processor is called
    a. Closing the file
    b. Exiting Works
    c. Opening the file
    d. Printing the file

14. How would you open a file that appears in the Existing Documents tab of the Works Task Launcher?
    a. Click the filename with the right mouse button.
    b. Click the Cancel button.
    c. Double-click the Help me find a document button.
    d. Double-click the filename.

15. What is the purpose of the ruler in the Word Processor?
    a. To measure the width of margins and text in the document
    b. To track available disk space
    c. To measure the width of the toolbar
    d. To control the scroll bars

16. After you open a file in the Word Processor, what information does the document window title bar contain?
    a. The name of the directory the file is stored in
    b. The filename associated with the document
    c. The number of characters in the file
    d. All of the above

17. What happens when you click the plus button in the Zoom Box?
    a. The insertion point moves up one line.
    b. Works adds a blank line to the top of your document.
    c. Your document view is magnified.
    d. You enter Print Preview.

18. Which keyboard key moves the insertion point to the end of the current line in a document?
    a. [Page Up]
    b. [Page Down]
    c. [Home]
    d. [End]

19. Which technique *cannot* be used to select text in the Word Processor?
    a. Double-click a word.
    b. Double-click the end-of-file mark.
    c. Hold down [Shift] and press an arrow key.
    d. Hold down the mouse button and drag the mouse pointer.

20. Which of these techniques *cannot* be used to move text from one location to another in the Word Processor?
    a. The [Del] and [Ins] keys
    b. Cut and Paste commands on the Edit menu
    c. The drag-and-drop technique
    d. The cut and paste buttons on the toolbar

21. When does the insertion pointer change to the line pointer?
    a. When you move the mouse pointer into the left margin of the document
    b. When you place the mouse pointer over a button on the toolbar
    c. When you use the scroll box on one of the scroll bars
    d. When you drag and drop text

22. Which of these document view commands is not listed on the Word Processor View menu?
    a. Normal
    b. Page Layout
    c. Zoom
    d. Print Preview

23. What is the purpose of the Zoom pointer in Print Preview?
    a. Adds page numbers to the document
    b. Prints the document
    c. Magnifies the page
    d. Speeds the editing process

24. What is the purpose of the Add button in the Spelling dialog box?
    a. Adds a corrected word to the document
    b. Adds a word to your personal dictionary
    c. Adds a synonym to the Thesaurus
    d. Activates the Always suggest check box

25. Which of these can you *not* do with the Print command?
    a. Determine the default printer on your system
    b. Determine the port the default printer is connected to
    c. Specify the number of copies to be printed
    d. View how different printers will print your document

SKILLS REVIEW

1. Plan the document, start Works, open the WKS 2-2 file, and save it as "Welcome."

    a. You need to change an existing letter. Do you start a new document, use a TaskWizard, or open an existing file and modify it?

b. Launch Microsoft Works.

c. In the Works Task Launcher, open the Existing Documents tab, if necessary.

d. Click Open a document not listed here.

e. Place your Student Disk in a floppy drive, then click the appropriate drive in the Look in list box.

f. Open the My Works Files folder in the list box.

g. Open the file WKS 2-2.

h. Save a copy of the file in the My Works File folder on your Student Disk under the name, "Welcome."

i. Identify the following elements in the document window: title bar, sizing buttons, ruler, scroll bars, and Control menu icon.

2 Add a paragraph to the document and save your changes when you finish.

a. Shrink the Help screen if necessary.

b. Move the insertion point to the blank line after the first paragraph.

c. Add a blank line to leave space between the paragraphs.

d. Type the following text:

"When you send along your reports, be sure to include a list of stores you visited this past month, how many square feet each store has devoted to merchandise, and a few words about any new businesses that opened in your territory."

e. Add a blank line between the second and third paragraphs.

f. Move the insertion point to end of the document with the arrow keys.

g. Delete the name "Melissa Cavenaugh" below the closing.

h. Type your name as the signature.

i. Click the Save button on the toolbar to save the memo.

3 Edit your document using [Backspace], [Delete], and the arrow keys; and fix any typing mistakes you made.

a. Use the arrow keys to move the insertion point to any apparent misspelled words.

b. Press [Backspace] to delete the mistakes, then type the corrections.

c. Move the insertion point to the left of the phrase "have just been hired as" in the third line of the first paragraph with the mouse.

d. Delete the phrase "have just been hired as."

e. Type the word "am" so the sentence begins "I am the Summer Intern."

f. Use the arrow keys to move to the left of the phrase "a few words" near the end of the second paragraph.

g. Highlight the phrase using the [Shift][→] key combination.

h. Delete the phrase "a few words."

i. Undo the deletion.

j. Save the document.

4 Move a sentence from the beginning of the third paragraph to the first. Copy a phrase from the first paragraph to the cc: line at the bottom of the memo. Use drag and drop to reorder a phrase.

a. Select the sentence "Welcome to the company!" at the beginning of the third paragraph.

b. Cut the text to place it on the Clipboard.

c. Move the insertion point to the beginning of the first paragraph.

d. Paste the sentence from the Clipboard as the first sentence of the paragraph.

e. Select "Sales and Marketing group" in the first paragraph with the mouse and copy the text to the Clipboard.

f. Move the insertion point to the end of the document so it blinks after the name "Sue Ellen" on the cc: line.

g. Type a comma and a space, then paste the text after the space.

h. Select the word "rapidly" in the first paragraph.

i. Drag the text so it follows "approaching"

j. Save your edits.

5 Select the paragraph you just added to the memo using the line pointer, then run the Spelling Checker to verify the spelling of the words you inserted.

a. Scroll left until you can see the left margin of the second paragraph.

b. Move the mouse pointer to the left margin to change the insertion pointer to the line pointer.

c. Select the lines in the second paragraph with the line pointer.

d. Start the Spelling Checker.

e. Make sure the Always suggest option is selected.

f. Correct any spelling the Spelling Checker identifies.

g. Check the spelling in the rest of the document.

h. Close the Spelling Checker dialog box.

i. Save your changes.

6 Practice viewing your document in different views. In Print Preview, use the Zoom pointer to magnify the text on the page. Use the Zoom Box in Page Layout view. In Normal view, examine your document without margins.

a. Switch your document view to Print Preview.

b. Enlarge the document by 50%, and look at the second paragraph.

c. Look at that paragraph in full size.

d. Return the document to Page Layout view.

e. Switch to Normal view.

f. Scroll to the top of the document; the margins are not visible on the page.

g. Switch to Page Layout view.

h. Shrink the document to 70% of its size; look at the layout of the letter.

i. Enlarge the document to 150% of its size; look at the design of the letterhead.

7 Print the letter with the Print command on the File menu.

a. Open the Print dialog box.

b. Verify that your printer is online and properly connected to your computer.

c. Open the Properties dialog box.

d. Check that your printer is set to print on 8 ½" × 11" paper.

e. Print the Welcome letter.

f. Save any changes you made to the letter.

g. Close the document.

h. Exit Works.

INDEPENDENT CHALLENGE 1

You're in charge of organizing a sales conference for the entire sales department of Wacky Words, a company that produces comic greeting cards. You need to prepare a letter welcoming the sales department and field sales representatives to the semi-annual Wacky Words Sales Conference on August 16. The conference will take place in Orange, New Jersey, at the Convention Center, from 10:00 a.m. until 5:00 p.m. Afterwards, there will be an awards ceremony and banquet, featuring speaker Pierre Maury, a noted French cartoonist, who frequently contributes art to Wacky Words. The president of the company has asked that attendees confirm their travel plans with you within the next three weeks.

To complete this independent challenge:

1 Open the file WKS 2-3 on your Student Disk and save it in the My Works Files folder as "Sales Conference Letter."

2 Remove the destination name and address so one copy can be sent to all conference attendees.

3 Delete the placeholder text "SUBJECT OF THE LETTER IN UPPERCASE" then type the subject of your letter in upper case.

4 Delete the placeholder text "Start typing your letter," then write a short letter inviting everyone to the conference; include all information listed in the paragraph of this exercise. Make sure you tell them to confirm their travel plans with you. At the bottom of the page, delete the placeholder text "YOUR NAME GOES HERE (Signature below)," and replace it with your name in uppercase.

5 After you enter all the text, check your spelling and save the letter on disk.

6 Use Print Preview or the Zoom Box when you're finished to see how the printed letter will look. When you're satisfied, print a copy, sign it beneath your name, and submit it for the president's review.

INDEPENDENT CHALLENGE 2

Joel Rubin runs a small steakhouse in Austin, Texas. He wants to attend a trade show showing the latest in grill pits, smoke ventilators, and other equipment he uses in his restaurant. He asked you to write a letter of inquiry to the coordinator of the trade show, which is held each fall in Denver, Colorado. He wants you to find out when the trade show is, what admission costs, how many people attend, and who the typical exhibitors are. In addition, he wants you to request any general literature distributed for the show, such as hotel information, past experiences, airline discounts, and so on. The letter should use the company letterhead and fit on one page.

To complete this independent challenge:

1. Open the WKS 2-4 letterhead file on your Student Disk and save it in your My Works Files folder as "Denver Show Inquiry."
2. Address the letter to the trade show coordinator: Maria Burgos, Grills and More Trade Show Coordinator, 4433 High Bluff Road, Denver, CO, 55555. Remember to delete the placeholder text.
3. Write a short letter to the trade show coordinator asking Joel's questions as listed in the paragraph before this step list. Use the Spelling Checker and Thesaurus to help you compose your document.
4. When you finish writing the letter, use Print Preview to see how the printed letter will look. When you're satisfied, print a copy of the letter.

INDEPENDENT CHALLENGE 3

As a receptionist for a wholesale pet supply store, your responsibilities include answering mail and phone requests for catalogs and other information provided by the Stuff for Pets sales staff. This morning, you received a letter from Seth Lightfoot, owner of a small pet store in Livingston, Montana. Seth wants the Stuff for Pets product catalog and the opportunity to talk with a sales rep about prices of animal collars and gourmet cat and dog foods. You need to compose a brief cover letter for your mailing and to let Seth know that Gerry Zell, the sales rep covering Montana, will call him shortly. Rather than create a cover letter from scratch, you decide to use a Works TaskWizard to create the letter from a template designed for sending company brochures. You need to run the TaskWizard, customize the template, and print a final copy.

To complete this independent challenge:

1. Start Works, click the TaskWizards tab in the Works Task Launcher dialog box, and double-click the Letterhead TaskWizard. You'll find it in the Common Tasks category.
2. Run the TaskWizard and specify a Professional letterhead style. Look at the design in the Letterhead box, and create a fictional company address for Stuff for Pets with the Address box.
3. Click the Contents box and double-click the Welcome and Company Brochure entry.
4. Complete the letterhead with the TaskWizard, and then use the Word Processor to edit the document with your specific information. Use the following address for the prospective customer: Seth Lightfoot, 7788 Sawmill Gulch Road, Livingston, Montana, 55555. Add your name at the end. Be sure to delete the template instructions when you finish. If you have trouble, try using the Help Index to pinpoint and solve the problem.
5. Preview the document, and then print it. Save the file as "Montana Catalog Request" in your My Works Files folder.

INDEPENDENT CHALLENGE 4

The Literary Loft sells gift certificates to customers who plan to use them as gifts. Kristine Moscallo, the owner, has asked you to create three $50 gift certificates for customers Claudia Borghese, Bill Brus, and Duncan Overstreet. Works includes a TaskWizard that creates gift certificates automatically in the Word Processor, so you'll be able to use this feature to get started. You'll need to run the Certificate TaskWizard, specify the Gift Certificate option, and customize the certificates to include the recipients' names, the amount, and the words "The Literary Loft."

To complete this independent challenge:

1. Start Works, click the TaskWizards tab in the Works Task Launcher dialog box, and double-click the Certificate TaskWizard. (You'll find it in the Correspondence category.)
2. Click the Gift Certificate option and complete the TaskWizard.
3. Customize the gift certificates by editing all amounts to $50, adding "THE LITERARY LOFT" before the words "GIFT CERTIFICATE," and inserting the recipient names listed in the paragraph before this step list.
4. Use Print Preview to verify that the three certificates all appear on one page. If not, widen the margins with the Page Setup command on the File menu.
5. When you finish, print the certificates and save the file as "Gift Certificates" in your My Works Files folder.

VISUAL WORKSHOP

Create the document shown in Figure 2-14 with the Works Word Processor. The letter is based on a Works letterhead style and a Works content template. When you finish, print the document and save it as Client Query on your Student Disk. *Hint: Use the Letterhead TaskWizard in the Common Tasks category.* (Only a few changes have been made to a document supplied by Works.)

FIGURE 2-14

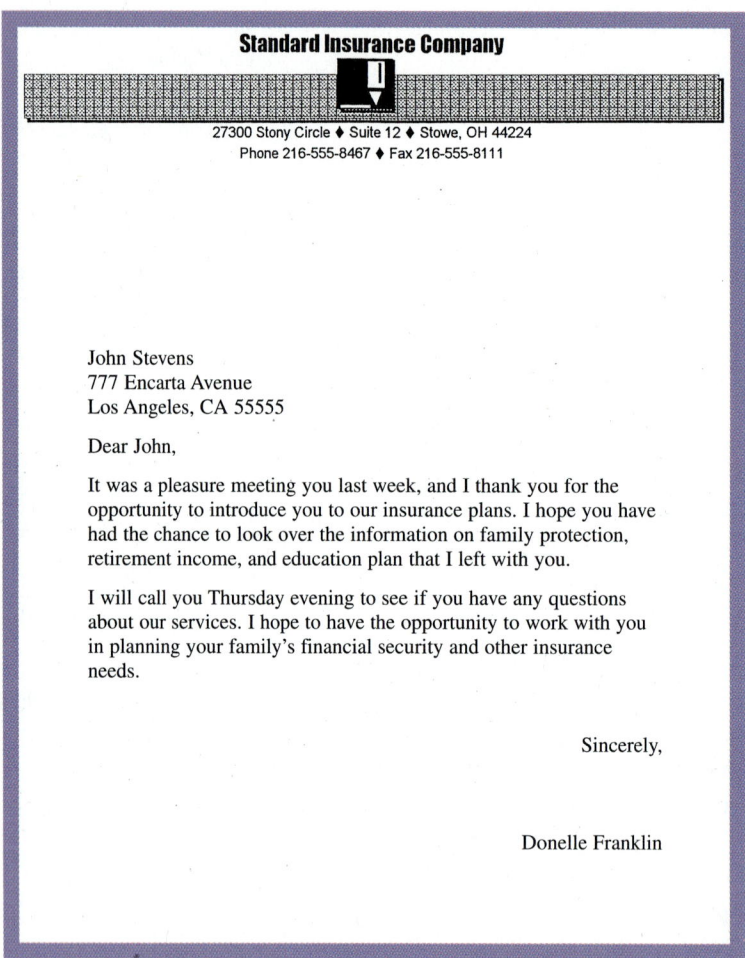

UNIT 3

OBJECTIVES

▶ Change font type and size

▶ Change font style

▶ Change alignment

▶ Change margin settings

▶ Change paragraph style

▶ Insert manual page breaks

▶ Insert headers and footers

Enhancing
A DOCUMENT'S APPEARANCE

Now you will use the Word Processor to **format**, or enhance, the way a document looks by changing fonts, font style, text alignment, and margin settings, and by adding bullets, page breaks, and a footer. ▶case Frasier, Outdoor Designs' marketing manager, gives you a product information sheet for the Cascade Ski Sack—Outdoor Designs' newest product—that he wants you to format. Sales reps and the public relations specialist will refer to the product information sheet to promote the ski sack when they call potential customers and local stores that carry their products. The more clearly formatted the sheet, the easier it will be for reps to find information when they need it. ▶

Changing font type and size

You can access many individual font and style commands (including list boxes for font type and font size, and buttons for bold, italic, and underline styles) from the Word Processor toolbar. Table 3-1 shows some font and style formatting samples. In this lesson you'll work with font type and size; in the next you'll change the font style as well. For more information about fonts, see the related topic, "Where do fonts come from?" ▶case After you open the product information sheet, you see that all text is the same font (Times New Roman) and size (12 points). First you want to change the title's font type and size so it stands out from the rest of the document.

1. Start **Works**, click the **Existing Documents tab** in the Works Task Launcher dialog box, then click **Open a document not listed here**
   The Open dialog box opens.

2. In the Look in list box, select the drive that contains your Student Disk, then double-click **WKS 3-1**
   The unformatted product information sheet opens.

3. Click **File** on the menu bar, click **Save As**, type **Ski Sack Sheet** in the File Name text box, double-click the **My Works Files folder**, then press **[Enter]**
   Works renames the file and saves it on your Student Disk in the My Works Files folder.

4. Click the **Shrink Help button** on the Help screen, if necessary
   The document window enlarges to fill the space left by the Help screen.

5. Click **View** on the menu bar, then click **Normal**, if it is not already checked
   The Normal command displays the document in Normal view. (The letters H and F appear at the top of the document to reserve space for the header and footer.)

6. Select **Outdoor Designs** and **New Product Information Sheet**, the first two lines of the Ski Sack Sheet document
   The highlighted lines are selected. You must select the text in a document in order to format characters (letters).

7. Click the **Font Name list arrow** on the toolbar, scroll to the top of the list, then click **Arial**
   The selected text changes to the Arial font, and Arial appears in the Font Name list box as the active font.

8. Click the **Font Size list arrow** on the toolbar, then click **18**
   The point size of the selected text changes to 18 and appears in the Font Size list box (1 point equals ½ of an inch). Figure 3-1 shows the selected text formatted in 18-point Arial.

9. Click the **Save button** on the toolbar to save your changes on disk

FIGURE 3-1: Selected text formatted with 18-point Arial

Click to change font type

Click to change font size

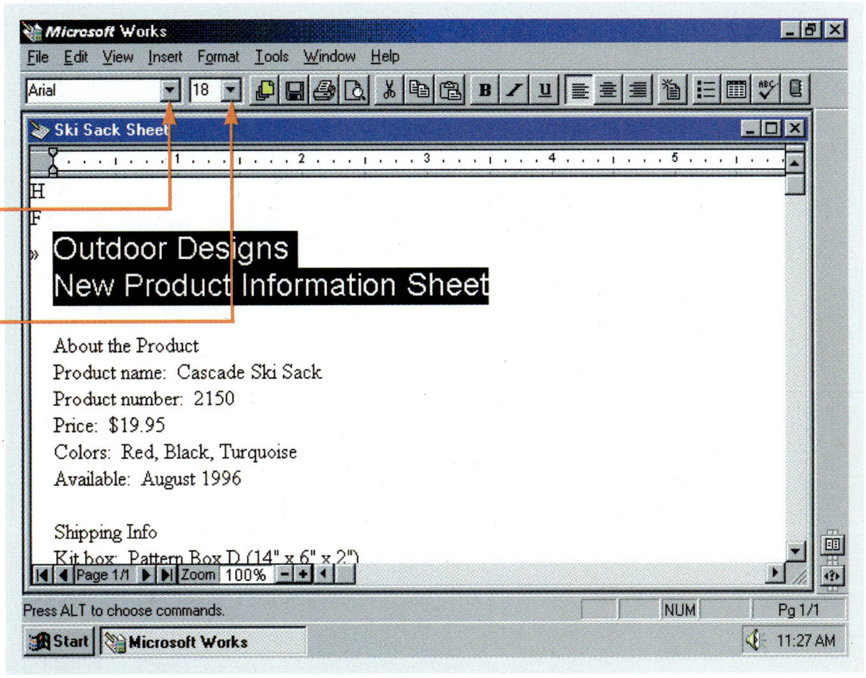

Where do fonts come from?

Font creation, or **fontography**, is an old business. In ancient times, scribes concerned with the uniformity of letters and symbols wrote in standard forms so future generations could easily understand their writing. Some of today's fonts descend from these earlier type styles; other type styles developed in modern times.

Before you can use fonts on a computer, they must be installed. The Windows operating system comes with several TrueType fonts, such as Arial and Times New Roman, preinstalled. **TrueType fonts** on your screen look just like they do on your printed page. The **T** symbol that appears in the Font Name list box identifies TrueType fonts. Your system might include other fonts supplied by the manufacturer of your printer or another company. Ask your instructor or technical support person for a list of fonts on your system, or click the Font Name list arrow on the toolbar and scroll through the list to see for yourself.

TABLE 3-1: Font and style formatting samples

FONT FORMATS	SAMPLES
Type	Arial, Courier, Times New Roman
Size	Six point, ten point, fourteen point
Style	**Bold**, *italic*, underline

QUICK TIP

The Help system usually opens whenever you start Works. Each time you start Works click  on the Help screen to minimize Help and make the document window as large as possible. Working on a document that fills the entire screen is much easier.

Changing font style

In many documents, you'll want to emphasize certain words or phrases or certain lines of text, to show readers their importance. You can use **font styles**, such as **bold** (darker type), *italics* (slanted type), and underlined, to add emphasis. Use these styles selectively: too much emphasis has the same effect as too little emphasis—nothing stands out. ▶case In the last lesson, you made the title of the product information sheet stand out from the rest of the document by changing the font type and size; now you'll change the font style to make it even more distinctive. Then you'll format other headings in the document to distinguish them from the rest of the text. The document includes two magazine names, which you'll italicize to indicate that they're publication titles.

1. Select the **first two lines** of the Ski Sack Sheet document with the mouse, if they're not selected

2. Click the **Bold button** [B] on the toolbar, then click the **Italic button** [/] on the toolbar
   The Bold and Italic buttons are pushed in, and the selected text is formatted for bold and italic. You like the way the title looks, but want to see how it looks with underlining as well.

3. Click the **Underline button** [U] on the toolbar, then click to the left of the letter **O** in Outdoor Designs
   The Underline button is pushed in and the first two lines are underlined, bolded, and italicized. With the underlining the text looks too busy, so you'll remove it. You could select the text and then click the Underline button again, but Works offers an even easier way to undo your last action—the Undo Editing command.

4. Click **Edit** on the menu bar, then click **Undo Editing**
   Works removes the underlining from the first two lines of the document and the Underline button is no longer pushed in. The **Undo Editing command** reverses or undoes your *last* formatting or editing action. Use the Undo Editing command if you notice a mistake right away or change your mind immediately after performing an action.

5. Select **About the Product**, then click [B]
   The heading becomes bold and distinct from the rest of the document.

6. Select each of the remaining four headings in the document **(Shipping Info, Description, Competitive Products, and Kit Promotions)**, and click [B]
   All headings in the document are boldface.

7. Under the heading Kit Promotions, select **Profitable Craft Merchandising**, then click [/]
   Figure 3-2 shows the italicized magazine title and the pushed-in Italic button on the toolbar.

8. Repeat Step 7 to italicize the magazine title, **Outside Magazine**, in that paragraph

9. Click the **Save button** [🖫] on the toolbar to save your style changes

FIGURE 3-2: Magazine name in italic

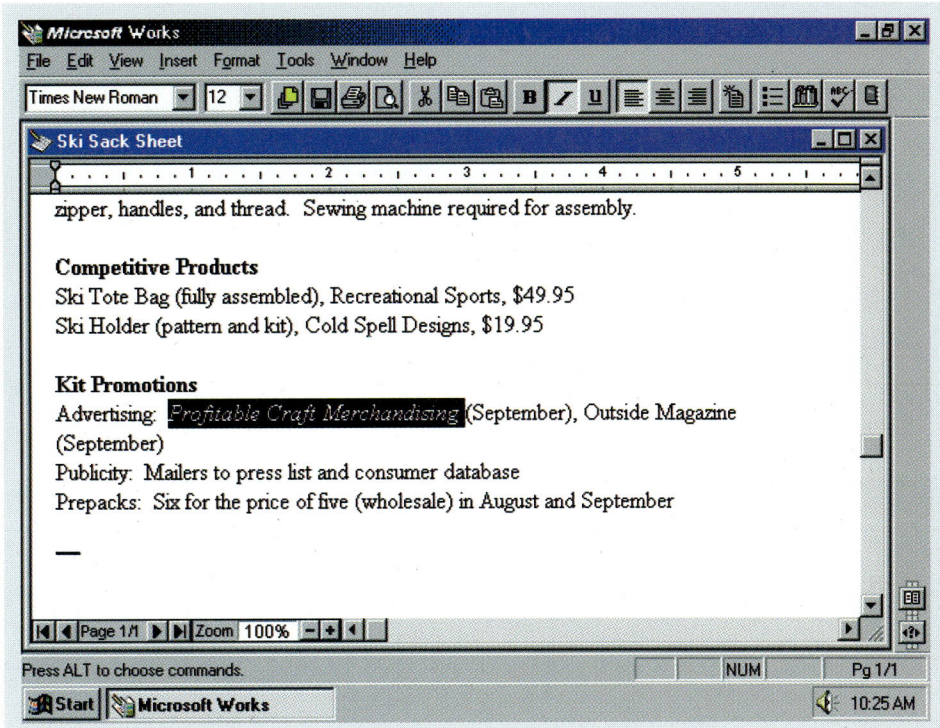

You can also use the keyboard shortcuts [Ctrl][B], [Ctrl][I], and [Ctrl][U] to format selected text in boldface, italic, and underline, respectively.

Changing alignment

You can change the **alignment**, or position, of text in relation to a document's margins with the alignment buttons on the toolbar. You can also **justify** text (align it at both the right and left margins) with the Paragraph command. For example, titles are often centered, headings left aligned, and paragraphs justified. For information about changing spacing between lines in a document, see the related topic, "Changing line spacing." **case** The product information sheet contains lots of important information; right now it all looks alike. You decide to use the Center and Justified alignments to format different types of information distinctly and make the document look more professional.

1. **Use the scroll bars to scroll to the top of the document**
   The window scrolls vertically until the top of the document is visible.

2. **Select the text, Outdoor Designs and New Product Information Sheet**
   The first two lines (formatted with Arial bold and italic) are highlighted.

3. **Click the Center Align button on the toolbar**
   Works centers the text. You decide to justify the product description text so it looks polished.

4. **Scroll down until you see the paragraph under the heading Description, then select the paragraph with the mouse**
   The paragraph under Description is highlighted.

5. **Click Format, then click Paragraph**
   The Format Paragraph dialog box opens. It contains two types of formatting options: Indents and Alignment, and Spacing.

6. **Click the Indents and Alignment tab if it is not already in front**
   The Indents and Alignment tab shown in Figure 3-3 appears. It offers different indent and alignment options. You can also select one of the alignment options listed in Table 3-2 from the toolbar. However, you must use the Format Paragraph dialog box to choose Justified alignment.

7. **Click Justified, then click OK**
   The Format Paragraph dialog box closes and the Description paragraph's alignment changes to Justified. Notice that the paragraph is aligned at both margins. When you select Justified alignment, the Word Processor adds or reduces the space between each word so that the text aligns along both the right and left margins.

8. **Click the Save button on the toolbar to save your formatting changes**

FIGURE 3-3:
Format Paragraph dialog box

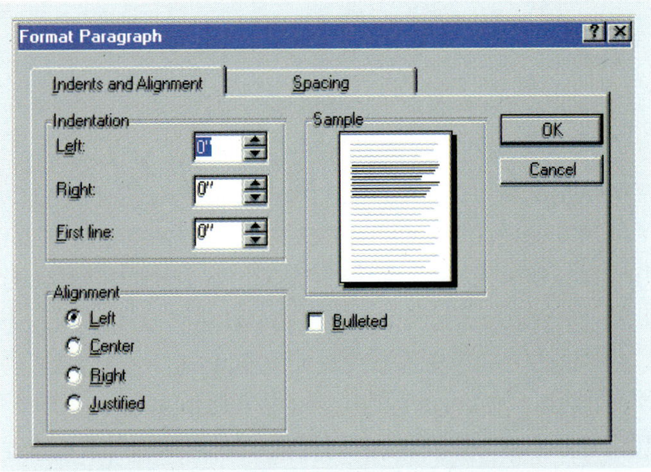

FIGURE 3-4:
Adjust line spacing with the Spacing tab

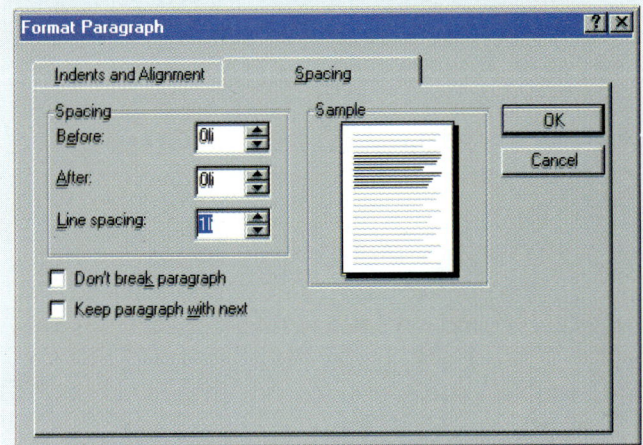

Changing line spacing

In the Word Processor, default spacing between lines in a document is one line **(single spacing)**. You can adjust line spacing in a paragraph or an entire document with the Spacing tab in the Format Paragraph dialog box, shown in Figure 3-4. The Spacing tab includes options for setting spacing between lines and before and after paragraphs. To double-space lines, select them, choose the Paragraph command from the Format menu, click the Spacing tab, type 2 in the Line spacing text box, then click OK. You can also protect paragraphs from breaking across pages by choosing the Don't break paragraph option, or you can keep a heading with the paragraph that follows it by choosing the Keep paragraph with next option.

TABLE 3-2: Alignment icons on the toolbar

ICON	DESCRIPTION
📄	Aligns text at the left margin
📄	Aligns text at the center of the page
📄	Aligns text at the right margin

QUICK TIP

To select the entire document, you hold down [Ctrl] and click in the left margin, making sure the pointer is a  when you do so.

Changing margin settings

The Word Processor sets default page margins at 1 inch from the top and bottom, and 1.25 inches from the left and right. You can change the margin settings using the Page Setup command on the File menu. When you change the margins, the Word Processor automatically adjusts line wrapping and repaginates your document. To evaluate what margin settings to use in a specific document, switch to Page Layout view to see the actual margins on the page. For more information about making other overall changes to your document, see the related topic, "Changing the paper source, size, and orientation." **case** Frasier used the Word Processor's default settings when he typed the Ski Sack product information sheet. Outdoor Designs' style guidelines indicate that all product information sheets should have 1-inch left and right margins. You'll change the margins now.

1. **Click File on the menu bar, then click Page Setup**
   The Page Setup dialog box opens. It contains three tabs: Margins, Source, Size, and Orientation; and Other Options.

2. **Click the Margins tab if it is not already in front**
   Figure 3-5 shows the Margins tab, which contains six margin text boxes (one for each margin on the page), a Sample window, two command buttons, and a Reset button (to restore default settings). The first text box, Top margin, is currently selected.

3. **Press [Tab] twice**
   The Left margin text box is selected. Notice that each time you press the Tab key in a dialog box, the insertion point moves from one text box to the next. In this case, the insertion point moved from the Top margin text box to the Bottom margin text box to the Left margin text box.

4. **Type 1 in the Left margin text box, then press [Tab]**
   The Left margin text box shows 1. (Don't worry about typing the inch symbol: Works adds it automatically when you close the Page Setup dialog box.) The Right margin text box is selected. The Sample window shows the new left margin.

5. **Type 1 in the Right margin text box, then click OK**
   The Page Setup dialog box closes, and the left and right margins in the product information sheet change to 1 inch. You can't see the margins in Normal view, so you decide to change to Page Layout view.

6. **Click View on the menu bar, then click Page Layout**
   The view switches to Page Layout, and you can see the document margins. If you scroll to the edge of the page using the horizontal scroll bar, you can verify the left and right margin measurements with the ruler.

7. **Click the left scroll arrow to scroll to the left edge of the page**
   Use the ruler to verify that the left margin is 1 inch from the left edge of the page. After you check the left margin's size, scroll to the right edge of the page and verify that margin's size.

8. **Click View on the menu bar, then click Normal**
   You see the document in Normal view.

9. **Click the Save button 💾 on the toolbar**
   Your document is saved with its new margins.

FIGURE 3-5:
Margins tab in Page Setup dialog box

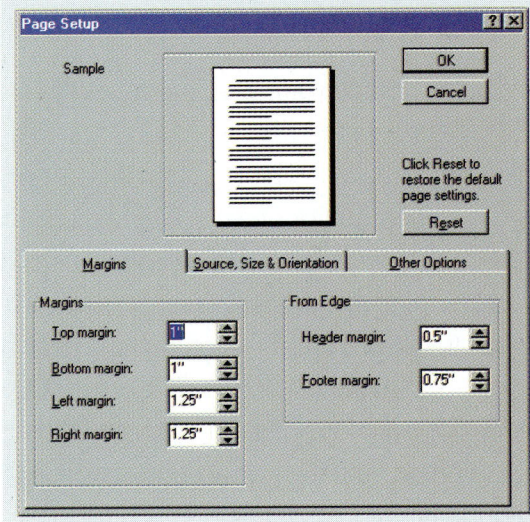

FIGURE 3-6:
Source, Size, and Orientation tab in Page Setup dialog box

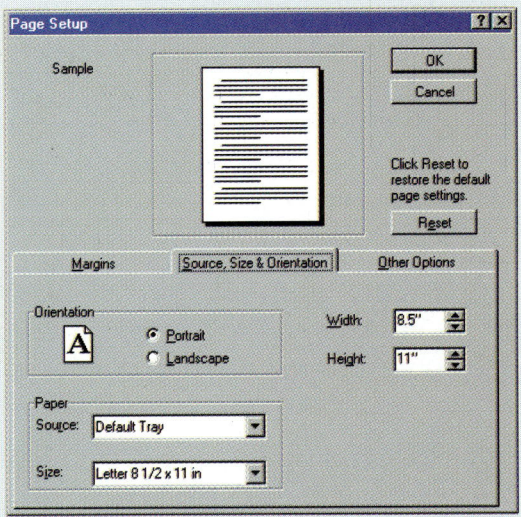

Changing the paper source, size, and orientation

The Word Processor's default paper settings are for an 8.5" × 11" sheet, oriented **portrait** style (meaning longer vertically, like a portrait painting), and stored in the printer's main paper tray. You can change these settings with the Source, Size, and Orientation tab in the Page Setup dialog box shown in Figure 3-6. The Source list box presents one or more paper source options, including manual feed and envelope, depending on the type of printer you have. The Size list box shows the paper types Works supports. Changing the paper size in this list box automatically changes your document's page size and also repaginates your document. Finally, the Orientation option buttons let you change the document from portrait to **landscape** (meaning longer horizontally) orientation, useful for a wide table or other information.

TROUBLE?

If you do not see the ruler on your screen, click View on the menu bar, then click Ruler.

QUICK TIP

For mechanical reasons, most printers require at least a ¼-inch margin around the page.

Changing paragraph style

In the last lesson you learned how to change an entire document's margins with the Page Setup command. You can also change margins, spacing, font style, and other aspects of individual paragraphs within the document, creating different **paragraph styles**. You can use the Word Processor's Easy Formats command to create many paragraph styles, including indented paragraphs, hanging indents, boxed text, and quotations. You can also modify text alignment within paragraphs with the Bullets and Tabs commands. To learn more about tabs, see the related topic, "Changing tab stops." **case** The Description paragraph still doesn't stand out the way you'd like. You decide to choose an existing paragraph style from Easy Formats and then place bullets before each competitor's product to show the reader that two competing products exist.

1. If necessary, select the paragraph beneath the heading **Description**; use the scroll bars to bring it into view

2. Click **Format** on the menu bar, then click **Easy Formats**
   The Easy Formats dialog box shown in Figure 3-7 opens. It offers a variety of predefined formatting styles and a Sample window so you can preview paragraph formatting. Easy Formats applies the selected style at the left margin unless you pressed the Tab key, in which case Easy Formats applies it to the current indent.

3. Click **Boxed text**
   A preview of the Boxed text style appears in the Sample window. The formatting details of the Boxed text style are listed below the window. The paragraph in Boxed text style seems to overpower other information on the page. You could alter the Boxed text style by clicking the Change button in the dialog box. Instead, you choose a more appropriate style from the Easy Formats list box.

4. Scroll down the Easy Formats list, then click **Indented Paragraph**
   As with the Boxed text style, a preview of the Indented Paragraph text style appears in the Sample window and formatting details (such as Left Aligned, First Line Indent 0.5", and so on) are listed below the window. The Indented Paragraph style seems appropriate for the Description paragraph.

5. Click **Apply**
   The Easy Formats dialog box closes, and the Description paragraph is formatted as an indented paragraph. Note that the left margin indicator on the ruler has split in half, and the top part has moved to the right ½ inch, showing that the paragraph is formatted for first line indent.

   A bulleted list better suits the information in the Competitive Products section, so you decide to reformat these lines as well.

6. Select the two lines under the Competitive Products heading, then click the **Bullets button** on the toolbar
   Bullets appear before each line, and each line is indented to add space between the bullets and the text. The Bullets button is a handy shortcut; however, you can also specify the bullet style and size you want with the Bullets command on the Format menu.

7. Click the **Save button** on the toolbar to save your paragraph formatting

FIGURE 3-7:
Easy Formats dialog box

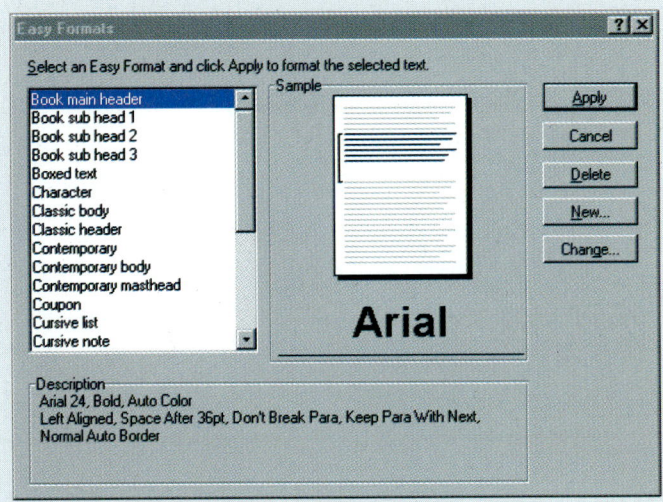

FIGURE 3-8:
Format Tabs dialog box

Indicates a default tab stop

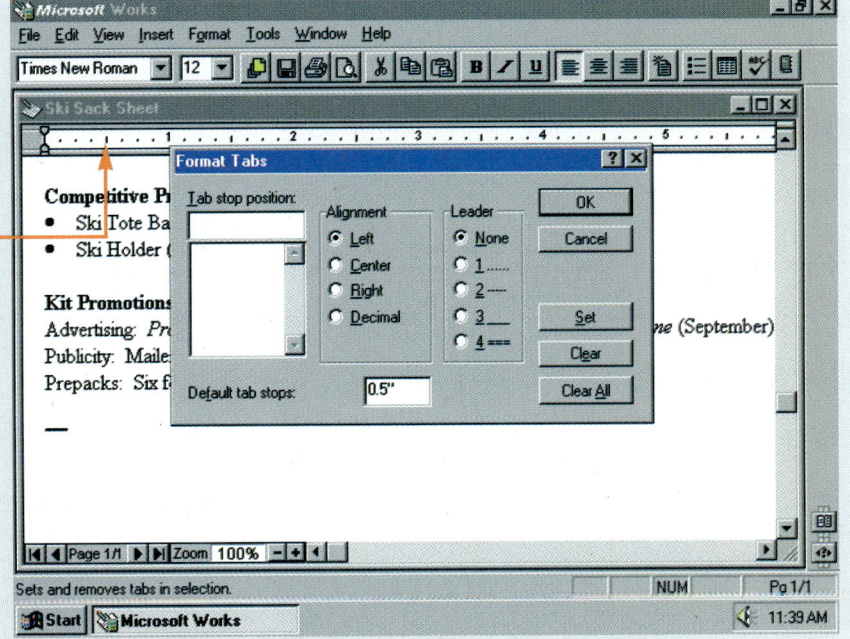

Changing tab stops

The Word Processor's default setting for tab stops is every ½ inch. This means that each time you press the Tab key in a paragraph, the insertion point moves one **tab stop**, or ½ inch to the right. (Gray dots on the bottom of the ruler indicate tab stops.) To change tab stops' frequency or spacing, choose the Tabs command from the Format menu to open the Format Tabs dialog box. You can use the Format Tabs dialog box, shown in Figure 3-8, to set a tab stop at a specific position in the document, change text alignment around a tab stop, place a leader line between tab stops, or clear unwanted tab stops. To customize more than one paragraph with the same tab stops you must select the paragraphs as a group before you choose the Tabs command.

QUICK TIP

You can also click the Easy Formats button  on the toolbar to choose predefined paragraph styles.

Inserting manual page breaks

The Word Processor automatically wraps text in a document to the next page when the last line of the current page is full. You can also manually insert a **page break**, forcing text to begin on a new page even if the current page is not full, using the Page Break command on the Insert menu. Before you print a document that has several pages you should preview it with the Print Preview command to determine whether you need to insert manual page breaks. ▶case The Outdoor Designs style guidelines suggest dividing product information sheets into two or more pages to separate different types of information and make information easier for salespeople to find. You'll add page breaks to the document now.

1. **Click the insertion point at the beginning of the line containing Description**
   The insertion point blinks at the left margin, just before the word "Description." You want the product description to start on a new page.

2. **Click Insert on the menu bar, then click Page Break**
   The page break inserted into the document before the Description heading is shown in Figure 3-9. The double arrow at the left margin marks the page break, and the dotted line extending across the screen indicates the page break is manual. (A double arrow appears at every page break; the dotted line appears only at manual page breaks.) The page number indicator in the lower-right corner of the screen tells that the insertion point is on the second of two pages (Pg 2/2).

3. **Repeat Steps 1 and 2 to insert a page break before the Competitive Products heading**
   The document is now three pages, with the Competitive Products and the Promotional Kits sections on the third page. You need to see how the information will look printed on three pages.

4. **Click the insertion point in the title, then click the Print Preview button on the toolbar**
   The document's first page appears in Print Preview, as shown in Figure 3-10.

5. **Click Next to view the document's second page, then click Next**
   The second and then the third page of the document appear in Print Preview. The third page is the last page of the document, so the Next button dims. You can view the previous pages, however, so the Previous button is darkened. Although you like the Description beginning on a new page, you decide that three short pages makes the document look too choppy.

6. **Click Cancel**
   The product information sheet returns to Normal view. Now you can delete the second page break from the document.

7. **Scroll to the Competitive Products paragraph and click in the left margin next to the line that indicates the second page break**
   The dotted line is highlighted.

8. **Press [Delete]**
   The dotted line and double arrow disappear from the document.

9. **Click the Save button on the toolbar to save your changes to the file**

FIGURE 3-9: Page Break command inserts a page break in the document

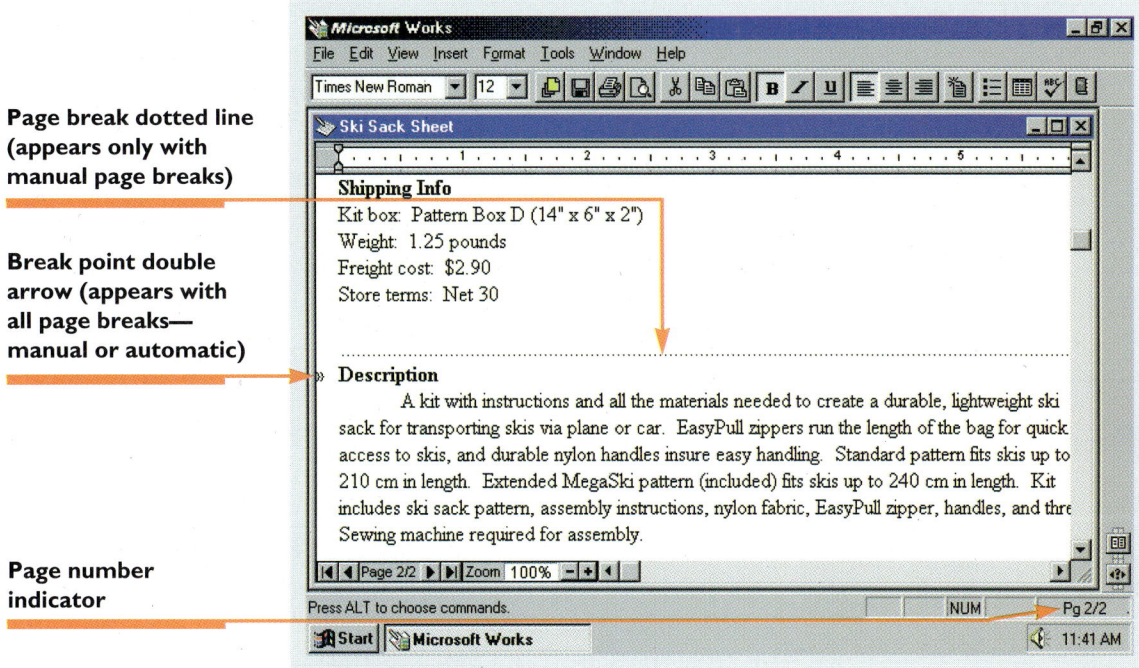

FIGURE 3-10: Three-page product information sheet in Print Preview

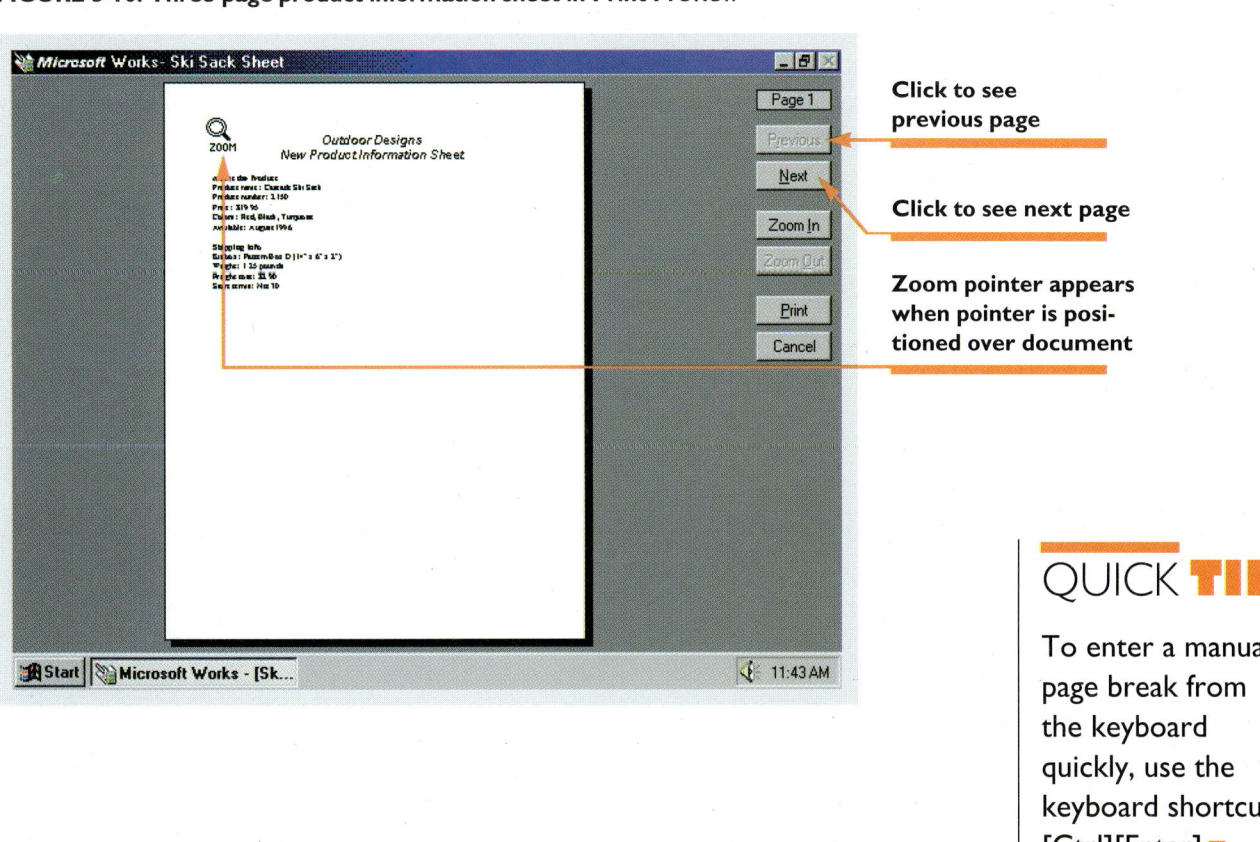

QUICK TIP

To enter a manual page break from the keyboard quickly, use the keyboard shortcut [Ctrl][Enter].

Inserting headers and footers

When you create a document, you might want to add page numbers, the print date, your name, or some other text to the top or the bottom of every page. You can add this information with the Headers and Footers commands on the View menu. In Works, a standard **header**, which appears just below the top margin, or **footer**, which appears just above the bottom margin, is one line long and can contain text or information added by the commands on the Insert menu. In Normal view, both the header and footer appear at the top of your document for easy editing and are identified by the letters H and F, respectively. ►**case** You'll add a header and footer based on Outdoor Designs' company guidelines now.

1. Click **View** on the menu bar, then click **Header**; if the First-time Help dialog box appears, click **OK**

   The insertion point moves to the header field at the top of the document, as shown in Figure 3-11. The text you enter in this field will appear at the top of every page in the document when you print it. You can also customize the header with character and alignment formatting or add special information with commands on the Insert menu.

2. Type **Outdoor Designs Confidential** in the header field, then click the **Center Align button** on the toolbar

   The header, Outdoor Designs Confidential, is centered at the top of the page. Although you need to select text to change character formats such as font size or font style, the insertion point just needs to be within the line to change most paragraph formatting, such as alignment or bullets.

3. Press **[Down Arrow]**, type **Printed on**, then press **[Spacebar]**

   The footer, Printed on, appears in the footer text field. Now you can insert the current date, so reps will know when the information was last updated.

4. Click **Insert** on the menu bar, click **Date and Time**, then double-click the **third date format** in the list

   The current date appears in the footer in the form of date, day, and year. The date will be updated automatically each time you print the document.

5. Press **[Spacebar]**, type **— Page**, press **[Spacebar]**, click **Insert** on the menu bar, then click **Page Number**

   A placeholder for the page number (*page*) appears in the footer. When you print the document, Works inserts the correct page number.

6. Click then click the **Print Preview button** on the toolbar

   The document opens in Print Preview so that you can review your work and see the header and footer positioned correctly.

7. Click the **header** with the Zoom pointer, then scroll to the bottom of the page to read the footer

   Both header and footer contain the text you typed, centered at the top and bottom of the page, respectively. The product information sheet is complete and you're ready to print.

8. Click **Print** on the Print Preview window

   The product information sheet prints. You have finished formatting the product information sheet for Frasier, so you can save your changes and exit Works.

9. Click the **Save button** on the toolbar, click **File** on the menu bar, then click **Exit Works**

   The Ski Sack sheet document and the Works program close.

FIGURE 3-11: Header and footer fields in Normal view

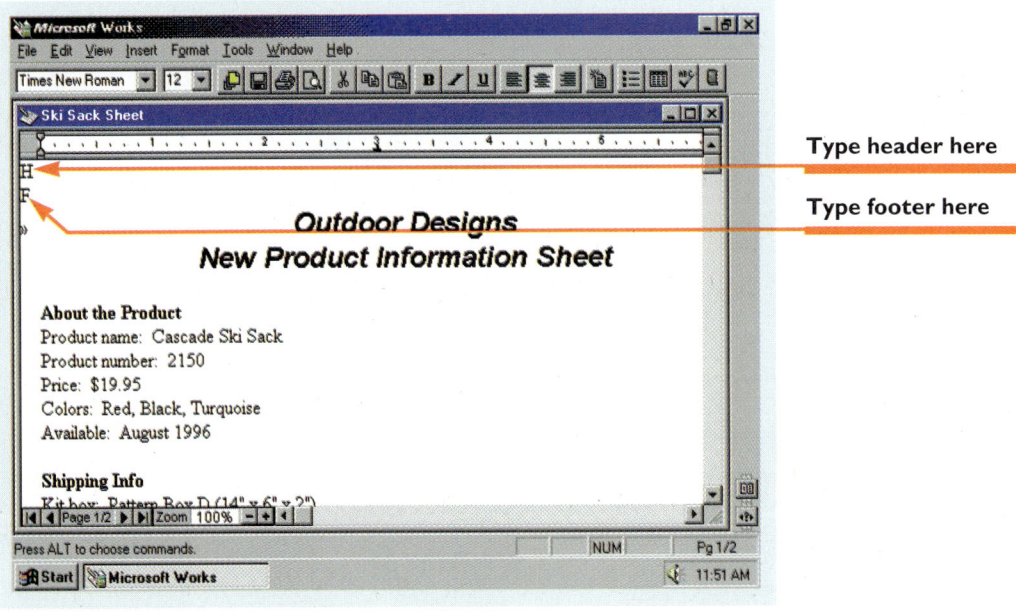

Type header here

Type footer here

FIGURE 3-12: Completed footer in Print Preview

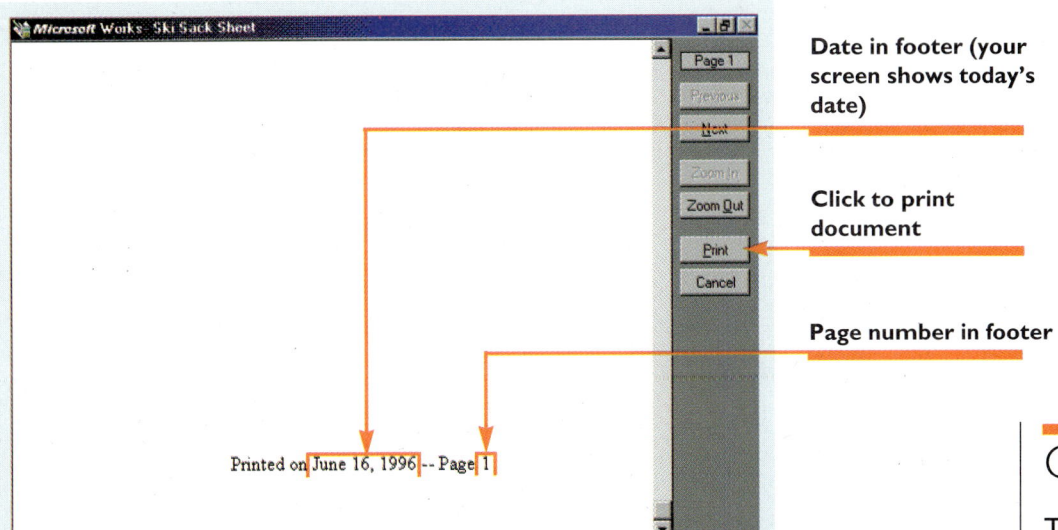

Date in footer (your screen shows today's date)

Click to print document

Page number in footer

QUICK TIP

To start numbering pages with a number other than 1, choose the Page Setup command from the File menu, click the Other Options tab, then enter the number you want to start with in the Starting page number text box.

TASK REFERENCE

TASK	MOUSE/BUTTON	MENU	KEYBOARD
Center align text	≡	Click Format, Paragraph	[Alt][O], [P]
Change font size	Click the Font Size list arrow	Click Format, Font and Style	[Alt][O], [F]
Change font type	Click the Font Name list arrow	Click Format, Font and Style	[Alt][O], [F]
Change margins		Click File, Page Setup	[Alt][F], [G], [M]
Format with bold style	B	Click Format, Font and Style	[Ctrl][B]
Format with italic style	I	Click Format, Font and Style	[Ctrl][I]
Format with underline style	U	Click Format, Font and Style	[Ctrl][U]
Insert footer	Click the footer field	Click View, Footer	[Alt][V], [F]
Insert header	Click the header field	Click View, Header	[Alt][V], [F]
Insert page break		Click Insert, Page Break	[Ctrl][Enter]
Left align text	≡	Click Format, Paragraph	[Alt][O], [P]
Right align text	≡	Click Format, Paragraph	[Alt][O], [P]
Set tab stops	Click or double-click the ruler	Click Format, Tabs	[Alt][O], [T]
Use an Easy Formats style		Click Format, Easy Formats	[Alt][O], [E]

CONCEPTS REVIEW

Figure 3-13 shows a document formatted with several Word Processor formatting commands. Match the commands from the Format list to the numbered elements in the document.

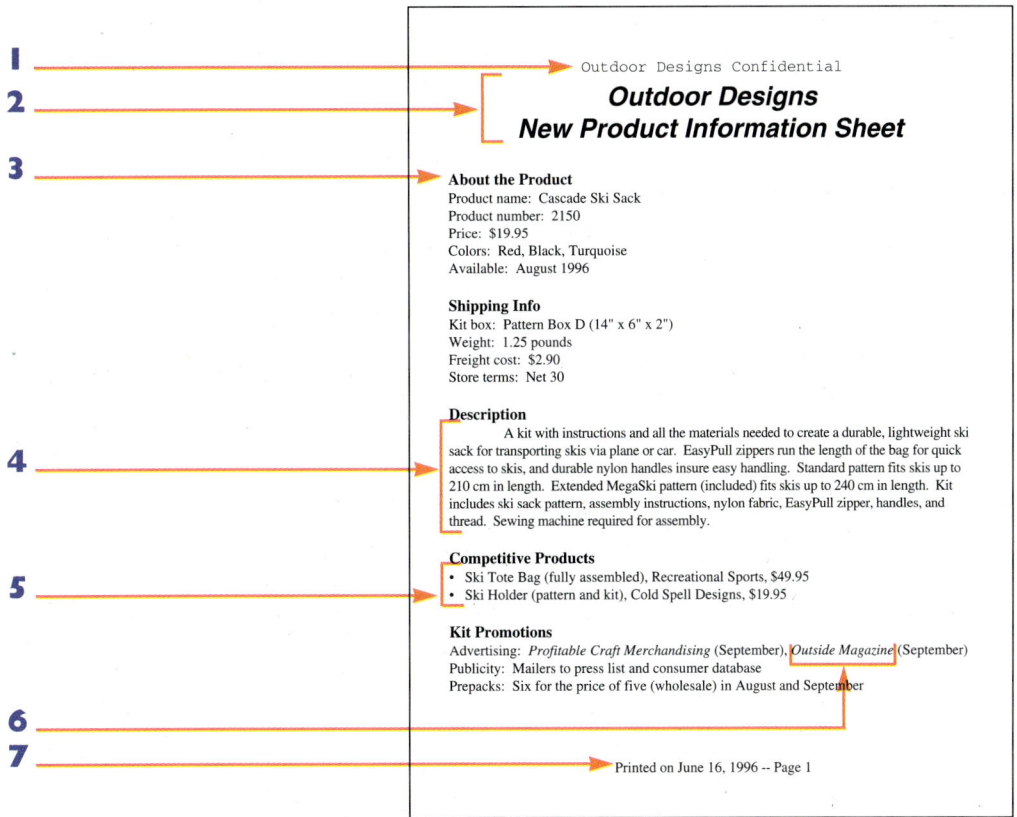

FIGURE 3-13

Format list

a. Indented paragraph style

b. Bulleted list

c. Center-aligned header

d. Footer with date and page number

e. 18-point Arial boldface italic, center alignment

f. 12-point Times New Roman boldface

g. 12-point Times New Roman italic

Match each toolbar button with the effect it creates.

8 **B**

9

10

11

12

a. Right align selected text

b. Left align selected text

c. Format paragraphs with bullets

d. Format text with bold

e. Display Easy Format options

Select the best answer from the list of choices.

13 Which of these is *not* an element in the Open dialog box?
   a. File name text box
   b. Recently used file list box
   c. Works Files in current folder
   d. Folders list box

14 Which of these is *not* a method for changing the style of selected text to boldface?
   a. Clicking the Bold button on the toolbar
   b. Holding down [Ctrl] and pressing [B]
   c. Changing the color of the text to blue
   d. Clicking the Bold check box in the Font and Style dialog box

15 What does the overlapping T symbol mean when it is listed next to a font in the Font Name list box?
   a. The font is a TrueType font.
   b. The font can only be displayed in Works.
   c. The font was designed by Technology Typeworks.
   d. The font works only with dot-matrix printers.

16 One point is equivalent to which of these measurements?
   a. 1 VGA screen pixel
   b. $\frac{1}{72}$ of an inch
   c. 210 centimeters
   d. 1 ounce

17 If the alignment of text in a paragraph is justified, what is true about the text?
   a. It is aligned at the right margin.
   b. It is aligned at the left margin.
   c. It is aligned at the center of the page.
   d. It is aligned at both the right and left margins.

18 Which of these commands would you use to change paragraph spacing from single spacing to double spacing?
   a. The Double Spacing command on the View menu
   b. The Paragraph command on the Format menu
   c. The Page Setup command on the File menu
   d. The Easy Formats command on the Format menu

19 What are the Word Processor's default page margin settings?
   a. ½ inch all around the document
   b. 1 inch all around the document
   c. 1.5 inches for the top and bottom margins, 2 inches for the left and right margins
   d. 1 inch for the top and bottom margins, 1.25 inches for the left and right margins

20 What is Easy Formats?
   a. Decorative document borders
   b. Predefined paragraph styles
   c. Predefined document styles
   d. Font styles

21 The default tab stops in the Word Processor are
   a. Every ½ inch
   b. Every inch
   c. Every 1.5 inches
   d. There are no default tab stops.

22 How do you insert a manual page break in a document?
   a. Choose the Page Break command from the Insert menu.
   b. Click Format on the menu bar, then click New Page.
   c. Hold down [Ctrl] and press [Shift].
   d. Double-click in the left margin.

23 How do you delete a manual page break?
   a. Double-click the page break.
   b. Click the left mouse button.
   c. Select the page break and press [Delete].
   d. Select the page break and press [PageDown].

24 How do headers and footers appear in the document when you're in Normal view?
   a. They appear just as they will be printed.
   b. In fields at the top of the document.
   c. In fields at the bottom of the document.
   d. With page numbers

25 How do you center a footer on the page?

   a. Click the Center Align button on the Formatting toolbar.

   b. Double-click the middle mouse button.

   c. Hold down [Ctrl] and press C.

   d. Click Format on the menu bar, then click Center Footer.

SKILLS REVIEW

1 Start Works, open the WKS 3-2 file, save it as Ski Sack Update, then change some font types and sizes.

   a. Launch Microsoft Works.

   b. Open the file WKS 3-2 on your Student Disk.

   c. Save the file as Ski Sack Update in the My Works Files folder.

   d. Switch to Normal view.

   e. Select the first three lines of the document.

   f. Change the font size to 14.

   g. Scroll until you see the lines "Outdoor Designs" and "Product Information Sheet UPDATE," then select them.

   h. Change the font type to Impact.

   i. Change the font size to 18.

   j. Save your changes.

2 Change some font styles and undo an action.

   a. Select the price "$22.75."

   b. Use the toolbar button to change the font style to underline.

   c. Underline the color Orange, then underline the freight cost $3.15.

   d. Select the lines, "Outdoor Designs" and "Product Information Sheet UPDATE."

   e. Use the toolbar button to bold the selection.

   f. Use the keyboard shortcut to italicize the selection.

   g. Select the bold heading "About the Product."

   h. Italicize the heading.

   i. Use Undo to remove the italic font style from the heading.

   j. Save your font style changes.

3 Change text alignment.

   a. Scroll to the top of the document.

   b. Select the first paragraph of Frasier's memo, which begins "The following is a new product information sheet…."

   c. Open the Format Paragraphs dialog box.

   d. Select the Indents and Alignment tab, if necessary.

   e. Change alignment to justified.

   f. Change line spacing of the paragraph to double spaced.

   g. Click OK.

   h. Scroll to and then select the lines "Outdoor Designs" and "Product Information Sheet UPDATE."

   i. Align text at the right margin using the toolbar button.

   j. Save your formatting changes.

4 Change the document's margins.

   a. Open the Page Setup dialog box.

   b. Select the Margins tab if necessary.

   c. Set the top and bottom margins to 1.5 inches.

   d. Set the left margin to 1.75 inches.

   e. Set the right margin to 1 inch.

   f. Click OK.

   g. Switch to Page Layout view.

   h. Use the ruler to verify that the left margin setting is 1.75 inches.

   i. Use the ruler to verify that the right margin setting is 1.5 inches.

   j. Save the new margin settings.

   k. Return to Normal View.

5 Change paragraph styles and add bullets to a list.

   a. Scroll to the top of the document and select the first paragraph in Frasier's memo, which begins "The following is a new…."

   b. Open the Easy Formats dialog box.

   c. Preview the Quotation style.

   d. Preview the Contemporary body style.

   e. Apply the Contemporary body style to the selected text.

   f. Select "new price" in the second paragraph, second line.

g. Add a bullet before the item, using the toolbar button.

h. Select the remaining two items Frasier updated ("additional color choice" and "increased freight cost").

i. Add bullets to these items.

j. Save your paragraph formatting changes.

6 Add page breaks to your document.

a. Move the insertion point before the heading "Outdoor Designs."

b. Add a manual page break to your document using the menu bar.

c. Move insertion point before "Description" heading.

d. Add a second manual page break to your document using the keyboard shortcut.

e. Switch to Print Preview.

f. Look at all three pages in the document.

g. Return to Normal view.

h. Select the page break line before the "Description" heading.

i. Delete the page break.

j. Save your new page breaks.

7 Add headers and footers to your document.

a. Move the insertion point into the header field at the top of the document.

b. Type the header "Outdoor Designs Confidential — Page."

c. Add a space and then add the page number placeholder from the menu bar.

d. Center the header.

e. Move the insertion point into the footer field.

f. Type the footer "Product Information Sheet Updated on."

g. Add a space and then add the current date using the menu bar.

h. Align the footer to the right margin using the toolbar button.

i. Preview and save your changes.

j. Print your document and exit Works.

INDEPENDENT CHALLENGE 1

Manuel Dominga, a sales representative at Wacky Words, asked you to format a letter and price sheet that he prepared for a customer. He used Wacky Words letterhead but didn't format anything else. If you can enhance the look of his materials, he's sure Samantha will put in a good-sized order for greeting cards.

To complete this independent challenge:

1 Open the file WKS 3-3 on your Student Disk, and save it in the My Works Files folder under the name Graduation Cards.

2 Scroll to the middle of page one, select "Wacky Words," and change it to 18-point Impact bold. Select the next line, change it to 14-point Impact italic. Center both lines. Left align the closing, signature, and title lines at the end of Manuel's letter.

3 Change the margin settings so the top, bottom, left, and right margins of the document are 1.5 inches.

4 Add bullets to the seven types of graduation cards listed in the second paragraph of the letter. Use Easy Formats to apply the Prestige header style to the headings "Subject of Greeting Cards," "Available Series," and "Prices," then apply the List with lines style to the text under the "Available Series" heading.

5 Separate the letter from the price sheet by adding a manual page break at the line beginning "Wacky Words" after the letter.

6 Save your changes, preview and then print the letter and price list.

INDEPENDENT CHALLENGE 2

Joel Rubin wants to create "Buy one dinner, get one free at The Steak Pit" certificates to donate to a local charity for its annual fund raiser. Last year, the group auctioned 15 certificates and raised $1,100 from his donation alone. Joel has written the text of the certificate and asks you to format it.

To complete this independent challenge:

1. Open the file WKS 3-4 on your Student Disk and save it in the My Works Files folder under the name Free Entree.

2. Change "The Steak Pit" to 48-point type, change the two address lines to 36-point type. Change the rest of the text to 14-point Mistral centered.

3. Underline the restaurant name in the first line of text. Bold the words "free" and "complimentary." Add bullets before the words "dessert" and "coffee or tea."

4. Change the top and bottom margins to 1.75 inches, and the left and right margins to 1 inch. Switch the paper orientation to Landscape.

5. Add a footer to the document that reads "The lesser-priced entree will be deducted from the final bill." in 10-point type. Left align the footer and italicize its text.

6. Preview the certificate, press [Enter] before or after lines until the main text is centered. Save your changes. Print your certificate, then close the document and exit Works.

INDEPENDENT CHALLENGE 3

Gerry Zell, the sales representative from Montana, calls and asks you to write a product description of the new pet collars being offered by Stuff for Pets and format it so he can send it out to his customers.

To complete this independent challenge:

1. Start Works and open a blank document. Save it as "Pet Collars" on your Student Disk.

2. Make up a name for the product. Type the name at the top of your document. Use any font you like. Center the text. Five lines below the product name, type the heading "Collar Description." On the next line, type a paragraph describing why these collars are better than any available on the market. Below that, list some benefits of using the collars.

3. Use Easy Formats to format the heading, paragraph, and list that you just typed. Then change line spacing for the entire document to double spacing. Italicize the product name every time it appears in your document.

4. Create a header that prints the company's name in 16-point boldface and right-aligned type. Create a footer that prints your name and today's date in 12-point, right-aligned type.

5. Preview your document. Make any formatting changes you like to improve your document's appearance. Save your changes. Print the document.

6. Close the document and exit Works.

INDEPENDENT CHALLENGE 4

The Literary Loft wants to provide a new customer service—book reviews. The owner, Kristine, asks each employee to write a brief synopsis of two books they've read and include a recommendation so customers can tell if they might like them.

To complete this independent challenge:

1. Start Works and open a blank document. Save the document as Book Reviews on your Student Disk.

2. Write a one-paragraph review of two books you've read and enjoyed. Write your recommendation in a new paragraph. Include each book's title on its own line before each review.

3. Format the text so that the title of each review is in a different font and size than the rest of the text. Italicize each book title. Use Easy Formats to format each review and recommendation. Place each review on its own page.

4. Add a header with your name. Add a footer with today's date and the page number.

5. Save your reviews, preview them, then print them. Close the document and exit Works.

VISUAL WORKSHOP

Create the document shown in Figure 3-14 with the Works Word Processor and save it as Product Sheet to the My Works Files folder on your Student Disk. *Hint: Use the Mountain Day Pack product information sheet (WKS 3-5) as your starting point, and review the formatting exercises you completed in this unit.* Don't worry if some lines wrap differently in your document than they do in Figure 3-14. This can occur due to differences in monitors and slight variations in computers.

```
          Outdoor Designs
      New Product Information Sheet
```

About the Product
Product name: **Mountain Day Pack**
Product number: **3350**
Price: **$29.95**
Colors: **Green, Red, Brown**
Available: **October 1996**

Shipping Info
Kit box: Pattern Box D (14" x 6" x 2")
Weight: 2.25 pounds
Freight cost: $3.00
Store terms: Net 30

Description
   A kit with instructions and all the materials needed to create a durable, lightweight backpack for light hiking, skiing, or mountain biking. EasyPull zippers run the length of the bag for quick access to gear, and comfortable shoulder straps insure miles of trail comfort. Standard pattern can be tailored to men, women, and children. Kit includes backpack pattern, assembly instructions, nylon fabric, EasyPull zipper, shoulder straps, and thread. Sewing machine required for assembly.

Competitive Products
- Back in the Saddle (mountain bike backpack), Team Encarta, Inc., $34.95
- Wild Women Wear (pattern and kit), Cold Spell Designs, $19.95

Kit Promotions
- Advertising: **Profitable Craft Merchandising** (October), **Outside Magazine** (January)
- Publicity: Mailers to press list and consumer database
- Prepacks: Six for the price of five (wholesale) in November and December

FIGURE 3-14

UNIT 4

OBJECTIVES

▶ Create multiple columns

▶ Place borders around text

▶ Insert WordArt

▶ Insert ClipArt

▶ Insert footnotes

▶ Replace text

▶ Verify page layout and printing

Getting Started
WITH DESKTOP PUBLISHING

This unit introduces you to **desktop publishing**, an advanced type of word processing that combines text, artwork, and other elements to create typeset-quality documents, such as product flyers and newsletters. Many dedicated desktop publishing programs are available on the market, but most word-processing programs, including the Works Word Processor, contain basic desktop publishing features. **case** You have been assigned the project of desktop publishing a one-page promotional flyer for Outdoor Designs' six kite kits. To make the flyer attractive and easy to read, you'll format the text of the flyer into columns. Then you'll place a decorative border around important information, insert graphic elements (called WordArt and ClipArt), and automatically replace some text in the flyer. Finally you'll verify the flyer's layout and print a final copy for distribution.▶

Creating multiple columns

Multiple **columns**, or vertical blocks of text in a document help readers scan a group of words rather than read individual letters, making it easier to absorb data quickly. For more information about dividing a document into columns, see the related topic, "Creating a multicolumn table." **case** To help you with your flyer project, Frasier gives you a file containing the flyer's text and suggestions for where to add borders and art to enhance the flyer's appeal. He also suggests that you begin by formatting the flyer into two columns to enhance its readability and provide some visual direction.

Steps

1. Start **Works**, click the **Existing Documents tab** in the Works Task Launcher dialog box, then click **Open a document not listed here**
   The Open dialog box opens.

2. Open the document **WKS 4-1** on your Student Disk, then save it as **Kite Flyer** in the **My Works Files folder**
   The promotional flyer opens in the Word Processor window. To separate his notes to you from the flyer text, Frasier enclosed them in double angle brackets, such as "<<Insert WordArt Title>>." These brackets help you find the suggestions quickly so you can respond to and then delete all his notes.

3. Click **Format** on the menu bar, then click **Columns**
   The Format Columns dialog box shown in Figure 4-1 opens. Note that the Columns command formats your entire document so you don't need to select the text before formatting it.

4. Type **2** then press **[Tab]**
   The Number of columns text box changes to 2, and a two-column document with a line between the columns appears in the Sample window. The highlight moves to the Space between text box. For this flyer, the default size is appropriate.

5. Press **[Tab]**
   The measurement between columns doesn't change, and the highlight moves to the Line between columns check box. You decide that a line between columns makes the document look too busy.

6. Click the **Line between columns check box**
   The check box is now empty, and the line between columns disappears from the Sample window.

7. Click **OK**
   The Format Columns dialog box closes, and another dialog box opens, recommending that you work with the document in Page Layout view so you can see how the columns will look in print. (In Normal view you don't see the columns side by side.)

8. Click **Yes**
   The dialog box closes and the document switches to the two-column format shown in Figure 4-2.

9. Click the **Save button** 💾 on the toolbar, then read the kite flyer
   Use the scroll bars to scroll through the entire document and read Frasier's notes.

FIGURE 4-1: Format Columns dialog box

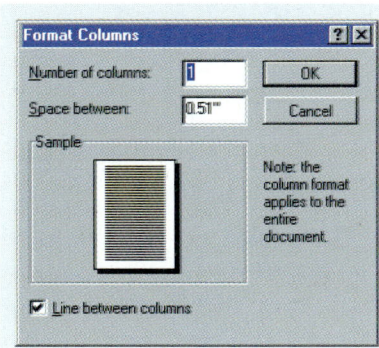

FIGURE 4-2: Kite flyer in two-column format in Page Layout view

New right margin of first column

Your screen view may vary slightly

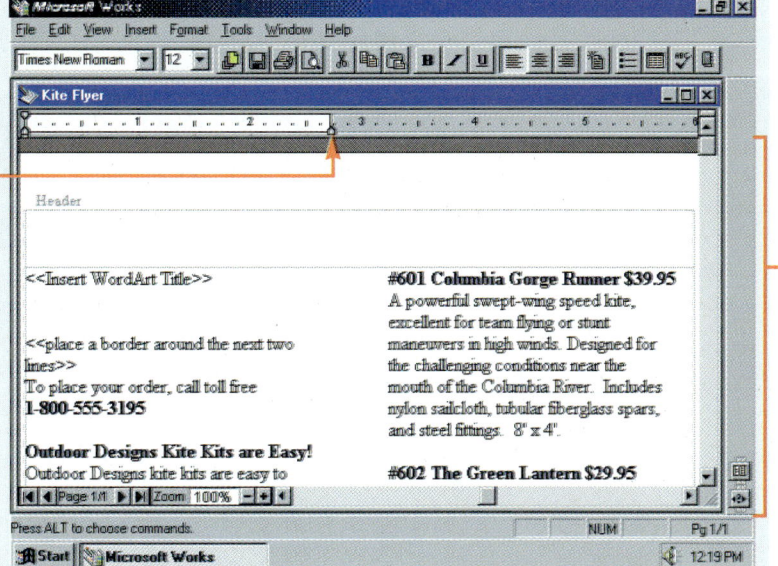

Creating a multicolumn table

Sometimes you might want only part of your document in a two- or more column format. For example, you might want to list the names, prices, and colors of products within a report. Instead of dividing your entire document into two or three columns, you can use the Table command on the Insert menu to divide a section of your document into rows and columns. The Insert Table dialog box lets you pick a predefined table format for the information you want to display and specify the number of rows and columns in the table. After you insert the table, you can add entries to it by highlighting individual table cells or by pressing the Tab key to move from one cell to the next. In many respects, a table functions like a spreadsheet, which you'll learn about later in this book.

Placing borders around text

The Word Processor lets you add decorative borders that emphasize words and paragraphs in your document. You can add one or more lines at the top, bottom, left, or right edges of selected text, or outline selected text with a frame. **case** You'll place a box around the two lines Frasier indicated at the top of the kite flyer, making it easy for customers to find the toll-free number when they want to place an order.

1. **Scroll to the top of the document if it is not already visible**
   Before you format text with a border, you should select all text you want included within the border. Table 4-1 shows some useful keyboard shortcuts for selecting text blocks.

2. **Select To place your order, call toll free 1-800-555-3195**
   The two lines are highlighted.

3. **Click Format on the menu bar, click Borders and Shading; then, if it is not already in front, click the Borders tab**
   The Borders and Shading dialog box opens with the Borders tab in front, as Figure 4-3 shows. In it, you can select styles of the border and line you want to place around the selected text. You can click one or more Border check boxes, but only one Line Style option button. Note that clicking the Outline check box is equivalent to clicking the Top, Bottom, Left, and Right check boxes.

4. **Click the Outline check box**
   A check mark appears in the Outline check box, and the highlight moves to the line style below None.

5. **Click the third line style button from the bottom left to select a medium-weight line style**

6. **Click OK**
   The Borders and Shading dialog box closes and a medium-weight line box surrounds selected text. The information stands out from the rest of the flyer, but you think the text will look better centered within the box.

7. **Click the Center Align button on the toolbar**
   The selected text aligns in the center of the column, which is also the center of the box. Now you need to delete Frasier's bracketed note above the box.

8. **Select <<place a border around the next two lines>>, then press [Delete]**
   Because you deleted Frasier's note, the rest of the text wraps back to fill the space. Figure 4-4 shows the completed text border.

9. **Click the Save button on the toolbar**

FIGURE 4-3: Borders tab in Borders and Shading dialog box

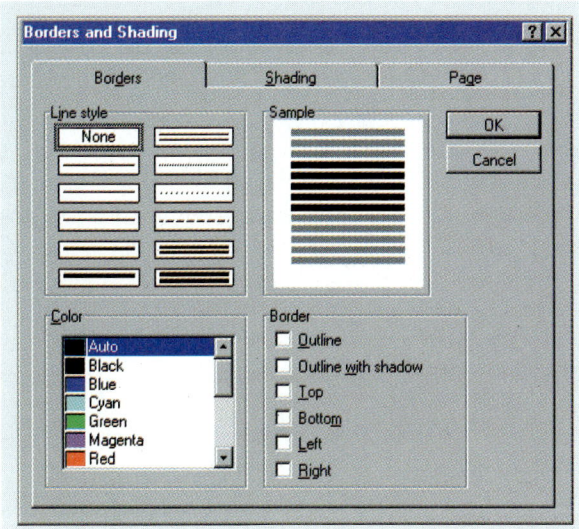

FIGURE 4-4: Text centered in medium-weight outline border

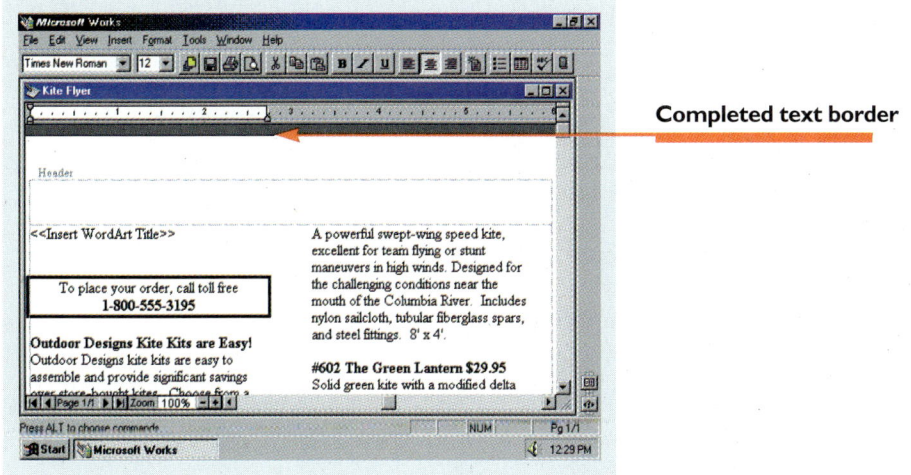

Completed text border

TABLE 4-1: Keyboard shortcuts for selecting text blocks

TO SELECT	PRESS
A word	[F8] twice
A sentence	[F8] three times
A paragraph	[F8] four times
The entire document	[F8] five times
Previous selection level	[Shift][F8]

TROUBLE?

If you've used [F8] to select the text and cannot deselect the text when you're done, just press [Esc] then click the pointer anywhere in the document to deselect the text.

QUICK TIP

The Borders tab includes a Color list box you can use to change the border color. This option is useful if you have a color printer or simply want to emphasize part of your document on the screen.

Inserting WordArt

You can insert several types of electronic art into your document from the Word Processor. One is **WordArt**, a type of stylized text created by the WordArt Accessory, which provides sophisticated text formatting features not available in the Word Processor. You'll learn to use some of these features in this lesson; to learn about all features WordArt Accessory offers, consult WordArt online help.

case As Frasier suggested, you'll use the WordArt Accessory to add a title to the Outdoor Designs kite flyer.

1. Select **<<Insert WordArt Title>>** then press **[Delete]**
   Frasier's suggestion disappears from the document, and the insertion point blinks on the blank line at the top of the flyer.

2. Click **Insert** on the menu bar, then click **WordArt**
   The WordArt Accessory starts and the Enter Your Text Here dialog box shown in Figure 4-5 opens. Notice that the WordArt menu bar and toolbar replace the Word Processor menu bar and toolbar. The WordArt Accessory elements are labeled in Figure 4-5. The Enter Your Text Here dialog box appears in the document near the insertion point, where the WordArt will be inserted. You'll type the text you want to use as a title for the flyer in this dialog box. The placeholder text in both the dialog box and your document is currently "Your Text Here."

3. Type **Outdoor Designs Kite Kits,** then click **Update Display**
   New text replaces placeholder text in the Enter Your Text Here dialog box and at the top of your document. You decide that the title needs to be more prominent to capture attention.

4. Click the **Bold button** on the WordArt toolbar
   The WordArt text style changes to boldface. Notice that because the insertion point is in the Enter Your Text Here dialog box, you don't need to select the text before you bold it.

5. Click the **Shadow button** on the WordArt toolbar, click the **third shadow style** from the left, then click **OK**
   A 3-D shadow appears behind the WordArt text. The title definitely looks more striking now, but it would stand out even more if it were a little larger than the rest of the text.

6. Click the **Font Size list arrow** on the WordArt toolbar, then click **16**
   The font size changes to 16 points and a dialog box asks if you'd like to resize the WordArt text frame to fit the enlarged text.

7. Click **Yes**
   The WordArt changes to 16 points, and the WordArt text frame enlarges at the top of the document to accommodate the larger font size. You are satisfied with the title's look and size.

8. Click in the flyer's text, anywhere outside the Enter Your Text Here dialog box and the WordArt text frame
   The Enter Your Text Here dialog box closes, and the Word Processor menu and toolbar return to the screen, as Figure 4-6 shows. Note that the WordArt text frame is still selected. If you wanted to continue working elsewhere in this document right now, you would need to click again anywhere in the document to deselect the text frame. If you wanted to edit or reformat the WordArt later, you would double-click in the WordArt text frame.

9. Click the **Save button** on the toolbar to save your changes

FIGURE 4-5: WordArt Accessory

- WordArt toolbar
- WordArt text frame
- WordArt placeholder text
- Click to change font size
- Click to add a shadow
- Bold button

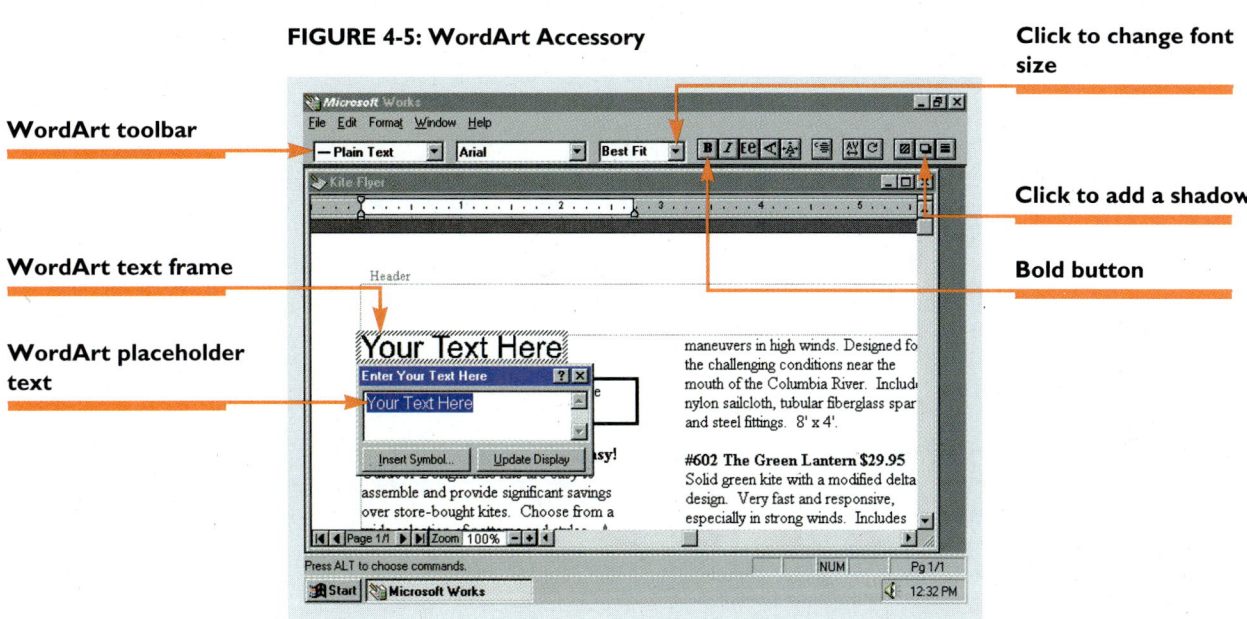

FIGURE 4-6: Completed WordArt in kite flyer

- WordArt is 16 point, bold font with a shadow

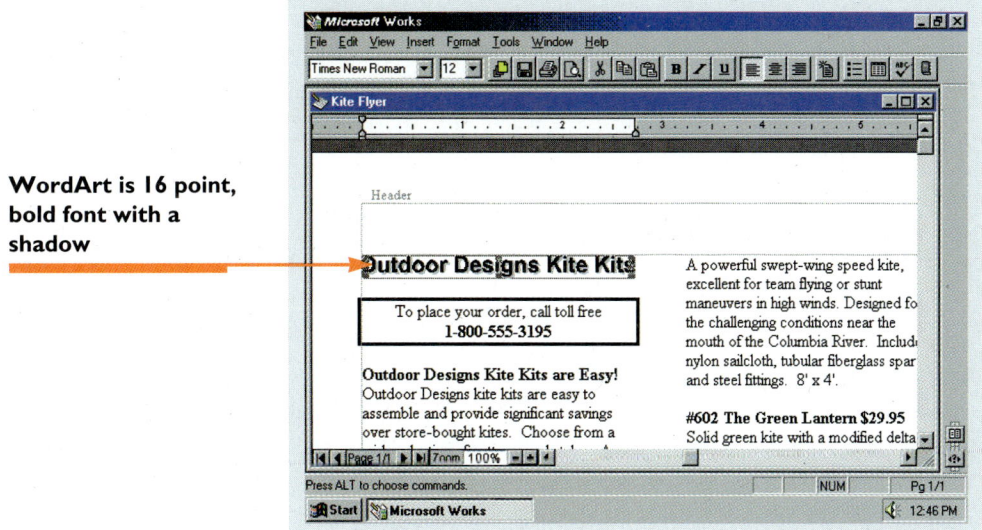

QUICK TIP

You can resize WordArt in a document by clicking the WordArt frame, then dragging the frame's right or left edge with the sizing pointer. To remove WordArt from a document, highlight the WordArt and press [Delete].

Inserting ClipArt

ClipArt, ready-to-use graphic images stored in the ClipArt Gallery, is another type of electronic art available in the Word Processor. The ClipArt Gallery includes many groups of ClipArt in different shapes, sizes, and colors. You can purchase additional ClipArt images and add them to the ClipArt Gallery. **case** Frasier suggested that you add ClipArt to the kites flyer to brighten the flyer and enhance its visual appeal.

1. If Frasier's note is not visible on the screen, scroll about one-third of the way down the first column until you see **<<Insert ClipArt>>**, select the text, then press **[Delete]**
   After you delete Frasier's note, the insertion point blinks on a blank line, with one blank line above it and one below it. (If your document does not look like this, change it so it does.) You need to find an appropriate ClipArt to illustrate the beginners' kite kits.

2. Click **Insert** on the menu bar, then click **ClipArt**; if the Add New Pictures dialog box opens, click **OK**
   The ClipArt Gallery shown in Figure 4-7 opens. It provides access to all ClipArt images stored on your hard disk. Works comes with more than 100 ClipArt images, and you may have access to additional images from other Microsoft programs or additional ClipArt packages installed on your computer. By default, the ClipArt Gallery displays the images in all subject categories, but you can focus the selection by choosing a specific category in the Category list box. Look in the Plants category for an appropriate illustration.

3. Click **Plants** in the Category list box
   All available ClipArt images in the Plants category appear in the Pictures list box. The big tree looks like a good choice because it might remind readers of parks, a place they would fly kites.

4. Double-click **big tree ClipArt**
   The ClipArt Gallery closes and the big tree ClipArt shown in Figure 4-8 appears in the document. The full-color image is left aligned in the first column (where the insertion point was), with text above and below it. (The image will print in black and gray shades, unless you have a color printer.) You can center or right align ClipArt in the column. You decide that the image will look better centered in the column.

5. Click the **Center button** on the toolbar
   The ClipArt image is centered within the first column. You think the first image looks good, and you're ready to add another ClipArt image to the kites flyer.

6. Scroll through the columns and select **<<Insert ClipArt>>**, then press **[Delete]**

7. Click **Insert** on the menu bar, then click **ClipArt**
   The ClipArt Gallery opens again. For this specialty product, a balloon image would look great.

8. Click the **Pictures down arrow** until you see the **balloon ClipArt**, then double-click it
   The ClipArt Gallery closes and the balloon ClipArt appears in the flyer at the top of the second column. You think this image would also look better centered.

9. Click , then click the **Save button** on the toolbar

FIGURE 4-7: ClipArt Gallery

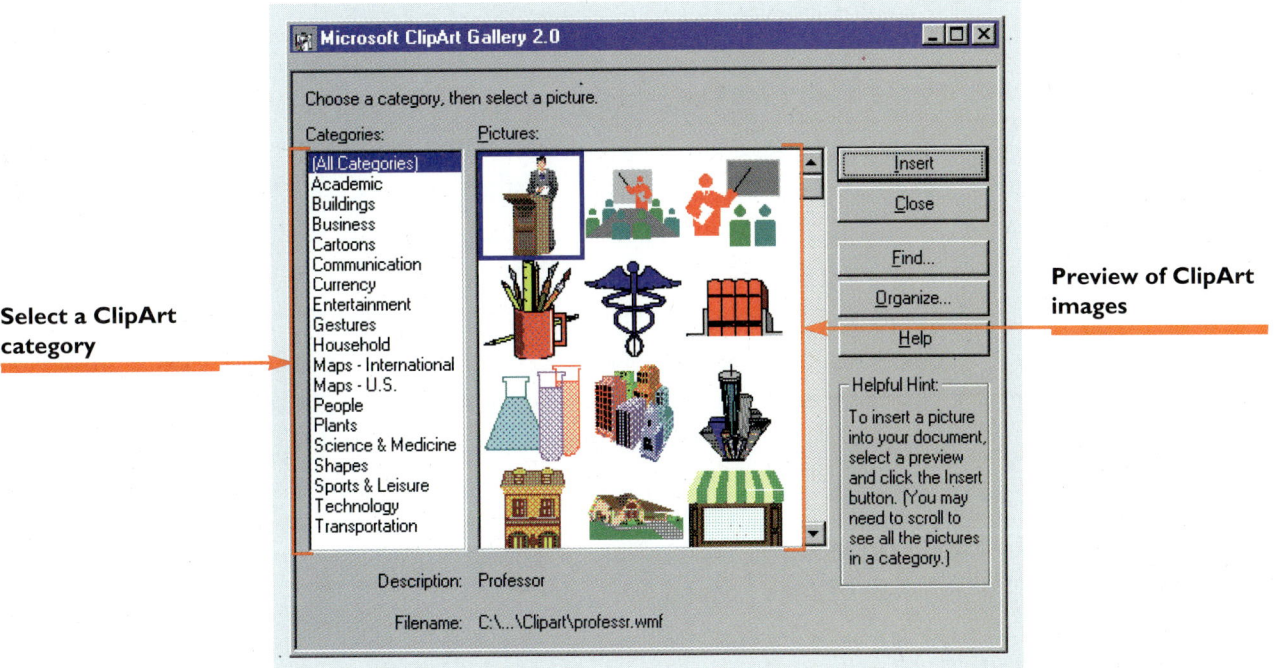

Select a ClipArt category

Preview of ClipArt images

FIGURE 4-8: Big tree ClipArt in Outdoor Designs kite flyer

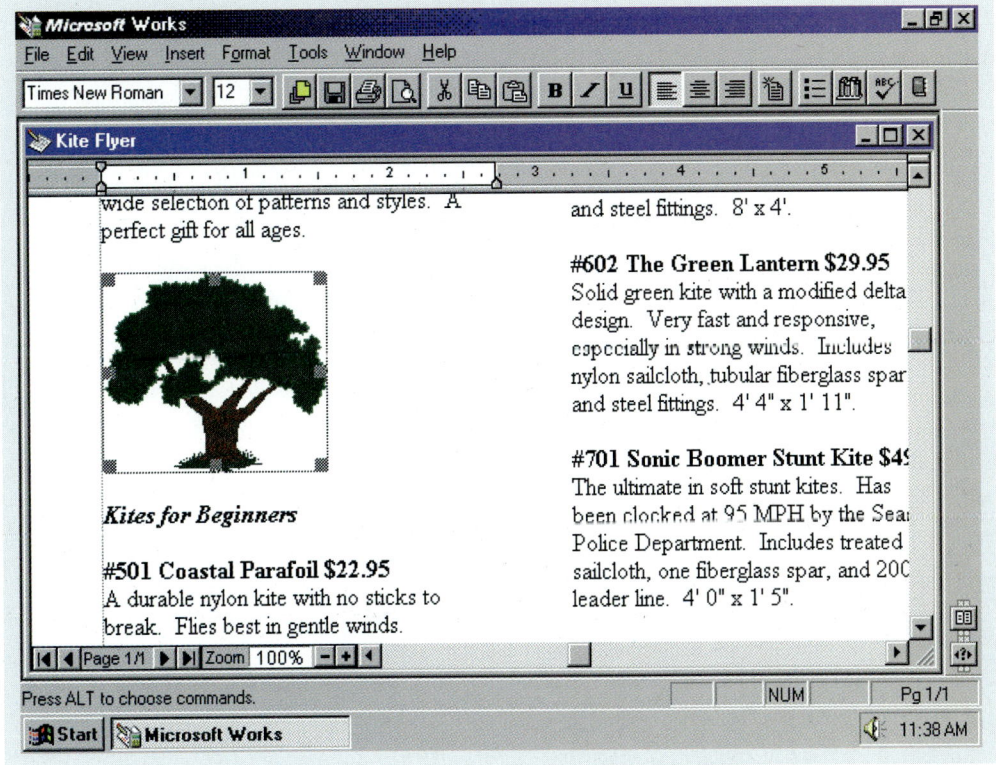

TROUBLE?

Your assortment of ClipArt might differ from that shown here, depending on the other Microsoft programs or ClipArt packages installed on your system.

QUICK TIP

You can insert your own original art in a document with the Microsoft Draw Accessory. You will learn more about Microsoft Draw later in this book.

Inserting footnotes

You can easily add footnotes with Works' Footnote command. Works automatically adds the footnotes to your document and handles all layout issues related to the footnote references in the text and the actual footnote text at the bottom of the page. Footnotes are like other text in that you can format their font and style in Page Layout view. Footnotes can also be printed as endnotes; see the related topic, "Printing Endnotes" for more information. **case** Lucinda in the Outdoor Designs legal department reviewed the text of the kite flyer. She is concerned that the statement "Has been clocked at 95 MPH by the Seaside Police Department" in the Sonic Boomer Stunt Kite description could be construed as a product endorsement by the Seaside Police Department and the City of Seaside. She asks you to add a footnote that clarifies the statement and acts as a disclaimer to the sentence.

1. Scroll until you see the Sonic Boomer Stunt Kite description, near the end of the second column

2. Click directly after the period following the word "Department" in the statement "Has been clocked at 95 MPH by the Seaside Police Department"
   The insertion point blinks after the period in the sentence.

3. Click **Insert** on the menu bar, then click **Footnote**
   The Insert Footnote dialog box opens. Because you're inserting only one footnote in the flyer, you'll use the Special mark option to insert a custom footnote reference. If you use numbered footnotes in a document such as a term paper, Works automatically numbers the footnotes for you.

4. Click the **Special mark option button,** then press **[Tab]**
   The Special mark option button is selected, and the insertion point moves to the Mark text box. You want to use an asterisk (*) as the footnote reference.

5. Type * and click **Insert**
   The Insert Footnote dialog box closes, and the insertion point moves to the bottom of the screen in the footnote area, where you'll enter your footnote text. (Note that you can see the footnote area only in Page Layout view and Print Preview.)

6. Type **Kite not endorsed by the Seaside Police Department.**
   The footnote text appears in the footnote area, with a small leading asterisk. You want to distinguish the footnote from the rest of the flyer and ensure that it doesn't distract from the main text, so you change the footnote size to 8 point and its style to italic.

7. Select the **footnote text**, then click the **Italic button** on the toolbar
   The footnote style changes to italic.

8. Click the **Size list arrow** on the toolbar, then click **8**
   The point size is reduced to 8 points. Figure 4-9 shows the completed footnote.

9. Click the **Save button** on the toolbar to save your changes on disk

FIGURE 4-9: Completed footnote in kite flyer

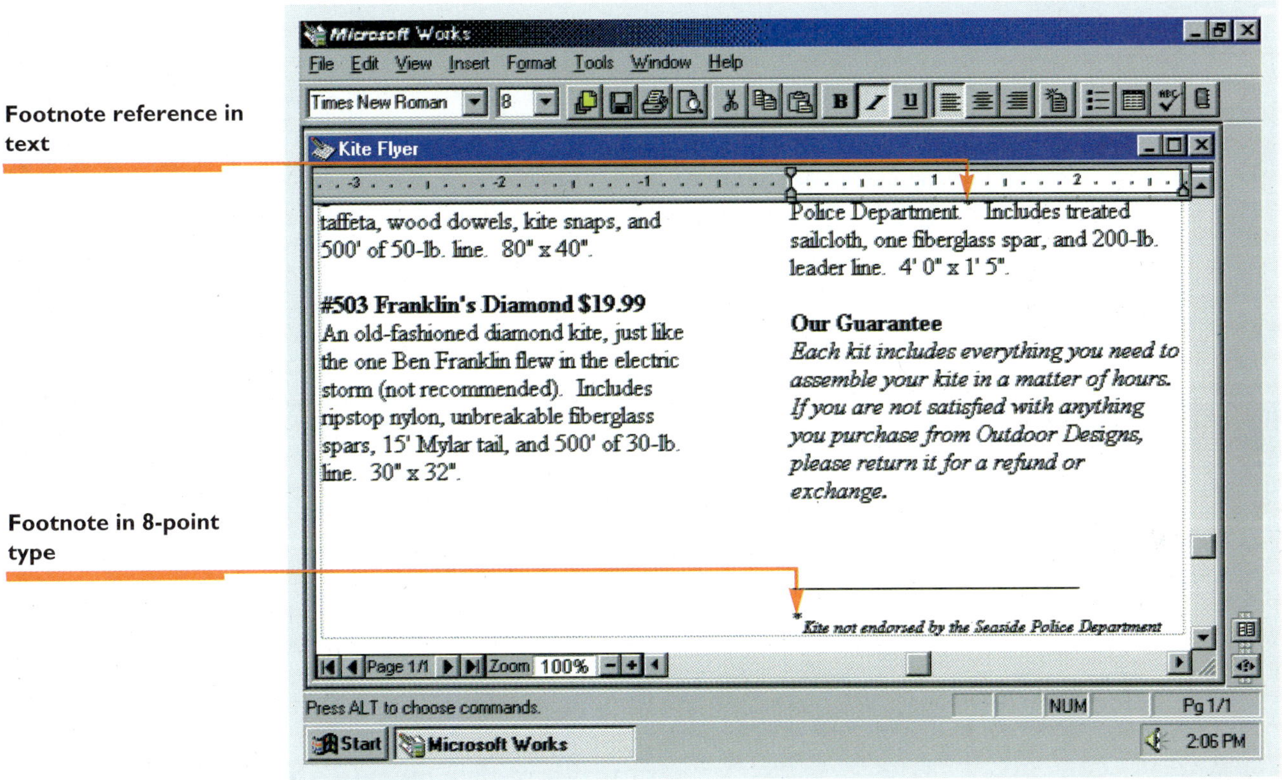

Footnote reference in text

Footnote in 8-point type

Printing Endnotes

Footnotes can also be printed as **endnotes** at the end of your document. Click Page Setup on the File menu, click the Other Options tab, then click the Print footnotes at end check box.

QUICK TIP

To delete a footnote from a document, select the footnote reference mark in the body of the text and delete it. The Word Processor deletes the corresponding footnote and renumbers the remaining footnotes automatically.

Replacing text

The **Replace command** helps you quickly and easily substitute one or more occurrence of a particular word or phrase in a document. First you tell Works what text you want to find, then you tell Works what text you want replaced. You can replace every occurrence of the text or you can choose specific occurrences. For more information about finding text, see the related topic, "Using the Find command." **case** Frasier decided to change pricing for all kite kits so their prices end with 99 cents, rather than 95 cents. He asks you to update pricing in the kite flyer. The Replace command makes it easy to find each 95 in the document and change it to 99.

1. Scroll to the top of the first column, then click before **Outdoor** in the WordArt title
   The insertion point blinks at the beginning of the kite flyer.

2. Click **Edit** on the menu bar, then click **Replace**
   The Replace dialog box opens. It contains the Find what and Replace with text boxes, plus check boxes for instructing Works to find whole words only and to match case (such as uppercase letters). You can also find and replace Tab and Enter characters by using the tab mark and paragraph mark buttons to insert these symbols in the text boxes. First, you need to tell Works what to search for.

3. Type **95** in the Find what text box, then press **[Tab]**
   The text you want to find or insert can be one or more words or just numbers.

4. Type **99** in the Replace with text box, then click **Find Next**
   Works starts searching the document from the insertion point. The first 95 it finds is in the phone number. If you had clicked the Find whole words only check box, Works would have skipped this 95 because it is part of a "word" (3195). You want to leave the phone number as is.

5. Click **Find Next** again
   Works leaves the phone number unchanged and locates the second occurrence of 95 in the description for the Coastal Parafoil kite shown in Figure 4-10.

6. Click **Replace**
   The price changes from $22.95 to $22.99, and Works highlights the next 95.

7. Click **Replace** five more times, verifying each time that you are changing only prices in the kite flyer
   After the last price change, Works highlights 95 in the phrase "95 MPH." You don't want to change this phrase, so you continue searching.

8. Click **Find Next**
   A dialog box opens, asking if you want to continue searching from the beginning of the document. This indicates that no more 95s appear between "95 MPH" and the end of the kite flyer. Because you already searched the document from the beginning, you want to end the search.

9. Click **No** in the dialog box, click **Close** in the Replace dialog box, then click the **Save button** 💾 on the toolbar
   The Replace dialog box closes, and the insertion point blinks at the beginning of the document.

FIGURE 4-10:
Changing 95 to 99 with the Replace dialog box

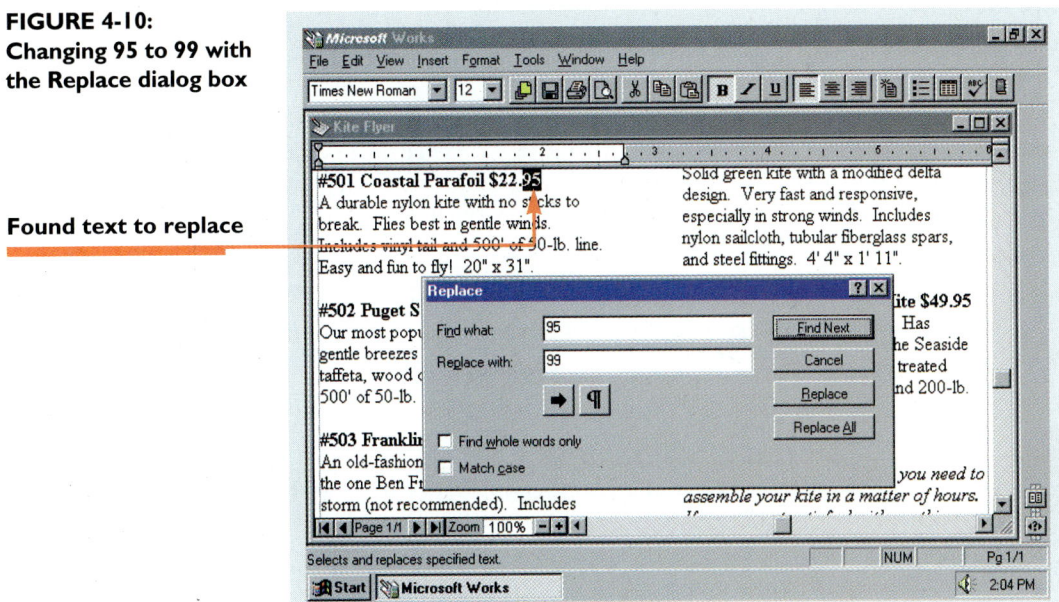

Found text to replace

FIGURE 4-11:
Searching for text with the Find dialog box

Found text

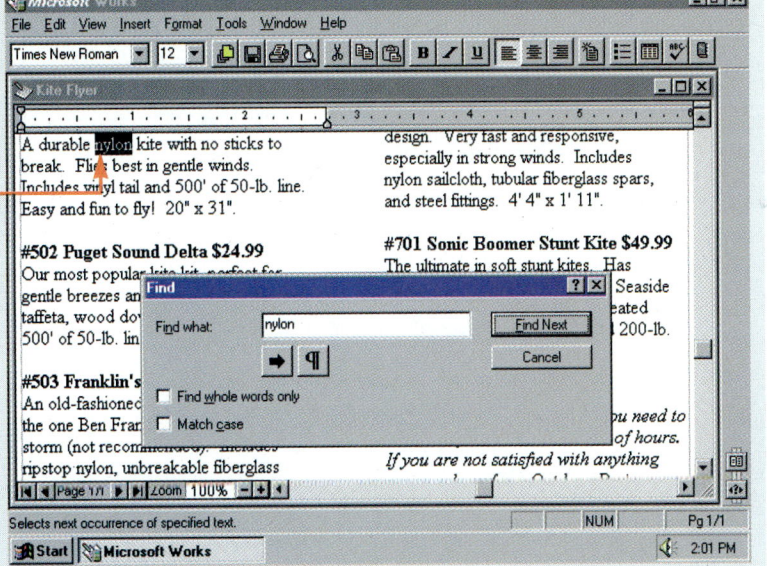

Using the Find command

The Find command on the Edit menu is similar to the Replace command, but the Find command searches for text without replacing it. The Find command is useful when you want to locate a particular word or phrase in a document, but you don't know where it is. To use the Find command, click Find on the Edit menu, type the word you're looking for in the Find what text box (for example, nylon), then click Find Next. If Works finds the word, it highlights it in the document window, as shown in Figure 4-11. To search for other occurrences of the word in the document, click Find Next again.

Be careful using the Replace All button in the Replace dialog box. When you click it, Works makes all substitutions in your document at once, without letting you preview them first.

Verifying page layout and printing

When you finish desktop publishing a document, it often helps to spend a few minutes checking page layout (line breaks, column breaks, and page breaks in the document), just to make sure that everything is exactly where you want it and that the document looks good. Sophisticated art, borders, and footnotes might take a few extra moments to print, so you want to make sure everything is correct before you print a final copy. **case** You'll verify the page layout of the finished kite flyer before you print a final copy for Frasier to review.

1. **Click the Print Preview button** ▣ **on the toolbar**
   The Outdoor Designs kite flyer appears in Print Preview, as shown in Figure 4-12.

2. **Verify that the entire flyer fits on one page**
   You want the contents of the kite flyer to fit on one page. Check the Next and Previous buttons. If they are dimmed, then the document is exactly one page long. If everything doesn't fit on the number of pages you want, now's a good time to edit, resizing graphic elements such as WordArt or ClipArt, or deleting unnecessary blank lines. If the kite flyer fits on one page, skip to Step 4. If your document is on more than one page, return to Page Layout view and delete extra lines before or after WordArt and ClipArt insertions. Check your document in Print Preview to see where extra lines might be.

3. **Click Cancel in the Print Preview window, delete any extra blank lines in the kite flyer, then click** ▣ **again**
   Your document should now be on one page. If not, repeat Step 3 until it is.

4. **Verify that the margins and columns are appropriate for the flyer**
   The kite flyer's margins and columns look good. If the text looks out of proportion on the page, you might want to change margin or column width. Changing these variables can also help fill up a short page or make room for extra text. To change document margins, use the Page Setup command; to change column margins, use the Columns command.

5. **Verify that footnotes and other items are correctly placed**
   The footnote should appear at the bottom right-corner of the flyer, with the footnote reference in the next to last paragraph of the right column.

6. **Be sure your printer is on line and ready to print**
   If necessary, ask your instructor or technical support person for help.

7. **Click Print in the Print Preview window**
   The final copy of the kite flyer prints, as shown in Figure 4-13.

8. **Click Cancel in the Print Preview window, then click the Save button** ▣ **on the toolbar**
   The flyer is finished and you stop working in Works for the day.

9. **Click File on the menu bar, then click Exit Works**
   The Kite Flyer document and the Works program close.

FIGURE 4-12: Final kite flyer in Print Preview

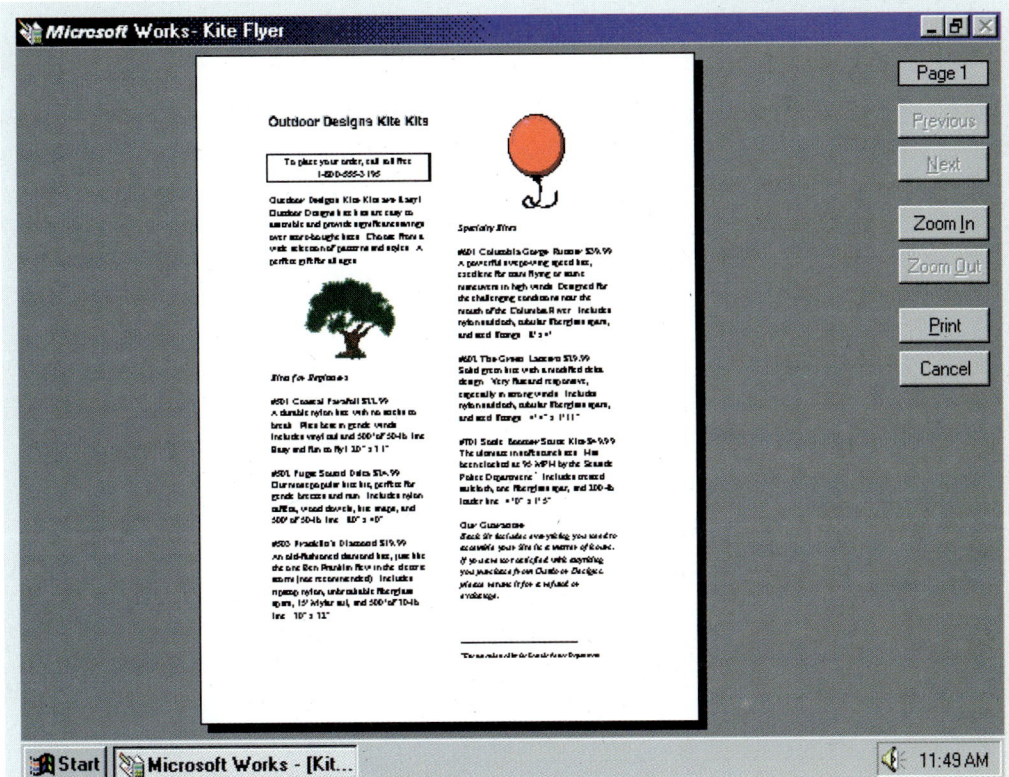

FIGURE 4-13: Printout of the Outdoor Designs kite flyer

To change the size of art in the Word Processor, select the art, then drag any gray square (called a **resize box**) bordering the art until the art is correctly sized.

TASK REFERENCE

TASK	MOUSE/BUTTON	MENU	KEYBOARD
Add a border	Right-click text, then click Borders and Shading	Click Format, Borders and Shading	[Alt][O],[B]
Adjust columns in document		Click Format, Columns	[Alt][O],[C]
Delete highlighted artwork	✂	Click Edit, Clear	[Delete]
Edit ClipArt	Double-click ClipArt		
Edit WordArt	Double-click WordArt text frame		
Find text		Click Edit, Find	[Ctrl][F]
Insert a table	▦	Click Insert, Table	[Alt][I],[T]
Insert ClipArt		Click Insert, ClipArt	[Alt][I],[A]
Insert footnote		Click Insert, Footnote	[Alt][I],[N]
Insert WordArt		Click Insert, WordArt	[Alt][I],[W]
Replace text		Click Edit, Replace	[Ctrl][H]
Select a word	Double-click the word		[F8] twice
Verify page layout	🔍	Click File, Print Preview	[Alt][F],[V]

CONCEPTSREVIEW

Label each element of the WordArt Accessory shown in Figure 4-14.

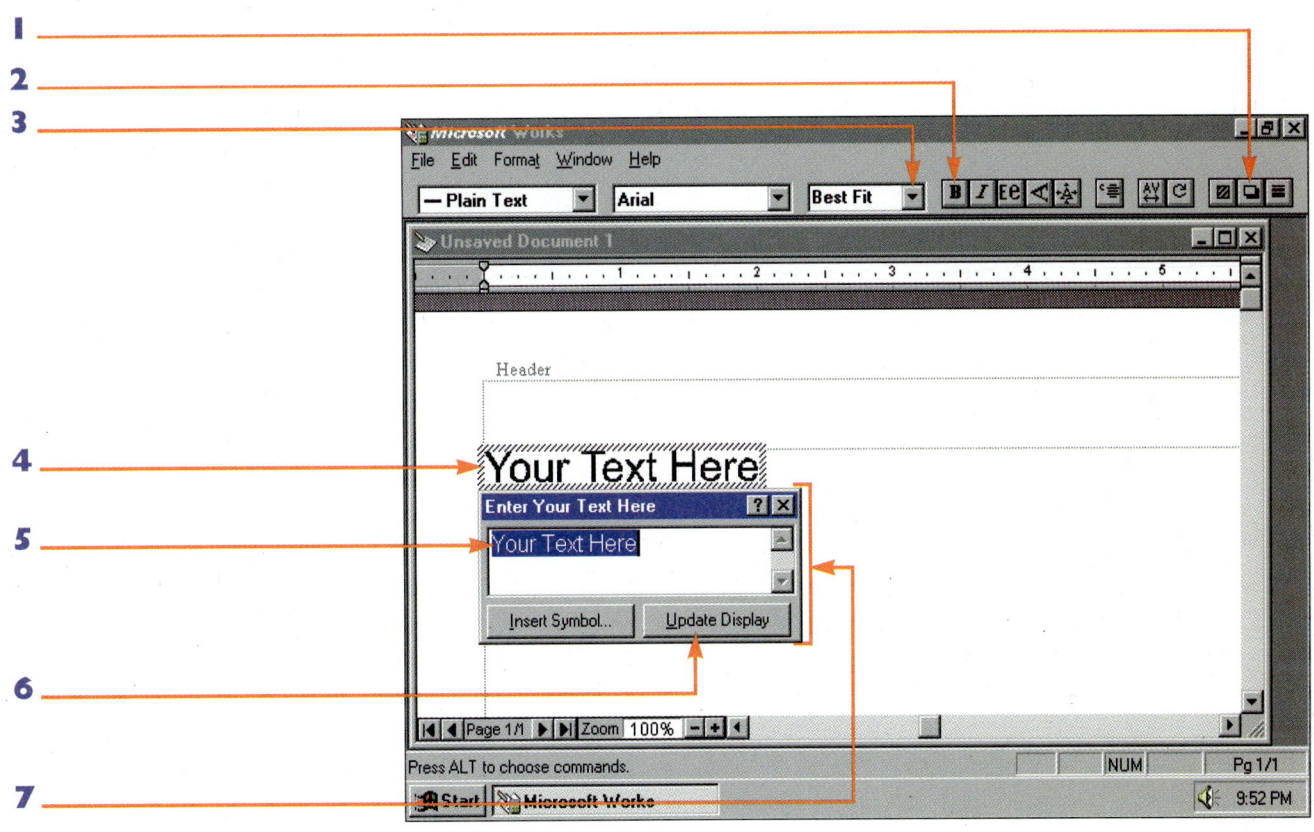

FIGURE 4-14

Match each keyboard operation with the amount of text it selects in the document window.

8 Press [F8] twice
9 Press [F8] three times
10 Press [F8] four times
11 Press [F8] five times
12 [Shift][F8]

a. A sentence
b. A paragraph
c. The previous selection level
d. The entire document
e. The word in which the insertion point is located

Select the best answer from the list of choices.

13 Which of these should *not* be considered a desktop publishing activity?

  a. Adding electronic art to a document
  b. Combining text, art, and footnotes in multiple columns
  c. Using Print Preview to verify page layout and design
  d. Opening a document created by another user

14 Which of these options *cannot* be set in the Insert Table dialog box?

  a. Number of rows
  b. Number of columns
  c. Number of dimensions
  d. Table format

15 Which of these column characteristics *cannot* be changed with the Format Columns dialog box?

   a. Number of columns in the document

   b. Distance between the outside column margins and the edge of the page

   c. Distance between the columns

   d. Presence of a dividing line between the columns

16 Which document view is best suited for working with multiple-column documents?

   a. Normal view

   b. Page Layout view

   c. Table view

   d. Print Preview

17 How would you place a box around selected text in the Word Processor?

   a. Click the Outline check box in the Borders tab.

   b. Click the Top check box in the Borders tab.

   c. Click the Bulleted check box in the Indents and Alignments tab in the Paragraph dialog box.

   d. Hold down [Shift] and click the Center Align button on the toolbar.

18 How many Line Style options (not including None) are in the Borders tab?

   a. 4

   b. 7

   c. 9

   d. 11

19 Which of these buttons would you click in WordArt to add shadow styling to text?

   a.

   b.

   c.

   d.

20 When you finish creating your WordArt, how do you return to your document?

   a. Double-click the WordArt window.

   b. Click in your document where you want to work next.

   c. Click Close on the File menu.

   d. Click Exit Works on the File menu.

21 Where does ClipArt appear in a document after you click Insert ClipArt?

   a. At the top of the document

   b. At the bottom of the document

   c. At the location of the insertion point

   d. At the location of a footnote

22 Which toolbar button would you click to center a ClipArt image in a column?

   a.

   b.

   c.

   d.

23 Which button would you click in the Footnote dialog box to specify a custom footnote reference character?

   a. The Numbered option button

   b. The Cancel button

   c. The Special mark option button

   d. The Insert option button

24 Which button would you click in the Replace dialog box to end a search-and-replace operation?

   a. Find Next

   b. Replace

   c. Replace All

   d. Cancel

25 How do the Find command and the Replace command differ?

   a. The Find command cannot be used to replace one word with another.

   b. The Find command works only with numbers.

   c. The Find command doesn't let you search for paragraph marks.

   d. The Find dialog box is bigger than the Replace dialog box.

SKILLS REVIEW

1 Start Works, open the WKS 4-2 file, save it as "Kite Newsletter," and format the document for two columns.

   a. Launch Microsoft Works.

   b. Open the file WKS 4-2 on your Student Disk.

c. Save the file as "Kite Newsletter" in the My Works Files folder.
d. Open the Format Columns dialog box.
e. Set the number of columns to 2.
f. Use the default space between columns.
g. Print a line between the columns.
h. Click OK to close the Format Columns dialog box.
i. Switch to Page Layout view if necessary.
j. Save the document.

2 Place a border around text.
   a. Use the line pointer to select all the text of the five bullets.
   b. Open the Borders and Shading dialog box.
   c. Click the Borders tab, if necessary.
   d. Click the Outline with shadow check box.
   e. Choose the double line style option at the top of the second column.
   f. Click OK to close the Borders and Shading dialog box.
   g. Select the heading "Our Guarantee" and the paragraph that follows.
   h. Open the Borders and Shading dialog box again, add a top and bottom border using the line weight below the None style.
   i. Click OK to close the dialog box.
   j. Save the borders you added to the document.

3 Insert WordArt at the top of the document.
   a. Select the middle blank line between "Outdoor Designs" and "Stock up on" at the top of the document.
   b. Start the WordArt Accessory.
   c. Type "Go Fly a Kite Sale."
   d. Click the Update Display button.
   e. Boldface the WordArt.
   f. Italicize the WordArt.
   g. Add shading to the WordArt; use the last shadow option.
   h. Exit the WordArt Accessory.
   i. Deselect the WordArt text frame.
   j. Save the document with the WordArt.

4 Insert ClipArt images in the document.
   a. Move the insertion point to the top of column two.
   b. Open the ClipArt Gallery.
   c. Select the Man Pointing ClipArt in the Cartoon category.
   d. Insert the ClipArt into your document and center it.
   e. Move the insertion point to the end of column two.
   f. Open the ClipArt Gallery.
   g. Select any ClipArt image you'd like.
   h. Insert the ClipArt in your document.
   i. Drag the horizontal resize box to make the image the full width of column one.
   j. Save your document with the ClipArt images.

5 Insert a footnote in the document.
   a. Move the insertion point to the end of the second line of text at the top of the document.
   b. Open the Insert Footnote dialog box.
   c. Use one asterisk (*) as the Special mark option, and click Insert to use the asterisk as the footnote reference.
   d. Type "Sale applies only to selected kite kits."
   e. Select the footnote text.
   f. Format the footnote for 8-point italic.
   g. Place the insertion point after the name "Ben Franklin" in the middle of the second column.
   h. Insert a footnote using two asterisks (**) as the Special mark option.
   i. Type "Kite not endorsed by the Franklin family." and format the text for 8-point italic.
   j. Save your document with the footnotes.

6 Change all prices in the document so that they end with 59 cents.
   a. Move the insertion point to the top of the document.
   b. Open the Replace dialog box.
   c. Type "95" in the Find What text box.
   d. Type "59" in the Replace with text box.
   e. Click the Find Next button.
   f. Replace only the prices with 59.
   g. Do not search again from the beginning of the document.
   h. Close the Replace dialog box to end the search.
   i. Save the new prices in your document.

7 Verify the document's page layout and print it.
   a. Switch to Print Preview.

b. Verify that the document fits on one page.

c. If the document doesn't fit on one page, exit Print Preview and then delete extra blank lines and resize the ClipArt until the document fits on one page.

d. Zoom in at the bottom of page one.

e. Examine the footnote to check your typing.

f. Print the document.

g. Exit Print Preview.

h. Save your changes.

i. Exit Works.

INDEPENDENT CHALLENGE 1

Dianne Finn in Human Relations asked you to prepare a flyer for Wacky Words annual Beach Bash on Saturday, June 14. The picnic will take place at Wildwood Park from 2 p.m. until dusk. The company will provide lobster and chicken dinners for adults, hot dogs and hamburgers for children, and build-your-own ice cream sundaes for all. Attendees can spend the day swimming, wind surfing, and playing volleyball. Other activities include a team sand castle building contest and a children's treasure hunt. The flyer should contain an RSVP section that asks for employee name, number of adults attending, and number of children attending.

To complete this independent challenge:

1 Prepare a one-page poster based on the information supplied. Use the toolbar or menus in the WordArt Accessory to rotate text, create shaped text or sideways text, adjust spacing between characters, and add shading, shadows, or borders.

2 Use Print Preview as you work to produce an effective layout.

3 Print a copy of your flyer, and save the file as "Beach Bash 96" to the My Works Files folder on your Student Disk.

INDEPENDENT CHALLENGE 2

Joel's friends have mentioned that the other three steak restaurants in town charge much more for the same steak, potato, and garden salad than The Steak Pit does. Because Joel is going to have new menus printed for The Steak Pit, he wants to compare his prices to other local restaurants. He asks you to create a simple quick reference sheet that he can use to compare the information he has gathered. He asks you to put all the information in tabular format, with separate columns for the restaurant name, steak size, price, and location.

To complete this independent challenge:

1 Open a new document in the Word Processor, and enter the title "The Steak Pit — A Quick Reference Sheet" at the top. Add three blank lines below the title.

2 Use the Table command on the Insert menu to insert a table at the location of the insertion point. Specify four columns, four rows, and the Classic Ledger table format. Click OK to create the table.

3 Enter the following information into the table one row at a time, starting with the column headings and moving down. Press [Tab] between entries to move the insertion point and watch as your entries are automatically formatted to match the table style. (If you make a mistake, click the entry you mistyped and edit it.)

For headings in row one, use: "Restaurant," "Location," "Steak Size," and "Price"

For row two use: "Broderick's," "in town square," "12 ounces, $17.99"

For row three use: "The Grill," "in mall," "8 ounces, $18.75"

For row four use: "Hunter's," "outskirts of town," "10 ounces, $16.95"

4 When you finish entering data, click outside the table to complete it and review its contents. Like a WordArt or ClipArt object, you can delete a table by highlighting it and pressing [Delete].

5 Save the document on your Student Disk as "Restaurant Comparisons" to the My Works Files folder on your Student Disk and print a copy.

INDEPENDENT CHALLENGE 3

Orders have been slow for Nibblets, the gourmet rabbit food that Stuff for Pets sells. Lee Janson in the marketing department has decided to send out a promotional flyer to help spur orders. Lee wants to send the flyer to all retail pet shops that order from Stuff for Pets, so they can post them in their shops and convince more rabbit owners to switch to Nibblets. She started putting together the flyer as a two-column document, with WordArt and ClipArt. Now she decides the flyer would look better in a single column format. She asks you to format the document so that it is in one column, not two. She also wants you to add an appropriate ClipArt image and center it at the top of the page.

To complete this independent challenge:

1 Open WKS 4-3 and save it as "Nibblets" to the My Works Files folder on your Student Disk.

2 Format the document for one column using the Columns command.

3 Move the ClipArt image to the end of the document using the drag-and-drop mouse technique. Delete the ClipArt image currently in the document and insert a more appropriate image. Resize the image to fill the rest of the page.

4 Change the font used in the WordArt to a font of your choice. Change the shadow selection to one of your choice.

5 Insert the footnote "Based on an informal survey of rabbits" at the end of the paragraph that begins "Your rabbit will nibble away" after the bordered text. Use the number 1 as the reference mark.

6 Remove any unnecessary blank spaces and examine the document in Print Preview to catch any layout problems.

7 Save your changes, then print the document.

INDEPENDENT CHALLENGE 4

Kristine has just hired Josh Turney as the assistant for The Literary Loft. She asks you to prepare a flyer to announce his hiring and to welcome him to the job. Kristine wants the entire staff to gather at noon for a company lunch on his first day, February 3. The company will provide pizza, salad, and assorted beverages. She also plans to announce the employee-of-the-month award, which comes with a gag gift. The flyer should contain an RSVP section that asks for employee name, department, and funny gift suggestions.

To complete this independent challenge:

1 Open a new document and save it as "New Hire" to the My Works Files folder on your Student Disk.

2 Type all the text described above.

3 Use WordArt, ClipArt, tables, and footnotes to communicate the necessary information.

4 Use Print Preview as you work to produce an effective and attractive layout.

5 Save your changes and print a copy of your flyer.

VISUAL WORKSHOP

Create the document shown in Figure 4-15 with the Works Word Processor and save it as Coffee to the My Works Files folder on your Student disk. *Hint: The artwork is located in the Sports and Leisure category in the ClipArt gallery.*

FIGURE 4-15

The Coffee Clubhouse

Daily Coffee Specials

Cafe Mocha with a Twist

A single shot of our rich dark espresso mixed with just the right amount of imported Belgian chocolate powder and a touch of mint flavoring.

Tall Dark Cooler

A tall glass filled with iced Hawaiian Kona coffee, brewed to dark and rich tasting perfection.

Pick your favorite type of milk: nonfat, skim, 2 percent, whole, half-and-half, or cream

---

Become a Member of *The Coffee Clubhouse* for the price of a cup of coffee.[1]

Just fill out a "I'm a regular" card. Ask the person behind the coffee pot to stamp your card for each cup of coffee you buy here. When the card is full (ten stamps) you're a member. That's it. No membership dues or other fees.

Once you're a Coffee Clubhouse member, you'll receive a 15% discount on every purchase of 1 or more pounds of coffee beans.

Save big bucks while making your own home a Coffee Clubhouse.

Clubhouse Coffees[2]
Sumatra
French Roast
Mocha Java
Special Blend
Espresso
Kona
and more

---

[1] Actually ten cups of coffee.
[2] All coffees available decaf.

UNIT 5

OBJECTIVES

- Start the Works Spreadsheet Tool
- Enter numbers and labels
- Save your work
- Change column width and row height
- Use formulas
- Edit the spreadsheet
- Change alignment and number format
- Change the font and the font style and add borders
- Print the spreadsheet

Building
A SPREADSHEET

This unit introduces you to the Works **Spreadsheet** tool, an electronic ledger you can use to organize rows and columns of information and create colorful business charts. The Spreadsheet is useful for financial planning, calculating, data analysis, and creating business forms. ▶**case** Outdoor Designs uses the Spreadsheet tool to track orders and sales. To help sales reps track their product orders, Frasier asked you to build a spreadsheet to record orders as they come in from sales reps. You'll also enter the order information, modify the spreadsheet so it is easy to use, and print out the final product for Frasier's review. ▶

Starting the Works Spreadsheet Tool

You start the Spreadsheet from the Works Task Launcher. The Spreadsheet's graphic interface is similar to the Word Processor's. If you worked through Units 2 through 4, you'll recognize many toolbar buttons and menu commands. Unlike the Word Processor, however, the Spreadsheet document window is divided into rows and columns that intersect to form **cells** that can contain numbers, text, and formulas. Figure 5-2 identifies important elements of the Spreadsheet interface, and Table 5-1 lists the buttons unique to the Spreadsheet toolbar.

▶case Launch Works and start the Spreadsheet tool now.

1. **Launch Works**
   The Works Task Launcher dialog box opens. It contains tabs that run TaskWizards, open existing documents, and start the four Works tools.

2. **Click the Works Tools tab**
   The Works Tools tab shown in Figure 5-1 appears. It contains buttons that launch the Word Processor, Spreadsheet, Database, and Communications program. This tab is most useful if you want to open a new, blank document in a Works program and create it from scratch.

3. **Click Spreadsheet**
   The Works Task Launcher disappears, and the Spreadsheet program opens in the window shown in Figure 5-2. The Spreadsheet contains interface elements found in every Works program: menu bar, toolbar, document window, scroll bars, toggle indicators, sizing buttons, control menu boxes, and (in the lower-right corner) Help buttons. The mouse pointer becomes a cross in the Spreadsheet. Unique to the Spreadsheet interface are a gridlike document window made up of cells; a **cell reference box**, which shows the currently highlighted cell; and a **formula bar** where you enter equations for spreadsheet calculations.

   Refer to Table 5-1 to identify toolbar buttons unique to the Spreadsheet program. Use Figure 5-2 to identify the Spreadsheet's interface elements.

TABLE 5-1: Toolbar buttons unique to the Spreadsheet tool

BUTTON	FUNCTION
Σ	Sums numbers in highlighted cells
$	Formats highlighted cells in currency format
🖩	Helps you create a spreadsheet formula (Easy Calc)
📊	Creates a chart using highlighted cells

FIGURE 5-1: Works Tools tab in Task Launcher dialog box

Spreadsheet button

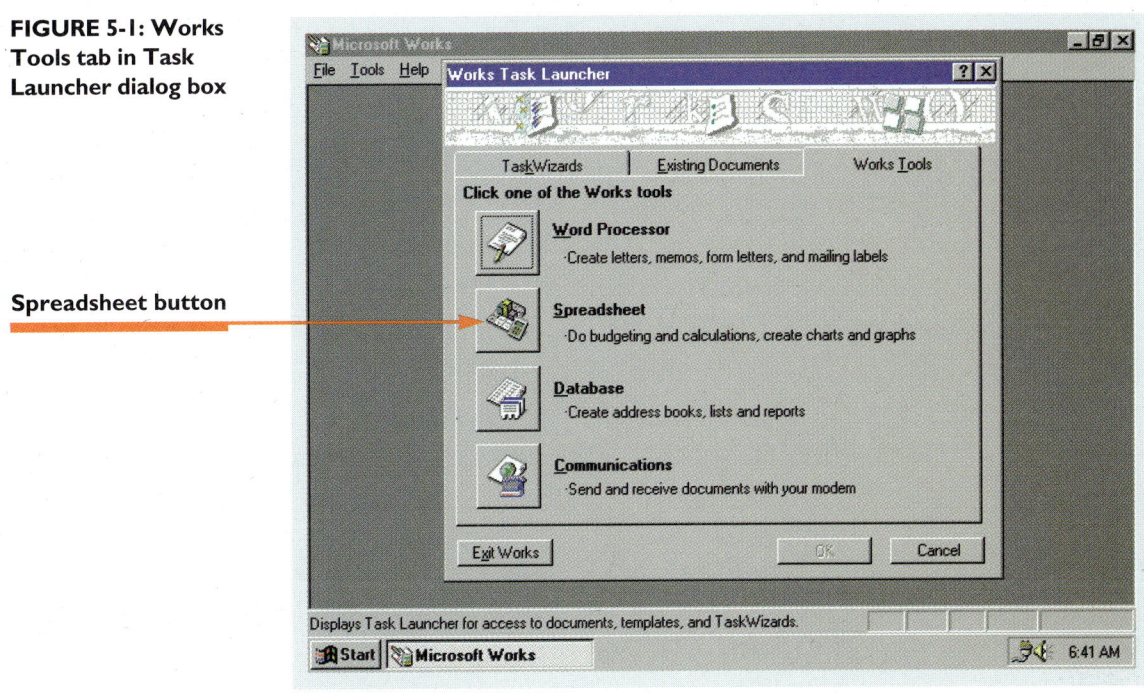

FIGURE 5-2: Works Spreadsheet with unique elements labeled

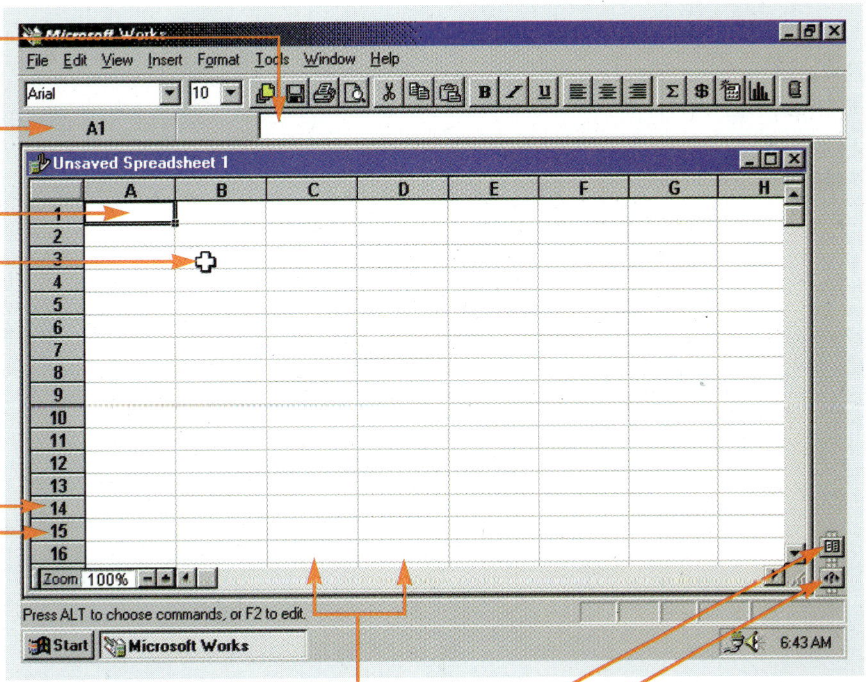

Formula bar

Cell reference box

Cell A1

Mouse pointer

Rows

Columns

Index button

Help button

WK 97

WORKS 4 UNIT 5 **BUILDING** A SPREADSHEET

QUICK TIP

Press F1 when the Spreadsheet is running for on-line Help on using the Spreadsheet program.

Entering numbers and labels

You enter numbers and labels in the Spreadsheet by typing in cells. As you learned in the previous lesson, a cell is the rectangular area formed where a row and a column intersect. When you open a new spreadsheet, Works highlights the cell in the upper-left corner of the document window. Referred to as "A1," this cell is where column A and row 1 intersect. You can move the highlight to other cells by clicking them with the mouse or by moving to them with the arrow keys. **case** Practice entering numbers and labels into the spreadsheet by typing in a product order from one of Outdoor Designs' sales reps. The completed product order serves as an internal tracking sheet that the Outdoor Designs fulfillment and billing staff will use to process the order.

1. **In cell A1, type Outdoor Designs Product Order**
   As you type, the text appears in cell A1 and in the formula bar.

2. **Press [Enter]**
   Works enters the text in the formula bar in the spreadsheet, as shown in Figure 5-3. Because the text you typed began with a letter (rather than a number), Works considers it a **label**, a piece of text used for description, not calculation. Works lets labels extend into neighboring cells that don't contain data, so the text "Outdoor Designs Product Order" extends into cells A1, B1, and C1. Works identifies the text as a label in the formula bar by adding a double quotation mark (") at the beginning of the formula bar.

3. **Press [↓] twice to move to cell A3**
   Cell A3 is highlighted and "A3" appears in the cell reference box, identifying your current location. You can use the arrow keys to highlight different cells in the spreadsheet and enter information in them, as you'll see in Step 4.

4. **Type these four lines, pressing [↓] after each line**
   Sales rep: Kimberly Ullom [↓]
   Store: Mountain Air, North Bend, WA [↓]
   Order date: June 30, 1996 [↓]
   Terms: Payment 30 days after receipt (Net 30) [↓]

5. **Press [↓] to move to cell A8, then type the following text in columns A through D of rows 8 through 13, pressing [→] and clicking the cells indicated in the far right column (see Figure 5-4)**

Kit num	Kit name	Price	Quantity	
#401	Cascade Ski Sack	19.95	5	[click cell A9]
#501	Coastal Parafoil Kite	22.95	1	[click cell A10]
#502	Puget Sound Delta Kite	24.95	2	[click cell A11]
#801	Olympic Rain Tent	79.95	2	[click cell A12]
#802	Tent Vestibule	19.95	1	[click cell A13]
				Press [Enter]

   Works enters the labels and numbers in the spreadsheet, as shown in Figure 5-4. The text in row 8 and in columns A and B are labels but do not extend into neighboring cells because those cells contain data. Works considers the numbers in columns C and D **numeric values**. You'll use these numbers in calculations later in the unit.

FIGURE 5-3: Spreadsheet text in formula bar and in neighboring cells

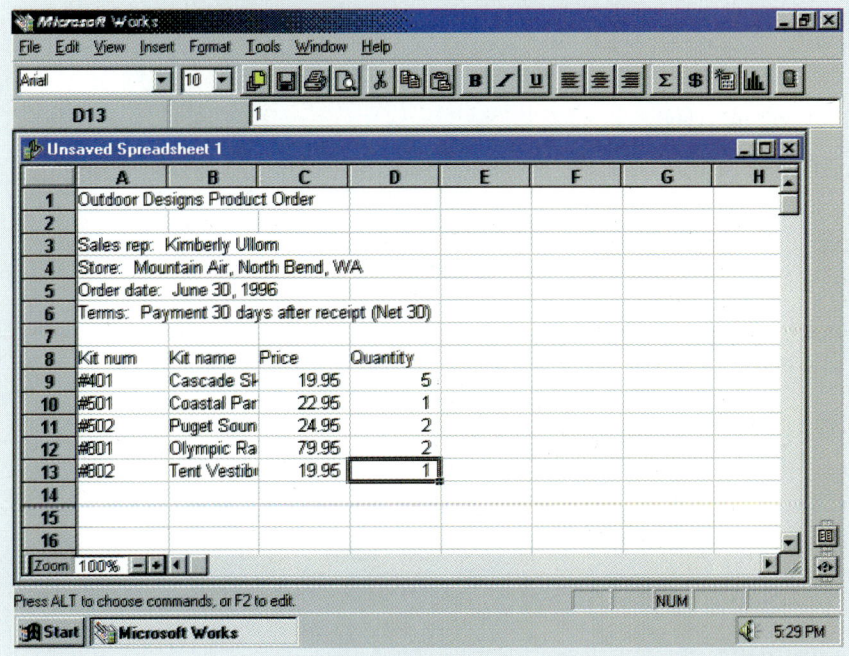

FIGURE 5-4: Spreadsheet after you enter product order data

QUICK TIP

Pressing [Tab] is the same as pressing [→] in the Spreadsheet. You might find it more convenient for entering multiple columns of data. ■

Saving your work

The process of saving a document in the Spreadsheet is identical to saving a document in the Word Processor. To save a new document and give it a unique filename on disk, use the Save As command on the File menu. To save changes to a document that has already been named and saved, use the Save command on the File menu or click the Save button on the toolbar. For information on checking spelling before saving a file, see the related topic, "Using the Spelling Checker." **case** Save the product order spreadsheet on your Student Disk now.

1. Place your Student Disk in the appropriate drive

2. Click **File** on the menu bar, then click **Save As**
   The Save As dialog box shown in Figure 5-5 opens. Several dialog box elements contain suggested or **default** values to help you save your file. You can request that Works save the file in another format in the Save as Type list box, so that you can use the file with other spreadsheet programs. Table 5-2 lists the spreadsheet file formats that Works 4.0 supports. To save your spreadsheet in another format, you click the Save as Type list box, then click the appropriate spreadsheet program. Employees of Outdoor Designs use this technique so they can give their spreadsheet files to a consulting accountant, who uses Lotus 1-2-3 for Windows. For your purposes, however, the Works format is fine.

3. Type **Product Order 6-30**
   The filename Product Order 6-30 appears in the File name text box. Now you need to save your product order spreadsheet on your Student Disk.

4. Click the **Save in list box**, then click the letter of the drive that contains your Student Disk
   A list of your Student Disk files appears in the list box, along with the My Works Files folder that you created in Unit 1.

5. Double-click the **My Works Files** folder in the list box
   The My Works Files folder opens, indicating that Works will save your file in this folder.

6. Click **Save**
   The Save As dialog box disappears, and the Spreadsheet window reappears with Product Order 6-30 in the title bar.

Using the Spelling Checker

After you save your spreadsheet, it is a good idea to check the spelling of the words and labels you entered. The Spelling Checker in the Spreadsheet is identical to the one in the Word Processor. (However, the Thesaurus is not available in the Spreadsheet.) To run the Spelling Checker in the Spreadsheet, click Spelling on the Tools menu. The Spelling dialog box opens, and Works starts checking the spelling of text in the spreadsheet, starting with cell A1. (The Spelling Checker ignores all numeric values.) Figure 5-6 shows the Spelling Checker at work in the Product Order 6-30 spreadsheet.

FIGURE 5-5:
Save As dialog box

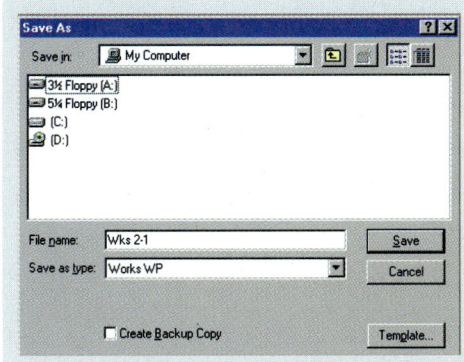

FIGURE 5-6:
Spreadsheet Spelling Checker

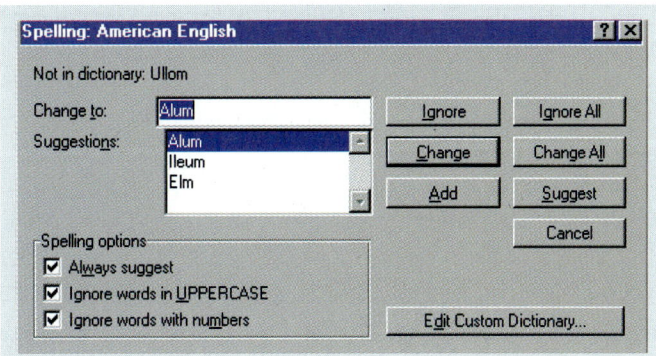

TABLE 5-2: Spreadsheet file formats included in the Save as Type list box

SPREADSHEET FORMAT	DESCRIPTION
Works for Windows 3.0	A format that version 3.0 of Works for Windows can read
Works for Windows 2.0/ Works for DOS	A format that either Works for Windows 2.0 or Works for DOS can read
Text and Commas	Unformatted spreadsheet with entries separated by commas
Text and Tabs	Unformatted Windows spreadsheet with entries separated by tabs
Text and Tabs (DOS)	Unformatted DOS spreadsheet with entries separated by tabs
Excel SS	A format that Excel for Windows versions 4.0 and later can read
Lotus 1-2-3	A format that Lotus 1-2-3 versions 2.0 and later can read
Works 3.0 for Macintosh SS	A format that Works 3.0 for the Apple Macintosh can read
Works 4.0 for Macintosh SS	A format that Works 4.0 for the Apple Macintosh can read

QUICK TIP

[Ctrl][S] is the keyboard shortcut for saving a Works file.

Changing column width and row height

You can adjust spreadsheet column widths and row heights by using the Format menu or by dragging the column or row borders with the mouse. You'll practice the first method next; for more information on dragging column or row borders, see the related topic, "Dragging column and row borders." **case** Spend a few minutes adjusting column width and row height in the Product Order 6-30 spreadsheet so that the information in the spreadsheet is more readable.

1 Click the letter **B** at the top of the column to select **column B** in the spreadsheet.
Works highlights column B. Before you resize or format one or more spreadsheet cells, you must first select it or them. Table 5-3 lists several methods for selecting spreadsheet cells with the mouse or keyboard.

2 Click **Format** on the menu bar, then click **Column Width**
The Column Width dialog box opens. It contains a Column width text box where you can specify column width (in characters) and a Best Fit button, which when pushed automatically resizes the column so that it is slightly wider than the longest item in the column. Because kit names vary in length, choose the Best Fit button — it takes the guesswork out of widening the column.

3 Click the **Best Fit button**
Works closes the Column Width dialog box and resizes column B. The complete kit names now appear in the column. Next you increase the height of row 7 to add a little more space between the two blocks of text in the spreadsheet.

4 Click the number **7** to the left of row 7 to select **row 7**
Works highlights the row.

5 Click **Format** on the menu bar, then click **Row Height**
The Row Height dialog box opens. Works automatically adjusts each row's height to be at least as large as the largest font in the row, so you only need to use the Row Height dialog box if you want to increase or decrease the row height. Here you change the height of the row to 20 points to add more space between the order data and the general order information.

6 Type **20** in the **Row Height text box,** and press **[Enter]**
The height of row 7 changes from 12 to 20 points, as shown in Figure 5-7.

FIGURE 5-7: Product order spreadsheet with row and column resized

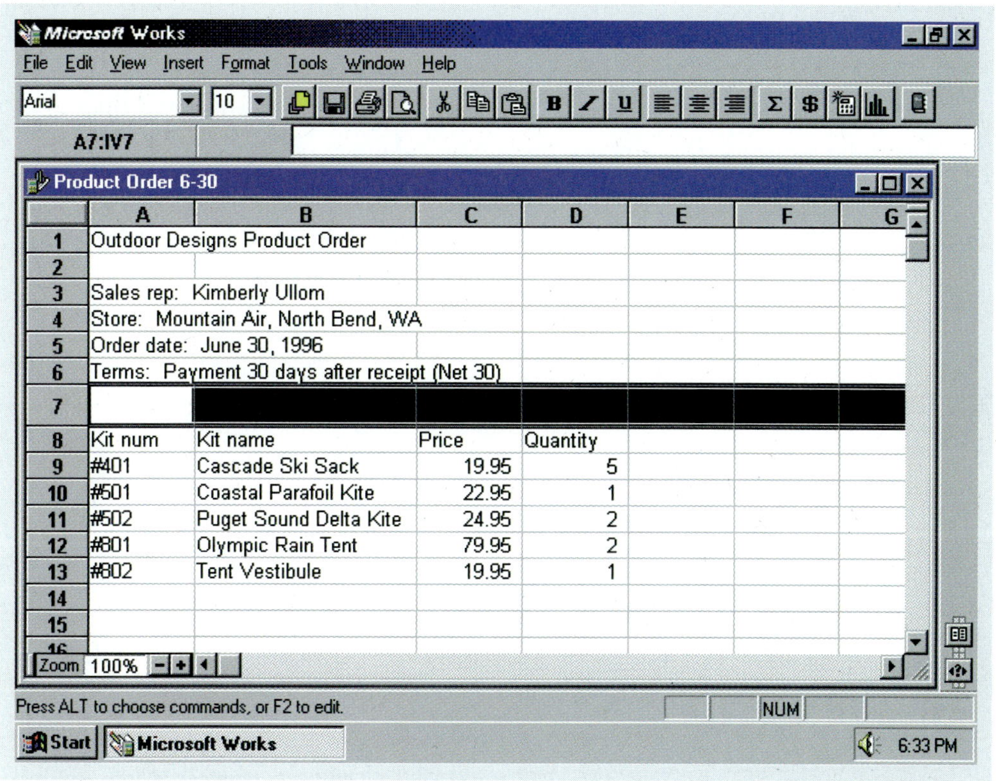

TABLE 5-3: Methods for selecting spreadsheet cells

TO SELECT	WITH THE MOUSE	WITH THE KEYBOARD
A cell	Click the cell	Use arrow keys
A row	Click the row number	Select a cell in a row, then press [Ctrl][F8]
A column	Click the column number	Select a cell in a column, then press [Shift][F8]
Group of cells	Drag across the cells	Press [F8], then use arrow keys
Spreadsheet	Click the box above row 1	Press [Ctrl][Shift][F8]

Dragging column and row borders

You can also change column width and row height by dragging the column or row border with the mouse. To drag a border, position the mouse pointer over the line to the right of a column heading or below a row number, until the mouse pointer changes shape and the word "Adjust" appears below it. When the pointer changes, drag the border in the direction you want to change. Changing column width and row height with the mouse is a fast but limited technique: you can only change one row or column at a time, and you can't specify an exact value.

QUICK TIP

If you make a mistake, press [Ctrl][Z] or click Undo on the Edit menu to cancel your most recent column width or row height adjustment.

Using formulas

Copying and Moving Cell Entries

To perform a calculation in the Spreadsheet, you enter a formula in a cell. A **formula** is an equation that calculates a new value from existing values. Formulas can contain numbers, mathematical operators, cell references, and built-in equations called **functions**. Table 5-4 lists some mathematical operators you can use in a formula. To learn more about how Works reads and evaluates formulas, see the related topic, "How Works calculates formulas." Also, be sure to view the CourseHelp called "Copying and Moving Cell Entries" before completing the steps below. **case** The product order spreadsheet should provide subtotals for each item ordered. Create a formula to calculate these subtotals.

1. Click **cell E8**, type **Subtotal**, then press **[↓]**

2. Type **=**
   The equal sign (=) tells Works you're about to enter a formula in cell E9. From this point on, Works will include in the formula any numbers, mathematical operators, cell references, or functions you type.

3. Press **[←]** twice to move to **cell C9**
   Works highlights cell C9, which appears as a **cell reference** in the formula, meaning that Works will use the number in cell C9 when it calculates the formula. To help you keep track of the formula as you build it, Works displays the formula in both the formula bar and in cell E9.

4. Type *****
   When calculating the formula, Works will use the asterisk to multiply the number in cell C9 by the next cell reference you select.

5. Press **[←]** once to move to **cell D9**
   Works highlights cell D9, which appears as the last cell reference in the formula. In calculating the formula, Works will multiply the product price in cell C9 by the quantity in cell D9.

6. Press **[Enter]**
   Works enters the formula, multiplies the two numbers, and displays the result (99.75) in cell E9. Notice that although the calculation's result appears in cell E9, the original formula still appears in the formula bar. Now you need to **replicate**, or copy, the formula you just created in cells E10 through E13 to calculate a subtotal for each item in the product order.

7. Select **cells E9** through **E13** with the mouse
   You select multiple cells, or **cell ranges**, in the Spreadsheet by dragging the mouse across the cells or holding down the Shift key and pressing the direction keys to highlight the cells. Now that you have selected the range of cells, you can use the Fill Down command to replicate the contents of the top selected cell in the other selected cells.

8. Click **Edit** on the menu bar, then click **Fill Down**
   Works replicates the subtotal formula in cells E10 through E13, and the subtotal for each product appears, as shown in Figure 5-8.

9. Click the **Save button** 💾 on the toolbar
   Works saves your changes to disk.

FIGURE 5-8: Subtotal formula replicated in cells E10 through E13

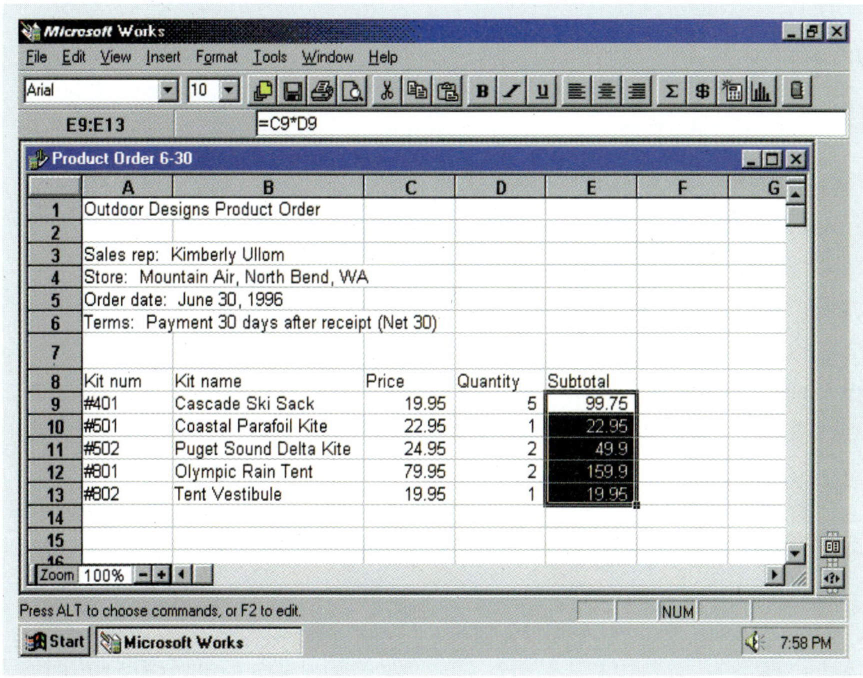

TABLE 5-4: Useful mathematical operators (in order of evaluation)

OPERATOR	DESCRIPTION	EXAMPLE	RESULT
( )	Parenthesis	(3+6)*3	27
^	Exponential	10^2	100
*	Multiplication	7*5	35
/	Division	20/4	5
+	Addition	5+5	10
–	Subtraction	12–8	4

How Works calculates formulas

When you enter a formula that contains more than one mathematical operator, Works follows standard algebraic rules to determine which calculation to accomplish first. First, Works evaluates the calculations between parentheses. Then the rules dictate that exponential calculations are performed first, multiplication and division calculations second, and addition and subtraction calculations last. If there is more than one calculation in the same category, Works evaluates them from left to right.

QUICK TIP

Use cell references, rather than actual numbers, in formulas so your calculations are easier to replicate.

Editing the spreadsheet

Copying and Moving Cell Entries

You can edit cells in a spreadsheet in several ways. You can revise a single cell by clicking it and editing its contents in the formula bar. You can cut, copy, and paste blocks of cells using the Edit menu or the toolbar. You can also move cells using drag-and-drop editing. Be sure to view the CourseHelp called "Copying and Moving Cell Entries" before completing the steps below. As in the Word Processor, you can use the Replace command to automatically change one word to another throughout the spreadsheet; for more information on this, see the related topic, "Making changes with the Replace command." **case** Mountain Air increased its order for Coastal Parafoil kites and renegotiated payment terms. Edit the product order spreadsheet to reflect these changes. You also can move the sales rep's name to give the store information more prominence.

1. Select **cell D10** and type **3**, then press **[Enter]**
   The number in cell D10 changes from 1 to 3, and the subtotal in cell E10 changes from 22.95 to 68.85. This feature applies to all Works applications: when you select text, new text replaces selected text as you type.

   The accounting department notified you that it extended the payment grace period for the Mountain Air store to 60 days, so now you need to edit the contents of cell A6 on the formula bar.

2. Select **cell A6**
   Works highlights the cell and the label "Terms: Payment 30 days after receipt (Net 30)" appears in the formula bar.

3. Position the mouse over the formula bar, select the first **3** in the label, then type **6**
   Works selects the number 3, then replaces it when you type the new number, 6.

4. Select the second **3** in the formula bar, then type **6**
   Works replaces the second number 3 with the number 6. The formula bar now contains "Terms: Payment 60 days after receipt (Net 60)."

5. Press **[Enter]** to confirm your formula bar edits
   The updated label appears in the spreadsheet in cell A6. Now you use drag-and-drop to move the sales rep's name from row 3 to row 6.

6. Select **row 3** in the spreadsheet by clicking the number **3** to the left of row 3

7. Move the mouse pointer to the bottom edge of the selected row until it changes to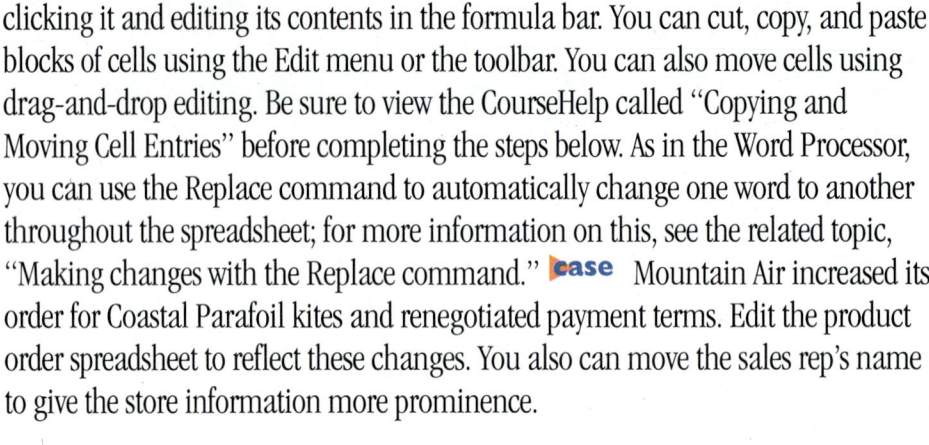
   The mouse pointer changes to the drag pointer.

8. Click the row, drag it down until the move bar is between rows 6 and 7, then release the mouse button
   The word "Move" appears beneath the mouse pointer, and the contents of row 3 move to row 6, as Figure 5-9 shows. Notice that the contents of rows 4, 5, and 6 each move up a row to fill the gap left by row 3. When you move a row or column in a spreadsheet, other rows and columns adjust after Works finishes the move (this ensures that the spreadsheet never has "missing" rows or columns). However, when you move individual cells, they replace the cells they move onto.

9. Click the **Save button** on the toolbar to save your editing changes

FIGURE 5-9: Product order spreadsheet after editing

Making changes with the Replace command

The Replace command in the Spreadsheet works just like it does in the Word Processor: you specify the text you want to search for in the Find what text box and the text you want to substitute in the Replace with text box, then click the Find Next button. You can replace one word at a time by clicking the Replace button or replace the word everywhere it appears in the spreadsheet at once with the Replace All button. Figure 5-10 shows the Replace command at work in the Spreadsheet.

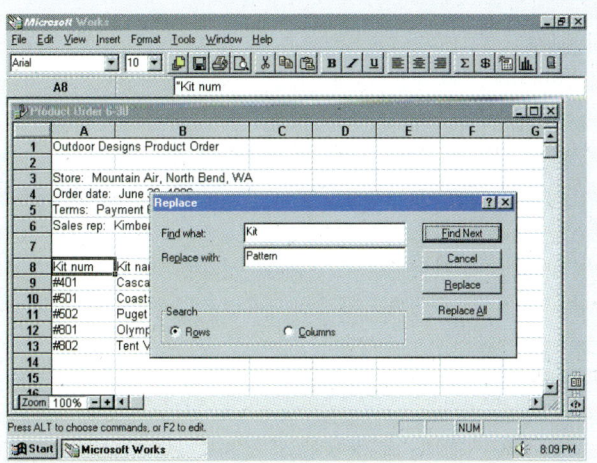

FIGURE 5-10: Replace command

QUICK TIP

To edit a cell from the keyboard, use the arrow keys to select the cell you want to edit, then press [F2] to move the edit cursor to the formula bar.

Changing alignment and number format

Works can right-align, center, or left-align information in cells, and it can format numbers to appear in one of several standard formats, including currency, percent, and exponential. For details about number format options, see the related topic, "Changing the number format." Changing alignment and number format can make your spreadsheet better looking and easier to read. **case** Now use the formatting options to improve the appearance of the product order spreadsheet.

1. Select **row 8** in the spreadsheet
   Works highlights the row of column labels.

2. Click **Format** on the menu bar, then click **Alignment**
   The Alignment tab in the Format Cells dialog box appears. It contains an option button for each cell alignment option available in the spreadsheet. General (the default) aligns labels at the left of the cell and numbers at the right, Left aligns everything at the left, Right aligns everything at the right, Center centers everything within the cell, Fill repeats the characters in the cell until the cell is full (this is useful for repeating a dash or another symbol), and Center across selection centers text horizontally across several selected cells.

3. Click the **Center option button**, then click **OK**
   Each label in row 8 is centered in its cell. Now you center the spreadsheet's title using the Center across selection option.

4. Select cells **A1** through **E1**
   Works highlights the title "Outdoor Designs Product Order."

5. Click **Format** on the menu bar, click **Alignment**, click the **Center across selection option button**, then click **OK**
   Works centers the spreadsheet title across the five highlighted cells. (Note that the cell reference of the title is still A1, however.) Now you change the alignment in two columns using the alignment buttons on the toolbar.

6. Select cells **A9** through **A13**, and click the **Center-align button** on the toolbar
   Works highlights the five cells in the Kit num column and centers the contents of the five cells in the column.

7. Select cells **D9** through **D13**, then click on the toolbar
   Works highlights the five cells in the Quantity column, and centers the contents of the five cells in the column. Now change the number format in two columns using the Currency button on the toolbar.

8. Select cells **C9** through **C13**, and click the **Currency button** on the toolbar
   Works formats the five cells in the Price column with currency (dollars and cents) format, as Figure 5-11 shows. The Currency button is a shortcut for the Number command on the Format menu.

9. Select cells **E9** through **E13**, click on the toolbar, then click the **Save button** on the toolbar
   Works formats the five cells in the Subtotal column with currency format and saves your changes on disk.

FIGURE 5-11: Formatting information in spreadsheet cells

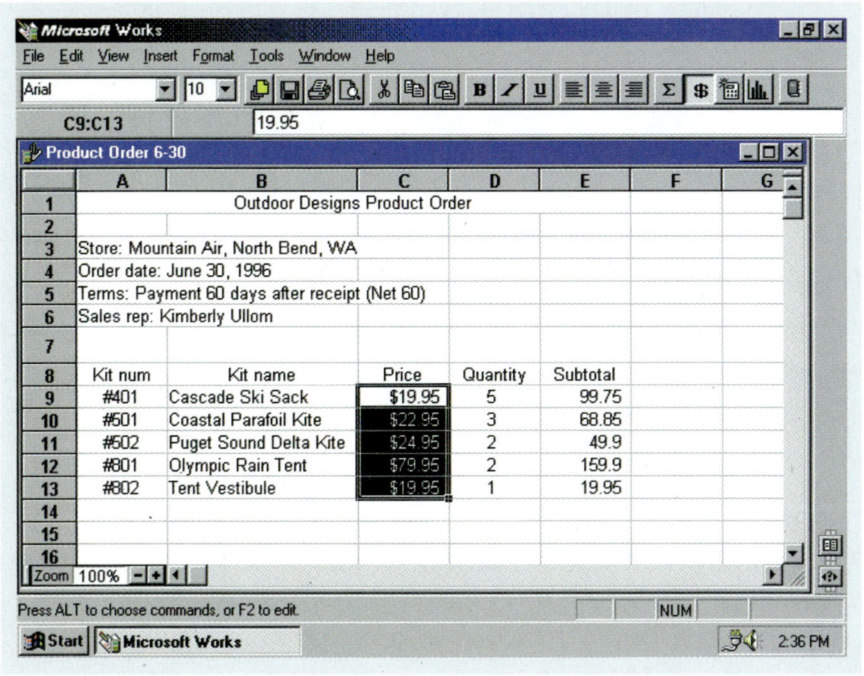

[Screenshot of Microsoft Works spreadsheet "Product Order 6-30" showing Outdoor Designs Product Order with columns for Kit num, Kit name, Price, Quantity, and Subtotal. Price column cells C9:C13 are selected showing $19.95, $22.95, $24.95, $79.95, $19.95.]

Changing the number format

To change the number format in a cell, click the Number command on the Format menu and click the format you want in the Number tab of the Format Cells dialog box, as shown in Figure 5-12. The most popular option is Currency. Because the Currency format is used so often, Works' designers placed a Currency button  on the toolbar to accomplish the task. Other useful number formats include Percent, which creates fractional values; Exponential, which formats numbers in scientific notation, Leading zeros, which creates numbers with a set number of digits; Date, which formats calendar dates in popular formats; and Time, which enters times in a consistent format.

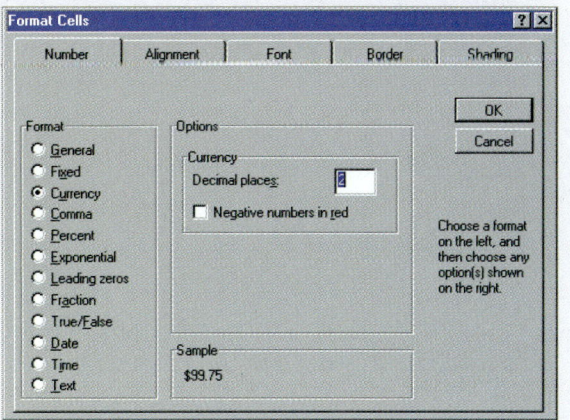

FIGURE 5-12: Number tab in Format Cells dialog box

QUICK TIP

When you see ######## in a cell, the cell is not wide enough to display information in the format you chose. Use the Column Width command on the Format menu to increase column width, or choose a different format.

Changing font and font style and adding borders

Works lets you change the font and font style of text in the spreadsheet and add borders and shading to make important information stand out. The font and font style commands are identical to the commands in the Word Processor, and several are also available as toolbar buttons. The Borders and Patterns commands on the Format menu help you take advantage of the unique rectangular design of spreadsheet cells and can produce impressive formatting effects. For more information about shading options, see the related topic, "Adding shading to cells." ▶case Try working with the font and Borders commands now, to enhance the product order spreadsheet.

1. Select **cell A1** and click the **Bold button** B and **Italic button** I on the toolbar
   The title "Outdoor Designs Product Order" appears in bold italic style.

2. Click the **Font size list box,** click **16,** then click the **Font name list box,** scroll down, and click **Times New Roman**
   The title's size changes to 16 points. The title's font changes from Arial to Times New Roman. Notice that the sizing buttons work exactly as they do in the Word Processor. You can also use the Font and Style command on the Format menu to make these formatting changes.

3. Select **row 8** in the spreadsheet, then click B
   The font style of the row of column labels changes to bold. Now you add a border around the sales information in rows 3 through 6.

4. Select cells **A3** through **C6** (a block of cells three cells wide and four cells long)
   Works highlights the block of cells, and the cell range A3:C6 appears in the cell reference box.

5. Click **Format** on the menu bar, then click **Border**
   The Border tab of the Format Cells dialog box appears. It presents border, line style, and color formatting options you can use to emphasize the selected block of cells.

6. Click **double line** (third from the bottom) under Line style, then click **OK**
   Works places a selection rectangle around the double line style, and a double line appears in the Outline Border option. (You want the outline style.) When you click OK, the dialog box closes and a double line border appears around the block of highlighted cells.

7. Select cells **A8** through **E13** (a block of cells five cells wide and six cells long), click **Format** on the menu bar, then click **Border**
   Works highlights the block of cells, and the cell range A8:E13 appears in the cell reference box. When you click Border, the Border tab of the Format Cells dialog box appears.

8. Click the **Top, Bottom, Left,** and **Right Border options,** click **OK,** then click elsewhere in the spreadsheet to see the new border clearly
   The dialog box closes and Works places a single line border around each cell in the selection, as Figure 5-13 shows.

9. Click the **Save button** 💾 on the toolbar to save your formatting changes

FIGURE 5-13: Spreadsheet after font style and border formatting

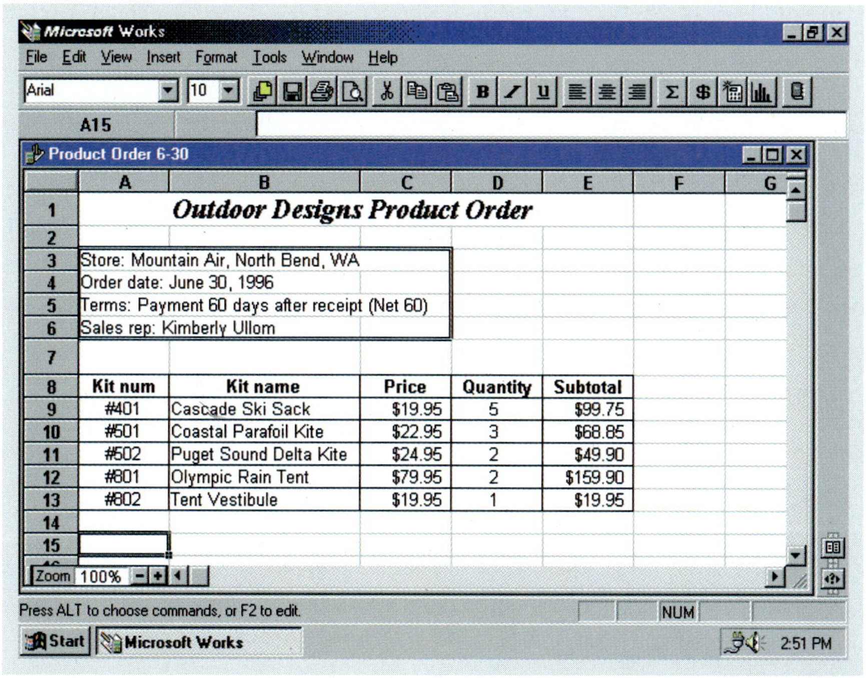

Adding shading to cells

You can fill one or more spreadsheet cells with a shading pattern using the Shading command on the Format menu. Shading formatting works like other types of formatting: first you select the cells you want to format, then you click the formatting options you want in the Shading tab of the Format Cells dialog box. The Patterns list box contains 14 different shading patterns for you to choose from. In addition, you can select foreground (i.e., text) or background color to complement the shading pattern. Figure 5-14 shows the Shading tab and a range of cells in column E formatted with 20% shading and a cyan background color.

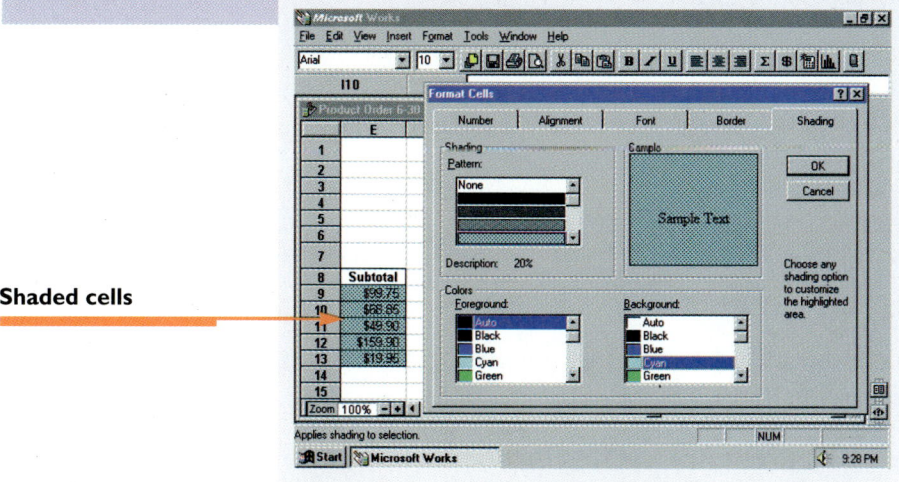

Shaded cells

FIGURE 5-14: Shading tab in Format Cells dialog box

QUICK TIP

The AutoFormat command on the Format menu combines several formatting operations in one command and can effectively format a range of cells in several different styles.

Printing the spreadsheet

When you finish working with your spreadsheet and have saved your work, you are ready to print. It is important to save your work before printing. That way, if you experience technical problems while printing, you will not lose your work. You can examine your document in Print Preview and verify the page layout with the zoom pointer. After you preview your document, you're ready to print a copy with the Print command. Ask your instructor or lab manager for specific instructions on how to print with your classroom printer. For information on adding headers and footers to a spreadsheet, see the related topic, "Adding headers and footers." **case** After you print the product order spreadsheet, you save your changes and exit Works.

1. **Click File on the menu bar, then click Print Preview**
   The Print Preview window opens, and the product order spreadsheet looks as it will on the printed page. Several command buttons that control the Print Preview window's operation appear on the right of the window.

2. **Move the mouse pointer onto the document page**
   The pointer changes to the **zoom pointer**, which you can use to examine parts of the document more closely.

3. **Click the top half of the spreadsheet with the zoom pointer**
   The document enlarges to half size in the Print Preview window.

4. **Click the title of the spreadsheet with the zoom pointer**
   The spreadsheet enlarges to full size in the Print Preview window, as Figure 5-15 shows.

5. **Click the Cancel button**
   The Print Preview window closes, and the product order spreadsheet reappears.

6. **Click File on the menu bar, then click Print**
   The Print dialog box opens. It lets you specify the printer you want to use, the printing page range (if you don't want to print the entire document), the number of copies you want to print, and whether the printing should be best quality (the default) or draft quality. (If you simply want to print one copy of the entire spreadsheet, you can also click the Print button on the toolbar.)

   Take a moment now to verify that your printer is on-line and properly connected to your computer. If you have questions, ask your instructor or lab manager for help.

7. **Click OK**
   The Print dialog box closes. After a few moments the completed product order emerges from your printer. You are now finished working for the day.

8. **Click the Save button on the toolbar, click File on the menu bar, then click Exit Works**
   The Product Order 6-30 spreadsheet and the Works program both close.

FIGURE 5-15: Spreadsheet in Print Preview

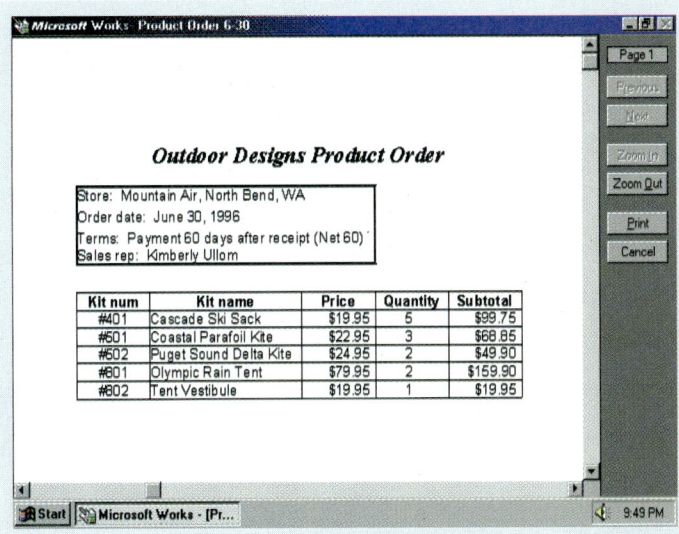

Adding headers and footers

When you print your spreadsheet, you may want to add page numbers, the current date, or some other text to the top or bottom of each page. You can add this information to your spreadsheet with the Headers and Footers command on the View menu. A standard header or footer in the spreadsheet is one line long and can contain one or several header and footer codes. **Header and footer codes** consist of an ampersand (&) and one of the formatting characters listed in Table 5-5. You won't see headers and footers in your document in Normal view, but you can examine them in Print Preview.

TABLE 5-5: Useful Spreadsheet header and footer codes

CODE	DESCRIPTION
&c	Centers the characters that follow on the page
&l	Aligns the characters that follow at the left margin
&r	Aligns the characters that follow at the right margin
&p	Prints the page number
&d	Prints the date when the file is printed
&t	Prints the time when the file is printed
&f	Prints the spreadsheet filename
&&	Prints a single ampersand character

Use the Page Setup command on the File menu to change page margins, paper orientation, and other printing options.

TASK REFERENCE

TASK	MOUSE/BUTTON	MENU	KEYBOARD
Center-align cell contents	Click ≡	Click Format, Alignment	
Change column width	Drag column border with mouse	Click Format, Column Width	
Change row height	Drag row border with mouse	Click Format, Row Height	
Check spelling		Click Tools, Spelling	[F7]
Format for currency	Click $	Click Format, Number	
Highlight a cell	Click the cell		Direction keys
Highlight a column	Click column letter	Click Edit, Select Column	[Shift][F8]
Highlight a row	Click row number	Click Edit, Select Row	[Ctrl][F8]
Highlight spreadsheet	Click selection box to the left of column 1	Click Edit, Select All	[Ctrl][Shift], [F8]
Move cell contents	Drag selected cells to new location	Select cells, click Edit, Cut, then highlight new cells and click Edit, Paste	Cut with [Ctrl][X] and paste with [Ctrl][V]
Print the spreadsheet	Click 🖨	Click File, Print	[Ctrl][P]
Save a file	Click 💾	Click File, Save As	[Ctrl][S]
Undo a mistake		Click Edit, Undo	[Ctrl][Z]
Use Bold	Click B	Click Format, Font and Style	[Ctrl][B]
Use Italic	Click /	Click Format, Font and Style	[Ctrl][I]
Use Underline	Click U	Click Format, Font and Style	[Ctrl][U]

CONCEPTS REVIEW

Label each spreadsheet element shown in Figure 5-16.

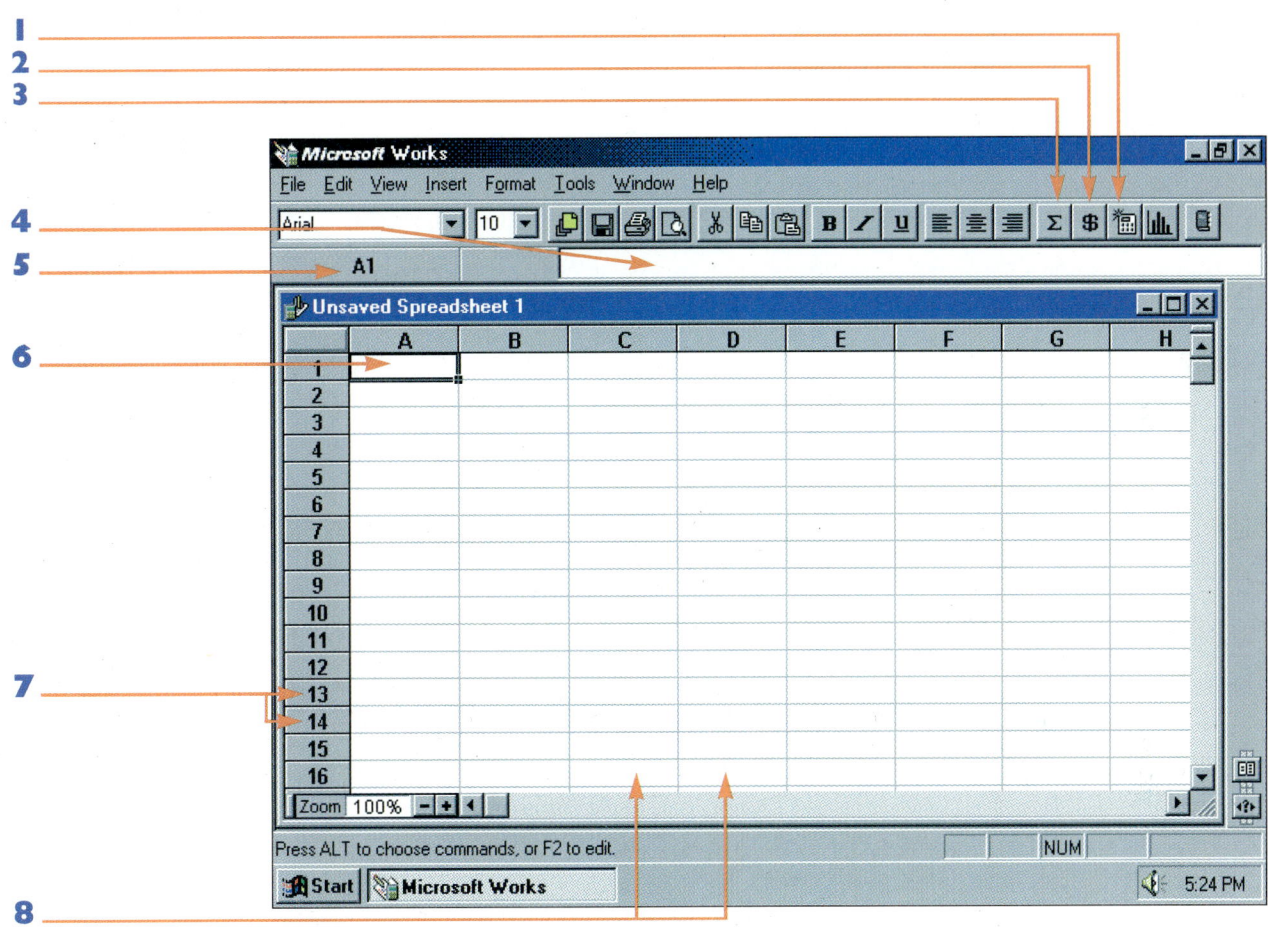

FIGURE 5-16

Match the mathematical operators with their uses in spreadsheet formulas.

9 ^
10 /
11 *
12 –
13 +

a. Multiplication
b. Division
c. Addition
d. Exponential
e. Subtraction

Select the best answer from the list of choices.

14 You start the spreadsheet application from the
   a. Windows 95 Start button
   b. Windows 95 desktop
   c. Help system
   d. Works Task Launcher dialog box

15 Spreadsheet rows and columns intersect to form
   a. The toolbar
   b. Cells
   c. Paragraphs
   d. Selected text

16 The name of a cell in column B and row 2 is
   a. A1
   b. 1A
   c. B2
   d. 2B

17 Text in the formula bar with a double quotation mark (") in front of it is a
   a. Label
   b. Number
   c. Formula
   d. Function

18 How do you select an entire column in the spreadsheet?
   a. Press [Esc].
   b. Press [Ctrl][B].
   c. Click the row number to the left of the column.
   d. Click the column letter at the top of the column.

19 What does the Best Fit button in the Column Width dialog box do?
   a. Lets you specify the width (in characters) of the column
   b. Automatically resizes the column so that it is slightly wider than the longest item
   c. Picks the best TrueType font for the cell
   d. Places a border around the column

20 Which of these items *cannot* be included in a spreadsheet formula?
   a. Mathematical operator
   b. Cell reference
   c. Built-in function
   d. Italic type

21 What answer would Works give after calculating the formula 4+3*2–2?
   a. 12
   b. 8
   c. 6
   d. 4

22 What word is part of the drag-and-drop pointer?
   a. Drag
   b. Drop
   c. Copy
   d. There is no word in the drag-and-drop pointer.

23 Which of these is *not* a horizontal alignment option in the Alignment tab of the Format Cells dialog box?
   a. Diagonal
   b. Left
   c. Right
   d. Center across selection

24 What does ######## mean when it appears in a cell?
   a. The cell has been formatted for currency.
   b. The cell contains shading.
   c. The cell is too narrow to display the information in the cell.
   d. The cell contains information that cannot be deleted.

25 Imagine that cell B5 is selected in your spreadsheet. What happens when you press [Shift][F8]?
   a. Row 8 is selected.
   b. Column B is selected.

    c. The entire spreadsheet is selected.

    d. The contents of cell B5 are formatted for italic.

SKILLS REVIEW

1. Start the Works Spreadsheet tool, and identify the elements of the spreadsheet screen.

    a. Click the Start button, point to the Programs folder, point to the Microsoft Works 4.0 folder, and then click the Microsoft Works 4.0 program icon.

    b. Click the Works Tools tab in the Task Launcher dialog box.

    c. Click Spreadsheet.

    d. Identify the spreadsheet screen elements, referring to Figure 5-2 and Table 5-1.

2. Enter numbers and labels.

    a. Type the following information (starting in cell A1), pressing ↓ as indicated, to create an Outdoor Designs shipping ticket.

    Outdoor Designs Shipping Ticket ↓↓

    Ship to: ↓

    Pam's Kites ↓

    21 Vose Road ↓

    Edmonds, WA ↓

    Date: June 29, 1996 ↓↓

Kit num	Quantity	Kit name	Price	
#401	2	Cascade Ski Sack	19.95	[click A10]
#501	2	Coastal Parafoil Kite	22.95	[click A11]
#503	3	Franklin's Diamond	19.95	[click A12]
#701	2	Sonic Boomer Kite	49.95	[click A13]
#801	1	Olympic Rain Tent	79.95	[click A14]
				[Enter]

3. Save your work in the My Works Files folder on your Student Disk with the name Shipping Ticket 6-29.

    a. Click File on the menu bar, then click Save As.

    b. Type "Shipping Ticket 6-29."

    c. In the Save in list box, click the letter of the drive that contains your Student Disk.

    d. Double-click the My Works Files folder in the Folders list box.

    e. Click Save.

4. Adjust column width and row height, so all the information appears in the spreadsheet. Then increase the space between the address and the data by increasing the height of row 8.

    a. Select column C.

    b. Click Format on the menu bar, then click Column Width.

    c. Click the Best Fit button.

    d. Select row 8.

    e. Click Format on the menu bar.

    f. Click Row Height.

    g. Type "20" in the Row height text box, and press [Enter].

5. Enter a formula in cell E10 that calculates the value of the product price times the product quantity, then replicate the formula in cells E11 through E14. Then enter a formula in cell B15 that calculates the total number of items shipped.

    a. Click cell E9.

    b. Type "Item Total," then press ↓.

    c. Type "=B10*D10" in cell E10, then press [Enter].

    d. Select cells E10 through E14.

    e. Click Edit on the menu bar, then click Fill Down.

    f. Click cell A15, type "# Items," then press →.

    g. In cell B15, type =B10+B11+B12+B13+B14, then press [Enter].

6. Practice editing the contents of cells in the formula bar and using the mouse to drag and drop text. What happens to the results of the formula in E10 when you edit the data?

    a. Select cell D10.

    b. Click the formula bar.

    c. Change 19.95 in the formula bar to 20.95, then press [Enter].

    d. Select rows 10 and 11.

    e. Drag the selected rows to row 14.

    f. Select row 7 and drag it to row 3.

    g. Click Tools on the menu bar, then click Spelling to run the Spelling Checker.

h. Verify spelling in the spreadsheet, and make changes if necessary.

i. Click OK when you finish the spelling check.

7 Change cell alignment and number formats.

a. Select row 9.

b. Click the Center-align button on the toolbar.

c. Select cells A1 through E1.

d. Click Format on the menu bar, then click Alignment.

e. Click the Center across selection radio button, then click OK.

f. Center-align the data in the Kit num and Quantity columns with the Center-align button on the toolbar.

g. Change the number format of the data in the Price and Item Total columns to currency with the Currency button on the toolbar.

h. Select cells E10 through E14.

i. Use the Shading command on the Format menu to add a 20% shading pattern to the cells in the Item Total column. See the Description to learn the percentage of each shading choice when you select it.

j. With cells E10 through E14 still selected, use the Shading command to change the background color to cyan.

8 Use font and border changes to emphasize and delineate information in the spreadsheet.

a. Select cell A1.

b. Click the Underline button on the toolbar.

c. Change the font to Impact and the font size to 18 point.

d. Select row 9 and change the font for the column labels to Impact.

e. Select cells A3 through C7.

f. Click Format on the menu bar, then click Border.

g. Click the last Line Style (the thickest), then click OK.

h. Select cells A9 through B14, click Format on the menu bar, then click Border.

i. Click the last Line style, then click OK.

j. Select cells A15 through B15.

k. Click Format on the menu bar, then click Border.

l. Click the last Line style, then click OK.

9 Add a footer, examine the spreadsheet in Print Preview, then print a final copy.

a. Click the View menu, then click Headers and Footers.

b. Type "&cPage - &P" in the Footer text box, and then click OK.

c. Click File on the menu bar, then click Print Preview.

d. Click the top of the spreadsheet twice with the zoom pointer, and verify the contents.

e. Click the Zoom Out button twice, then click the spreadsheet footer. Verify that the footer is centered in the bottom margin and reads "Page - 1."

f. Click the Cancel button.

g. Save changes to the file.

h. Click File on the menu bar, then click Print.

i. Verify your printer is turned on and ready to print, then click OK to print the spreadsheet.

j. Exit Works.

INDEPENDENT CHALLENGE 1

At Wacky Words, Karl Edwards requires you to provide the sales and marketing department with a monthly order summary. The summary includes the order number, account name, order date, order total, and whether or not the order has been paid for. It also provides a monthly sales total and indicates what percentage of the year's sales-to-date the month's orders represent. It's time to create the order summary for August.

To complete this independent challenge:

1 Enter the title "August Order Summary" in cell A1.

2 Enter the following information, starting in cell A3.

Order #	Account	Date	Total	Paid
600	Britts Books & Cards	8/5/96	1501	0
601	Songs and Such	8/10/96	950	950
602	Stationery Plus	8/7/96	2005	0
603	Cards-n-More	8/25/96	1261	0
604	Rita's Gift Shop	8/14/96	1800	1800
	Monthly Total			
	Percent of year-to-date		.09	

3 Widen and narrow each column as necessary so that the data in each column fits comfortably.

4 Drag rows 9 and 10, which contain the Monthly Total and Percent of year-to-date information down to rows 10 and 11. Reduce the row height of row 9, which is now blank, to 6.

5 Enter a formula in cell D10 that adds the figures in the Total column. Then change the amount in cell D4 from 1501 to 1400.

6 Format the order numbers in A4 through A8 for Leading Zero format and center them in the column. What is the format option for the dates in the Date column? Format the numbers in D4 through D8 as Comma format with no decimal places. Format the numbers in E4 through E8 for True/False format. Format cell D10 for Currency with no decimal places and cell D11 as Percent with no decimal places.

7 Center the title between columns A and E. Change the font to 18-point bold Arial Narrow. Center the column labels in row 3; make them bold, and change the font to Arial Narrow. Change the labels in cells B10 and B11 to bold Arial Narrow as well.

8 Add a border line at the top and bottom of the column labels in cells A3 through E3. Choose the second line thickness from the top, and change the line color to blue. Add the same type of line above cells A10 through E10 and below cells A11 through E11.

9 Preview and save the spreadsheet as August Order Summary in the My Works Files folder on your Student Disk, then print it.

INDEPENDENT CHALLENGE 2

Joel Rubin asked you to compare sales for the four menu items featured during the past month at The Steak Pit. He wants to determine whether featuring menu items has affected sales appreciably.

To complete this independent challenge:

1. Open a new spreadsheet. In cell A1, type "Featured Menu Items Comparison" as the spreadsheet title.

2. Enter the following information, starting in cell A3.

Featured Item	Price	Last Month	Total	This Month
12 oz. Sizzler	18.00	353		478
Chicken Sizzler	15.00	321		398
Roast Beef	20.00	349		403
Filet	23.00	314		378

3. Adjust column widths so that the data fits comfortably within the columns.

4. Add a formula to cell D4 that calculates the total amount for last month for the first item, 12 oz. Sizzler. Copy this formula down the column for the other items. Then repeat the process for column F, to calculate totals for this month as well.

5. Change the title's font to 18-point bold italic Times New Roman, and center it across columns A through F. Center the column labels in row 3, and make them 12-point bold Times New Roman. Center the numbers in the Last Month and This Month columns. Adjust column width as necessary.

6. Format the data in the Price and Total columns for Currency with two decimal places. Then add shading to the two Total columns. Finally, add a border around the spreadsheet data (cells A3 through F7).

7. Preview and save the spreadsheet as Items Comparison in the My Works Files folder on your Student Disk, then print it.

INDEPENDENT CHALLENGE 3

Stuff for Pets market research coordinator Rachel Palmer asked you to create a spreadsheet containing company sales figures for the last two quarters. Create a spreadsheet that presents the data for the third and fourth quarters attractively.

To complete this independent challenge:

1. In cell A1, type "Stuff for Pets," and in cell A2, type "Third and Fourth Quarter 1996 Sales Data."

2. Enter the following information, starting in cell A4.

Region	3rd Quarter	4th Quarter
Northeast	80,000	85,000
South	62,000	60,000
Midwest	56,000	71,000
West	100,000	110,000
Totals		

3. Change the two rows of the spreadsheet title so that the first is 14-point bold Arial Narrow and the second is 18-point bold Arial Narrow. Then change the column labels in row 4 to bold Arial Narrow.

4. Widen row 3 to add more space between the title and the data.

5. Add formulas that calculate each quarter's totals. Format the quarterly data in cells B5 through C9 for Comma with no decimal places. Adjust column widths if necessary.

6. Edit A5 so that it reads "East" instead of "Northeast."

7. Change the "Total" label and numbers in row 9 to bold Arial Narrow.

8. Add a border around the spreadsheet data, including the row and column labels (cells A4 through C9). Then add shading to the column labels in row 4 and the label and numbers in row 9.

9. Add a footer to the page that includes the words "Company Confidential" on the left, centers the page number, and right-aligns the current date.

10. Preview and save the spreadsheet as Quarterly Sales in the My Works Files folder on your Student Disk, then print it.

INDEPENDENT CHALLENGE 4

Clayton Warren, owner of Clayton's Clayworks, asked you to develop a spreadsheet that will help him take telephone orders. Create this spreadsheet using some sample data.

To complete this independent challenge:

1 Enter the following information beginning in cell A1.

Customer Order	100
Date:	8/18/96
Name:	Fred Laske
Address:	2310 Lockhaven Dr.
City/State:	Springdale, CA 99090

Item #	Description	Price	Quantity	Total
179	Mountain mugs	12.50	8	
156	Teapot Deluxe	49.95	1	
168	Cereal/Soup bowls	15.95	12	

2 Adjust column widths so that all information fits comfortably. Adjust row heights to add extra space between the spreadsheet's sections.

3 Add formulas to column E that calculate the total for each row. Add the word "Order Total" in C11 and a formula in E11 that calculates the total for the whole order.

4 Format the numbers in A7 through A9 for Leading zero with four digits and center them. Format the Price and Total columns for Currency with two decimal places. Center the figures under Quantity.

5 Change the column labels to bold italic. Change the "Order Total" label to bold italic. In the top portion of the spreadsheet, change the labels in column A to bold italics. Increase the font size of Customer Order to 14 point and make it bold.

6 Add a border around the customer information in the top portion of the spreadsheet. Add a thin line above and below cells A6 through E6, which contain the column labels, and cells A11 through E11, which include the order total.

7 Preview and save the spreadsheet as Order Form in the My Works Files folder on your Student Disk, then print it.

VISUALWORKSHOP

Create the sales analysis shown in Figure 5-17 using the commands and techniques you learned in this chapter. Save it as Ticket Sales Analysis to the My Works Files folder on your student disk.

FIGURE 5-17

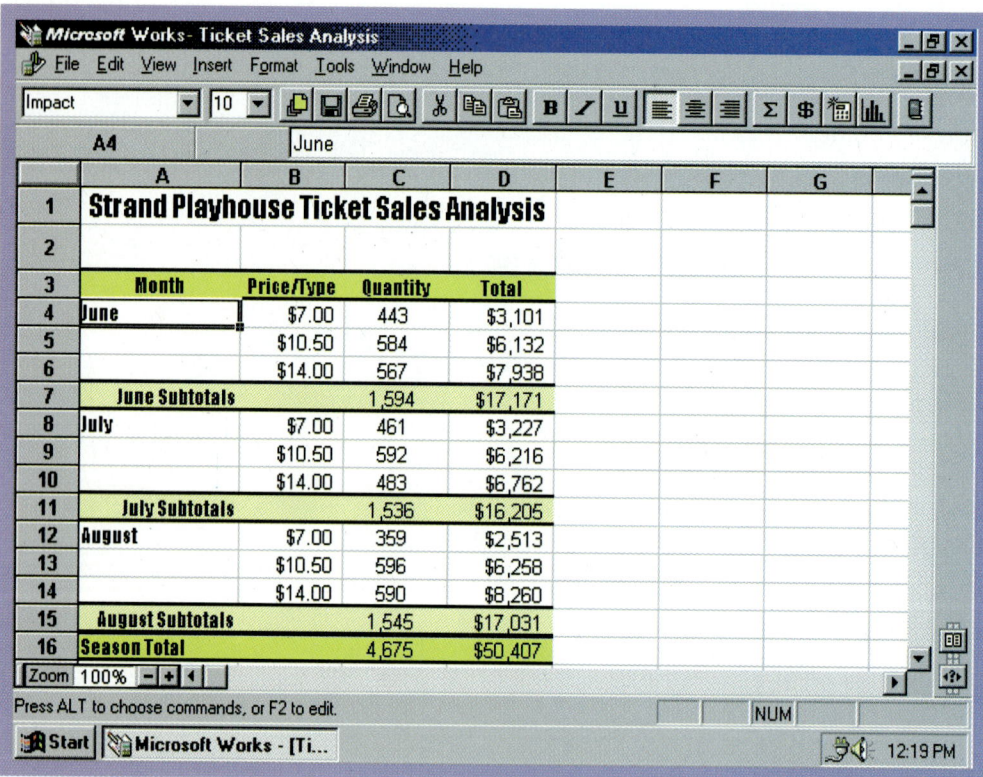

UNIT 6

OBJECTIVES

▶ Learn about functions

▶ Use the SUM function

▶ Use date and time functions

▶ Use statistical functions

▶ Use financial functions

▶ Use text functions

▶ Sort rows and print

Working
WITH SPREADSHEET FUNCTIONS

*I*n this unit you'll learn about **functions**, built-in calculations you can use in spreadsheet formulas. Spreadsheet functions help you accomplish sophisticated numerical and text processing operations automatically. For example, you can use a function to find the average of a group of numbers or to calculate monthly loan payments. **case** Working for Outdoor Designs, you'll use functions to finalize the product order spreadsheet so that it provides meaningful sales and account data for the marketing and accounting departments. When you finish, you'll print a copy of the document for the order processing department. ▶

Learning about functions

A **function** is a calculation used in a formula. Each function includes the function name, a set of parentheses, and function arguments separated by commas and enclosed in parentheses. **Arguments** are information a function needs to perform a task. Figure 6-1 shows the anatomy of a Works function named AVG, used to calculate the average of a set of numbers contained in cells in a spreadsheet. AVG accepts one or more cells, referred to as a **reference** or a **range reference**, as arguments. Table 6-1 lists the categories of functions that you can use in the Spreadsheet. The related topic, "Planning to use functions," discusses what to consider when you prepare to use functions in a spreadsheet.

case Sue Ellen asked you to add more information to the Outdoor Designs product order spreadsheet. She and Frasier will use this information when evaluating product sales.

1. Make sure your Student Disk is in the appropriate drive, start Works, click the **Existing Documents tab,** and click **Open a document not listed here**

   The Open dialog box appears, showing the current folder's contents in the list box.

2. Open the spreadsheet **WKS 6-1.WKS** on your Student Disk, then save it as **Function Practice** in the My Works Files folder

   The Outdoor Designs Product Order spreadsheet opens in a window in the Spreadsheet tool. You are now ready to enhance your spreadsheet with functions. You add totals to row 14 for the Quantity and Subtotal columns using the SUM function. In rows 16 through 22, you add functions to calculate the current date, payment due date, average price per item in the order, and payment due if Outdoor Designs has extended credit to a store.

FIGURE 6-1: Anatomy of AVG function

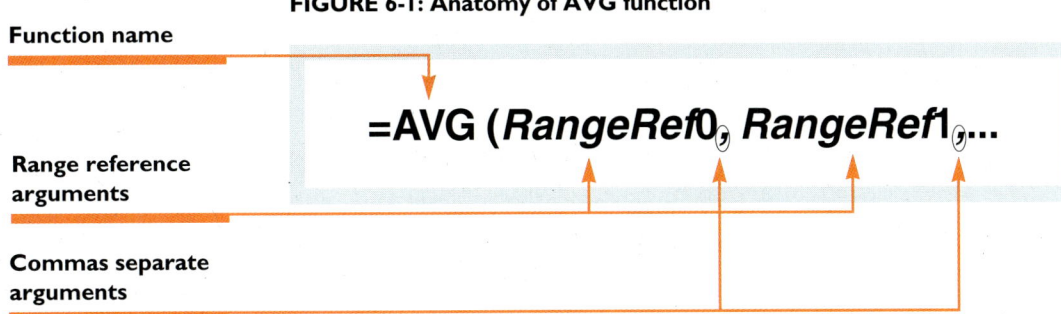

Function name

Range reference arguments

Commas separate arguments

Planning to use functions

Using functions in a spreadsheet takes advance planning, because many arguments used in functions come from spreadsheet cells. Because you can include spreadsheet ranges as arguments, organize your rows and columns when building a spreadsheet so you can select and include them in functions. Before you start creating formulas from scratch, also determine what results you want from your spreadsheet data and examine the list of Works functions in on-line Help to see if any can handle your calculations.

QUICK **TIP**

Many of the 75 Spreadsheet functions can also be used in the Database application.

TABLE 6-1: Categories of Spreadsheet functions

CATEGORY	USED FOR
Date and time	Calculations involving dates and times
Financial	Loan payments, appreciation, and depreciation
Statistical	Average, sum, variance, and standard deviation calculations
Mathematical	Mathematical and trigonometric calculations like those found on a scientific calculator
Informational	Determining if an error occurred in a calculation
Lookup and reference	Calculations involving tables of data
Logical	Calculations that produce the result TRUE or FALSE
Text	Comparing, converting, and reformatting text in cells

Using the SUM function

The most frequently used spreadsheet function, SUM totals all numbers and cell references included as function arguments. To add the SUM function to a formula, choose the Function command on the Insert menu, select the SUM function, then edit the function arguments in the formula bar. You can also sum selected cells by clicking the AutoSum button on the toolbar. For more information on shortcuts for creating formulas, see the related topic, "Building formulas with the Easy Calc command." **case** The Product Order form would not be complete without the total dollar amount and the total number of items to be shipped. Use the SUM function to total the Quantity and Subtotal columns.

1. Click cell **C14**, type **Totals,** press **[Enter]**, then click the **Right Align button** and the **Bold button** on the toolbar
   Works enters the label "Totals" in cell C14, then formats it with right alignment and boldface.

2. Click **cell D14**, then type =
   An equals sign (=) appears in the formula bar, indicating you're about to enter a formula.

3. Click **Insert** on the menu bar, then click **Function**
   The Insert Function dialog box opens. It contains Category radio buttons that let you select the type of function you want to insert, a Choose a function list box that lets you select a template for the function, and a Description window that describes the function highlighted in the Functions list box.

4. Click the **Statistical radio button**, then double-click **SUM(RangeRef0,RangeRef1,...)** in the Choose a function list box
   The Insert Function dialog box closes, and the SUM function template appears in the cell and in the formula bar. The template lists the arguments that the SUM function requires. You now replace these arguments with the actual cell references from the product order spreadsheet.

5. In the formula bar, select the text **RangeRef0,RangeRef1,...** and press **[Del]**
   Works deletes the arguments for the SUM function and displays =SUM( ) in the formula bar.

6. Select the range **D9** through **D13** in the spreadsheet, then press **[Enter]**
   After you select the five cells in the Quantity column, the range D9:D13 appears in the cell and in the formula bar as the argument in the SUM function. When you press [Enter], Works enters the formula in the spreadsheet, calculates the sum of cells D9 through D13, and displays the result, the number 13, in cell D14. Next you use AutoSum, an alternative method for calculating sums, to total the dollar amounts in the Subtotals column.

7. Click cell **E14**, then click the **AutoSum button** on the toolbar
   The AutoSum button automatically places the SUM function in the cell and in the formula bar. To complete the function, you simply need to select the range of numbers you want to total.

8. Select the range **E9** through **E13**, then press **[Enter]**
   Works enters the range in the SUM function and calculates and displays the result, 398.35, in cell E14. See Figure 6-2. Next format the cells containing the SUM formulas.

9. Click **cell D14** and click the **Center align button** on the toolbar, then click cell **E14** and click the **Currency button** on the toolbar, then click the **Save button**

FIGURE 6-2: Product order spreadsheet with column totals

- Function in formula bar
- AutoSum button
- Result calculated by SUM function

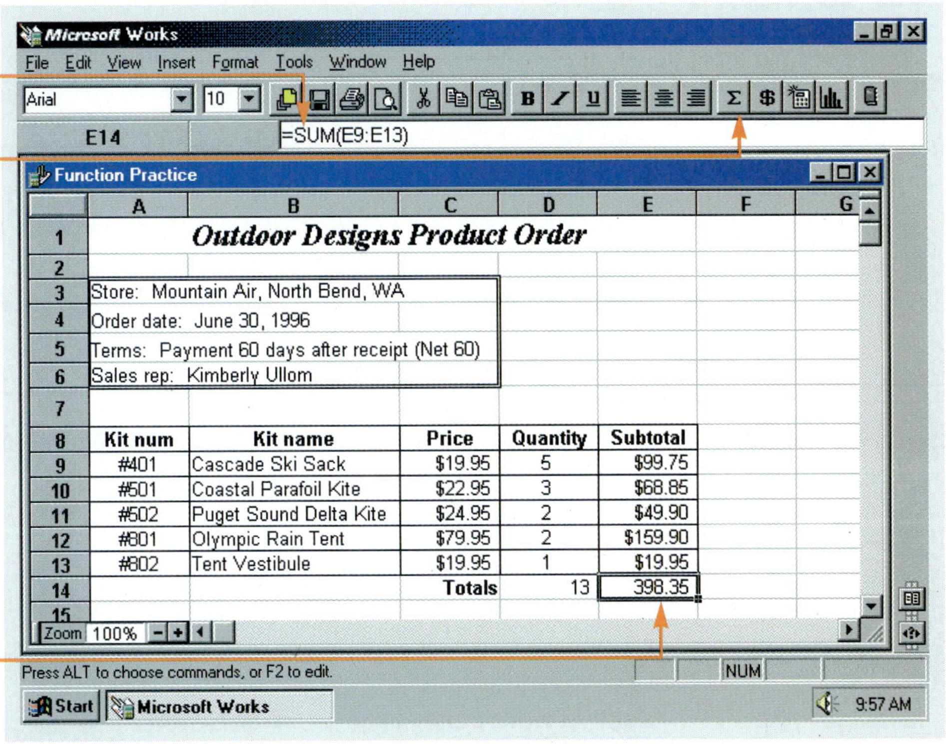

Building formulas with the Easy Calc command

If your formula is basic, you can build it quickly with the Easy Calc command. To use this timesaver, click Tools on the menu bar and then click Easy Calc, or click the Easy Calc button on the toolbar. The Easy Calc dialog box shown in Figure 6-3 opens. Simply click the button associated with the calculation you want and follow the on-screen instructions. Although you may need to drag the Easy Calc dialog box out of the way to click the cells in your formula, you won't need to type anything or worry about function syntax; Easy Calc handles it for you.

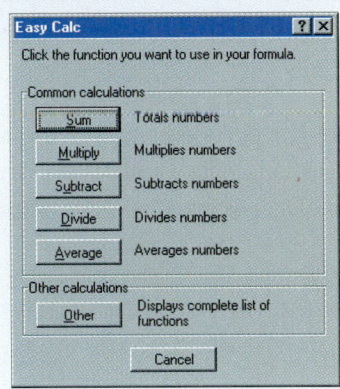

FIGURE 6-3: Easy Calc command

QUICK TIP

[Ctrl][M] is the keyboard equivalent of the AutoSum button.

Using date and time functions

The Works date and time functions let you display the current date and time in your spreadsheet and can help you calculate the time between important events. Table 6-2 lists the date and time functions with their respective arguments and briefly describes each. ▶case Sue Ellen asked you to add a formula to the product order spreadsheet that calculates payment due dates for the store placing the order. Use the NOW function to enter the current date in the spreadsheet, and use the Number command to format the date's style. Then enter a formula that uses the current date to calculate when payment is due.

1. Scroll down, if necessary, to see cell A16, click **cell A16**, type **Ship date:**, then press **[→]**
   Works enters the label "Ship date:" in cell A16 and highlights cell B16.

2. Type **=NOW( )** and press **[Enter]**
   Works enters the NOW function in the spreadsheet and places a serial number representing the current date and time in cell B16. Because NOW doesn't require any arguments, typing the function is easier than inserting it with the Function command. Works uses a special number called a **serial number** to store dates and times internally. To change the serial number to a date people can understand, you need to format it with the Number command.

3. Click **Format** on the menu bar, then click **Number**
   The Number tab of the Format Cells dialog box appears.

4. Click the **Date radio button**
   Today's date appears in seven different formats in the Options list box. You can convert the serial number to any of these formats.

5. Double-click the **fourth date format** in the list
   The Number dialog box closes, and today's date appears in cell B16, with the month spelled out, followed by the day and year. Now calculate the day when full payment is due from the store, assuming a 60-day payment grace period.

6. Click **cell A17**, type **Pmt due:**, then press **[→]**
   Works enters the label "Pmt due:" in cell A17 and highlights cell B17.

7. Type **=**, press **[↑]** to highlight cell **B16**, type **+60**, then press **[Enter]**
   The formula =B16+60 appears in the formula bar, and a date serial number appears in cell B17. Next format the serial number with the same date format you used in cell B16.

8. Click **Format** on the menu bar, click **Number**, click the **Date radio button**, then double-click the **fourth date format**
   The payment due date shown in Figure 6-4 appears in cell B17. Works determines the payment due date by adding 60 days (net 60) to the current date. Works considers the number of days in each month as it calculates.

9. Click the **Save button** 🖬 on the toolbar
   Your additions to the spreadsheet are saved.

FIGURE 6-4: Product order spreadsheet after date calculations

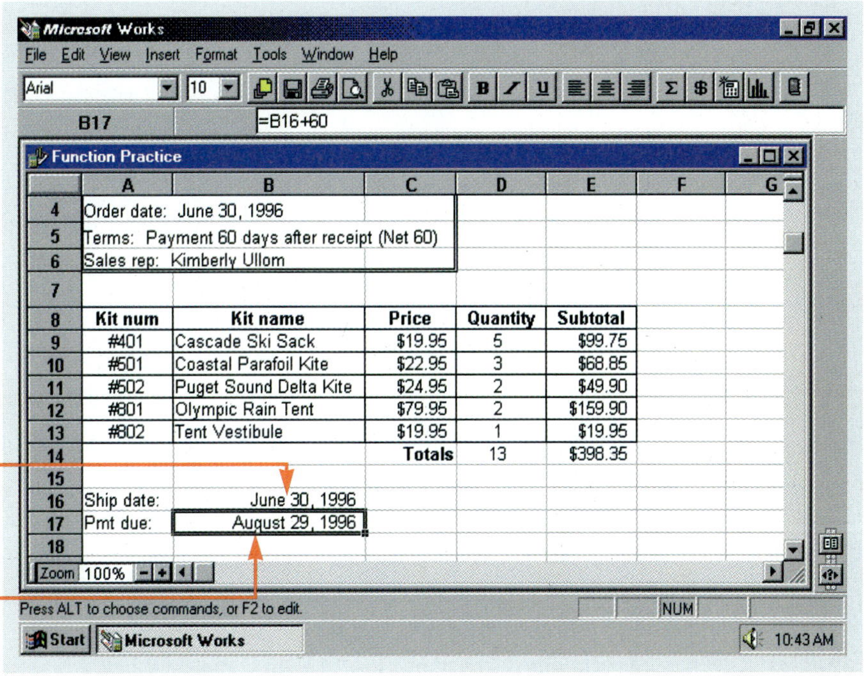

Result of NOW( ) function

Result of formula =B16+60

TABLE 6-2: Works date and time functions

FUNCTION	DISPLAYS
NOW( )	Serial number for the current date and time
DATE(*Year,Month,Day*)	Serial number of the specified date
DAY(*SerialNumber*)	Day of the month using the specified serial number
MONTH(*SerialNumber*)	Month using the specified serial number
YEAR(*SerialNumber*)	Year using the specified serial number
TIME(*Hour,Minute,Second*)	Serial number of the specified time
SECOND(*SerialNumber*)	Seconds using the specified serial number
MINUTE(*SerialNumber*)	Minutes using the specified serial number
HOUR(*SerialNumber*)	Hour using the specified serial number

The valid range for dates in Works 4.0 is January 1, 1900, through June 3, 2079.

Using statistical functions

Works' statistical functions let you assemble, classify, and tabulate numeric data in your spreadsheet. Table 6-3 lists the statistical functions with their respective arguments and briefly describes each function. For information about another useful set of functions, see the related topic, "Mathematical functions." **case** Sue Ellen and Frasier want to evaluate how order amount influences orders. You can use the AVG function to find the average dollar amount for each item in the product order.

1. Click **cell A19**, type **Ave order:**, and press **[→]**
   Works enters the label "Ave order:" in cell A19, and highlights cell B19.
2. Click **Insert** on the menu bar, then click **Function**
   The Insert Function dialog box opens.
3. Click the **Statistical radio button**, then double-click **AVG(RangeRef0,RangeRef1,...)**
   The Insert Function dialog box closes, and the AVG function template appears in the cell and in the formula bar. AVG determines the average of all arguments within the parentheses. You can specify numbers, cell names, or cell ranges.
4. Select the arguments **RangeRef0,RangeRef1,...** inside the parentheses, then press **[Del]**
   Works deletes the template part of the AVG function.
5. Select the range **E9** through **E13**, then press **[Enter]**
   Works enters the range E9:E13 as an argument in the AVG function in the formula bar. When you press [Enter], Works enters the formula in the spreadsheet, calculates the average of cells E9 through E13, and displays the number 79.67 in cell B19.
6. Click the **Currency button** 💲 on the toolbar
   Works formats the cell for currency, as shown in Figure 6-5.
7. Click the **Save button** 💾 to save your changes

TABLE 6-3: Works statistical functions

FUNCTION	DISPLAYS
AVG(*RangeRef0,RangeRef1,...*)	Average of the specified arguments
COUNT(*RangeRef0,RangeRef1,...*)	Number of arguments in the list
MAX(*RangeRef0,RangeRef1,...*)	Largest number in the list
MIN(*RangeRef0,RangeRef1,...*)	Smallest number in the list
STD(*RangeRef0,RangeRef1,...*)	Standard deviation of the arguments
SUM(*RangeRef0,RangeRef1,...*)	Total of the arguments
VAR(*RangeRef0,RangeRef1,...*)	Variance of the arguments

FIGURE 6-5: Product order spreadsheet with AVG function

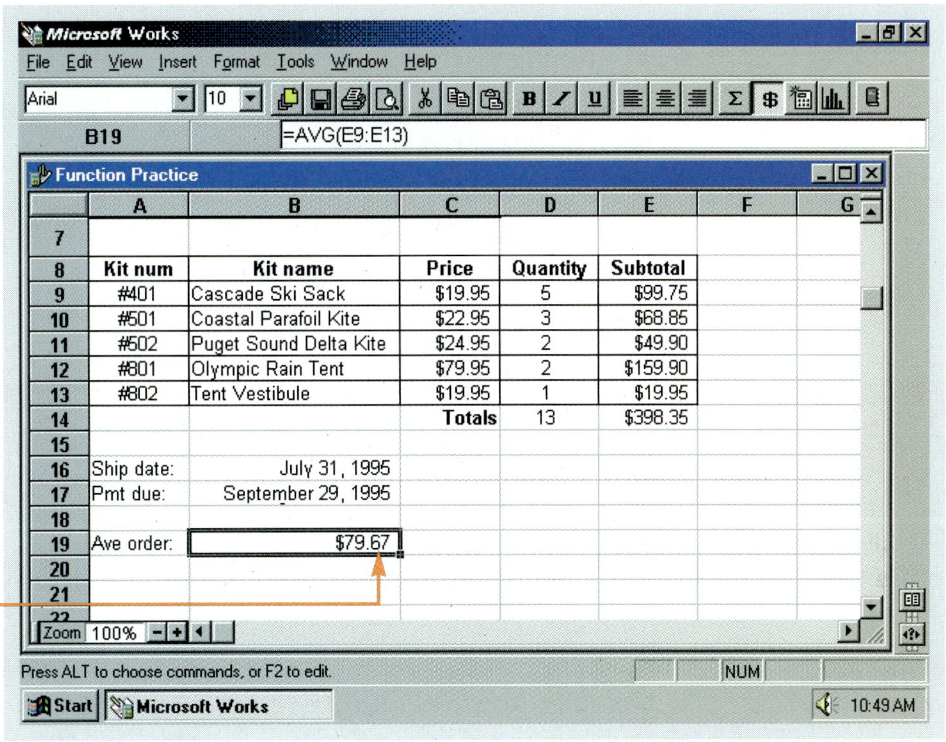

	A	B	C	D	E	F	G
7							
8	Kit num	Kit name	Price	Quantity	Subtotal		
9	#401	Cascade Ski Sack	$19.95	5	$99.75		
10	#501	Coastal Parafoil Kite	$22.95	3	$68.85		
11	#502	Puget Sound Delta Kite	$24.95	2	$49.90		
12	#801	Olympic Rain Tent	$79.95	2	$159.90		
13	#802	Tent Vestibule	$19.95	1	$19.95		
14			Totals	13	$398.35		
15							
16	Ship date:	July 31, 1995					
17	Pmt due:	September 29, 1995					
18							
19	Ave order:	$79.67					
20							
21							

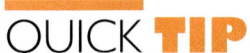

Result of AVG function

Mathematical functions

Another useful category of functions that produce numbers as results are the mathematical functions. These functions perform many mathematical and trigonometric calculations found on a standard scientific calculator, including ABS (absolute value), COS (cosine), LOG (logarithm), and SQRT (square root). Most mathematical functions take a single number as an argument and produce a single number as a result. For more information about using the mathematical functions in the Spreadsheet, search for "mathematical functions" in the Works Help Index.

QUICK TIP

You can include one function as an argument in another function if the result is compatible. For example, the formula =SUM(5, SQRT(9)) adds the number 5 to the square root (SQRT) of 9 and displays the result (8).

Using financial functions

The Works financial functions help you calculate loan payments, appreciation, and depreciation using spreadsheet data. Table 6-4 lists the most useful financial functions with their respective arguments and briefly describes each. See the related topic, "Using the Mortgage and Loan Analysis TaskWizard," for more information. **Case** Outdoor Designs extends credit to approved wholesale customers who want to pay for their purchases over a two-year period. Use the PMT function to determine what the monthly payment would be if the Mountain Air store chooses to finance its outstanding balance.

1. Click cell **A20**, type **24 pmts:**, and press **[→]**
   Works enters the label "24 pmts:" in cell A20 and highlights cell B20.

2. Click **Insert** on the menu bar, then click **Function**
   The Insert Function dialog box opens.

3. Click the **Financial radio button**, then double-click **PMT (Principal, Rate, Term)**
   The Insert Function dialog box closes, and the PMT function template appears in the cell and formula bar. PMT determines the periodic payment for a loan based on the principal loan amount, the interest rate charged, and the payment term (number of payments). You can specify the function arguments as numbers or cell references.

4. Select **Principal, Rate, Term** inside the parentheses, then press **[Del]**
   Works deletes the template arguments of the PMT function.

5. Click cell **E14**, then type **,** (a comma)
   Works enters the cell reference E14 (representing the amount financed) as the *Principal* argument in the formula bar. Next you'll specify the *Rate* and *Term* arguments, which must use the same time period, in this case months. To find the monthly rate, divide the annual rate, 19%, by 12, the number of months in a year.

6. Type **19%/12,24** and press **[Enter]**
   Works enters a 19% interest rate (divided by 12 months) and a 24-month payment term as arguments and then calculates the monthly payment. The result, 20.08027266, appears in cell B20. You want it formatted as currency.

7. Click the **Currency button** 💲 on the toolbar
   A monthly payment of $20.08 appears in the cell, as shown in Figure 6-6. Mountain Air would pay this amount monthly for two years if it chose to finance its purchase.

8. Click the **Save button** 💾 on the toolbar to save your changes

TABLE 6-4: Useful financial functions

FUNCTION	DISPLAYS
PMT(*Principal,Rate,Term*)	Periodic payment of an investment
FV(*Payment,Rate,Term*)	Future value of an investment
SLN(*Cost,Salvage,Life*)	Depreciation for an item using the straight-line method
SYD(*Cost,Salvage,Life,Period*)	Depreciation for an item using the sum-of-the-year's-digits method

FIGURE 6-6: Product order spreadsheet with the PMT function

Result of PMT function

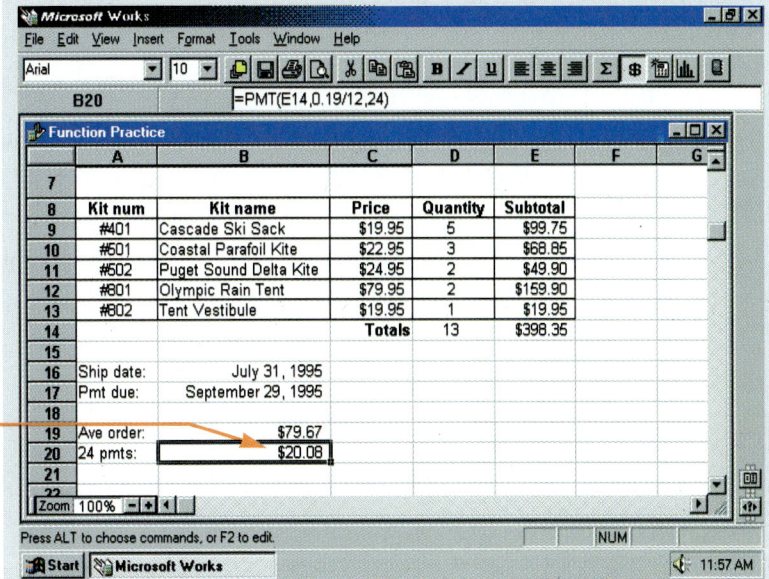

Using the Mortgage and Loan Analysis TaskWizard

Works includes a Mortgage/Loan Analysis TaskWizard to help you calculate principal and interest payments for home and auto loans. To use the TaskWizard, choose the New command from the File menu, and then click the TaskWizard Tab to display the TaskWizard categories. Click Business Management in the list box, double-click Mortgage/Loan Analysis, and then click Yes, Run the TaskWizard. The Mortgage/Loan Analysis TaskWizard opens with a window that explains your options. Double-click Standard Loan to display the basic loan spreadsheet, and then enter values in the Amount financed, Annual interest, and Duration of Loan cells, as shown in Figure 6-7.

FIGURE 6-7: Mortgage and Loan Analysis TaskWizard

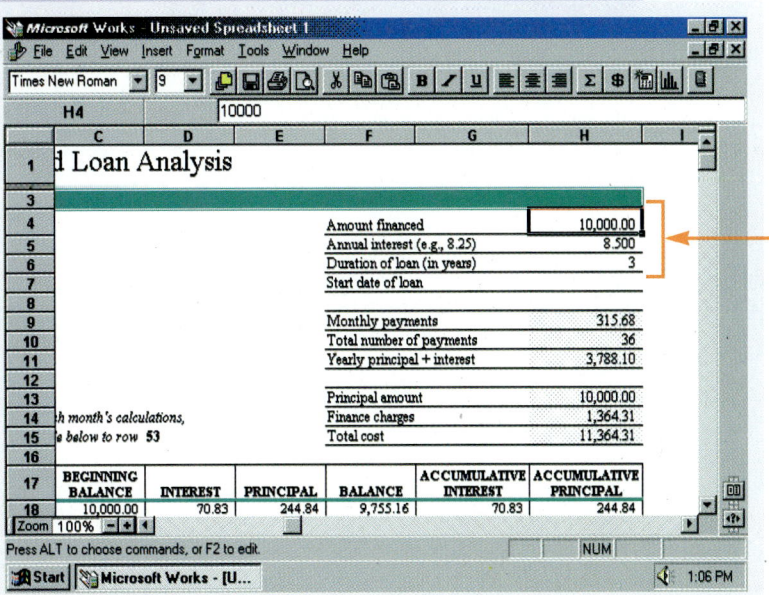

Enter loan data in these 3 cells

Using text functions

The Works text functions let you compare, convert, and manipulate the text in your spreadsheet. For example, you can use a text function to see if two pieces of text are the same or to convert all letters in a piece of text to lowercase. Table 6-5 lists the most useful text functions with their respective arguments and briefly describes each. ▶case To give the product order some visual interest, you can use the REPEAT function to repeat the words "Outdoor Designs" across the bottom of the spreadsheet.

1. Click cell **A22**

2. Click **Insert** on the menu bar, then click **Function**
   The Insert Function dialog box opens.

3. Click the **Text radio button**, then double-click **REPEAT(TextValue,Count)**
   Works closes the Insert Function dialog box and places the REPEAT function template in the cell and in the formula bar. REPEAT replicates text in a cell the number of times you specify. REPEAT requires a *TextValue* argument, which is the text you want repeated and which can be a word enclosed in quotation marks or a cell reference, and a *Count* argument, which is the number of times you want the *TextValue* repeated.

4. Select **TextValue,Count** inside the parentheses, then press **[Del]**
   Works deletes the template part of the REPEAT function. Now you replace it with the name "Outdoor Designs" and an asterisk, to form a decorative border across the bottom of the spreadsheet.

5. Type **"Outdoor Designs * "**,4, then press **[Enter]**
   Be sure to type the quotation marks and comma exactly as shown, and type a space on either side of the asterisk. Figure 6-8 shows the text "Outdoor Designs *" repeated four times at the bottom of the spreadsheet.

6. Click the **Save button** 🖬 on the toolbar to save your changes

FIGURE 6-8: Product order spreadsheet with REPEAT function

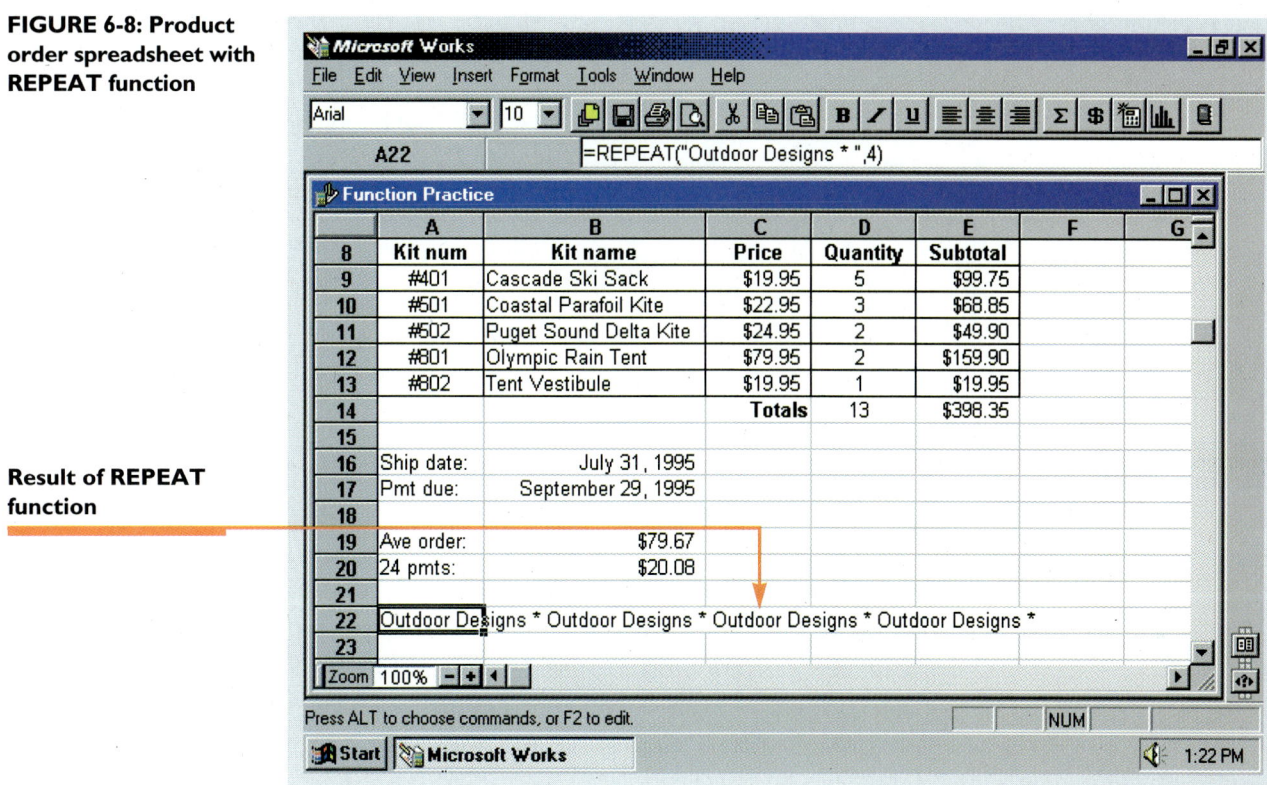

Result of REPEAT function

TABLE 6-5: Useful text functions

FUNCTION	DESCRIPTION
REPEAT(*TextValue,Count*)	Repeats text the specified number of times
UPPER(*TextValue*)	Capitalizes every letter of the specified text
LOWER(*TextValue*)	Makes every letter of the specified text lowercase
PROPER(*TextValue*)	Capitalizes the first letter of each word in the specified text
TRIM(*TextValue*)	Removes blank spaces from the specified text
VALUE(*TextValue*)	Converts the specified label to a number
LENGTH(*TextValue*)	Displays the number of characters in the specified text
MID(*TextValue,Offset,Length*)	Extracts one or more characters from *TextValue*

QUICK TIP

The UPPER, LOWER, and PROPER functions help you standardize your spreadsheet's appearance and are especially useful for formatting arguments in other functions.

Sorting rows and printing

The Sort command sorts rows in the spreadsheet by comparing values in one or more columns. You can sort rows alphabetically or numerically, and in ascending or descending order. See the related topic, "Sorting by more than one column," for more information about using multiple sort criteria. ▶case You added to the product order spreadsheet all the information Sue Ellen requested. Before you print a final copy, use the Sort Rows command to organize the information so that the lowest-priced item is listed first and the highest-priced item is listed last.

1. **Select rows 9 through 13**
   Works highlights rows 9 through 13.

2. **Click Tools on the menu bar, then click Sort; click OK to close the First time help dialog box if it opens**
   The Sort dialog box opens. It contains a Sort By list box to let you pick the column to be compared in the sort, Ascending and Descending radio buttons to let you choose the order of the sort, and two radio buttons that indicate the presence of a header in the selection. First move the dialog box out of the way, so you can see the selected rows clearly. To move a dialog box, drag its title bar.

3. **Drag the Sort dialog box title bar down until the dialog box is near the bottom of the screen**

4. **Click the Sort By list box, click the list box down arrow, and then click Column C**
   You indicated you want to use column C as your primary sort criteria (Price) for the sort. Your screen should look like Figure 6-9.

5. **Click Sort**
   The Sort dialog box closes and Works sorts rows 9 through 13 according to kit price, as shown in Figure 6-10.

6. **Click the Save button 💾 on the toolbar**
   Works saves your changes on disk, and you are ready to print a final copy of the product order spreadsheet for Sue Ellen's review.

7. **Click the Print button 🖨 on the toolbar**
   Turn on your printer first, if necessary. After a few moments the final product order spreadsheet emerges from your printer, ready for the order processing department. Congratulations! You completed another useful business document and finish working in Works for the day.

8. **Click File on the menu bar, then click Exit Works**
   The Function Practice spreadsheet and the Works program both close.

FIGURE 6-9: Sorting rows with the Sort command

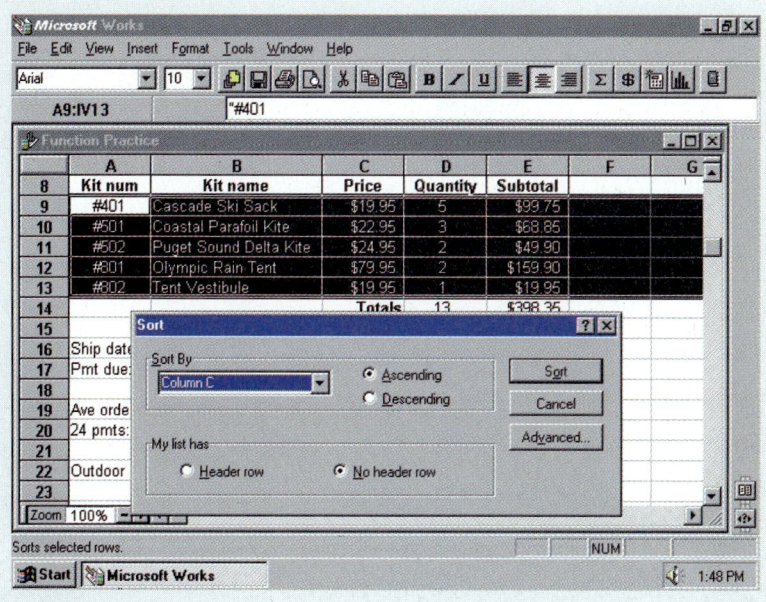

FIGURE 6-10: Order information sorted by kit price (column C)

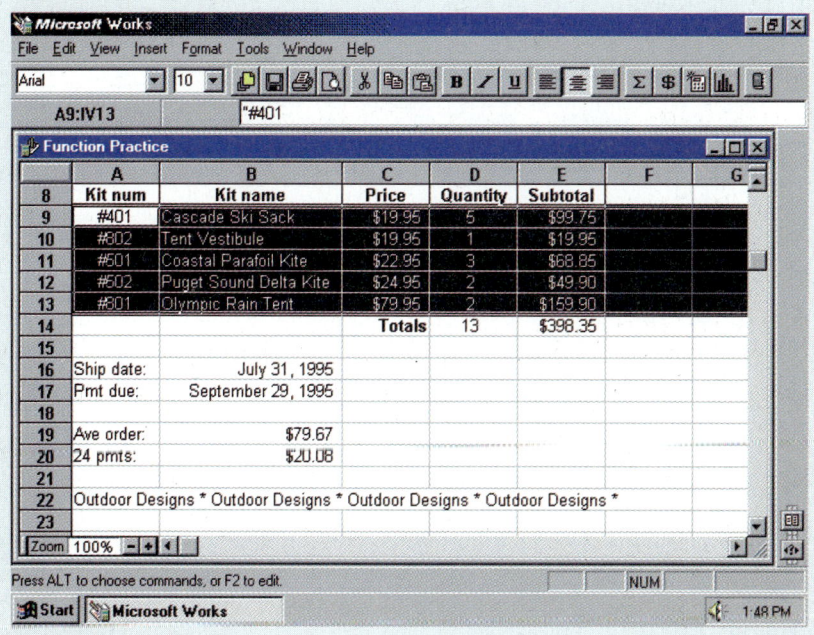

Sorting by more than one column

If more than one row contains the same value in the column you are sorting by, the sort results in a "tie." For example, if you sort by Sales Region, more than one row may list the same sales region. To break ties, you can sort by more than one column. Click the Advanced button in the Sort dialog box, and use the Then By list boxes to specify additional columns for the sort. You can sort by up to three columns this way.

You can sort the rows in your spreadsheet any number of times, depending on the order in which you want your information presented. To undo a sort's results, choose the Undo command from the Edit menu.

TASK REFERENCE

TASK	MOUSE/BUTTON	MENU	KEYBOARD
Add currency formatting to totals	Click [$]	Click Format, Number, Currency	
Create formulas with Easy Calc	Click [📆]	Click Tools, Easy Calc	[Alt][T], [E]
Format serial numbers as dates		Click Format, Number, Date	
Insert a function in a formula		Click Insert, Function	[Alt][I], [F]
Sort spreadsheet rows		Click Tools, Sort	[Alt][T], [R]
Total a range of cells with AutoSum	Click the cell that will contain the total, then click [Σ]		[Ctrl][M]

CONCEPTS REVIEW

Match components of the formula =SUM(5,SQRT(9)) with their descriptions.

1. SUM
2. 5
3. SQRT(9)
4. =
5. ,

a. Symbol used to separate arguments in functions
b. Function name
c. Function used as argument in function
d. Number used as argument in function
e. Symbol indicating the following text is a formula

Select the best answer from the list of choices.

6. Which answer best describes a function argument?
   a. A number, cell reference, or expression that helps a function make its calculation
   b. The result of a function calculation
   c. The abbreviated name of the function
   d. The parentheses following the function name in the formula bar

7. Which answer best describes the purpose of the statistical functions?
   a. Functions used for loan payments, appreciation, and depreciation
   b. Functions used for average, sum, variance, and standard deviation calculations
   c. Functions used for mathematical and trigonometric calculations
   d. Functions involving tables of date and time calculations

8. Many Spreadsheet functions can also be used in which Works application?
   a. Communications
   b. Word Processor
   c. WordArt
   d. Database

9. Which Spreadsheet function can you access through the toolbar?
   a. SUM function
   b. PMT function
   c. AVG function
   d. REPEAT function

10. Which menu do you open to execute the Function command?
    a. Edit
    b. Format
    c. Insert
    d. Tools

11. What answer does Works calculate for the formula =SUM(5,3,1)?
    a. 7
    b. 8
    c. 9
    d. 10

12. What is a function serial number?
    a. A special number used to identify the function a result comes from
    b. A special number Works uses to store dates and time internally
    c. The time difference between your time zone and Greenwich Mean Time
    d. The column number of the highlighted cell

13. What type of argument do you use with the NOW( ) function?
    a. A text string
    b. A cell reference
    c. A cell range
    d. The NOW( ) function doesn't have arguments.

14. How do you format date and time serial numbers so people can understand them?
    a. With the Number command
    b. With the NOW( ) function
    c. With the Alignment command
    d. With the SUM button on the toolbar

15. What does E9:E12 represent in the formula =SUM(E9:E12)?

    a. A range of five cells

    b. A range of four cells

    c. Two cell references

    d. The average of cells E9 and E12

16. Which of these functions would you use to display the largest number in a cell range?

    a. The AVG function

    b. The STD function

    c. The MAX function

    d. The MIN function

17. How would Works evaluate the formula =SUM(2,SQRT(16))?

    a. 2

    b. 4

    c. 6

    d. 8

18. What does the Rate argument represent in the PMT function?

    a. The interest charged

    b. The principal loan amount

    c. The number of payments

    d. The monthly payment

19. What does the formula =REPEAT("**", 2) display?

    a. **

    b. ***

    c. ** **

    d. ****

20. What is the purpose of the Advanced button in the Sort dialog box?

    a. To sort rows in ascending order

    b. To customize your printer

    c. To add numbers with the SUM function

    d. To let you specify additional columns to sort on and resolve "ties" in the sort

SKILLS REVIEW

1. Start Works and open the file WKS 6-2 on your Student Disk.

   a. Start Works.

   b. Click the Existing Documents tab in the Works Task Launcher dialog box.

   c. Click Open a document not listed here, and place your Student Disk in the appropriate drive.

   d. In the Open dialog box, click Look in, then click 3½ Floppy (A:).

   e. Double-click WKS 6-2 to open the spreadsheet in Works.

   f. Use the Save As command to save the file as August Sales in the My Works Files folder on your Student Disk.

2. Use the SUM function to total the Amount column and calculate the Monthly Total.

   a. Click cell D15, then type "=" (an equals sign).

   b. Click Insert on the menu bar, then click Function.

   c. Click the Statistical radio button under Category.

   d. Double-click SUM(RangeRef0,RangeRef1,...).

   e. Delete the arguments between the parentheses.

   f. Select cells D5 through D13, then press [Enter].

   g. Format cell D15 for Currency with two decimal places.

   h. Widen column D so that the Monthly Total number fits.

   i. Click the Save button to save your changes.

3. Look at the Order Date entries, then calculate the payment date considering a 45-day payment grace period.

   a. Click cell E5.

   b. Click Format on the menu bar, then click Number. What format does the cell have?

   c. Click OK.

   d. Click cell F5 and enter the formula =E5+45, then press [Enter].

   e. Select cells F5 through F13.

   f. Click Edit on the menu bar, then click Fill Down.

   g. With F5 through F13 still selected, click Format on the menu bar, then click Number.

h. Click the Date radio button, and then click the first data format.

i. Click OK to format the serial numbers as dates.

4 Use the AVG function to determine the average order amount for the month.

a. Scroll down until you see cell D17.

b. Click cell D17.

c. Click Insert on the menu bar, then click Function.

d. Click the Statistical radio button.

e. Double-click the AVG(RangeRef0,RangeRef1,...).

f. Delete the arguments inside the parentheses.

g. Select cells D5 through D13, and press Enter.

h. Click the Currency button to format the cells in currency format.

i. Click the Save button on the toolbar to save your changes.

5 Use the PMT function to determine monthly payments for the orders, using a 14% annual interest rate and a 6-month term.

a. Click cell G5.

b. Click Insert on the menu bar, then click Function.

c. Click the Financial radio button.

d. Double-click PMT(Principal,Rate,Term).

e. Delete the arguments in parentheses.

f. Click cell D5, then type ",14%/12,6" and press Enter.

g. Click the Currency button to add currency formatting.

h. Select cells G5 through G13.

i. Click Edit on the menu bar, then click Fill Down.

6 Use the REPEAT function to repeat the phrase "August Sales" across row 2.

a. Click cell A2.

b. Click Insert on the menu bar, then click Function.

c. Click the Text radio button.

d. Double-click REPEAT(TextValue,Count).

e. Delete the arguments between the parentheses.

f. Type "August Sales ** ",4" between the parentheses, and press Enter.

g. Click the Save button on the toolbar to save your changes.

7 Use the Sort Rows command to sort the sales information by Region and then by Amount.

a. Select rows 5 through 13.

b. Click Tools on the menu bar, then click Sort.

c. Click Column B in the Sort By list box to specify the Region column.

d. Click the Advanced button.

e. Click the first Then By list box.

f. Click Column D to specify the Amount column.

g. Click Sort.

h. Verify the sorting order in rows 5 through 13. (The spreadsheet should be sorted by Region and then by Amount.)

i. Click the Print button to print a copy of the final spreadsheet.

j. Save your changes and exit Works.

INDEPENDENT CHALLENGE 1

The Wacky Words card company is thinking about raising the prices of its cards and wants to know how this change will affect its bottom line. The sales director thinks the price of cards should jump from $1.50 to $2.25 but estimates that orders will drop by 15% as buyers adjust to the new pricing. Create a spreadsheet that demonstrates the effect of the proposed pricing change on gross income.

To complete this independent challenge:

1. Open a new spreadsheet and save it as Card Price Hike in the My Works Files folder on your Student Disk. Place the label "Price Increase Analysis" in cell A1.

2. In cells A3, B3, and C3, create the column labels "Cards Produced," "Price," and "Sales." Widen column A so that the labels fit comfortably.

3. In rows 4 and 5, enter card quantities of 5000 and 10000, each at a price of $1.50. Add formulas to cells C4 and C5 that compute estimated sales at existing prices.

4. In rows 6 and 7, enter quantities of 4250 and 8500 (85% of the existing levels), priced at $2.25. Add formulas to cells C6 and C7 that compute estimated sales at the new levels.

5. Format B4 through C7 for Currency with two decimal places. Widen the columns if necessary.

6. Which price level generates more money? Print the Price Card Hike spreadsheet and save your changes.

INDEPENDENT CHALLENGE 2

The veterinary clinic you work for, Palmer's Pet Hospital, decided to sell a small collection of pet products and supplies. Your boss asked you to prepare a price list based on the information given below.

To complete this independent challenge:

1. Run the Price List TaskWizard in the Business Management category of the TaskWizards tab. Select the Standard Price List template.

2. Customize the price list with the name, address, and phone number of the clinic:

   Palmer's Pet Hospital
   32 North Street
   West Springs, CO 80502
   303-555-3433

3. Fill in the ordering information with the hours, phone number, and fax number:

   9-5, Monday through Saturday
   303-555-3433
   303-555-3434

4. Save the price list as Pet Supply List in the My Works Files folder on your Student Disk.

5. Add prices to the list using the information in the table.

Item Number	Name	Price
101	Nylon Dog Bone	$ 7.95
102	Dog Dish	$19.95
103	Pet Blanket	$24.95
201	Cat Collar	$ 9.95
205	Fish Food	$ 6.95
301	Cat Toys (misc.)	$ 6.95
401	Dog Leash	$12.95

6. Print the spreadsheet and then save your changes before closing the file.

INDEPENDENT CHALLENGE 3

A local art gallery, working with travel guides from Outdoor Designs, is marketing guided outdoor adventures—including helicopter skiing, orienteering, hang gliding, ballooning, trail riding, and backpacking. Outdoor Designs assigned you the task of reviewing last year's trip data to determine the most popular trips, how long it takes to save for trips, and other variables.

To complete this independent challenge:

1 Open the file WKS 6-2a on your Student Disk. This file contains the data on the number of trips sold for each sport by month for 1995. Save the file as Art Trips 1996 in the My Works Files folder on your Student Disk.

2 Use statistical functions to analyze the data. Use the SUM function to find the total number of trips taken each month. Enter these totals in cells B11 through M11. Also use the SUM function to enter a grand total in cell N11.

3 Use the MAX function to identify the most popular trip, based on the totals in cells B14 through B19. Enter the label "Most Popular" in cell A21 and the function in cell B21.

4 Use financial functions for estimating costs. Use the TERM function to find how long it will take to save $1,950 for a balloon vacation in France if you put $150 per month into a savings account earning 4 1/2% interest compounded monthly. Enter the label "Save 150/month for" in cell A22 and the function in cell B22. (You can use Works on-line Help to learn about the TERM function. The *Payment* is the amount you save each month, *Rate* is the percentage rate, and *Future Value* is the total amount you want to save.) Format B22 for Fixed format with 1 decimal place. You can add the word "months" in cell C22.

5 Use the PMT function to find the monthly payment if you borrowed the $1950 at 14% annual rate with 12 months to repay. Enter the label "Monthly Payment" in cell A23 and the function in cell B23.

6 Print the spreadsheet and then save your changes before closing the file.

INDEPENDENT CHALLENGE 4

Joel Rubin of The Steak Pit is creating a spreadsheet to analyze business expansion with the addition of another restaurant. He started the spreadsheet but wants you to complete it.

To complete this independent challenge:

1 Open the file WKS 6-3 on your Student Disk. Save the file as Expansion Analysis in the My Works Files folder on your Student Disk.

2 Use the text function REPEAT to add a decorative heading across row 2. Enter the function in A2. The text "— The Steak Pit —" should repeat 3 times. Format cell A2 for 12-point bold text.

3 Use the NOW function to add the current date to cell B4. Format the cell for Date format using the first date option.

4 Use the SUM function to calculate totals for each year in row 10. Format the cells for Currency with no decimal places.

5 Use the AVG function to calculate the yearly average amount in cell B13. Format the cell for Currency with no decimal places.

6 In cell B14, enter a formula to calculate the loan amount, which is half the amount needed to cover costs in the first year. The formula is =B11/2. Then use the PMT function to calculate the monthly payment for the loan, using a 12% annual interest rate and a 60-month (5-year) term.

7 Print the spreadsheet and then save your changes before closing the file.

VISUALWORKSHOP

Create the spreadsheet in Figure 6-11 using commands and techniques you learned in this chapter. Save the spreadsheet as Playhouse Analysis in the My Works Files folder on your Student Disk.

FIGURE 6-11

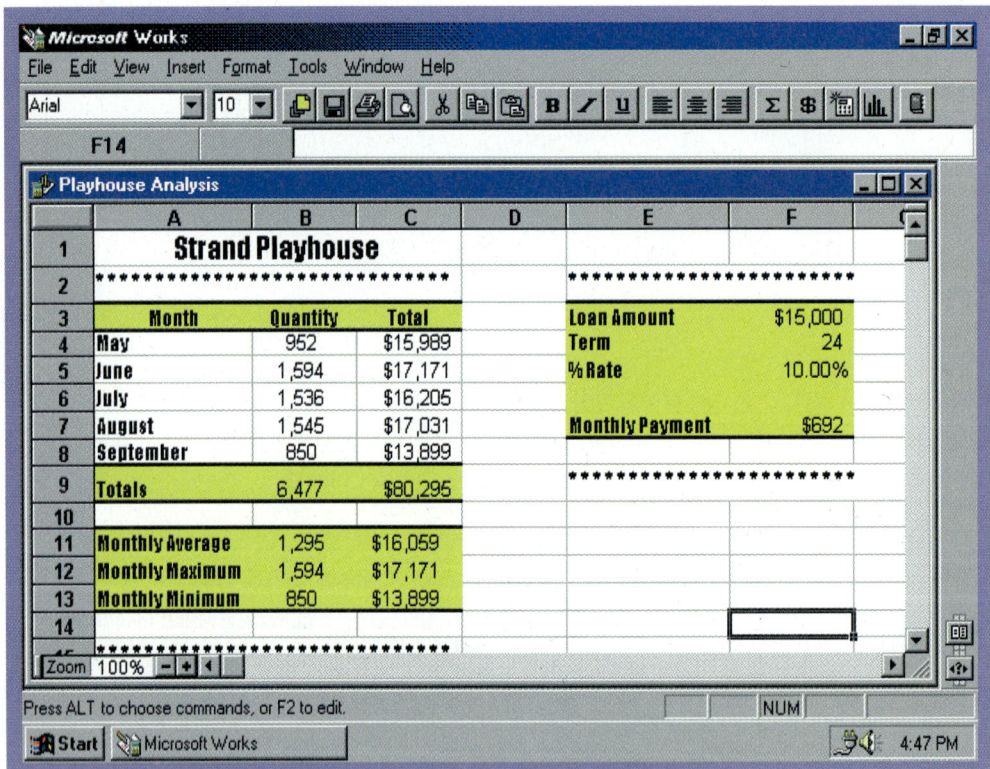

UNIT 7

OBJECTIVES

▶ Plan a chart

▶ Create a chart

▶ Change the chart type

▶ Add a subtitle and gridlines

▶ Change fonts and colors

▶ Paste a spreadsheet table into the Word Processor

▶ Paste a chart into the Word Processor

Creating CHARTS WITH THE SPREADSHEET

In this unit you'll learn to display spreadsheet information graphically using charts. A chart transforms data into a picture. If a picture is worth a thousand words, then a well-organized chart may be worth at least a thousand numbers. A chart can present the number of kite kits sold in a month or the amount of water consumed each summer, in a format that's easy to understand and remember. **case** In this unit you will create a chart to graphically show the Outdoor Designs regional sales figures for the first and second quarters of 1996. Then you'll customize the chart using Outdoor Designs information. Finally you'll paste the spreadsheet and the chart in a sales memo in the Word Processor and print a final copy to distribute to the sales force. ▶

Planning a chart

Displaying Data as a Chart

The Works Chart accessory is designed to perform several different charting operations. Figure 7-1 shows the eight chart types available in Works, and Table 7-1 describes the most popular use for each chart type. For more information, view the CourseHelp called "Displaying Data as a Chart" before completing the steps below.

case Before you create a chart, you need to do some general planning. The steps in this lesson show the kinds of questions you need to ask as you plan to create Outdoor Designs regional sales chart for Sue Ellen, as well as when you plan future charting projects.

- **Plan your presentation**
  What data are you including in the spreadsheet? How will the data fit in the report or memo you're creating? What data would you like to highlight with a chart? For example, the sales and marketing group will use the chart that you create for Sue Ellen to evaluate how business is growing and to determine which regions need special attention.

- **Determine the chart type**
  Consider the eight chart types shown in Figure 7-1 and described in Table 7-1. What chart type will best represent data you want to include? Do you want to show one category of data or make comparisons between two categories? Several chart types are appropriate for the regional sales figures; however, Sue Ellen's preference for 3-D bar charts may influence your final decision.

- **Design the spreadsheet so Works will create the chart you want**
  Group your data into logical rows and columns. As you'll learn in the next lesson, Works uses the spreadsheet row and column labels to create labels and other identifiers for the chart. The spreadsheet data from Sue Ellen is likely to be designed appropriately since she uses many of her own spreadsheets for charts.

Now you're ready to choose the chart type you want, create the chart, and edit it.

You'll start the Chart accessory and create your first chart in the next lesson.

FIGURE 7-1: Works chart types

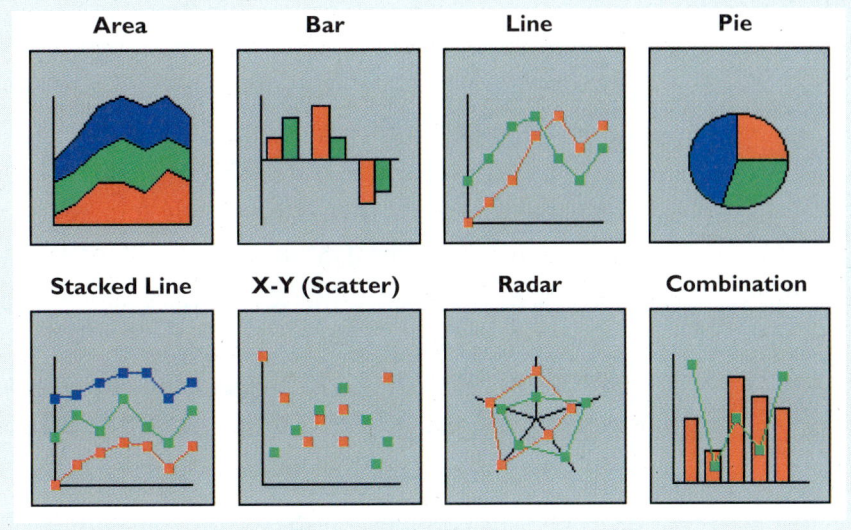

TABLE 7-1: Chart types available in Works and common use of each

CHART TYPE	DESCRIPTION
Area	Shows relative importance of values over a period of time
Bar	Compares categories of data to each other
Line	Shows trends by category over a period of time
Pie	Describes relationship of the parts to the whole
Stacked line	Shows relationship of values in each category to total in that category
X-Y (scatter chart)	Shows relationship between two kinds of related data
Radar	Shows changes in data or data frequency relative to a center point
Combination	Includes both line and bar graphs in single chart

In addition to the eight chart types Figure 7-1 shows, Works provides 3-D versions of the area, bar, line, and pie charts.

Creating a chart

Creating a Works chart is simple. You open the spreadsheet file that contains the data you want to chart, select just those cells that contain relevant data, and then plot the data by choosing one of the eight chart types in the Chart accessory. **case** The spreadsheet you will use to create the Outdoor Designs sales chart contains sales figures for the past two quarters for the four sales territories in the United States: Northeast, South, Midwest, and West. Sue Ellen provided a file containing sales data, so you have everything you need to create the chart she requested.

1. Start Works, click the **Existing Documents tab** in the Works Task Launcher, and click **Open a document not listed here**
   Works launches and the Open dialog box opens.

2. Open the spreadsheet **WKS 7-1** on your Student Disk, then save the spreadsheet as **Sales Chart** in the **My Works Files folder** on your Student Disk
   Take a moment to review the sales data in the spreadsheet. In the next step you select data for the bar chart.

3. Select cells **A5** through **C9**
   Works highlights the cell range A5:C9 in the spreadsheet, as Figure 7-2 shows. Works will use this information to create the bar chart. Notice that you selected the row and column labels, but not the column totals.

4. Click the **New Chart button** on the toolbar; if a First-time Help dialog box opens, click **OK** to close it
   The New Chart dialog box opens. It includes a selection of chart types that you can choose from; a Finishing touch area that lets you add a title, border, or gridlines to the chart; and a preview window where you can experiment with different chart styles. Bar chart is the default chart type, and its default format options are fine for your report, so you won't customize the chart now.

5. Press **[Tab]** and type **Outdoor Designs—Regional Sales 1996** in the Title text box, then click **OK**
   The dialog box closes and a new window presents the sales data bar chart shown in Figure 7-3. The Chart Accessory's interface elements appear, including a new menu bar and toolbar, and the title bar identifies the new chart as Chart1. Notice that the region names from the spreadsheet are on the chart's x-axis and that the sales amounts from the spreadsheet are on the chart's y-axis. Sales data are graphically displayed in the chart; the red and green bars correspond to the first quarter and second quarter, respectively.

   Refer to Figure 7-3 for a moment to identify the Chart Accessory's elements and the sales data chart.

6. Click the **Save button** on the toolbar
   Works saves the bar chart as part of the Sales Chart file. (Works does not save Charts separately, but saves them as part of the spreadsheet file.)

FIGURE 7-2: Chart data selected

New Chart button

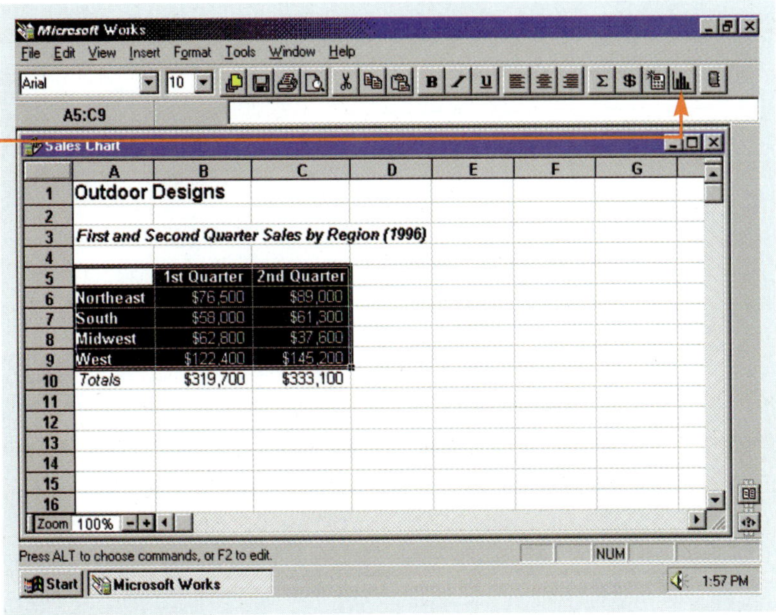

FIGURE 7-3: Chart accessory and bar chart in a window

Title

Y-Axis

X-Axis

Legend

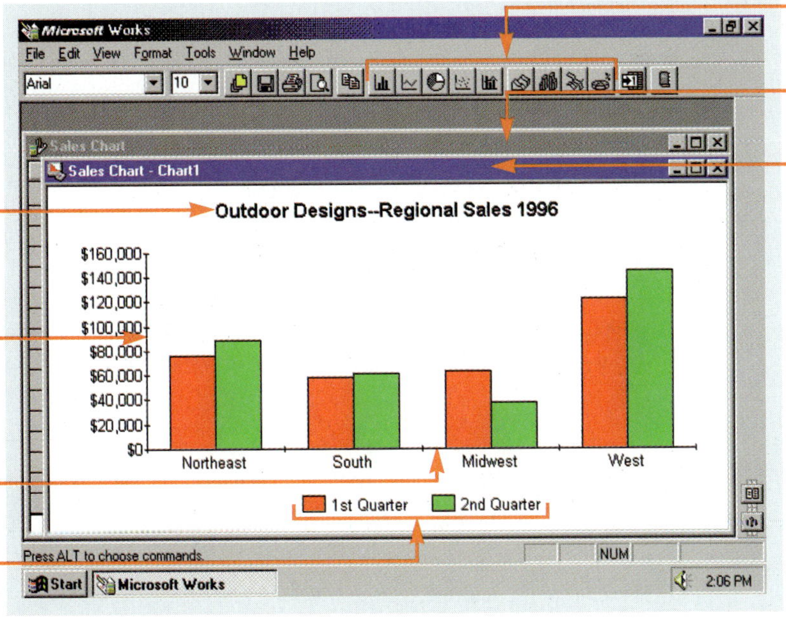

Charting buttons

Spreadsheet window

Chart Window

TABLE 7-2: Common charting terms

TERM	DEFINITION
X-axis	Horizontal line in a chart containing a series of related values from the spreadsheet
Y-axis	Vertical line in a chart containing a series of related values from the spreadsheet
Labels	Text describing data in the chart
Legend	Box explaining what labels, colors, and patterns in the chart mean
Gridlines	Horizontal and vertical lines connecting to the x-axis and y-axis

Click the Help button in the lower-right corner of your screen for useful information about menus and commands in the Chart accessory.

Changing the chart type

The Chart accessory's toolbar includes nine different charting buttons. You can change the chart type by clicking one of the charting buttons or by picking a new chart in the Chart Type dialog box. In addition, you can display each chart type in one of several variations, depending on how you want to present the information. Table 7-3 describes the different charting buttons on the toolbar. ▶**case** Experiment with some different chart types to add flair to your presentation. Use the 3-D Bar Chart button to change the appearance of your Outdoor Designs chart.

1. **Click the 3-D Bar Chart button** on the toolbar, then click the **Variations tab** in the Chart Type dialog box
   The Variations tab of the Chart Type dialog box shown in Figure 7-4 appears. It contains six different 3-D Bar chart styles. Experiment to see what these variations look like. First, try using the second style, a stacked bar chart.

2. **Double-click the second style**
   Works transforms the chart in the window into a 3-D bar chart. Because you chose a stacked bar chart, sales numbers for the two quarters are stacked together in segmented bars. This chart highlights the West region's leadership in year-to-date sales, with combined sales totaling between $250,000 and $300,000. Try another chart type, this time using the preview in the Chart Type dialog box to determine whether it is a good choice.

3. **Click the 3-D Bar Chart button** again, click the **Variations tab**, and then click the **second style**
   The preview area displays your chart as a 3-D bar chart with the second quarter data series (green bars) behind the first quarter data series (red bars). You can see that because sales in the Midwest declined, the Midwest bar for the first quarter partially obscures the second quarter bar. Side-by-side bars for both quarters present the data better, so restore the chart to the first style.

4. **Double-click the first style**
   The dialog box closes and the chart in the window is the 3-D bar chart shown in Figure 7-5. The first and second quarter sales figures display as separate bars, so you can compare each quarter's results as well as overall results. This chart emphasizes that each region experienced growth in sales except the Midwest region, whose sales declined by approximately 40%. The sales and marketing group will probably find this trend *very* interesting.

5. **Click the Save button** on the toolbar to save your changes to the bar chart

FIGURE 7-4: Variations for 3-D bar charts

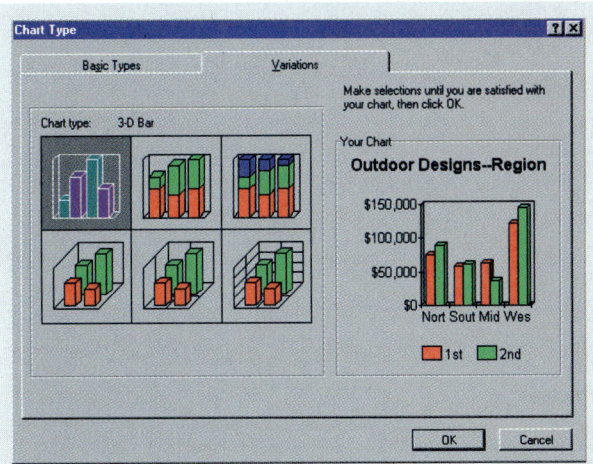

FIGURE 7-5: Sales chart

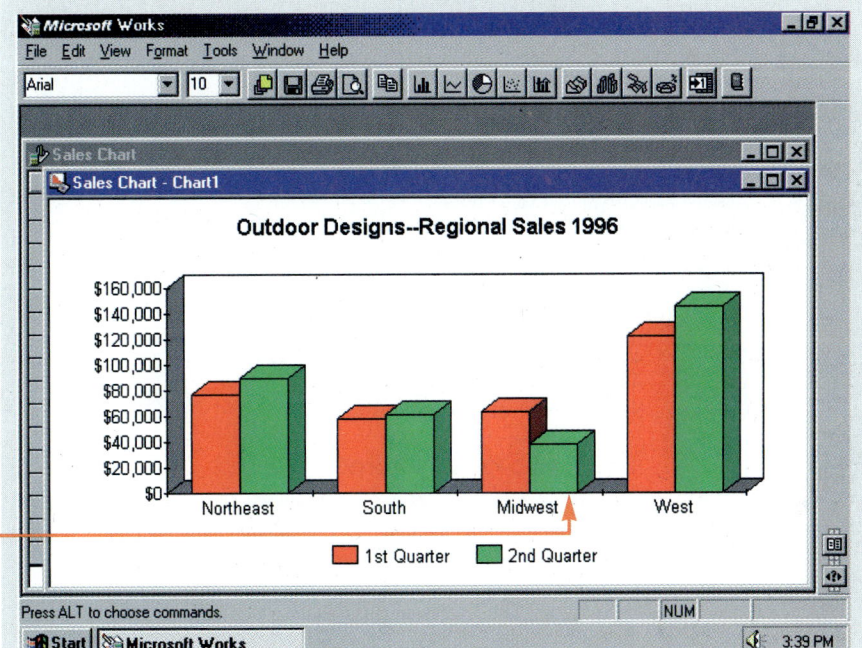

This bar shows a 40% decline in sales

TABLE 7-3: Charting buttons on Chart Accessory toolbar

ICON	CREATES	ICON	CREATES
	Bar chart		3-D area chart
	Line chart		3-D bar chart
	Pie chart		3-D line chart
	Scatter chart		3-D pie chart
	Combination (Mixed) chart		

The Basic Types tab in the Chart Type dialog box lets you try out other chart types with the data you select. Don't be afraid to experiment; you can always go back to your first choice.

Adding a subtitle and gridlines

Now that you have created a chart in the spreadsheet, you can customize it. Works lets you add subtitles and axis titles to clarify the chart data. You can also format each axis, adding gridlines, changing the placement of tickmarks, controlling label placement, and so on. You can also change the chart legend; see the related topic, "Changing the chart legend," for more information. **case** To clarify data in the regional sales data chart, add a subtitle and gridlines. These changes will also make the chart match the standard 3-D Bar chart style used at Outdoor Designs.

1. **Click Edit on the menu bar, then click Titles**
   The Titles dialog box opens. It contains text boxes for a chart title, a subtitle, a label for the x-axis, a label for the y-axis, and a label for the right vertical axis (not applicable in this situation). In the Chart title text box, Works has highlighted the chart title you entered earlier.

2. **Press [Tab], type First and Second Quarters in the Subtitle text box, then click OK**
   The subtitle "First and Second Quarters" appears below the chart title. Next you add horizontal and vertical gridlines to the chart.

3. **Click Format on the menu bar, then click Horizontal (X) Axis**
   The Horizontal Axis dialog box shown in Figure 7-6 appears. It contains options for controlling the frequency of x-axis labels, the position of axis labels, the display of a gridline between items on the x-axis, the appearance of droplines in area charts, and whether or not the x-axis appears.

4. **Click the Show gridlines check box, then click OK**
   Gridlines appear between the four regions listed along the x-axis. If you're confused because vertical gridlines come from the Horizontal (X) Axis command, you're not alone. To understand this better, think about which axis the gridlines connect to. Because gridlines come from the x-axis, they are x-axis gridlines.

5. **Click Format on the menu bar, then click Vertical (Y) Axis**
   The Vertical Axis dialog box opens. It lets you change the minimum, maximum, and interval of the numbers along the y-axis, and the style of chart displayed; it also lets you show gridlines, use a logarithmic scale, and remove the vertical axis. Change the Interval (set automatically based on the values being charted) to 25000 so that the y-axis is less cluttered with labels.

6. **Press [Tab] twice, then type 25000 in the Interval text box**
   The value 25000 appears in the Interval text box, indicating you want amounts listed in multiples of $25000 on the y-axis. Finally, add gridlines for the y-axis to complete the gridlines for the chart.

7. **Click the Show gridlines check box, then click OK**
   Works extends gridlines from the y-axis and lists amounts in multiples of $25000, as Figure 7-7 shows. The gridlines make the sales totals the bars in the chart represent easier to read.

8. **Click the Save button 🖫 on the toolbar to save your changes**

FIGURE 7-6: Horizontal Axis dialog box

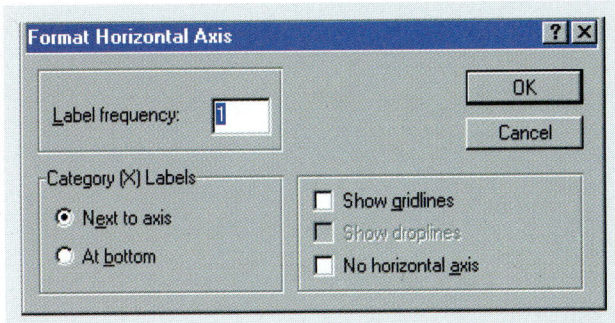

FIGURE 7-7: Sales chart with subtitle and gridlines

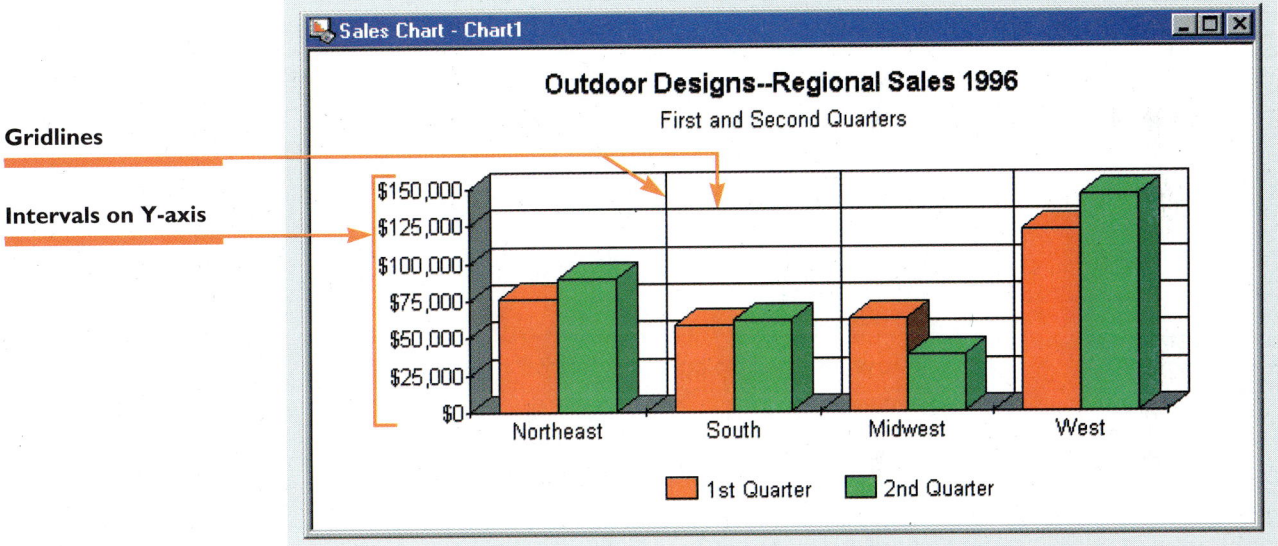

Gridlines

Intervals on Y-axis

Changing the chart legend

The chart legend, a collection of boxes and labels beneath the chart, explains what colors, patterns, and markers in the chart mean. In the Outdoor Designs sales chart, the legend text comes from the column labels "1st Quarter" and "2nd Quarter" in cells B5 and C5, respectively. When you selected these labels with the sales data, Works automatically used them to create a chart legend. To change text in a legend, you choose Edit, Legend/Series Labels and specify different cells in the dialog box (or type new text for legend labels). To remove a legend, you click the Don't use option button in the Edit Legend/Series Labels dialog box and click OK.

TROUBLE?

If you make a mistake while formatting your chart, choose the Undo command from the Edit menu.

Changing fonts and colors

Works lets you customize the font and style of chart text and the color and pattern of bars in the chart. As in the Word Processor, to change fonts and colors, select the item you want to adjust first and then choose the right command. Control over fonts and colors lets you create effective, readable charts. **case** Outdoor Designs traditionally uses Times New Roman for subtitles and labels, and Arial for chart titles. Change the fonts used in the chart, and then change the chart's colors to match the colors in next month's campaign.

Steps

1. Click a label on the vertical axis, click **Format** on the menu bar, then click **Font and Style**

   The Format Font and Style dialog box opens. The title of this dialog box changes depending on the text currently selected in the chart. By default, when you select a label in the chart or legend, all text in the chart *except* the title and subtitle are selected.

2. Scroll down in the Font list box until **Times New Roman** appears, then double-click it

   The dialog box closes and the sales chart appears. The text in the x-axis, y-axis, and legend changes to Times New Roman. Next, change the subtitle font to match the Outdoor Designs standard. As in the Word Processor, you can also use the toolbar to change font.

3. Click the subtitle **First and Second Quarters**, click the **Font Style list arrow** on the toolbar, then scroll down the list and click **Times New Roman**

   The highlighted subtitle in the chart changes to Times New Roman. Now use the toolbar to increase the chart title's size.

4. Click the title **Outdoor Designs—Regional Sales 1996**, click the **Font Size list arrow** on the toolbar, click **14**, then click elsewhere in the chart to remove the selection handles

   Works increases the title's size to 14 points. Next, change the bar colors in the chart to match the colors in next month's campaign.

5. Click **Format** on the menu bar, then click **Shading and Color**

   The Shading and Color dialog box opens. It lets you change the colors and patterns of the series—in this case, the bars—in your chart. Because your chart only contains two series (1st Quarter and 2nd Quarter), option buttons representing the 3rd through 6th series appear dimmed in the dialog box. The Markers list box is empty, because it applies only to line charts.

6. Click **Blue** in the Colors list box and **Dense** in the Patterns list box, then click the **Format button**

   The 1st quarter bars and the 1st quarter legend box change from solid red to shaded blue.

7. Click the **2nd series option button**, click **Yellow** in the Colors list box, scroll down and click **Dark ** in the Patterns list box, then click **Format**

   The 2nd Quarter bars and the 2nd Quarter legend box change from solid green to yellow striped.

8. Click the **Close button** to close the Shading and Color dialog box, then click the **Save button** on the toolbar

   Figure 7-8 shows the completed chart.

FIGURE 7-8: Sales chart with font and color changes

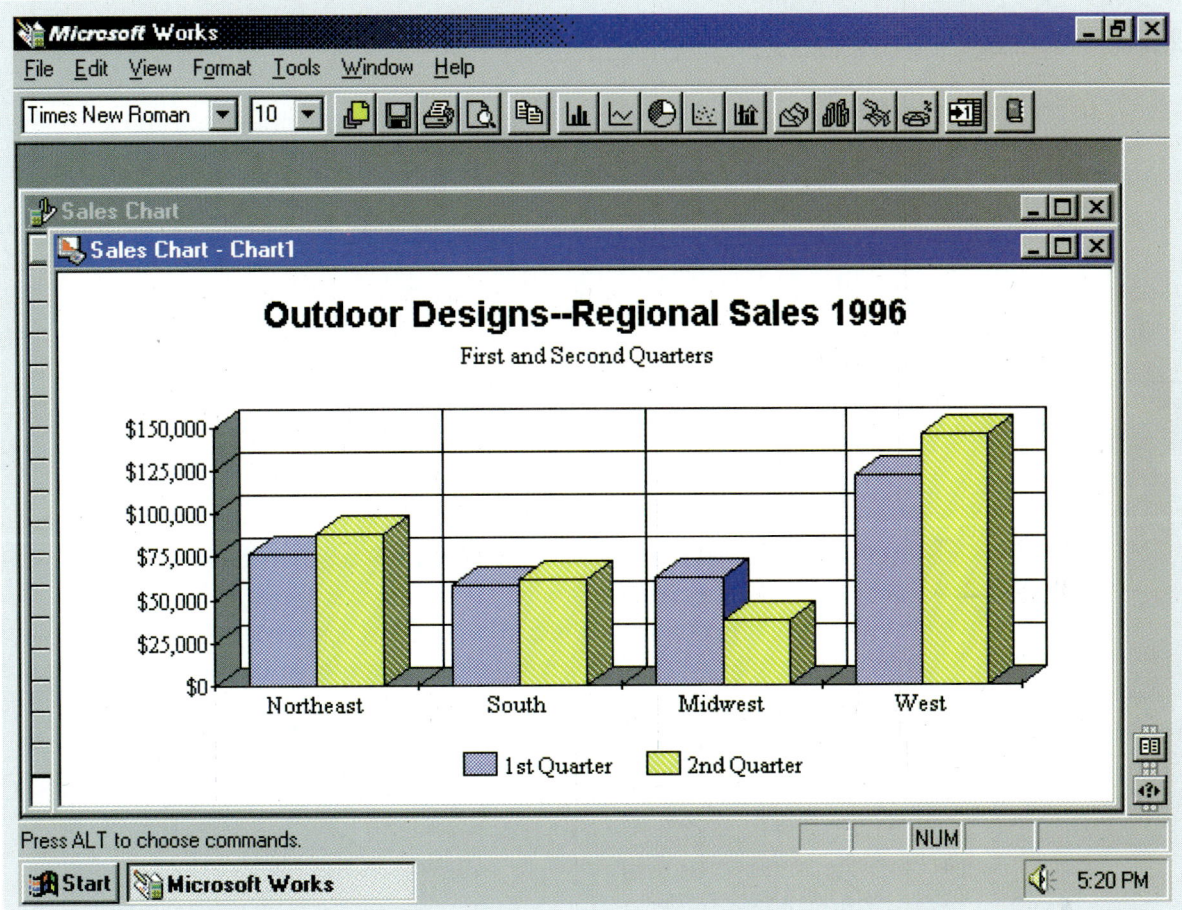

QUICK TIP

If you don't have a color printer attached to your computer, choose the Display as Printed command from the View menu to see how the chart will look printed.

Pasting a spreadsheet table into the Word Processor

After you complete a spreadsheet and a chart, you could print them and staple them together with a quick note. Wouldn't everything look nicer neatly arranged on one page? Combining the output of different Works tools is easy, because all were designed to be used together. You simply copy the cells from one file and paste them in another file. **case** In this lesson you'll paste part of the sales information spreadsheet in a memo in the Word Processor. To begin, you need to make the Sales Chart file the active file, so that you can copy the necessary cells from it.

1. Click **Window** on the menu bar, then click **Sales Chart**
   The Sales Chart spreadsheet window moves in front of the chart window.

2. Select cells **A5** through **C10** in the spreadsheet, then click the **Copy button** on the toolbar
   Works highlights the cell range A5:C10 and then copies it to the Windows Clipboard. You want to paste this spreadsheet data in a blank document, so you need to create one.

3. Click the **Task Launcher button** on the toolbar, click the **Works Tools tab**, then click the **Word Processor button**
   You follow this procedure to open a new, blank word processing document in Works.

4. Save the blank document as **Chart Memo** in the My Works Files folder on your Student Disk
   Before pasting the data into the file, type a short memo to the sales and marketing staff.

5. Type this text at the top of the new document:
   To: Sales and marketing staff [Enter]
   Fm: Melissa Cavenaugh [Enter]
   Date: July 12, 1996 [Enter]
   Re: Sales figures are in [Enter]
   [Enter]
   [Enter]
   Here are sales figures for the first two quarters of 1996: [Enter]
   [Enter]

6. Click the **Paste button** on the toolbar to insert the spreadsheet data; if the First-time Help dialog box opens, click **OK** to close it
   Works pastes cells A5 through C10 in the Word Processor, as Figure 7-9 shows. The cells appear as a table in the Word Processor, maintaining their row and column organization. For more information on working with spreadsheet tables in a Word Processor file, see the related topic, "Working with tables in the Word Processor."

7. Click the **Save button** on the toolbar to save your changes

FIGURE 7-9: Spreadsheet table in Word Processor document

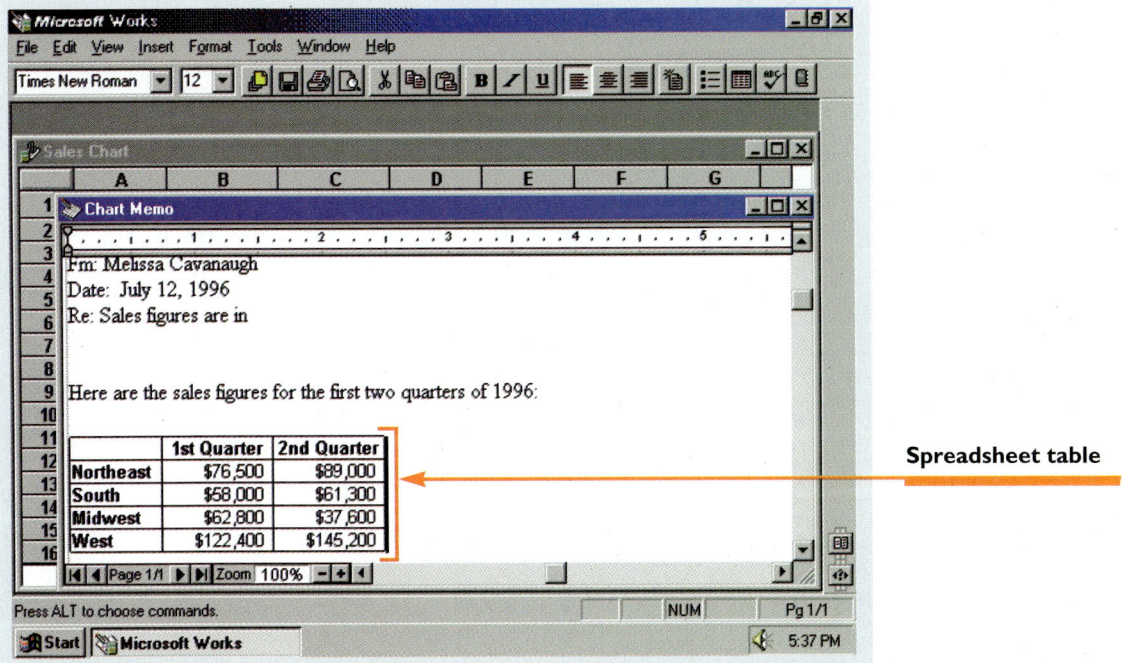

Spreadsheet table

Working with tables in the Word Processor

After you enter a spreadsheet table in a Word Processor document, it becomes an **object** that you can resize, edit, or delete. To resize a table, you would select it, then drag one of its edges until the table is the shape you want. You could also drag the selected table to another location, change its alignment, or delete it by pressing [Del]. (In these ways the table object is just like any other selected item in the Word Processor.) To edit a table you double-click it; this starts the Spreadsheet application and places a cursor in the table. You then edit the table as you would any Works spreadsheet. After editing, you click anywhere in the document to return to the Word Processor.

You can insert a new spreadsheet table in the Word Processor by choosing the Spreadsheet command from the Insert menu. Then you can select, resize, and edit it just like a pasted table from a spreadsheet.

Pasting a chart into the Word Processor

Pasting a chart in the Word Processor is similar to pasting a spreadsheet table. Because charts contain color, however, it's a good idea to use Print Preview to examine your document before printing, even if you don't have a color printer. That way, if the chart shading is not to your liking, you can double-click the chart and change the patterns before you print. ▶case You now have a memo that contains the sales data in spreadsheet form. After you pasted the chart in the memo, you can preview the entire document and then print it for distribution to the sales and marketing department.

1 Click **Window** on the menu bar, then click **Sales Chart - Chart1**
   The sales chart window displays in front of the spreadsheet and memo windows.

2 Click the **Copy button** on the toolbar
   Works copies the chart to the Clipboard.

3 Click **Window** on the menu bar, then click **Chart Memo**
   The Word Processor window displays in front of other windows.

4 Press **[Enter]** three times
   Works inserts two blank lines below the spreadsheet table.

5 Type this text:
   And here is the same information in visual form: [Enter] [Enter]

6 Click the **Paste button** on the toolbar to insert the chart
   Works inserts the sales chart in the Word Processor document, as Figure 7-10 shows. The chart appears as an object in the Word Processor, and you can select, resize, align, delete, and edit it just like a spreadsheet table. For more information, see the related topic, "Establishing a link between documents."

   Congratulations! You completed the sales memo. Next you examine it in Print Preview and print a final copy for distribution.

7 Click the **Print Preview button** on the toolbar
   The memo displays in Print Preview. Use the zoom pointer to examine the spreadsheet table and the chart closely. If part of the spreadsheet or chart has been cut off or is the wrong size, return to Normal view, select the object, then resize it. If a chart bar doesn't look right in black and white, you can return to Normal view, double-click the chart object, then modify the bar with the Shading and Color command. When the memo looks just right, you're ready to print.

8 Click the **Print button** on the right side of the Print Preview window
   Turn on your printer first if necessary, and be sure it is ready to print. After a few moments, you have a final printed copy of the memo.

9 Click the **Save button** on the toolbar to save your changes, click **File**, then click **Exit Works**
   The Word Processor, Spreadsheet, and Chart windows close, and you exit Works.

FIGURE 7-10: Sales chart in memo

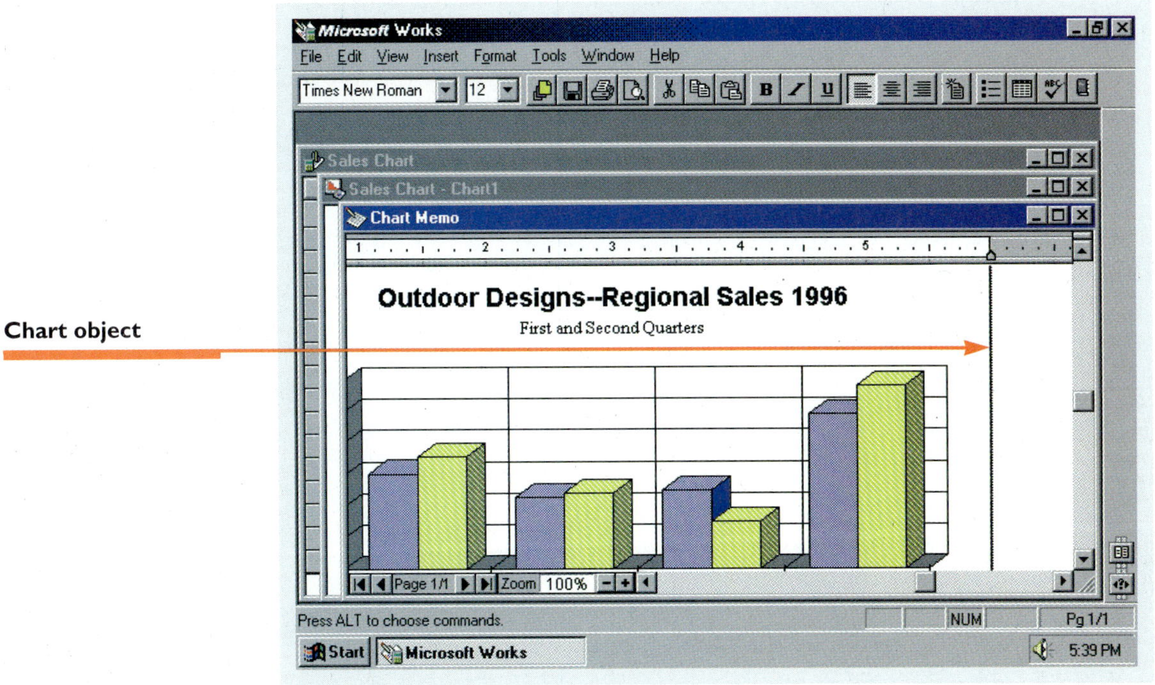

Chart object

Establishing a link between documents

The copy-and-paste technique you used in this unit to exchange information is called **embedding an object**. An embedded object "remembers" how to run the application that created it. Embedding lets you edit the spreadsheet table and the chart you pasted in the Word Processor by simply double-clicking the table or chart object.

Another type of information exchange is called **linking documents**. When you link documents, any changes you make to the original, or **source**, document are automatically made in the linked document. This technique is useful when you want to pass data from one key source document to one or more linked documents. To link data to a document in the Word Processor, you select data from the source document, copy it to the Clipboard, start the Word Processor, and then choose Paste Special from the Edit menu. In the Paste Special dialog box, you click the Paste Link button, then click OK. Works links the two documents and updates the linked document to include all changes made to the source document from that point on.

QUICK TIP

To display an existing chart in a spreadsheet file, choose the Chart command from the View menu, then double-click the chart number in the View Chart dialog box.

TASK REFERENCE

TASK	MOUSE/BUTTON	MENU	KEYBOARD
Add a title or subtitle to the chart		Click Edit, Titles	[Alt][E], [T]
Change chart type	Click one of the nine charting buttons on the toolbar	Click Format, Chart Type	[Alt][O], [C]
Change fonts in the chart	Select the title or label and use a formatting command	Click Format, Font and Style	[Alt][O], [F]
Copy a chart to the Clipboard	Click	Click Edit, Copy	[Ctrl][C]
Create a chart from spreadsheet data	Select spreadsheet cells and click	Click Tools, Create New Chart	[Alt][T], [N]
Open a new word processing window	Click , click	Click File, New, Word Processor Tool	[Ctrl][N], [Enter]
Preview a chart before printing	Click	Click File, Print Preview	[Alt][F], [V]
Save a chart with the spreadsheet	Click	Click File, Save	[Ctrl][S]

CONCEPTS REVIEW

Label each element of the Chart Accessory window shown in Figure 7-11.

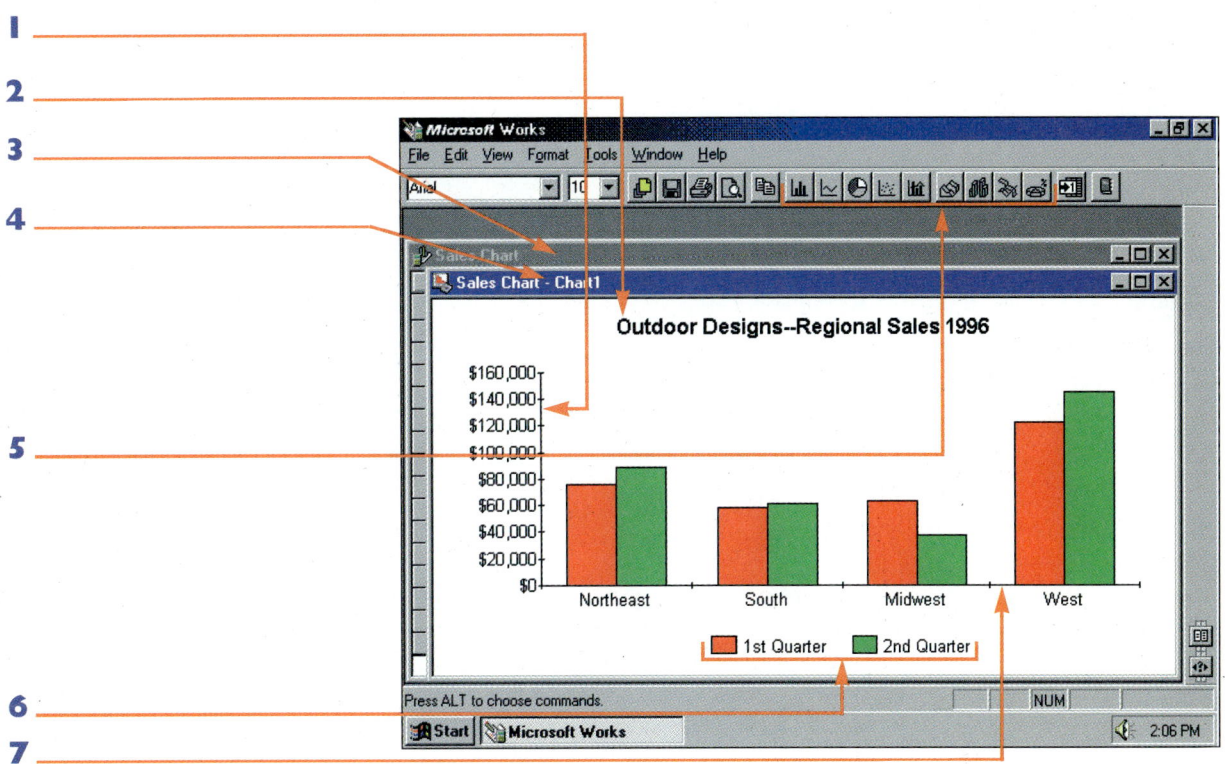

FIGURE 7-11

Match each charting button on the toolbar to the chart type it creates.

8.
9.
10.
11.
12.
13.
14.
15.
16.

a. 3-D Pie chart button
b. 3-D Line chart button
c. 3-D Bar chart button
d. 3-D Area chart button
e. Mixed chart button
f. Scatter chart button
g. Pie chart button
h. Line chart button
i. Bar chart button

Select the best answer from the choices listed.

17 Which definition best describes the x-axis in a Works chart?

a. The vertical line that contains a series of related spreadsheet values

b. The horizontal line that contains a series of related spreadsheet values

c. A box that explains what the labels, colors, and patterns in the chart mean

d. Horizontal and vertical lines that connect to the x-axis and y-axis

18. Which steps do you follow to create a new chart in the Spreadsheet?

    a. Click the Chart icon in the Works Task Launcher dialog box.

    b. Click the New Chart button, then select the spreadsheet data you want to chart.

    c. Select the spreadsheet data you want to chart, then click the New Chart button.

    d. Click the Print Preview button, then click Zoom In.

19. Which of these is *not* a valid way to select the chart type you want?

    a. Select the chart type in the New Chart dialog box.

    b. Choose the Chart Type command from the Format menu.

    c. Click a charting button on the toolbar.

    d. Select the chart type in the Shading and Color dialog box.

20. Which of these *cannot* be set with the Vertical (Y) Axis command?

    a. Chart colors

    b. Tick labels on the y-axis

    c. Interval between numbers on the y-axis

    d. Gridlines

21. How do you change the color of a bar in a chart?

    a. Click the bar, then choose a new color from the Color list box on the toolbar.

    b. Choose a new color from the Color list box in the Font and Style command.

    c. Choose a new color for the bar series in the Shading and Color dialog box.

    d. Choose the Display as Printed command from the View menu.

22. What steps do you follow to copy a Spreadsheet table to the Word Processor?

    a. Copy the data in the Spreadsheet, then paste it in the Word Processor.

    b. Copy the data in the Spreadsheet, then paste it in the Chart Accessory.

    c. Double-click a range of spreadsheet cells.

    d. Paste the data in the Word Processor, then copy it from the Spreadsheet.

23. A Spreadsheet table inserted into the Word Processor becomes

    a. A table with entries separated by tabs

    b. Regular text that you can format

    c. A chart that you can print

    d. An object that you can resize, edit, or delete

24. How do you change the font size in a chart that you inserted in the Word Processor?

    a. Select the chart, then change the font size with the Font Size list box.

    b. Select the chart, choose Page Layout view, then press [F1].

    c. Double-click the chart, then change the font size in the Chart Accessory.

    d. After you insert the chart, you cannot change its font size.

25. How does an embedded object differ from a linked object?

    a. An embedded object is not updated automatically; a linked object is.

    b. A linked object is the only object that you can resize, edit, or delete.

    c. Embedded objects must be inserted into documents with the Paste Special command.

    d. The Word Processor only accepts linked objects.

SKILLS REVIEW

1. Open the file WKS 7-2 and create several charts of the trip information it contains.

    a. Start Works and open the file WKS 7-2.

    b. Save the spreadsheet as Adventure Chart in the My Works Files folder on your Student Disk.

    c. Select the cell range A4 through C10, then click the New Chart button.

d. Click Bar in the chart type box.
   e. Press Tab to move the cursor to the Title text box.
   f. Type "Total Trips."
   g. Click Border to add a border to the chart.
   h. Click OK to create the chart.

2. Experiment with different chart types.
   a. Click the Mixed Chart button, and then click OK.
   b. Click the Line Chart button, click the Variations tab, and double-click the second chart style.
   c. Click the 3-D Bar Chart button, click the Variations tab, and double-click the fourth chart style.
   d. Click Window on the menu bar, then click Adventure Chart.
   e. Select cells A5 through B10, then click the New Chart button.
   f. Click 3-D Pie chart.
   g. Press [Tab] and type "Total Trips," the chart title.
   h. Click OK to create the chart.
   i. Click the 3-D Bar chart button on the toolbar.
   j. Click the Variations tab.
   k. Double-click the sixth chart style to add labels with text and percentages.

3. Add a subtitle to the pie chart and gridlines to the bar chart.
   a. With the pie chart open, click the Edit menu, then click the Titles command.
   b. Press [Tab], type "1995" in the Subtitle text box, then click OK.
   c. Click Window on the menu bar, then click Adventures Chart - Chart1.
   d. Click Format on the menu bar, then click Horizontal (X) Axis.
   e. Click Show gridlines, then click OK.
   f. Click Format on the menu bar, then click Vertical (Y) Axis.
   g. Click Show gridlines, then click OK.
   h. Click the Save button to save your changes.

4. Modify fonts for two charts and the colors for the pie chart.
   a. For the bar chart, click the chart title.
   b. Click Format on the menu bar, then click Font and Style.
   c. Click Times New Roman in the Font list box.
   d. Click 14 in the Size list box, then click OK.
   e. Click an axis label.
   f. Click Arial Narrow on the Font list on the toolbar.
   g. Click 8 on the Font Size list on the toolbar.
   h. Click Window on the menu bar, then click Adventure Chart - Chart2.
   i. Click the pie chart title, and change it to 14-point bold Times New Roman.
   j. Click the pie chart subtitle, and change it to 12-point Times New Roman.
   k. Click an axis label and change all axis labels to 10-point Arial Narrow.
   l. Click Format on the menu bar, then click Shading and Color.
   m. Change the pie slices to colors you like.
   n. Click the Save button to save your changes.

5. Paste the spreadsheet data and charts into a new memo file in the Word Processor.
   a. Click the Window menu, then click Adventure Chart to display the spreadsheet.
   b. Select the cell range A4 through C10.
   c. Click the Copy button to copy the cell range to the Clipboard.
   d. Click the Task Launcher button on the toolbar.
   e. Click the Works Tools tab.
   f. Click the Word Processor button to open a new document.
   g. Save the file as Adventure Memo.
   h. Type the following lines:

      To: Brenda Miller [Enter]

      Fm: Ernie Starr [Enter]

      Re: Last year's data and next year's projections [Enter]

      [Enter] [Enter]

      Here are the trip data for last year and projections for this year. [Enter]

      [Enter]

i. Click the Paste button to insert the spreadsheet table as an object in the Word Processor.

j. Click the Save button to save your changes.

6 Paste the charts into the Word Processor, then print the memo.

a. Click Window on the menu bar, then click Adventure Chart - Chart1.

b. Click the Copy button.

c. Click Window on the menu bar, then click Adventure Memo.

d. Press [Enter] twice, then type this text:

Here is a chart of the data. [Enter]

[Enter]

e. Click the Paste button to insert the chart as an object in the Word Processor.

f. Press [Enter] twice.

g. Click Window on the menu bar, then click Adventure Chart - Chart2.

h. Click the Copy button.

i. Click Window on the menu bar, then click Adventure Memo.

j. Click the Paste button to insert the chart.

k. Click the Print Preview button on the toolbar.

l. Use the zoom pointer to verify that everything in the memo looks right before you print.

m. Click the Print button to print a final copy of the memo.

n. Click the Save button to save your final document.

o. Close the file and exit Works.

INDEPENDENT CHALLENGE 1

The Wacky Words card company is evaluating last year's Christmas card sales, hoping to spot important selling trends. Use the WKS 7-3 spreadsheet on your Student Disk to create a line chart that graphically depicts Christmas card sales from October through January. Experiment with line chart variations to create a chart that looks ready for distribution.

To complete this independent challenge:

1 Open the file WKS 7-3 on your Student Disk, and save it as Card Chart in the My Works Files folder on your Student Disk.

2 Create a chart of data for October through January. Be sure to include card types in column A and to exclude totals.

3 Experiment with three different chart types. Which types did you try? Would they be appropriate or inappropriate for card sales data? Why?

4 Make the chart a line chart. Add the title "Christmas Card Sales" and put a border around the chart.

5 Add the subtitle "October - January." Then add gridlines for both axes.

6 Change the line colors and marker shapes for the lines.

7 Print the chart, save your changes, and then close the file.

INDEPENDENT CHALLENGE 2

Palmer's Pet Hospital is evaluating its January business. Ellen Smith, the office manager, wants to know what percentage of time employees spend treating each type of animal. This information will be useful when it's time to hire additional staff. Using the WKS 7-4 spreadsheet on your Student Disk, create a pie chart that shows what percentage of visits each animal type accounts for in January. Also use the chart to settle a bet you have with Ellen that pigs accounted for more than 10% of the total January business.

To complete this independent challenge:

1 Open the file WKS 7-4 on your Student Disk, and save it as Animal Chart in the My Works Files folder of your Student Disk.

2 Create a 3-D Pie chart of the data. Be sure to include row labels and to exclude column labels.

3 Add the title "Treatment by Animal Type," and put a border around the chart.

4. Use pie chart variations to label each pie slice with the animal type and the percentage it represents.

5. Explode the Pigs pie slice using the Format Shading and Color dialog box. The Pig slice is the fifth series.

6. Reduce the font size of the pie slice labels so that they do not overlap.

7. Use the Word Processor to create a note that tells Ellen Smith she lost the bet: pigs represent over 10% of the business.

8. Copy and paste the chart into the note. Resize the chart in the note so that it is smaller.

9. Print the note and save it as Animal Memo in the My Works Files folder of your Student Disk. Close Animal Memo. Then save the changes to Animal Chart, and close it as well.

INDEPENDENT CHALLENGE 3

The local art gallery is conducting research to determine how many people viewed a recent art exhibit. They want you to create an area chart that depicts the number of people who attended over a six-month period and includes a breakdown of men, women, and children under 10 who attended. The attendance data is already in the WKS 7-5 spreadsheet; you just need to create the chart.

To complete this independent challenge:

1. Open the file WKS 7-5 on your Student Disk, and save it as Attendance Chart in the My Works Files folder on your Student Disk.

2. Create a stacked area chart of the data. How does this chart type meet the art gallery's needs?

3. Add the chart title "Gallery Attendance." Change it to 14-point Impact. Add the subtitle "March - August." Change it to 12-point Impact.

4. Format the x-axis with drop lines.

5. Add a centered footer to the page that includes the text "1996 Gallery Attendance Page" and a page number.

6. Preview the chart and then print it. Save your changes and close the file.

INDEPENDENT CHALLENGE 4

For its study on advertising's effect on meal revenues, The Steak Pit has asked you to create a chart to show the relationship (if any) between increased advertising costs and increased revenues. Has advertising directly affected revenues, or has its effect been nonlinear? WKS 7-6 on your Student Disk has the data you need to make an initial analysis.

To complete this independent challenge:

1. Open the file WKS 7-6 on your Student Disk, and save it as Advertising Chart in the My Works Files folder of your Student Disk.

2. Create a line chart of the data. Be sure to include row and column labels. Add a border to the chart.

3. Add the chart title "Advertising vs. Revenue" in 14-point bold Arial Narrow. Change the chart labels to 10-point bold Arial Narrow.

4. Make the chart an area chart, and format its Horizontal axis so that only every second axis label appears.

5. Examine the chart. Is there a correlation between advertising and revenue?

6. Print the chart, save your changes, then close the file.

VISUAL WORKSHOP

Create the chart in Figure 7-12 using commands and techniques you learned in this unit. Save it as the name of your choice in the My Works Files Folder on your Student Disk.

Approximate numbers as best you can using the chart shown. To prepare the chart for printing, click the Page Setup command on the File menu, click the Other Options tab, and then click the Screen Size option button.

FIGURE 7-12

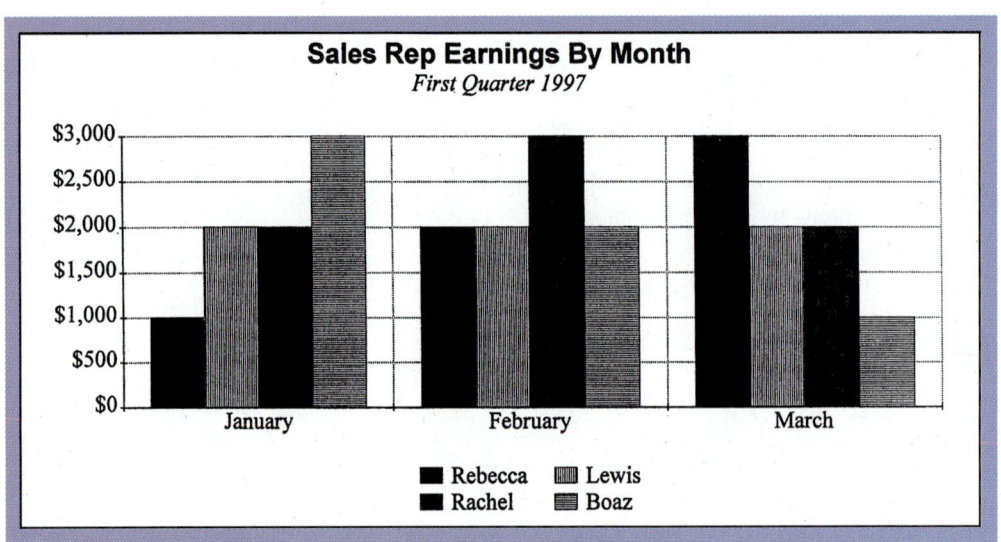

UNIT 8

OBJECTIVES

▶ Plan a database

▶ Create fields

▶ Build a data-entry form

▶ Enter data into fields

▶ Add records to the database

▶ Edit data in fields

▶ Manage fields

▶ Change font size and style

▶ Print the database

Building
A DATABASE

You have already learned how to use the Works Word Processor and Spreadsheet. In this unit you'll learn about the Works Database tool. Think of a **database** as an organized collection of information stored electronically in a file. A database can contain information of any kind, from sales and financial records about your business, to lists of school friends and associates, and even the compact discs in your music collection. ▶case In this unit you'll use the Database tool to create a database to help Outdoor Designs keep track of customers. After you create the database, you'll practice editing and manipulating data in it and then learn to print the database. ▶

Planning a database

Planning a Database

Before you create a new database, you should analyze your needs. Consider what type of information the database will contain and how you need to work with that information. A well-designed database saves you time and effort in the future and requires less maintenance. Be sure to view the CourseHelp entitled "Planning a Database" before you begin this lesson. ▶case Sue Ellen assigned you the task of creating a database to keep track of the name, address, phone number, and fax number of each Outdoor Designs customer. You will use the following guidelines to define your database.

1 Determine the purpose of the database
You need to create a database to store information about each Outdoor Designs customer. Each customer's information will be stored in a record. A **record** contains all information pertaining to a person or business. A record consists of **fields**, specific categories of information in a database such as name, address, and phone number.

2 Determine potential uses for the database
You will use this database to locate and update information on a customer or group of customers, perform sales comparisons, and produce various reports. A **report** is a summary of database information specifically designed for printing.

3 Collect all the information needed to produce the results you want, talking to all possible database users to gather additional ideas that might enhance the design
At this time, all your customer data is on index cards. You meet with Sue Ellen and other coworkers who will also use the database. Current customer information cards, like the one shown in Figure 8-1, provide the information Outdoor Designs wants to store in the database for each customer. You all decide that the cards are a good basis for the database form you will create. A database **form** is where Works displays the database fields one record at a time so you can enter the information as if you were filling in a form.

4 Sketch the form's structure, including each field's format
Using all the information on the original customer information cards, you plan your form and the fields it will contain as shown in Figure 8-2. Choosing the right fields for your database is an important task. Fields affect how Works enters data in the database, as well as how it sorts, searches, and reports on the database later. It's usually better to create specific fields, including enough fields so that you can break out important information, but not so many that using the forms becomes a burden. For example, using separate fields for city, state, and zip code elements is usually better than combining them in a single field because you can later search for records about a particular city, state, or zip code individually.

FIGURE 8-1: Original customer information card

FIGURE 8-2: Planned form and fields

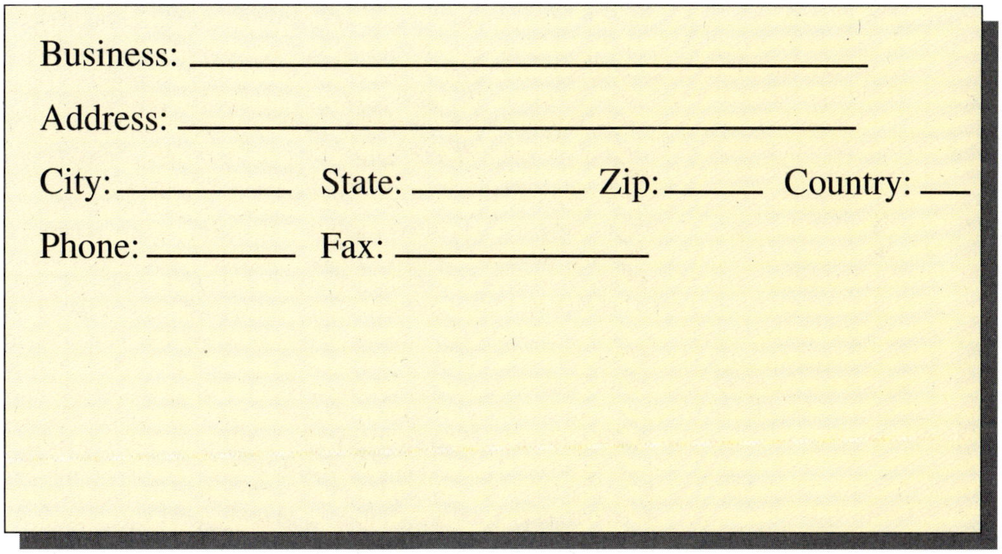

Business: _____

Address: _____

City: _____ State: _____ Zip: _____ Country: ___

Phone: _____ Fax: _____

Creating Fields

Now that you've planned the structure of the Outdoor Designs database, you are ready to start the Database tool and create the necessary fields. The Database tool's graphical interface is similar to those of the Word Processor and Spreadsheet. Figure 8-3 identifies unique elements of the Database interface. **case** With your plan completed, you are ready to create the fields Sue Ellen specified.

1. Launch Works and if the First-time Help dialog box appears, click **OK**, then click the **Works Tools tab** in the Works Task Launcher dialog box, and click the **Database button**

   The Database tool starts and the Create Database dialog box opens, as shown in Figure 8-4. A Works database can contain up to 256 fields with names up to 15 characters in length. You can choose from seven field formats, detailed in Table 8-1, to format the data you plan to place in a field. According to your planning sketch, you decided that you need to create eight fields for your database. The first field identifies the name of the Outdoor Designs customer.

2. In the Create Database dialog box, be sure that **General format** is selected, type **Business** in the Field name text box, then click **Add**

   Works places the Business field in your database in the default General format, and the temporary name for the second field appears in the Field name text box. Now add the remaining fields.

3. Type **Address**, click **Add**, type **City**, click **Add**, type **State**, click **Add**, type **Zip**, click **Add**, type **Country**, click **Add**, type **Phone**, click **Add**, type **Fax**, click **Add**, then click the **Done button**

   Works adds each field to the database in General format. Then the Create Database dialog box closes, and Works displays your database fields in List view, one of three views available in the Database tool. In **List view**, you see information arranged in the spreadsheet format. Field names appear as column headings across the top and a list of check boxes appear along the left edge.

4. Take a moment to identify the elements of the user interface

   The Database contains many components found in every Works tool: a menu bar, a toolbar, scroll bars, toggle indicators, title bar buttons, and Help buttons. The Database interface has an **entry bar** where you enter and edit field entries in the database. Each row in the spreadsheet represents one record. You are finished adding fields so now you can save your new database.

5. Click the **Save Button** on the menu bar, then in the Save As dialog box, specify the **My Works Files folder** on your Student Disk, type **Customer Database** in the File name text box, and click **Save**

   Works saves your database on disk and places the filename you specified in the title bar.

FIGURE 8-3: Works Database in List view

- Menu bar
- Toolbar
- Formula bar
- Fields
- Records
- Toggle indicators
- Title bar buttons
- Help buttons

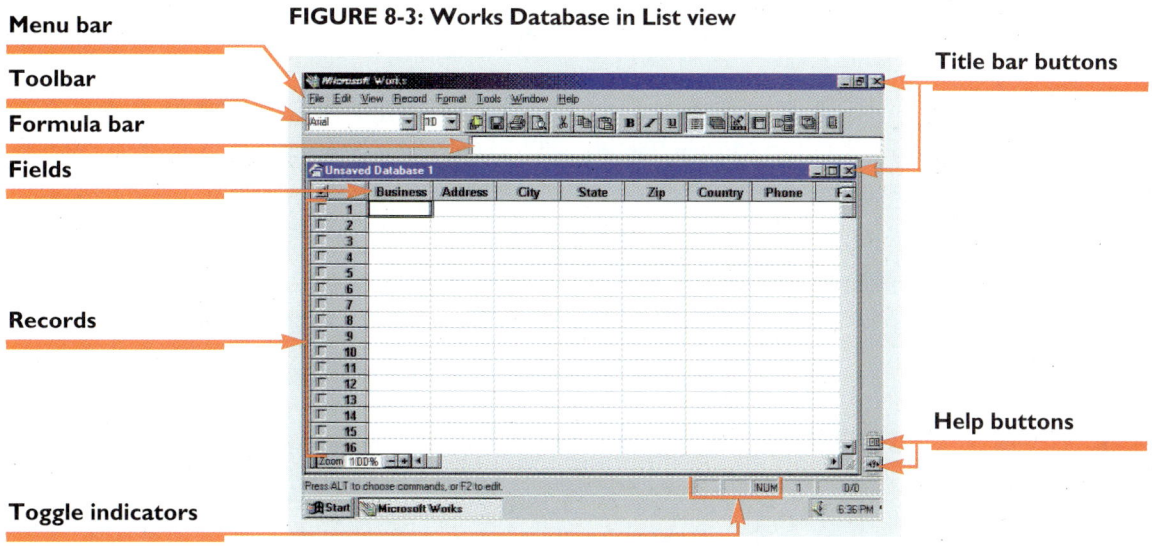

FIGURE 8-4: Create database dialog box

- Type your field names here
- Default format
- Provides details and/or options about specified format

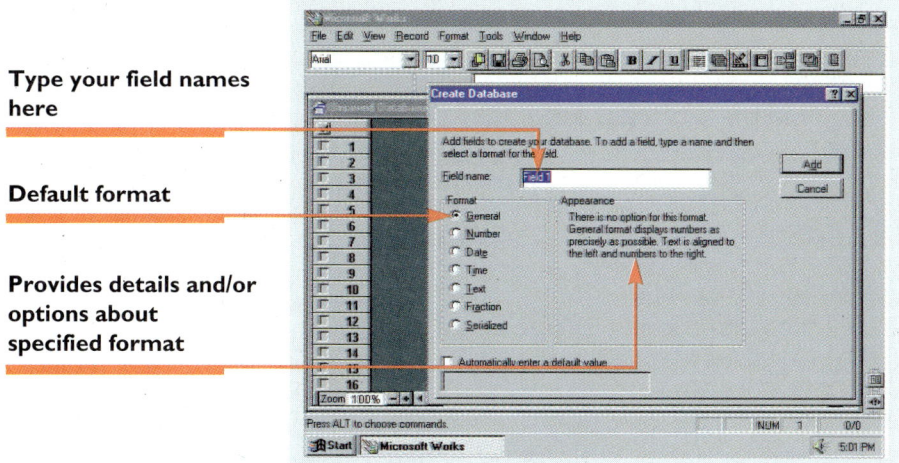

QUICK TIP

To get online help as you work with the Database tool, click the Help button in the lower-right corner of the program window.

TABLE 8-1: Field formats

TYPE	DESCRIPTION
General	Default format. Uses integer (123), decimal fraction (1.23), or exponential notation (123E+75).
Number	Currency symbols and separators, percent signs, leading zeros, true/false, and exponential notation.
Date	Day of the week, month, and year. Choose from a list of predefined formats.
Time	Hours, minutes, and seconds. Choose from a list of predefined formats.
Text	Alphanumeric characters.
Fractions	Fractions rounded or reduced to the number you specify. When you type a fraction, first type 0, for example: 0 1/32.
Serialized	A numbered sequence, such as serial numbers, ID numbers, or index numbers.

Building a data-entry form

If you want, you can enter database information directly into the rows and columns of the List view spreadsheet. However, working in Form view makes entering database information easier. To facilitate the often repetitive process of entering data, a Works form displays the fields for one record at a time, with fields arranged and formatted as you wish. **case** You and other colleagues will enter data on hundreds of customers before completing the Outdoor Designs database. Build an Outdoor Designs form to make this process easier.

1. **Click the Form Design button on the toolbar**
   Works opens in Form Design view and places the eight fields you defined on a blank data-entry form. The Form Design button is one of six buttons unique to the Database toolbar. Table 8-2 lists the complete set of buttons. To customize your data-entry form, you simply drag the fields to the desired location and lengthen or shorten them with the sizing handles. You can also use a TaskWizard to automate form creation; see the related topic, "Using the Customers or Clients TaskWizard." You decide that a standard business letter layout is the most logical layout for entering data.

2. **Click and hold the Address field, then drag it under the Business field**
   The word Move appears beneath the mouse pointer when you drag the field. The moved Address field is a little too short, so you resize it to hold any long customer addresses. When you resize, your mouse pointer changes to RESIZE.

3. **Click the right-top sizing handle shown in Figure 8-5, and drag it to the right until the Address field is large enough to accommodate a long address**
   The field is now correctly positioned. To complete the business letter layout, you now move the other fields to new positions.

4. **Reposition and resize the City, State, Zip, Country, Phone, and Fax fields, then resize the Business field so they look like Figure 8-5**
   You rearranged and resized the fields, allowing adequate room for data. Now you add a **label** containing descriptive text about your form.

5. **Click at the top left of your form (above the fields) to mark the starting point for a descriptive label on your form**
   The cursor blinks where you click.

6. **Click Insert on the menu bar, then click Label**
   The Insert Label dialog box opens, prompting you for a descriptive label.

7. **Type Outdoor Designs Customer Database, and press [Enter]**
   Works adds the label "Outdoor Designs Customer Database" to the form. In Form view, a double quotation mark in the entry bar identifies a label. Now save the database on your Student Disk.

8. **Click the Save button on the Database toolbar**
   Your changes are saved.

FIGURE 8-5: Customer Database form in Form Design view

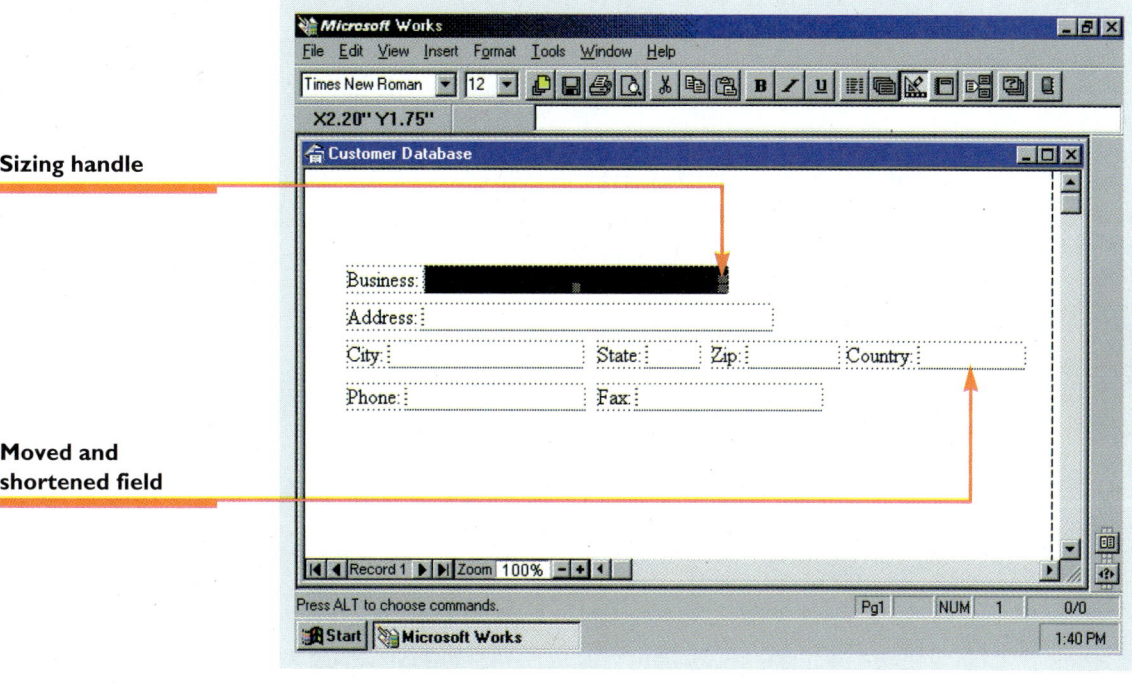

Sizing handle

Moved and shortened field

Using the Customers or Clients TaskWizard

You can also create a customer database with the Customers or Clients TaskWizard. To use this TaskWizard, choose New from the File menu, click the TaskWizards tab in the Works Task Launcher dialog box, click the Names and Addresses category, and then double-click Customers or Clients.

TABLE 8-2: Toolbar buttons unique to the Database

BUTTON	FUNCTION
	Displays the database in List view
	Displays the database in Form view
	Displays the form in Form Design view
	Creates a report summarizing database information
	Inserts a new record into the database
	Filters the database to display specific records

Entering data into fields

After you create a database form, you can enter information in it. To enter information in a field, you select the field, then type the appropriate data. You can enter text, numbers, or a formula in a field. Table 8-3 lists useful keys for working with fields. To enter data, you can be in Form view or List view; it's easier to work in Form view. **CASE** Enter a record in the Outdoor Designs database now for the company Cambridge Kite Supplies.

1. **Click the Form View button on the toolbar**
   Works highlights the data-entry portion of the Business field. This part of the field is called the **field value**. The first part of the field (the word "Business" and the colon) is called the **field name**. See Figure 8-6. You can start entering a company name in the highlighted first field, Business.

2. **In the highlighted Business field, type Cambridge Kite Supplies and press [Tab]**
   Works enters Cambridge Kite Supplies in the Business field and highlights the Address field. Pressing the [Tab] key confirms your entry and moves you to the next field, in this case the Address field.

3. **Type 1437 Wednesday Street, press [Tab], type Cambridge, press [Tab], then type MA and press [Tab]**
   Works enters the company's street address, city, and state in the appropriate fields, and highlights the Zip field.

4. **Type 02142, then press [Tab]**
   Works highlights the Country field, but notice the correct zip code does not appear in the Zip field. Works automatically deleted the leading zero because you did not choose a specific zip code format when creating the field. To correct the format, return to the Zip field, switch back to Form Design view, and change the field's formatting.

5. **Press [Shift][Tab] to return to the Zip field, click the Form Design View button on the toolbar, click Format on the menu bar, then click Field**
   The Format dialog box appears with the Field tab selected.

6. **Click the Number radio button, click 01235 (the zip code entry) at the bottom of the Appearance list box, click OK, and then click the Form View button on the toolbar**
   The number 02142 now appears in the Zip field. You can use the Field command to change the number format of any field in the database. You can now move to the Country field and finish entering your information in the database.

7. **Press [Tab], type USA, press [Tab], type (617) 275-3333, press [Tab], type (617) 275-3344, press [Enter], then save your work**
   Works enters the remaining fields in the database, as shown in Figure 8-6. Pressing the [Enter] key after the last field confirms your entry; pressing the [Tab] key after the last field would have created a new record. You will learn more about creating new records in the next lesson.

FIGURE 8-6:
Cambridge Kite Supplies record

Label

Field name

Field value

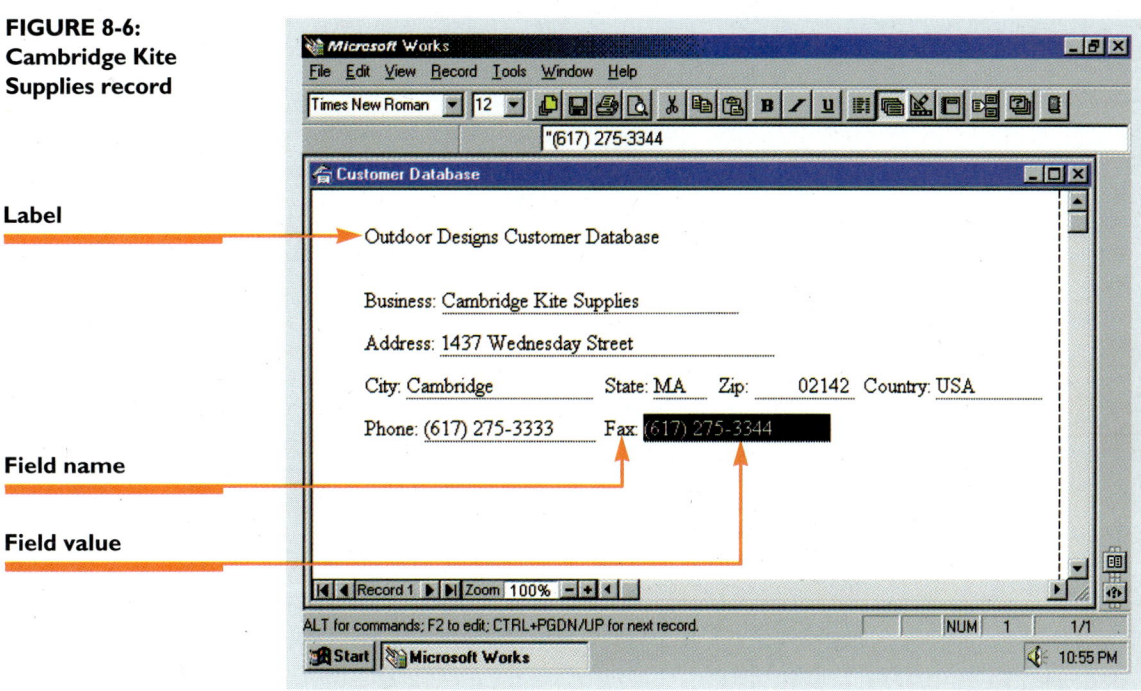

TABLE 8-3: Useful keys for working with database fields

KEY	FUNCTION
[Tab]	Highlights the next field in the database
[Shift][Tab]	Highlights the previous field in the database
[F2]	Lets you edit the highlighted field in the entry bar
[Del]	Deletes the contents of the highlighted field

QUICK TIP

A heavily used database can quickly grow to hundreds of records and become an important asset. Keep a backup copy in a safe place to avoid losing valuable information. ■

TROUBLE?

If any text you type is obscured, the field value is not long enough. To fix this, click the Form Design View button on the toolbar, resize the field value, then click the Form View button. ■

Adding records to the database

To add a new record to a database you can either click the Insert Record button on the toolbar or press [Tab] when the last field in the last record is highlighted. When your database contains more than one record, you can scroll through the database using the **record navigation buttons** located just above the status bar. See Figure 8-7. **case** You are now ready to add more clients to the Outdoor Designs database.

1. Verify that the last field value on the form is highlighted, then press **[Tab]**
   Works adds a new, blank record to the database and hides the Cambridge Kite Supplies record from view. The Business field highlights and Record 2 appears in the **record number indicator**, a marker of your position in the database, located in the lower-left corner of the screen.

2. Type the following customer data, pressing **[Tab]** between fields:
   Mountain Air [Tab] 10 Blaine Street [Tab] North Bend [Tab] WA [Tab] 98045 [Tab] USA [Tab] (206) 888-1541 [Tab] (206) 888-1532 [Enter]
   Your new record is complete. Pressing the [Enter] key lets you review your record before you create another one. Continue now and add another record.

3. Press **[Tab]** to add a new record, then type the following customer data:
   Ken's Outdoor Gear [Tab] 4545 64th Ave. SE [Tab] Olympia [Tab] WA [Tab] 98503 [Tab] USA [Tab] (206) 491-2222 [Tab] (206) 491-2255 [Enter]
   You added another record to your database. You can view your records by clicking the record navigation buttons.

4. Click the **inside-left record navigation button**, shown in Figure 8-7, twice
   The second and first records in the database appear as you click. The inside navigation buttons let you scroll through the database one record at a time. The left and right outside navigation buttons move you to the first and last records of the database, respectively. You can add your next customer to the beginning of your database.

5. Click the **Insert Record button** on the toolbar
   A new, blank record appears at the beginning of the database. As you add records to the database you can add them to the end of the list with the [Tab] key, or between existing records with the Insert Record button. Some people prefer to add new records while in List view; to learn why, see the related topic, "Working in List view."

6. Click the **Business field value**, then type the following customer data:
   The Essential Surfer [Tab] 100 Seawind Drive [Tab] Newport Beach [Tab] CA [Tab] 92660 [Tab] USA [Tab] (714) 837-4444 [Tab] (714) 837-4436 [Enter]
   Your screen should look like Figure 8-7.

7. Click the **Save button** on the toolbar
   Works saves your new records in your My Works Files folder.

FIGURE 8-7: New record inserted

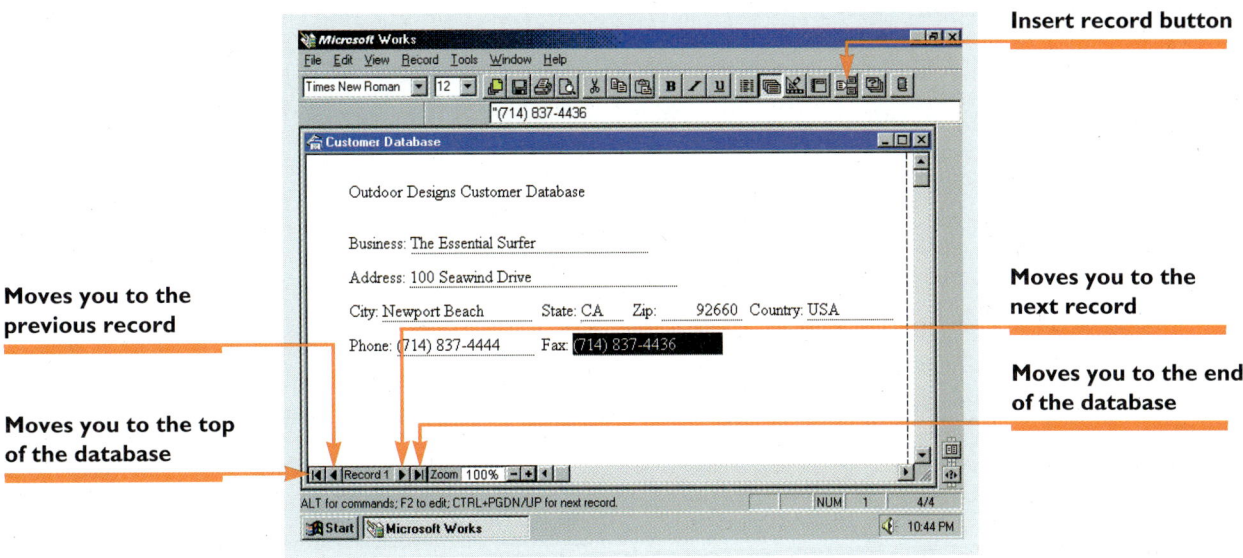

FIGURE 8-8: Database in List view

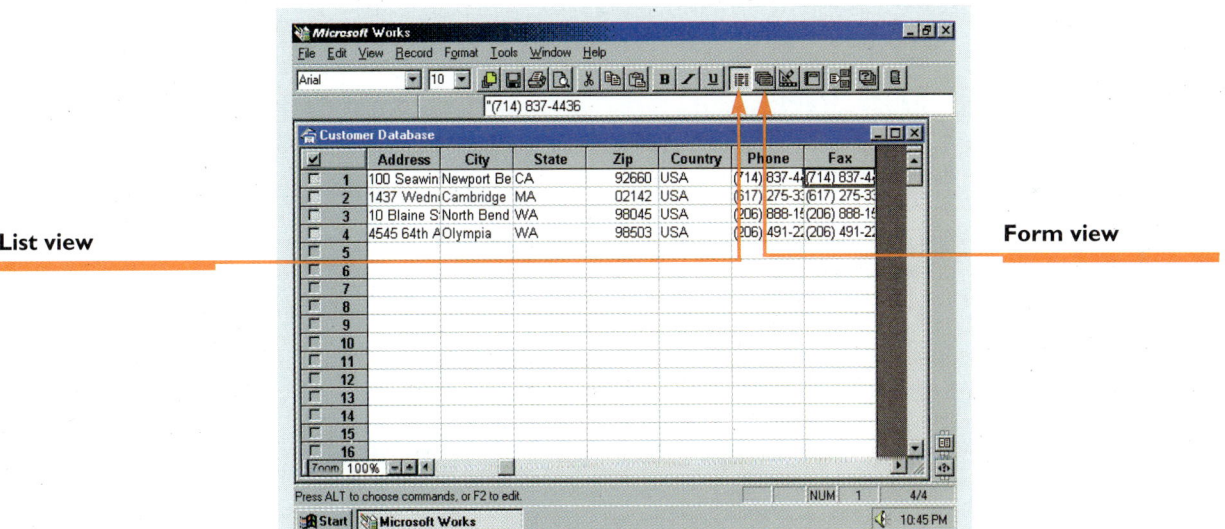

Working in List view

When you click the List View button  on the toolbar, the database appears in its original spreadsheet format, shown in Figure 8-8. In this format, you can compare different database records for overall consistency, quickly search for individual records, and easily edit existing records. You can also add new records anywhere in the database by using the Insert Record command or Insert Record button. To widen a column of cells (so that you can read a field's entire contents), click the title of the column you want to adjust, click Format on the menu bar, click Field Width, then click Best Fit.

QUICK TIP

In Form view, [Ctrl][PgUp] and [Ctrl][PgDn] move you to the previous and next records in the database, respectively.

Editing data in fields

Almost inevitably the data you enter in a database needs correcting or revising. Fortunately, you can replace the information stored in a field by highlighting the field, typing the new entry, and pressing [Enter]. You can also edit a field value on the entry bar by highlighting the field and pressing [F2]. Table 8-4 lists several useful keys for editing text in the entry bar. In addition to these techniques, you can use the Cut, Copy, and Paste toolbar buttons to delete and replicate field entries in the database. ▶case Sue Ellen brought you a correction memo indicating that some customer data needs updating. Cambridge Kite Supplies has changed its name, and Ken's Outdoor Gear has disconnected its separate fax line. You'll make those database corrections now.

1. **Verify that you are in Form view, then click the inside-right record navigation button to scroll to Record 2 in the database**
   The customer record for Cambridge Kite Supplies appears.

2. **Click the Business field and press [F2]**
   The text "Cambridge Kite Supplies" appears in the entry bar, along with a blinking cursor. The new name of the business is "Cambridge Kite Supply."

3. **Press [Backspace] three times, then type y and press [Enter]**
   Works enters the revised business name in the database. Now you need to delete the fax number for Ken's Outdoor Gear.

4. **Click the inside-right record navigation button twice to scroll to Record 4**
   The record for Ken's Outdoor Gear appears. Sue Ellen informed you that this business now receives faxes on their voice line, so you copy the value in the Phone field to the Fax field. To speed your work, you use the shortcut buttons on the toolbar.

5. **Click the Fax field, then click the Cut button ✂ on the toolbar**
   Works deletes the old fax number from the record.

6. **Click the Phone field, then click the Copy button 📋 on the toolbar**
   Works copies the value in the Phone field to the Windows Clipboard.

7. **Click the Fax field, then click the Paste button 📋 on the toolbar**
   Works replicates the phone number (206) 491-2222 in the Fax field, as shown in Figure 8-9. Note that the Cut, Copy, and Paste commands on the Edit menu are the menu command equivalents to the Cut, Copy, and Paste buttons. You can use any combination of these buttons and commands to edit your database.

8. **Click the Save button 💾 on the toolbar**
   Works saves your edits on disk.

FIGURE 8-9: Record for Ken's Outdoor Gear after editing

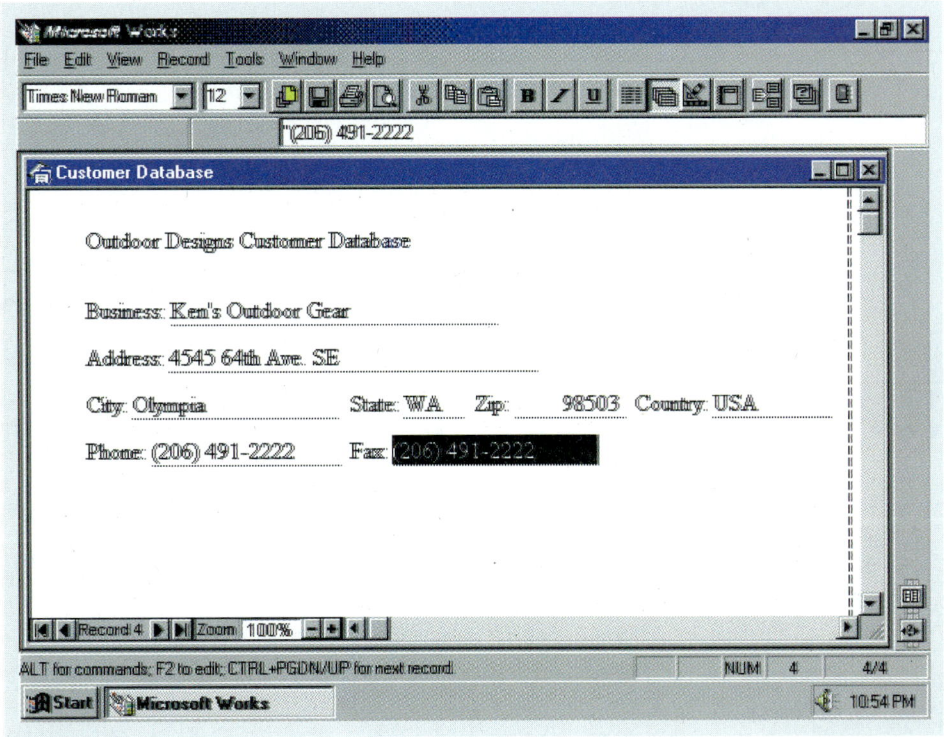

TABLE 8-4: Useful keys for editing text on the entry bar

KEY	FUNCTION
[←]	Moves the cursor one character to the left
[→]	Moves the cursor one character to the right
[Home]	Moves the cursor to the beginning of the text
[End]	Moves the cursor to the end of the text
[Shift][←]	Selects the character to the left of the cursor
[Shift][→]	Selects the character to the right of the cursor
[Del]	Deletes the selected text

QUICK TIP

To reverse an editing change you mistakenly made, press [Ctrl][Z] or choose the Undo command from the Edit menu.

Managing fields

You can add new fields or delete unwanted fields if you switch from Form view to Form Design view. You can also move, resize, or set the alignment to make existing fields more appropriate for the information stored in the database. For more information about setting the alignment for fields, see the related topic, "Changing the alignment in a field." **case** As you review Outdoor Designs' customer information cards, you notice that all customers are based in the U.S. Sue Ellen suggests that you delete the Country field, move the Fax field, and then add a Comments field for additional, miscellaneous information about each customer.

1. Click the **Form Design button** on the toolbar, then click the **Country field name** on the form
   You can click the Country field in any record. However, be sure to click the field name (Country), not the field value (USA).

2. Press **[Del]**, then click **OK**
   Works deletes the Country field from the form and from each record in the database. Next, move the Fax field below the Phone field so it's visible in the layout.

3. Drag the **Fax field name** below the Phone field, as shown in Figure 8-10, then release the mouse button
   If you have trouble moving the field to the correct spot, choose Undo from the Edit menu and try again. Next you add a Comments field to the form.

4. Click directly below the Fax field

5. Click **Insert** on the menu bar, then click **Field**
   The Insert Field dialog box opens.

6. Type **Comments** and press **[Enter]**
   Works adds a field named "Comments" to the form. Because you need plenty of space in the Comments field for miscellaneous notes on customers, you need to resize the field so that it is two lines high.

7. Click and drag the **right-top sizing handle** of the Comments field to the right side of the form, then drag the **bottom-middle sizing handle** of the Comments field so that it is two lines high
   Works widens and extends the field to two lines, as shown in Figure 8-11. Works has replicated each change you made to the form in this lesson in every record in the database.

8. Click the **Save button** on the toolbar
   Works saves your changes.

FIGURE 8-10: Moving Fax field

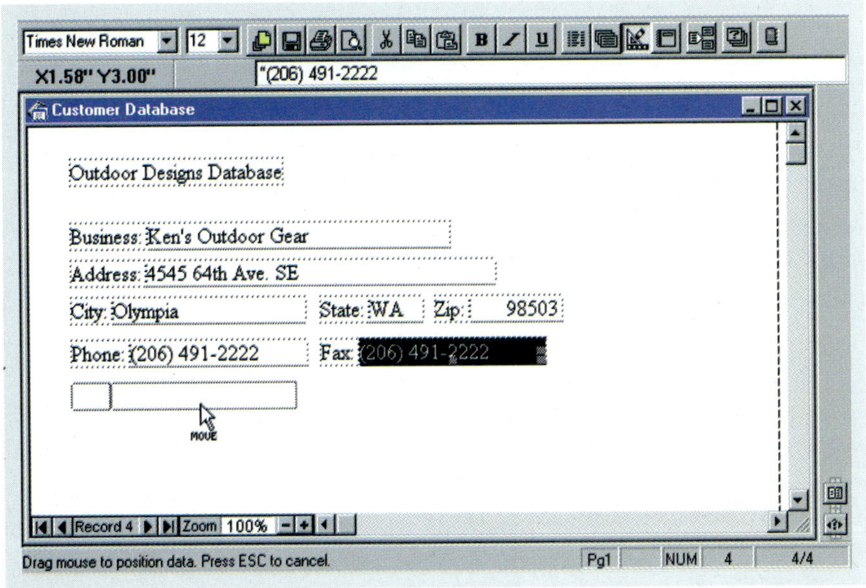

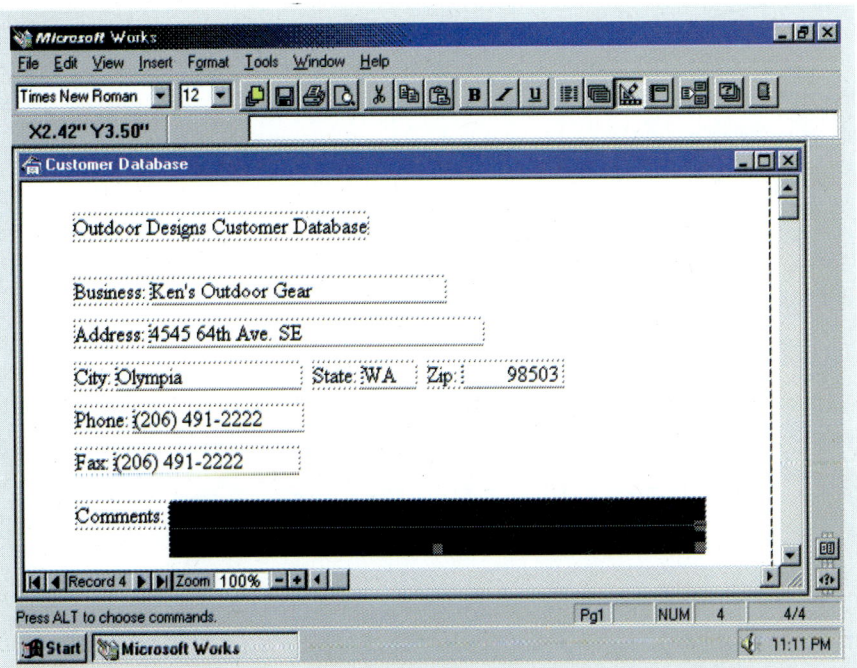

FIGURE 8-11: Database form after field changes

Changing the alignment in a field

You can change a field value's alignment in Form Design view. The alignment options are General, Left, Right, and Center. **General alignment**, the default, aligns text at the left of the field and numbers at the right of the field. A popular alignment option for zip codes is left alignment. To left-align a field, you click the field, click Format on the menu bar, click Alignment, click the Left option button, and press Enter.

TROUBLE?

Be careful when you delete fields from a form. Works removes deleted fields from every record in the database, and you cannot reverse the deletion with the Undo command.

Changing font size and style

You can easily dress up your database with formatting. You can change the font and style of labels and fields in your new database, and you can also add borders and shading to emphasize special information. The Border and Shading commands on the Format menu help you take advantage of the unique rectangular design of database fields and produce impressive formatting effects; see the related topic, "Adding shading and borders to fields" for more information about these commands. **case** You will now add larger fonts and color to your database to make entering information easier and to make the database look more appealing.

1. Make sure you are in Form Design view, then click the label **Outdoor Designs Customer Database** at the top of the form

2. Click the **Font Size list box**, click **16**, then click **Arial**
   The label's size changes to 16 points, and the font changes from Times New Roman to Arial. Notice that the toolbar elements work exactly as they do in the Word Processor and Spreadsheet. You can also use the Font and Style command on the Format menu to accomplish these formatting changes.

3. Click the **Bold button** on the toolbar
   The label's style changes to boldface. Now you add color to both parts of the Business field. Using a second color draws attention to the Business Field in the database and helps you scroll to and find the name of a particular customer more easily.

4. Click the **Business field name**, hold down **[Ctrl]** and click the **Business field value**, then release **[Ctrl]**
   Works highlights Business and Ken's Outdoor Gear. (Which record Works currently displays doesn't matter: font and style formatting applies to all records.) Holding down [Ctrl] lets you select more than one field at a time.

5. Click **Format** from the menu bar, click the **Font and Style command**, then click the **Font tab** if it doesn't open in front.

6. Click the **Color list box**, then scroll down the list and click **Red**
   You selected red as the font color, and text in the sample rectangle appears in red.

7. Click **OK**, then click the **Address field** (or anywhere on the form)
   Now the Business field appears in red, as shown in Figure 8-12.

8. Click the **Form View button** on the toolbar, then click the **Save button** on the toolbar
   Works saves your font changes and returns to Form view. Notice the font size and color changes also appear in this view.

FIGURE 8-12: Database after font and style changes

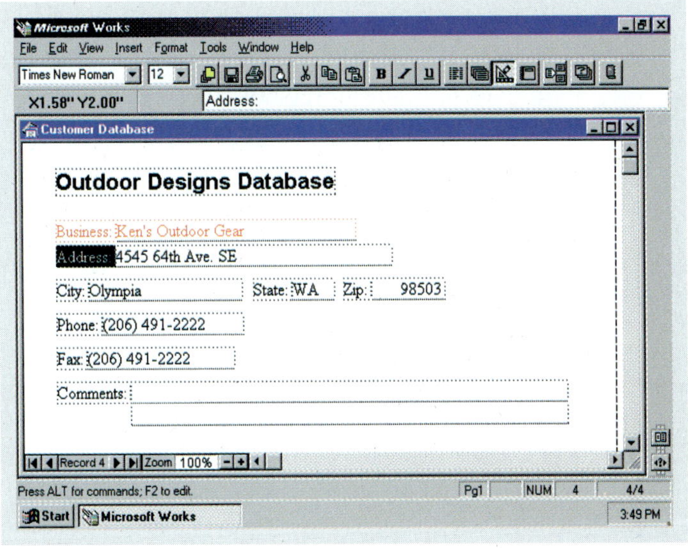

Adding shading and borders to fields

To add shading or borders to a field, you must be in List view or Form Design view. To add shading, you click the field, click Format on the menu bar, then click the Shading command. A Format dialog box tab appears with Pattern, Foreground, and Background list boxes. The Pattern list box contains 14 different shading patterns, ranging from slight shading to solid black. To outline a field with a border, you click the field, click Format on the menu bar, then click the Border command. A tab appears displaying Outline, Color, and Line style elements. To add a thin border you click the Outline button, then click OK. Figure 8-13 shows a database with light shading and a thin border added to a field.

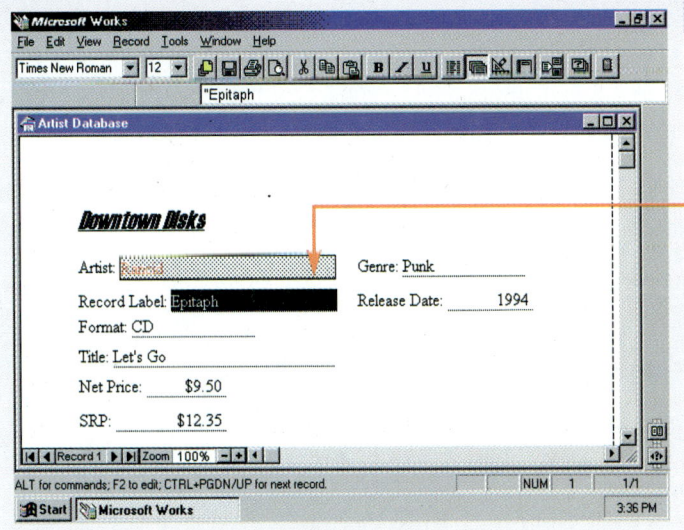

Shading and border formatting

FIGURE 8-13: Field with shading and border

QUICK TIP

You can add WordArt to a database form by choosing the WordArt command from the Insert menu.

Printing the database

Entire databases are rarely printed because they usually contain hundreds or even thousands of records; printing them all can be very time-consuming and impractical. However, printing one or more records for quick reference or mailing information is often useful. Inserting a header or footer in your printed record(s) is also useful; see the related topic, "Adding headers and footers," for more information.

▶ case Print the Cambridge Kite Supply record now for Sue Ellen so she can use it for an upcoming account call.

1. **Make sure you're in Form view, then click the Print Preview button on the toolbar**

   The Print Preview window opens, and the first record in the database appears as it will print. (By default Works prints one record per page in landscape orientation.) Several command buttons that control the operation of the Print Preview window appear on the window's right side. If you receive a warning message that some of your fields are past the printing range, go back to Form Design view and reduce the size of some fields a little.

2. **Click Zoom In**

   The record enlarges to half-size in the Print Preview window, as shown in Figure 8-14.

3. **Click Previous**

   The first record (Cambridge Kite Supply) appears in the Print Preview window. You'll print this record and give it to Sue Ellen for her upcoming account call.

4. **Click Cancel**

   You can print from Print Preview, but that would print the entire database. The File menu Print command lets you select records for printing.

5. **Click File on the menu bar, then click Print; if a First-time Help dialog box opens, click OK**

   The Print dialog box opens. It lets you specify the number of copies you want to print, the printing page range (if the form is longer than one page), and whether to print all records or only the current record.

   Take a moment now to verify that your printer is online and properly connected to your computer. If you have any questions, ask your instructor or lab manager for help.

6. **Click Current record only in the What to Print section, then click OK**

   The Print dialog box closes. After a few moments the database record for Cambridge Kite Supply emerges from the printer. Now save any changes you made, and exit Works.

7. **Click the Save button on the toolbar**

   Works saves your changes. You are now finished working for the day.

8. **Click File, then click Exit Works**

   The Customer Database file and the Works program close.

FIGURE 8-14: Examining second database record in Print Preview

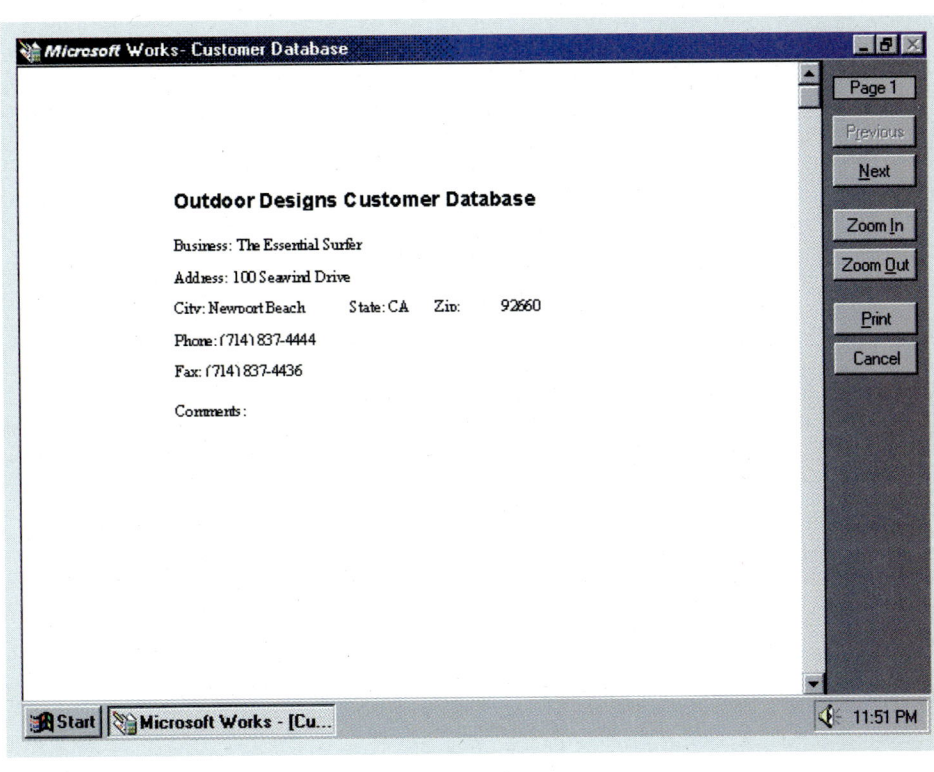

Adding headers and footers

When you print your records, you may want to add page numbers, the current date, or other text to the top or bottom of each page. You can add this information to your form with the Headers and Footers command on the View menu. Figure 8-15 shows the Headers and Footers dialog box. A standard header or footer in Works is one line long and can contain one or several header and footer codes, identical to the Spreadsheet tool's header and footer codes. Headers and footers don't appear in Form view, but you can examine them in Print Preview.

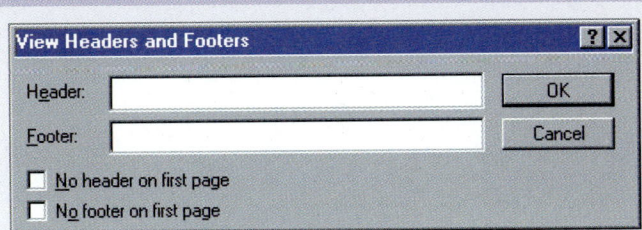

FIGURE 8-15: Headers and Footers dialog box

You can print a table containing some or all of your database records by switching to List view before printing. This saves lots of paper if you're printing several records.

TASK REFERENCE

TASK	MOUSE/BUTTON	MENU	KEYBOARD
Add a record to the database	Click	In Form view, click Record, Insert Record	Press [Tab] when last field is selected
Build a data-entry form	Click and arrange fields by dragging	Click View, Form Design	[Ctrl][F9]
Create database fields	Type field name in Create Database dialog box and click Add	In Form Design view, click Insert, Field	[Alt][I], [F]
Display the database as it will be printed	Click	Click File, Print Preview	[Alt][F], [V]
Format numbers in fields		In Form Design view, click Format, Field	[Alt][O], [L]
Insert a descriptive label on the form		Click Insert, Label	[Alt][I], [L]
Switch between database fields	Click the next field		[Tab]
Switch to Form view for data entry	Click	Click View, Form	[F9]
Switch to List view	Click	Click View, List	[Shift][F9]

CONCEPTSREVIEW

Label each element of the Database Tool, as shown in Figure 8-16.

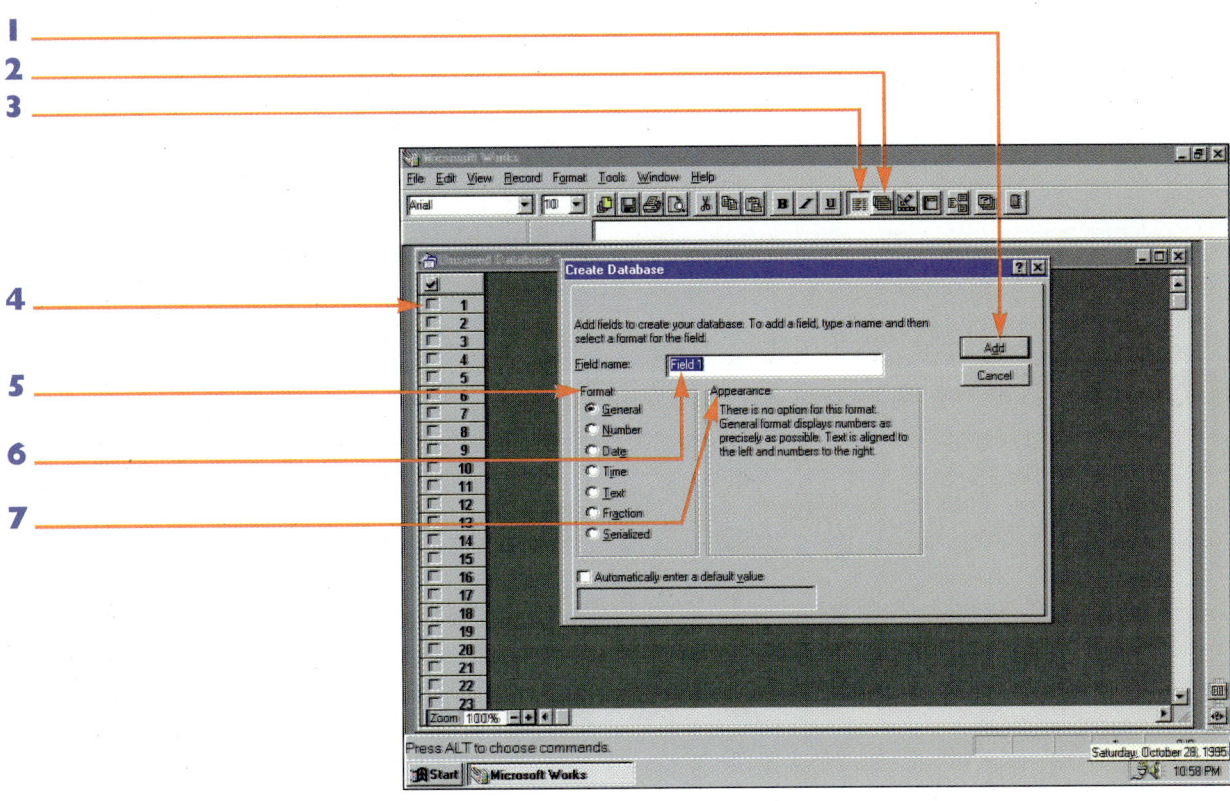

FIGURE 8-16

Match each of the buttons on the Database toolbar with their names.

8.
9.
10.
11.
12.
13.

a. Filters
b. List View
c. Report View
d. Insert Record
e. Form View
f. Form Design

Select the best answer from the list of choices.

14 A database is

    a. An organized collection of information

    b. Stored electronically

    c. Can contain information of any kind

    d. All of the above

15 List View displays the records in a format resembling

    a. A word processing document

    b. A spreadsheet

    c. A form filled out on paper

    d. A Fax cover sheet

16 Form View displays the records in a format resembling
   a. A word processing document
   b. A spreadsheet
   c. A form filled out on paper
   d. A Fax cover sheet

17 If you want to use the keyboard to move between fields on a database form, you would use
   a. [Tab]
   b. [Enter]
   c. [Esc]
   d. [F1]

18 If you wanted to edit the contents of a field on the formula bar, you would use
   a. [Tab]
   b. [F1]
   c. [F2]
   d. [Esc]

19 To add a new record to the database, you would
   a. Press [Tab] when the last field in the last record is highlighted
   b. Click the Insert Record button on the toolbar
   c. Choose the Insert Record command from the Record menu
   d. All of the above

20 Fields in a database can be
   a. Deleted
   b. Moved
   c. Sized
   d. All of the above

21 Fields deleted from a database
   a. Can be restored with the Undo command
   b. Are removed from every record in the database
   c. Cannot be restored with the Undo command
   d. Answers b and c

22 To select more than one field at a time in Form View
   a. Hold down the [Alt] key, then click the fields
   b. Hold down the [Ctrl] key, then click on the fields
   c. Drag the mouse across the fields
   d. Press [F8] two times

23 When there is more than one record in the database, you can move to other records, using the
   a. record navigation buttons
   b. scroll bars
   c. the [Enter] key
   d. All of the above

24 You can add records or edit records in
   a. Form View
   b. List View
   c. ReportCreator
   d. Answers a and b

SKILLS REVIEW

1 Start the Database tool and create an inventory database.
   a. Start Works.
   b. Start the Database tool.
   c. In the Create Database dialog box, type Department and click the Add button.
   d. Type "Item" and click the Add button.
   e. Type "Color" and click the Add button.
   f. Type "Size" and click the Add button.
   g. Type "Description" and click the Add button.
   h. Type "Cost", choose the Number format, select the second number Appearance, and click the Add button.
   i. Type "On-Hand" and click the Add button.
   j. Click the Done button to display the database fields in List View.

2 Using Form View.

a. Click the Form View button.

b. Click the Insert Record button.

c. Type "Camping", press [Tab], type "Tent", press [Tab], type "blue", press[Tab], type "11 x 14", press [Tab], type "dome", press [Tab], type "259.00", press [Tab], type "7".

d. Press [Tab] to insert a new record.

e. Type "Clothing", press [Tab], type "Shirt", press [Tab], type "green", press [Tab], type "L", press [Tab], type "pull-over", press [Tab], type "9.99", press [Tab], type "30".

f. Press [Tab] to insert a new record.

g. Type "Camping", press [Tab], type "Stove", press [Tab], type "green", press [Tab], type "2-burner", press [Tab], type "propane", press [Tab], type "29.99", press [Tab], type "15".

h. Press [Tab] to insert a new record.

i. Type "Shoes", press [Tab], type "Hiking Boots", press [Tab], type "brown", press [Tab], type "7", press [Tab], type "high-top", press [Tab], type "39.99", press [Tab], type "4".

j. Press [Tab] to insert a new record.

k. Type "Clothing", press [Tab], type "Shirt", press [Tab], type "maroon", press [Tab], type "L", press [Tab], type "pull-over", press [Tab], type "19.99", press [Tab], type "24", press [Tab].

l. Choose File, Save As to save the database to the My Works Files folder on your Student Disk, giving it the name Inventory.

3 Add records to the database in List View.

a. Click the List View button and go to the last record.

b. Type "Camping", press [Tab], type "sleeping bag", press [Tab], type "red", press [Tab], type "single", press [Tab], type "light weight", press [Tab], type "19.99", press [Tab], type "20", press [Tab].

c. Click the Insert Record button.

d. Type "Shoes" press [Tab], type "Running", press [Tab], type "white", press [Tab], type "9", press [Tab], type "full-support", press [Tab], type "19.99", press [Tab], type "15", press [Tab].

e. Click the Insert Record button.

f. Type "Boats", press [Tab], type "canoe", press [Tab], type "green", press [Tab], type "15" foot, press [Tab], type" 2-person", press [Tab], type "109.99", press [Tab], type "3", press [Tab].

g. Click the Insert Record button.

h. Type "Accessories", press [Tab], type "knife", press [Tab], type "red", press [Tab], type "20" , press [Tab], type "Swiss Army", press [Tab], type "29.99", press [Tab], type "40", press [Tab].

i. Click the Save button to save your changes to the file.

4 Edit the contents of the database.

a. Be sure you are in List view.

b. Move to the first record.

c. Move the pointer to the Cost field.

d. Type 299.99.

e. Press [Tab].

f. Move to the last record.

g. Move the pointer to the Size field.

h. Press the [Delete] key.

i. Type 25 feature.

j. Click the Save button to save changes to the file.

5 Edit the Fields.

a. Click the Form Design button.

b. Place the pointer on the last field.

c. Click Insert on the menu bar.

d. Choose Field from the Insert menu.

e. In the Insert Field dialog box, type Supplier, and click OK.

j. Click and drag the field to the bottom of the list of fields on the form.

g. Click the List View button to view the new field.

h. Click the Form Design button.

i. Click the Supplier field.

j. Press the Delete key.

k. In the Delete field dialog box, click OK.

6 Adding a Label and Changing the Font Size and Style.

  a. Click the Form Design button.

  b. Starting with the On-Hand field, drag each field down in the form so that you have about an inch of white space at the top of the form.

  c. Click the insertion point in the blank space you created at the top of the box.

  d. Click the Insert menu.

  e. Choose the Label command.

  f. In the Insert Label dialog box, type "Outdoor Designs Inventory".

  g. Click the Insert button.

  h. With the label selected, click the Format menu.

  i. Choose the Font and Style command.

  j. In the Font list, choose Arial and in the Size list choose 18 and click OK.

  k. Drag the label to the center top of the screen.

  l. Save the file to the My Works Files Folder on your Student Disk.

7 Preview the Inventory database and print it.

  a. From List View, click the File menu.

  b. Choose the Print Preview command.

  c. Verify that your fields and records look correct on the page.

  d. Click Cancel to return to the database.

  e. Click the File menu.

  f. Choose the Print command.

  g. Verify the correct printer.

  h. Click OK to print.

  i. After the printing is complete, click the File menu.

  j. Choose the Close command to close the Inventory file, clicking yes to save changes when prompted.

INDEPENDENT CHALLENGE 1

In order to analyze pet sales at Stuff for Pets, you decide to create a database of animals which have been for sale in the store this year. You will need to include information on each animal so that you can look at sales trends for the store.

To complete this independent challenge:

1 Create a new database which includes the following fields. Format the fields as indicated.

Field Name	Format	Appearance
Category	General	
Breed	General	
Gender	General	
DOB	Date	10/15/96
Time	General	
Cost	Number	1,234.56
Retail	Number	1,234.56

2 Add the following records to the database.

Category	Breed	Gender	DOB	Time	Cost	Retail
Dog	Poodle	F	3/7/95	120	125.00	499.99
Dog	Collie	M	4/1/95	60	110.00	459.99
Cat	Persian	F	2/3/95	30	120.00	299.99
Dog	Yorkie	M	3/1/95	30	100.00	359.99
Bird	Parrot	M	5/15/94	90	150.00	659.99

3 Save the database in the My Works Files folder on your Student Disk as Star.

4 Print the database.

INDEPENDENT CHALLENGE 2

As part of a long-term marketing strategy at Stuff for Pets, you are charged with creating the database of customers who have purchased animals at the store. You will use the database to notify customers with information of interest to them.

To complete this independent challenge:

1 Create a new database that includes the following fields. Format the fields as indicated.

Field Name	Format	Appearance
Type	General	
Breed	General	
First	General	
Last	General	
Address	General	
City	General	
State	General	
Zip	General	

2 Add the following records to the database:

Type	Breed	First	Last	Address	City	State	Zip
Dog	Yorkie	Sue	Jones	987 Lincoln Ave.	Seattle	WA	98701
Dog	Poodle	Mary	Miller	717 Adams Ave.	Bellingham	WA	98551
Cat	Calico	Jerry	Smith	789 Old Mill Ln.	Snohomish	WA	98456
Turtle	Box	Larry	Hill	654 Riverview Rd	Seattle	WA	98765
Dog	Mixed	Linda	James	345 Augusta Rd	Seattle	WA	98765

3 Save the database in the My Works Files folder on your Student Disk as Customer.

4 Print the database.

INDEPENDENT CHALLENGE 3

As Human Resources Manager for Washington County, you are responsible for tracking all employee records. You decide to create an electronic database of all full-time and part-time employees. This database will help you create reports for the managers and county commissioners.

To complete this independent challenge:

- **1** Create a new database which includes the following fields. Format the fields as indicated.

Field Name	Format	Appearance
First Name	General	
Middle	General	
Last Name	General	
Hire Date	Date	10/15/95
Salary	Number	1,234.56
Gender	General	
Status	General	
Dept	General	

- **2** Add the following records to the database.

First Name	Middle	Last Name	Hire Date	Salary	Gender	Status	Dept
Mary	S.	Walker	10/1/89	28,000.00	F	Full	PW
James	W.	Miller	5/7/92	30,000.00	M	Full	Safety
Sherry	M.	Adams	6/4/85	32,000.00	F	Full	Safety
Linda	E.	Simms	9/9/95	15,000.00	F	PT	PW
James	W.	Johnson	5/10/90	17,500.00	M	PT	Legal

- **3** Save the database in the My Works Files folder on your Student Disk as County.

- **4** Print the database.

INDEPENDENT CHALLENGE 4

As manager of the Quick Stop Video Store, you are responsible for creating the electronic database of movies that are for sale in the store. You will use this data to track video sales for the store.

To complete this independent challenge:

- **1** Create a new database that includes the following fields. Format the fields as indicated.

Field Name	Format	Appearance
Category	General	
Movie Name	General	
Release Date	Date	10/15/96
Rating	General	
Cost	Number	1,234.56
Sold	General	

- **2** Add the following records to the database.

Category	Movie Name	Release Date	Rating	Cost	Sold
Adventure	Speed	10/1/94	R	10.99	123
Childrens	Splash	3/6/89	G	15.99	150
Comedy	Tommy Boy	10/15/95	PG-13	12.99	70
Comedy	Casper	11/1/95	PG	12.99	45
Childrens	Pocahontas	1/1/96	G	24.99	400

- **3** Save the database on your Student Disk in the My Works Files folder as Movies.

- **4** Print the database.

VISUALWORKSHOP

Create the database shown below. Save the file as Run in the My Works Files folder on your Student disk. Print the database.

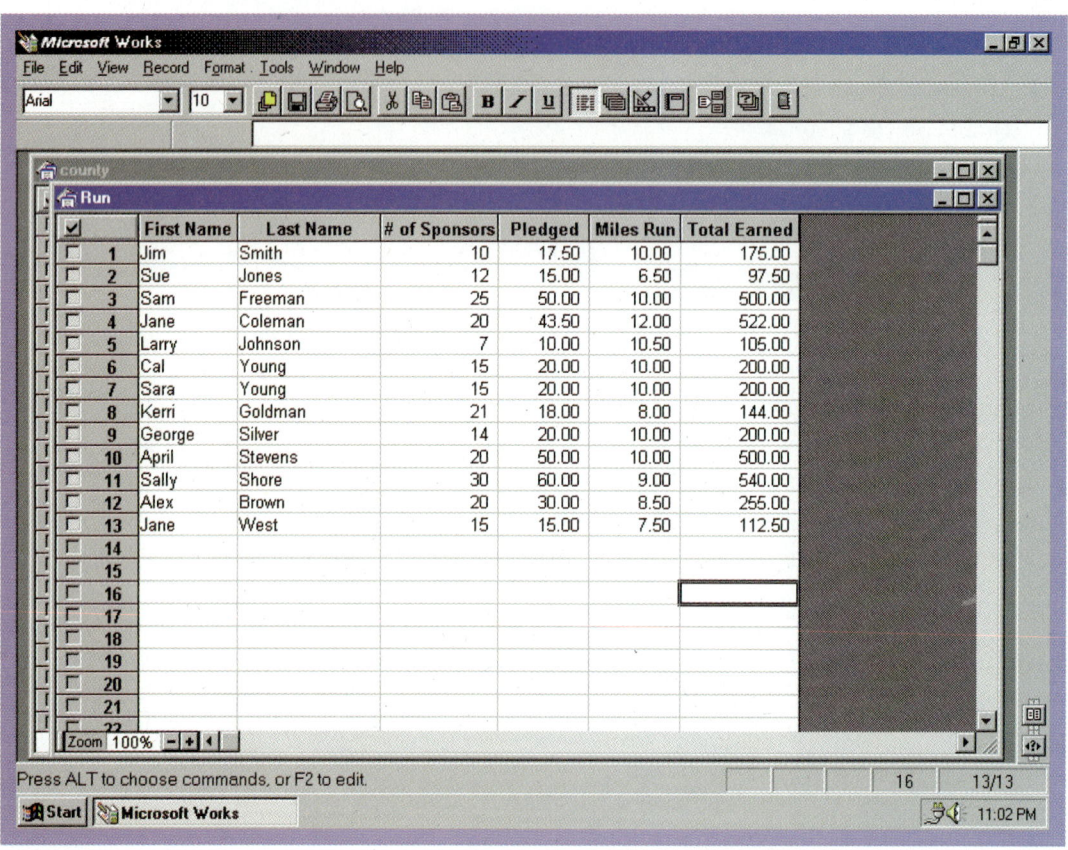

FIGURE 8-17

UNIT 9

OBJECTIVES

- Open an existing database
- Add ClipArt to a database form
- Use field entries in formulas
- Sort database records
- Filter a database
- Use advanced filters
- Protect a database
- Print envelopes from a database

Working
WITH AN EXISTING DATABASE

Now that you know how to create a database you are ready to add more information to it and start working with the information in creative ways. In this unit, you'll learn how to add ClipArt to a database form, how to search a database with helpful commands called **filters**, how to protect a database, and how to print envelopes using records from a database file. ▶ **case** You have been charged with customizing the Outdoor Designs database so that Sue Ellen and Frasier can use it to track sales and to calculate sales reps' commissions. You'll update the data-entry form so that it contains artwork, two new fields, and formulas that will help employees who use it regularly. You'll also protect the database from unauthorized use and print envelopes for a mailing. ▶

Opening an existing database

Works lets you open an existing database at any time and start working with it. To open an existing database, you need to know where to find the database file on disk. If you used the file recently, you can double-click its name in the Existing Documents tab in the Works Task Launcher dialog box. If the file's name doesn't appear in the Existing Document tab, you can search for it by clicking the Open a document not listed here button. **case** Sue Ellen asked you to open the existing Outdoor Designs database and add several items to it. Open the Works 9-1 file now on your Student Disk, and save it under a new name to protect the original.

1. **Start Works**
   The Works Task Launcher dialog box opens.

2. Put your Student Disk in the appropriate drive, then click the **Existing Documents tab** in the Works Task Launcher dialog box

3. Click the **Open a document not listed here button**
   The Open dialog box, shown in Figure 9-1, lets you locate and open files stored on your computer disks. You use the Open dialog box now to open the database named Works 9-1 on your Student Disk.

4. Click the **Look in list box**, then the letter of the drive containing your Student Disk
   The names of files and folders on your Student Disk appear in the Open dialog box.

5. Double-click **WKS 9-1**
   The dialog box closes. After a moment the Outdoor Designs customer database shown in Figure 9-2 opens in a window. Similar to the file you created in Unit 8, this file contains a few new business records. Before you start to modify the database, save the file on your Student Disk with a different name to protect the original.

6. Click **File** on the menu bar, then click **Save As**
   The Save As dialog box opens.

7. Type **Sales Data** in the File name text box

8. Double-click the **My Works Files folder** in the list box, then click **Save**
   Works saves the file Sales Data in the My Works Files folder on the Student Disk.

FIGURE 9-1: Open dialog box

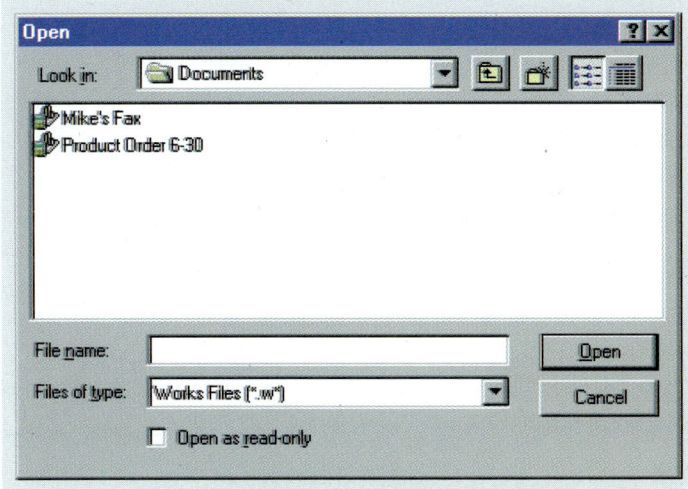

FIGURE 9-2: Use database to track sales commissions

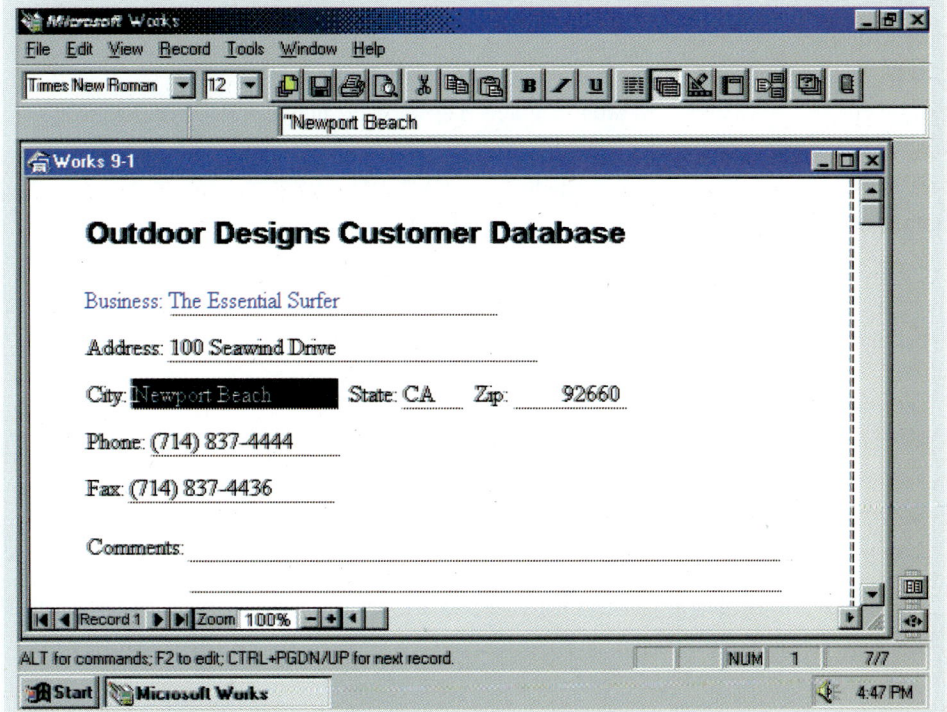

When you open an existing database, Works displays the record that was open when the file was last saved on disk.

Adding ClipArt to a database form

Works lets you add artwork and other types of information to your database with several Insert menu commands. Adding ClipArt to your data-entry form can make a database easier and more fun to use. For more information, see the related topic, "Working with ClipArt objects." **case** Sue Ellen asked you to add a piece of ClipArt to the Outdoor Designs database form to add visual interest to the information. To give your database an outdoor theme, try adding the Big Tree ClipArt to your form now.

1. Click the **Form Design button** on the toolbar
   Your database form appears in Form Design View.

2. Click your form, just to the right of the label "Outdoor Designs Customer Database"
   The cursor blinks on your form. (If the label highlights, you clicked too close to it. Click again to deselect it, and try again.) When you insert ClipArt in your form, the cursor location marks the upper-left corner of the artwork.

3. Click **Insert** on the menu bar, then click **ClipArt**
   The Microsoft ClipArt Gallery shown in Figure 9-3 opens. The ClipArt Gallery gives you access to all ClipArt images stored on your hard disk. The standard Works installation includes about 100 pieces of electronic artwork, but if other Microsoft programs are installed on your system, such as Microsoft Office, you have additional images. The Big Tree ClipArt is in the Plants category.

4. Click the **Plants category** in the Categories list box, and then click the **tree**
   The filename C:\Msworks\Clipart\Bigtree.wmf appears at the bottom of the ClipArt Gallery dialog box. This is the name of the Big Tree ClipArt on your hard disk.

5. Click **Insert**
   The ClipArt Gallery closes and the Big Tree artwork displays on the form. The image appears in the upper-right corner of the form (where the cursor is) and is currently selected. Works selects ClipArt when you insert it so you can move or resize it if you want. If the image on your screen is larger than the one shown in Figure 9-4, follow steps 6 and 7. Otherwise, skip to Step 8.

6. Scroll down and to the right, until you see the lower-right corner of the image
   The small squares on the border of the image are **sizing handles**. You drag them to resize the image.

7. Drag the sizing handle in the lower-right corner of the image up and to the left, until the image size matches that shown in Figure 9-4.
   The cursor changes to a sizing pointer, and the word "Resize" appears below it. Note that in the figure, the right edge of the image is to the left of the record's dotted-line border.

8. Click the **Form View button** on the toolbar to lock in the ClipArt
   The ClipArt appears in its final position, as shown in Figure 9-4. The tree will now appear in each database record, just as the labels and fields do.

9. Click the **Save button** on the toolbar to save the ClipArt in the database

FIGURE 9-3: ClipArt Gallery dialog box

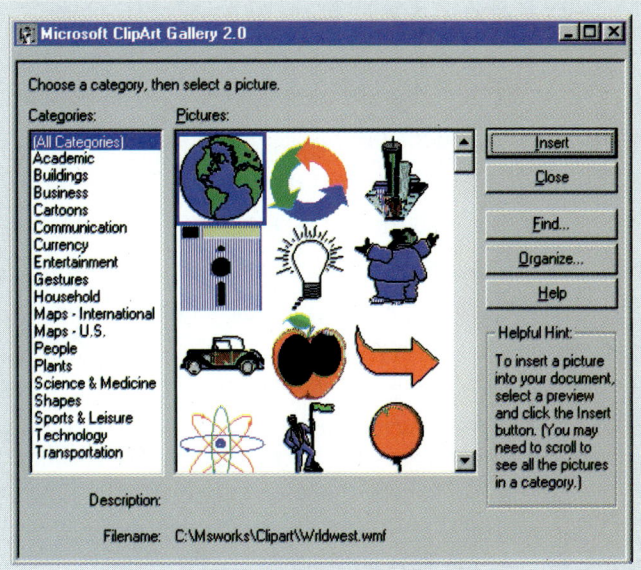

FIGURE 9-4: Big Tree ClipArt in database form

Clipart

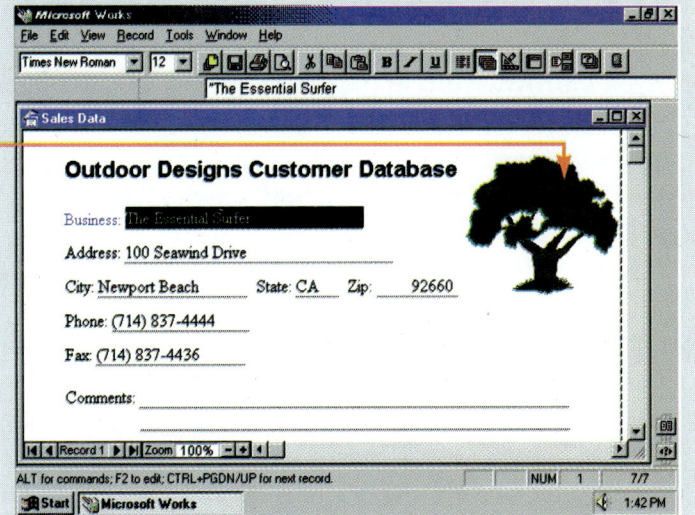

Working with ClipArt objects

ClipArt images are called **objects** in the Database tool. ClipArt objects can be selected, moved, copied, pasted, and deleted like any other element of the database form. You can use menu commands, keyboard keys, or the toolbar to perform these basic operations. In addition, you can resize a ClipArt object by clicking it, then dragging it to the right or left edge of the ClipArt frame with the sizing pointer.

QUICK TIP

In Form Design View you can also add a pop-up note to your form with the Note-It command on the Insert menu. This is useful for including instructions or messages in your database.

Using field entries in formulas

To perform a calculation in the Database, you enter a formula in a field. As you learned in Unit 5, a formula is an equation that calculates a new value from existing values. In the Database, formulas can contain numbers, mathematical operators, field names, and functions. Table 9-1 lists some mathematical operators that you can use in a formula. **case** Sue Ellen wants you to add a year-to-date sales field to a form and a commission field that calculates commissions. She and Frasier will use this information to evaluate sales of Outdoor Designs products and to calculate sales reps' commissions.

1. Click the **Form Design button** on the toolbar
   To enter new fields, you need to be in Form Design View.

2. Click to the right of the Phone field, click **Insert** on the menu bar, click **Field**, type **YTD Sales**, then press **[Enter]**
   A field named "YTD Sales" is added to the form where you clicked. You'll use this field to store year-to-date sales for each database record.

3. Click to the right of the Fax field, click **Insert** on the menu bar, click **Field**, type **Commission** in the Insert Field dialog box, then press **[Enter]**
   A field named "Commission" appears on the form. Now specify currency formatting for the two new fields.

4. Click the Commission field, hold down **[Ctrl]**, click the **YTD Sales field**, click **Format** on the menu bar, and click **Field**
   (Be sure to click the fields, not their descriptions.) Works selects the two new fields on your form and opens the Field tab in the Format dialog box.

5. Click the **Number option button**, click the **currency style** (the third item) in the Appearance list box, then click **OK**
   The YTD Sales and Commission fields appear with currency formatting. Next you enter a formula that calculates the commission for Outdoor Designs' sales reps.

6. Click the **Form View button** on the toolbar, click the **Commission field**, type **=YTD Sales*0.15**, then press **[Enter]**
   As in the Spreadsheet tool, the equals sign (=) lets Works know you're about to enter a formula in the field. The formula multiplies the value in the YTD Sales field by the 15% sales commission rate. When you press [Enter], zero ($0.00) appears in the field, because no sales totals have been entered on the form yet. Now you'll add sales information to each database record.

7. Scroll to the **first record** (The Essential Surfer) in the database if it is not already active, click the **YTD Sales field**, type **5500**, then press **[Enter]**
   $5,500.00 appears in the YTD Sales field, and $825.00 appears in the Commission field, as shown in Figure 9-5.

8. In records **2** through **7** of the database, enter these values in the YTD Sales field: **8230, 1600, 2450, 4000, 7200, 3650**
   Remember to press Enter after each entry. Use the record navigation buttons to move to each record quickly.

9. Click the **Save button** on the toolbar to save your changes

FIGURE 9-5: Database form with new formatted fields

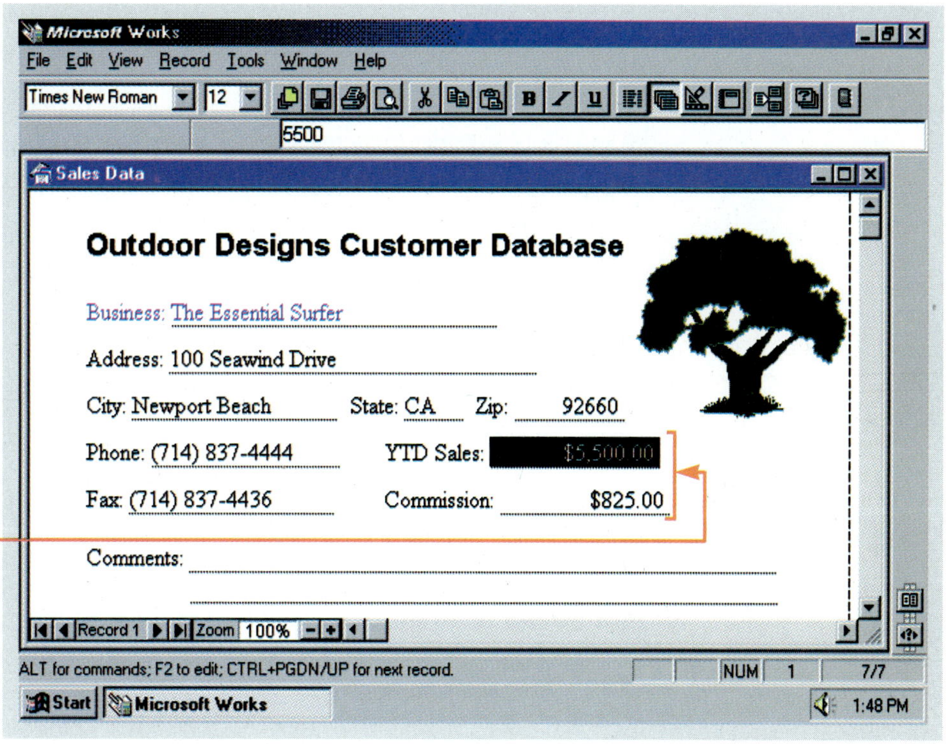

Fields with currency formatting

TABLE 9-1: Useful mathematical operators (listed in order of evaluation)

OPERATOR	DESCRIPTION	EXAMPLE	RESULT
( )	Parentheses	(3+6)*3	27
^	Exponential	10^2	100
*	Multiplication	7*5	35
/	Division	20/4	5
+	Addition	5+5	10
–	Subtraction	12–8	4

QUICK TIP

You can also use Works functions, which you worked with in the Spreadsheet tool, in database formulas. ■

Sorting database records

Works lets you rearrange or **sort** the records in your database in alphabetical or numerical order. When you sort your database, you need to specify a key field for the sort. For example, in a customer database you could sort records by the Business, Zip, or YTD Sales field. ▶case Sue Ellen asked you to sort the database in alphabetical order by business name, to match other records in the Outdoor Designs office. You try sorting alphabetically now.

1. Click the **Business field value** on the database form, then click the **List View button** on the toolbar
   The database appears in List View, and Works places the cursor in the Business field. The first several fields of the database appear in columns across the screen. (You can view the remaining fields by clicking the right scroll arrow.) Because the default column width in List View is only 10 characters, several field entries are only partially visible. Before you sort the database, you adjust each field's column width with the Field Width command, so you can read each fully.

2. Click the **Select All rectangle** above the first row and to the left of the Business column
   The entire database highlights.

3. Click **Format**, click **Field Width**, then click the **Best Fit button**
   The column width of each field in the database adjusts to fit the data. (Note that this command affects List View only.) Now you sort the seven records in the database alphabetically by business name.

4. Click **The Essential Surfer**, click **Record** on the menu bar, then click the **Sort Records** command
   The Sort Records dialog box shown in Figure 9-6 appears. (If you see a First-time Help dialog box, click OK.) It contains list boxes for the first, second, and third field names you want to use to sort the database with, respectively. The Sort By list box already contains the name of the Business field, because you chose it before the sort. You'll specify a second field name in the first Then By list box next, to resolve any ties (in this case, identical company names) that occur during the sort.

5. Click the first **Then By list box**, then click **City**
   The City field appears in the 2nd Field list box.

6. Click **OK**
   Works sorts the records and the result appears in the List View window shown in Figure 9-7. Ballard Boats and Kites is now the first record in the database.

7. Click the **Save button** on the toolbar
   You save your changes on disk.

FIGURE 9-6: Sort Records dialog box

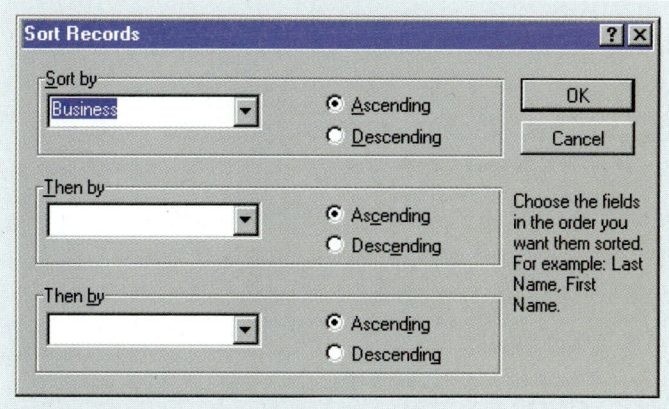

FIGURE 9-7: Customer records, sorted alphabetically by business name

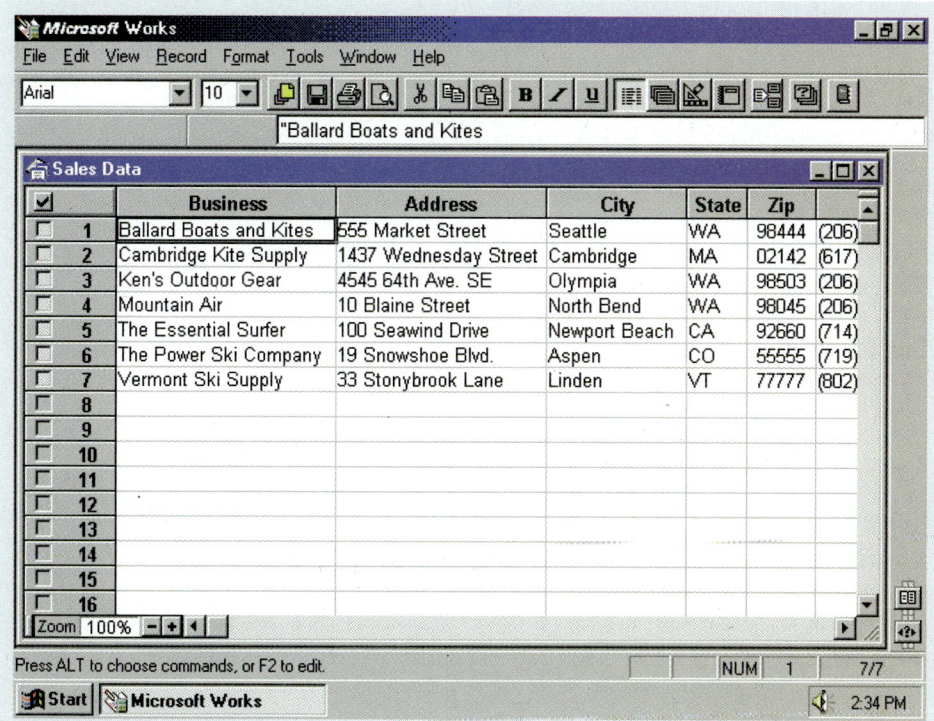

To sort database records in descending order, click the Descending option button to the right of each field list box you use in the Sort Records dialog box.

Filtering a database

As in the Word Processor, the Find command on the Edit menu searches for a specific item in the database. However, you'll often find that you want to locate a group of records that match a certain criterion, such as all businesses in the state of California or all addresses with the zip code 98503. In these instances you use a database **filter** in a search that compares one or more fields in the database with one or more values. ▶case To help Sue Ellen and Frasier determine their best customers this year, use a filter now to determine which businesses purchased at least $5,000 worth of Outdoor Designs products.

1. Verify that you are still in **List View**
   This view is best for seeing a filter's results.

2. Click **Tools** on the menu bar, then click **Filters**; if a First-time Help dialog box opens, click **OK**
   A Filter Name dialog box opens, prompting you for your new filter's name.

3. Type **$5000 in Sales**, then click **OK**
   The Filter dialog box shown in Figure 9-8 opens. It contains a Filter name text box you can use to switch between filters; a series of Field name list boxes, where you specify which field you want to use in the filter; a series of Comparison list boxes, where you specify a comparison operator; and a series of Compare To text boxes, where you type a value to compare. Now you compose a filter to identify all businesses that purchased at least $5,000 worth of products from Outdoor Designs this year.

4. Click the **list arrow** in the first Field name list box, scroll down and click the **YTD Sales field**
   YTD Sales is selected as the field for the filter.

5. Click the **list arrow** in the Comparison list box, then click **is greater than or equal to**
   You selected Is greater than or equal to as the comparison operator for the filter.

6. Type **$5000** in the Compare To text box, then click **Apply Filter**
   Works runs the filter, and the names of three businesses with sales greater than or equal to $5,000 appear in the window shown in Figure 9-9.

7. Click **Record** on the menu bar, point to **Show**, then click **All Records**
   The Show command cancels the $5,000 in sales filter. Although the filter disappears from the screen, it still exists in your computer's memory. Save your file on disk, so the filter is there when Sue Ellen and Frasier ask for it.

8. Click the **Save button** 💾 on the toolbar
   You saved the changes to the Sales Data file on disk.

FIGURE 9-8: Filter dialog box

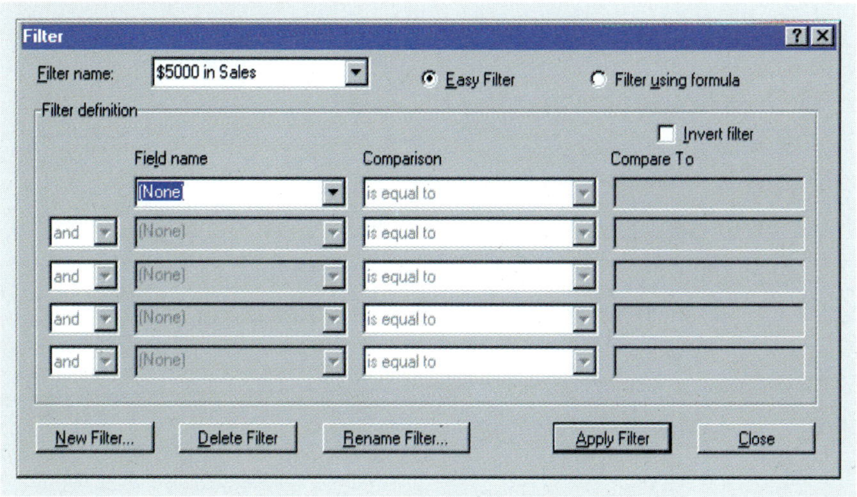

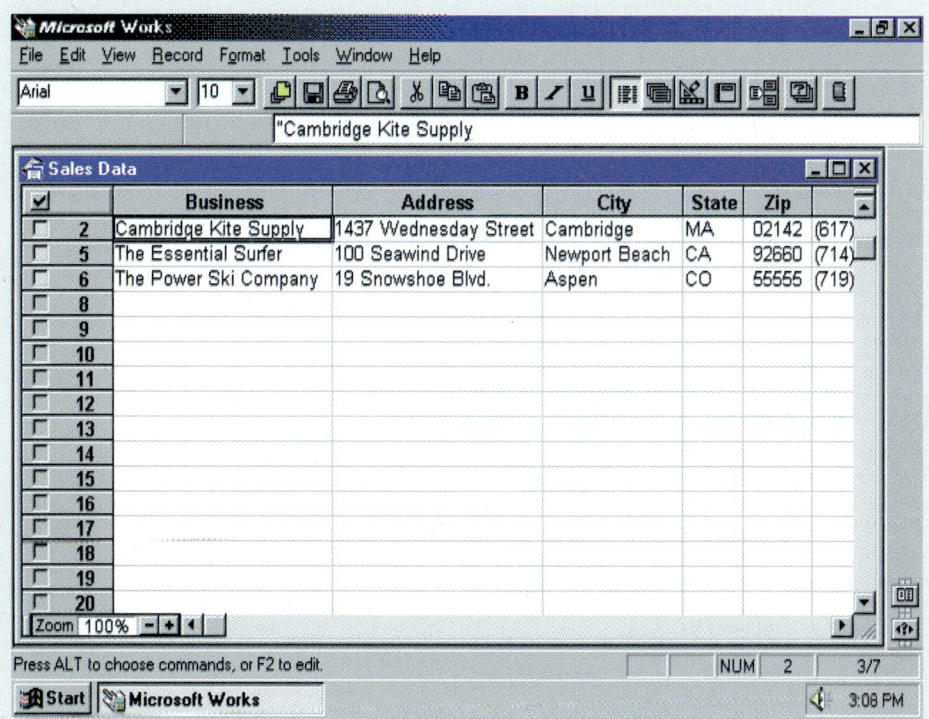

FIGURE 9-9: Works displays records that match filter in List View

QUICK TIP

To rerun a filter later, click Record on the menu bar, point to Apply Filter, and click the filter's name on the sub-menu that opens.

Using advanced filters

You can use the Filter dialog box to conduct a search based on more than one criterion. Filters with more than one criterion are linked with the **And** or **Or conjunctions**. You use the And conjunction when you want both comparisons to be true in the filter for a record to be selected. You use the Or conjunction when either criterion can be true in the filter for a record to be selected. ►case To highlight noteworthy sales activities in California, enter a filter now that searches for businesses that purchased at least $5,000 worth of products this year and are located in California.

1. Verify that you are in **List View**
   You learned in the last lesson that List View is best for reviewing a filter's results.

2. Click **Tools** on the menu bar, then click **Filters**
   The Filter dialog box opens, and the $5,000 in Sales filter appears in the dialog box.

3. Click the **New Filter button**, then type **$5000 in CA** in the Filter Name dialog box and click **OK**
   $5,000 in CA is the name of your new filter, and the Filter dialog box is empty, so you can define the new filter.

4. Click **YTD Sales** in the Field name list box, click **is greater than or equal to** in the Comparison list box, and type **$5000** in the Compare To text box
   So far, your filter is identical to the one you used in the last lesson. Now add a second comparison.

5. Click **State** in the second **Field name list box**, press **[Tab]** twice, then type **CA** in the Compare To text box
   Because the And conjunction is selected in the list box to the right of your second search, it's linked to the search on the first line when you run the filter. Your two-part filter should look like the one shown in Figure 9-10.

6. Click **Apply Filter** to run the search
   Works displays the filter's results in the window shown in Figure 9-11. Adjust your view with the horizontal scroll bar if necessary. The Essential Surfer, with purchases of $5,500, is the only record matching the filter.

7. Click **Record** on the menu bar, point to **Show**, then click **All Records**
   The Show command cancels the $5,000 in CA filter. If necessary, use the vertical scroll bar to see all your records. Although the filter disappears from the screen, it still exists in your computer's memory. Save the file on disk, so that the new filter is saved for Sue Ellen's use. (You can view it again with the Apply Filter command on the Record menu.)

8. Click the **Save button** 🖫 on the toolbar
   You saved the changes to the file on disk.

FIGURE 9-10: Use the And conjunction to link two filters

And conjunction →

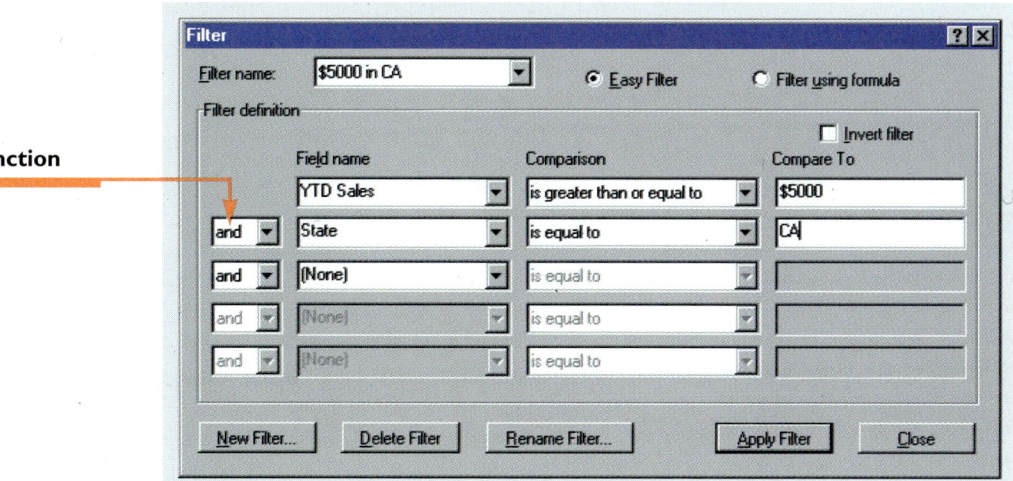

FIGURE 9-11: The Essential Surfer is the only record matching this advanced filter

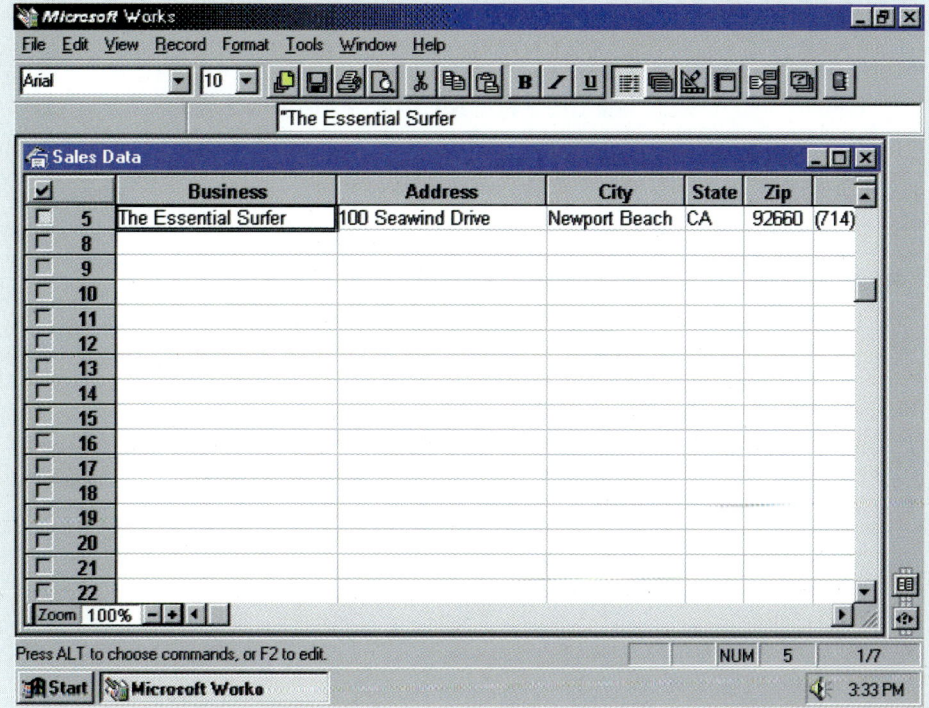

QUICK TIP

To delete a filter from the database, click the Delete Filter button in the Filter dialog box when the filter is open. ■

Protecting a database

After you complete a database form and enter several records, you should protect the data from accidental changes or deletion. Works lets you protect part or all of a database with the Protection command, so you control just what information users of your database can change. **case** Sue Ellen asked you to protect all fields in the database except the Comments field, so that employees cannot change the important fields but can include notes about customers.

1. Click the **Form Design button** on the toolbar
   It's easiest to protect your data in Form Design View, where you can specify each field you want to protect.

2. Hold down **[Ctrl]**, click each field value in the database form except the Comments field, then release **[Ctrl]**
   Nine fields are highlighted. (Be sure to select field values, not field names.)

3. Click **Format** on the menu bar, then click **Protection**
   The Protection dialog box shown in Figure 9-12 opens.

4. Click the **Protect field check box**, then click **OK**
   The dialog box closes and Works locks every database field, except Comments. To unlock the fields later (so you can change the data), you select the fields you want to unlock in Form Design View, then click the Protection command and remove the x from the Protect field check box. Now type some text in the unprotected Comments field.

5. Click the **Form View button**

6. Use the record navigation buttons to scroll to the first record in the database (**Ballard Boats and Kites**)

7. Click the **Comments field**, type **Account started by Jud Keim on 5/7/96**, then press **[Enter]**
   Figure 9-13 shows the text displayed in the Comments field.

8. Click the **Save button** on the toolbar
   You saved the changes to the form and the data protection options on disk in the file.

9. Click the **File menu**, then click **Close**
   The Database closes and the Works Task Launcher dialog box opens.

FIGURE 9-12: Protect your database with the Protection command

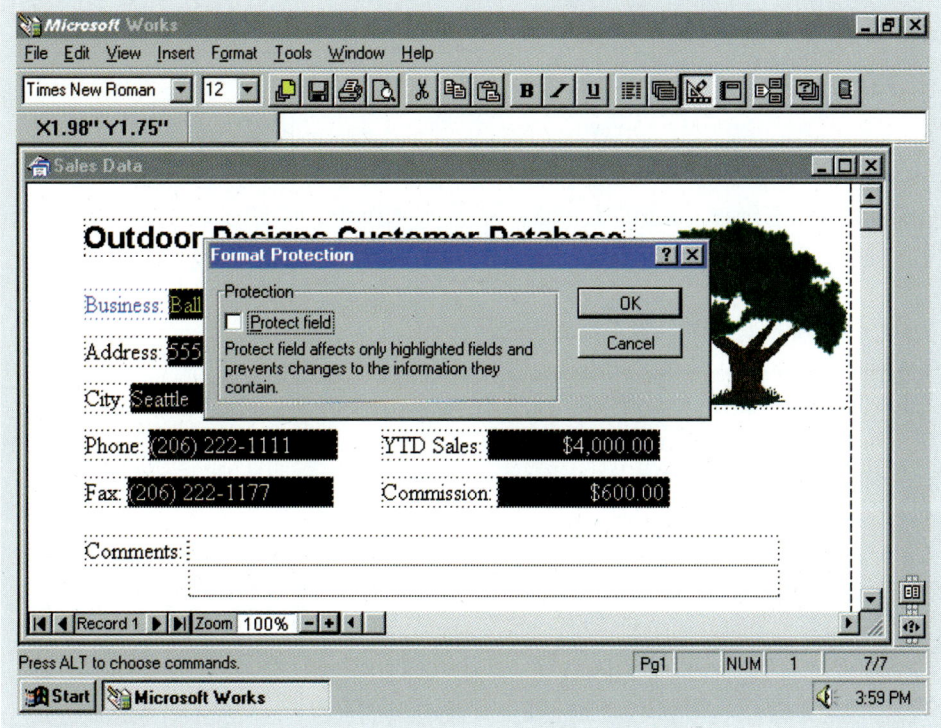

FIGURE 9-13: Comments field has been left unprotected for notes

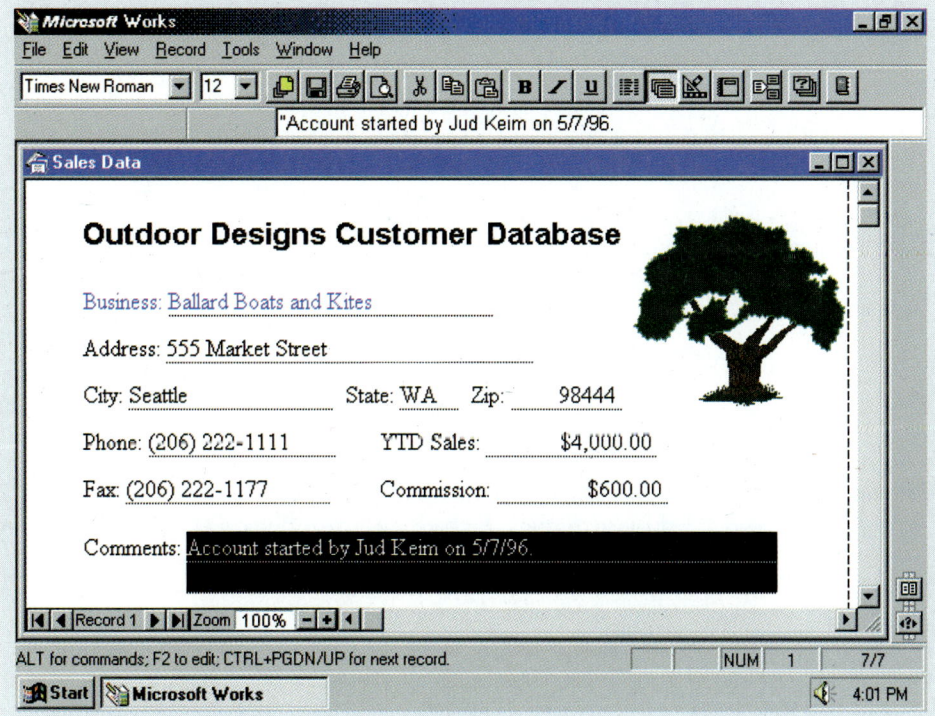

QUICK TIP

Press [Tab] to move to the next unprotected field in a database.

Printing envelopes from a database

You print envelopes from a Works database in three steps: first you design the envelope in the Word Processor; then you insert fields from your database with the Fields command; finally, you load envelopes into your printer and print the mailing list. ▶case Sue Ellen asked you to print envelopes for Outdoor Designs customers that have bought at least $5,000 worth of products this year. Complete this lesson even if your lab printer can't print envelopes.

1. Start the **Works Word Processor tool**
   The Word Processor opens in a window.

2. Click **Tools** on the menu bar, click **Envelopes**
   (If a First-time Help dialog box opens, click OK.) The Envelopes dialog box opens, and a seven-step instruction tab appears to guide you through the process of creating envelopes. (A check mark appears next to each step when you complete it.)

3. Click the **Next button**, choose the envelope size you want to use (choose Size 10 for business envelopes), then click the **Next button**
   Works records your selection and displays the instruction tab again.

4. Proceed through each instruction, clicking **Next** to open the next tab as in Figure 9-14, entering the appropriate information according to the table below

In this tab…	Do this…
Database	In the Choose a database list box, click **Sales Data.wdb**
Recipients	Click the **Filtered records in the database option button**, then click the **$5000 in Sales filter** in the Current Filter list box
Return Address	Type **Outdoor Designs**, press **[Enter]**, type **1820 Big Timber Drive**, press **[Enter]**, then type **Seattle, WA, 98555**
Main Address	Click the **Business field** in the Choose a field list box, then click **Add Field**, press **[Enter]**, click the **Address field** in the list box, click **Add Field**, press **[Enter]**, click **City**, click **Add Field**, type a **comma (,)**, press **[Spacebar]**, click **State**, click **Add Field**, press **[Spacebar]** twice, click **Zip**, then click **Add Field**
Printing	Click **Print** if envelopes are loaded in your printer; otherwise click **Preview**, then click **OK** to confirm the filter (see Figure 9-15)

5. When you finish previewing or printing, click **Close**
   You can save this template just like any other Works file so that you can print the envelopes in this filter any time Sue Ellen or Frasier requests them.

6. Click **File, Save As**, type **Customer Envelopes** in the File name text box, click the letter of the drive that contains your Student Disk in the Save in list box, double-click the **My Works Files folder**, then click **Save**
   You finish working on the database and are ready to exit Works.

7. Click the **File** menu, then click **Exit**

FIGURE 9-14: Main address tab

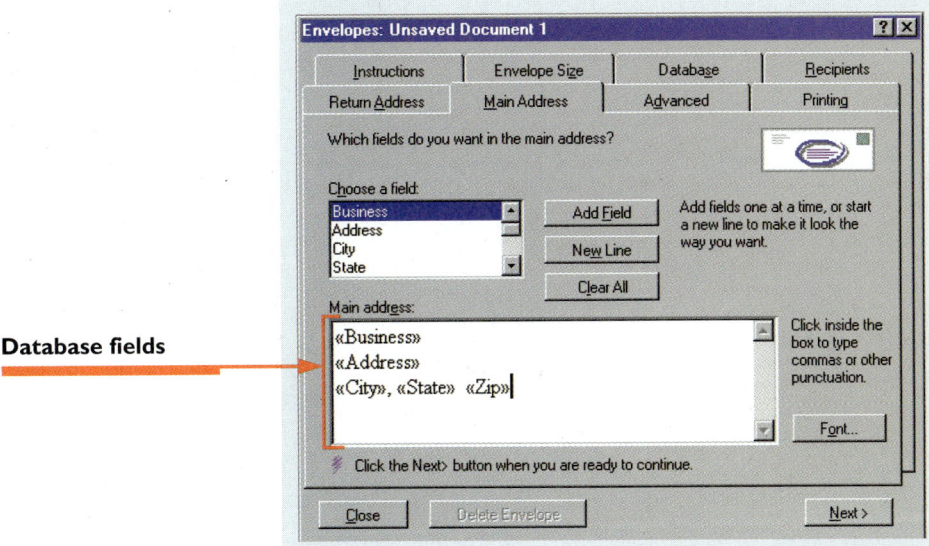

Database fields ▶

FIGURE 9-15: Completed envelope

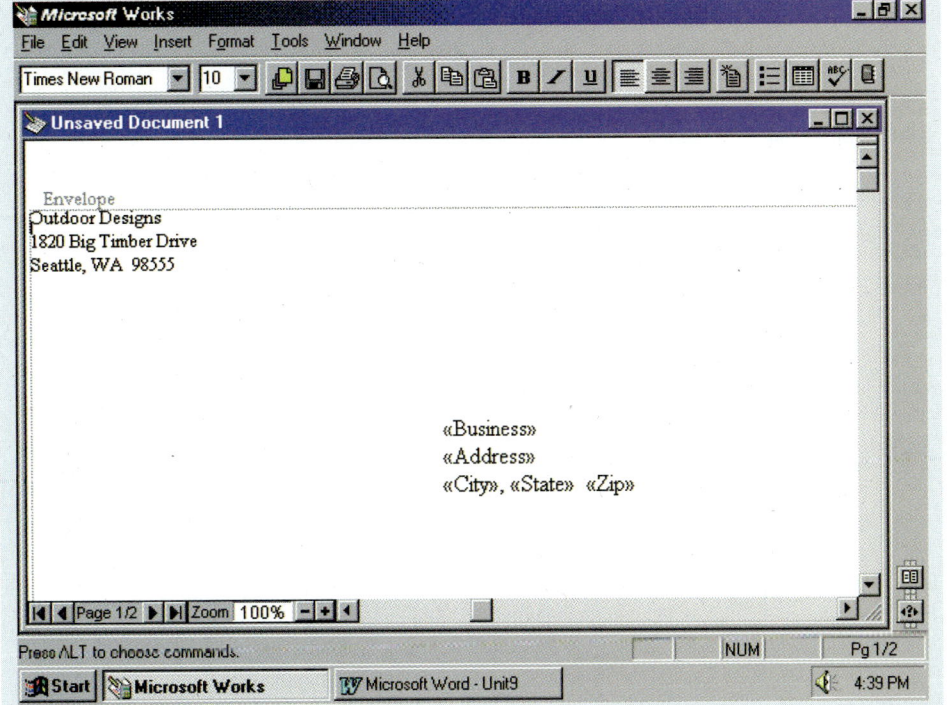

In Print Preview, you can preview how each envelope will look printed. Click the Next button to move from one envelope to the next.

TASK REFERENCE

TASK	MOUSE/BUTTON	MENU	KEYBOARD
Add ClipArt to a database form		Click Insert, ClipArt	[Alt][I],[A]
Apply a filter		Click Record, Apply Filter, then enter name of filter	[Alt][R],[F]
Cancel a filter		Click Record, Show, All Records	[Alt][R],[O],[I]
Create a filter		Click Tools, Filters	[Alt][T],[F]
Perform a calculation		Click Insert, Field, then enter a formula	[Alt][I],[F], then enter a formula
Print envelopes		In Word Processor, click Tools, Envelopes	[Alt][T],[E]
Protect a database		Click Format, Protection	[Alt][O],[R]
Resize ClipArt	Drag sizing handles with sizing pointer		
Sort Records		Click Record, Sort Records	[Alt][R],[S]

CONCEPTSREVIEW

Label each element of the Database Tool, as shown in Figure 9-16.

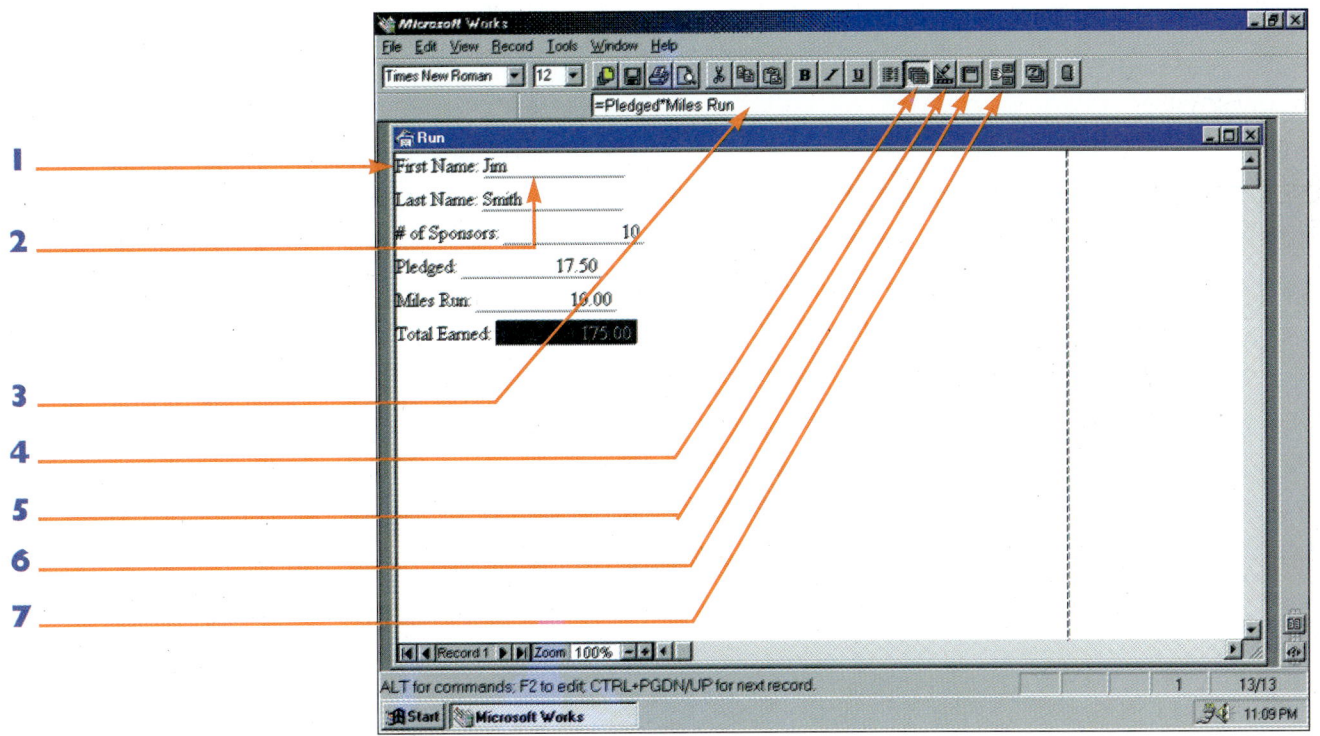

FIGURE 9-16

Select the best answer from the list of choices.

8 A formula can contain

   a. Numbers

   b. Field names

   c. Operators

   d. All of the above

9 To format a field for currency, you would click the

   a. Currency button

   b. Number button

   c. Format button

   d. Field button

10 You begin formulas with which character

   a. !

   b. &

   c. =

   d. $

11 To delete, copy, or move clip art on a form, you must

   a. Drag it

   b. Select it

   c. Paste it

   d. View it

12 You can sort a database

   a. In ascending order

   b. In descending order

   c. In alphabetical or numerical order

   d. All of the above

13 To subtract Cost from Sales, you would use which of the following formulas

   a. &Cost–Sales

   b. =Sales–Cost

   c. =Cost–Sales

   d. =Cost/Sales

14 You can protect

   a. The entire database

   b. Certain fields in the database

   c. Records

   d. Answers A and C

15 To print envelopes to clients in a database file, you would

   a. Type each envelope individually

   b. Insert database fields on the envelope

   c. Filter the records

   d. Sort the records

16 To multiply Price times Quantity, you would use which of the following formulas

   a. =Price/Quantity

   b. &Price*Quantity

   c. =Price*Quantity

   d. =Price^Quantity

17 To see records sorted on the screen, you would use

   a. Form View

   b. List View

   c. Sort View

   d. Report View

18 You would use which feature to compare one or more fields in the database with one or more values

   a. Formula

   b. Filter

   c. Sort

   d. Protection

19 To add Tax to Total, you would use which of the following formulas

   a. =Tax–Total

   b. =Tax*Total

   c. =Tax+Total

   d. =Tax/Total

20 A filter can use which of the following operators

   a. =

   b. >

   c. <

   d. All of the above

SKILLS REVIEW

1 Open an existing file and add a field.

   a. Start Works.

   b. In the Works Task Launcher, choose the Existing Document tab.

   c. Open the WKS9-2 file on your Student Disk and save it in the My Works Files folder under the name Invested.

   d. Click the Form Design button.

   e. Move to the last field in the database.

   f. Choose Field from the Insert menu.

   g. In the Insert Field dialog box, type Invested and click OK.

   h. Drag the field to the bottom of the database.

   i. Save the file.

2 Adding Art to a Form.

   a. Click the Form Design button.

   b. Click the mouse to the right of the Item field.

   c. Click the Insert menu.

   d. Choose the ClipArt command.

   e. In the Microsoft ClipArt Gallery, choose the Shapes Category.

   f. Select the graphic image of the check mark.

   g. Click the Insert button.

h. Drag the handle on the bottom-right corner then enlarge the size of the box.

i. Click the Form View button.

j. Save the file.

3 Use Field Entries in formulas.

a. Click the List View button.

b. Click the Field name Invested.

c. Choose Field from the Format menu.

d. Choose Number Format and select the second Appearance.

e. Click the Form View button.

f. With the pointer in the Invested field, type =Cost*On-Hand.

g. Click the List View button to look at the calculations.

h. Save the database.

4 Sort the database by the Invested field and then re-sort by Department.

a. In List View, click the Record menu.

b. Choose the Sort Record command.

c. In the Sort Records dialog box, select Invested from the Sort by list.

d. Select the Descending choice and click OK.

e. Click the Record menu.

f. Choose the Sort Record command.

g. In the Sort Records dialog box, select Department from the Sort by list.

h. Select the Ascending choice and click OK.

i. Save the database.

5 Use a Filter to find any kind of Shirts in the database.

a. Click the Tools menu.

b. Choose the Filters command.

c. In the Filter Name dialog box, type Shirts and click OK.

d. In the File name text box in the Filter dialog box, choose the Item field.

e. Click the mouse in the Compare To and type Shirt.

f. Click the Apply Filter button, and the database displays the matching records.

g. Click the Record menu.

h. Choose the Show command.

i. Choose All Records, and the filter is canceled.

6 Use a Filter to find any records with an On-Hand of greater than or equal to 24.

a. Click the Tools menu.

b. Choose the Filters command.

c. In the Filter dialog box, choose the Rename Filter button.

d. Type On-Hand >=24, and click OK.

e. Choose the On-Hand field in the Field Name box.

f. In the Comparison box choose "is greater than or equal to."

g. In the Compare To box delete shirt and type 24.

h. Click the Apply Filter button, and the database displays the matching records.

i. Choose the Show command.

j. Choose All Records, and the filter is canceled.

7 Use a Filter to find any records the Cost of which is less than $10 and On-Hand is greater than 15.

a. Click the Tools menu.

b. Choose the Filters command.

c. In the Filter dialog box, choose the Rename Filter button.

d. Type C<10 & On-H>15, and click OK.

e. Choose the Cost field in the Field Name box.

f. In the Comparison box choose "is less than."

g. In the Compare To box delete 24 and type 10.

h. Choose On-Hand in the Field Name box, leaving the And operator.

i. In the Comparison box choose "is greater than."

j. In the Compare To box type 15.

k. Click the Apply Filter button, and the database displays the matching records.

l. Choose the Show command.

m. Choose All Records, and the filter is canceled.

8 Protect the database.

a. Click the Form Design button.

b. Hold down the Ctrl key and click all the fields.

c. Click the Format menu.

d. Choose the Protection command.

e. In the Format Protection dialog box, click the Protect field option and click OK.

f. Click the List View button.

g. Try to type data in any field.

h. In the Protected field dialog box, click OK.

i. Click the Form Design button.

j. Hold down the Ctrl key and click all the fields.

k. Click the Format menu.

l. Choose the Protection command.

m. In the Format Protection dialog box, click the Protect field option to remove the check mark, and click OK.

n. Save the database.

INDEPENDENT CHALLENGE 1

In preparation for a Stuff for Pets marketing meeting, you need a database formula to automatically calculate the profit generated by each animal.

To complete this independent challenge:

1 Open the file WKS 9-3 on your Student Disk and save it in the My Works Files folder under the name "Profit."

2 Add a field to the database named "Profit."

3 Enter a formula in the Profit field which subtracts Cost from Retail for each animal.

4 Sort the database in descending order on the Profit field.

5 Protect the database from changes.

6 Save the database.

7 Print the database.

INDEPENDENT CHALLENGE 2

Stuff for Pets recently purchased a large quantity of dog beds. The store is also over-stocked on a book about Persian cats. You decide to use the customer database to send flyers to dog owners and Persian cat owners advertising specials on these products.

To complete this independent challenge:

1 Open the file WKS 9-4 on your Student Disk and save it in the My Works Files folder under the name "Owners."

2 Use a filter to locate customers who have purchased a dog.

3 Create envelopes for the customers who purchased a dog.

4 Preview the envelopes.

5 Print the envelopes.

6 Delete the filter.

7 Use a filter to locate customers who have purchased a Persian cat.

8 Create envelopes for the customers who purchased a Persian cat.

9 Save the file and print the envelopes.

INDEPENDENT CHALLENGE 3

As Human Resources Manager for Washington County, you are creating the database form for your assistant to use. You decide to include a pop-up note as a way to include instructions on the form.

To complete this independent challenge:

1 Open the file WKS 9-5 on your Student Disk and save it in the My Works Files folder as "Note."

2 Place the database in Form view.

3 Select one of the yellow road signs as the note picture.

4 Type the caption "More Information."

5 Type the note "Use the following abbreviations: PW for Public Works, Safety for Public Safety, Legal for County Courts."

6 Save the file.

7 Print the form.

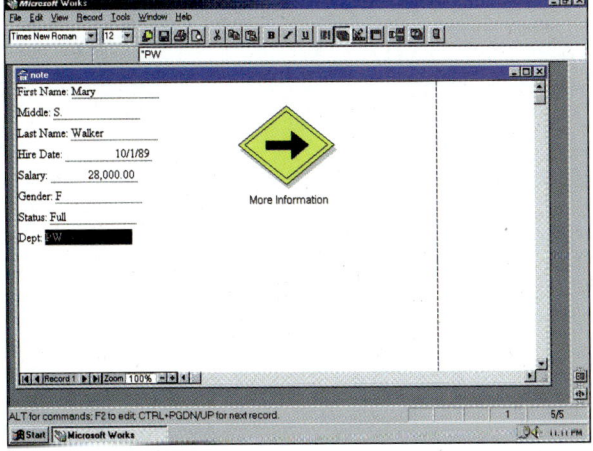

FIGURE 9-17

INDEPENDENT CHALLENGE 4

As manager of the Quick Stop Video Store, you are interested in learning what video categories you should focus on in the coming year. You can gain valuable insights into your customers' habits by tracking recent video sales for the store, using the sort and filter features.

To complete this independent challenge:

1 Open the file WKS 9-6 on your Student Disk and save it in the My Works Files folder as "Tracking."

2 Use a filter to find all movies that sold more than 100 copies.

3 Sort the results in descending order by the Sold field.

4 Print the results.

5 Use a filter to find only Children's movies that sold more than 120 copies.

6 Sort the results by Movie Name.

7 Save the file and print the results.

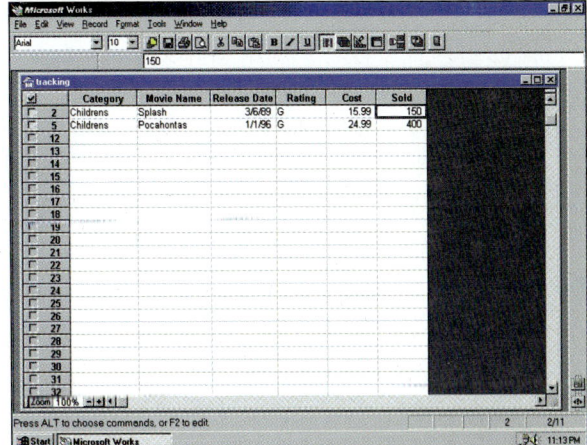

FIGURE 9-18

VISUAL WORKSHOP

Open the file WKS 9-7 on your Student Disk and save it in the My Works Files folder as Hunger. Then add ClipArt to the database form, as shown in Figure 9-19. You will find the picture of the runner under the Sports & Leisure category in the Microsoft ClipArt Gallery. If the picture doesn't appear in the location shown below, move it there. Print the form.

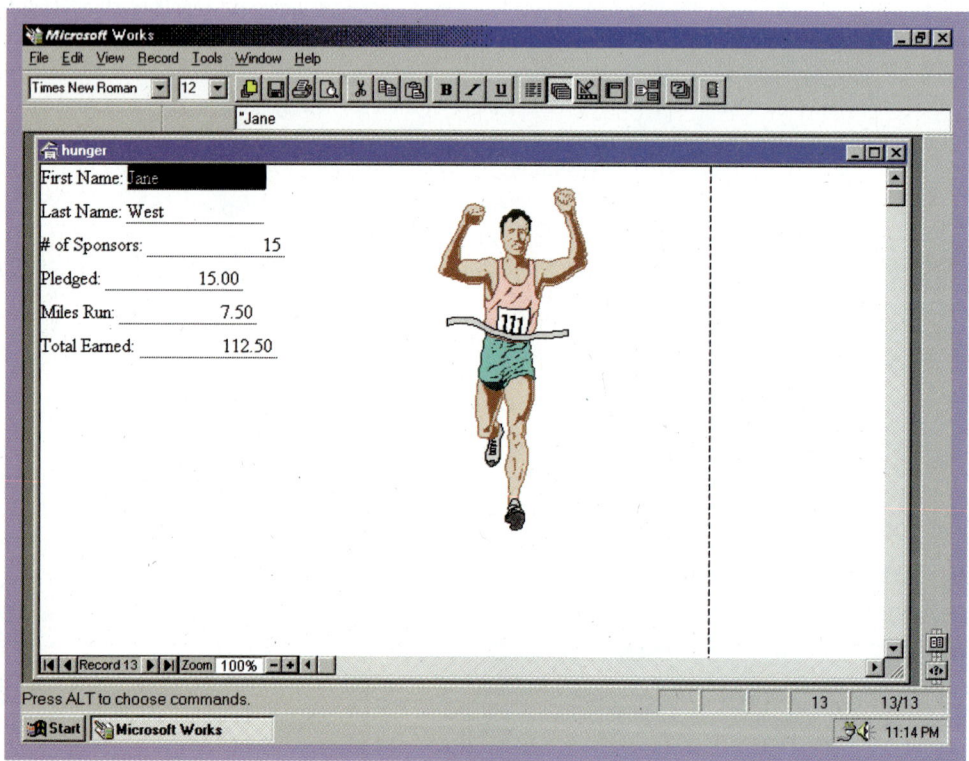

FIGURE 9-19

UNIT 10

OBJECTIVES

▶ Create a new report

▶ Add summary information

▶ View a report in Print Preview

▶ Edit in Report view

▶ Print a report

Creating DATABASE REPORTS

In this unit you'll learn to organize the fields of a database in reports. A **report** is a summary of database information specifically designed for printing. A report can include one or more database fields, summary information, and descriptive labels. ▶case Sue Ellen asked you to create a sales and commission report containing summary information from the Outdoor Designs customer database. She wants you to create the report, add some statistical data to it, and print a copy for distribution to the Outdoor Designs sales staff. You'll create the report using skills you learn in this unit. ▶

Creating a new report

When a database grows large, spotting statistical trends in the data can be difficult. For example, if a sales database contains hundreds of records, it's hard to determine the average sale, or the total sales. Works solves this problem by letting you create summary reports of your database. You define new reports with the ReportCreator command, and Works stores each report in your database file so that you can print it or refer to it later. **case** Sue Ellen requested that you create a new report with the Outdoor Designs customer database that presents the total of all year-to-date sales recorded, the average of all sales, and the total commission sales reps earned. Start working on the report now by creating the report and adding fields to it.

1. Launch Works

2. Put your Student Disk in the appropriate drive, open the file **Works 10-1** on your Student Disk, then save it as **Sales Report** in the **My Works Files folder**
   The Outdoor Designs customer database (the database you created in Unit 9) opens in a window. (To review how to open and save a file in the Database tool, see "Opening an Existing Database" in Unit 9.) Now you'll create a report with the ReportCreator command.

3. Click **Tools** on the menu bar, then click **ReportCreator**; if a First-time Help dialog box opens, click **OK**
   The Report Name dialog box opens, prompting you to name the report.

4. Type **1996 YTD Sales** and click **OK**
   The ReportCreator dialog box shown in Figure 10-1 opens. It contains six tabs where you define your report's contents, and a Next button that moves you through each tab in order. (Filling out the tabs in left-to-right order is the method recommended for creating reports in Works.) The first tab, Title, contains a text field where you can modify the default report title and options that control the report's orientation and fonts used. Now you add database fields to the report.

5. Click **Next** to display the Fields tab, then click **Add** to add the highlighted field in the Fields Available list box to the report
   The Business field appears in the Fields in Report list box.

6. Click **City**, click **Add**, click **YTD Sales**, click **Add**, click **Commission**, then click **Add**
   The four fields display in the Fields in Report list box shown in Figure 10-2. To delete a field you mistakenly added, click the incorrect field in the list box, then click the Remove button.

FIGURE 10-1: ReportCreator dialog box

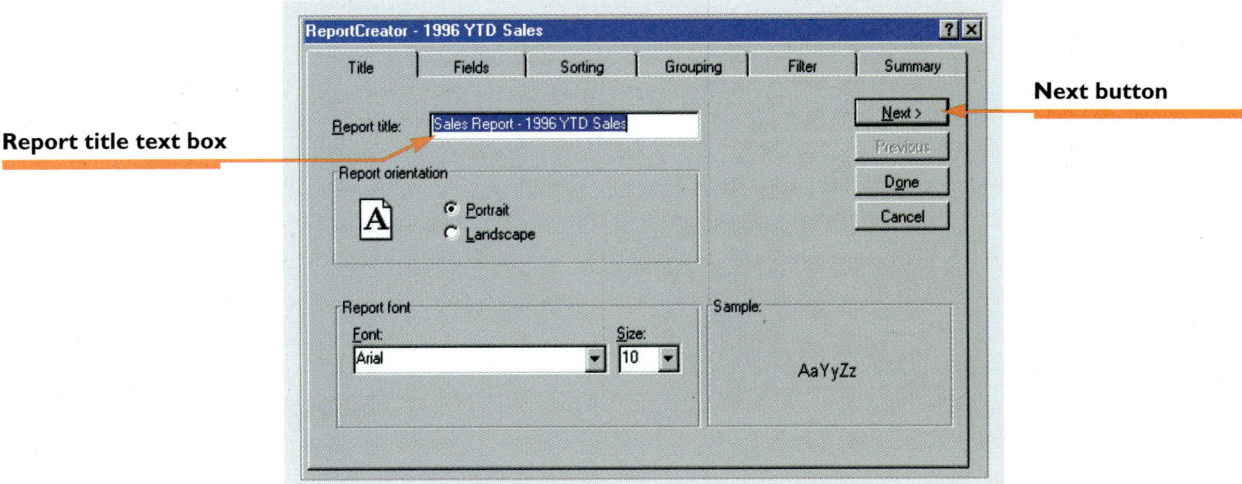

FIGURE 10-2: Adding database fields to a report

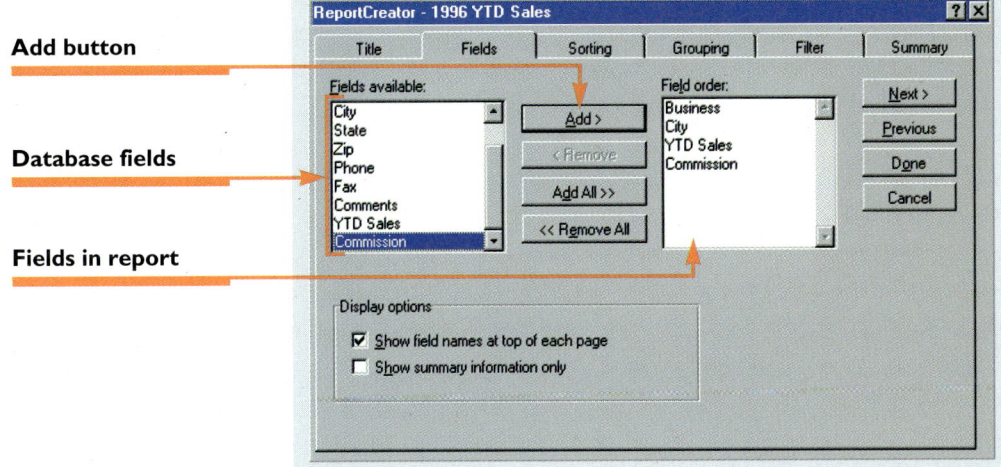

QUICK TIP

You can also click the Report view button  on the toolbar to create a new report. This button is the toolbar equivalent of the ReportCreator command.

Adding summary information

Several tabs in the ReportCreator dialog box are useful, but the Summary tab lets you add the most interesting information to your report. Summary information consists of statistics about one or more fields in the report. For example, you can display the average, sum, or count of one or more database fields. Table 10-1 lists statistical operations you can use in Database reports. **case** To display the summary information Sue Ellen wants for her financial report, you'll specify the Average and Sum statistics for the YTD Sales field and the Sum statistic for the Commission field.

1. **Click Next four times**
   You scroll through the Sorting, Grouping, and Filter tabs, which control which records the report includes and their display. Sue Ellen wants all Outdoor Designs customers included in the report, so you don't adjust the defaults in these tabs. Finally the Summary tab shown in Figure 10-3 opens. It contains a list box for selecting fields for the report, seven Statistics check boxes for specifying the statistics you want included, and several options for controlling the placement of summary information.

2. **Click YTD Sales in the Fields Available list box, then click the Sum and Average check boxes**
   The check mark in the Sum and Average check boxes tells Works to calculate the sum and average of all YTD Sales fields in the database, then to place these values in rows in the report.

3. **Click Commission in the Available Fields list box, then click the Sum check box**
   The check mark in the Sum check box tells Works to calculate the sum of all Commission fields in the database, then to place this value in a row in the report.

4. **Click Done**
   Works creates the report and displays it in Report view. The dialog box shown in Figure 10-4 opens, tells you that the report instructions or **definitions** are complete, and gives you the option of previewing the report or modifying the report definition. In the next lesson, you'll preview the report and try to spot any problems before you print a final version for the sales department.

FIGURE 10-3: Summary tab

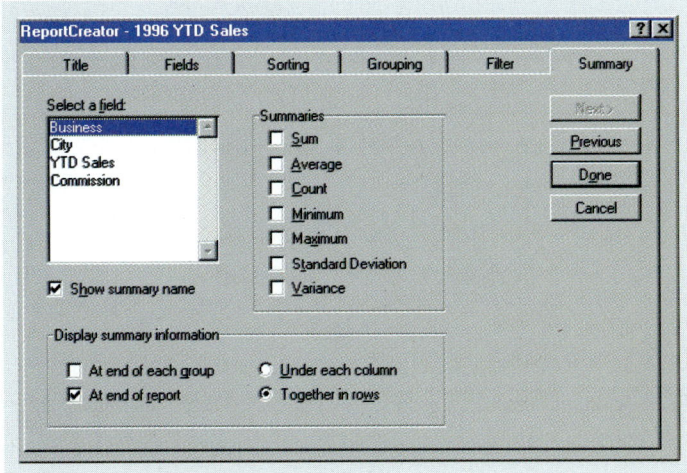

FIGURE 10-4: ReportCreator dialog box

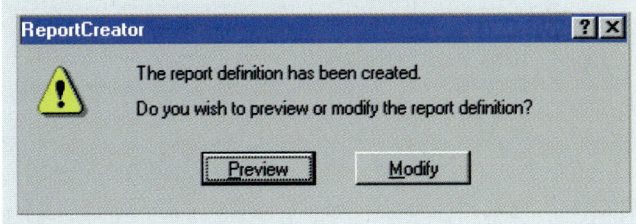

TABLE 10-1: Statistical calculations available in database reports

STATISTIC	CALCULATES
Sum	Total of all values in the field
Average	Average of all values in the field
Count	Number of records in the database
Minimum	Smallest value in the field
Maximum	Largest value in the field
Standard deviation	Standard deviation of values in the field
Variance	Variance of values in the field

QUICK TIP

The Filter tab in the ReportCreator dialog box lets you use a filter to display a subset of records in your database.

Viewing a report in Print Preview

To view a report as it will be printed you need to preview it. Print Preview displays the report with the title, headings, records, and summary information you specified in place. Examining the report in Print Preview is an important step, because you can catch any formatting problems before you print. **case** To verify that you created a professional-looking report for your colleagues, examine the sales and commission report in Print Preview now.

1. **Click Preview in the ReportCreator dialog box**
   The report appears in the special preview window shown in Figure 10-5. Print Preview shows the report on a simulated page exactly as it will look when printed. Six buttons on the right side of the window control the operation of Print Preview. To zoom in to look closely at parts of the report, you can click the Zoom In button or click the report with the zoom pointer. The Zoom pointer appears whenever the mouse pointer is over the simulated page.

2. **Click Zoom In**
   The top part of the report enlarges to half-size in the Print Preview window. At this magnification you can begin to see the information in the report, but a closer view would be more clear.

3. **Click between the City and YTD Sales columns with the Zoom pointer**
   The report enlarges to full size in Print Preview, as shown in Figure 10-6. At this magnification the title, headings, records, and summary information are clearly visible. Works has inserted the seven database records in the report with their respective year-to-date sales and commission totals. Three statistics appear at the bottom of the report: Total YTD Sales, Average YTD Sales, and Total Commission. However, the report's title ("Sales Report - 1996 YTD Sales") is right-aligned at the top of the document, so you want to adjust the title's placement before you finalize the report. You'll do so in the next lesson.

4. **Click Cancel**
   The Print Preview window closes, and the **report definition**, the set of definitions that create the report, appears in Report view. If a First-time Help dialog box opens, click OK.

FIGURE 10-5: Print Preview screen

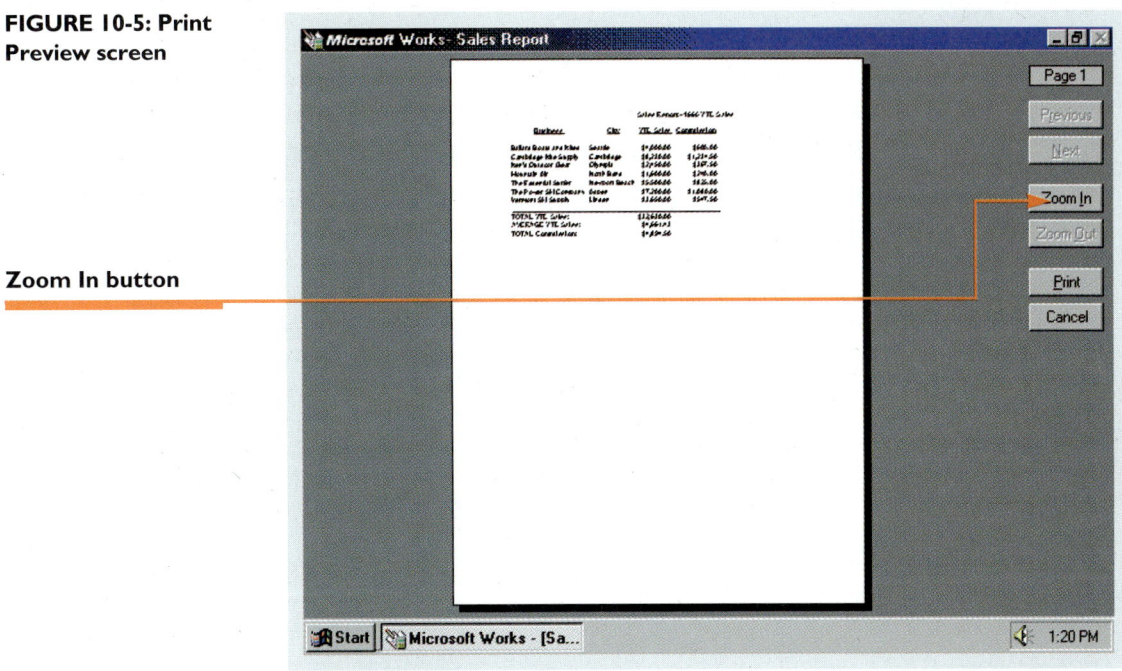

Zoom In button

FIGURE 10-6: Report in full size

Report title

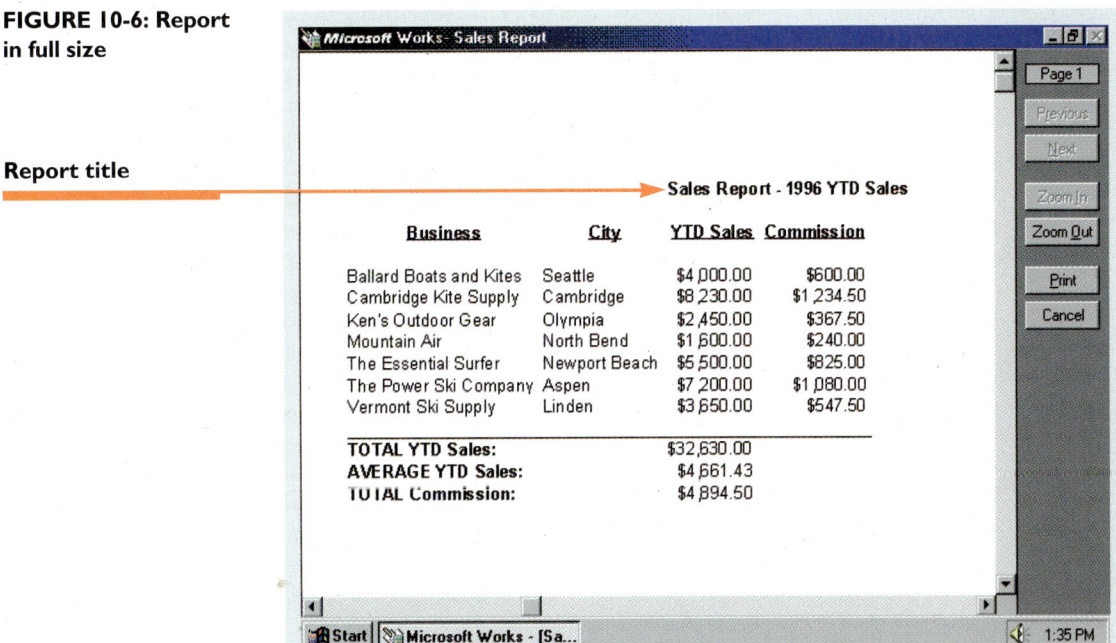

QUICK TIP

The keyboard shortcut for the Print Preview command is [Alt][F], [V]. You can also click the Print Preview button  on the toolbar.

Editing in Report view

Report view is a special view in the Database tool that lets you edit the report definition. Similar to list view, Report view contains special headings that identify how your report will print, as well as a few new menu commands. In Report view, you can fix layout problems or customize your report by changing the font or adding new information. ▶case To create a professional-looking report for the sales group, you'll left-align the report's title and insert more white space between the title and the headings. After these edits, you'll be ready to print.

1. **Verify that your database is in Report view**
   In Report view, the Report view button on the toolbar appears to be pushed in. The 1996 YTD Sales report definition appears on your screen, as shown in Figure 10-7. Field names and fields are arranged as they will be on the final report. Row names are to the left of column A.

2. **Click the first cell in column C to select the report title**
   The title "Sales Report - 1996 YTD Sales" appears in the formula bar. Now you move the title left two cells to align at the left margin.

3. **Click the Cut button on the toolbar**
   Works removes the report title from the report definition and places it in the Clipboard. Now you paste the title in column A.

4. **Click the first cell in column A, then click the Paste button on the toolbar**
   Works copies the report title to the first cell in column A. To give the title more impact, increase the font size to 14 points.

5. **Click the list arrow in the Font Size list box, then click 14**
   The title's font size increases to 14 points. Now place another blank line below the title to add some more white space to the report.

6. **Click the second Title row name (the blank line located in the second row, left of column A)**
   To insert another blank line between the report title and the row heading, you need to insert an extra Title row in the report definition.

7. **Click Insert on the menu bar, then click Insert Row**
   The Insert Row dialog box opens. You use it to identify the type of row you want to insert.

8. **Double-click Title in the list box**
   Works inserts the blank Title row shown in Figure 10-8 in the report.

9. **Click the Save button on the toolbar**
   Works saves the 1996 YTD Sales Report with the Sales Report database.

FIGURE 10-7: 1996 YTD Sales report definition in Report view

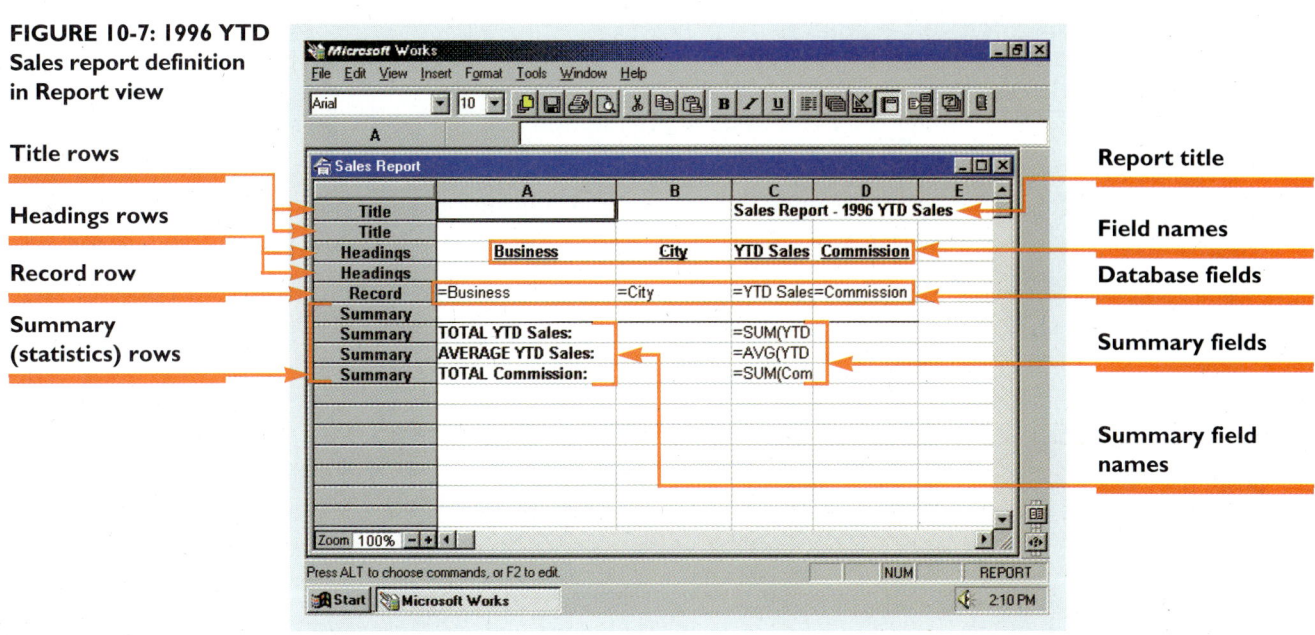

FIGURE 10-8: Sales report definition after editing and formatting changes

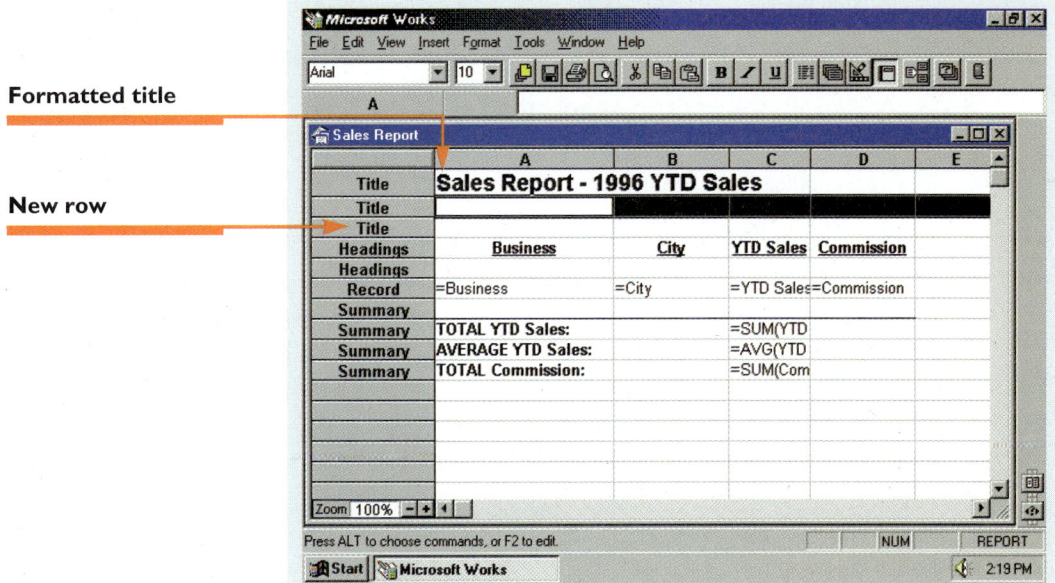

QUICK TIP

To change the font or style of the text in the report, highlight the cell containing the text, then choose the Font and Style command from the Format menu.

Printing a report

After you edit a report definition, you're ready to print a final copy of the report. Before you do, you preview the report one last time to see the results of editing the report definition. You also look at your statistics to verify that they produce the results you want. **case** Sue Ellen requested a sales report with two totals and one average, so after you verify your information, you print a copy for her review. For information on changing a report after you close the file, see the related topic, "Opening an existing report."

1. **Click the Print Preview button on the toolbar**
   The report opens in Print Preview. Before you print, use the zoom pointer to verify the changes you made to the report's format.

2. **Click the report twice with the Zoom pointer**
   The report enlarges to full size in Print Preview, as shown in Figure 10-9. Examine the new title position and point size. Is it a good introduction to the report? Examine the blank line you added between the title and column headings. Does it help set off the information in the report? Should you make other formatting changes? To make additional changes, click Cancel, edit the report definition in Report view, then click the Print Preview button again.

3. **Verify that your printer is ready, then click the Print button on the toolbar**
   After a few moments, your report emerges from your printer, ready for Sue Ellen's review.

4. **Click the Save button on the toolbar**
   Congratulations! You created a useful report and finished your work with the Database tool. Exit from Works using a keyboard shortcut.

5. **Press [Alt][F4]**
   The Sales Report file and Works both close.

FIGURE 10-9: Your final report in Print Preview

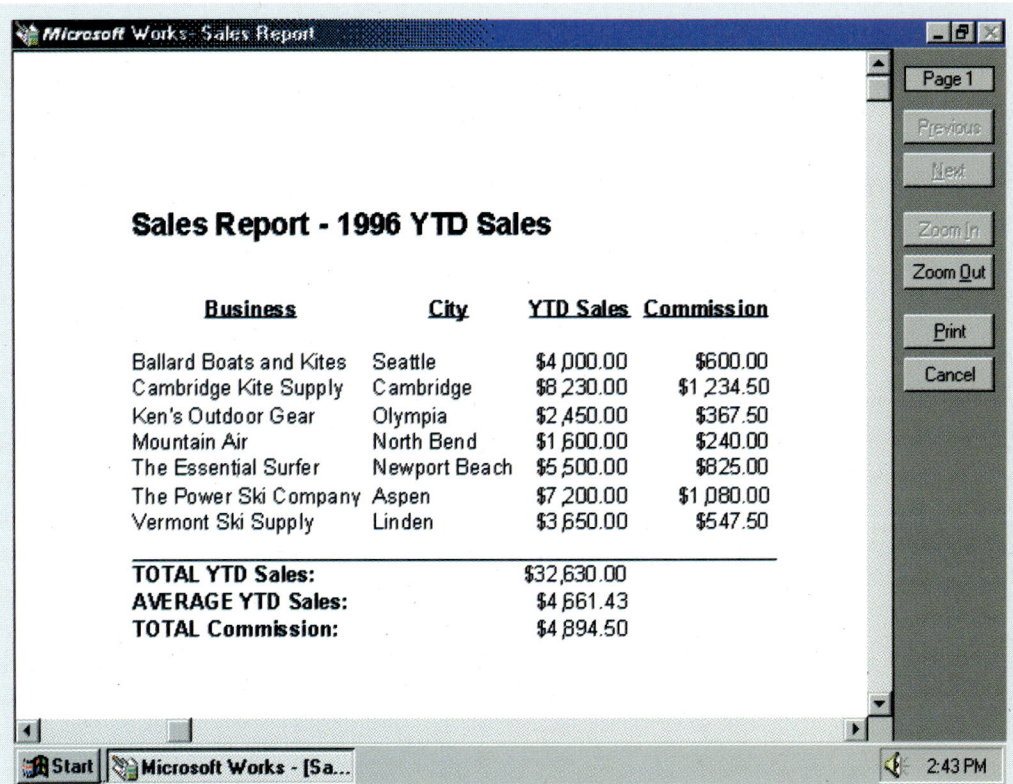

Opening an existing report

Because Works saves your report with the database for which you created it, you can open an existing report any time you open the original database file. For example, to open the 1996 YTD Sales report you created in this unit, start Works, open the Sales Report database, then choose the Report command from the View menu. The View Report dialog box opens, as shown in Figure 10-10. Highlight the 1996 YTD Sales report, and then click Preview to examine the report in Print Preview or Modify to edit the report in Report view.

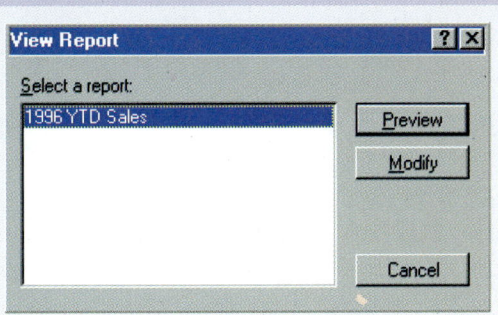

FIGURE 10-10: View Report dialog box

QUICK TIP

To delete a report from the database, choose Delete Report from the Tools menu, highlight the report you want to delete, then click the Delete button.

TASK REFERENCE

TASK	MOUSE/BUTTON	MENU	KEYBOARD
Copy selected text in a report	🗎	Click Edit, Copy	[Ctrl][C]
Create a new report	🗎	Click Tools, ReportCreator	[Alt][T],[R]
Cut selected text in a report	✂	Click Edit, Cut	[Ctrl][X]
Delete a report		Click Tools, Delete Report	[Alt][T],[T]
Delete a row in a report		Click Insert, Delete Row	[Alt][I],[D]
Insert a blank row in a report		Click Insert, Insert Row	[Alt][I],[R]
Paste selected text in a report	🗎	Click Edit, Paste	[Ctrl][V]
Preview a report	🔍	Click File, Print Preview	[Alt][F],[V]
Print a report	🖨	Click File, Print	[Ctrl][P]

CONCEPTSREVIEW

Label each element of the Report view, as shown in Figure 10-11.

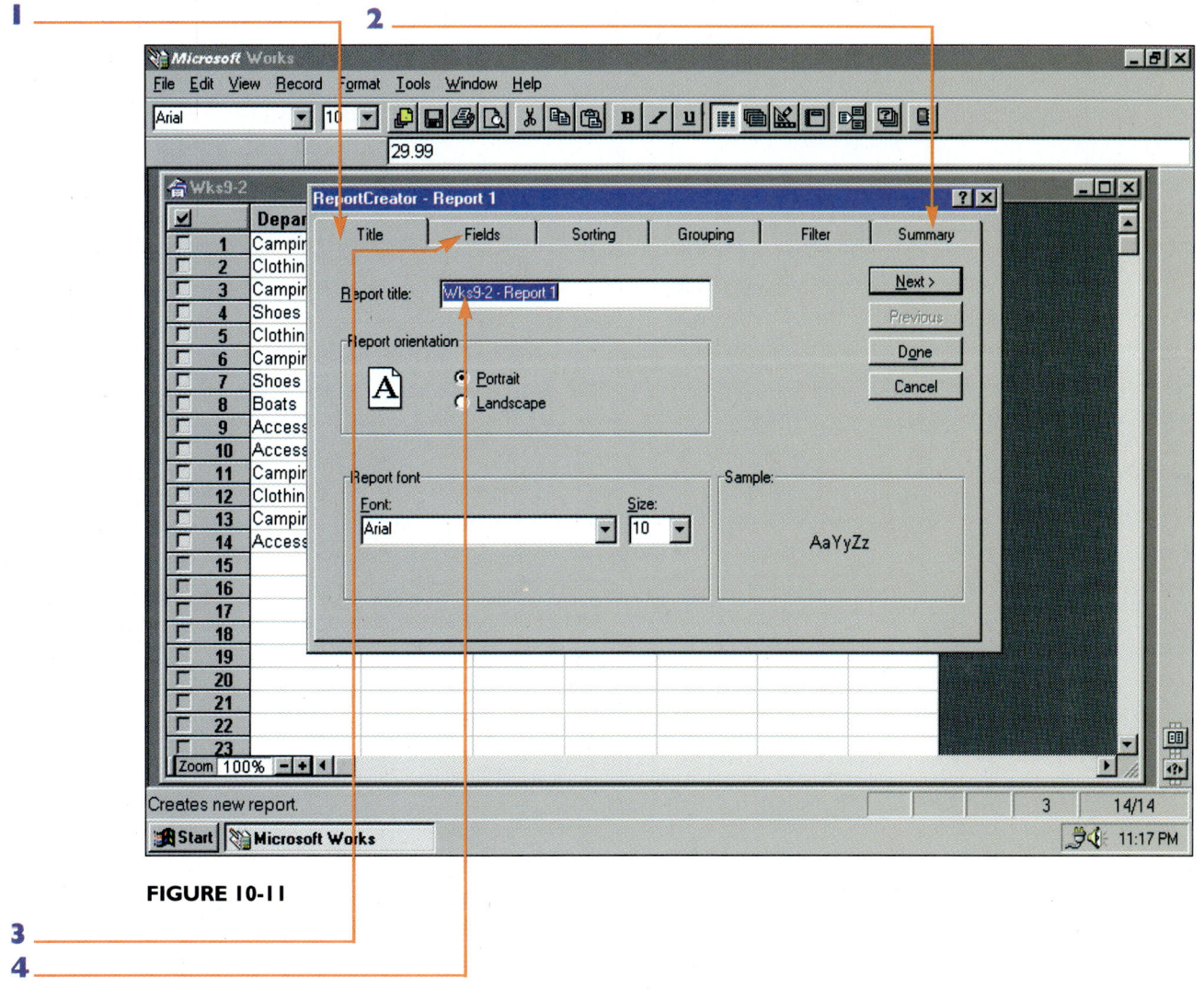

FIGURE 10-11

WK 230   WORKS 4   UNIT 10 CREATING DATABASE REPORTS

Match the statistical calculations with their descriptions.

5 Sum
6 Average
7 Count
8 Minimum
9 Maximum

a. Largest value in the field
b. Total of all values in the field
c. Smallest value in the field
d. Number of records in the database
e. Average of all values in the field

Select the best answer from the list of choices.

10 A report is a summary of database information specifically designed for
    a. Searching
    b. Sorting
    c. Examining in Form view
    d. Printing

11 Which of these elements cannot be included in a database report?
    a. Fields
    b. Statistics
    c. ClipArt
    d. Column headings

12 Which of the following calculations is not available in a Summary report?
    a. Variance
    b. Net present value
    c. Standard Deviation
    d. All of the above

13 When you are finished defining the report, Works displays
    a. The report definition
    b. The database
    c. List view
    d. The database form

14 Works includes which of the following rows in the report definition?
    a. Title
    b. Headings
    c. Record
    d. All of the above

15 If you see ######## instead of data for a field in Print Preview, you know that
    a. The field is not available in the database
    b. The field contains a negative number
    c. The column is not wide enough in the report definition
    d. Works is busy calculating the statistic

16 Works reports can
    a. Be sorted on three fields
    b. Filter data
    c. Summarize data
    d. All of the above

17 If you want to show data in a report that matches a certain value, you would use
    a. A filter
    b. A variance
    c. A summary
    d. A Standard Deviation

18 To view the actual report on the screen, you would use
    a. Form view
    b. Print preview
    c. List view
    d. Report view

19 When working in the report definition, you can
    a. Change fonts
    b. Align titles
    c. Insert blank rows
    d. All of the above

20 To create a report, you choose
    a. View, Report
    b. Tools, ReportCreator
    c. Report view button
    d. Both b and c

SKILLS REVIEW

1. Create a report, using some of the database fields.
   a. Open the WKS10-2 file on your Student Disk and save it in the My Works Files folder under the name Report.
   b. Click the Tools menu.
   c. Choose the ReportCreator command.
   d. In the Report Name dialog box, delete any text and type Inventory and click OK.
   e. On the Title tab in the Report title text box, delete any text and type 1996 Inventory.
   f. On the Title tab, select a different font and enlarge the size to 16.
   g. Click the Next button.
   h. Select the Item field and click the Add button.
   i. Select the Cost field and click the Add button.
   j. Select the On-Hand field and click the Add button.
   k. Click the Done button.
   l. Click the Preview button.
   m. Click the Cancel button.

2. Create a report which totals the Cost field and averages the On-Hand field and Preview the report.
   a. Click the Tools menu.
   b. Choose the ReportCreator command.
   c. In the Report Name dialog box, delete any text and type Inventory Info and click OK.
   d. On the Title tab in the Report title text box, delete any text and type Inventory Summary.
   e. Click the Next button.
   f. On the Fields tab, click the Add All button.
   g. Click the Next button 4 times.
   h. On the Summary tab, click the Cost field and click Sum.
   i. Click the On-Hand field and click Average.
   j. Click the Done button.
   k. Click the Preview button.
   l. Click the Cancel button.

3. Edit the Report Definition.
   a. In the report definition, select the title of the report.
   b. Click the Format menu.
   c. Choose the Font and Style command.
   d. Choose a font from the font list.
   e. Change the size to 16.
   f. Select the Bold style and click OK.
   g. Place the pointer on the first Summary row.
   h. Click the Insert menu.
   i. Choose the Insert Row command.
   j. In the Insert Row dialog box, click the Insert button.
   k. Click the File menu.
   l. Choose the Print Preview command.
   m. Click Cancel.

4. Print the current report and a previously created report.
   a. Click the File menu.
   b. Choose the Print Preview command.
   c. Click the Print button.
   d. When the report is finished printing, click the View menu.
   e. Choose the Report command.
   f. Select the Inventory report and click the Preview button.
   g. Click the Zoom In button.
   h. Click the Print button.

5. Use a Filter with a report.
   a. Make the Inventory Info report the active report.
   b. Click the Tools menu.
   c. Choose the Report Filter command.
   d. Click the Create New Filter button.
   e. In the Filter Name dialog box, type Department and click OK.
   f. In the Filter dialog box, select Department from the Field name list.
   g. In the Compare To box, type Camping and click OK.
   h. Click the Done button.
   i. Click the Print Preview button.
   j. Click the Zoom In button to see the Camping data.

6. Delete a report.
   a. Click the Tools menu.
   b. Choose the Delete Report command.
   c. In the Delete Report dialog box, select the Inventory report.
   d. Click the Delete button and click OK.
   e. In the OK to delete dialog box, click OK.
   f. Save the file.

INDEPENDENT CHALLENGE 1

Lee Janson, in the marketing department at Stuff for Pets, asks for your help with some sales research. She needs you to create a report of all animals that have been sold in the store.

To complete this independent challenge:

1. Open the file WKS 10-3 on your Student Disk and save it in the My Works Files folder under the name "Pets."
2. Give the report the title "Pet Sales Year to Date."
3. Include only the following fields in the report: Category, Breed, Gender, Time
4. Sort by Category and then by Breed.
5. Group by Category and then by Breed.
6. Preview and save the report.
7. Print the report.

INDEPENDENT CHALLENGE 2

Now that you've embarked on sales research at Stuff for Pets, your interest is piqued. You want to look at trends in sales of animals in the store. You decide to use the summary feature in your reports.

To complete this independent challenge:

1. Open the file WKS 10-3 on your Student Disk and save it in the My Works Files folder under the name "Summary."
2. Create a report with the title "Number of Animals by Category."
3. Use the report summary feature to count the number of animals by category.
4. Print the report.
5. Create a report with the title "Profit by Category."
6. Use the report summary feature to sum the Profit field by category.
7. Print the report.

INDEPENDENT CHALLENGE 3

As Human Resource Manager for Washington County, you need to make reports that provide your supervisors with statistical data about employment trends. You decide to use the summary feature.

To complete this independent challenge:

1. Open the file WKS 10-4 on your Student Disk and save it in the My Works Files folder under the name "Trends."
2. Create a report with the title "Female Employees Who Earn More than $30,000."
3. Use the summary feature to count the number of female employees by department.
4. Print the report.
5. Create a report with the title "Average Salary of Employees by Department."
6. Use the report summary feature to average the Salary field by department.
7. Print the report.

INDEPENDENT CHALLENGE 4

As manager of the Quick Stop Video Store, you want to provide the owner with a report that shows the number of movies sold in each main category.

To complete this independent challenge:

1. Open the file WKS 10-5 on your Student Disk and save it in the My Works Files folder under the name "Sold."
2. Create a report with the title "Movies Sold by Category."
3. Include only the Movie Name and the Sold fields.
4. Sum the Sold field by Category.
5. Sort by the Category field.
6. Preview the report.
7. Print the report.

VISUALWORKSHOP

Open the file WKS 10-6 on your Student Disk and save it in the My Works Files folder under the name Runners. Then create the report shown below and print it.

FIGURE 10-12

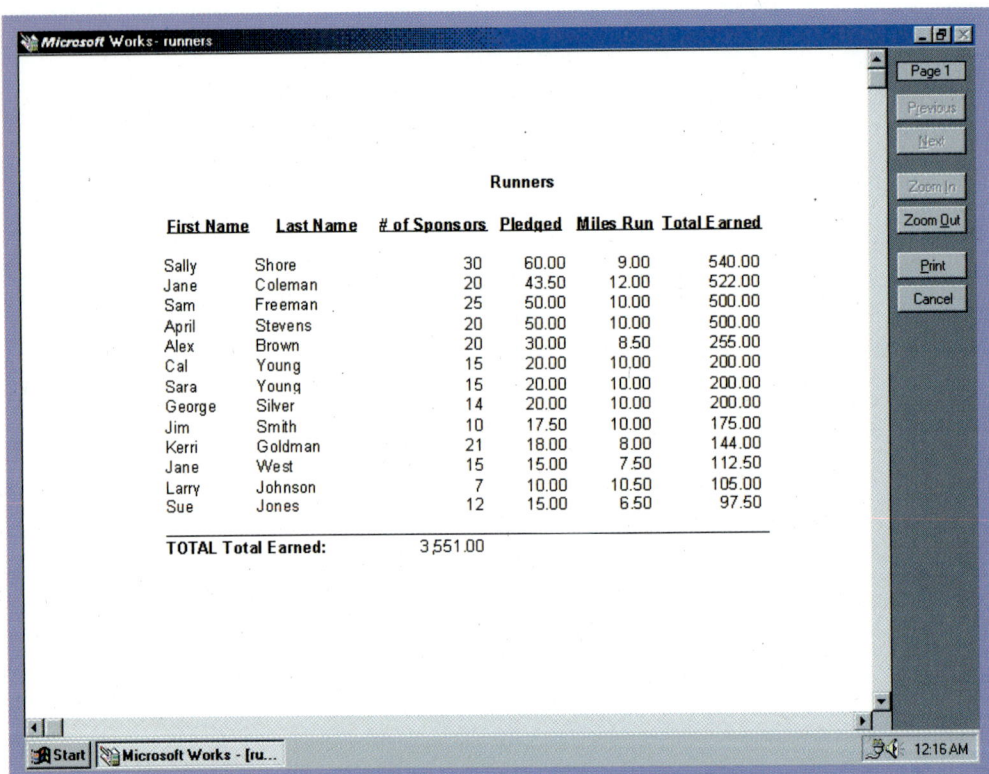

UNIT 11

OBJECTIVES

▶ Plan a telecommunication session

▶ Start the Communications tool

▶ Set communications parameters

▶ Connect to a remote computer

▶ Search an online database

▶ Send e-mail on the Internet

▶ End your communications session

Exploring TELECOMMUNICATIONS

In this unit you will learn to use the Works Communications tool. Communicating with another computer over phone lines is called **telecommunicating**. Through telecommunication you can connect to the computers in your school or business, use sophisticated electronic services such as CompuServe or The Microsoft Network, or explore a global network of computers known as the **internet**. **case** Frasier, the Outdoor Designs marketing manager, asked you to connect to the University of Washington computer facility and search for books relating to outdoor sports in the library database. When you find a suitable book, Frasier wants you to send an electronic message to a person at the university who can send you the book directly. Because each online service is different, your instructor will provide customized instructions for your telecommunication session. ▶

Planning a telecommunication session

Before you start telecommunicating, you need to do some planning. Telecommunication requires a computer, a modem, and a phone line connecting your modem to the phone jack. In addition, you need to know the phone number of the computer or service you'll be connecting to and any necessary communication settings or **parameters**. Finally, you need a communications program, such as Microsoft Works, to connect the two computers and manage the telecommunication session.  Frasier suggests you use your computer account at the local university for your database search. Ask your instructor now for the service, phone number, and parameters you'll use to connect to a local service with Works.

■ Check your hardware

Before you telecommunicate, you need to verify that your computer has the hardware necessary to link to another computer. A computer supports telecommunication through one of its **serial ports**. The actual work of telecommunication is done by a special peripheral called a **modem** that fits inside the computer or attaches to one of the serial ports on the back of the computer. The modem is then connected to a standard phone jack with a phone line, as shown in Figure 11-1. For more information see the related topic, "What is a modem?". If you're using a computer in a lab, ask your instructor or lab manager if your computer has the necessary hardware to telecommunicate. If you're working on this unit at home, check with an experienced friend or your computer dealer to see if your computer has the hardware you need to go online.

■ Learn about the service you'll be using

When you're sure your computer has the necessary hardware, you need to determine what remote computer or service you'll connect to. There are dozens of options; some are free of connect charges, and some will cost you money. You can connect to a comprehensive online service such as CompuServe, The Microsoft Network, or America Online, or you can connect to a special-interest bulletin board, university computing facility, or electronic mail system. Several services require you to sign up in advance and issue you a user name and password that you can use to access the system. (To access a few services, such as The Microsoft Network, you also need a special communications program, so you can't make the connection with Works.) Ask your instructor for details, then learn what you can about the service you'll use.

■ Verify the phone number and communications parameters

Finally, get the phone number and the communications parameters for the service you'll connect to. Be sure to get a local phone number for the service, so you can avoid long-distance phone charges. The communications parameters you need relate to how your modem transmits the data and include the baud rate, data bits, parity, stop bits, and terminal setting. (We'll discuss these terms later in the unit.) Your instructor will provide you with details. You can also find these parameters in your telecommunication service documentation.

After you've checked your hardware and know the necessary details about your telecommunication service, you're ready to connect with the Works Communications tool. You'll start the program in the next lesson.

FIGURE 11-1: Hardware components in a typical telecommunication session

[Diagram showing two computers connected via modems, wall jacks, and phone lines on telephone poles. Left side labeled "Your computer" and right side labeled "Remote computer or on-line service".]

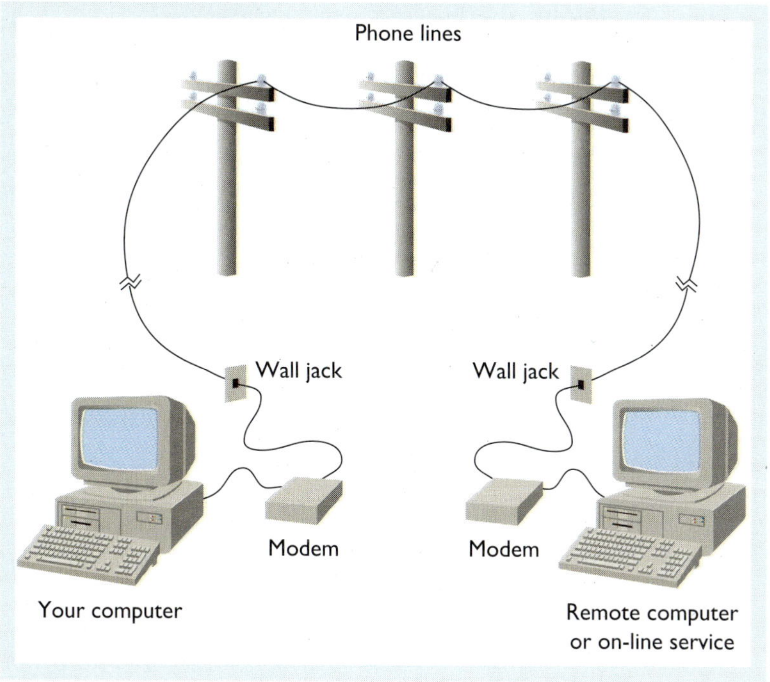

What is a modem?

A **modem** is a communications device that lets a computer transmit information over a standard telephone line. Modem is short for modulator/demodulator, which means that a modem can convert the digital signals in your computer to the analog signals phone lines use and vice versa. When you telecommunicate, your modem converts digital instructions from your computer and sends them over phone lines to a remote computer's modem. The remote modem then converts the analog signals to digital signals and passes them to the remote computer for processing.

TROUBLE?

If you have Call Waiting, disable it before you telecommunicate. Incoming calls during a telecommunication session can break the phone link between computers or cause data loss.

Starting the Communications tool

With the Works Communications tool you can communicate with an online service, a university computing facility, or a computer belonging to a friend or colleague. The Communications tool uses the modem to connect to the remote computer and handles the details of the telecommunication session. Figure 11-3 shows the elements of the Communications tool, and Table 11-1 lists the most useful toolbar buttons. **case** Start the Communications tool now, and prepare to make a telecommunication connection for your Outdoor Designs research.

1. **Launch Works**
   The Works Task Launcher dialog box opens and displays three tabs.

2. **Click the Works Tools tab**
   The four Works tool icons shown in Figure 11-2 appear in the tab. Now start the Communications tool.

3. **Click the Communications button**
   The Communications tool shown in Figure 11-3 opens in a window and displays an Easy Connect dialog box, which prompts you for the phone number and name of the service you'll connect to. The Communications tool contains interface elements found in every Works tool: a menu bar, a toolbar, a document window, scroll bars, toggle indicators, sizing buttons, and two Help buttons. Two boxes are unique to the Communications interface: the **connect time box** shows how long you have been connected to a remote computer, and the **connect status box** displays messages about your telecommunication session.

4. **Click Cancel to close the Easy Connect dialog box**
   In the future, you'll use the Easy Connect dialog box to connect to services you use regularly. However, because this is your first telecommunicating session, you'll specify the communications parameters manually with buttons on the toolbar.

TABLE 11-1: Useful toolbar buttons

BUTTON	FUNCTION
	Change communications settings
	Change terminal settings
	Change phone settings
	Change file transfer settings
	Display Easy Connect dialog box
	Dial remote computer or (if a connection exists) hang up

FIGURE 11-2: Start Communications tool from the Works Tools tab

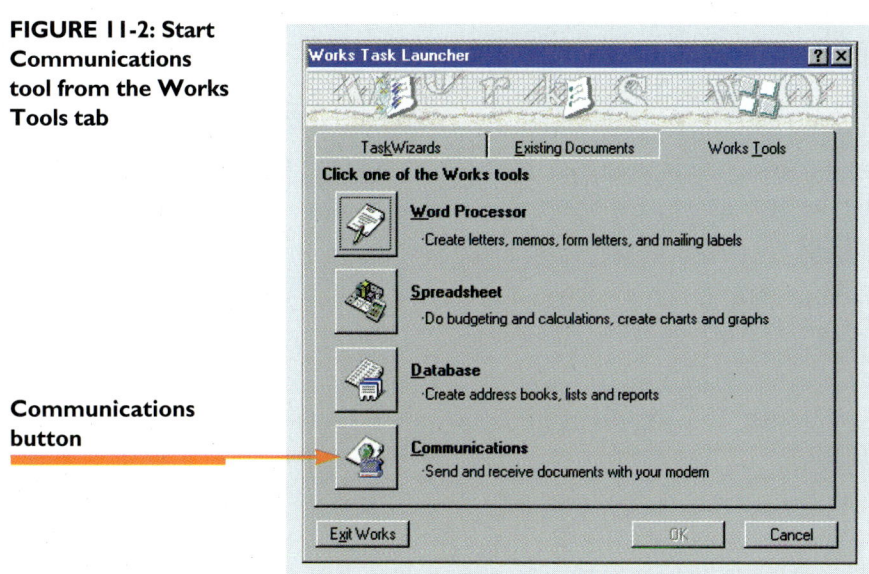

Communications button

FIGURE 11-3: Communications tool with unique elements labeled

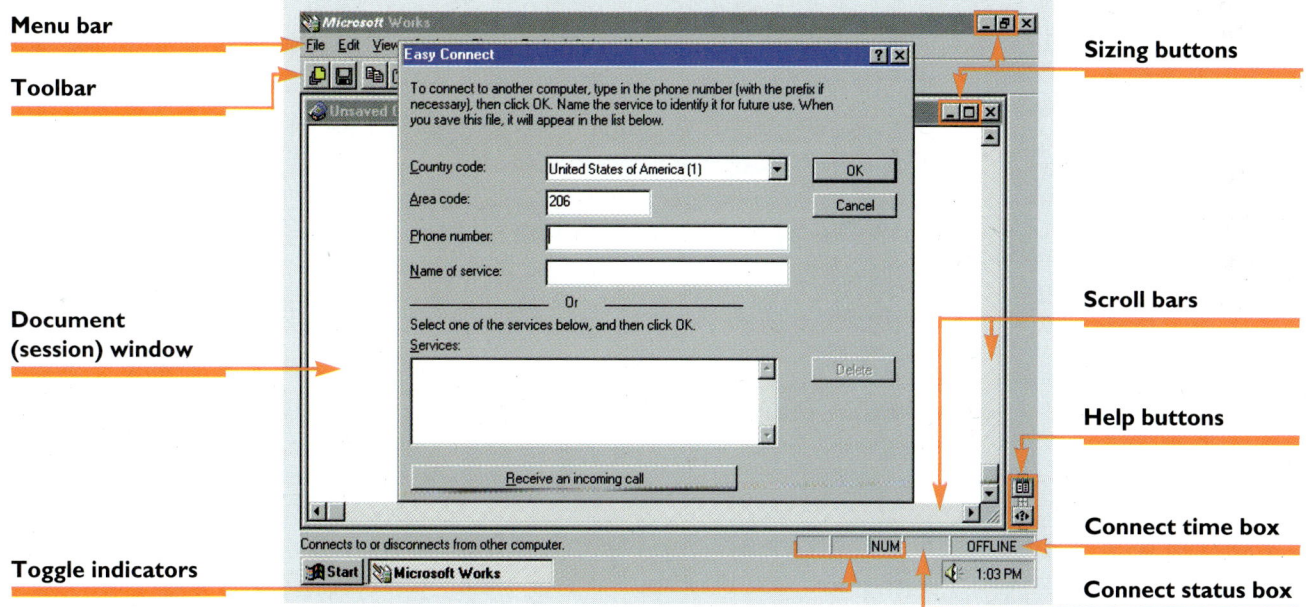

Menu bar
Toolbar
Document (session) window
Toggle indicators

Sizing buttons
Scroll bars
Help buttons
Connect time box
Connect status box

QUICK **TIP**

To save on connect charges, don't call an online service until you're ready to work. Many services charge by the minute.

Setting communications parameters

In this lesson you'll set the communications parameters for your telecommunication session. When you do, you'll encounter several special terms. **Baud rate** is the speed at which data is transferred, and **data bits**, **parity**, and **stop bits** are technical terms describing how data is transmitted. For more information on baud rate, see the related topic, "What is baud rate?" ▶**case** Frasier asked you to connect to the University of Washington computer facility, so you need to prepare the Communications tool with communications parameters that the university computer recognizes. Ask your instructor for the parameters your class uses.

1. **Click the Communication Settings button 🖥 on the toolbar**
   The Communication tab shown in Figure 11-4 opens in the Settings dialog box. It lets you select the hardware component or **device** that will manage the communications session in your computer and adjust other settings. If your modem is internal, Works identifies its manufacturer in the Available devices list box. In Figure 11-4, for example, the modem name is Practical Peripherals PM144HCII.

2. **If your modem is internal, click your modem in the Available devices list box (or, if an external modem is connected to your primary serial port, click Direct Connection on COM1), then click the Properties button**
   A dialog box opens, listing your modem's current settings. (If you click a modem name, the dialog box looks like Figure 11-5; if you click Direct Connection on COM1, the dialog box looks slightly different.) The General tab lets you set the communications port, the speaker volume, and the maximum modem speed (baud rate). You set modem speed to 9600, the default for the University of Washington.

3. **Click the Maximum speed list box, then click 9600**
   You set the baud rate to 9600. (You may need to set a different speed.) Now adjust the transmission protocols using the Connection tab.

4. **Click the Connection tab, select 8 in the Data bits list box, select None in the Parity list box, and select 1 in the Stop bits list box**
   These settings control how your modem transmits data to the online service or remote computer. (Your modem may already contain these default values.) Again, your instructor will tell you what settings to use. Now examine the terminal emulation settings for your online session.

5. **Click OK, then click the Terminal tab in the Settings dialog box**
   The Terminal tab opens, as shown in Figure 11-6. It contains settings that control the configuration of your monitor and keyboard. (Some services require a specific type of hardware configuration for the connection.) Check with your instructor or refer to your telecommunication service manual for the proper settings in this dialog box tab. The University of Washington dial-in service is best suited for VT100 terminal emulation, listed third in the Terminal list box.

6. **Click the VT100 option in the Terminal list box, then click OK**
   Congratulations! You set your communication parameters. In the next lesson you'll connect.

FIGURE 11-4:
Communication tab in Settings dialog box

Internal modem

Properties button

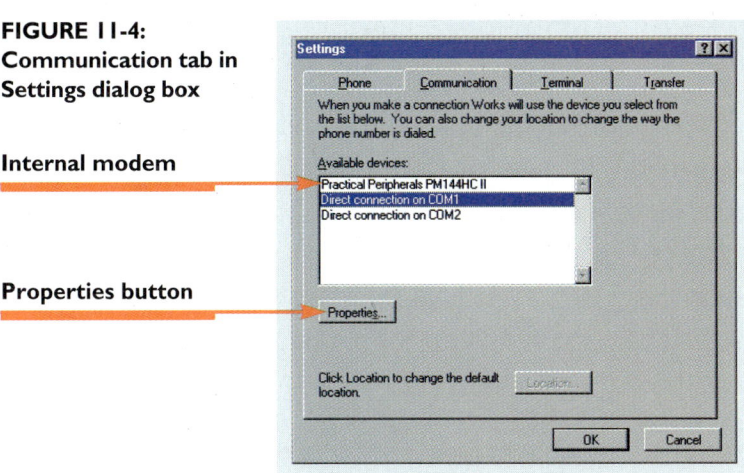

FIGURE 11-5:
General tab in Properties dialog box

Baud rate

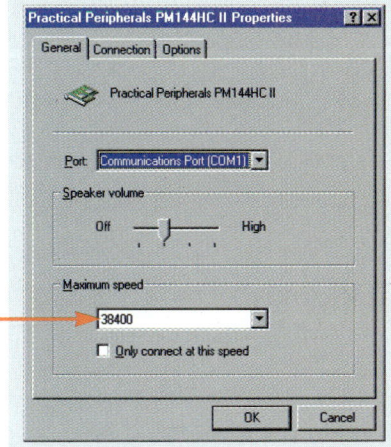

FIGURE 11-6:
Terminal tab in Settings dialog box

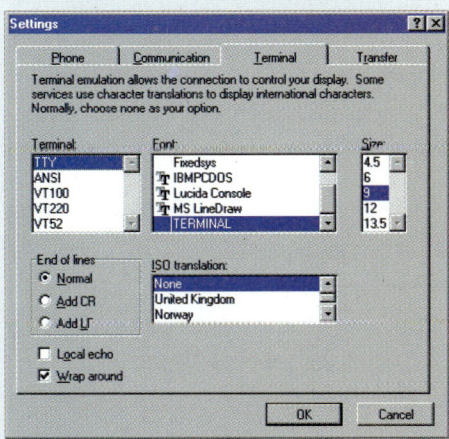

What is baud rate?

Baud rate is the rate at which your modem transfers data over the phone lines. Technically, it refers to the number of times a circuit can switch its electrical state each second. Typical baud rates are 2400 and 9600. The higher the baud rate, the faster the data transfer.

QUICK TIP

To control how your modem dials the remote computer, click the Phone Settings button  on the toolbar.

Connecting to a remote computer

After setting your communication parameters, you're ready to connect to the remote computer. To make the connection you click the Easy Connect button on the toolbar and enter the online service's name and phone number. Your modem dials the remote computer and, if the computer is available, makes the connection. The remote computer then prompts you through the **login** process, which validates you as an authorized user of the system. ▶case Complete your Outdoor Designs work now by connecting to your university dial-in facility or online service.

1. **Make sure you have the account information for your service handy**
   This information typically includes a computer name, a user name, and a password. Ask your instructor for this information if you do not have it.

2. **Click the Easy Connect button on the toolbar**
   The Easy Connect dialog box opens, prompting you for a phone number and service name.

3. **Type the number for the service you'll use in the Phone number text box**
   This number varies depending on your location and the service you use. Ask your instructor for the proper information.

4. **Press [Tab], then type the name of the service you'll use**
   The service name also varies with your situation. Ask your instructor for help. Proceed when you are ready to connect.

5. **Click OK, then click Dial in the Dial dialog box**
   Works dials the phone number you specified in the Settings dialog box and attempts to connect with the remote computer. You see some technical information on the screen as your modem and the remote modem interact. Works then prompts you for your login information. Figure 11-7 shows an example; note that your screen and login information will differ. If the connection is not made for some reason, Works displays a message telling you why. (Two common reasons are that the line is busy or you forgot to turn on your external modem.)

6. **Enter your computer name, user name, and password as directed, pressing [Enter] after each item**
   The remote computer validates your responses and, if you are an authorized user, admits you to the system. A welcome message usually appears, along with any instructions or announcements from the **system administrator**, the person in charge of the service. Figure 11-8 shows what the screen looks like for a fellow employee, Melissa Cavenaugh, after she connects to the University of Washington computing facility to conduct her Outdoor Designs research.

Notice that Works now displays the total connect time in the connect time box. You can use this information to track how long you are connected to the remote computer or service. If you need to disconnect from the remote computer for any reason, you can click the Dial/Hangup button on the toolbar to break the connection. However, you should always log out from the remote computer first, if possible. We'll cover this process later in the unit.

FIGURE 11-7: Remote computer prompts login information

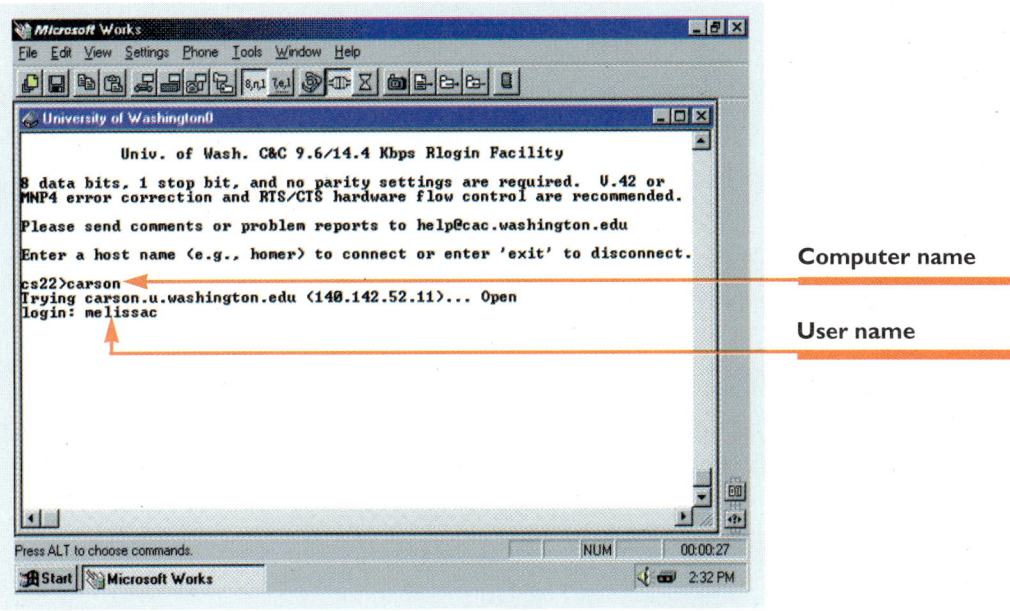

FIGURE 11-8: Typical telecommunication screen after login process

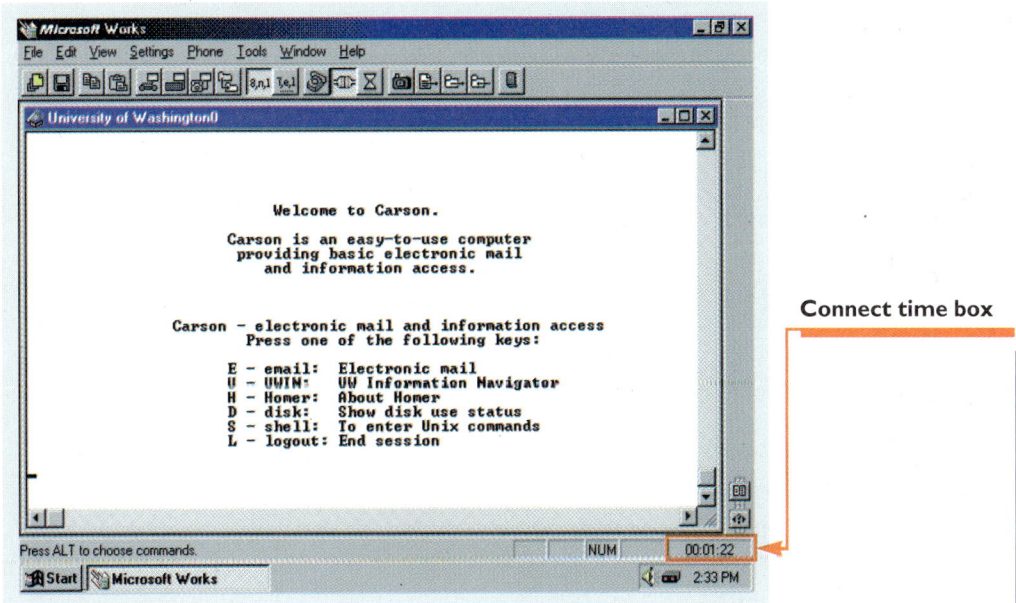

TROUBLE?

If you can't connect to the remote computer, or if you established a connection but strange characters clutter your screen, you may need to adjust your communication or terminal settings. Ask your instructor for help or call a support person at your online service. ■

Searching an online database

Now that you're connected to the remote computer, you can begin to access its resources. **case** Frasier has asked you to search for books relating to outdoor sports in the university library database. Follow along as Melissa Cavenaugh searches for the books in the University of Washington library database. If you can search for the books on your remote computer or service also, do it now. Most services provide this facility, but the commands you need to access your service database probably differ.

1. **Run the program that lets you access the library database**
   The command you type to run this program varies from system to system. Ask your instructor or check your service documentation for details. Melissa types "u," to run the University of Washington Information Navigator, a special program that helps students access university records and materials.

2. **Run the search option in the library database**
   This option, which varies from system to system, displays a dialog box that helps you search for books in the database. Figure 11-9 shows the University of Washington search dialog box. It contains Title, Author, Subject Heading, and Call Number text boxes, and one Keywords text box.

3. **Type outdoor sports in the Title text box (the name of your text box may differ)**
   The remote computer uses these words to search through its library database and retrieve matching titles.

4. **Press [Enter] to run the search (you may need to press a different key)**
   The remote computer searches the library database and displays a list of matching titles. Spend a few minutes examining the books that would help the Outdoor Designs marketing staff with their upcoming fall promotion. Melissa picks the book shown in Figure 11-10.

5. **Write down the book's citation, then exit the library search program**
   The system menu reappears.

Next you send a person at the University of Washington some electronic mail and ask him to send you the book.

FIGURE 11-9: Typical library search dialog box

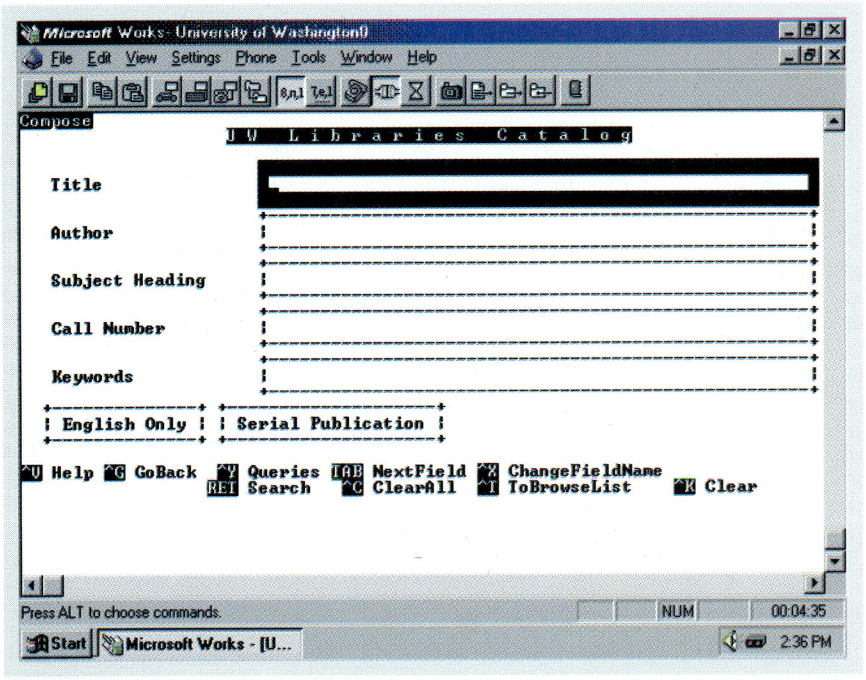

FIGURE 11-10: Online record for outdoor sports book

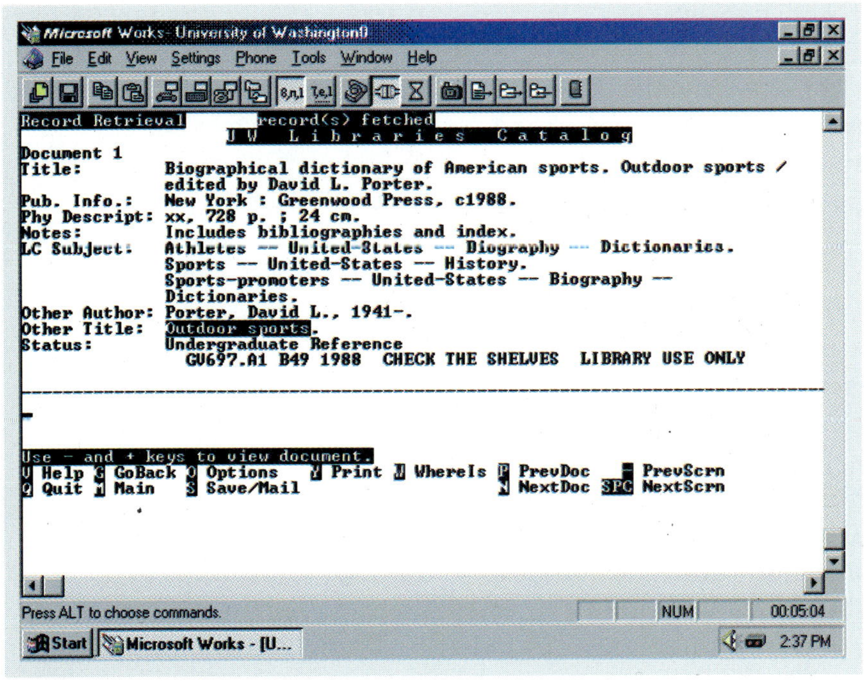

QUICK TIP

You can make more room for information on your screen by clicking the Maximize button in the upper-right corner of the document window and choosing the Hide Help command on the Help menu.

Sending e-mail on the Internet

One of the best reasons for connecting to an online service is to send electronic mail to another computer user. **Electronic mail**, or **e-mail**, is a computer-to-computer version of interoffice mail or the postal service. Each online service has its own program for controlling electronic mail, but services are often linked together in a network to exchange mail and other information. One such network is called the Internet. ►case Use electronic mail now to check out your Outdoor Designs library book and have it sent to you.

1. **Run the program in your service that lets you send electronic mail**
   The commands you type to run this program vary from system to system. Ask your instructor or check your service documentation for details. Melissa types "e," to run the Pine electronic mail program at the University of Washington, as shown in Figure 11-11.

2. **Run the compose message option in the electronic mail program**
   This option, which varies from system to system, displays a dialog box that lets you enter the contents of your electronic mail message. In most electronic mail programs, you press [Tab] to move from one prompt to the next.

3. **Type a friend's internet address after the To: prompt**
   Every user with access to the Internet has a different call name or **address**, depending on the user's location and the remote computer or service the user receives mail from. Ask your instructor or system administrator for the Internet address of a user to whom you can send a test message. (If you don't want to bother anyone with a test message, you can send a test message to your own Internet address.)

4. **Type Looking for library book after the Subject prompt**

5. **Type the following in the Message Text area, pressing [Enter] as indicated (Do not press [Enter] within the paragraph if your program does not require it)**
   **Can you send me the book Biographical Dictionary of American Sports, [Enter]
   edited by David L. Porter? I think it might be just the thing [Enter]
   for an upcoming promotion we're doing this fall at Outdoor Designs. [Enter]
   The book is in the Odegaard Undergraduate Library, and its call [Enter]
   number is GV697.A1 B49. [Enter]
   [Enter]
   Please use my student number for the checkout. [Enter]
   Thanks a million! [Enter]
   [type your first name here]**

   Figure 11-12 shows the message Melissa typed.

6. **Type the command to send the message, then exit the e-mail program**
   The mail program closes and the system menu reappears.

FIGURE 11-11:
University of Washington electronic mail

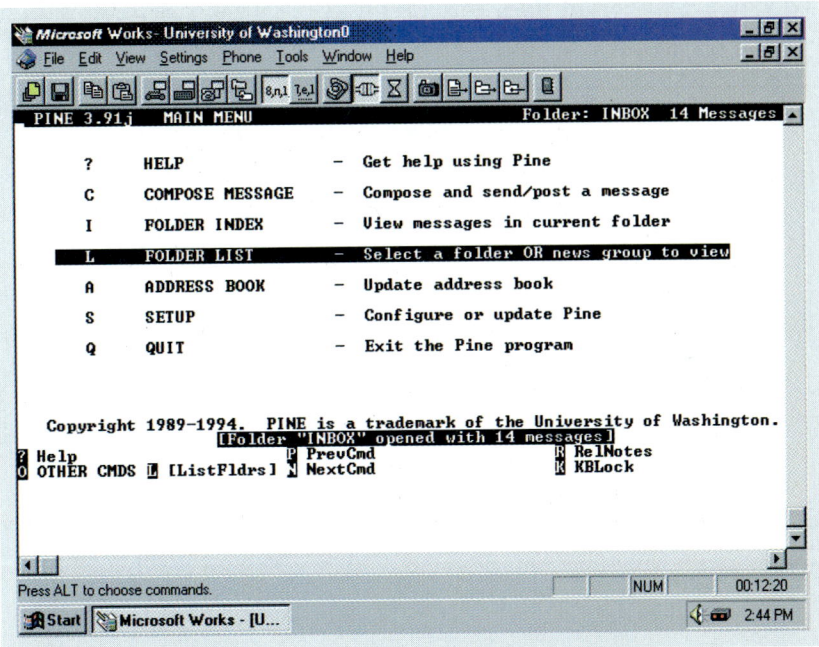

FIGURE 11-12: Composing an electronic mail message

Internet address

Subject

Message text

Electronic mail commands

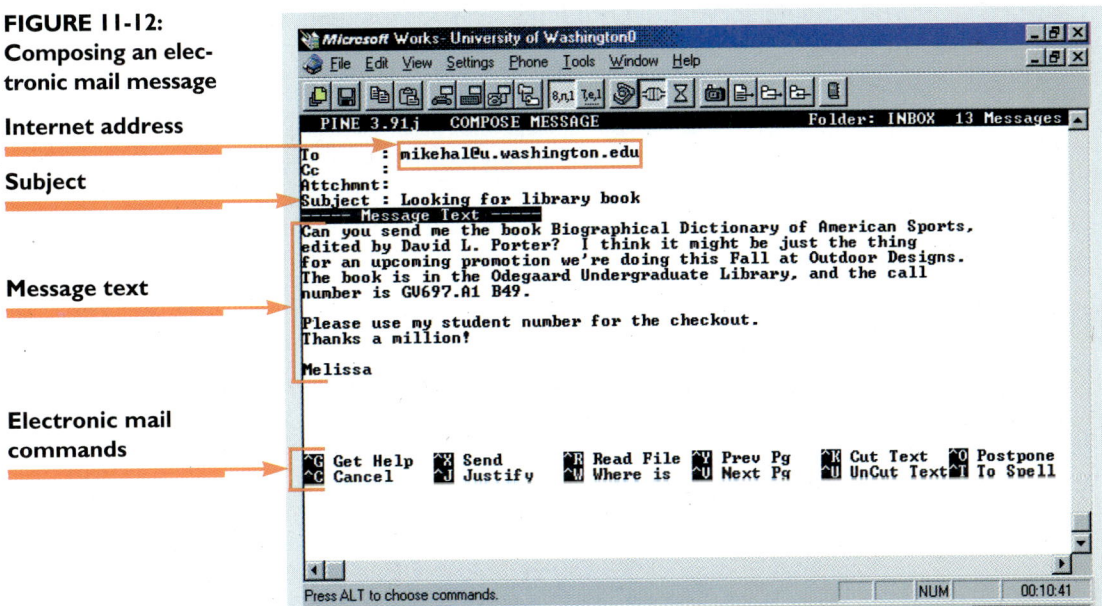

You can also use your e-mail program to read, forward, and delete mail that others send you. Check your online service documentation for details.

Ending your telecommunication session

When you finish working with the remote computer, you're ready to end your telecommunication session, or **log out**. Logging out entails two basic steps: first you log out from the remote computer, then you disconnect your phone connection. After you log out you can save your communications settings in a file, so you won't have to enter them again the next time you telecommunicate. ▶**case** Log out from the remote computer now, and save your connection settings so you can do additional research for Outdoor Designs in the future.

1 **Type the command to log out from your online service**
The command you type to log out varies from system to system. Ask your instructor or check your service documentation for the exact command. Melissa types "l" to log out of the Carson computer, then she types "logout" to terminate the connection, as shown in Figure 11-13.

2 **If your online service did not hang up your modem, click the Dial/Hangup button on the toolbar**
Some online services hang up your modem automatically, others do not. If the service did hang up your modem, the Dial/Hangup button appears pushed out, and you see OFFLINE in the Connect Time box. (You may also hear a click when the modem hangs up.)

3 **If Works asks you if you want to end the active session, click OK**
Works hangs up your phone line, and you can now safely use it for voice calls. Now that you are offline, save your communication settings on your Student Disk so you can use them later at Outdoor Designs.

4 **Insert your Student Disk in the appropriate drive, click File on the menu bar, then click Save As**
The Save As dialog box opens.

5 **Click the letter of the drive that contains your Student Disk in the Save in list box, then double-click the My Works Files folder**

6 **Click Save to save your communication settings on disk under the default name (University of Washington)**
Works automatically uses the service name you specified in the Easy Connect dialog box for your file name, unless you specify otherwise. The next time you want to use these settings, simply double-click the filename in the Easy Connect dialog box. See the related topic, "Using the Easy Connect dialog box," for more information.

7 **Click File on the menu bar, then click Exit Works**
The Works program closes.

FIGURE 11-13: Logging out from the remote computer

Dial/Hangup button

Logout command

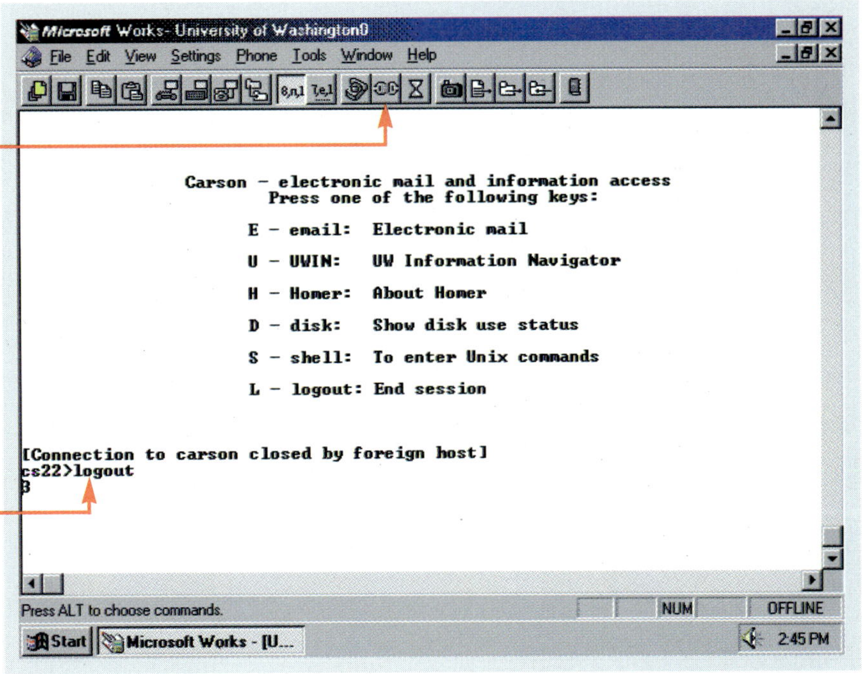

Using the Easy Connect dialog box

The next time you start the Communications tool, the name of the service you just used will appear in the Easy Connect dialog box, as shown in Figure 11-14. To connect to this service again, put your Student Disk in the appropriate drive, then double-click the service name in the dialog box. Works will load the settings from your Student Disk into Works automatically and dial the service. You only need to enter communication settings for your service the first time. After that Works loads them directly from disk.

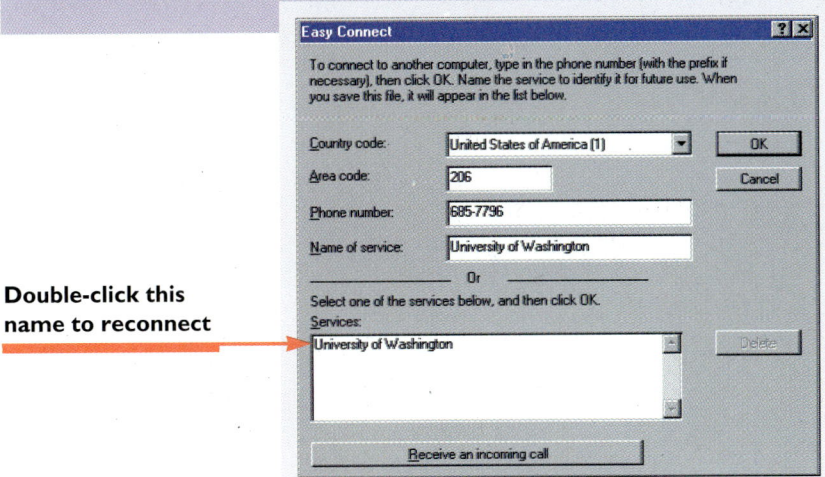

Double-click this name to reconnect

FIGURE 11-14: Easy Connect dialog box

TROUBLE?

Don't try to use your phone for calls while you are telecommunicating. Picking up the phone (even another extension) may break your phone link with the remote computer. ■

WORKS 4 UNIT 11 EXPLORING TELECOMMUNICATIONS

TASK REFERENCE

TASK	MOUSE/BUTTON	MENU	KEYBOARD
Change communications settings	🖥	Click Settings, Communication	[Alt][S],[C]
Change file transfer settings	📇	Click Settings, Transfer	[Alt][S],[R]
Change phone settings	📞	Click Settings, Phone	[Alt][S],[P]
Change terminal settings	⌨	Click Settings, Terminal	[Alt][S],[T]
Connect to a remote computer using Easy Connect	🔗	Click Phone, Easy Connect	[Alt][P],[C]
Dial a remote computer	☎		
End a communications session	☎	Click Phone, Hang Up	[Alt][P],[H]
Exit from Communications tool		Click File, Exit	[Alt][F4]
Start the Communications Tool	Click the Communications Tool in the Task Launcher		

CONCEPTSREVIEW

Label each element of the Communications tool shown in Figure 11-15.

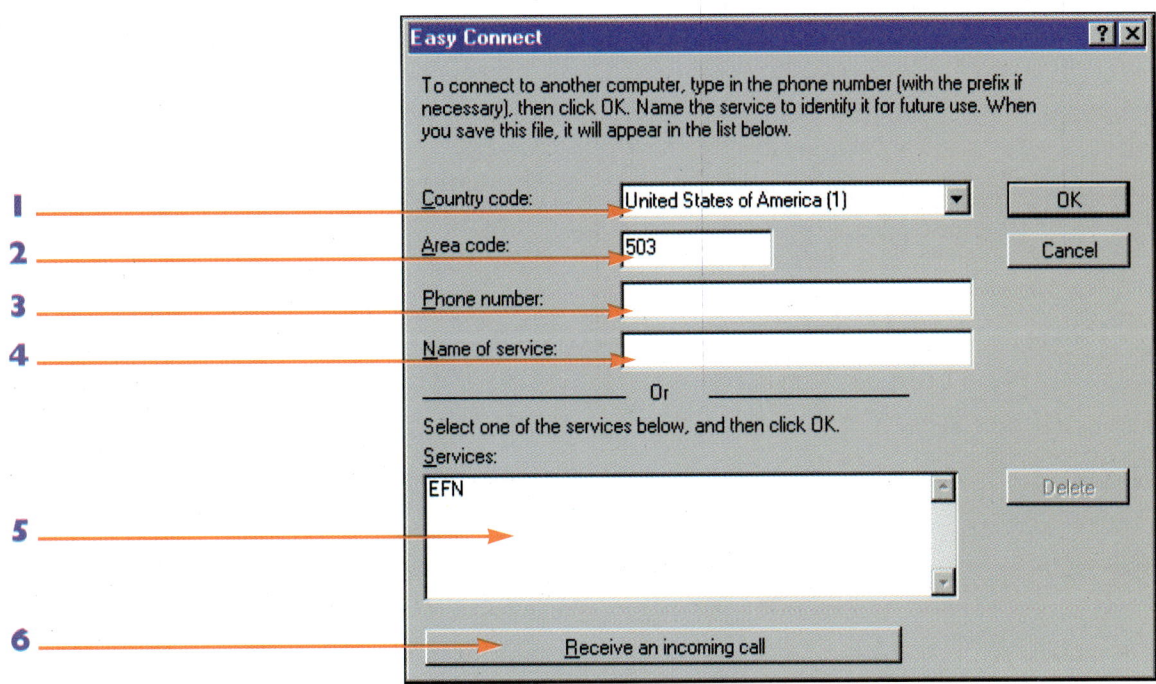

FIGURE 11-15

Match the toolbar buttons with their descriptions.

7.
8.
9.
10.
11.
12.

a. Change file transfer settings
b. Change communications settings
c. Display Easy Connect dialog box
d. Change terminal settings
e. Dial remote computer or (if a connection exists) hang up
f. Change phone settings

Select the best answer from the list of choices.

13 To use your computer to communicate over phone lines, you need a
   a. Modem
   b. Phone line
   c. Serial port
   d. All of the above

14 Which of these is usually required to access an online service?
   a. User name and password
   b. Photo identification
   c. A spreadsheet
   d. All of the above

15 If you have Call Waiting on the phone line you want to use your modem with, you should

  a. Enable it before using the modem

  b. Discontinue the service

  c. Disable it before using the modem

  d. Not use the phone line

16 When you telecommunicate, your modem

  a. Converts analog signals from your computer into digital signals and sends them over phone lines

  b. Converts digital signals from your computer into analog signals and sends them over phone lines

  c. Is unnecessary

  d. Acts like a terminal

17 Modem is short for

  a. Motion Over Dense Electronic Media

  b. Mode em frequency

  c. University of Montana Wireless Experiment

  d. Modulator/demodulator

18 The Internet is

  a. A library database that you can search for books by title, author, or keyword

  b. A university computing facility located in Washington, DC

  c. A global network of computers that exchanges electronic mail and other information

  d. An electronic mail program developed at the University of Washington

19 The process of disconnecting from a remote computer is called

  a. Rebooting

  b. Logging out

  c. Shutting down

  d. Stopping

SKILLS REVIEW

1 Try a new online service provider.

  a. Locate one of the many offers to connect to Prodigy, America Online, CompuServe, or any other service that provides a free trial service period.

  b. Follow the instructions on the disk to connect to the service.

  c. Have your VISA or MasterCard handy so that you can sign up for your free time. (Most services want you to provide a major charge card number.)

  d. After successfully logging on to your new service, explore the many options.

  e. Use any Help options, frequently asked questions options, or user information to make the most of your time.

  f. When you finish, exit from the service so that Works hangs up the phone.

2 Use the Easy Connect dialog box to reconnect to your communication service.

  a. Verify that your hardware is ready.

  b. Check the phone number, settings, and login information for your service.

  c. Start the Communications tool.

  d. Put your Student Disk in the appropriate drive.

  e. Double-click the service name in the Easy Connect dialog box.

  f. Enter your user name and password as required to gain admittance to the system.

3 Send e-mail.

  a. Before connecting to your service provider, get an e-mail address for a person or an institution you want to communicate with. For example, if you don't know an individual with a computer and a modem, you could listen to National Public Radio and send e-mail to one of the program addresses that are announced daily.

  b. Connect to your service provider, using Microsoft Works.

c. When connected to your service provider, select the program option that provides electronic mail.

d. After the To prompt, type the e-mail address of the person or institution with whom you want to communicate.

e. Compose the message.

f. Follow the on-screen instructions to send the message.

g. Exit from the mail program.

h. Log out from the online service.

4 Check for a response to your e-mail.

a. Connect to your service provider, using Microsoft Works.

b. When connected to your service provider, select the program option that provides electronic mail.

c. Select your in-box.

d. If necessary, select the e-mail message.

e. After reading the message, you can delete it if you are finished with it or you can simply close it if you want to keep it.

f. Exit from the mail program.

g. Log out from the online service.

INDEPENDENT CHALLENGE 1

The best way to learn about the Microsoft Works' communications features and communications in general is to connect to a local bulletin board system or to use a local Internet service provider. You should use the library in your area as a resource. Many schools and private individuals maintain bulletin board systems for public use. Find out about all the bulletin boards and service providers in your area and get both their voice phone and modem phone numbers.

After you have the names and numbers of bulletin boards or other service providers, you can call them on your regular voice phone first to ask about pricing details, communication parameters, and services provided. Then use Microsoft Works to dial their numbers and connect to their computers.

INDEPENDENT CHALLENGE 2

After deciding on an Internet service provider in your area and signing up for service, you can use e-mail. Many people have considerably reduced their long-distance telephone bills by using e-mail. You simply connect to your service provider with Microsoft Works and compose letters to friends and relatives anyplace in the world who have access to computers and modems. Send the letters to the correct e-mail addresses, and your mail will await them the next time they connect to their service.

INDEPENDENT CHALLENGE 3

After signing up for an Internet service provider in your area, you can subscribe to newsgroups that interest you. You can find general newsgroups or specialized groups. Sometimes you will receive more mail than you have time to read, so you can withdraw from any group at any time.

INDEPENDENT CHALLENGE 4

America Online, CompuServe, Prodigy, and The Microsoft Network compete to offer the best features for the best prices. Use the periodical section of the library to research each information service. Write a two-page paper comparing and contrasting the four services.

VISUAL WORKSHOP

Windows 95 comes with the capability to use the information service Microsoft provides called The Microsoft Network. This service provides online assistance for Microsoft Works users. To use this service, see your instructor or lab technician for access information. Then, simply connect to The Microsoft Network, as shown in Figure 11-16. Click Tools from the menu bar, then click Find. From the Find menu, click On The Microsoft Network. Type "Works Forum" in the text box, then click the Find Now button. Works will provide you with a list of Works Forum files that you can download onto your computer and read after you sign off the network. These files contain interesting and valuable information about the software you are using.

FIGURE 11-16

UNIT 12

OBJECTIVES

▶ Start Draw

▶ Work with the Draw tools

▶ Create a drawing

▶ Add text to a drawing

▶ Save and format a drawing

▶ Print a drawing

Creating ILLUSTRATIONS WITH DRAW

Now that you know how to add ClipArt to documents you are ready to create original drawings with the Draw accessory. You can use Draw to create company logos, decorative artwork, technical illustrations, and other useful drawings to insert in your documents. Best of all, Draw contains several tools that create shapes automatically, so you don't have to be artistic to produce successful visuals. ▶case A large part of Outdoor Designs' business is kite kits and supplies. President Rebecca Singer is preparing a letter to the company's investors and asked you to create a kite illustration that she can use in the mailing and in future reports and brochures. Create the drawing by following the instructions in this unit. ▶

Starting Draw

You start the Draw accessory from inside the Word Processor or Database tool. Draw has a graphic interface similar to other Works tools and accessories you've used. In Draw the document window where you create your illustration is called the **canvas**. Along the left edge of the canvas are the **drawing tools**, which you use to create the lines, shapes, and text of your illustration. Near the bottom of the screen are **Line** and **Fill palettes**, which let you change the colors of lines and shapes in your illustration. Figure 12-2 identifies the Draw interface's unique elements, and Table 12-1 describes the drawing tools.  Start Works and the Draw accessory now.

1. Launch Works, then click the **Works Tools tab** in the Works Task Launcher dialog box
   The four Works tool buttons appear on your screen.
2. Click the **Word Processor button**
   You'll create your Outdoor Designs kite illustration from within the Word Processor.
3. Click **Insert** on the menu bar, then click **Drawing**
   The Draw accessory shown in Figure 12-1 opens in a window. Notice the shaded area in the upper-left corner of the Word Processor window. (You may have to move the Draw window to see this area.) Works reserves this space for the illustration you are about to create with Draw. When you finish your illustration and exit Draw, Works puts the drawing in this space. Now you maximize the Draw window so you can see all elements of the Draw interface.
4. Click the **Maximize button** in the Draw window
   The Draw accessory expands to full size, as shown in Figure 12-2. Take a moment to identify the elements of the Draw accessory, referring to Table 12-1 to identify the drawing tools. You'll use the drawing tools in the next lesson.

TABLE 12-1: Drawing tools in the Draw accessory

TOOL	FUNCTION
▶	Selects objects in an illustration. Also used for moving objects.
🔍	Enlarges part of an illustration for close-up viewing.
╲	Creates a straight line.
○	Creates an ellipse. (Hold down [Shift] to create a circle.)
▢	Creates a rectangle with rounded edges. (Hold down [Shift] to create a square with rounded edges.)
▭	Creates a rectangle. (Hold down [Shift] to create a square.)
◜	Creates an arc or "pie slice."
⌇	Creates polygons. (Hold down the mouse button to create freeform lines.)
A	Inserts text (or labels) in the illustration.

FIGURE 12-1: Start Draw, Database, or Word Processor tool

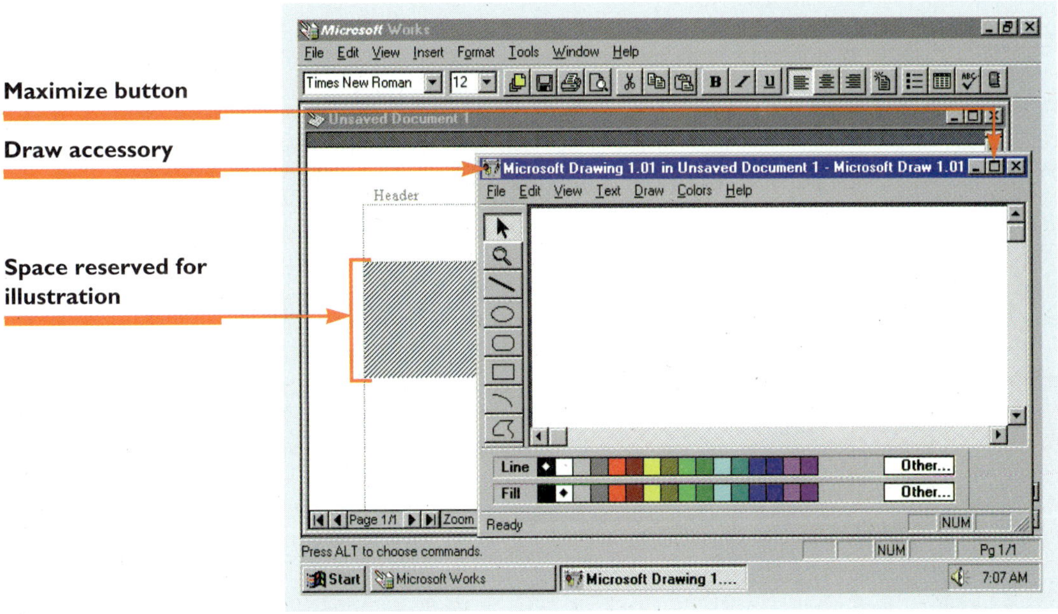

- Maximize button
- Draw accessory
- Space reserved for illustration

FIGURE 12-2: Important elements in the Draw accessory interface

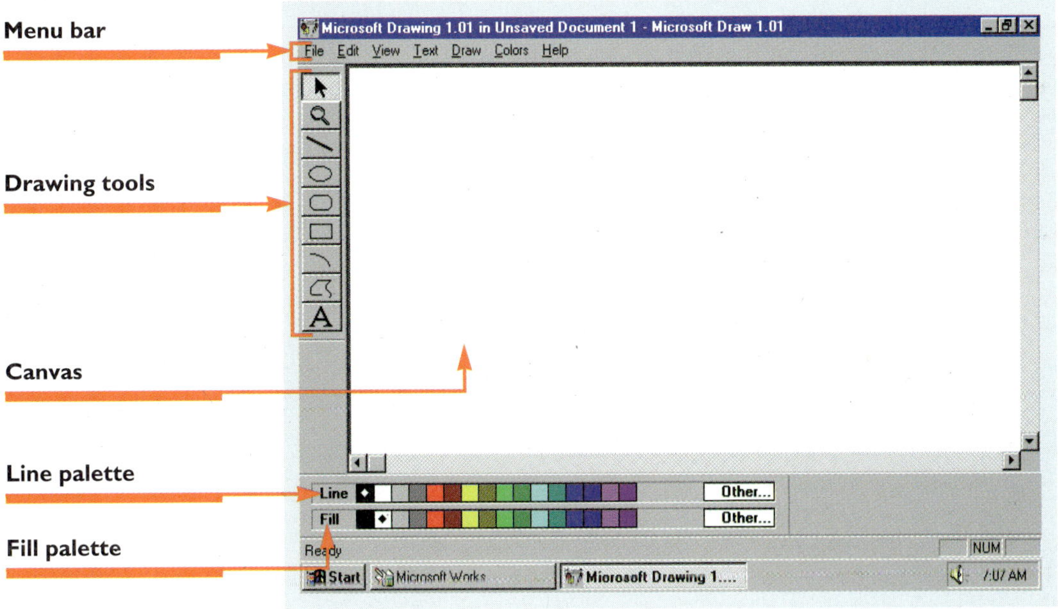

- Menu bar
- Drawing tools
- Canvas
- Line palette
- Fill palette

QUICK TIP

You can learn more about drawing tools by choosing the Tools command from the Draw accessory's Help menu.

Working with the Draw tools

The drawing tools help you create your illustration or modify it later. Creating an illustration is easy, because Draw lets you build it one object, or piece, at a time. Each object remains a single entity that can be selected, moved, or deleted at any time. (This means one mistake cannot ruin an entire illustration.) **case**
Because you don't want to present your first attempts at creating an illustration to Outdoor Designs' President, take this opportunity to practice using the drawing tools. To learn the basics, create an abstract face using a few commands. Feel free to experiment—you'll erase your creation at the end of the lesson.

1. **Click the Ellipse tool**
   The Ellipse tool highlights and the mouse pointer changes to crosshairs. You try using the Ellipse tool to draw an ellipse on the left side of the canvas.

2. **Position the Ellipse tool on the canvas,** *hold down the mouse button,* **drag the crosshairs down and to the right,** *then release the mouse button*
   An ellipse appears on the canvas, surrounded by four selection rectangles. These rectangles, called **handles**, indicate an object is selected and you can cut, copy, paste, or move it like any highlighted object in Works. Cut the ellipse object now.

3. **Click Edit on the menu bar, then click Cut**
   Works removes the object from the canvas and places it in the Windows Clipboard. Now you paste it with the Paste command.

4. **Click Edit on the menu bar, then click Paste**
   Works pastes the object back on the canvas. Now move the object to the right.

5. **Click the Arrow tool**
   The Arrow tool highlights and the mouse pointer changes to an arrow.

6. **Click the ellipse object,** *hold down the mouse button,* **drag the object to the right,** *then release the mouse button*
   The object moves to the right. You can use the Arrow tool to drag any object on the canvas. Now fill a shape with color.

7. **Click the dark green box in the Fill palette**
   The ellipse fills with dark green color, as shown in Figure 12-3, and Works places a check mark in the dark green square on the palette. You can add color to any geometric shape with the Fill palette. To change the color of an object's lines, you click any color box in the Line palette.

8. **Experiment with the Ellipse tool, Rectangle tool, Rounded Rectangle tool, and Arc tool on your own to create an abstract face similar to the one shown in Figure 12-4**
   If you want, you can place one object on top of another. When you finish, delete all objects and clear the canvas.

9. **Click Edit on the menu bar, click Select All, then press [Delete]**
   Draw deletes all objects in the drawing.

FIGURE 12-3: Ellipse created with the Ellipse tool

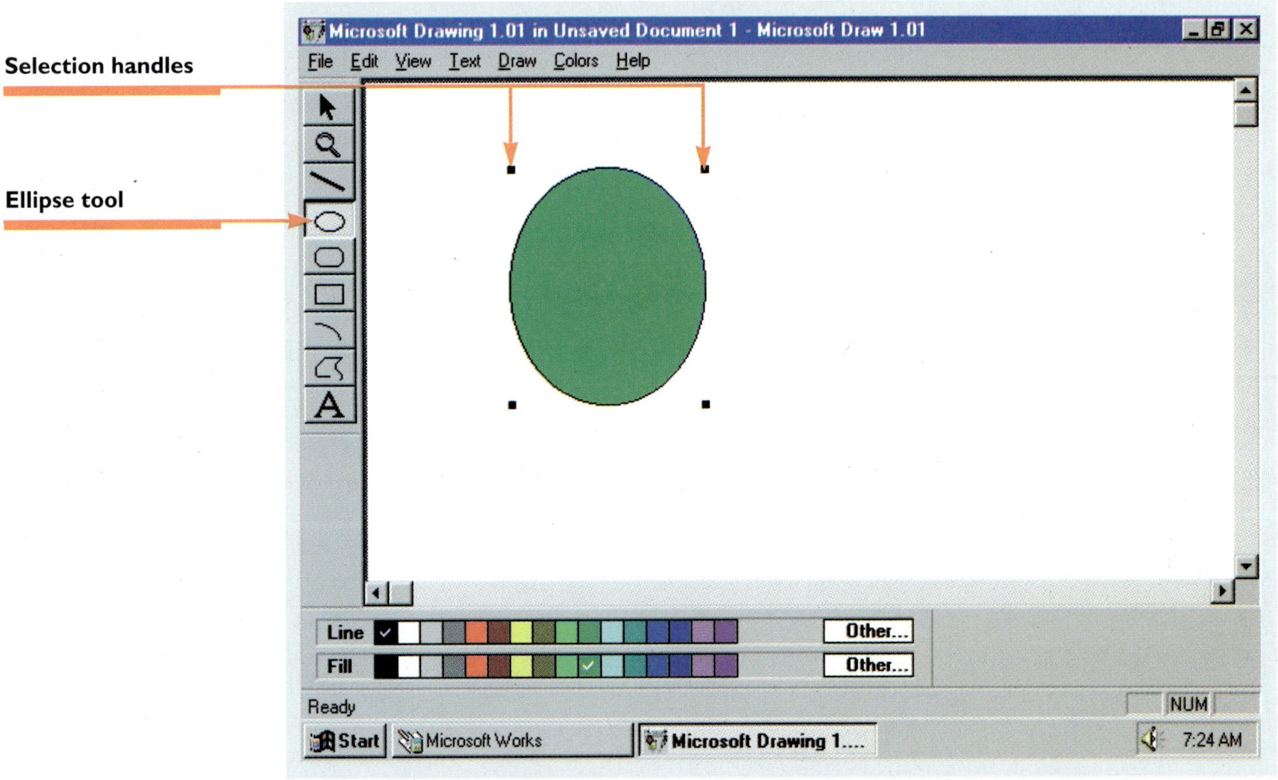

Selection handles

Ellipse tool

FIGURE 12-4: Abstract face created with several drawing tools

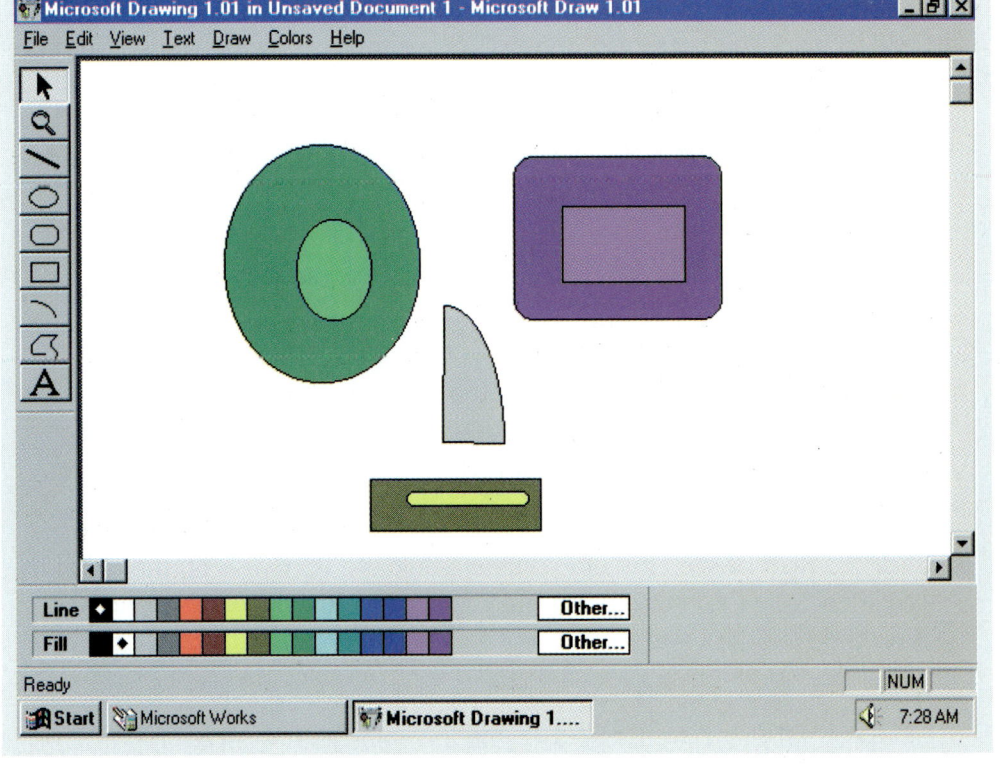

QUICK TIP

The Select All command on the Edit menu lets you perform several operations on all objects on a canvas, including dragging all the parts as a single entity.

Creating a drawing

Using the Freeform and Rectangle tools, you can build most shapes you want to create with the Draw accessory. You gained experience with the Rectangle tool in the last lesson. The **Freeform tool** lets you create polygons (many-sided objects) and freehand drawings. ▶case Use the Freeform and Rectangle tools now to create a diamond-shaped kite with a tail for President Singer's sales report.

1 Click the **Freeform tool**
The Freeform tool highlights and the mouse pointer changes to crosshairs. You can use the Freeform tool to create polygons (such as triangles and diamonds) by moving the mouse to each **vertex** (corner) of the shape and clicking, then double-clicking the last corner. Or you can create a freehand drawing (such as a signature or a jagged line) by holding down the mouse button and moving the crosshairs, then double-clicking when you finish.

Now try creating the diamond for the kite illustration with the Freeform tool, referring to Figure 12-5 for the proper shape. If it takes you a while to get the hang of it, don't worry. You can always select the diamond, delete it, and start again.

2 Click near the top of the canvas with the **Freeform tool**, then move the crosshairs down and to the left
A line extends from the Freeform tool to the point you clicked. This is the upper-left edge of the four-sided diamond kite.

3 Click to mark the kite's left corner, then move the crosshairs down and to the right to mark the bottom of the kite
A line extends from the kite's left corner down to the bottom of the kite.

4 Click to mark the bottom of the kite, move the crosshairs to the right edge and click, then move the crosshairs to the top of the kite and double-click where the first line begins
The kite's diamond shape is complete, as shown in Figure 12-5. If your diamond doesn't look quite right, select it, delete it, then try again.

5 Click the **yellow color box** in the Fill palette
The diamond kite fills with yellow color. Now use the Freeform tool to draw a tail for the kite, referring to Figure 12-6 for the proper shape. (You'll add the bows in Step 7.)

6 Click the **Freeform tool**, then click the bottom of the diamond, hold down the mouse button, draw a wavy line, then double-click the end of the line
A tail appears below the kite. Again, if you're not happy with the object you created, select it, delete it, and try again.

7 Click the **Rectangle tool** create a tiny kite rectangle on the tail of the kite, then copy the rectangle to the Clipboard and paste it several times along the tail of the kite
The tiny rectangles give the impression of small bows decorating the kite tail.

8 Fill the rectangles with different colors using the **Fill palette**
When you finish, your kite should look like the one shown in Figure 12-6.

FIGURE 12-5: Create kite diamond with Freeform tool

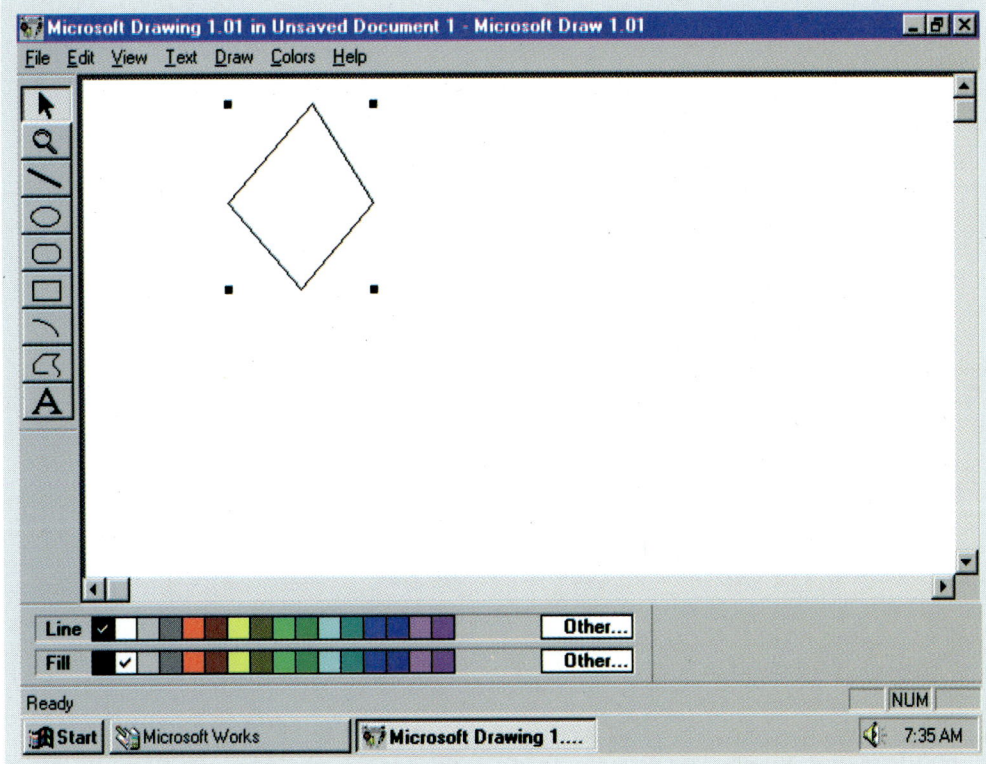

FIGURE 12-6: Add bows and color to kite

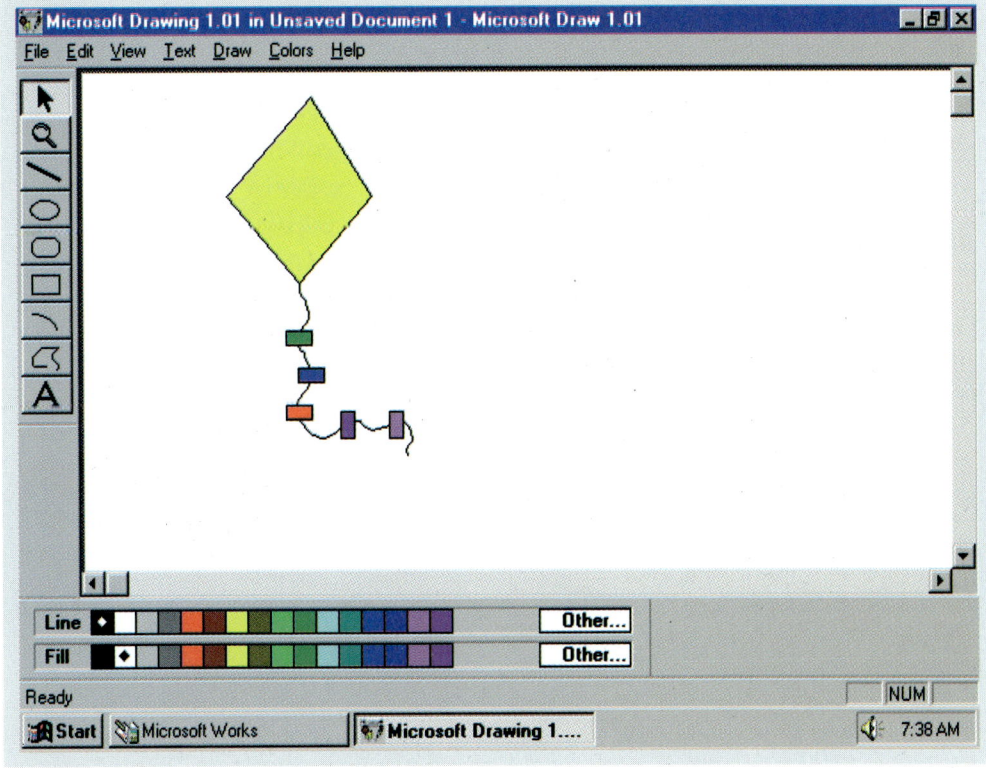

QUICK TIP

You can rotate drawn objects, such as the kite bows, with the Rotate/Flip command on the Draw menu.

Adding text to a drawing

The Text tool lets you place the cursor anywhere in a drawing and type characters to add information. After you enter text, you can select it, move it with the Arrow tool, and format it with the Text menu commands. **case** Use the Text tool now to place the words "Outdoor Designs" in the kite you are creating for Rebecca's sales report.

1. **Click the Text tool A and click inside the kite near the top**
   See Figure 12-7 for guidance. The Text tool highlights and the mouse pointer changes to a blinking insertion pointer (similar to the insertion pointer in the Word Processor).

2. **Type Outdoor and press [Enter]**
   Works adds the word "Outdoor" to the illustration and selects it.

3. **Click the Text tool, then click inside the kite below the word Outdoor**

4. **Type Designs and press [Enter]**
   Works adds the text "Designs" to the illustration, as shown in Figure 12-7.

5. **If necessary, reposition the words with the Arrow tool so they're neatly centered in the kite**
   Now you change the font of the two words to Times New Roman and their style to boldface. Before you can make these changes, you need to select the text you want to modify. Because it is the last text you typed, "Designs" is already selected.

6. **Hold down [Shift] and click Outdoor in the kite**
   Now you've selected both words in the illustration.

7. **Click Text on the menu bar, click Font, then scroll to and click Times New Roman in the Font list box**
   The Font dialog box opens, and the font setting for the kite text changes to Times New Roman.

8. **Click Bold in the Font style list box, then click OK**
   The Font dialog box closes, and the two words are formatted with boldface Times New Roman type. Congratulations! You've finished creating the kite. It should look similar to the one shown in Figure 12-8.

FIGURE 12-7: Entering text in illustration with Text tool

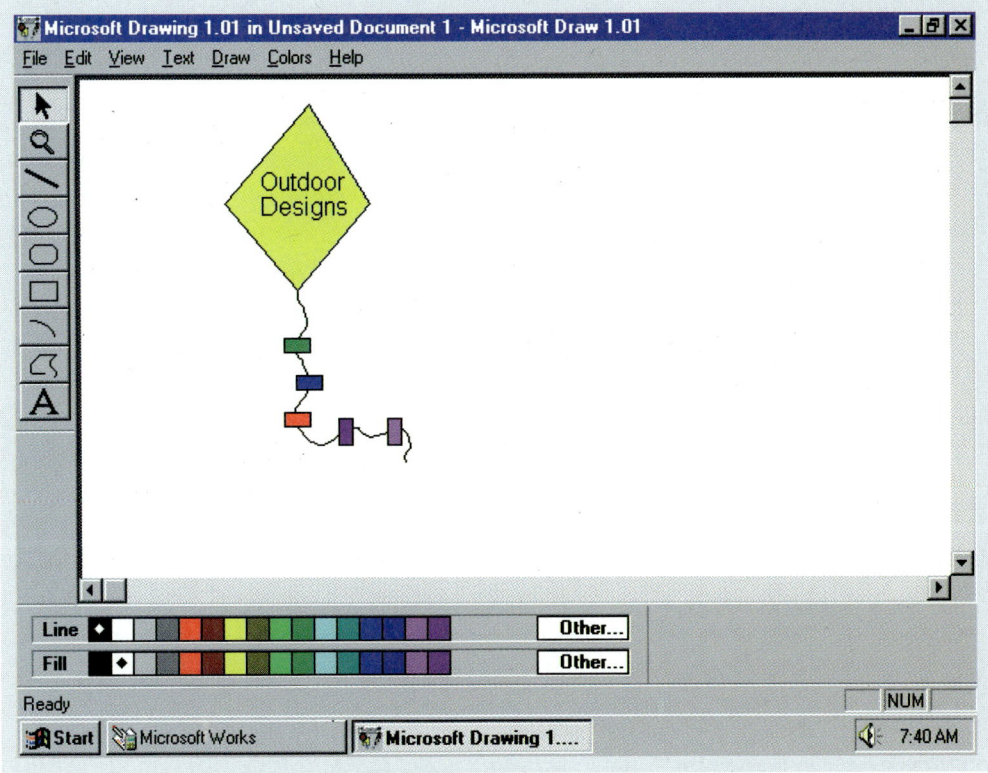

FIGURE 12-8: Final kite illustration

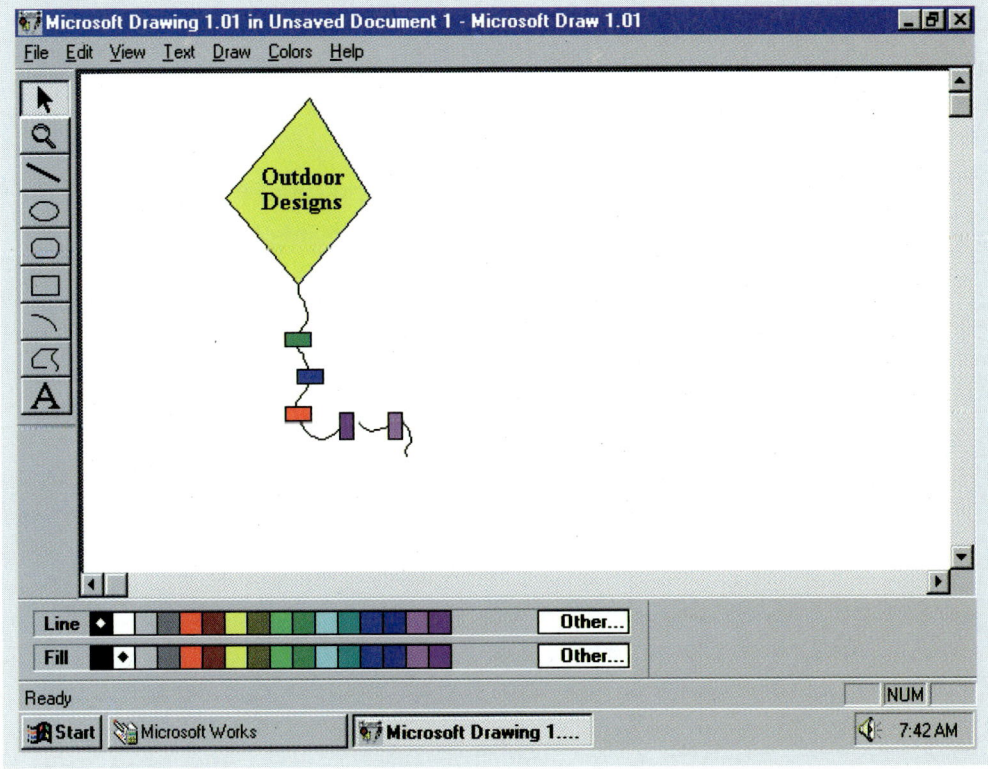

QUICK TIP

Zooming in on your illustration with the Zoom tool  as you work, and using the sizing commands on the View menu can make your work easier. ∎

Saving and formatting a drawing

To save a Draw illustration you need to return to the Word Processor and save the illustration in a file. You can store a Draw illustration by itself in a file, or store it with text and other graphics in a word-processing document or database form. After you place the drawing in a document, you can change its size, alignment, and border formatting. ▶**case** Finalize your Outdoor Designs kite illustration now by returning to the Word Processor and formatting the picture. Then save the kite on your Student Disk so you can use it later in the sales report.

1   Click **File** on the menu bar, then click **Exit and Return**
    A Works dialog box asks if you want to update the open document in the Word Processor. This is an opportunity to discard your illustration if you want, but in this case, you want to save it.

2   Click **Yes**
    The Draw accessory closes and the kite illustration appears in the Word Processor, as shown in Figure 12-9. Eight selection handles appear around the illustration, indicating that it's selected. (As with text, a drawing must be selected before you can format it.) Now center-align and enlarge your kite so it has more impact.

3   Click the **Center-align button** on the toolbar
    The illustration moves to the center of the document. You can also use the Left- and Right-align buttons to change an illustration's alignment. Now increase the kite's size.

4   Click **Format** on the menu bar, then click **Picture**
    The Picture dialog box opens, and the Size tab appears. The Size tab lets you control the selected picture's exact size or its scaling percentage. You use the Width and Height scaling options now to enlarge the picture to 120% of its original size.

5   Select the text in the Scaling Width text box, and replace it with **120**; then select the text in the Scaling Height text box, and replace it with **120**; then click **OK**
    You'll typically want to scale the picture width and height equally to avoid distorting the image. When the dialog box closes, your slightly enlarged illustration appears, as shown in Figure 12-10. (To restore the picture's original size, you open the Size tab again and return the scaling percentages to 100.) Now save the kite illustration on your Student Disk.

6   Insert your Student Disk in the appropriate drive, click **File** on the menu bar, then click **Save As**
    The Save As dialog box opens.

7   Select the **My Works Files folder** on your Student Disk, then type **Kite Artwork** in the File name text box and click **Save**
    You saved the kite illustration on your Student Disk under the name "Kite Artwork."

FIGURE 12-9: Kite illustration in Word Processor

Selection handles

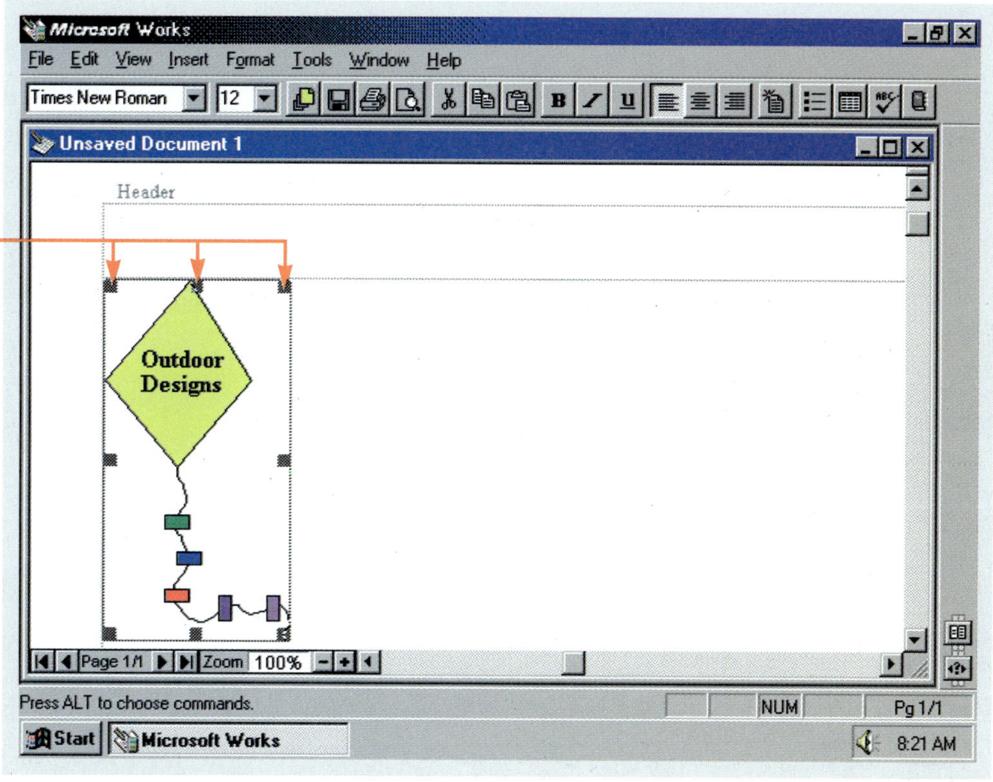

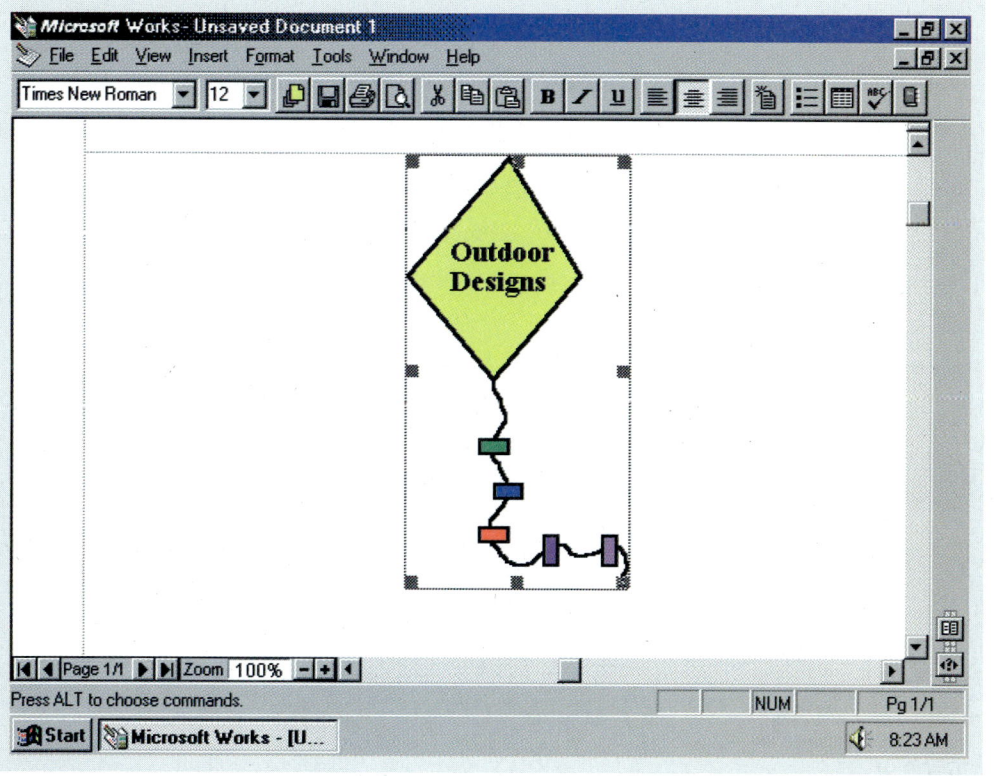

FIGURE 12-10: Kite illustration enlarged to 120% of its original size

QUICK TIP

You can move an illustration in a document with the drag-and-drop technique or by cutting and pasting. To delete an illustration select it and press [Delete].

Printing a drawing

When you finish creating a drawing and place it in your document, you can print it with the Print command. As usual, it's a good idea to examine your illustration in Print Preview before you print to identify any sizing or layout problems. If you don't have a color printer, your drawing appears in black and white. **case** Print your kite illustration now and give Rebecca Singer a copy to review. Be sure to tell her that you can resize the artwork so that it neatly fits in any presentation. See the related topic, "Editing ClipArt in Draw," for information on customizing ClipArt illustrations.

1. Click the **Print Preview button** on the toolbar
   The kite illustration in Print Preview looks as it will when printed.

2. Click the **kite** twice with the **Zoom pointer**
   The full-size kite appears, as shown in Figure 12-11. The kite looks good.

3. Verify that your printer is ready, then click the **Print button** in the Print Preview window
   Works sends the document to the printer. After a few moments, the final kite illustration emerges.

4. Click the **Save button** on the toolbar
   Any changes you've made are saved on disk.

5. Click **File** on the menu bar, then click **Exit Works**
   The Works program closes.

FIGURE 12-11: Kite illustration in Print Preview

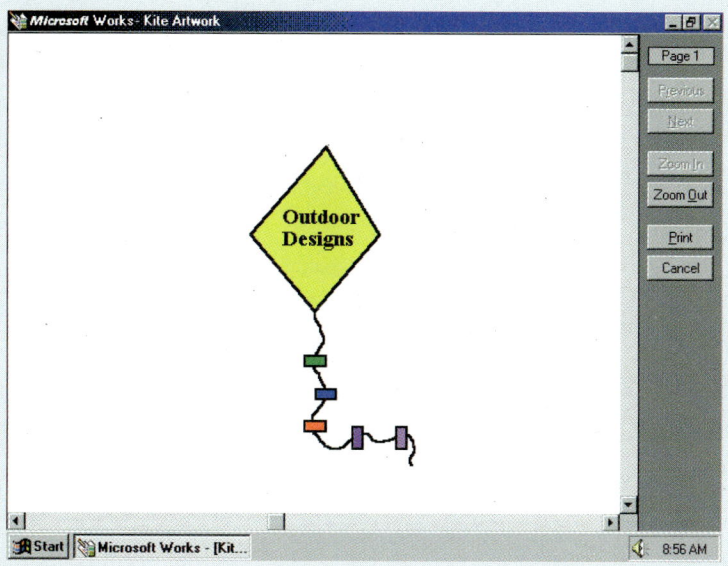

Editing ClipArt in Draw

Have you seen a piece of ClipArt in the ClipArt gallery that would be perfect with a few changes? You can make those changes by editing the ClipArt in Draw and then paste the art in your document. Here's the procedure: Start in the Word Processor. Choose the ClipArt command from the Insert menu, and double-click the ClipArt you want to modify. Next, click the ClipArt, then choose the Cut command from the Edit menu, then choose the Drawing command from the Insert menu. Maximize the Draw accessory, choose the Paste command from the Edit menu to paste the ClipArt, then edit the artwork as you like. See Figure 12-12. When you finish, exit the Draw program and click Yes to update the document. Works pastes the revised ClipArt in the Word Processor document.

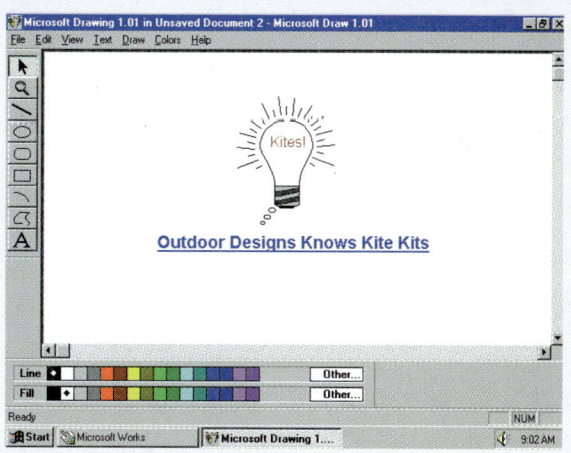

FIGURE 12-12: Editing light bulb ClipArt in Draw accessory

You cannot print from the Draw accessory. You must print your illustration from the tool where the artwork is located.

TASK REFERENCE

TASK	MOUSE/BUTTON	MENU	KEYBOARD
Align a drawing in the Word Processor	[icon]	Click Format, Paragraph	[Alt][O],[P]
Change a line color	Select object, click color in Line palette		
Create a freeform shape or polygon	[icon]		
Create a rectangle	[icon]		
Create a rectangle with rounded edges	[icon]		
Create a straight line	[icon]		
Create an arc	[icon]		
Create an ellipse	[icon]		
Delete a drawing in the Word Processor			Select drawing, then press [Del]
Delete an object			Select object, then press [Del]
Edit ClipArt		Click Insert, ClipArt, then select ClipArt and click Edit, Cut, then click Insert, Drawing, then click Edit, Paste	
Fill an object with color	Select object, click color in Fill palette		
Insert text	[icon]		
Move an object	Click [icon] and drag		
Print a drawing in the Word Processor	[icon]	Click File, Print	[Ctrl] [P]
Resize a drawing in the Word Processor	Select drawing, then drag one of the sizing handles	Click Format, Picture	[Alt][O],[R]
Save a drawing		Click File, Exit and Return	[Alt][F],[X]
Select an object	[icon]		
Start Draw Accessory		Click Insert, Drawing	[Alt][I],[I]
View part of an illustration close up	[icon]	Click View, then click desired percentage	[Alt][V],[2] or [4] or [8]

CONCEPTSREVIEW

Label each element of the Draw tool, as shown in Figure 12-13.

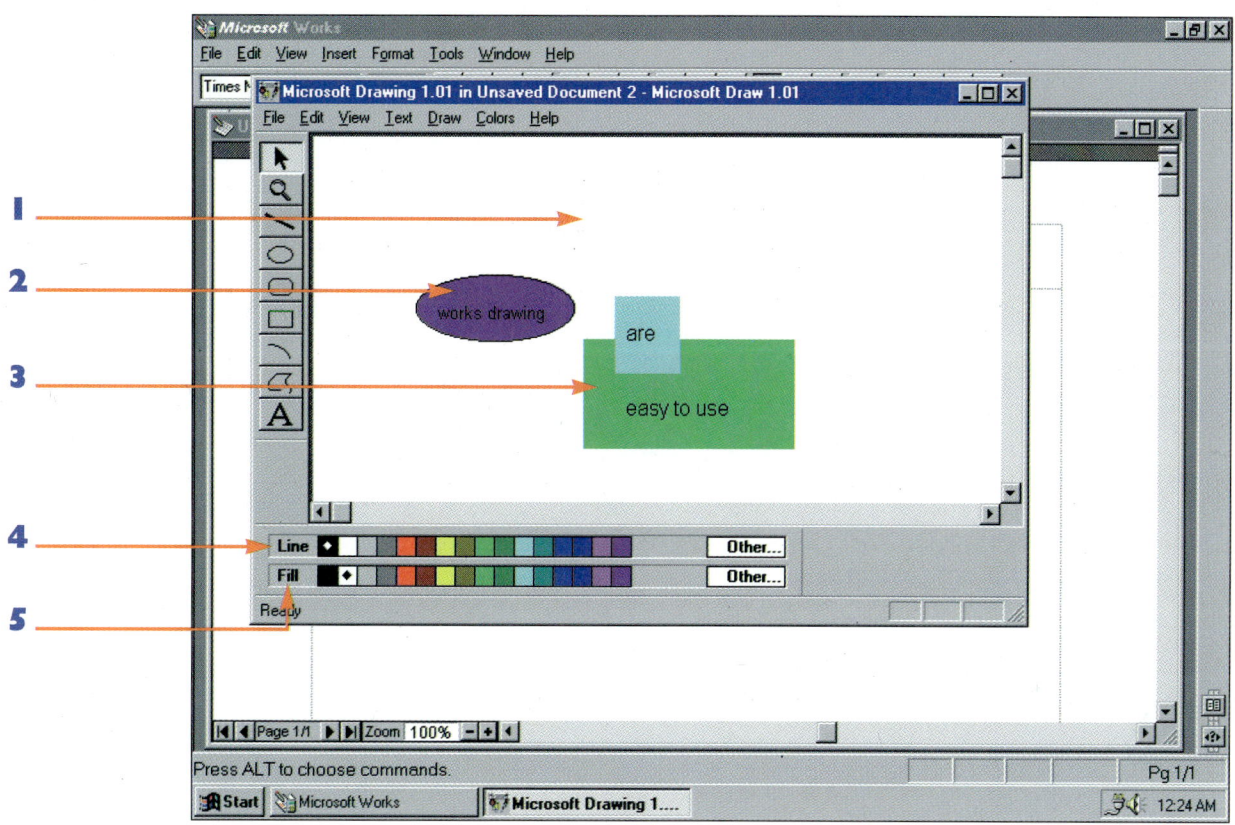

FIGURE 12-13

Match the drawing tools with their functions.

6.
7.
8.
9.
10.
11.
12.
13.
14.

a. Creates polygons
b. Creates an ellipse
c. Creates an arc
d. Enlarges part of the illustration for up-close viewing
e. Inserts text in the illustration
f. Creates a rectangle with square edges
g. Selects objects in the illustration
h. Creates a rectangle with round edges
i. Creates a straight line

Select the best answer from the list of choices.

15. In the Draw tool, the document window is called the
    a. Document
    b. Canvas
    c. Form
    d. Easel

16. The arrow tool
    a. Creates a straight line
    b. Creates an arrow
    c. Selects objects in the illustration
    d. Enlarges part of the illustration

17. To add color to the inside of a rectangle, you would
    a. Click the Edit Palette command on the Colors menu
    b. Click the rectangle object, then click a color in the Fill palette
    c. Click the rectangle object, then click the color in the Line palette
    d. Double-click inside the object

18. To create a circle, you would
    a. Use the circle tool
    b. Use the arc tool
    c. Hold down the [Shift] key while using the ellipse tool
    d. Use the freehand tool

19. To move an object you have drawn, you would
    a. Use the Tools Move command
    b. Use the Selection tool to drag the object
    c. Choose the Move Object tool
    d. All of the above

20. When an object is selected, it appears with
    a. Color
    b. Handles
    c. A pointer
    d. An ellipse

21. To print the drawn object, you would
    a. Choose the Print tool from within the Drawing tool
    b. Choose File, Print from within the Drawing tool
    c. Close the Drawing tool and print from the word processor
    d. All of the above

SKILLS REVIEW

1. Create a drawing and add it to a database form.
   a. Open the WKS 9-2 file on your Student Disk and save it in the My Works Files folder under the name Form2.
   b. Click the Form Design button.
   c. Click the mouse in the blank area next to the Size field.
   d. Click the Insert menu.
   e. Choose the Drawing command.
   f. Click the Line tool and draw a tent.
   g. Click the Text tool and type the name Outdoor Designs on the tent.
   h. Close the Drawing tool to view the artwork.
   i. Save the file.
   j. Click the Form View button to return to form view.

2 Resize and Move a drawing.
   a. Click the Form Design button.
   b. Click the drawing of the tent so that handles appear.
   c. Click and drag the handle in the bottom right corner to size the drawing.
   d. Click and drag the drawing to move it (click in the drawing not on a handle).
   e. Double-click the drawing to return to the Drawing tool.
   f. Click the text you typed, and choose the green box from the Line palette.
   g. Choose Exit and Return from the File menu.
   h. Click Yes to save the changes.
   i. Click the Form View button.
   j. Save and close the file.

3 Create a drawing and add it to a document.
   a. Start the Word Processing tool.
   b. Click the Insert menu.
   c. Choose the Drawing command.
   d. Draw the body of a truck with the Rectangle tool.
   e. Draw the wheels of the truck with the Ellipse tool (hold down [Shift] for circles).
   f. Draw additional details—antennas, mirrors, etc.—as desired.
   g. Fill the truck body and wheels with a color using the Fill palette.
   h. Use the Text tool to write the name Joe's Garage on the body of the truck.
   i. Change the font and size of the font.
   j. Click the File menu.
   k. Choose the Exit and Return command.
   l. Save the file as Truck in the My Works Files folder on your Student Disk, then close it.

4 Create a drawing of your choice.
   a. Start the Word Processing tool.
   b. Click the Insert menu.
   c. Choose the Drawing command.
   d. Use any of the drawing tools to create a drawing of your choice.
   e. Use Fill to change parts of the drawing.
   f. Use the Text tool to add text to the drawing.
   g. Click the File menu.
   h. Choose the Exit and Return command.
   i. Size or move the graphic as necessary.
   j. Save the file.
   k. Print the graphic.

INDEPENDENT CHALLENGE 1

Joel Rubin at the Steak Pit is looking for an attractive design to use on napkins and matchbooks at the restaurant. Create an abstract design that will add a touch of class to the decor. Fill in some of the images, changing colors and patterns to see some of the effects that are provided.

INDEPENDENT CHALLENGE 2

The marketing director at Wacky Words is looking for a new logo for the company. She has looked through all of the ClipArt in Works, but nothing is exactly perfect. She asks you to find an image and jazz it up to suit the playful mood the company wants to communicate. Use the Draw tool to edit the ClipArt image so that it is perfect for your needs.

To complete this independent challenge:

1 Find a ClipArt image that has some promise as a Wacky Words logo, and retrieve it.

2 Rotate the image.

3 Add elements to the picture using the drawing tools.

4 Add text to the picture.

5 Save the drawing under a new name to the My Works Files folder on your Student Disk.

6 Print the drawing and close the file.

INDEPENDENT CHALLENGE 3

The Stuff for Pets store wants you to create a graphic of a cat that they can use for promotions.

To complete this independent challenge:

1 Use the Draw tools to create a simple drawing of a cat; see Figure 12-14 as a guide.

2 Use any of the fill tools to try filling in the drawing.

3 Add the text "Cats of All Kinds" to the drawing.

4 Save the drawing as "Catart" to the My Works Files folder on your Student Disk.

5 Print the drawing.

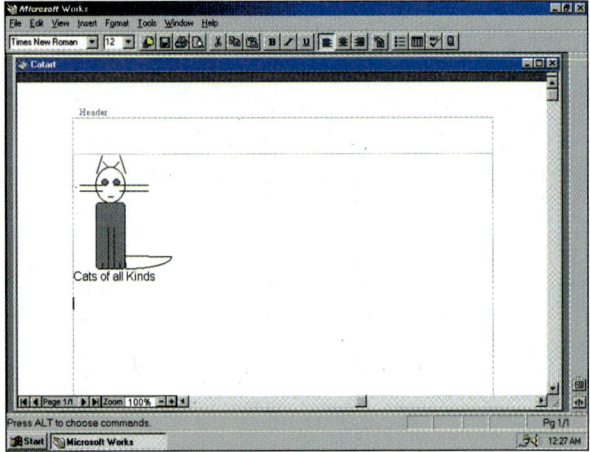

FIGURE 12-14

INDEPENDENT
CHALLENGE 4

As manager of the Quick Stop Video Store, you want to create the picture of a video tape for use in your logo.

To complete this independent challenge:

1 Use the Draw tools to create the image of a video tape; use Figure 12-15 as a guide.

2 Include text with the drawing that could be used as part of a logo.

3 Move the picture to a suitable location on the page.

4 Save the logo file as Videotape to the My Works Files folder on your Student Disk.

5 Print the file.

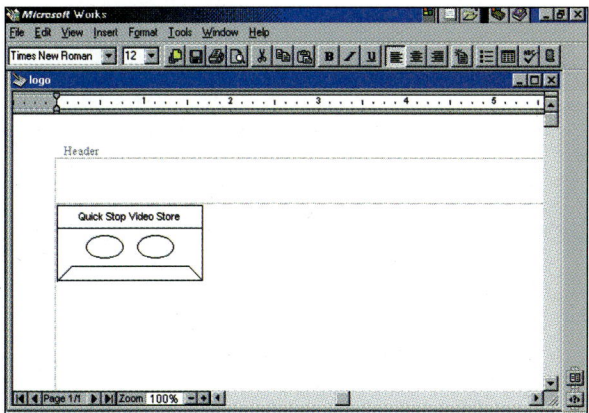

FIGURE 12-15

VISUAL WORKSHOP

Create the image shown in Figure 12-16 by editing an existing ClipArt image to meet your needs. Use the Draw tools to edit the ClipArt image as shown below. Save the file as RunArt to the My Works Files folder on your Student Disk.

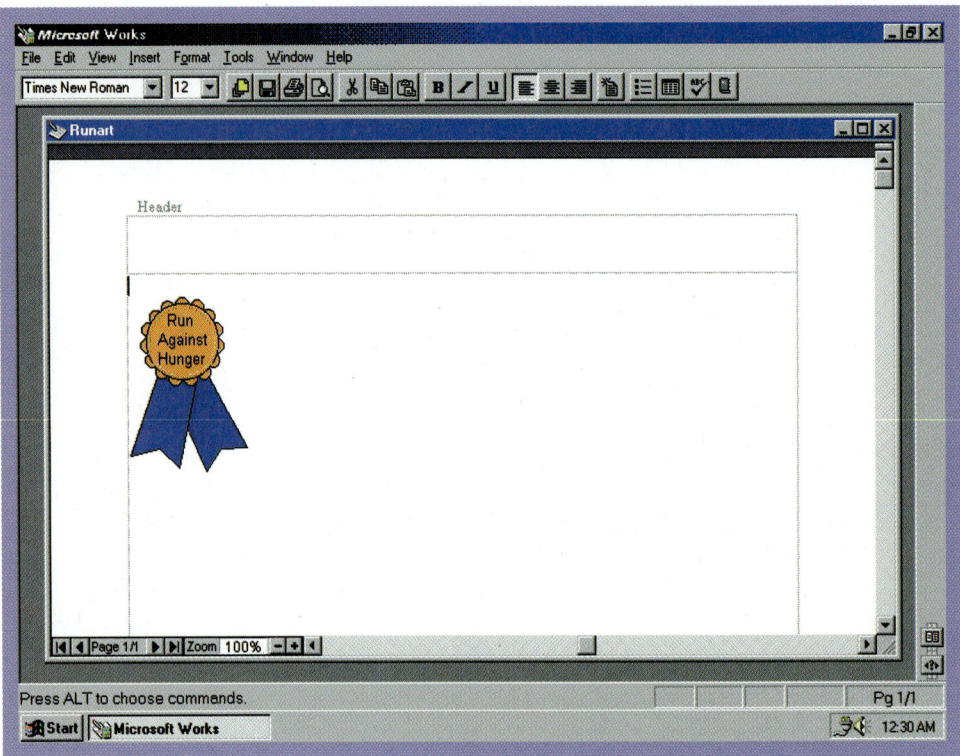

FIGURE 12-16

UNIT 13

OBJECTIVES

- Create a cover letter
- Insert an illustration
- Insert spreadsheet data
- Insert database fields
- Print a form letter

Combining
WORKS APPLICATIONS

As you have learned, you can complete many tasks with individual Works tools; sometimes using the Works tools together to create a report or presentation containing a variety of elements makes more sense. **case** As your final project, you'll prepare the Outdoor Designs six-month sales summary that contains financial information created with the Works Word Processor, Spreadsheet, and Database applications, and artwork created with the Microsoft Draw accessory. You'll create the report with the Word Processor. Your last task will be to make the report a **form letter**, a document with standard body text that contains a custom address header for each recipient. ▶

Creating a cover letter

It is professional to create a cover letter for a report. The cover letter often contains a return address, a business address, a date, and a one- or two-paragraph introduction. **case** Create a cover letter now for Outdoor Designs' six-month sales summary using a file Rebecca supplies.

1. Start Works, open the file on your Student Disk named **WKS 13-1**, and save the file as **July Report** in the My Works Files folder on your Student Disk
   Works displays Rebecca's personal correspondence template in the Word Processor, as shown in Figure 13-1. Rebecca customizes this document when she prepares a business letter. It already contains the Outdoor Designs address. Now type the date and the letter's contents.

2. Select the label **[Today's Date]**, then type **July 29, 1996**
   Works automatically deletes the label when you begin typing.

3. Select the label **[Letter Text]**, then type the text that follows, pressing **[Enter]** to add a blank line as directed
   I am pleased to send you Outdoor Designs' financial summary for the first six months of calendar year 1996. The past two quarters have been an exciting time for our business. We have added several new products to our growing outdoor equipment line, including a high-country backpacking tent kit and several new kite kits. Our sales representatives have established new accounts in several important areas in the United States and our total sales volume rose 4% between the first and second quarters. We also experienced strong growth in every region except the Midwest, where we are currently restructuring our operations. Our combined sales figures for the first two quarters of 1996 are shown in Figures 1 and 2 on the next page. [Enter]

   [Enter]

   I'd like to thank everyone who has helped make the first half of 1996 such a success, including the dedicated employees at Outdoor Designs, our valued suppliers, our retail partners, and especially our investors, who have supported us since the beginning. We look forward to a strong summer and another record-breaking six months this year. [Enter]

   Text in each paragraph wraps automatically when it reaches the right margin. Your screen should look like Figure 13-2.

4. Click the **Spelling Checker button** on the toolbar to check the spelling in the letter
   Fix any spelling mistakes, if necessary. If the Spelling Checker flags any graphic elements, click Ignore.

5. Click the **Save button** on the toolbar
   You saved your changes on disk.

FIGURE 13-1: Rebecca Singer's correspondence template

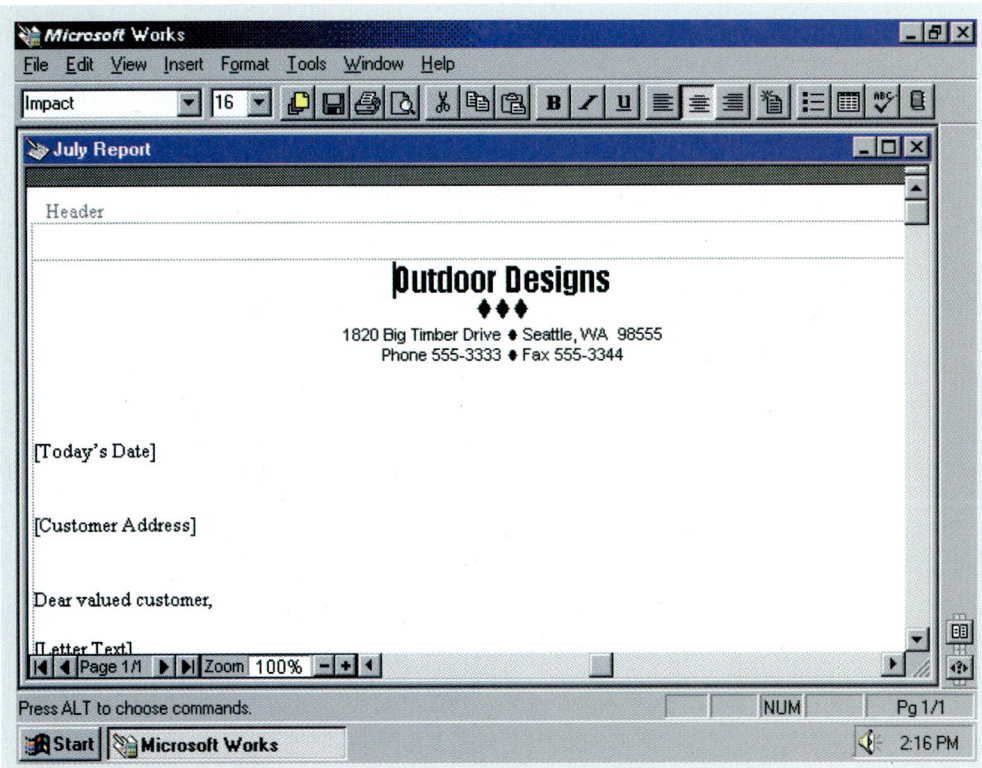

FIGURE 13-2: Six-month sales summary letter

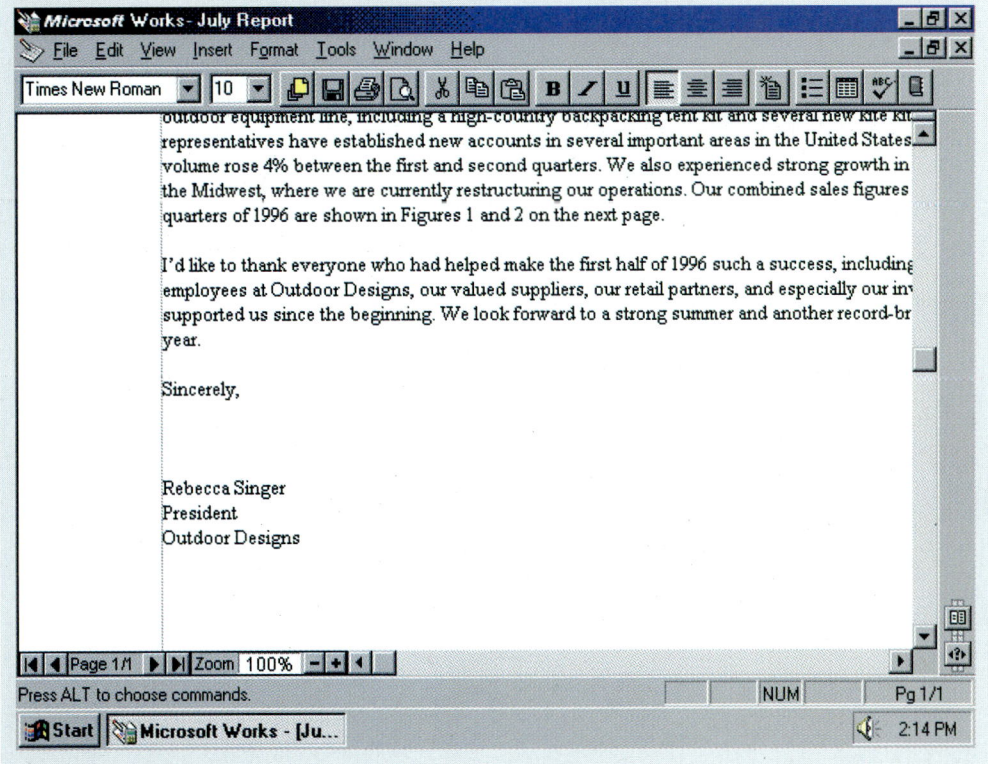

A typical business cover letter includes the recipient's name and address at the top. You'll add these later with database fields.

Inserting an illustration

Works lets you add electronic artwork to a document in several locations. You can position the illustration **inline**, so that it moves when the text around it moves, or in **absolute position**, so that it remains in its original location on the page. ▶case Rebecca asked you to add the kite illustration you created to the cover letter of Outdoor Designs' sales report and to place the artwork in absolute position along the right margin so that text wraps around it.

1. Click the **Task Launcher button** on the toolbar, then open the artwork file **WKS 13-2** on your Student Disk
   The Works 13-2 document opens, and the Outdoor Designs kite illustration appears in a window.

2. Click the illustration, then click the **Copy button** on the toolbar
   Works copies the illustration to the Clipboard.

3. Click **File** on the menu bar, then click **Close**, saving changes to the file when prompted
   The kite illustration document closes, and the cover letter reappears.

4. Press **[Ctrl][End]** to move the cursor to the bottom of the cover letter, then click the **Paste button** on the toolbar
   Works pastes the kite illustration in the cover letter. Now you select the illustration and center it on the page along the right margin. If First-time Help appears, click ok.

5. Click the **kite**, click **Format** on the menu bar, then click **Text Wrap**
   The Text Wrap tab of the Format Picture dialog box shown in Figure 13-3 opens. It lets you specify how text wraps around your illustration and your illustration's position on the page.

6. Click the **Absolute button**
   You selected absolute positioning, placing your kite in a specified location on the page so everything else wraps around it.

7. Click the **list arrow** of the Horizontal list box, click **Right**, click the **list arrow** of the Vertical list box, click **Center**, then click **OK**
   The illustration aligns at the center of the right margin, as shown in Figure 13-4. The cover letter text wraps around the illustration automatically. The kite illustration is positioned absolutely and will remain in the same place even if you add text above or below it.

8. Click the **Save button** on the toolbar
   You saved your changes to the cover letter on disk.

FIGURE 13-3: Format Picture dialog box

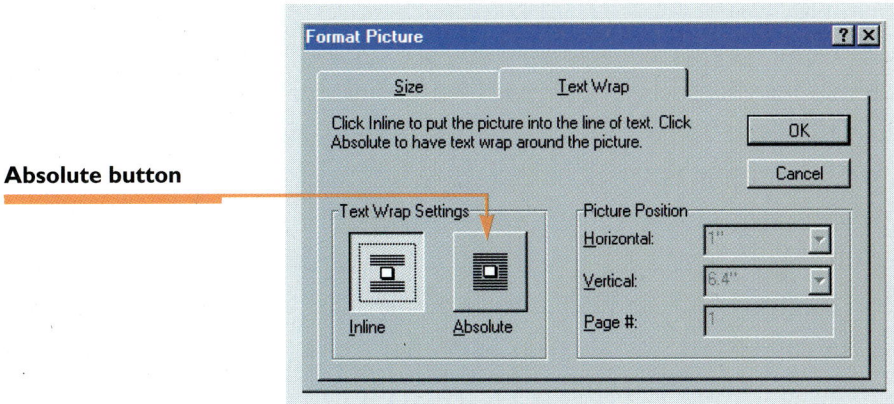

Absolute button

FIGURE 13-4: Absolute positioning: text wraps around illustration

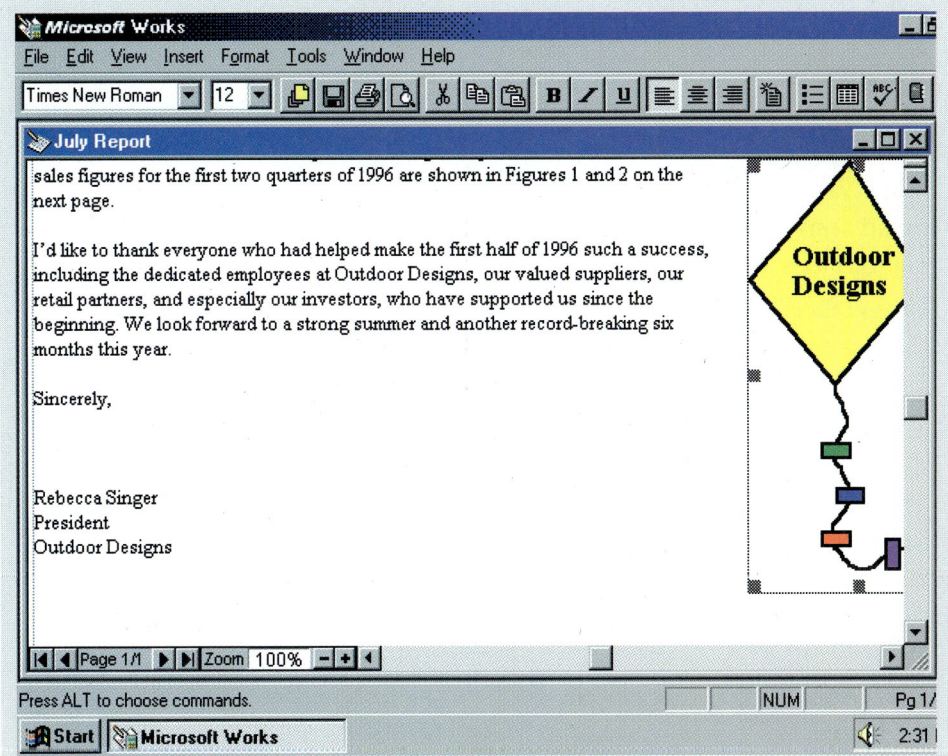

QUICK TIP

To edit a drawing in the Word Processor, double-click it. You return to the Draw accessory.∎

Inserting spreadsheet data

Works lets you combine spreadsheet information with text in the Word Processor to create truly integrated letters and reports. You can also insert charts into the Word Processor using the same copy-and-paste technique you used in the last lesson. As you learned earlier in this book, several Works files can be open at once. You use the Window menu to switch from open file to open file to create an integrated document. ▶case Rebecca asked you to insert a spreadsheet and a chart in your report showing the Outdoor Designs regional sales data for the first six months of 1996. The data you add will make up the heart of the report and support your cover letter with facts and figures.

1. Click the **Task Launcher button** on the toolbar, then open the spreadsheet **WKS 13-3** on your Student Disk
   The spreadsheet opens in a new window and the Outdoor Designs sales data appears.

2. Select the cell range **A5** through **C10**, then click the **Copy button** on the toolbar
   Works copies the sales spreadsheet to the Clipboard. You leave this file open because you'll use it again soon.

3. Click **Window** on the menu bar, then click **July Report** (the first filename listed at the bottom of the window)
   The cover letter document window moves in front of the sales spreadsheet window.

4. Press **[Ctrl][End]**, press **[Ctrl][Enter]** to insert a page break, type **Figure 1: Outdoor Designs sales totals**, then press **[Enter]** twice
   Works inserts a page break at the bottom of the cover letter and a figure caption at the top of the new page.

5. Click the **Paste button** on the toolbar
   The sales spreadsheet appears in the sales summary, as shown in Figure 13-5. Now add a chart to the report.

6. Press **[Enter]** four times, type **Figure 2: Outdoor Designs sales by region**, then press **[Enter]** twice
   The chart's caption appears in the document. Now copy and paste the chart. You return to the open spreadsheet file to copy the chart.

7. Click **Window** on the menu bar, click **WKS 13-3**, click **View** on the menu bar, click **Chart**, then double-click **Chart1**
   The sales chart appears in the Chart accessory window.

8. Click **Edit** on the menu bar, click **Copy**, then click **File** on the chart window's menu bar, click **Close**, click **File** on the spreadsheet window's menu bar, and click **Close**
   Works copies the chart to the Clipboard and closes both the Chart accessory window and the WKS 13-3 file.

9. Click, then maximize the document window (if it is not already maximized), then click the **Save button** on the toolbar
   Works pastes the sales chart into the six-month summary, enlarges the screen for easier viewing, as shown in Figure 13-6, and saves your changes on disk.

FIGURE 13-5: Sales spreadsheet in six-month summary

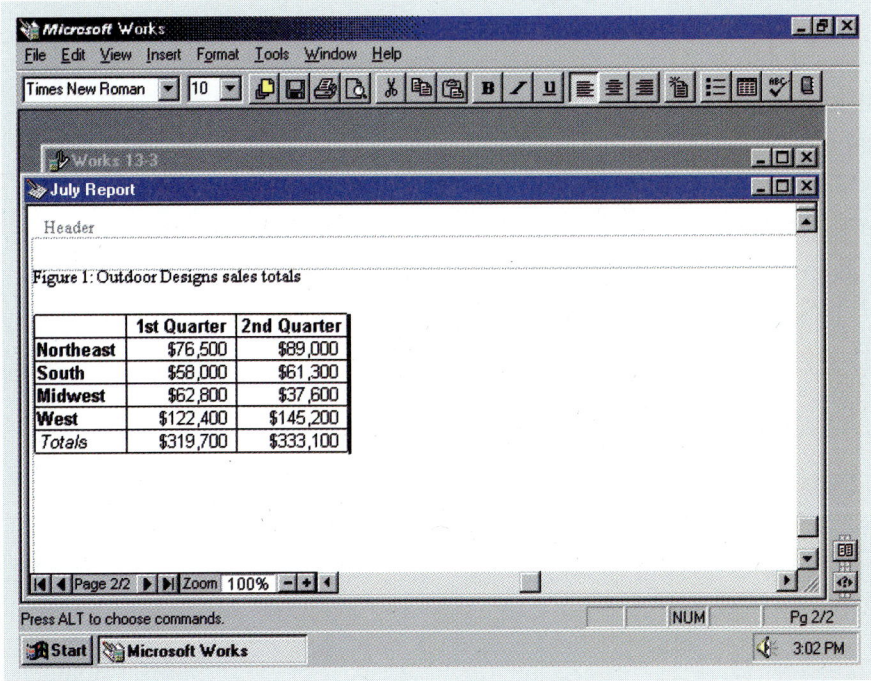

FIGURE 13-6: Adding a chart

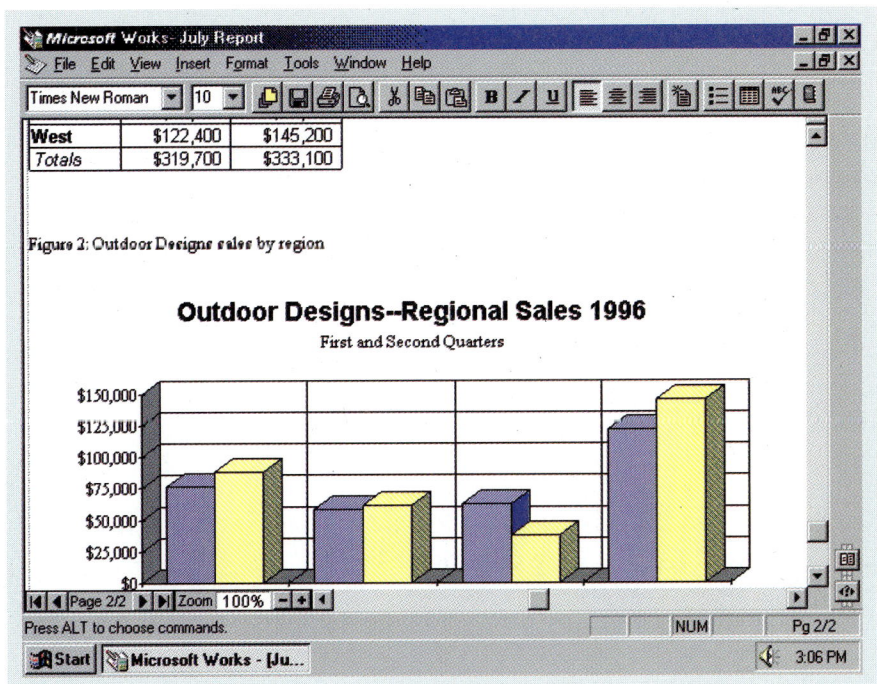

TROUBLE?

Saving your sales summary on a floppy disk takes some time because the file contains large artwork and application objects. Saving it on your hard disk is much faster but might not be practical in your lab setting.

Inserting database fields

Understanding Mail Merge

After you combine data from different Works applications, you need to insert database fields to make your document a form letter. A **form letter** is a document that contains standard body text and a custom header for each recipient. The Works Word Processor lets you create form letters in which you insert fields from the database. This process is known as **mail merge**. Be sure to view the CourseHelp called "Understanding Mail Merge" before completing the steps below.

case Rebecca asked you to insert fields from the Outdoor Designs database now, so that you can print a custom copy of the report for each customer. This will add a personal touch to the mailing.

1. Press **[Ctrl][Home]** to move to the top of the report, select and delete the label **[Customer Address]**
   This is where you will insert the database fields that automatically print customer addresses in your letter.

2. Click the **Insert** on the menu bar, then click **Database Field** (If a First-time Help dialog box opens, click **OK**.)
   The Insert Field dialog box opens.

3. Click the **Use a different database button**, then double-click **WKS 13-4** in the list box
   If this file's name does not appear in the list box, click the Open a database not listed here button and locate the file on your Student Disk. When you double-click the file's name, the database opens and its fields appear in a list box, as shown in Figure 13-7.

4. Click the **Business field** in the database list box, then click the **Insert button**
   Works inserts the Business field in the form letter and surrounds it with chevrons (« »). The chevrons indicate that Works will insert field values from the database into the Word Processor when you print the form letter.

5. Click **Insert** four more times to insert the Address, City, State, and Zip fields, then click the **Close button**
   Works enters the Address, City, State, and Zip fields in the letter and closes the dialog box. Now you arrange the fields so they look like a mailing address.

6. Edit the fields so the Business and Address fields are on separate lines, and the City, State, and Zip fields are on a single line

7. Type a **,** (comma) after the City field, and type a **space** between the State and Zip fields
   When you finish, the fields should look like those in Figure 13-8. Congratulations! Your form letter is finished. In the next lesson you'll add a footer and print it.

8. Click 🖫 to save your changes

FIGURE 13-7: Insert Field dialog box

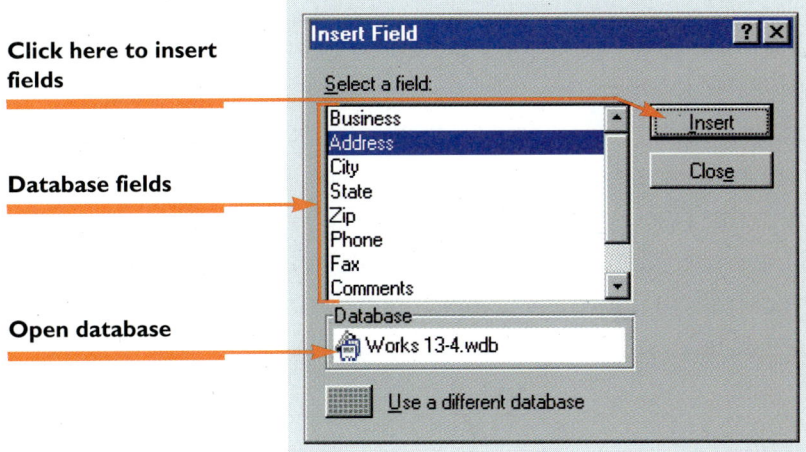

Click here to insert fields

Database fields

Open database

FIGURE 13-8: Form letter database fields

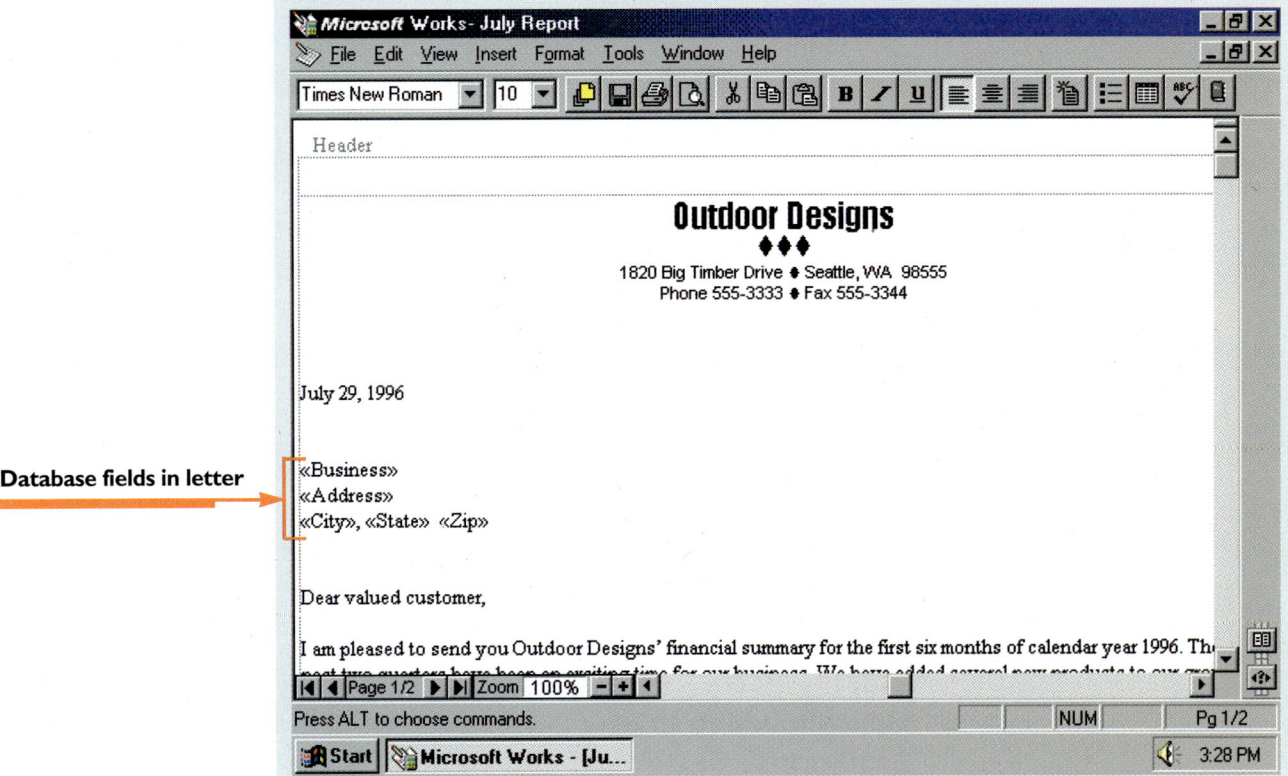

Database fields in letter

QUICK TIP

You can also use the Form Letter TaskWizard to create form letters.

Printing a form letter

After you create a form letter using mail merge, you should examine it in Print Preview to verify that the fields you inserted actually produce recognizable addresses from the database. (You need to examine addresses from the database in Print Preview; Works doesn't display them in Page Layout view.) **case** To give your report a polished look, you decided to add a footer containing the report title, printing date, and page number. Finish your report now by adding the footer, examining your fields in Print Preview, and printing a copy of the report for each person in the database.

1. Click **View** on the menu bar, then click **Footer**; if First-time Help appears, click **OK**.
   Works displays the Footer area of your document and places the cursor in the left margin.

2. Type **Six-month Summary**, press **[Tab]**, type **July 1996**, press **[Tab]**, type **Page**, then press **[Spacebar]**
   The footer that appears in your document has an empty spot for the current page number.

3. Click **Insert** on the menu bar, then click **Page Number**
   The placeholder for the page number appears in the footer, as shown in Figure 13-9. Now examine the report in Print Preview.

4. Click the **Print Preview button** on the toolbar
   A dialog box asks if you want to **merge** (include) all records in the database.

5. Click **OK**
   The dialog box closes and you see the first page of the document in Print Preview.

6. Click the **Zoom In button** twice
   Notice that mailing information from the first record in the WKS 13-4 database replaces the database fields in the document, as shown in Figure 13-10.

7. Click the **Next button** to review the seven addresses in the mailing list
   Because each summary is two pages, you'll preview a total of fourteen pages. Use the scroll bars to view the rest of the document and verify that the text, artwork, figures, and footers are in the right places.

8. Verify that your printer is ready, click the **Print button** to print the documents, and click **OK** in the Print all records dialog box.
   After a few minutes, the completed six-month summary reports emerge from the printer. Congratulations! You finished your final project and the documents are ready for Rebecca to sign. She's impressed with how much you learned in such a short time.

9. Click the **Save button** on the toolbar, then exit Works
   You save your changes on disk. The Sales Report file and the Works program closes.

FIGURE 13-9: Add a footer

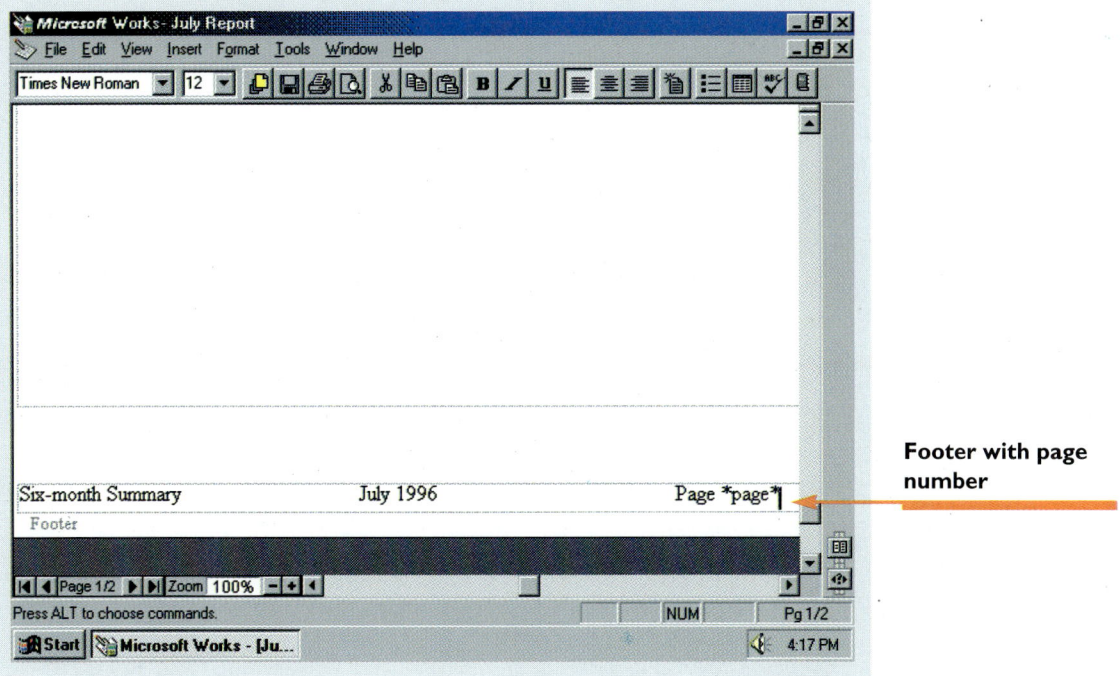

Footer with page number

FIGURE 13-10: Mail merge addresses in Print Preview

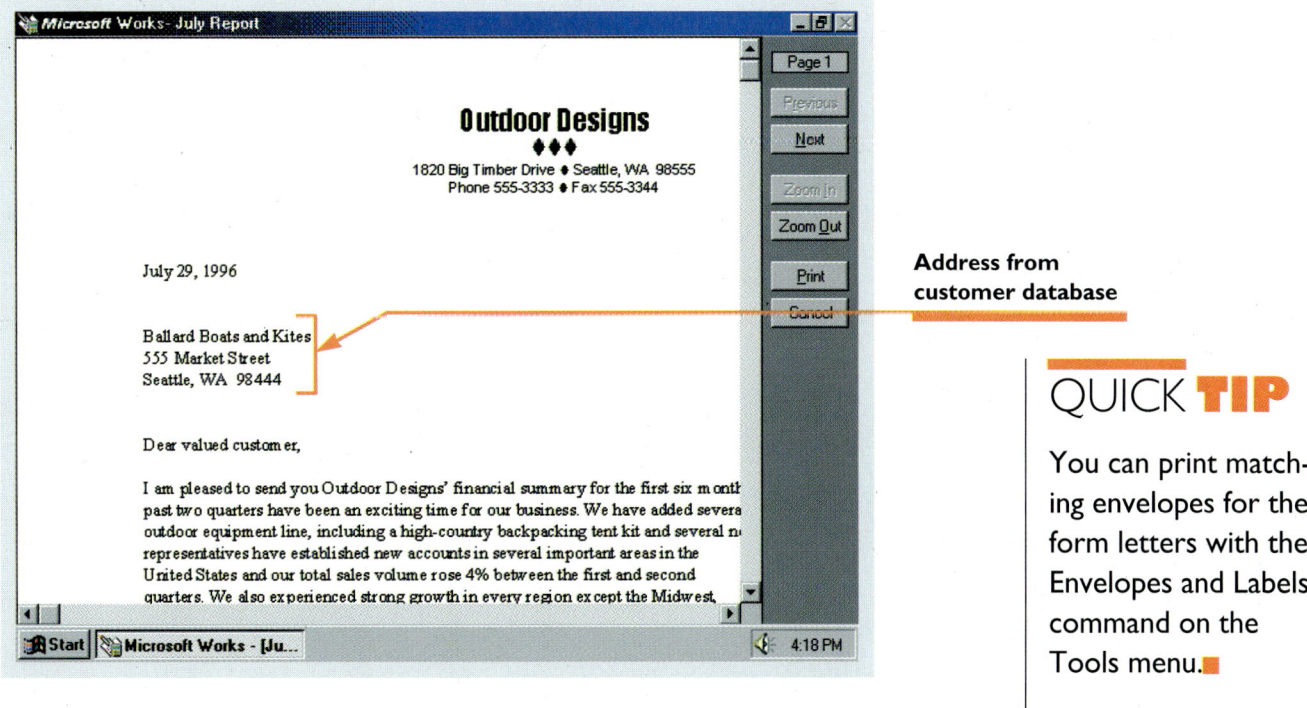

Address from customer database

QUICK TIP

You can print matching envelopes for the form letters with the Envelopes and Labels command on the Tools menu.

TASK REFERENCE

TASK	MOUSE/BUTTON	MENU	KEYBOARD
Edit an illustration in the Word Processor	Double-click drawing		
Insert a chart in a document	Copy chart to Clipboard, then click 📋 in target document	Click Insert, Chart	[Alt][I],[C]
Insert a database field in a word processing document		Click Insert, Database Field	[Alt][I],[F]
Insert an illustration in a document	Copy illustration into Clipboard, then click 📋 in target document	Click Insert, Drawing	[Alt][I],[W]
Insert spreadsheet data in a document	Copy selection to Clipboard, then click 📋 in target document	Click Insert, Spreadsheet	[Alt][I],[R]

CONCEPTS REVIEW

Label each element of the dialog box as shown in Figure 13-11.

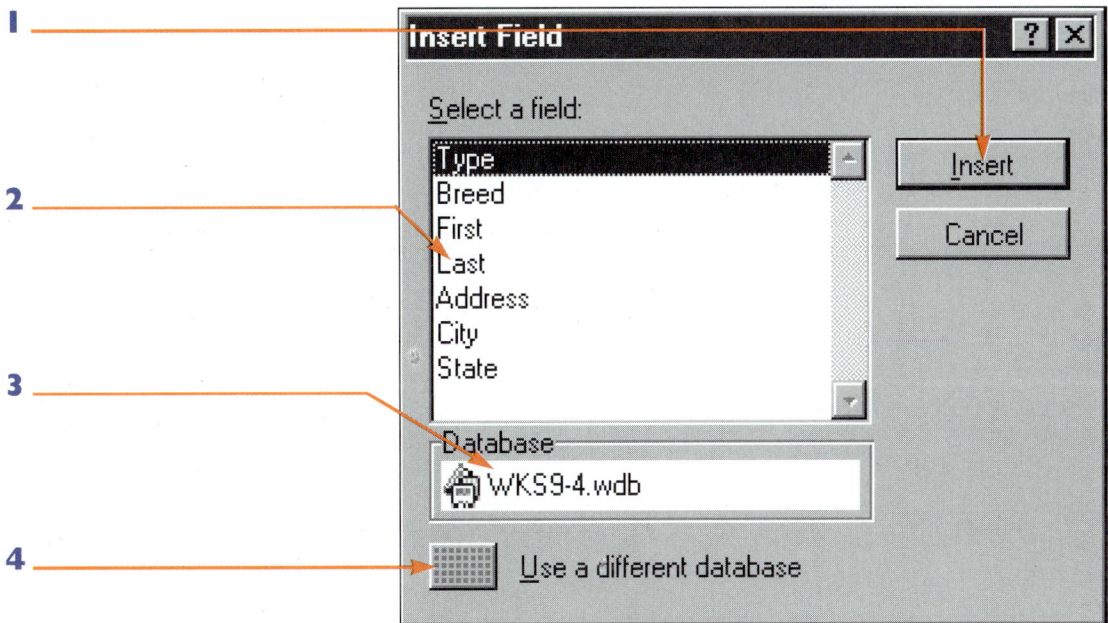

FIGURE 13-11

Select the best answer from the list of choices.

5 To move to the bottom of a Word Processor document, you would use

   a. [Ctrl][Home]

   b. [Ctrl][End]

   c. [Ctrl][PgDn]

   d. [Shift][Enter]

6 Works temporarily stores information that is copied from one document onto the

   a. Windows clipboard

   b. ClipArt gallery

   c. Floppy disk

   d. Control panel

7 Artwork that moves with the text around it is positioned

   a. In an absolute position

   b. Inline

   c. Above line

   d. In a relative position

8 Artwork that is placed in a specific location and everything else wraps around it is called

   a. Absolute

   b. Inline

   c. Above line

   d. Relative

9 To edit an illustration that has been pasted into the word processor, you would

   a. Choose the Drawing command from the Insert menu

   b. Double-click the illustration

   c. Change to Print Preview, then click the illustration with the zoom pointer

   d. Select the illustration, then press [F1]

10 Works lets you combine text in the word processor with

   a. Spreadsheet information

   b. Charts

   c. Database fields

   d. All of the above

11 To switch between active Works documents, you use which of the following menus?

   a. File

   b. View

   c. Tools

   d. Window

12 To enter a page break into a document, you would use

   a. [Ctrl][Home]

   b. [Ctrl][End]

   c. [Ctrl][Enter]

   d. [Ctrl][PgDn]

13 A document that contains a standardized text body and a customized header is called a

   a. Six-month summary

   b. Form letter

   c. Spreadsheet

   d. Footer

14 A mail merge

   a. Inserts fields from a database into a form letter

   b. Prints formatted letters

   c. Merges ClipArt into a document

   d. Merges spreadsheets and charts

15 A database field in a document is identified by

   a. Parentheses

   b. Square brackets

   c. Chevrons

   d. Selection rectangles

16 What does the &p code do in a footer?

   a. Prints the filename

   b. Prints the page number

   c. Centers the text

   d. Right-aligns text

17 To verify the database addresses inserted into the documents you are printing, you would

   a. Examine the database fields in Print Preview

   b. Double-click the addresses in the document

   c. Click the Print button on the toolbar

   d. Examine the records in the database

18 You can send merged letters to everyone in the database, or you can use one of the following to send letters to selected people

   a. Merge

   b. Print preview

   c. Filter

   d. Sort

19 Besides letters, you can also merge to

   a. ClipArt

   b. Envelopes and labels

   c. Spreadsheets

   d. Databases

SKILLS REVIEW

1 Inserting a Drawing into a letter.

   a. Open a new word processing document.

   b. Open the file Form2 which you created in Chapter 12 and click the Form Design button.

   c. Select the drawing you drew of the tent.

   d. Click the Copy button.

   e. Click the File menu.

   f. Choose the Close command and don't save any changes.

   g. When the blank word processing document appears, click the Center Align button.

   h. Click the Paste button.

i. Select the drawing of the tent.
  j. Size the tent to fit on the letterhead.
  k. Save the file as Tent in the My Works Files folder on your Student Disk.

2 Creating the body of the letter and inserting spreadsheet data.
  a. Make sure the text is not selected (or you will delete it), then move below the drawing, and type:

  Outdoor Designs
  1820 Big Timber Drive
  Seattle, Washington 98765

  b. Press the Enter key 2 times.
  c. Click the Right Align button.
  d. Type the current date.
  e. Press the Enter key 2 times.
  f. Click the Left Align button.
  g. Type the body text shown:

  Outdoor Designs is a company to watch. It has expanded into new areas in the last year and has plans to expand even further over the next few months. As a person who has expressed an interest in becoming an investor in our growing company, we wanted to provide you with the following confidential information.

  h. Press the Enter key twice.
  i. Click ▨.
  j. Choose the Existing Document tab, and open WKS13-5.
  k. Select the cell range A1 through F7.
  l. Click the Copy button ▨.
  m. Click the Window menu.
  n. Click the Tent file.
  o. Click the Paste button ▨.
  p. Save the file.

3 Inserting a Chart.
  a. Click the Window menu.
  b. Choose WKS13-5.
  c. When the chart displays, click the Copy button ▨.
  d. Click the Window menu.
  e. Choose the Tent document.
  f. Click the Paste button ▨.
  g. Save the file.

4 Inserting database fields.
  a. Place the insertion point at the left margin below the current date.
  b. Click the Insert menu.
  c. Choose the Database Field command.
  d. In the Insert Field dialog box, click the Use a different database button.
  e. Select WKS13-7 and click OK.
  f. Highlight Title and click Insert.
  g. Highlight each field and click the Insert button, and then click the Close button.
  h. Move the insertion point between the Last field and Address field and press the Enter key.
  i. Move the insertion point between the Address field and the City field and press the Enter key.
  j. Move the insertion point between the City field and the State field and type a comma.
  k. Move the insertion point after the Zip field and press the Enter key twice.
  l. Type "Dear," and press the spacebar.
  m. Click the Insert menu.
  n. Choose the Database Field command.
  o. Highlight Title and click the Insert button, and highlight Last and click the Insert button, then click the Close button
  p. Save the file.

5 Adding a footer, finishing the letter, and previewing the letter.
  a. Click the View menu.
  b. Choose the Footer command.
  c. Type "Proposed."
  d. Click the mouse back into the document window below the chart.
  e. Type the following:

  Thank you for your interest in our company. Please let us know if you have any questions.

  Sincerely,

  Rebecca Singer

  President

f. Run the Spell Checker.
g. Click the Print Preview button.
h. Save the file.
i. Print the document.

INDEPENDENT CHALLENGE 1

As an owner of two miniature poodles with chronic eye problems, you are very excited about a new product that Stuff for Pets has begun stocking. You decide to send a letter to all customers who purchased miniature poodles informing them of the new eye medication especially for that breed of dogs.

To complete this independent challenge:

1 Open the file WKS 13-4 on your Student Disk and save it in the My Works Files folder on your Student Disk under the name "Poodles."

2 Replace the label [Today's Date] with the current date.

3 Replace the label [Letter Text] with the following:

Our records show that you recently purchased a poodle from our store. As an owner of a breed which sometimes can develop eye problems, we wanted to inform you about a new medication that just came on the market. This new medication is called Clear Eyes and was especially developed to clear up eye disorders in poodles.

We will be keeping a limited supply of Clear Eyes in stock, but we can always special order it for you.

We appreciate your business and hope to see you soon.

Sincerely,

The Staff at Stuff for Pets

4 Run the Spelling Checker.

5 Insert the fields from the database file WKS 9-4 to create an inside address and a personalized salutation.

6 Merge the letter with customers who purchased poodles.

7 Print the letters.

8 Print envelopes.

INDEPENDENT CHALLENGE 2

The Steak Pit has done extensive expansion analysis, using the Works spreadsheet. Joel Rubin asks you to write a letter that he can send to potential investors in the expansion. Include the expansion analysis along with a chart of the data to prospective investors.

To complete this independent challenge:

1 Open a new word processing document.

2 Type the following:

The Steak Pit restaurant has been serving the best grilled steaks and sea food in our area for over 30 years. We have been awarded many honors over the years, and we feel that it is time to expand our operation. We are looking for investors who want to grow with us as we open a second location.

Our accounting staff has compiled the following budget based on extensive analysis.

3 Open the Expansion Analysis file

4 Select the data in cells A6 through E15

5 Paste the spreadsheet data into the document below the text that you typed.

6 Using the spreadsheet, create a chart of costs

7 Insert the chart into the letter below the spreadsheet data

8 Select the chart and size it so that it fits into the document

9 Below the chart type

Please call if you have any questions.

Sincerely,

Joel Rubin

10 Save the letter as Steaks to the My Works Files folder on your Student Disk and print it.

INDEPENDENT CHALLENGE 3

Jim Smith, an assistant manager of the Stuff for Pets store, is a serious cat lover. He wants to be sure cat-owning customers at Stuff for Pets are getting adequate attention from the store's marketing department. He asks you to contact all customers who purchased cats to inform them of an upcoming cat show.

To complete this independent challenge:

1 Open the file WKS 13-6 on your Student Disk and save it in the My Works Files folder on your Student Disk under the name "Cats."

2 Replace the label [Today's Date] with the current date.

3 Insert the drawing of the cat you created and saved under the name Catart.

4 Replace the label [Letter Text] with the following:

Our records show that you are the proud owner of one of Stuff for Pets prize cats. Because we know you are a cat lover, we wanted to inform you of the statewide cat show to be held in our town next May 23 and 24. We know you will want to participate by showing your cat or by simply admiring others, so mark your calendars. The show is sponsored by Feline Foods and they will provide many of the prizes.

See you there,

Sincerely,

Jim Smith

Assistant Manager

5 Run the Spelling Checker.

6 Insert the fields from the database file WKS 9-4 to create an inside address and a personalized salutation.

7 Merge the letter with customers who purchased cats.

8 Print the letters.

9 Print envelopes.

INDEPENDENT CHALLENGE 4

The Steak Pit investment letter needs a letterhead, and it also needs to be addressed to the specific individuals, using database fields. Using Works you can accomplish these tasks easily, so that Joel Rubin has a professional-looking mailing to send to investors.

To complete this independent challenge:

1 Open the file you created above and named Steaks.

2 Place the insertion point at the top of the document and press the Enter key twice.

3 Move back to the top and insert the ClipArt of the handshake under the Gestures category.

4 Center the graphic.

5 Change fonts and size and center the letterhead:

Steak Pit

1298 West River Avenue

Seattle, WA 98765

6 Insert the date at the right margin.

7 Use the WKS 9-4 database to insert fields for the inside address and salutation.

8 Run the Spell Check.

9 Preview and print the letters.

VISUAL WORKSHOP

Create the form letter shown below. Save the letter as Run Letter in the My Works Files folder on your Student Disk. Merge the form letter with the Runners database and print all the letters.

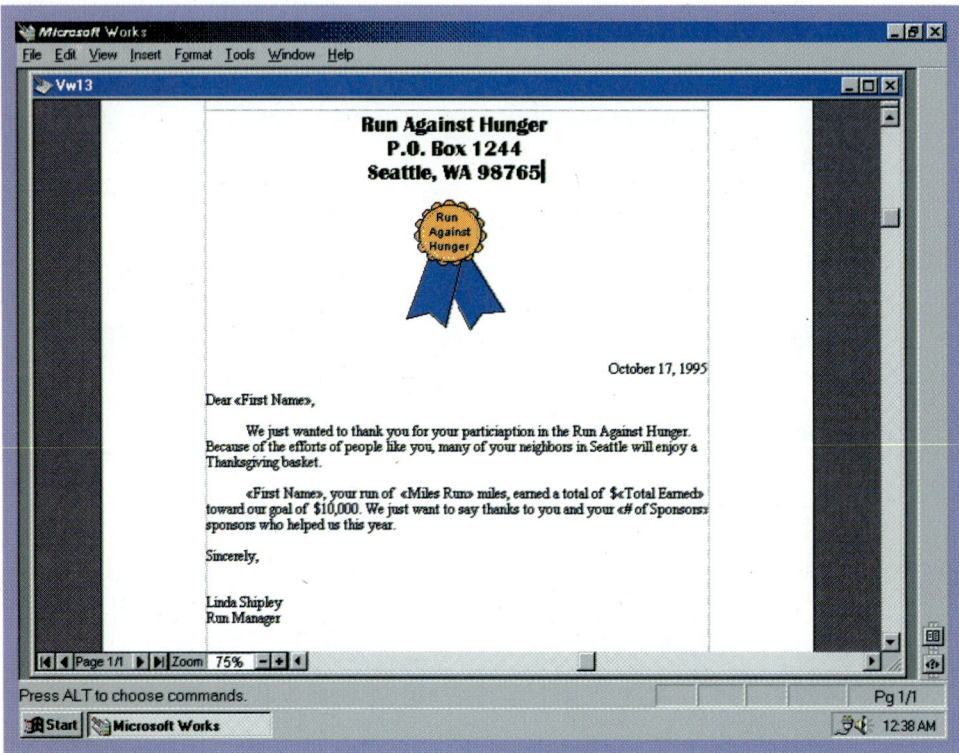

FIGURE 13-13

Glossary

Absolute positioning Placing an object in a specified location in a Works document. Used when you want to wrap text around an object.

Accessory A supplementary software tool in Microsoft Works, such as the Draw accessory.

Active program The program that is running (that is, open).

Active window A window that you are currently using. If a window is active, its title bar changes color to differentiate it from other windows and its program button in the taskbar is highlighted.

Alignment The horizontal placement of numbers or text, relative to the page margins. For example, right, center, and left alignment.

Application A term for a software program, such as Microsoft Excel, or for a module in an integrated software program, such as the Works Database. Works applications are called tools in the Works Task Launcher dialog box.

Area chart A line chart in which each area is colored or patterned to emphasize the relationships between pieces of charted information.

Argument A value, cell reference, or text used in a function. Commas separate arguments and parentheses enclose them; for example, AVE(A1,10,5).

Arial A TrueType font supplied with Microsoft Windows for use in Works documents.

Baud rate The rate at which your modem transfers data over phone lines.

Bold A font style used to emphasize text in Works documents.

Cancel A command button that voids dialog box selections.

Canvas The document window in the Draw accessory.

Cell The intersection of a row and a column in a spreadsheet.

Cell range A collection of adjacent cells.

Cell reference The name of a spreadsheet cell; for example, A1.

Cell reference box A box in the Works Spreadsheet that shows the currently highlighted cell.

Chart A graphic representation of selected spreadsheet information. Chart types include bar, pie, area, and line.

Chart title The name assigned to a chart.

Check box Clicking this square box in a dialog box turns an option off or on.

Clicking Quickly pressing and releasing the mouse button.

ClipArt Ready-to-use artwork accessed through the ClipArt accessory.

Clipboard A temporary storage area in Windows for items that have been cut or copied and may be pasted.

Close Use to quit a program or remove a window from the desktop. The Close button usually appears in the upper-right corner of a window.

Command Directive that provides access to a program's features.

Command button In a dialog box, a button that carries out an action. A command button usually has a label that describes its action, such as Cancel or Help. If the label is followed by an ellipses, clicking the button displays another dialog box.

Context-sensitive help Help information related to your current task. An example of context-sensitive help in Windows is the What's This? feature.

Control Panel A Windows utility for changing computer settings, such as desktop colors or mouse settings.

Copy A command that copies selected information from the document to the Clipboard.

Currency format A type of formatting that adds a dollar sign ($) and two decimal places to a number.

Cursor A blinking vertical bar indicating the insertion point in a program.

Cut A command that removes a selected object from a Works program and places it in the Clipboard.

Database An organized collection of information stored electronically in a file.

Default A value or setting that is assumed by Works in a program. For example, the default left margin setting in the Word Processor is 1.5 inches.

Desktop An on-screen version of a desk that provides workspace for different computing tasks.

Desktop publishing A type of word processing that combines text, artwork, and other elements to create professional-looking documents.

Dialog box A window that appears when Works needs more information to execute a command.

Directory An older term for the section of a disk used to store files and other directories. In Windows 95, directories are called folders. (See also Folder.)

Disk label Name that you assign to a disk using the Properties dialog box.

Document window Displays the current document.

Double-clicking Quickly pressing and releasing the left mouse button twice.

Dragging Holding down the left mouse button and moving the mouse pointer to a new location.

Draw accessory A Works tool used to create original illustrations and artwork.

Drawing tools The electronic tools used to create and edit an illustration in the Draw accessory.

Drive A disk or area of a network used for storing files. Drives are organized by folders.

GLOSSARY

Edit   To change the contents of a file without having to recreate it.

Electronic mail (e-mail)   A computer-to-computer version of interoffice mail or the postal service.

Embedding an object   Pasting an object from another program in a Works document. To edit an embedded object you double-click it.

End-of-file mark   A horizontal bar indicating the end of a Word Processor document in Normal view.

Field   A category of information in a database. Each field in a Works database has a unique name.

File   A collection of information that has a unique name, distinguishing it from other files.

File hierarchy   A logical order for folders and files that mimics how you would organize files and folders in a filing cabinet.

File management   A skill to organize and keep track of files and folders.

Filename   A unique name assigned to a Works document on disk.

Fill palette   A palette in the Draw accessory used to change the colors of shapes in your illustration.

Filter   A question that compares one or more fields in the database with one or more values.

Find   A command that searches for a word or phrase in a Works document.

Font   A typeface used to display and print text in a Works program.

Folder   A storage location on a drive or disk used to hold files and other folders.

Footer codes   Special codes in a footer, prefaced by an ampersand (&) symbol, that format text in a Spreadsheet or Database header or footer.

Footnote   A note or citation placed at the bottom of a Works document page.

Form   The window in the Database tool where information is entered and displayed.

Format   To change the appearance of information but not the actual content.

Form letter   A document that contains standard body text and a customized header for each recipient.

Formula   An equation that calculates a new value from existing values. Works formulas can contain numbers, mathematical operators, cell references, field names, and functions.

Formula bar   A bar in the Spreadsheet and Database tools where you enter or edit formulas.

Function   A built in formula that can be used alone or in another formula. Works includes dozens of useful functions.

Graphical user interface (GUI)   An operating environment, such as Microsoft Windows 95, that uses meaningful pictures and symbols to replace hard-to-remember commands.

Gridlines   Horizontal and vertical lines that connect the x-axis and y-axis in a chart.

Help   A feature that lets you search for help on a specific topic, review basic skills, and run the Works online tutorial.

Help button   A button in a Help window that when clicked jumps to a dialog box or opens a program to answer your question.

Highlight   When an icon is shaded differently indicating it is selected. Also see Select.

Horizontal scroll bar   Moves your view from side to side in a window.

Icon   A picture or symbol that represents a command or identifies an object on the Windows desktop.

Insertion point   The blinking cursor in a Works tool or accessory; indicates where in a document text will be inserted.

Internet   A global network of computers and telecommunication services.

Internet address   A unique name used to identify a user on the Internet, for example, mikehal@carson.u.washington.edu.

Italic   A font style used to emphasize text in Works documents.

Justified text   Text aligned at both the right and left margins.

Keyboard shortcut   A keyboard alternative for executing a menu command (i.e., [Ctrl][X] for Cut).

Label   Descriptive text used to identify spreadsheet data.

Launch   To start a software program, so you can use it.

Legend   A key explaining the information that colors or patterns in a chart represent.

Line chart   A graph of data mapped by a series of lines. Because line charts show changes in data or categories of data over time, they can be used to document trends.

Line palette   A palette in the Draw accessory used to change the colors of lines in your illustration.

Line pointer   The shape of the mouse pointer when it is in the left margin in the Word Processor; used to select more than one line at a time.

Linking documents   Connecting documents so that information can pass between them automatically. The Paste Special command links documents in Works.

List box   A box in a dialog box containing a list of items. To choose an item, click the list arrow, then click the desired item.

List view   A way to examine records in a database. In List view, a database is formatted in rows (fields) and columns (records).

Log out   To disconnect from a remote computer.

Mail merge   A process that automatically inserts mailing addresses into form letters from a Works database.

Maximize   To enlarge a window so it takes up the entire screen. There is usually a Maximize button in the upper-right corner of a window.

Menu A list of available commands in a program.

Menu bar The area under the title bar on a window. The menu bar provides access to most of a tool's commands.

Minimize To reduce the size of a window. There is usually a Minimize button in the upper-right corner of a window. Clicking the Minimize button shrinks the window to an icon.

Modem A communications device that enables a computer to transmit information over a standard telephone line.

Mouse The hand-held input device that you roll on your desk to position the mouse pointer on the Windows desktop.

Mouse buttons The two buttons on the mouse (right and left) that you use to make selections and issue commands.

Mouse pointer The arrow-shaped cursor on the screen that follows the movement of the mouse as you roll the mouse on your desk. You use the mouse pointer to select items, choose commands, start programs, and edit text in applications. The shape of the mouse pointer changes depending on the program and the task being executed.

My Computer Use to view the files that are available on your computer and how they are arranged. The icon appears on the desktop.

Note-It accessory A Works accessory that adds notes to your documents.

Numeric value A number in a spreadsheet cell.

Object An item (such as a file or folder) in a window. In task-oriented programs, objects are also graphics or text from another program.

OK A command button that confirms selections in a dialog box.

On-line services Telecommunication services such as CompuServe, Genie, or The Microsoft Network.

Open Action which describes starting a program or displaying a window that was previously closed. Also used to describe a program that is currently running, but not necessarily displayed in an active window.

Operating system A comprehensive control program such as Windows 95 that helps you run programs and manage your computer.

Operator A symbol used in formulas, such as + or -.

Page break The point at which text in a document flows to the top of a new page.

Page layout view A document view in the Word Processor that displays artwork, columns, and footnotes as they will be printed.

Parameters Settings required in a telecommunication session; for example, baud rate, data bits, and parity.

Password A secret combination of letters and numbers used to gain admittance to an on-line service or remote computer.

Paste A command that moves information from the Clipboard into a Works window.

Pattern A design that will display as your desktop background.

Pie chart A circular chart that displays data as slices of a pie. A pie chart is useful for showing the relationship of parts to a whole.

Point A unit for measuring fonts and row height. One inch equals 72 points.

Pointing Positioning the mouse pointer over an icon or object on the Windows desktop.

Pop-up menu The menu that appears when you right-click an item on the desktop. Also known as the shortcut menu.

Print Preview The command in a Works tool that shows how a document will look when it is printed.

Printer port A special connector on the back of a computer that connects the computer to the printer.

Program Task-oriented software that you use for a particular kind of work, such as word processing or database management. Microsoft Access, Microsoft Excel, and Microsoft Word are all programs.

Program button The button that appears on the taskbar, representing a minimized (but still running) program.

Properties The characteristics of a specific element (such as the mouse, keyboard, or desktop display) that you can customize.

Radio button A small circle in a dialog box that you click to select an option.

Random Access Memory (RAM) A temporary storage area in a computer whose contents are erased each time the computer is turned off or whenever power fluctuates. When a program is launched, it is loaded into RAM so you can work with that program.

Range A selected area of adjacent cells.

Record All information in a database pertaining to a single business or other entity.

Recycle Bin An icon that appears on the desktop that represents a temporary storage area for deleted files. Files will remain in the Recycle Bin until you empty it.

Replace A command that searches for a word in a Works document, deletes it, and inserts another word.

Replicate To copy a cell to one or more adjacent cells with the Fill Down or Fill Right command in the Spreadsheet tool.

Report A summary of database information specifically designed for printing.

Report definitions The instructions that create a database report.

Restore To reduce the window to its previous size before it was maximized. There is usually a Restore button in the upper right corner of a window.

Right-click To press and release the right mouse button once quickly.

Row height A cell's vertical dimension.

Ruler A measuring tool in a Works program below the title bar.

Run To start or operate a program.

Screen saver A moving pattern that fills your screen after your computer has not been used for a specified amount of time.

GLOSSARY

Scroll bars Bars on the right and bottom of a window on the desktop that give you access to information not currently visible in the window.

Scroll box Located in the vertical and horizontal scroll bars and indicates your relative position in a window. *Also see* Horizontal scroll bar and Vertical scroll bar.

Select When you click and highlight an item in order to perform some action on it. *Also see* Highlight.

Selected The state of a highlighted object in a Works tool or accessory.

Selection handles Boxes that surround a selected object in a Works tool. You can use the selection handles to enlarge or shrink the size of an object by dragging them.

Serial number A special number Works uses to store dates and times internally.

Serial port A communications port on the back of a computer. Suitable for connecting a modem, mouse, or printer.

Shading A pattern of dots or lines placed in a spreadsheet cell or database field to emphasize it.

Shortcut A link that you can place in any location that gives you instant access to a particular file, folder, or program on your hard disk or on a network.

Shortcut menu The menu that appears when you right-click an item on the desktop. Also known as a popup menu.

Shut down The action you perform when you are finished your Windows work session. After you perform this action it is safe to turn off your computer.

Sizing buttons Buttons in the upper-right corner of a window that can be used to minimize, maximize, or close a window.

Sort To arrange contents of a database or selected range in a particular sequence.

Sorting Alphabetically or numerically ordering information in a Works file.

Spell Checker A tool that checks the spelling in a document.

Spreadsheet An electronic ledger you use to organize rows and columns of information and create charts.

Start Button A button on the Taskbar that you use to start programs, find files, acccess Windows Help and more.

Statistics Descriptive calculations used in database reports, such as sum, average, or count.

Superscript A font style that places text above the line in Works documents.

Synonym A word that has a meaning similar to another word. The Works Thesaurus lists synonyms.

System administrator The person in charge of a network, remote computer, or on-line service.

Tabs The name of the windows in a dialog box that contain multiple screens of options.

Taskbar A bar at the bottom of your screen that lets you switch between programs running under Windows.

Task Launcher dialog box The dialog box in Works where you can open existing files, Works tools, and TaskWizards.

TaskWizard A tool that structures and formats a Works document automatically.

Telecommunicating Communicating with another computer over phone lines.

Template A standard document, such as a letterhead file, that can be used as the basis for many new files.

Text box A box in a dialog box in which you type text.

Thesaurus A tool in the Word Processor that lists one or more synonyms for a word.

Times New Roman A TrueType font supplied with Windows and available in Works tools.

Title bar The area along the top of the window that contains the filename and program used to create it.

Toggle indicators Indicators near the lower-right corner of the screen for the Num-lock, Caps-lock, and Insert toggle keys.

Tool A graphic representation of a command in a software program. Also, Works software modules, such as the Spreadsheet and the Word Processor, are called tools.

Toolbar The row of drop-down list boxes and command buttons beneath the menu bar in a Works tool or accessory.

ToolTip A description of a toolbar button that appears on your screen.

Triple-click In some programs, this action causes an entire line to be selected.

User name A unique name used to identify the user of an on-line service while telecommunicating.

Vertical scroll bar Moves your view up and down through a window.

Wallpaper An image that is in the same format as Windows 95 Paint files that will display as your desktop background.

Window A framed area on the screen in a graphical user interface. Each Works tool runs in a window.

Windows desktop The entire screen area in Windows; an electronic version of a desk with workspace for different computing tasks.

Windows Explorer Use to manage files, folders, and shortcuts; more powerful than My Computer and allows you to work with more than one computer, folder, or file and once.

Word Processor A Works tool that creates and manipulates text-based documents, such as a memo, newsletter, or term paper.

WordArt A type of stylized text created by the Works WordArt accessory.

X-axis The horizontal line in a chart.

X-axis label A label describing the x-axis of a chart.

Y-axis The vertical line in a chart.

Y-axis label A label describing the y-axis of a chart.

Zoom pointer The mouse pointer in Print Preview; used to magnify a document in Print Preview.

APPENDIX

OBJECTIVES

- What's new in Works 4.5
- Use new Works templates
- Explore new templates for civic and volunteer projects
- Explore new templates for home and education productivity
- Explore new clip art
- Learn about Internet Explorer
- Practice using Internet Explorer

Upgrading TO MICROSOFT WORKS 4.5

Microsoft Works 4.5 contains some new features and enhancements to Works 4.0, but it is not a major upgrade. Software publishers periodically revise programs. Sometimes, they **upgrade** the product, altering the look and feel of the program, procedures for completing tasks, and basic functionality of major features; other times, the changes result in an **update**, meaning that minor improvements have been made in key areas of the program to increase user satisfaction and productivity. The version number of a program tells whether it is an upgraded or an update. A whole number change, say from 3.0 to 4.0, indicates an upgrade. A decimal number change, such as Works 4.0 to 4.5, indicates an update. ▶case This appendix introduces the new features and improvements in Works 4.5, such as the new templates, new clip art and Clip Art Gallery 3.0, and Internet Explorer.

What's new in Works 4.5

Version 4.5 of Microsoft Works for Windows offers a host of new features to improve productivity and enhance the look of your documents. The look and feel of the program has not changed, but new features help speed up document creation, add more clip art, surf the Internet, and more. In the following lessons, you'll become familiar with these new tools. ▶ Works 4.5 now includes:

- **One-hundred new templates** for creating home, volunteer and civic activities, and education-related documents. You'll find these new templates in the TaskWizards tab of the Works Task Launcher dialog box, under the User Defined Templates category. Figure A-1 shows one of the templates available.

- **Microsoft Clip Gallery 3.0.** This new version of the ClipArt Gallery contains more than 7,000 clip art images. You still follow the same procedures to insert a piece of clip art in your document. Now, though, instead of choosing from 107 pre-installed images, you can browse through more than 7,000! You can access many more images by connecting to the World Wide Web (the Web) through Clip Gallery.

- **Microsoft Internet Explorer.** This popular Web browser program makes it easy to surf the Web, where you can visit sites such as the Works forum, the New York Times online, or any Web site of your interest. Figure A-2 shows just one of the many pages available on the Microsoft Web site.

- **Complete file compatibility.** Because Works 4.0 files are compatible with Works 4.5 files, you don't need to update your old files.

FIGURE A-1: A new Works 4.5 template

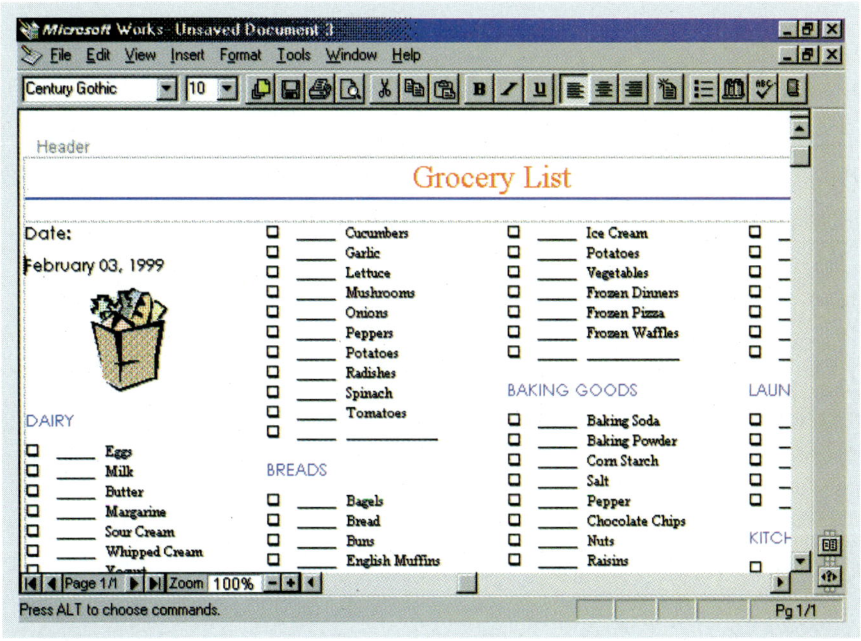

FIGURE A-2: Surfing the Internet with Internet Explorer

Find out more about Works 4.5 on the Works home page

The Works home page contains information, helpful tips, feedback from other users, and additional resources such as education templates, just for Works users. If you have Internet access, you can visit the Works home page at http://www.microsoft.com/works/.

Using new Works templates

As you have learned, a TaskWizard is an automated tool that structures and formats a document, so that all you have to do is add the necessary text. A new assortment of user-defined templates allows you to start a new document with the click of a button. When you use a **User Defined Template**, you do not run a TaskWizard to complete the document; the new document simply opens on your screen, and you customize it by selecting existing text and replacing it with your own. ▶case Review the steps for starting a new document using a TaskWizard, and explore the new templates now.

1. Click the **Start button** on the taskbar, point to the **Programs folder**, point to the **Microsoft Works folder**, then click **Microsoft Works**
   The Works Task Launcher dialog box opens.

2. If necessary, click the **TaskWizards tab**
   The new templates are located in the User Defined Templates category, so you need to scroll down the TaskWizards list to reach them.

3. Scroll down the TaskWizards list until you see the User Defined Templates category

4. Click **User Defined Templates**
   See Figure A-3. The templates available in this category include documents for home projects, education projects, and more. See Table A-1 for an overview of what's available.

5. Scroll through the list of templates
   Notice that the Preview window to the right of the list does not provide preview information about user-defined templates when you click them; to learn what each template provides, you need to open it.

6. Scroll to and double-click **Home Budget, Monthly**, then maximize the document window
   A new document opens based on this template.

7. Close the document without saving changes
   In the following lessons, you will create some documents based on User Defined Templates.

FIGURE A-3: User Defined Templates category of TaskWizards list

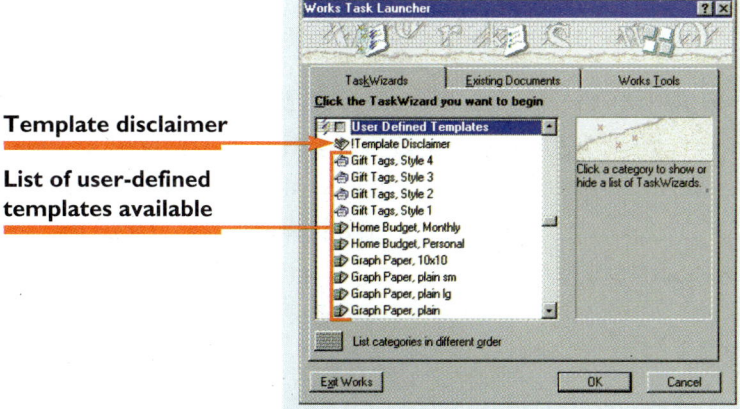

Template disclaimer

List of user-defined templates available

TABLE A-1: Overview of User Defined Templates

TYPE OF PROJECT	TEMPLATES AVAILABLE
Certificates	Certificate of Membership, Certificate of Merit, Certificate of Achievement
Correspondence	Envelopes, Mailing Labels, Stationery
Entertaining	Greeting Card Register, Place Cards, Menu Cards, Party Planner
Gift Giving	Gift Tags, Sizes and Favorites, Gift Certificates
Home Productivity	Home Budgets, Fitness Trackers, Lawn and Garden, Move Planners, Chore Lists, Meal Planner, Recipe Forms, Grocery List, Credit Card Log, Insurance Policy Log, Babysitter Notes, Eldercare Notes, Daily Instruction Sheet, Home Improvement Record, Home Maintenance Checklist
Mathematical	Graph Paper, Conversion Tables
Medical and Dental	Medication Record, Hospital & Illness Record, Family Medical History, Dental Record, Personal Medical History
Special Events	Recital Flyer, Garage Sale Flyer, Programs
Sports	Game Schedule, Team Standings, Training Record, Team Roster, Coach Letter, Performance Record
Travel	Travel Planners
Vehicle Care	Vehicle Details, Vehicle Repair Log, Vehicle Road Trip Log, Vehicle Maintenance Log
Volunteering and Civic Activities	Donation and Volunteer Pledge Forms, Donation Receipt, Fundraising Worksheets and Logs

TROUBLE?

If this is the first time you have started Works 4.5, you may see an introductory dialog box instead; in that case, read the contents of the dialog box and then close it.

QUICK TIP

The Template Disclaimer template is not a usable template; open it to read an informative disclaimer from Microsoft.

QUICK TIP

Remember that you can shrink the Help window by clicking the **Shrink Help button** below the Help list.

Exploring new templates for civic and volunteer projects

Works 4.5 offers several templates for civic and volunteer projects. You will find volunteer pledge forms, to-do lists, budget worksheets, certificates of membership, and many other useful documents. ▶case Familiarize yourself with one of these templates now. The Task Launcher dialog box should be open on your screen.

1. If necessary, click the **Task Launcher button** on the toolbar, then, if necessary, click the **TaskWizards tab**

2. If necessary, scroll to and click **User Defined Templates**, scroll through the list of templates in the TaskWizards list, click the **Fundraising, Project Task List template**, then click **OK**
   A new document based on this template opens in the document window, as shown in Figure A-4. This document was created using the spreadsheet tool, so you use spreadsheet navigation tools to select and enter information. Take a moment to scroll through the document and see what types of information are suggested for this project.

3. Scroll to the right, if necessary, then scroll down to read the complete contents of the document
   This document lists several activities that are essential to successfully planning a fundraising event. The columns under DATE, VOLUNTEER, and DONE prompt you to assign a date and a volunteer, and mark off which activities are necessary to ensure each task gets completed. It's always a good idea to scroll through a template document before you begin completing it.

4. Save this document as **Spring Fundraiser Tracker**
   Now, you are ready to complete the worksheet. Cell A1 is currently selected. You want to change part of this entry to reflect the name of the event, a spring fundraiser for your favorite charity.

5. In the Entry bar, select the text **[Event name]**, type **Spring Fundraiser**, then press **[Enter]**

6. Click **Cell B3** to select it, replace the text **TASK** with the text **5K Run in the Sun**, then press **[Enter]**

7. Click **Cell C5**, and replace the contents with a new date, **3/15/99**

8. If you wish, continue practicing your editing skills by changing the contents of **Cells C7, C9,** and **C11** to reflect the year **1999**

9. Close the spreadsheet, saving changes when prompted

FIGURE A-4: New document created based on Fundraising, Project Task List template

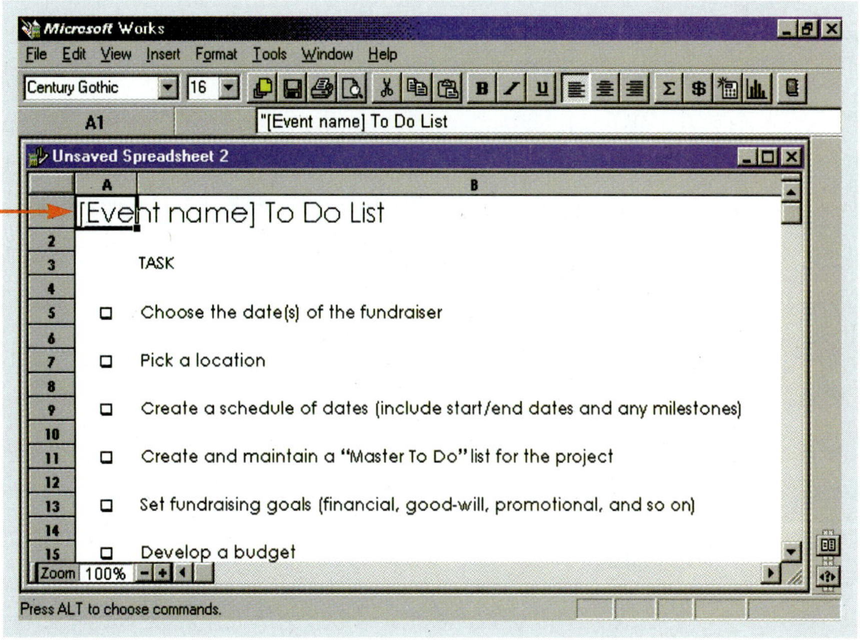

Cell A1

User Defined Templates help with planning and writing

As you explore User Defined Templates in Works 4.5, you will find them invaluable for helping you to think through many new projects. In the area of fundraising, for example, you might need to create a budget for an event. If you've never created this type of budget before, the prospect could be overwhelming. How can you anticipate all the possible costs for a new event? What if you forget an important entry? However, by using the Fundraising, Budget Worksheet template as shown in Figure A–5, you'll find placeholder entries for almost every budget item you might need to include.

You'll probably find a few, such as postage, lighting, or gratuities that you might never have thought of.

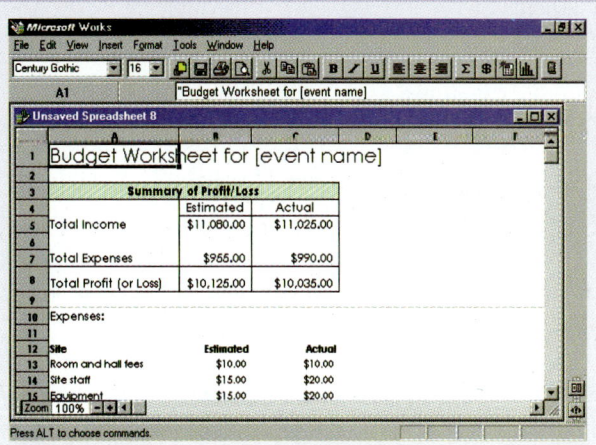

FIGURE A-5: Fundraising, Budget Worksheet template

TROUBLE?

Remember that in order to enter data in a spreadsheet document, you need to click the appropriate cell of the spreadsheet. The contents of the selected cell appear in the Entry bar. After entering or editing the entry, press [Enter].

Exploring new templates for home and education productivity

Works 4.5 offers several templates for home and education projects. Whether you want to create a budget, plan a party, recognize a student's outstanding achievement, or challenge yourself with a fitness project, you can find a predesigned document that gets you off to the perfect start. ▶case   See for yourself how easy it is to create a great-looking document by using one of the home productivity templates.

1. In the User Defined Templates list, scroll to and click **Recipe, full-page**, then click **OK**
   A new document based on the Recipe, full-page template opens in the document window. See Figure A-6. To customize a template-based document, you simply select placeholder text and replace it with your own. Practice replacing template text with your own by creating a recipe for scalloped potatoes.

2. Select the text **Recipe Name**, then type **Scalloped Potatoes**
   The placeholder text is replaced with the text "Scalloped Potatoes," but the formatting and alignment remain. Not every part of a template document contains placeholder text. In some cases, you simply click in an appropriate area, and type the necessary information. Try that now.

3. Click after the text **From the kitchen of:**, type your name, click after **Preparation time:**, type **1 hour**, click after **Number of servings:**, then type **4-6**
   Remember that to replace text, you can also select text and simply begin typing new text. You'll try that now.

4. Scroll down to the **INGREDIENTS** area if necessary, then select the word List and type **5 Idaho potatoes**

5. Complete the ingredients listing by replacing the rest of the placeholder text with the following information:

1 onion sliced thin	1 cup whole milk
1 garlic clove	1 cup cheddar cheese (shredded)
	1 cup Asiago cheese (shredded)

6. Scroll down to the INSTRUCTIONS area and select the text **Recipe Instructions go here**, press **[Delete]**, then enter the instructional text shown in Figure A-7
   As you have learned, saving a document created with a TaskWizard involves the same steps as those for saving any document; you open the Save As dialog box, choose a name and location for the file, then click Save.

7. Click the **Save button** on the toolbar, save the document as **Scalloped Potatoes** in the folder of your choice, then click **Save**
   In just a few minutes, you've completed a professional-looking recipe that you can share with friends and family or further customize to suit your needs and tastes.

FIGURE A-6: New document based on Recipe, full-page template

Insert recipe name here

FIGURE A-7: Completed Scalloped Potatoes recipe

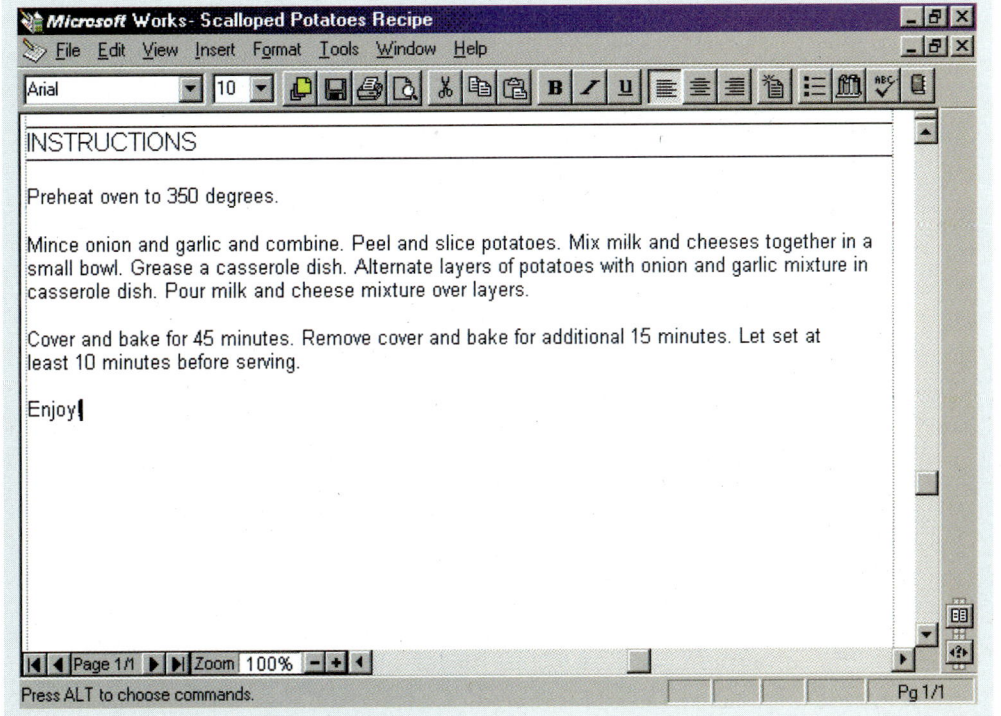

QUICK TIP

Remember that you can shrink the Help window by clicking the Shrink Help button below the Help list.

TROUBLE?

If you accidentally delete a Tab stop between the ingredient lists, simply type [Tab] to enter a new Tab, so that the ingredients line up attractively in two columns.

Exploring new clip art

In Works 4.0, you worked with Microsoft ClipArt Gallery 2.0. Microsoft Clip Gallery 3.0 offers some exciting improvements. Instead of choosing from 107 preinstalled images, you have more than 7,000 at your immediate disposal. **case** You familiarize yourself with Clip Gallery 3.0 by choosing a clip art image to insert in the Scalloped Potatoes recipe. This document should still be open.

1. Click after the word **Enjoy!**, press **[Enter]** twice, click **Insert** on the menu bar, then click **ClipArt**

   The Microsoft Clip Gallery 3.0 opens, as shown in Figure A-8. It provides access to all clip art images stored on your hard disk and also lets you surf the Web for additional images, pictures, sounds, and videos. In place of the Helpful Hint area is a Magnify check box. You can click to see a larger view of the selected clip art, helpful information if available, and a Connect to the Web button. Look for a fun, food-related image to insert at the end of your recipe.

2. Click **Food & Dining** in the Category list box, scroll through the list, when you see an interesting image, click the **Magnify check box** to see a larger view

   If you want to look for additional clip art choices on the Web, the Connect to the Web button in the Clip Gallery dialog box links you to a special Web page that contains additional images, sounds, and videos. If you have Web access, continue with Step 3; if not, select any image from the Clip Gallery, read Steps 3 through 6, then continue with Step 7.

3. Click the **Connect to the Web button** in the dialog box

   A dialog box opens, explaining that you need Internet access to connect to the Web page and also explaining that every clip you select will be added to your Clip Gallery.

4. Click **OK**

   You are connected to Microsoft Clip Gallery Live, a Web site that Microsoft constantly updates.

5. Read the contents of the Welcome screen, then click **Accept** to accept the terms of the license agreement

   A navigation pane opens on the left side of the screen, as shown in Figure A-9. Here, you can choose to search for specific images, pictures, sounds or videos using keywords, or browse by category much as you do in the Clip Gallery. In the right-hand pane are the images in the currently selected category, with filename and file-size information below each one.

6. Click the **Select a category list arrow**, click **Food & Dining**, click **Go**, then browse through the files, when you find an image you like click the **file name**, in the File Download dialog box click the **Open the file from its current location option button**, then click **OK**

   The file is saved in the Downloaded category of the Clip Gallery.

7. When you are finished searching for images in Clip Gallery Live, click **File** on the menu bar, click **Close**, then in the Clip Art Gallery select the image you downloaded

8. Click **Insert**, then drag a sizing handle of the selected image, if necessary, to resize the image attractively

9. Save changes, close your document, then exit Works

FIGURE A-8: Microsoft Clip Gallery 3.0

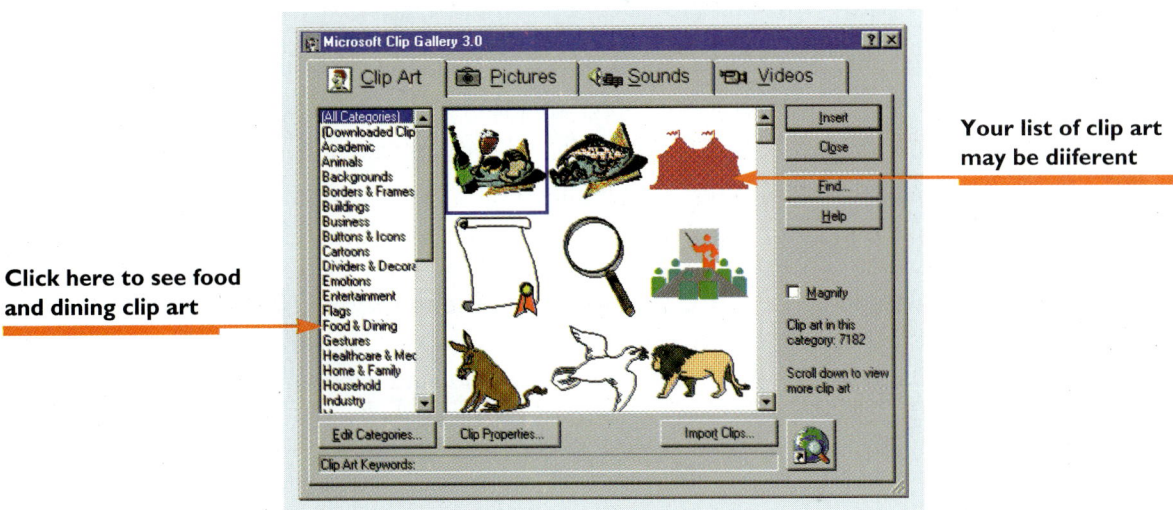

Click here to see food and dining clip art

Your list of clip art may be different

FIGURE A-9: Microsoft Clip Gallery Live 1.2

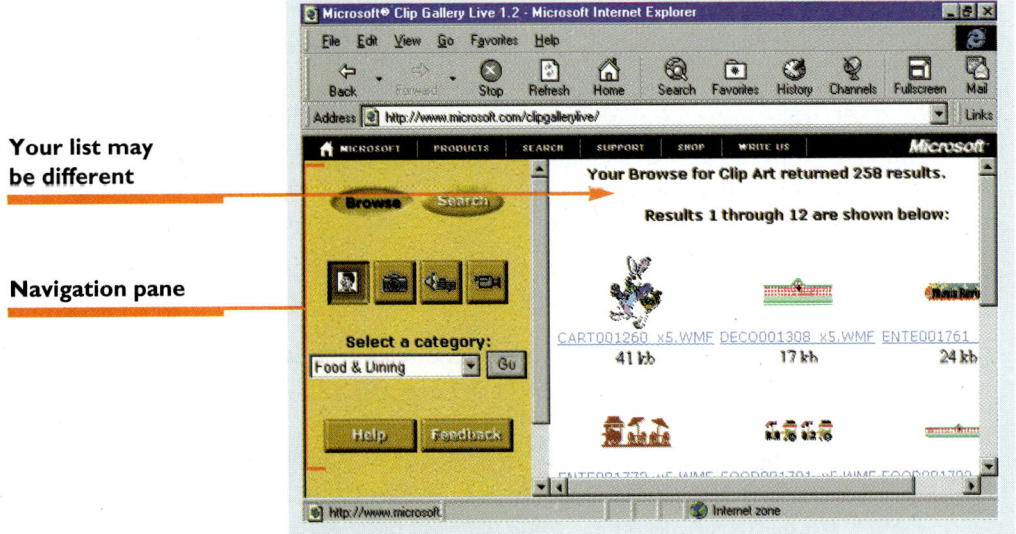

Your list may be different

Navigation pane

QUICK TIP

You can leave the Magnify check box selected at all times, so that each image you click appears in a larger view, or you can deselect it so that you can move more quickly through the list.

QUICK TIP

Check with your instructor or technical support person for permission to download additional images.

Learning about Internet Explorer

You may already be familiar with Internet Explorer, the popular Web browser software from Microsoft. This program now comes included with Microsoft Works 4.5, so that you can use it to browse the Web, send and receive e-mail, and join newsgroups. **case** Using Microsoft Internet Explorer, you can:

- Access the **Internet**, a huge network of more than 40 million computers and computer networks throughout the world. Through telephone lines, satellites, and other media, people around the world can exchange information in the form of text, pictures, sound, and even video quickly and easily.

- Browse the Web, the most popular part of the Internet. The Web consists of a network of pages, called **Web sites**, that are linked together to make it easy to move from one to another. To visit any Web site, you simply enter the **URL**, which is the Internet address of the Web site, in the Internet Explorer address text box.

- Use menus, toolbar buttons, and on-screen links to navigate quickly. As shown in Figure A-10, Internet Explorer looks similar to the Works program window, to make finding commands and choosing options easy. See Table A-2 for a description of Internet Explorer toolbar buttons.

- Click **links**, which can be a word, a phrase, or a picture on any Web site, to move to a related page or Web site.

- Search for sites that match your interests. Internet Explorer contains a search button that connects you to popular search engines. If you don't know the Internet address of the site you want to visit, or if you are simply interested in a topic and want to find out whether any related Web sites exist, you can enter a keyword in a search engine. Then you can read the results of your search and click any sites that interest you.

- Save or print Web pages. If you want a hardcopy of any content you find on the Web, you can save the file to your hard disk, or print a hardcopy to take along with you.

- Publish Web documents. You can publish documents you create on the Web by following the steps in Internet Explorer's Web Publishing Wizard.

- Send and receive e-mail. Outlook Express is an easy-to-use mail server program that allows you to send e-mail messages, read messages, keep an address book, attach files (including Works files) to your messages, and manage your online correspondence.

FIGURE A-10: Internet Explorer program window

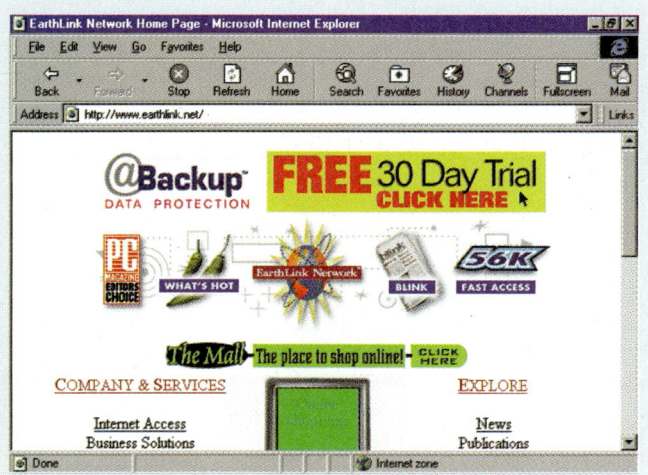

Connecting to the Internet

You also need a modem or network connection, an Internet Service Provider (ISP) such as The Microsoft Network, AT&T WorldNet, or another service, and your computer must be configured for a TCP/IP network. If you do not currently have a working Internet connection, see your instructor or technical support person for assistance.

TABLE A-2: Internet Explorer toolbar buttons

BUTTON	DESCRIPTION
Back	Opens the previous page; list arrow opens a list of recently viewed pages
Forward	Opens the next page; list arrow opens a list of recently viewed pages
Stop	Stops loading the current page
Refresh	Reloads the current page
Home	Opens the home page
Search	Opens a Search engine page
Favorites	Opens the Favorites list
History	Opens a list of recently viewed pages so you can open one
Channels	Opens a list of available channels, or pages
Fullscreen	Displays the current window in full page view, so it fills the screen
Mail	Starts Outlook Express or the default mail viewer

Practice using Internet Explorer

The Web offers information resources and ideas to suit almost any interest. If you have an Internet account and Internet Explorer is your Web browser, take a few minutes to familiarize yourself with some of the resources for Works users.

1. Click the **Start button** on the taskbar, point to **Programs**, point to **Internet Explorer**, then click **Internet Explorer**
   Internet Explorer starts your ISP and connects you to your home page. The program window contains a menu bar that organizes commands by category plus a toolbar with buttons for the most common commands. The **Address bar**, located below the toolbar, is the place where you enter the Internet address of the site you want to visit. You can also click the Address bar list arrow to select a recently visited site.

2. Click in the Address bar text box, then type **http://www.microsoft.com**
   As shown in Figure A-12, the Microsoft home page contains links to useful information for users of all Microsoft products, including Works. The table of contents at the top of the site contains links to major pages within this site.

3. Click **PRODUCTS**
   The Microsoft Products page opens. From this page, you can search for and connect to sites containing information on all Microsoft products. Use the alphabetical list at the top of the page to search for information about Microsoft Works.

4. Click the **Select from an alphabetical list of all products list arrow**, scroll to and click **Works 4.5 for Windows**, then click **go**
   The Works 4.5 for Windows Overview page opens.

5. Scroll through the page to read its contents
   The Contents list contains links to more detailed information about Works. Click any topic that interests you and read the related page. When you are finished, you can visit the Works home page, a more interactive source of information and resources for Works users.

6. Click in the **Address Bar text box**, type **http://www.microsoft.com/works/**, then press **[Enter]**
   The Microsoft Works home page opens, as shown in Figure A-12.

7. Click the **links** that interest you
   The Insiders Update newsletter, Works Education side, and archive categories are particularly useful if you want to use Works for home, business, or educational purposes.

8. When you are finished, click **File** on the menu bar, then click **Close**
   Remember to disconnect, if necessary, from your ISP.

The Works Forum

The Works Forum offers another source of information and advice for Works users. If The Microsoft Network is your ISP, you can visit the Works Forum. The Works Forum contains information, templates, and other software to facilitate working in Works. You can also give feedback about the product, make suggestions for future upgrades, get answers to technical questions, and communicate with other Works users. To access the Works Forum, click Help on the Works menu bar, then click Launch Works Forum.

FIGURE A-11: Microsoft home page

Your page may look different

FIGURE A-12: Microsoft Works home page

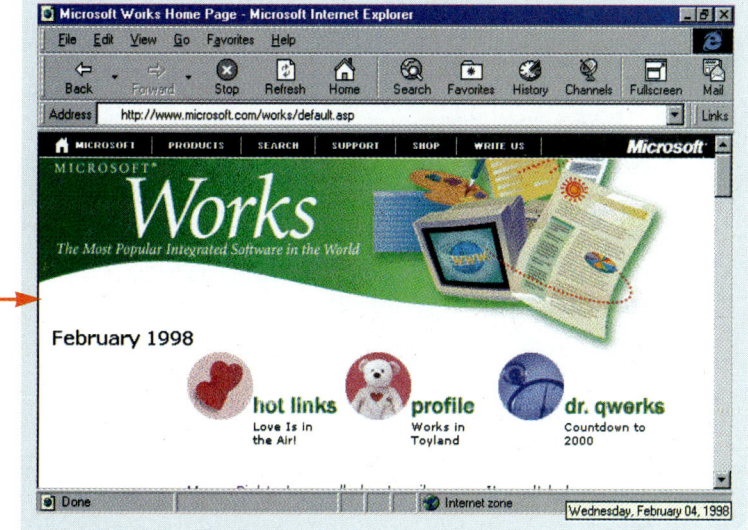

Your page may look different

TROUBLE?

If you're not sure whether you have Internet access, or if a different Web browser is configured as your default browser, see your instructor or technical support person for assistance.

QUICK TIP

To learn what parts of a Web page are links to other pages, point with your mouse; when the pointer changes to a 👆, you know you are pointing to a link.

TROUBLE?

Sites on the Web are constantly being updated and restructured, so the pages on your screen may not match those shown here. If the Microsoft and Works Web sites no longer contain the links shown here, click any links that interest you.

VISUAL WORKSHOP

Create the document shown in Figure A-13 and save it as "New Address Card." (*Hint:* The TaskWizard used to create the document is contained in the User Defined Templates category of the TaskWizards tab.) To work in the Database, remember that you click the field you want to edit, delete and insert text in the Entry Bar, and then press [Enter] to complete your entry.

FIGURE A-13: Completed address card

Glossary

Links A word, a phrase, or a picture on any Web site, that moves to a related page or Web site when clicked.

Update Minor improvements made to increase user satisfaction and productivity of a product; indicated by a decimal-point change (i.e., 4.0 to 4.5).

Upgrade Alters the look and feel of a program, procedures for completing tasks, and basic functionality of major features, indicated by a full number change (i.e., 5 to 6).

URL (Uniform Resource Locator) The address of a Web site.

Web sites Pages on the Internet that are linked.

World Wide Web (WWW) The most popular part of the Internet; consists of a network of pages, linked to make it easy to move from one to another.

Index

Special Characters
" (double quotation mark), WK 98
\# (hash mark), WK 109
& (ampersand), WK 113
( ) (parentheses), WK 105, WK 199
* (asterisk), WK 104, WK 105, WK 199
+ (plus sign), W 42, WK 105, WK 199
– (minus sign), W 42, WK 105, WK 199
/ (slash), WK 105, WK 199
= (equal sign), WK 104, WK 126
^ (caret), WK 105, WK 199
... (ellipsis), W 13, W 14
triangle, W 13

A
ABS function, WK 131
absolute position, WK 278
Accessories menu, W 8
active document, WK 18
active program, W 10
  buttons, W 8
  displaying, W 4
Add button, W 47
addition operator (+), WK 105, WK 199
Address bar, Internet Explorer, AP 14
addresses
  Internet, WK 246
  mail merge, WK 285
alignment
  fields, WK 181
  spreadsheet cells, WK 108, WK 109
  text, WK 56-57
Alignment tab, WK 108
America Online, WK 236
ampersand (&), header and footer codes, WK 113
And conjunction, WK 204, WK 205
Apple Macintosh computers, W 5
applications. *See* active program; programs; Works tools; *specific applications*
Apply button, W 14
area charts, WK 147
arguments, functions, WK 124, WK 125, WK 131
arrow keys, WK 32

art. *See also* ClipArt; Draw accessory; drawings; WordArt
  inserting in documents, WK 278-279
  original, WK 81
  resizing, WK 87
Ascending radio button, Sort dialog box, WK 136
asterisk (*), multiplication operator, WK 104, WK 105, WK 199
AutoFormat command, WK 111
AutoSum button, WK 127
Average statistic, reports, WK 221
AVG function, WK 124, WK 125, WK 130, WK 131

B
Back button, WK 12
Backspace key, WK 178
backup copies, databases, WK 175
bar charts, WK 147
Basic Types tab, Chart Type dialog box, WK 151
baud rate, WK 240, WK 241
Bold button, W 33, WK 10, WK 11, WK 182
bold type, WK 54, WK 55
Border command, WK 182, WK 183
borders
  documents, WK 76-77
  fields, WK 183
  spreadsheets, WK 103, WK 110, WK 111
Borders and Shading dialog box, WK 76, WK 77
Borders command, WK 110
Borders tab, Borders and Shading dialog box, WK 76, WK 77
Border tab, Format Cells dialog box, WK 110, WK 111
Boxed text style, WK 60
Browse button, W 47
Brush tool, W 31
Budget Worksheet template, AP 7
bulletin boards, WK 236
Bullets command, WK 60
buttons, WK 10, WK 11. *See also specific buttons*
  command, W 14, W 15
  displaying function, WK 11
  indented, W 8, W 9, WK 10
  mouse. *See* mouse buttons
  navigation, WK 31
  open programs, W 8
  removing, WK 13

sizing. *See* sizing buttons
taskbar, W 8
toolbars, W 12. *See also* toolbars; *specific toolbars*
ToolTips, W 12, W 13
Word processor toolbar, WK 37
Buttons tab, W 14

C
calculations. *See also* formulas
  interest payments, WK 133
  reports, WK 221
Calculator program, W 9
Calendar program, W 9
Call Waiting, telecommunication, WK 237
Cancel button, W 14
canceling
  actions. *See* undoing
  TaskWizards, WK 15
canvas, WK 256
capacity
  disks, W 29
  hard drive, W 42
  Recycle Bin, W 45
Capacity option, formatting disks, W 29
Cardfile program, W 9
caret (^), exponential operator, WK 105
cascading menus, W 8, W 9
Category radio buttons, Insert Function dialog box, WK 126
cell ranges, WK 104
cell reference box, WK 96, WK 97
cell references, WK 104, WK 105
cells, spreadsheets. *See* spreadsheet cells
Center-align button, WK 10, WK 11
characters, filenames, W 32
Chart accessory, WK 146. *See also* charts
  Help system, WK 149
  toolbar buttons, WK 151
Chart command, WK 159
charts, WK 145-160
  axes, WK 149
  changing type, WK 150-151
  colors, WK 154-155
  creating, WK 148-149
  displaying, WK 159

INDEX

fonts, WK 154-155
gridlines, WK 149, WK 152-153
labels, WK 149
legends, WK 149, WK 153
pasting into Word Processor, WK 158-159
planning, WK 146-147
subtitles, WK 152-153
3-D, WK 147
types, WK 147
Chart Type dialog box, WK 150, WK 151
check boxes, W 14, W 15, W 8, W 9
check marks, menus, W 12
circles, drawing, W 30, W 31
civic and volunteer projects, templates for, AP 5, AP 6-7
clicking, W 6, W 7
clip art, AP 2, AP 10-11
ClipArt
    adding to database forms, WK 196-197
    inserting in documents, WK 80-81
ClipArt Gallery, WK 80, WK 81, WK 196, WK 197
ClipArt Gallery dialog box, WK 197
Clipboard, W 34, WK 36, WK 37, WK 159
Close All command, W 21
Close button
    Control Panel window, W 20
    My Computer window, W 6
    program windows, W 21
Close command, WK 18, WK 19
    File menu, W 20
closing
    files. *See* closing files
    Help window, WK 31
    programs, W 20, 21
    windows, keeping program running, W 10
closing files, WK 18, WK 19
    all open files, W 21
    multiple files, simultaneously, W 21
codes, headers and footers, WK 113
Color list box, WK 8, WK 9, WK 77
    Font and Style command, WK 182
colors
    charts, WK 154-155
    Paint program, W 30, W 31
columns. *See* spreadsheet columns; text columns
Columns command, WK 74
Column Width dialog box, WK 102
combination charts, WK 147
combining Works applications, WK 275-286
    creating form letters, WK 276-277
    inserting database fields, WK 282-283
    inserting illustrations, WK 278-279
    inserting spreadsheet data, WK 280-281
    printing, WK 284-285
command buttons, W 14, W 15
commands. *See also specific commands*
    descriptions, W 12, W 13
    dimmed, W 13
    Edit menu, W 40, W 41
    ellipsis (...), W 13, W 14
    keyboard to carry out. *See* keyboard
    menus, W 12, W 13
    MS-DOS, W 5
    pop-up menus, W 6, W 7
    selecting, W 6, W 12
    Start menu, W 8
    underlined letters, W 12, W 13
Communications button, WK 238, WK 239
Communication Settings button, WK 240
communications parameters, WK 236, WK 240-241

communications programs, WK 236.
    See also Communications tool; telecommunication
Communications tool. *See also* telecommunication
    document types, WK 4
    starting, WK 238-239
    toolbar buttons, WK 238
Communication tab, Settings dialog box, WK 240, WK 241
Compare To text boxes, Filter dialog box, WK 202
Comparison list boxes, Filter dialog box, WK 202
CompuServe, WK 235, WK 236
computer, turning off, W 20, W 28, WK 19
Confirm Folder Delete dialog box, W 44, W 45
connect charges, online services, WK 239
connection status box, WK 238
Connection tab, WK 240
connect time box, WK 238
control menu icon, WK 31
Control Panel toolbar, W 12, W 13
Control Panel window
    Close button, W 20
    dragging border to display buttons, W 13
Copy button, W 40, W 41, WK 36, WK 178
Copy command, Edit menu, W 40, W 41
copying
    files. *See* copying files
    folders, W 42, W 43
    objects to Clipboard, W 34
copying files, W 36
    Edit menu, W 40, W 41
    keyboard shortcut, W 41
    My Computer, W 40, W 41
    system files, W 29
Copy System Files Only option, formatting disks, W 29
correcting errors. *See* error correction; spelling checker; undoing
COS function, WK 131
COUNT function, WK 130
Count statistic, reports, WK 221
CourseHelps, WK 37
Create Database dialog box, WK 170, WK 171
Create Shortcut dialog box, W 47
criteria, multiple, filtering databases, WK 204-205
Currency format, WK 109
current document, WK 18
cursor, W 34, WK 10, WK 32
Curved line tool, W 30, W 31
Customers or Clients Task Wizard, WK 173
customizing desktop, W 47
Cut button, W 40, W 41, WK 10, WK 11, WK 36, WK 178
Cut command, Edit menu, W 40, W 41
cutting. *See also* deleting; removing
    files, W 41
    text in documents, WK 36

D

data
    editing in fields, WK 178-179
    entering in fields, WK 174-175
    loss. *See* data loss
database forms, WK 168
    adding ClipArt, WK 196-197
    adding notes, WK 197
    adding WordArt, WK 183
databases, WK 167-186, WK 193-210
    backup copies, WK 175
    building data-entry forms, WK 172-173
    Database toolbar, WK 172, WK 173
    fields. *See* fields
    filtering. *See* filtering databases
    font size and style, WK 182-183
    footers, WK 185

forms. *See* database forms
    headers, WK 185
    navigating, WK 176, WK 177, WK 207
    online, searching, WK 244-245
    opening, WK 194-195
    planning, WK 168-169
    printing, WK 184-185
    printing envelopes, WK 208-209
    protecting, WK 206-207
    records. *See* records
    reports. *See* reports
Database tool. *See also* databases
    document types, WK 4
data bits, WK 240
data-entry forms, WK 172-173
data loss
    previous versions of files to protect against, W 36
    turning off computer, W 20
date and time functions, WK 125, WK 128-129
Date format, WK 109, WK 171
DATE function, WK 129
dates, valid range, WK 129
DAY function, WK 129
default categories, Start menu, W 8
default values, WK 100
definitions, reports, WK 220, WK 222
Delete button, WK 227
Delete Filter button, Filter dialog box, WK 205
Delete Report command, WK 227
deleting. *See also* cutting; removing
    fields, WK 180, WK 181
    files. *See* deleting files
    filters, WK 205
    footnotes, WK 83
    reports, WK 227
    text, WK 32, WK 34
deleting files, W 36
    floppy disks, W 45
    hard disk, W 44, W 45
    restoring deleted files, W 44, W 45
    undoing deletions, W 44
deleting shortcuts, W 46
Descending option, Sort Records dialog box, WK 201
Descending radio button, WK 136
deselecting text, WK 77
desktop, W 4, W 5
    customizing, W 47
    elements, W 4
    file management, W 46-47
desktop publishing, WK 73-88
    borders around text, WK 76-77
    inserting ClipArt, WK 80-81
    inserting footnotes, WK 82-83
    inserting WordArt, WK 78-79
    multiple columns, WK 74-75
    printing, WK 86, WK 87
    replacing text, WK 84-85
    verifying page layout, WK 86, WK 87
Details button, W 38
Details view, W 38, W 39
devices, telecommunication, WK 240
Dial/Hangup button, WK 248, WK 249
dialog boxes, W 14-15, WK 8-9. *See also specific dialog boxes*
    elements, W 15
    ellipsis (...), W 13
    Help system, W 19
    keyboard to carry out commands, W 15
    moving, WK 9, WK 136
    navigating, WK 9
    tabs, WK 4, WK 5

dictionary, personal, WK 38
dimensions, windows, W 10, W 11
dimmed commands, W 13
disks
    floppy. *See* floppy disks
    hard. *See* hard disk
    saving files to, WK 16-17, WK 281
    saving space, W 44
Display as Printed command, WK 155
displaying
    charts, WK 159
    drive or folder contents, W 38, W 39
    files, W 42, W 43
    folders, W 42, W 43
    font names, WK 8, WK 9
    help information, W 8
    hierarchy of files and folders, W 36, W 37
    list box functions, W 11
    names of files being moved, W 40
    previewing file contents, W 36, W 42, W 43.
        See also Print Preview
    Recycle Bin contents, W 44
    ruler, WK 59
    Task Wizards, WK 14
    tool functions, WK 11
    window contents, W 16-17
division operator (/), WK 105, WK 199
documents. *See also* files
    current (active), WK 18
    desktop publishing. *See* desktop publishing
    editing, WK 34-35
    entering text, WK 32-33
    formatting. *See* formatting documents
    inserting database fields, WK 282-283
    inserting illustrations, WK 278-279
    inserting spreadsheet data, WK 280-281
    linking, WK 159
    planning, WK 28-29
    printing, WK 42-43, WK 86, WK 87
    saving, WK 281
    selecting, WK 57, WK 77
    source, WK 159
    text. *See* text
    types, WK 4
    viewing, WK 40-41
    Word Processor tool. *See* Word Processor tool
Documents command, W 8
document windows, W 8, W 9, WK 6, WK 7
    maximizing, WK 31, WK 53
    Word Processor tool, WK 31
double-clicking, W 6, W 7
double quotation mark ("), labels, WK 98
downloading, images, AP 10-11
drag and drop method, WK 36, WK 37, WK 265
dragging, W 6, W 7
    column and row borders, WK 103
    files, W 40, W 45, W 46
    folders, W 42
    highlighting text, WK 34
    scroll boxes, W 16
    window borders, W 10
Draw accessory, WK 81, WK 255-268. *See also* drawings
    starting, WK 256-257
drawings. *See also* art; ClipArt; Draw accessory; Paint program; WordArt
    adding text, WK 262-263
    creating, WK 260-261
    drawing tools, WK 256, WK 258-259
    editing in Word Processor, WK 279
    formatting, WK 264, WK 265
    printing, WK 266-267
    saving, WK 264, WK 265
drawing tools, WK 256, WK 258-259
drive list arrow, W 38
drives. *See also* disks; hard disk
    saving files, WK 16

E

Easy Calc button, WK 127
Easy Calc command, WK 127
Easy Connect dialog box, WK 238, WK 242, WK 248, WK 249
Easy Formats button, WK 61
Easy Formats command, WK 60
Easy Formats dialog box, WK 60, WK 61
edit cursor, moving, WK 107
editing
    data in fields, WK 178-179
    documents, WK 34-35
    drawings in Word Processor, WK 279
    Report view, WK 224-225
    spreadsheets, WK 106-107
    tables, WK 157
    undoing changes, WK 35, WK 54
Edit menu
    commands, W 40, W 41
    Undo command, W 31
education templates, AP 8-9
electronic mail, WK 236, WK 246-247, AP 12
Ellipse tool, W 30, WK 258, WK 259
ellipsis (...), menus, W 13, W 14
e-mail, WK 236, WK 246-247, AP 12
embedding objects, WK 159
enabled features, W 12
endnotes, printing, WK 83
entering
    data in fields, WK 174-175
    labels in spreadsheets, WK 98, WK 99
    numbers in spreadsheets, WK 98, WK 99
    text in documents, WK 32-33
Enter Your Text Here dialog box, WK 78, WK 79
entry bar, WK 170
envelopes
    printing for form letters, WK 285
    printing from databases, WK 208-209
Envelopes dialog box, WK 208
equal sign (=)
    formulas, WK 104
    functions, WK 126
equations. *See* formulas; functions
Eraser/Color Eraser tool, W 31
error correction
    data in fields, WK 178
    formatting charts, WK 153
    restoring accidentally deleted files, W 44, W 45
    spelling errors. *See* spelling checker
    undoing actions. *See* undoing
Existing Documents tab, WK 30
Exit command, File menu, W 20
exiting
    Word Processor tool, WK 7
    Works 4 for Windows 95, WK 18, WK 19
expanding folders, W 42
Explorer. *See* Windows Explorer
Exponential format, WK 109
exponential operator (^), WK 105

F

Field name list boxes, Filter dialog box, WK 202
fields, WK 168
    adding, WK 180
    alignment, WK 181
    borders, WK 183
    creating, WK 170-171
    deleting, WK 180, WK 181
    editing data, WK 178-179
    entering data, WK 174-175
    formats, WK 171
    formulas, WK 198-199
    highlighted, keyboard keys, WK 175
    inserting in documents, WK 282-283
    moving, WK 180, WK 181
    name, WK 174, WK 175
    shading, WK 183
Fields in Report list box, ReportCreator dialog box, WK 218, WK 219
field values, WK 174, WK 175
    size, WK 175
file compatibility, AP 2
file management. *See also* copying files; files; moving files
    desktop, W 46-47
    folders, W 36, W 37
    locating files, W 36
    My Computer, W 36-41
    previewing file contents, W 36
File menu, W 20, WK 18, WK 19
File Name box, W 32
filenames, W 32, W 36, W 42, W 43, WK 16, WK 17
    selecting, W 33
File name text box, Open dialog box, WK 30, WK 31
files, W 3
    closing. *See* closing files
    cutting, W 41
    deleted, W 4
    deleting. *See* deleting files
    displaying, W 42, W 43
    displaying names of files being moved, W 40
    finding, W 4, W 8, W 36
    folders. *See* folders
    moving. *See* moving files
    opening, W 30-31
    pasting, W 40, W 41
    previewing, W 36, W 42, W 43. *See also* Print Preview
    restoring. *See* restoring files
    saving, W 28, W 32, W 33, WK 16-17, WK 33
    selecting, W 40, W 41
    viewing with My Computer, W 38, W 39
Files of type list box, Open dialog box, WK 30, WK 31
file windows, sizing buttons, W 11
Fill palette, WK 256
Fill With Color tool, W 30, W 31
Filter dialog box, WK 202, WK 203, WK 205
filtering databases, WK 193, WK 202-205
    advanced filters, WK 204-205
    deleting filters, WK 205
    rerunning filters, WK 203
Filter Name dialog box, WK 202
Filter tab, ReportCreator dialog box, WK 221
financial functions, WK 125, WK 132-133
Find command, W 8, WK 85, WK 202
Find dialog box, WK 85
Find feature, W 36
finding. *See also* searching online databases
    files, W 4, W 8, W 36
    Help topics, WK 13
    records. *See* filtering databases
    text, WK 85

First-time Help dialog box, WK 42, WK 200, WK 208
floppy disks
    deleting files, W 45
    formatting, W 28-29
    saving documents, WK 281
    saving files, W 28
    Work Disk, W 28, W 42, W 43
    write-protected, W 29
    write-protect tabs, W 29
folders, W 36, W 37
    copying, W 42, W 43
    creating, W 38, W 39, W 40, W 41
    displaying, W 42, W 43
    expanding, W 42
    hierarchy. *See* hierarchy of folders
    selecting, W 41
Folder tab, W 37
Font and Style command, WK 182, WK 225
font box, W 33
Font list box, WK 8, WK 9
fontography, WK 53
fonts
    charts, WK 154, WK 155
    creation, WK 53
    listing names, WK 8, WK 9
    reports, WK 224, WK 225
    size. *See* font size
    spreadsheets, WK 110, WK 111
    style. *See* font style
    type, documents, WK 52, WK 53
font size
    databases, WK 182, WK 183
    documents, WK 52, WK 53
font style
    databases, WK 182, WK 183
    documents, WK 53, WK 54-55
    reports, WK 224, WK 225
    spreadsheets, WK 110, WK 111
Font tab, Font and Style command, WK 182
font type, documents, WK 52, WK 53
footer codes, WK 113
footers
    databases, WK 185
    documents, WK 64-65
    reports, WK 284, WK 285
    spreadsheets, WK 113
Footnote command, WK 82
footnotes
    deleting, WK 83
    inserting in documents, WK 82-83
    numbering, WK 83
format, numbers, WK 108, WK 109
Format Cells dialog box, WK 108, WK 109, WK 110, WK 111, WK 128
Format Columns dialog box, WK 74, WK 75
Format dialog box, W 28, W 29, WK 183
Format Font and Style dialog box, WK 8, WK 9, WK 154
Format menu, WK 8
Format Paragraph dialog box, WK 56, WK 57
Format Picture dialog box, WK 278, WK 279
formats
    fields, WK 171
    spreadsheets, WK 101
Format Tabs, dialog box, WK 61
formatting
    disks. *See* formatting disks
    documents. *See* formatting documents
    drawings, W 32, W 33, WK 264-265

formatting disks, W 28-29
    options, W 29
formatting documents, WK 51-66
    alignment, WK 56-57
    font style, WK 54-55
    font type and size, WK 52-53
    headers and footers, WK 64-65
    manual page breaks, WK 62-63
    margin settings, WK 58-59
    paragraph styles, WK 60-61
    predefined styles, WK 60, WK 61
Form Design button, WK 172, WK 175
Form Design view, WK 183, WK 197
form letters, WK 282-283
    creating, WK 276-277
    printing, WK 284-285
    printing envelopes, WK 285
Form Letter TaskWizard, WK 283
forms. *See* database forms
formula bar, WK 96, WK 97
formulas, WK 104-105
    field entries, WK 198-199
    order of precedence, WK 105
    replicating, WK 104, WK 105
Form view, WK 177
Form View button, WK 175
Fractions format, WK 171
Free-Form Select tool, W 31
Freeform tool, WK 260, WK 261
free space, W 42
Full option, Format dialog box, W 28, W 29
Function command, WK 126
functions, WK 104, WK 123-135
    as argument in another function, WK 131
    arguments, WK 124, WK 125, WK 131
    AVG, WK 124, WK 125
    building, WK 127
    categories, WK 125
    date and time, WK 125, WK 128-129
    financial, WK 125, WK 132-133
    informational, WK 125
    logical, WK 125
    lookup and reference, WK 125
    mathematical, WK 125, WK 131
    planning use, WK 125
    references, WK 124, WK 125
    statistical, WK 125, WK 130-131
    SUM, WK 126-127
    text, WK 125, WK 134-135
FV function, WK 132

G

General alignment, WK 181
General format, WK 171
General tab, W 42
    Properties dialog box, WK 240, WK 241
graphical user interface (GUI), W 3, W 5
gridlines, charts, WK 149, WK 152, WK 153

H

handles, WK 258
hard disk
    capacity, W 42
    deleting files, W 44, W 45
    saving documents, WK 281
    saving files, W 28
hardware, telecommunication, WK 236
hash mark (#), spreadsheet cells, WK 109

header codes, WK 113
headers
    databases, WK 185
    inserting in documents, WK 64-65
    spreadsheets, WK 113
Headers and Footers command, WK 113, WK 185
height, windows, W 10
Help buttons, W 19, WK 6, WK 7
    Spreadsheet tool, WK 97
Help command, W 8
help information, displaying, W 8
Help system, W 4, W 18-19, WK 12-13
    Chart accessory, WK 149
    dialog boxes, W 19
    Spreadsheet tool, WK 97
Help Topics button, W 18
Help Topics dialog box, W 18, W 19
Help Topics window, W 18, W 19
Help window, WK 12, WK 13
    closing, W 31
    minimizing, W 53
Hide Help command, WK 13, WK 245
hierarchy of folders, W 38
    displaying, W 36, W 37
highlighting. *See also* selecting
    selected icons, W 6
home productivity templates, AP 8–9
Horizontal Axis dialog box, WK 152, WK 153
HOUR function, WK 129

I

icons, W 3, W 4, W 5. *See also specific icons*
    highlighted, W 6
    moving, W 6
    selecting, W 6, W 7
    shortcuts, W 46, W 47
images, downloading from Microsoft Clip Gallery Live, AP 10-11
    Microsoft ClipArt Gallery 2.0, AP 2, AP 10-11
indented buttons, W 8, W 9
Indented Paragraph text style, WK 60
Indents and Alignment tab, Format Paragraph dialog box, WK 56, WK 57
Index button, WK 13
    Spreadsheet tool, WK 97
informational functions, WK 125
inline position, WK 278
Insert Field dialog box, WK 180, WK 282, WK 283
Insert Footnote dialog box, WK 82
Insert Function dialog box, WK 126, WK 130, WK 132, WK 134
inserting
    ClipArt in documents, WK 80-81
    database fields in documents, WK 282-283
    footnotes in documents, WK 82-83
    headers and footers in documents, WK 64-65
    illustrations in documents, WK 278-279
    manual page breaks, WK 62-63
    spreadsheet data in documents, WK 280-281
    WordArt in documents, WK 78-79
insertion point, W 34, W 10, W 32
    moving, WK 32
Insert Label dialog box, WK 172
Insert Record button, WK 177
Insert Record command, WK 177
integrated software packages, WK 3
interest payments, calculation, WK 133
Internet, WK 235
    addresses, WK 246
    connecting to, AP 13, AP 15

INDEX

defined, AP 12
e-mail, WK 246-247
Internet Explorer. *See* Microsoft Internet Explorer
Italic button, W 33
italic type, WK 54, WK 55

J
justifying text, WK 56

K
keyboard
    accessing menu commands, W 12, W 13
    commands in dialog boxes, W 15
    copying files, W 41
    cutting files, W 41
    editing data in fields, WK 179
    error correction, WK 178
    highlighted fields, WK 175
    naming files, W 42, W 43
    navigation keys, WK 32
    pasting files, W 41
    shortcuts, W 13
    switching between programs, W 34, W 35

L
Label option, formatting disks, W 29
labels
    charts, WK 149
    date-entry forms, WK 172
    spreadsheets, WK 98, WK 99
landscape orientation, WK 59
Large Icons button, W 38
Leading zeros format, WK 109
Left-handed radio button, W 14
legends, charts, WK 149, WK 153
LENGTH function, WK 135
Letterhead TaskWizard, WK 14, WK 15, WK 32
line charts, WK 147
Line palette, WK 256
lines, drawing, W 30, W 31
line spacing, WK 57
line wraps, WK 32, WK 33
linking documents, WK 159
links, AP 12
list boxes, W 15, W 8, W 9
    displaying function, W 11
listing. *See* displaying
List view, WK 170, WK 177, WK 183, WK 185
List View button, WK 177
locating files, W 4, W 8, W 36
LOG function, WK 131
logging out, WK 248-249
logical functions, WK 125
login process, WK 242
Look in list box, Open dialog box, WK 30, WK 31
lookup and reference functions, WK 125
LOWER function, WK 135

M
Magnifier tool, W 31
mail merge, WK 282-283
manual page breaks, WK 62-63
margins
    printer requirements, WK 59
    settings, WK 58-59
    spreadsheets, WK 113
Margins tab, Page Setup dialog box, WK 58, WK 59
mathematical functions, WK 125, WK 131
mathematical operators, WK 104, WK 105, WK 199

MAX function, WK 130
Maximize button, W 10, W 31
maximizing windows, W 10, W 31
maximum speed list box, WK 240
Maximum statistic, reports, WK 221
menu bars, W 12, W 13, WK 6, WK 7
Menu button, WK 12
menus, W 12, W 13. *See also specific menus*
    cascading, W 8, W 9
    check marks, W 12
    commands, W 12, W 13
    ellipsis (...), W 13, W 14
    naming files, W 42, W 43
    pop-up, W 6, W 7, W 46, W 47
    submenus, W 8
    triangle, W 13
    underlined letters, W 13
merging records, WK 284, WK 285
Microsoft Clip Gallery 3.0, AP 2, AP 10-11
Microsoft Clip Gallery Live, AP 10-11
Microsoft homepage, AP 14-15
Microsoft Internet Explorer, AP 2-3, AP 12-15
    Address bar, AP 14
    features, AP 12
    practice using, AP 14-15
    program window, AP 13
    starting, AP 14
    toolbar buttons, AP 13
Microsoft Network, WK 235, WK 236
    Works Forum, AP 14
Microsoft Works 4.0 program icon, WK 4
Microsoft Works 4.5, file compatibility, AP 2
    home page, AP 14-15
    new features, AP 2-3
    updating to, AP 1
    upgrading to, AP 1
    Works Forum, Microsoft Network, AP 14
    Works Task Launcher dialog box, AP 4, AP 5
Microsoft Works home page, AP 3
MID function, WK 135
MIN function, WK 130
Minimize button, W 10
minimizing windows, W 10, W 11
Minimum statistic, reports, WK 221
minus button, Zoom Box, WK 40
minus sign (–)
    subtraction operator, WK 105, WK 199
    Windows Explorer window, W 42
MINUTE function, WK 129
misspellings. *See* spelling checker
mistakes. *See* error correction; spelling checker; undoing
modems, WK 236, WK 237, WK 240
MONTH function, WK 129
Mortgage/Loan Analysis Task Wizard, WK 133
mouse
    clicking, W 6, W 7
    double-clicking, W 6, W 7
    moving, W 6
    right-clicking, W 6, W 7
    techniques, W 6-7. *See also* drag and drop method; dragging
mouse buttons, W 6
    Help system, W 19
mouse pointer, W 4, W 5
    shapes, W 7, W 19
    trails, W 14
Mouse Properties dialog box, W 14, W 15
moving. *See also* navigating
    dialog boxes, W 9, WK 136
    edit cursor, WK 107

fields, WK 180, WK 181
files. *See* moving files
icons, W 6
illustrations, WK 265
insertion point, WK 32
mouse, W 6
selection box between programs, W 34, W 35
text in documents, WK 36-37
between windows, W 17
windows, W 10
moving files, W 36, W 40, W 41, W 45, W 46
    displaying names of files being moved, W 40
    Edit menu, W 40, W 41
    My Computer, W 40, W 41
Moving window, W 40
MS-DOS, W 5
multiple programs, running simultaneously, W 34-35
multiplication operator (*), WK 104, WK 105
My Computer, W 36-43
    browsing using single window, W 37
    copying files, W 40, W 41
    creating folders, W 38, W 39
    moving files, W 40, W 41
    previewing documents, W 42, W 43
    viewing files, W 38, W 39
    window, W 28, W 29
My Computer icon, W 4, W 28
My Computer window, Close button, W 6
My Folder window, W 40

N
names
    fields, WK 174, WK 175
    files. *See* filenames
navigating
    databases, WK 176, WK 177, WK 207
    dialog boxes, W 9
    spreadsheets, WK 99
    windows, W 16-17
    Word Processor documents, WK 31, WK 33
New Chart dialog box, WK 148
Normal view, WK 40, WK 41
Note-It command, WK 197
notes, adding to database forms, WK 197
Now function, WK 128, WK 129
Number command, WK 109
Number format, WK 171
numbering
    footnotes, WK 83
    pages, WK 65
numbers
    entering in spreadsheets, WK 98, WK 99
    format, WK 108, WK 109
    serial, WK 128
Number tab, Format Cells dialog box, WK 109, WK 128

O
objects, WK 157
    ClipArt, WK 197
    drawn. *See* Draw accessory
    embedding, WK 159
    selecting, W 34
OK button, W 14
online databases, searching, WK 244-245
on-line Help system. *See* Help system
online services, WK 235, WK 236
Open dialog box, WK 30, WK 31, WK 74, WK 148, WK 194, WK 195
Open Existing File command, WK 30

INDEX

opening
    databases, WK 194-195
    existing files, WK 30-31
    reports, WK 227
    View menu, W 12
    windows, W 6
operating systems, W 3, W 5. *See also* Windows 95
option buttons, W 9
Options dialog box, W 37
Or conjunction, WK 204
order of precedence, WK 105
orientation, paper, WK 59, WK 113
Orientation option, Page Setup dialog box, WK 59
OS/2, W 5
Outline button, WK 183
Outlook Express, AP 11

P

Page Break command, WK 62, WK 63
page breaks, manual, WK 62-63
page layout, verifying, WK 86, WK 87
Page Layout view, WK 40, WK 41
page navigation buttons, WK 31
page number indicator, WK 31, WK 62, WK 63
page numbering, WK 65
Page Setup command, WK 113
Page Setup dialog box, WK 58, WK 59
Paint program, W 9, W 30-33
    creating files, W 30-33
    drawing circles, W 30, W 31
    drawing lines, W 30, W 31
    formatting drawings, W 32, W 33
    saving files, W 32, W 33
    tools, W 30, W 31, W 32, W 33
Paint window, W 30, W 31
panes, Windows Explorer window, W 42, W 43
paper
    orientation, WK 113
    source, size, and orientation, WK 59
paragraphs, selecting, WK 77
paragraph styles, WK 60-61
parameters, telecommunication, WK 236, WK 240-241
parentheses (( )), mathematical operator, WK 105, WK 199
parity, WK 240
passwords, W 4
Paste button, W 40, W 41, WK 36, WK 158, WK 178
Paste command, Edit menu, W 40, W 41
Paste Link button, WK 159
Paste Special dialog box, WK 159
pasting
    Clipboard contents, W 34
    files, W 40, W 41
    text in documents, WK 36
pattern list box, Format dialog box, WK 183
Patterns command, WK 110
Patterns list box, Format Cells dialog box, WK 111
Pencil tool, W 31
Percent format, WK 109
personal dictionary, WK 38
phone lines, telecommunicating, WK 236
Phone Settings button, WK 241
Pick Color Tool, W 31
pie charts, WK 147
planning
    charts, WK 146-147
    databases, WK 168-169
    documents, WK 28-29
    function use, WK 125
    telecommunications sessions, WK 236-237
plus button, Zoom Box, WK 40

plus sign (+)
    addition operator, WK 105
    Windows Explorer window, W 42
PMT function, WK 132, WK 133
pointer. *See* mouse pointer
pointing, W 6, W 7, WK 4
pop-up menus, W 6, W 7, W 46, W 47
portrait orientation, WK 59
ports, WK 42
Position indicator, WK 8, WK 9
pound sign (#), spreadsheet cells, WK 109
Preview feature, W 36
Preview window, templates, AP 4
previewing file contents, W 36, W 42, W 43
Print button, WK 43, WK 158
Print command, WK 112, WK 266
Print dialog box, WK 42, WK 43, WK 112, WK 184
printers, WK 42
    margin requirements, WK 59
printing
    databases, WK 184-185
    documents, WK 42-43, WK 86, WK 87
    drawings, WK 266-267
    endnotes, WK 83
    envelopes for form letters, WK 285
    envelopes from databases, WK 208-209
    form letters, WK 284-285
    reports, WK 226-227
    spreadsheets, WK 112-113, WK 136, WK 137
    Web pages, AP 12
    Word Processor documents, WK 42-43
Print Preview, WK 158
    databases, WK 184
    drawings, WK 266, WK 267
    envelopes, WK 209
    mail merge addresses, WK 285
    reports, WK 222-223, WK 226, WK 227
    spreadsheets, WK 112, WK 113
    Word Processor documents, WK 40-41
Print Preview button, WK 223
Print Preview command, WK 223
programs, W 4
    active. *See* active program
    closing, W 20, 21
    communications, WK 236.
        See also Communications tool; telecommunication
    document types, WK 4
    moving selection box between, W 34, W 35
    multiple, running simultaneously, W 34-35
    running. *See* running programs
    starting, W 4, W 8-9
    switching among, W 34, W 35, WK 4, WK 7
    Windows 95, W 9. *See also* Paint program; WordPad program
Programs command, W 8
program windows
    Close button, W 21
    sizing buttons, W 11
progress bar, W 15
PROPER function, WK 135
Properties dialog box, W 42, WK 42, WK 43, WK 240, WK 241
protecting databases, WK 206-207
Protection command, WK 206, WK 207
Protection dialog box, WK 206, WK 207
publishing, Web pages, AP 12

Q

Quick (erase) option, formatting disks, W 29
Quick View command, W 42, W 43
quitting Works 4 for Windows 95, WK 7

R

radar charts, WK 147
radio buttons, W 14, W 15
random access memory (RAM), W 28
range references, functions, WK 124, WK 125
Recipe template, AP 8-9
record navigation buttons, WK 176
record number indicator, WK 176
records, WK 168
    adding to databases, WK 176-177
    finding. *See* filtering databases
    merging, WK 284, WK 285
    sorting, WK 200-201
Rectangle tool, W 32, W 33
Recycle Bin, W 44-45
    emptying, W 44
    full, W 45
    size, W 45
Recycle Bin icon, W 4, W 44
Recycle Bin window, W 44, W 45
references. *See* cell references; range references
remote computer, connecting to, WK 242-243
removing. *See also* cutting; deleting
    buttons, WK 13
    WordArt from documents, WK 79
Rename command, W 42, W 43
renaming files, W 36, W 42, W 43
REPEAT function, WK 134, WK 135
Replace All button, WK 107
    Replace dialog box, WK 85
Replace button, WK 107
Replace command, WK 107
Replace dialog box, WK 84, WK 85
replacing text, WK 84-85
replicating formulas, WK 104, WK 105
Report command, WK 227
ReportCreator dialog box, WK 218, WK 219, WK 220, WK 221
Report Name dialog box, WK 218
reports, WK 168, WK 217-228
    adding summary information, WK 220-221
    creating, WK 218-219
    definitions, WK 220, WK 222
    deleting, WK 227
    editing, WK 224-225
    footers, WK 284, WK 285
    opening, WK 227
    printing, WK 226-227
    statistical calculations, WK 221
    viewing in Print Preview, WK 222-223
Report view, editing, WK 224-225
Report View button, WK 219
resize box, WK 87
resizing. *See* sizing
Restore button, W 10
restoring files
    floppy disks, W 45
    hard disk, W 44, W 45
restoring windows, W 10, W 11
right-clicking, W 6, W 7
Rotate/Flip command, WK 261
rotating drawn objects, WK 261
Row Height dialog box, WK 102
rows, spreadsheets. *See* spreadsheet rows
ruler, WK 31, WK 35
    displaying, WK 59
Run command, W 8
running programs, WK 4
    multiple programs, W 34-35

INDEX

S

Save As command, W 32, WK 16, WK 100
Save As dialog box, W 32, W 33, WK 16, WK 17, WK 30, WK 100, WK 101, WK 264, AP 8
Save as Type list box, WK 100, WK 101
Save button, WK 100
Save changes dialog box, WK 18, WK 19
Save command, WK 16, WK 100
Save In list arrow, W 32
saving
    documents, WK 281
    drawings, WK 264-265
    files, W 28, W 32, W 33, WK 16-17, WK 33
    spreadsheets, WK 100-101
    Web pages, AP 12
scatter charts, WK 147
scroll arrows, W 17
scroll bars, W 16-17, WK 6, WK 7
scroll boxes, W 16, W 17, WK 31
    dragging, W 16
searching, for Web pages, AP 12
searching online databases, WK 244-245
SECOND function, WK 129
Select All command, WK 259
selecting
    commands, W 6, W 12
    documents, WK 57, WK 77
    filenames, W 33
    files, W 41
    folders, W 41
    icons, W 6, W 7
    objects, W 34
    spreadsheet cells, WK 103
    text, WK 10, WK 11, WK 34, WK 35, WK 76, WK 77
selection box, moving between programs, W 34, W 35
selection rectangles, WK 258, WK 259
Select Program Folder dialog box, W 47
Select tool, W 31, W 34
sentences, selecting, WK 77
Serialized format, WK 171
serial numbers, WK 128
serial ports, WK 236
Settings command, W 8
Settings dialog box, WK 240, WK 241
shading
    fields, WK 183
    spreadsheet cells, WK 111
Shading command, WK 111, WK 182, WK 183
Shading tab, Format Cells dialog box, WK 111
shortcuts, W 46, W 47
    adding to Start menu, W 47
    creating, W 46, W 47
    deleting, W 46
    keyboard, W 13. See also keyboard
Shortcut to Microsoft Works 4 icon, WK 4, WK 5
Show command, WK 204
Show pointer trails check box, W 14
Shrink Help button, WK 12, WK 13, AP 5
Shut Down command, W 8, W 20
Shut Down Windows dialog box, W 20, W 21
shutting down Windows 95, W 8, W 20, 21
single spacing, WK 57
size. See also capacity; sizing
    field values, WK 175
    fonts, WK 52, WK 53, WK 110, WK 111
size box, W 33
Size list box, Page Setup dialog box, WK 59

sizing
    art in Word Processor, WK 87
    tables, WK 157
    WordArt, WK 79
sizing buttons, W 10, W 11, WK 6, WK 7
    files, W 11
    programs, W 11
sizing handles, WK 172, WK 173, WK 196
sizing windows, W 10-11
slash (/), division operator, WK 105, WK 199
slider, W 14, W 15
SLN function, WK 132
Small Icons button, W 12, W 38
Sort By list box
    Sort dialog box, WK 136
    Sort Records dialog box, WK 200
Sort command, WK 136
Sort dialog box, WK 136, WK 137
sorting
    database records, WK 200-201
    by multiple columns, WK 137
    spreadsheet rows, WK 136, WK 137
Sort Records dialog box, WK 200, WK 201
Sort Rows command, WK 136
Source, Size, and Orientation tab, Page Setup dialog box, WK 59
source document, WK 159
Source list box, Page Setup dialog box, WK 59
spacing, text lines, WK 57
Spacing tab, WK 57
Special mark option button, Insert Footnote dialog box, WK 82
spelling checker
    Spreadsheet tool, WK 100, WK 101
    Word Processor tool, WK 38-39
Spelling command, WK 38
Spelling dialog box, WK 38, WK 39, WK 100
spin box, W 15
spreadsheet cells, WK 96
    alignment, WK 108, WK 109
    ranges, WK 104
    selecting, WK 103
    shading, WK 111
    width, WK 109
spreadsheet columns
    multiple, sorting by, WK 137
    width, WK 102, WK 103
Spreadsheet command, WK 157
spreadsheet rows, WK 97
    height, WK 102, WK 103
    sorting, WK 136, WK 137
spreadsheets, WK 95-114
    alignment and number format, WK 108-109
    borders, WK 110, WK 111
    cells. See spreadsheet cells
    charts. See charts
    columns. See spreadsheet columns
    editing, WK 106-107
    entering data in, AP 7
    entering numbers and labels, WK 98-99
    font and font style, WK 110, WK 111
    formats, WK 101
    formulas, WK 104-105
    functions. See functions
    inserting data in documents, WK 280-281
    navigating, WK 99
    pasting tables into Word Processor, WK 156-157
    printing, WK 112-113, WK 136, WK 137
    rows. See spreadsheet rows
    saving, WK 100-101
    spell checking, WK 100, WK 101
    starting, WK 96-97

Spreadsheet tool, WK 95. See also spreadsheets
    document types, WK 4
    on-line Help, WK 97
    toolbar, WK 96
SQRT function, WK 131
stacked line charts, WK 147
Standard deviation statistic, reports, WK 221
Start button, W 4, W 5, W 8, WK 4, WK 5
starting
    programs, W 4, W 8-9
    Windows 95, W 4, W 5
    Works 4 for Windows 95, WK 4-5
    Works tools, WK 6-7, WK 238-239, WK 256-257
Start menu, W 8, W 20
    adding shortcuts, W 47
    commands, W 8
    default categories, W 8
Start Menu Programs tab, W 47
statistical calculations, reports, WK 221
statistical functions, WK 125, WK 130-131
status bar, W 12, W 13
STD function, WK 130
Step-by-Step tab, WK 12
stop bits, WK 240
submenus, W 8
subtitles, charts, WK 152, WK 153
subtraction operator (−), WK 105, WK 199
SUM function, WK 126-127, WK 130
summary information, adding to reports, WK 220-221
Summary tab, ReportCreator dialog box, WK 220, WK 221
Sum statistic, reports, WK 221
switching between programs, W 34, W 35
    Windows programs, WK 7
    Works programs, WK 4
SYD function, WK 132
synonyms, WK 39
system administrator, WK 242

T

Tab keys, dialog boxes, WK 58
Table command, WK 75
tables
    editing, WK 157
    multicolumn, WK 75
    pasting into Word Processor, WK 156-157
    sizing, WK 157
tabs, W 14, W 15, AP 9
    dialog boxes, WK 4, WK 5
Tabs command, WK 60
tab stops, WK 61
taskbar, W 4, W 5
    buttons, W 8
Taskbar Properties dialog box, W 47
TaskWizards, WK 4, WK 14-15, AP 4
    canceling, WK 15
    Form Letter, WK 283
    Letterhead, WK 14, WK 15, WK 32
telecommunication, WK 235-250
    Call Waiting, WK 237
    connect charges, WK 239
    connecting to remote computer, WK 242-243
    devices, WK 240
    ending sessions, WK 248-249
    Internet. See Internet
    parameters, WK 236, WK 240-241
    planning sessions, WK 236-237
    searching online databases, WK 244-245
    sending e-mail, WK 246-247
    starting Communications tool, WK 238-239
Template Disclaimer template, AP 5

templates, AP 2, AP 4-9, AP 16
    civic and volunteer projects, AP 5, AP 6-7
    education, AP 8-9
    home productivity, AP 5, AP 8-9
    new in Works 4.5, AP 2-3
    opening, AP 4-5
    Preview window, AP 4
    recipes, AP 8-9
    selecting, AP 4
    types available, AP 5
Terminal tab, WK 240
text. *See also* documents; Word Processor tool
    adding to drawings, WK 262-263
    alignment, WK 56-57
    deleting, WK 32, WK 34
    deselecting, WK 77
    entering in documents, WK 32-33
    finding, WK 85
    formatting, W 32, W 33
    justifying, WK 56
    line spacing, WK 57
    moving in documents, WK 36-37
    replacing, WK 84-85
    selecting, WK 10, WK 11, WK 34, WK 35, WK 76, WK 77
text boxes, W 15, WK 9
text columns, multiple, WK 74-75
Text format, WK 171
text functions, WK 125, WK 134-135
Text tool, W 30, W 31, WK 262, WK 263
Text toolbar, W 32, W 33
Text Wrap tab, Format Picture dialog box, WK 278, WK 279
Then By list box, Sort Records dialog box, WK 200
Thesaurus, WK 38-39, WK 39
Thesaurus dialog box, WK 39
3-D charts, WK 147
3+Floppy (A:) icon, W 28
Time format, WK 109, WK 171
TIME function, WK 129
time functions. *See* date and time functions
title bar, dragging, W 10
Titles dialog box, WK 152
toggle indicators, WK 6, WK 7
toolbars, W 12, W 13, W 38, W 39, WK 6, WK 7, WK 10-11.
    See also specific toolbars
        alignment icons, WK 57
        buttons, W 12
        Spreadsheet tool, WK 96
        Word Processor tool, W 37
tools, WK 3. *See also* programs; Works tools; *specific tools*
    Paint program, W 30, W 31, W 32, W 33
Tools command, WK 257
ToolTips, W 12, W 13
trails, mouse pointer, W 14
triangle, menus, W 13
TRIM function, WK 135
True Type fonts, WK 53
turning off computer, W 20, W 28, WK 19

U

underlined letters, commands, W 12, W 13
underlining, WK 54, WK 55
Undo command, W 31, WK 103, WK 137, WK 153, WK 179

Undo Delete command, W 44
Undo Editing command, WK 54
undoing, WK 103, WK 153, WK 179
    commands, W 31
    editing changes, WK 35, WK 54
    file deletions, W 44
    sorting, WK 137
UNIX, W 5
Up One Level button, W 38
updating, AP 1
upgrading, AP 1
UPPER function, WK 135
URLs, AP 12
User Defined Templates. *See* templates

V

VALUE function, WK 135
values. *See* field values; numbers
VAR function, WK 130
Variance statistic, reports, WK 221
Variations tab, Chart Type dialog box, WK 150, WK 151
vertex, WK 260
Vertical Axis dialog box, WK 152
viewing. *See* displaying; Print Preview
View menu, W 12, W 13
    opening, W 12
View Report dialog box, WK 227

W

Web Publishing Wizard, AP 12
Web sites, defined, AP 12
    printing pages, AP 12
    publishing, AP 12
    saving pages, AP 12
    searching for, AP 12
windows. *See also specific windows*
    browsing My Computer using single window, W 37
    changing dimensions, W 10
    closing, W 10
    displaying contents, W 16-17
    minimizing, W 10, W 11
    moving, W 10
    moving between, W 17
    navigating, W 16-17
    opening, W 6
    resizing, W 10-11
    restoring, W 10, W 11
    sizing buttons, W 11
Windows 95, W 4
    accessories, W 9
    shutting down, W 8, W 20, 21
    starting, W 4, W 5
Windows Explorer, W 42-43
    copying folders, W 42, W 43
    file management, W 36
    previewing documents, W 42, W 43
Windows Explorer window, W 42, W 43
WordArt
    adding to database forms, WK 183
    inserting in documents, WK 78-79
    resizing, WK 79
WordArt command, WK 183

WordArt frames, WK 79
WordPad program, W 9
    starting, W 8, W 9
WordPad program button, W 10
Word Processor tool, 27-44. *See also* documents
    desktop publishing. *See* desktop publishing
    document window, WK 31
    editing drawings, WK 279
    exiting, WK 7
    maximizing document window, WK 31
    moving text, WK 36-37
    opening existing files, WK 30-31
    pasting charts into, WK 158-159
    pasting tables into, WK 156-157
    saving and formatting drawings, WK 264-265
    spell checking, WK 38-39
    starting, WK 6, WK 7
words, selecting, WK 77
Work Disk, W 28
    displaying contents, W 42, W 43
Works. *See* Microsoft Works 4.5
Works Forum, Microsoft Network, AP 14
Works 4 for Windows 95
    applications. *See* combining Works applications;
        Works tools; *specific tools*
    exiting, WK 18, WK 19
    quitting, WK 7
    starting, WK 4-5
Works Task Launcher, WK 4, WK 30, WK 96
Works Task Launcher dialog box, WK 4, WK 5, WK 6, WK 7,
    WK 14, WK 96, WK 97, WK 238, WK 239, AP 4, AP 5
Works tool icons, WK 238, WK 239
Works tools
    interface elements, WK 6, WK 7
    starting, WK 6-7
Works Tools tab, Works Task launcher dialog box, WK 238,
    WK 239
write-protect tabs, W 29

X

X-axis, WK 149
X-Y charts, WK 147

Y

Y-axis, WK 149
YEAR function, WK 129

Z

Zoom Box, WK 40
Zoom Indians button, WK 222, WK 223
zooming in/out, WK 40
zoom pointer, WK 222, WK 226
Zoom tool, WK 26